ISRAEL AND THE MIDDLE EAST

P9-CKR-392

AZERBAIJAN

★ Baku

TURKMENISTAN

Caspian Sea

★ Ashkgabat

★ Tehran

AFGHANISTAN

I R A N

UWAIT

★ Kuwait

Arabian Gulf

★ Al Manamah

BAHRAIN   QATAR

★ Ad Dawhah

★ Riyadh   Abu Dhabi ★

UNITED ARAB
EMIRATES

OMAN

YEMEN

LEBANON   *Mt. Hermon* ★

Mediterranean Sea   *GOLAN HEIGHTS*

Haifa ●   *GALILEE*   SYRIA

Caesarea ●   *SAMARIA*

Tel Aviv ●   Amman ★

Jerusalem ★

GAZA   *JUDEA*   *Dead Sea*

NEGEV   JORDAN

I S R A E L

EGYPT   N

0 Mi.   50

0 Km.   50

Sinai Desert

Eilat ● ● Aqaba

BIBI

My Story

BENJAMIN NETANYAHU

THRESHOLD EDITIONS

NEW YORK   LONDON   TORONTO   SYDNEY   NEW DELHI

Threshold Editions
An Imprint of Simon & Schuster, Inc.
1230 Avenue of the Americas
New York, NY 10020

Copyright © 2022 by Benjamin Netanyahu

Interior maps: Original concept design by Doron Goldberg; Updated map design by Jeffrey L. Ward

First Threshold Editions hardcover edition November 2022

THRESHOLD EDITIONS and colophon are trademarks of Simon & Schuster, Inc.

For information about special discounts for bulk purchases, please contact Simon & Schuster Special Sales at 1-866-506-1949 or business@simonandschuster.com.

The Simon & Schuster Speakers Bureau can bring authors to your live event. For more information, or to book an event, contact the Simon & Schuster Speakers Bureau at 1-866-248-3049 or visit our website at www.simonspeakers.com.

Interior design by Jaime Putorti

Manufactured in the United States of America

10 9 8 7 6 5 4 3 2 1

Library of Congress Cataloging-in-Publication Data

ISBN 978-1-6680-0844-7
ISBN 978-1-6680-0846-1 (ebook)

CONTENTS

AUTHOR'S NOTE

Some details of military and Mossad operations described in the book are excised due to Israeli national security requirements. For the same reason, other such operations, as well as details of certain diplomatic missions, are excluded in their entirety.

PART I

FOOTHILLS

1

BROTHERS

1972

I n 1972 I served as an officer in Sayeret Matkal,[1] an elite special forces unit of the Israeli army. Late one night my team and I returned to the Unit from an exercise near the Dead Sea. The base was practically empty.

"They've all gone to the airport," the lone remaining guard said. "There's been a plane hijacking. The hijackers landed the plane in Israel and they're going to kill all the passengers."

We quickly joined the rest of the Unit at Lod Airport near Tel Aviv, a ten-minute drive from our base. Earlier that day four Palestinian terrorists, two men and two women, had hijacked a Sabena airliner bound for Israel from Belgium. Landing at the airport, the terrorists demanded that Israel release 315 jailed terrorists who would be flown on the hijacked plane to an Arab country. If Israel didn't comply, they would blow up the plane with ninety-four passengers and crew on board.

The plane was wheeled to a corner of the airfield where, unseen by the terrorists, soldiers from the Unit punctured its tires.

Defense Minister Moshe Dayan started negotiating terms. This was meant to give the Unit time to improvise a rescue operation. But how do you storm a hijacked aircraft? Despite the rash of hijacking attempts worldwide at the time (326 in a four-year period between 1968 and 1972),[2] no one had tried anything like this before. In an airport hangar we practiced storming an identical aircraft. We learned that it had a sur-

prising number of entrances and that the emergency doors on the wings
could be opened by striking them from the outside.

We practiced using low-caliber Beretta pistols and were told to hide
them in our boots. The weapons we normally used, Kalashnikov assault
rifles and Uzi submachine guns, were too big to conceal and their fire-
power would endanger the passengers.

Dayan told the terrorists that Israel yielded to their demands. It would
release the jailed terrorists and send mechanics to prepare the plane for a
flight to an Arab country of their choice. The plan was simple and ingenious: Sixteen of the Unit's soldiers would be dressed in white mechanic's
overalls. We would pretend that we had come to prepare the plane for take-
off while assuming our positions at the various entry points to the aircraft.
We would then storm the entrances, kill the terrorists and free the hostages.

Each entrance had a Unit team commander responsible for breaking into the plane. As a senior team commander, I was assigned to storm
through a wing entrance with two of my men.

During the preparations, my older brother, Yoni, approached me.
Like me, he was an officer in Sayeret Matkal, but he had also fought
in the Six-Day War as a paratroop officer and had taken part in other
battles. Three years my senior, he was a proven warrior under fire, and he
outranked me.

"I'm going too," he said. "I have more combat experience than anyone in the Unit."

True, I thought, but irrelevant. Standing orders in the Israel Defense
Forces (IDF) and common sense dictated that two brothers should not
participate in the same high-risk operation, especially when it involved
such a small number of fighters in extremely close quarters.

"You *can't* go," I said, "because I'm already going!"

"Then I'll take your place," he said.

"You can't replace me. These are my soldiers."

"So we'll both go," he insisted.

"Yoni," I shot back in despair, "what are you saying? What if something happens to both of us? Think of Father and Mother."

Then he said something I will never forget.

"Bibi," he said, emphasizing each word, "my life is my own and my
death is my own."

I was stunned. Nine years earlier, as a seventeen-year-old, Yoni had written to a friend: "Death does not frighten me. I don't fear it because I attribute little value to a life without a purpose. And if I should have to sacrifice my life to attain its goal, I will do so willingly."[3] Even though I would read this letter only after Yoni's death, I sensed that same iron determination during those moments in the airport.

Regaining my composure, I pushed back.

"I'm not leaving and you're not going!" I said.

Deadlocked, we went to the Unit's commander, Ehud Barak. He sided with me. I rejoined my men to prepare for the assault.

An IDF film clip from the staging area in the airport shows Yoni pacing back and forth, frowning, a young lion caged. While he waited in the staging area with Moshe Dayan, Transportation Minister Shimon Peres, and others, we sixteen "mechanics" boarded a baggage train and made our way to the hijacked plane. We stopped about one hundred meters away at a checkpoint manned by Red Cross personnel. It had been agreed that the Red Cross would conduct body checks to assure the terrorists that the mechanics were unarmed. This was a trick Dayan had prepared, along with several buses brought in full view of the plane and packed with the terrorists' supposedly released comrades.

As the hijackers watched from the cockpit and the plane's front door, a Red Cross official frisked us. Feeling the weapon in my boot, he whispered "Mon Dieu" ("My God"), but he did not alert the terrorists. Contrary to later descriptions, I did not pull out the pistol from my boot, but merely responded "Dieu est grand" ("God is great") in my elementary French.

We were let through.

My men and I climbed onto our wing. We waited for Barak—who stood on the tarmac below—to blow a whistle, our signal to storm the aircraft. My wing members included my able soldier Arik Gerstel and a Unit veteran who was an air marshal.

Air marshals had expert training in handguns and planes, so we incorporated as many of these specially trained Unit veterans as we could find in the airport into the storming party. One of them was the Unit veteran Mordechai Rachamim, who had courageously thwarted a terrorist attack in 1969 against an El Al plane at Zurich International Airport.[4]

Just as we were set to storm into the cabin, the air marshal attached to my team tapped me on the shoulder.

"Bibi," he said, "tell Ehud to stop the operation."

"Why?" I asked. "What's the problem?"

"There's no problem," he explained. "I flew in from London. The plane was packed and I couldn't get to the toilet. As soon as I landed in the airport, you guys picked me up and I never had a chance to go."

"You have to go *now*?" I asked.

"Now," he answered emphatically.

"Big or small?" I asked.

"Big," he said.

I jumped off the wing and explained the situation to Barak. He held off blowing the whistle; the veteran went under the fuselage to relieve himself and then resumed his position on the wing.

Barak blew the whistle. We struck the door from the outside. It bounced outward. A terrorist in the aisle opposite our entrance fired several shots at us and ran toward the front of the plane. He was cut down by one of our men coming in from the other wing. Another terrorist in the front of the plane was killed by Rachamim as he stormed the cockpit.

One of the bullets fired at us hit the forehead of a young woman sitting next to the door. She slumped forward dead. I rushed past her and searched for the two female terrorists.

"Here's one of them!" shouted a passenger, pointing to a woman sitting in one of the seats. I yanked at her hair, only to have her wig come off. Grabbing her by her real hair, I pulled her to her feet.

"Where are the charges?" I shouted, fearing they would be detonated and blow up the plane. Seeing this, Marco Ashkenazi, another Unit veteran and air marshal, ran toward us shouting, "Bibi, let me deal with her!"

Before I could stop him, Marco slapped the woman's face with his pistol, releasing a single shot in the process.

The bullet tore through the woman and lodged itself in my left arm. It felt like I'd been hit with a sledgehammer.

The whole operation took less than two minutes. The two male terrorists were killed, the two women captured. The only civilian casualties were the young woman killed next to me and a passenger who rushed toward my fellow officer Uzi Dayan, the defense minister's nephew and a team commander in the Unit, who had rushed in from another entrance. Taking the passenger for a terrorist, Uzi shot him several times in the stomach. Thankfully, he survived. The only other casualty was me. I was taken off the plane and laid out on the tarmac. A medic gave me a shot of morphine to ease the pain. I saw Yoni running toward me from a distance, a look of terrible anxiety on his face. As he approached he saw that I was alive and fully conscious. Standing over me, he took in the red splatter of blood on the white sleeve of my mechanic's overalls.

A big grin spread on his face.

"See, Bibi," he said. "I told you not to go."

I was lucky. The bullet hit neither nerve nor bone. Once the doctors took it out, all that was left was a scar. I resumed my service as a team commander in the Unit and was released from military service a year later.

Four years after the Sabena rescue, on July 4, 1976, the American Bicentennial, my brother Yoni, by then a lieutenant colonel and commander of the Unit, led his men to rescue hostages from another hijacked aircraft. This time Palestinian and German terrorists hijacked an Air France plane bound from Tel Aviv to Paris after they boarded it in a stopover in Athens. They diverted the plane to Entebbe, Uganda, in the heart of Africa. Having learned their lesson from Sabena, the terrorists were certain they were now beyond Israel's reach.

They were wrong.

Landing in the dead of night at Entebbe Airport, Yoni's force killed the terrorists and the Ugandan troops aiding them, destroyed the MiG fighter jets that could give chase to the force's return flight to Israel and liberated 102 hostages. A few of the Unit's storming party sustained slight wounds. One brave soldier, Surin Hershko, was wounded in the neck, leaving him paralyzed for life. Two Israeli civilians, Jean-Jacques Maimoni and Ida Borochovitch, were killed in the crossfire. A third, Pasco Cohen, was seriously wounded and later died from his wounds. Dora Bloch, an elderly woman taken to hospital before the raid, was murdered the next day by orders of Uganda's dictator Idi Amin. The only military fatality in the mission was Yoni, who fell while leading his men in storming the terrorists. In his honor the Rabin government officially renamed the historic raid "Operation Jonathan."

The raid on Entebbe would become perhaps the most celebrated rescue mission in modern times. Drew Middleton, the military analyst at the *New York Times*, described it as an "operation with no precedent in military history."[5] The paper ran an editorial the day after Entebbe titled "A Legend Is Born." And indeed, that is what the raid on Entebbe would become. Yoni, too, instantly emerged from anonymity to fame. In military circles he was already known as an outstanding commander, a person of exceptional intelligence and dedication to Israel, a decorated soldier who put himself in the line of fire again and again. Moshe Dayan wrote in his autobiography six months before Yoni fell: "I do not know how many young men there are like Yoni. But I am convinced that there are enough to ensure that Israel can meet the grim tests which face her in the future."[6]

Yoni was my extraordinary older brother, and for my younger brother Iddo and me he was our North Star, guiding us through life's labyrinthine paths and serving as a model to be emulated. In so many crossroads in my life, I benefited from his advice and support. Yet his influence on me was even deeper than that. Israel's very existence was continuously challenged. I felt that as long as Yoni was alive, he would rise to great heights and help secure its future.

When the news reached me that Yoni had died in Entebbe, I felt as if my life had ended. I was certain I would never recover. To understand why I felt this way I will share with you the events in my life that led me to that point. Then I will tell you how Yoni's sacrifice and example helped me overcome inconsolable grief, thrust me into a public battle against terrorism, and led me to become Israel's longest-serving prime minister.

Asked in a 2011 television interview how I wished to be remembered, I answered simply: "That I helped secure the life of the Jewish state and its future."[7]

2

ROOTS

1949–1957

W hat do I remember from my earliest years?

Our house on the corner of Ein Gedi Street in the garden neighborhood of Talpiot in South Jerusalem. It was a one-story home with tall ceilings, shaded by cypress trees. These were the years of spartan austerity that followed the end of Israel's War of Independence in 1948, a year before I was born. Determined to ensure that our family would have enough to eat, my mother raised chicks in our backyard. They were soon devoured by weasels. She found other ways to pamper us. In this she was helped by her friend Tessie from New York, who sent us food packets. What a wonder it was for me as a toddler and my brother Yoni to peer through those packages and discover glistening chocolate bars embedded in nylon stockings, along with other bounties sent to us from that magical land across the sea, America.

Soon, when I was three years old, my brother Iddo arrived. I vividly recall him confined in his crib, wailing in protest as his older brothers played freely around him. Perhaps some constraints on Yoni and me should have been in order: in one of my forays I explored an electrical socket with my mouth and the electrical current tore my upper lip, leaving a permanent scar. Often asked about it, I never claimed it was a battle scar. Those would come later.

Jerusalem in those days resembled more a sleepy town than the sprawling, vibrant metropolis it is today. The quiet Talpiot neighborhood where we lived was home to a few prominent intellectuals, writers and scholars, of which my father, Benzion Netanyahu, was one. As early as I can remember I knew my father worked on something called "the sicklopedia."

A historian by profession, Father was the editor of the *Encyclopedia Hebraica*, which he modeled on the *Encyclopaedia Britannica*.

We led a comfortable life by Israeli standards because he was handsomely paid for producing a new volume each year. By 1959 the encyclopedia was purchased by 60,000 families out of Israel's roughly 450,000 households,[1] an impressive 14 percent, meriting our reputation as the People of the Book. My father broadened the orientation of the encyclopedia from a narrow Jewish one to one of general knowledge with emphasis on Jewish subjects. Families would wait for the next volume to come out, perusing the entries for their own erudition. The secret to the encyclopedia's great success, my father said, was *clarity*. Eighth graders and doctoral students, he said, should be able to read and understand with equal ease complex entries made simple by his rigorous editing. And they did.

Father had a decidedly empirical approach to the search for truth and an intimate familiarity with Jewish history. He once asked his science editor, Professor Yeshayahu Leibowitz, to review an entry on the origin of the universe submitted to the encyclopedia by a British scholar. Leibowitz, later an icon of the Israeli left, was my father's friend. An eccentric who visited our home frequently, he combined devout religiosity with scientific expertise.

Sometime after my father requested the entry, Leibowitz submitted his edited version of the British scholar's essay on the various theories of the universe's creation. My father read it with great interest.

"Leibowitz," he said, "you crossed out the theory that the universe was created by an omnipotent force. To me that makes as much sense as the other theories. You are, after all, a religious man. Don't you believe in this possibility?"

"My dear Netanyahu," Leibowitz said, "from a religious point of view of course I believe it. But scientifically? It doesn't hold."

Like his prolific mathematician brother, Professor Elisha Netanyahu, who was among the founding members of the math department at the Technion (Israel's MIT), Father retained an unquenchable intellectual curiosity until the end of his life. In his nineties, he gave me two books he had just read, the first describing the development of the atom bomb and the second a biography of Richard Feynman, the Nobel Prize–winning physicist.

In many ways he was an intellectual descendant of our distant relative, the Vilna Gaon, the great Jewish sage who two hundred years earlier instructed yeshiva students to add mathematics and physics to the study of the Scriptures.

As a historian, Father sought the unvarnished truth and went where the facts took him. He would study historical developments with great depth, balancing conflicting theories and data, and only then make up his mind. But once he did, he was fearless in defending his views.

My father's mentor, Professor Joseph Klausner, lived on a hill around the corner from our house in Talpiot. Klausner was a world-renowned historian of Second Temple Jewish history. He had written two definitive works on the origins of Christianity, *Jesus of Nazareth* and *From Jesus to Paul*. He was also a great expert on modern Hebrew literature. A linguist, he had invented the modern Hebrew words for "shirt," "pencil," and many other terms. The rebirth of the Jewish state required the revival and modernization of ancient Hebrew, a task undertaken by several ingenious scholars, including Klausner.

As small children, Yoni and I of course knew none of this as each Sabbath we made our way to Klausner's house, on whose door mantel he had inscribed the words "Judaism and Humanism," the title of one of his books.

Crossing a field, we would pick flowers along the way, which we would give the professor in a fixed ritual. Klausner would greet us at the door, a kindly bespectacled man in his late seventies with a white goateed beard. A widower with no children and living alone, he would always greet us warmly.

"Welcome children," Klausner would say.

"Shalom Professor Klausner," Yoni would respond for both of us.

Klausner would then pose the obligatory question: "Tell me, Jonathan, did you come to see me or did you come for the chocolates?"

"Oh no, Professor Klausner," Yoni would unerringly respond, "I came to see you."

Klausner would then usher us to the living room, where he would pull out a box of chocolates from a heavy Central European cabinet. We would pick our choices.

Time after time, this procedure guaranteed success. Then a mishap occurred. One Saturday after Yoni assured the professor of the purpose of our visit, Klausner suddenly turned to me and asked, "And what about you, Benjamin? What did you come for?"

Three years old, I had never been confronted by such a question. Totally disoriented, I covered my eyes with my forearm to shield my bewilderment. For lack of a better answer I kept silent, stuck my other hand into my pocket, and thrust a bunch of crumpled flowers at my interrogator.

Klausner smiled. We got the chocolates.

This was not our only encounter with the great minds of the day. Next to our house was a green wooden shack that served as the neighborhood synagogue. As I peered from the outside through the slats, I saw Yoni join the other worshippers who included Klausner, the writer Shai Agnon, who would later receive the Nobel Prize in literature, and others.

"Why are you here alone, Jonathan?" they would ask Yoni.

"I am *Aduk*," Yoni answered, using an arcane Hebrew word for ultra-Orthodox.

"And where is your father?" they pressed.

"He is not *Aduk*."

That was definitely true, yet although we were a secular family, throughout most of our childhood my parents made Kiddush, kept Shabbat dinner and celebrated all the major Jewish holidays.

The affection that Yoni received from adults was mirrored by the respect he received from the children in the neighborhood. In the face of the unique, children often respond with either extraordinary cruelty or extraordinary respect. In Yoni's case it was the latter.

I remember him as a small boy surrounded by children almost twice his age. Quiet and serious, he was totally lacking in bravado. He never posed. Yet older children strangely looked up to him in a manner that would follow him throughout his life, until his tragic death.

Unaccompanied, my six-year-old brother would board the city bus each day to a school in another part of Jerusalem. Years later as a teenager

I would regularly take bus line No. 15, driven by Yitzchakof, the driver who earlier had driven Yoni on No. 7. Yitzchakof, whose arm was marked by a concentration camp number, would recognize me as I boarded his bus and ask me, "How is your brother? I never met a boy like him."

After the War of Independence in 1948, Israel enjoyed little quiet. It suffered Fedayeen (guerrilla) terrorist attacks from the Sinai Peninsula, then controlled by Egypt, and sniper fire from the Arab side of a divided Jerusalem, then controlled by Jordan. On September 23, 1956, Jordanian snipers killed four and injured sixteen Israelis at an archaeological dig in Ramat Rachel, a kibbutz that adjoined Talpiot. But our years in Talpiot in the early 1950s were tranquil.

Strolling with my mother down Ein Gedi Street, I could see soldiers training in the Allenby Camp, a military facility left to us by the British.

The soldiers were jumping over barbed wire.

"*Imma*," I anxiously said to my mother, "I could never do that."

Instead of saying something reassuring like, "By the time you grow up we'll have peace, so you won't need to," my mother said, "Oh, you'll do fine, Bibi. You'll grow up and you'll be able to do it."

Still, I doubt she could have imagined that eighteen years later her three sons would simultaneously serve in the same elite unit in Israel's special forces and tackle obstacles far greater than barbed wire.

My older cousin Binyamin Ronn, named like me and several cousins after my grandfather Benjamin, would play as a child in the fields near my aunt Zipporah's home by the sea. His younger sister Daphna would call after him, "Bi, Bi, where are you?" From that point on he was called Bibi. The name stuck in the family, even when my cousin became one of the first pilots in Israel's young air force. His nickname was passed on to me.

When I was three years old, we left Talpiot for a more spacious house in Jerusalem's Katamon neighborhood. Bullet holes from the War of Independence pockmarked the front of the house and the door handle. One of the few single-family homes in a neighborhood of apartment buildings, it was built in the 1930s and had served as a British officers' club.

While we children played in the back rooms, my parents would receive guests in the front part of the house, including leading scholars who had penned entries for the Hebrew encyclopedia. When we got too noisy my mother would come to the back and whisper, "Children, we have guests," as if this would convince us to quiet down. It did not. We would often crowd the neighborhood kids into one of the rooms, shut the blinds to create total darkness, smash anything that moved with pillows and then turn on the lights to see who was left standing. Our home was a battlefield in which childhood play clashed with scholarship. We delighted in it.

My parents have often been portrayed as harsh disciplinarians. Nothing could be further from the truth. Far from disciplining us, they let us wield a degree of independence virtually unimaginable today. If discipline was in order, it was usually provided by Yoni, who intervened to keep the peace between Iddo and me.

Being the middle child, I sometimes felt wedged in between my two brothers. On one occasion, I complained to Yoni that he was unfairly dividing a tray of homemade ice cream my mother had prepared for us.

"You and Iddo always get the bigger portions," I protested.

"Okay, Bibi," he said, a ten-year-old Solomon. "You divide it. But Iddo and I get to choose first!"

Gradually, Yoni oversaw a permanent peace between Iddo and me and our childish squabbles evaporated.

I was lucky to be surrounded by a loving family: a father of inordinate intellect, a mother of inordinate pragmatism and intelligence, a brother of inordinate character. And now I even got along with my younger brother, who grew more thoughtful and mature with each passing month.

Life was made even happier when our veterinarian uncle gave us Bonnie, a boxer dog named after Bonnie Prince Charles. My father, who had never had a dog, insisted that we wash our hands after each time we played with Bonnie. My mother, who grew up among orange groves and walked barefoot as a child, couldn't have cared less.

With great skill, my mother steered the obstacle course of raising three active boys and enabling my father to pursue his scholarly and editorial work, which he often did at home. She had a wonderful earthy sense of humor and established an easy and warm rapport with everyone, from the maid to the most uppity visitors. She also had an unerring sense for the practical. Her friends would always say, "Ask Cela. Cela knows what to do."

My father was smitten with the pretty and vivacious Cela Segal when they were students in 1930 at the newly established Hebrew University, located on Mount Scopus in Jerusalem. Consumed by the intellectual and political pursuits of Zionism, the movement to establish a Jewish state in our ancient homeland, he could hardly compete with a charming fellow student, Noach Ben Tovim, who courted her more effectively.

She proceeded to marry Noach and joined him as Zionist emissaries to Finland. Years later, on a visit to Helsinki, I met members of the Jewish community there who told me that they had learned Hebrew from my mother. The couple later went to London, where she began studying law at Gray's Inn.

Noach was heartbroken when she later divorced him.

Some years later, in the United States during World War II, she met my father again when he was there on a Zionist mission. He hadn't married and had never stopped longing for her. She decided to give him another chance.

My mother told me she always knew she wanted to have children with him.

A brilliant woman in her own right, she would add with a sigh, "I married a genius, but even a genius needs to have his socks laundered." Which is just as well, because until he married my mother my father would often wear socks of a different color on each foot.

When Father's great historical work, *The Origins of the Inquisition in Fifteenth Century Spain*, was published in 1995, it garnered exceptional praise and is now considered a standard work on the subject.

Father ended the book with an acknowledgment to Cela. "She was my first research assistant," he wrote, "my first reader, and my first critic, whose astute judgement I always valued. . . . Judging by the sheer volume of her work, it took a good part of her life. And who can find words adequate enough to express due gratitude for such an effort? Nor can I duly acknowledge her support in times of travail and tragedy. Yet here are my thanks, inexpressible as they are."[2]

He loved her dearly.

Father combined an incredibly incisive mind with the habits of an absentminded professor. Sometimes he would dial himself on our phone, one of the few in the neighborhood. When no call came through, he would call my mother for help.

My mother often said that her real name was "Cela Where." As in, "Cela, where are my glasses? Cela, where did I leave my book?" and so on. She was wonderfully attentive to his needs and yet she was no pushover. She spoke her mind and put her foot down firmly when necessary. She was the pivot of our family and the final authority in our home.

"Mother," I complained one rainy winter day, "you force me to wear rubber soles to cover my shoes. But all the other kids don't wear shoes. They just wear rubber boots over their socks."

"Bibi," she said firmly, "you're not like the other kids."

At times, when my brothers and I got too raucous even for her, she tried in vain to harness my father's paternal authority. I was often the source of the problem, being known in my childhood as the *akshan*, or the "stubborn one." On one exasperating occasion, after my mother despaired of her efforts to quiet me down, she said to my father, "Benze, you deal with him."

My father dutifully got up from the sofa to discipline me. Alarmed, I ran to the other side of the room and suddenly turned and faced him, a five-year-old with arms akimbo.

"Just because you're bigger than me doesn't mean you have the right to hit me," I lectured him, my first attempt at speaking truth to power. My father stopped dead in his tracks and pondered this.

"Cela," he said, "the boy is right," and excused himself from a task he wasn't planning to undertake anyway.

Despite his taxing workload, he was a doting father. A lover of Westerns, he sought to entice Yoni and me in our early childhood to eat breakfast by entertaining us with stories of how we galloped in the prairies of the Wild West on our two horses, Lolo and Pico, with him playing the role of Gary Cooper. Try as we might, we couldn't recall that we took part in these adventures, but Father assured us that they really happened, as long as we kept on eating. He clearly had a hidden adventurous streak.

Next to the Hebrew encyclopedia's office there was a bicycle shop where he brought Yoni's bike for repair. The neighborhood kids were shocked to see the distinguished Professor Netanyahu racing down Palmach Street on the bicycle one day, his tie flailing in the wind behind him.

Years later I found my elementary school notebooks with homework from history class. They were packed with immaculate compositions about historical episodes I studied at school. Though written in a child's handwriting, they were clearly dictated to me by him. Naturally, my grades in history were excellent.

As I got older, my father gradually weaned me from the practice of relying on him for composition. "Write it yourself first, I'll edit it later," he'd say. This was followed by, "Now edit it yourself."

From a very early age he would ask me, "What are you trying to say?" When I told him he would say, "So write exactly that." He would trim the fat, eliminating unnecessary words to enhance the core idea. He also inspired me with unique insights into the history of our people. I could ask for no better teacher.

It took years for the full weight of my father's influence to dawn on my brothers and me. Years later, in one of his letters to me from Harvard University, Yoni wrote, "The more I talk with Father, the more I value him as a thinker and an educator. He is a great man with enormous capacities in many, many areas."

Guided by Father, I gradually became aware of the unprecedented historical time my generation was living through. It wasn't initially obvious. We were "normal" children living in a "normal" country, well adjusted, outgoing, confident in our patrimony, no different from children growing up in America, France, or Sweden.

It gradually dawned on me that Israel was unlike any other country. For one thing, it had to constantly defend itself against the repeated attempts of its Arab neighbors to destroy it. For another, the Jewish people had an utterly unique history. Time and again we had come back from the dead, most recently from the worst horror ever inflicted on any people. I was part of a new generation of Jewish children coming into its own in the Jewish state a mere few years after the slaughter of a million and a half Jewish children in the Holocaust. This was anything but normal. It was miraculous.

My brothers and I relished the outdoor life that characterized children's society in Jerusalem during the 1950s and early 1960s. We would light campfires in the Katamon fields and in the Valley of the Cross, next to the fifth-century monastery that tradition marked as the place the tree used in the crucifixion was taken from. We played soldiers on the hill studded with olive trees that now houses the Israel Museum and pretended we were Maccabees fighting Greeks with makeshift bows and arrows in the small wood next to our home.

Tellingly, in our school play, Theodor Herzl's *Solon in Lydia*, Yoni was dressed up as a stalwart military commander. Even at eleven, he looked the part.

My father would periodically go to the great libraries of Spain as part of his research into the history of the Jews in medieval Spain. His interest in this subject was piqued by his previous work on Don Isaac Abravanel, the leader of Spanish Jewry during the expulsion of the Jews from Spain in 1492.

When my mother joined him on his visits, they would send us postcards with ornate pictures of the gardens of the Spanish palaces I would later see for myself at the Madrid Peace Conference in 1991.

During one of their visits in 1956, the Suez Crisis broke out. Seven years after Israel's independence, Egypt's dictator Gamal Abdel Nasser nationalized the Suez Canal, built and owned by the French and British, and closed the Strait of Tiran, choking Israel's essential maritime gateway to Asia. In the intervening years he launched Fedayeen attacks from the Sinai into Israel's southern communities. He vowed to unite the newly independent countries of the Arab world and destroy Israel.

Israel secretly colluded with France and Britain to break the stranglehold. Britain and France would send paratroopers to seize the Suez Canal Zone, while Israeli paratroopers would seize the strategic Mitla Pass, thirty-two kilometers east of the canal. Other IDF forces would destroy the Egyptian army and terrorist bases in the Sinai.

The British and French seized the canal. The IDF seized the Mitla Pass, smashed the Egyptian army and conquered the Sinai within days. While the plan worked, the military gains were soon rolled back by a joint US-Soviet ultimatum to Britain, France and Israel to withdraw from the Canal Zone and the Sinai. In exchange for its withdrawal, the US gave Israel a guarantee that the Strait of Tiran would always remain open.

In Madrid, my parents heard dispatches from Cairo that described the Israeli army's "humiliating defeat" by the Egyptian army and the impending conquest of Israel. They didn't buy it, but nevertheless headed home to be with their children. That took a few days. In the meantime, we children helped maintain the mandatory blackout by plastering the windows in the neighbor's house where we were staying. Many of my friends' fathers were mobilized for military duty in the reserves during the Sinai operation. One of them rolled into the neighborhood in a dusty Jeep and handed us candy he brought from the captured Egyptian town of El Arish.

"I paid for them," he pointedly told us.

Even if my father had been present in Israel during the Suez operation, it is unlikely that he would have been drafted for reserve duty. His sole experience with the military was brief. Like all Israeli men in their forties, he had been summoned to reserve duty.

After a night in one of the Jerusalem outposts overlooking Jordanian positions on the other side of the divided city, he caught a terrible cold. In a live drill before assuming his watch, he pointed the gun he was given in every possible direction but the target. His superiors never called him up again.

Other than the blackouts, my memories of the brief war consisted of listening to the radio reports on the latest advances of our troops, the exhibits of captured military hardware at the Independence Day celebrations after Suez, and the playing cards that we children exchanged with each other that bore the pictures of tanks, warplanes and the like. These were our baseball cards.

3

AMERICA

1957–1959

In 1957, my parents told us that we were going to America for a few years. My father had taken an extended leave from editing the encyclopedia to pursue his historical research in the great libraries of New York. He also traveled twice a week to Philadelphia, where he taught at Dropsie College.

Remembering the care packages sent by my mother's friend Tessie from New York, we were filled with anticipation. The first part of the odyssey was an exciting sea voyage on the ocean liner *Theodor Herzl*. We cruised past the Strait of Messina and the Stromboli volcano and cheered the dolphins racing alongside the ship.

After ten days we sailed past the Statue of Liberty and gazed at the skyscrapers of New York. Such buildings hardly existed in embryonic Israel. No wonder I would always identify with the stories of new immigrants arriving in America through that mythic port, which I later learned included my forebears on my mother's side of the family.

My parents rented an apartment in the Kimberly Hotel in Manhattan. Its mildewed lobby was graced with a manually operated elevator attended by a uniformed bellboy, as well as a Coke machine. I recall my amazement holding the dark greenish bottle glazed with frosting as it came out of the dispenser. Until we were placed in Manhattan schools, my brothers and I had a grand time. At night we could see the street-cleaning machines from the hotel window; by day we would go up and down the escalators at Macy's or visit the rooftop terrace of the Empire State Building, built twenty-six years earlier. What marvels New York had in store for us!

There was more. In Israel we had no lack of uncles, aunts, and cousins. Not surprisingly, many on my father's side were named Nathan, after my paternal grandfather. But in America we were introduced to uncles, aunts and cousins we had never met before. These were the families of four of my father's eight siblings who made their fortune in the steel business in America. Being business oriented, they found it hard to thrive in the socialist economy of early Israel.

Coming to the US, these four uncles found a niche in the global steel trade and prospered. They lived in the affluent suburbs of New York and New Haven and Hartford in Connecticut. We roamed their spacious homes and played with our cousins on immaculate green lawns. The oldest among them was fifteen-year-old Nathan Mileikowsky, with whom I later formed a lifelong bond.

Yoni, Iddo and I raced on my uncle Hovav's speedboat on Long Island Sound and watched the wondrous device called television for the first time. But the parade of wonders ceased when I entered Manhattan Public School 166 in the third grade.

Thrust into a strange tribe with unfamiliar customs, I hardly knew a word of English. I disliked the mandatory drinking of a carton of milk at 10 a.m. and the strange game of baseball, played in a fenced-in concrete yard that contrasted so sharply with the open spaces of Jerusalem.

My teachers sat me next to a little Jewish girl named Judy. Her job was to teach me a few words of English each day. She did so diligently, using picture books with explanatory words printed in large letters, the foundations of my early English education.

"See Spot. Spot is a dog. Run, Spot, run."

Thus, at the age of eight, I began to simultaneously speak and read the language. My mother ensured rapid progress by teaching me how to pronounce English words, especially how to say *the* as opposed to *zee*, as pronounced by most Israelis.

"Press your tongue to the palate of your mouth behind your upper teeth," she said along with other trade secrets.

She had been spared this learning experience because at home her mother spoke English to her. At the end of World War I, when she was six years old, her own parents had taken her from Petach Tikva to Minnesota, where she perfected her flawless English. I grew up with "An apple a day keeps the doctor away" and the like, thinking that this was part of our Jewish heritage. I later learned that she absorbed such pithy sayings from her Scandinavian neighbors.

At the close of the nineteenth century and in the first decades of the twentieth, my mother's family migrated in stages from America to Zion. My mother's maternal grandfather, Abraham Marcus, had migrated to America from Lithuania in the 1870s. Trading furs with Native Americans in Minnesota, he amassed enough money to finally realize his dream to settle in the Land of Israel.

In 1896, the year Theodore Herzl wrote *The Jewish State*, Zionism's foundational text, Abraham came to the Holy Land and became a farmer in the early proto-Zionist community of Rishon LeZion (First of Zion). One of the few Jews to emigrate to the Holy Land from America, he was called "the Amerikaner" by the other Jewish settlers, who came mostly from Eastern Europe and Russia with no American detour.

Abraham was good-natured and well liked. He entertained the children of Rishon by letting them take turns riding his trained mule to which he gave commands in English, eliciting squeals of delight.

But Abraham was to run afoul of the older residents. Unlike the other Jewish farmers who employed cheap Arab labor, he employed newly arrived Yemenite Jews. What's more, he planned to donate part of his homestead to build a new synagogue for Yemenite Jews. This aroused vehement opposition from his neighbors.

The chairman of the community council, Aharon Mordechai Freeman, convened a special meeting on November 7, 1910.

"A rumor has reached us that the honorable gentleman, Abraham Marcus, is building on his lot in Jerusalem Street a special house of prayer for the Yemenite *Olim* [immigrants]," Freeman began.

"The neighbors Mr. Mordechai Branitzky and Mr. Menashe Meirovich have complained that the prayers and customs of Yemenite Jews are noisy and different from those of Ashkenazi Jews. They say this will disturb their rest and annoy them. They've asked us to convene this special meeting to prevent this from happening."

Council member Meirovich pitched in: "I tell my distinguished colleagues that this is unheard-of. No house of prayer with strange customs was ever built on our land."

Chairman Freeman disagreed: "The honorable gentleman is wrong. I built on my land a synagogue for Jews from Spain to commemorate the soul of my dearly departed wife."

Another council member, Yaakov Medalia, objected: "This is different. Our Spanish brothers are civilized."

The entire committee decided against the chairman to "prohibit the honorable settler, Mr. Marcus, to erect on his home lot a synagogue for Yemenites."

Abraham Marcus was not a man who gave up easily. He mobilized the Governing Committee of the Jewish Communities in Eretz Israel (the Land of Israel) and even turned for help to the Governing Committee of Hovevi Zion (Lovers of Zion) in Odessa. In the next meeting of the Rishon Council, this time in the presence of the public, Abraham rose to his feet and demanded to annul the previous decision. A big commotion broke out, which almost turned into a brawl.

The experienced chairman, Freeman, offered a compromise: "The honorable donor will sell the intended lot to one of his neighbors. With the proceeds received from the sale, he will purchase even more land at the edge of the community where he can build with full honors the synagogue for our Yemenite brothers."[1]

This solution was unanimously adopted. The neighbor Barnitisky immediately paid the required sum.

Abraham quickly went to inform his Yemenite friends of this development but was met with a stiff refusal. The proud Yemenites had had enough. They told Abraham that they would raise the funds among themselves and build their synagogue with their own means.

It didn't end there. Abraham received money to build a new synagogue for his brethren and he was determined to do so. One day he noticed in the synagogue where he prayed a member of the Suleiman family, Urphalim Jews who came from Aleppo in Syria after fleeing the town of Urpha in southern Turkey in 1896.[2]

Being a member of one of the few Urphalim Jewish families in Rishon at the time, Joseph Suleiman would crouch in the corner of the Ashkenazi synagogue silently reciting his prayers alone. He could not join the rest of the congregation because he followed the Urphalim prayer order, which was different from the Ashkenazi one.

Abraham solved the problem. He contributed the money to the Suleiman family to buy a lot in Rishon on condition that "they build on the lot a house of prayer at which they could pray in the custom of their community, the Urphalim."

In Passover of 1912, Abraham was invited as the guest of honor to the newly erected synagogue. On that very lot, No. 3 Molcho Street in Rishon LeZion, stands a synagogue today that serves Sephardi Jews.

Evidently my great-grandfather, like me, identified with *all* "Twelve Tribes" of Israel and stood up to condescension by one group toward another. I encountered in my life many similar situations.

When some people patronize me and ask, "How is it possible that a highly educated Ashkenazi Jew like you, coming from a well-to-do home, the son of a renowned historian, an officer in an elite unit and a graduate of the best schools in the world, could be the leader of a party supported by so many from the lower classes?" I reply with two words: "Abraham Marcus."

Then I add, "Oh, and they are *not* lower classes."

When he came to the Holy Land, Abraham left his daughter Mollie (Malka) behind in Minneapolis. At the age of seventeen she married my twenty-year-old grandfather Benjamin "Simon" Segal (no relation to the infamous Benjamin "Bugsy" Siegel). Childless for thirteen years, the couple then had seven children in quick succession. My mother was the youngest.

Born in Kovno, Lithuania, in 1867, Benjamin Segal escaped conscription at the age of sixteen to the tsarist army, where multitudes of young Jews often faced forced conversion, illness and death. Arriving penniless at Ellis Island in New York, he ended up in Minneapolis and ran a successful scrap iron and real estate business. Within a few years he was recognized by the city leaders as one of a handful of businessmen who changed the economic landscape of the city. My grandfather became especially innovative in advancing trade, connecting rail links and developing real estate projects.

A devout Jew like his father-in-law and an active Zionist, Benjamin was influenced by Abraham's example to migrate to the Holy Land. He sold his business and took Mollie and their six children to Petach Tikva (Gate of Hope), another early Zionist community. My mother was born there in 1912.

Before the family left Minneapolis, the local paper ran a big story celebrating this eminent member of the community who decided to follow his "life's dream" by going to the Holy Land to live there "the remainder of his days."[3]

Hundreds of people gathered at the railroad station in North Minneapolis to see them off. Some were brothers, sisters and relatives. Most were well-wishing friends.

Rabbi Shlomo Mordechai Silver greeted the carriage as forty-five-year-old Benjamin sprang out. The rabbi helped Malka and the six children disembark, led the crowd into the packed station, and gave an impassioned speech. It was cut short by the hooting of the locomotive as it slowly entered the station. The crowd broke ranks and ran to embrace the Segal family with hugs, kisses and tears. The family waved a moving good-bye as the train slowly departed the station on the long journey to Zion.[4]

This unusual and emotional send-off can only be understood in view of the rarity of the occasion. In the early twentieth century, Jews immigrated *to* America, not emigrated *from* America.

Conditions in Petach Tikva were harsh. Soon the money ran out and Benjamin decided to replenish the family fortune. He would return to Minneapolis, accumulate money and then rejoin his family.

But then World War I broke out and all passage was blocked to Turkish-controlled Palestine. Turkish soldiers chopped up the trees of the family's orange groves for firewood. They forcibly transferred the Jews of Jaffa to Petach Tikva.

Since the Turkish authorities suspected the local Jewish population of sympathizing with Britain, there was talk of a potential Turkish massacre against the Jews similar to the Armenian genocide of 1915. Fear was abundant, food was scarce. One of the first words my mother learned as a child was "ekmek," Turkish for bread.

Benjamin lost contact with his family during the war and was sick with worry. When the war ended, he was one of the first civilians to cross the Atlantic from America, using resourceful connections. Reunited with Mollie, they went back to Minneapolis, where my mother would spend a few years.

After Benjamin died of cancer in 1923, Mollie took her seven children and returned to their home in the orange groves of Petach Tikva. An outgoing girl, my mother was reunited with her childhood friends, who remained devoted to each other until the end of their lives.

Speaking accentless Hebrew and English and completely at ease in America and Israel alike, my mother was now in 1957 my indispensable guide to America.

She often took my brothers and me to Central Park to make up for Manhattan's confining spaces. We chased squirrels, rowed boats and played soccer with my father, who showed glimmers of a missed athleticism. He was broad-shouldered and most of his life had an athlete's pulse but he seldom exercised.

When he was thirteen, he broke his leg in a soccer game in the city of Safed, in the Upper Galilee. His younger brothers present on that occasion later told me that they hovered above him as he lay on the ground. Twisting in pain, he cried out, "Oh children, children! How great is the agony!" Quintessential Benzion, they would chuckle.

In all the years that I knew my father, I heard him rail occasionally against injustice and folly, but I never heard him utter an obscenity, which is what I would have done had I broken my leg on a soccer field.

Father's proclivity for poetry and immaculate Hebrew as a university student won him first place in a 1931 poetry contest sponsored by the newly established Hebrew University. When he went to receive the prize, meant to be an astronomical ten British pounds, the clerk gave him only five pounds.

"Why five?" my father asked.

"It's a short poem," the clerk answered.

Protesting this injustice, Father went to see his teacher Klausner, who was one of the judges of the poetry contest. Klausner patiently listened to my father's protest at being shortchanged.

"Young man," he said, "in all the long history of Hebrew poetry, no one ever received five pounds for a poem. I advise you to take the prize."

He did.

Nearly a hundred years later, I was given a copy of my father's poem from Israel's National Archives. Along with it was a letter by Judah Magnes, president of the university, to Lord Rothschild, the recipient of the historic Balfour Declaration fourteen years earlier and the scion of the Rothschild family, which for decades had almost single-handedly funded the renascent Jewish communities in Israel.[5] Magnes informed Rothschild that "the winner of the poetry competition is 21-year-old Benzion Netanyahu, a student of history and philosophy."[6]

In New York, we moved to the less mildewed Cameron Hotel, but the awkwardness of being cooped up for hours on end remained.

One evening my parents went out, leaving Yoni in charge. Always the bigger eater among my brothers, I headed straight for a packet of marshmallows, an American snack for which I had developed a strong craving. Knowing this, my mother hid the marshmallows in the top cabinet of the apartment's small kitchenette, well beyond my reach. Ingenuity was required to overcome this obstacle. I opened the metal door of the bottom cupboard and stepped on it to extend my height. Suddenly I slipped and slid on the sharp-edged corner of the metal door. It cut a deep gash in my thigh. Blood squirted out like a crimson fountain. I screamed in pain and panic.

There followed a scene I will never forget. Yoni, twelve years old, immediately took charge. He spoke with such calm authority that I immediately stopped crying. He spread a big towel on the bed and had me lie on it. He instructed Iddo to fetch more towels and told him to help him put pressure on the wound to stop the bleeding. Afterward he cleaned the wound and bandaged it. When my parents returned, they were astonished by what Yoni had done.

And I had earned another nonbattle scar for life.

After six months in Manhattan, my parents decided to move for a year to Long Beach, Long Island. Here Yoni, Iddo and I could sit on a small pier and try our hand at fishing or skate in an outdoor skating rink, all dutifully recorded by my mother's home movie camera. As in Manhattan, my parents insisted on sending us to a regular American school as opposed to Hebrew school. Hebrew, they figured, we already knew. They wanted us to perfect our English and learn about America.

4

BACK IN ISRAEL:
BLISSFUL YEARS

1959-1963

In 1959, Father ended his leave from the encyclopedia. We made the sea voyage back to Israel on the ocean liner *Israel*, stopping in Gibraltar to feed the monkeys and in Athens to tour the Acropolis. The Katamon neighborhood kids greeted us like returning heroes. Unfortunately for me, the language problem resurfaced, this time in reverse. In America I had to learn English; in Israel I had to recover my Hebrew, which had fallen behind. When my report card showed average grades, my mother looked at it and said, "You know, Bibi, you can do better." It was the only time in my life that I can recall even the mildest pressure for performance from my mother.

Biographies of me often include descriptions of my parents supposedly pushing Yoni, Iddo, and me to excel. This was simply not true. Our parents didn't need to push us. We were competitive by nature.

Yoni set the standard. By his early teens he was brown-haired and handsome, of medium height and athletic build, with high cheekbones, a captivating grin, and penetrating brown eyes. He was a star pupil, much admired by teachers and peers alike.

Taking my cue from him, I quickly improved my grades. Visiting my elementary school some fifty years later, I was presented with the evaluation of Mrs. Ruth Rubenstein, my sixth-grade teacher. She characterized me (as she must have characterized many others) as someone who "grasps things fast, is active, civil and responsible, reads, carries out his duties with precision and timeliness, is socially integrated, happy, brave."

Where she got "brave" from I have no idea, because I don't remember anything in those years that required courage. But I was sufficiently "socially integrated" to attempt my first, and for the next twenty-six years my only, venture into politics. I was elected class president at the grand age of twelve. It was, I remember, astonishingly easy to get elected. All you had to do was be nice to everyone.

Though I was socially accepted, certain qualities separated me from my peers. I was bigger and matured earlier than most of my classmates (a gap that eventually corrected itself), and almost none of them had lived or even traveled abroad.

I briefly joined but never immersed myself in the Israeli branch of the international scouts movement, unlike Yoni, who had become a devoted scout leader, idolized by the youngsters in his charge. When I was twelve, Yoni, relying on my drawing skills, asked me to design a pennant for his troop. He was delighted by what I produced, and when the kids in Yoni's scout troop saw the pennant, they asked me why I didn't rejoin. I answered in jest that I was afraid I'd fail the test of knotting ropes. They didn't get the joke. "No, Bibi, you don't have to worry. You're sure to pass it."

Some of my friends had parents with concentration camp numbers tattooed on their forearms. This was seldom spoken of in the open, until the capture of the Nazi war criminal Adolf Eichmann. Seized by Mossad agents in Argentina in 1960, Eichmann was brought to Israel to stand trial.

"What do you think is the best punishment for him?" Mrs. Rubenstein asked our class.

She heard us out and then answered her own question: "The best revenge is to take him around the country and show him what we've done here."

The court thought otherwise. Eichmann was sentenced to death, the only person in Israel's history to be executed.

Years later I would offer a different answer to Mrs. Rubenstein's question. The most important response to Eichmann and his boss Hitler was to ensure that such a horror never befalls the Jewish people again.

My standing with my classmates took a hit when some of them received acceptance letters to an elite junior high school to which we had all applied. I had not received such a letter. Noticing my somber mood, my mother asked me what the problem was.

"Nothing," I said.

She persisted. Finally, I revealed the source of my misery.

"Oh my God," she said. "You mean this envelope? It's been lying here for weeks."

Thus I entered the prestigious Leyada School.[1] In those days most Israeli children studied the same core curriculum, consisting of Bible study (more historic and literary than religious), Hebrew, math, history, geography, science, some sampling of the Jewish Oral Law, and English (a freebie for me).

Although most of my friends came from homes that supported the Labor Party in politics, there was no palpable divide among us children. Besides, though my father had decidedly conservative leanings, he didn't belong to any party and we never discussed party politics at home. He certainly didn't disparage Israel's government in front of his children.

I distinctly remember one telling exception that occurred soon after we moved to our new home in Haportzim Street in 1953. Our house adjoined a beautiful Arab-style residence that the government had requisitioned to serve as the home of Finance Minister Levi Eshkol, who later replaced David Ben Gurion as prime minister. One day a caravan of government cars stormed into the neighborhood and stopped in front of the residence. All the neighborhood children flocked to see the spectacle of VIPs coming out of those limousines. My father and I went out to the porch to take in the scene.

After a moment Father dismissively uttered one word, "Pkidim" (bureaucrats), and went back inside the house.

This was undoubtedly the germination of a lifelong skepticism toward bureaucracy that I've carried with me ever since.

Yet I remember this incident precisely because it was so rare. If my parents' ideological beliefs were evident at all, it was only during family occasions like my Bar Mitzvah party, which was held in our Haportzim Street home. Among the guests were many prominent right-of-center writers and intellectuals, some of whom, like the great poet Uri Zvi Greenberg, have since assumed legendary fame and whose inscriptions I cherish in the books they gifted me.

My Bar Mitzvah was marred by my father's acute appendicitis. His fiercely loyal brothers filled his place and accompanied me to the President's Synagogue in the Rehavia neighborhood to read the customary portion of the Bible, where I had to deal with another challenge. The reading that week was from [The Book of] Kings 1, describing how the aging King David took Avishag, the Shunammite woman, to warm his bed. Somehow I made it through the embarrassing text. In this and in so many other events of my early years, Yoni always stood by my side.

He continued to be admired by all. In an athletic competition between high schools in Jerusalem, he won the broad jump for his school and twisted his ankle on the landing. His schoolmates, elated by the victory he gave them, carried him on their shoulders all the way home.

I was reminded of this incident years later, when Yoni was still alive, when I read A. E. Housman's poem "To an Athlete Dying Young":

The time you won your town the race
We chaired you through the market-place;
Man and boy stood cheering by,
And home we brought you shoulder-high.[2]

After Entebbe, when Yoni was carried home by his grieving soldiers, this poem echoed in my mind with its full tragic force.

While Yoni and I were as close as two brothers could be, he cared with equal devotion for Iddo. One day, as seven-year-old Iddo walked home from school, he saw a bent old lady dressed in black walking toward him with what looked to him like a stove on her back and a cane in her hand. Reminded of a Grimm fairy tale, he decided she was a witch out to hunt little boys.

Seeing Yoni with a group of his friends not far away, Iddo ran to them.

"What's the matter, Iddo?" Yoni asked him. "What happened to you?"

"A witch," Iddo panted, pointing breathlessly to the nearby field. "I see a witch!"

Howls of laughter erupted from Yoni's friends.

"A witch, he sees a witch," they taunted. Iddo grew ever more dejected for not being believed.

Yoni remained quiet. Seeing this, his friends stopped laughing. Yoni put his arm around Iddo's shoulders and walked his little brother home.

A short time later a friend gave Iddo a little sparrow he found in the woods. Iddo was delighted with his newfound pet. He put it in a cardboard box with a screen, padded the cage with dry grass, scattered bread crumbs in it and put in a tiny dish of water.

"You know what *dror* [sparrow in Hebrew, also the word for 'liberty'] means?" Yoni gently asked Iddo. "It means freedom. That's why this bird is called 'freedom.' Because it can't live without it."

Iddo set the bird free.

The next year, the three of us were sitting in the long entrance hall of our home.

"You're in the desert with another person, and you only have one canteen of water," I said, presenting Yoni with the classic Talmudic dilemma. "Either of you would need to drink all the water in the canteen to save himself. You can't split it. What would you do, take it for yourself or give it to the other person?"

Yoni thought a moment before answering. Then he said, "It would depend on who the other person was. If it were Iddo, let's say, I'd give him the water."

Iddo and I looked at our fifteen-year-old brother and we knew: he would do it.

One afternoon in 1962, my parents announced that our blissful years in Israel were coming to an end. They brought all three of us into our dining room to break the news that we would go to America once again for a few years so Father could again pursue his historical research while teaching graduate and doctoral students at Dropsie College in Philadelphia (it later became part of the University of Pennsylvania).[3]

We broke into tears. Our world collapsed. Yoni was an ardent scout leader and class president. Iddo and I would have to leave our classmates again. Our second journey to America had none of the excitement of our first visit. We knew America, we liked many things in America, but America was not our *home*. Yoni considered staying in Israel for his remaining year and a half in high school but decided against it. He gritted his teeth and came along.

Yoni knew that at eighteen he would leave home and go to the army. "This," he explained, "is the last time I would live with Father and Mother."

5

AMERICA AGAIN: NERDS AND JOCKS

1963–1967

Our second sojourn in America brought us three brothers even closer. My mother used to say that we were a mutual admiration society. Now we were brothers in misery.

My parents set up house in the well-to-do suburb of Elkins Park, in Cheltenham County north of Philadelphia. They chose to live there because it had good schools. Elkins Park's most notable landmark was a leaking pagoda-style synagogue built by the great Frank Lloyd Wright, not one of his better designs which I later learned to admire.

I attended Ogontz Junior High School, where I could communicate but not connect. Every morning when the students would recite the Pledge of Allegiance, I would stand respectfully silent. It was by no means an act of protest but a quiet affirmation of my Israeli identity, which was understood and accepted by students and teachers alike. I was an outsider.

Every student had to take on a sport. I played on the soccer team, a freebie for me since at the time soccer was relatively unknown in the United States. Coming from Israel, where we played soccer in the streets, it wasn't hard to excel. But one sport wasn't enough.

"Why don't you take on wrestling?" the gym teacher urged me. "You're a big guy."

Regrettably, my first attempt at wrestling pitted me against tristate champion Albert Betesh, who was in my weight category. Pinned to the mat and lacking any wrestling training, I tried too hard to forcibly unlock his hold and broke my ankle. I was consigned to stay home in a cast for three months. This was no boon to my social life, but it did wonders for my studies. The school sent my teachers to our home to ensure that I wouldn't fall behind, and by receiving one-on-one instruction, I ended up surging ahead.

Taking a foreign language was mandatory, and I chose French. My teacher, Mrs. Leventhal, was from Paris. My mother spoke some French, and bought me language tapes that, paired with Mrs. Leventhal's home visits, provided me with the rudimentary French that I would dredge up in later years during visits to Paris and the Francophile countries of Africa, and in my encounter with the Red Cross official during the Sabena rescue.

A year and a half after our arrival in America, Yoni graduated from Cheltenham High School and returned to Israel to enlist in the army. Our only contact with him was through the extraordinary letters he wrote during his basic training and his subsequent service as a paratroop officer. Even in the midst of military hardships, he never neglected the two brothers he left behind in America, often encouraging us to focus on our studies.

On August 1, 1964, a day before he joined the army, he wrote a note to Iddo.

"Congratulations Iddo on your twelfth birthday," he began. "Succeed and excel in all you do. Just as Father offers me advice, let me suggest something to you—learning is important above all else. The desire to study and acquire knowledge, to solve problems, to read and understand—these are the things that make a man great. At the same time you have to get along with the society in which you live—with your friends and most of all with Father and Mother. Be a good son and don't upset them. Actually, you have always been good, and it seems that I'm the one, more than any of us, who used to irritate them sometimes. Learn from my experience, Iddo."[1]

Those last lines were not true. My parents took immense pride and comfort in Yoni and in the way he treated Iddo and me. A month later he wrote my parents, Iddo and me after reading an essay I wrote for school: "Bibi wrote a really *extraordinarily* good composition. In my opinion it can be published anywhere."[2] Just to make sure I got the point, he followed up in a second letter to me: "You have an uncommon gift of expressing yourself in writing. I wish I knew half the English you do. You appear able to make use of all the English at your disposal. If you continue along these lines you'll be producing marvelous things. If you are capable of composing an essay like this in the tenth grade, who knows what you will write in the twelfth, and afterwards." [3]

He sometimes expressed the bond between us to others. "Today I received a letter from Bibi," Yoni wrote to his girlfriend Tuttie, later his wife. "It was quite unexpected, and you don't know how happy I was to receive it! I think I love him more than anyone else in the world. I didn't take my correspondence with him as something particularly important. Bibi exists, and that was enough for me. He knows me better than anyone else does. When Bibi writes about home, our parents and Iddo, I *believe* him. I feel as though I had actually been there and seen everything that was going on and had reported it to myself." [4]

After Mother, Iddo and I visited him in Israel in the summer of 1965, he wrote to my parents of the three of us: "No one could wish himself a better, more complete triumvirate." [5]

Our entire family waited with great anticipation for each new letter from Yoni. Iddo and I were intrigued by every military detail, including mention of his first battle in the Jordanian village of Es-Samu, from which terrorists had attacked Israel. It was the largest Israeli military operation since the 1956 Suez Crisis.

Emerging from the battle, Yoni observed that "there are people who lose all sense of reality under fire and don't know what they're doing, while others feel no change at all. I felt the same degree of concentration and judgement, the same grip on reality and the same level of tension I usually feel." [6]

Though Iddo and I couldn't get enough of these letters, they sometimes depressed us. While Yoni was doing these marvelous things in the army, we were stuck in American schools. Yoni tried to console me.

"Look," he wrote, "I can't go back to high school whereas you'll be able to jump from a plane if that's what you decide. Maybe you don't really understand the importance of doing your best in what you are engaged in at the present. And if you do understand this, as your successes indicate, then how on earth can you belittle your activities? I don't think

I learned half of what you are learning. If we were both students in the same class right now, I believe you'd outshine me in many areas."[7]

This hardly comforted me. He wrote similar encouragements to Iddo, but they didn't console him either. Iddo's classmates urged him, "Why don't you play baseball, Iddo? Don't you want to be popular?"

"No I don't," he replied dryly. Another outsider.

Though never completely shedding my sense of alienation, my own circumstances gradually improved. Cheltenham High School, which I attended after Ogontz, was a public school with high standards (though it was eventually best known as the alma matter of the baseball star Reggie Jackson). Of the 550 students in my grade, roughly a dozen were chosen for each of the special honors classes in math, social studies, science and English. I was among the lucky five who were chosen for honors classes in all four subjects.

Teenagers in Cheltenham High School at the time were sharply divided into nerds and jocks. Scholastically I definitely belonged to the nerds, but being athletically inclined I was also considered, if not a jock, at least a semi-jock. I earned the respect of the other side of the social divide.

This was buttressed by my decision to earn my lunch money by clearing dishes from the school cafeteria dishwasher. I didn't need the money, but I thought the act of earning it was important. My coworkers were mostly students who came from blue-collar homes and did need the money. They were astonished to see a nerd working alongside them.

Except for a non-Jewish student who ran marathons in high school and later became a neurosurgeon, a charming Catholic girl of Polish origins, and a Japanese American boy who told me about his Quaker family's troubling experiences in internment camps during World War II, most of my friends were Jewish. They were highly cerebral and well-read, swept by the intellectual currents of the day, idealizing Bob Dylan, analyzing Jean-Paul Sartre and other intellectual icons fashionable at the time.

They formed an informal debating society in which I became fairly adept. I joined the high school's official debate team and never lost a match.

I read voraciously, devouring Machiavelli, Hemingway and the American historian Will Durant, whose voluminous *Story of Civilization* I discovered through my father. I made a point to add new words to my vocabulary each day. I thoroughly enjoyed my classes. My teachers were exceptional. I owe them a great deal.

Mrs. Jane Balsham, my English teacher, asked me about Yoni, whom she had also taught. "He was always inquiring, always curious," she said. Yoni had written a short story, his first attempt at literary writing in English. Mrs. Balsham was so impressed that she stopped the press for the school magazine to include Yoni's composition.

Nearly half a century later, in 2011, Elizabeth Gentieu, another English teacher who taught Yoni, described how a boy in the class, "dark, handsome, thoughtful and reserved," read her Ze'ev Jabotinsky's Hebrew translation of Edgar Allan Poe's "The Raven" and "Annabel Lee." "He was from Israel," she wrote, "in the US to complete his education, but he was longing to return to Israel. 'But surely there must be some advantages to life here,' I said. He gestured with his hand as though advantages were a gnat and then uttered a sentence that has stayed with me: 'Here in America my classmates don't know what they are living for, but in Israel, we know.' "[8]

Throughout my years in America I yearned to see my friends in Israel, whom I joined only on summer vacations. As I went back to school in Philadelphia at the end of each summer, a clear dichotomy developed in my life. America became the province of the mind, Israel the province of the heart.

This sentiment became stronger when I was fifteen. I had a girlfriend in Jerusalem, Miki (Miriam) Weissman, who had joined my close circle of childhood friends. I spent all my summers with her and them. Eight years later, in 1972, we married.

Each summer I joined Miki and my friends for a few weeks' work on kibbutzim. After laboring in banana fields or pruning vineyards, we were given a free bus trip to a destination of our choice. It was summer camp without counselors, awash in adolescent camaraderie and infatuation.

On one of these visits, when I was seventeen, I joined my mother in the Negev city of Arad. She had recovered from an illness and loved Arad's dry desert air. By chance, Yoni, by then an officer, was stationed a few kilometers away. I walked to the wadi (valley) where he was training his platoon. He asked me to sit aside until he finished the exercise.

One by one Yoni asked his soldiers to conduct a live-fire drill. He walked behind them issuing orders. Suddenly one of them pointed his weapon in the wrong direction, endangering the other soldiers. Yoni sharply rebuked him, too sharply for my ears. The soldier melted under his criticism.

"Did you really have to come down on him so hard?" I asked him after the exercise.

He winked at me and replied, "That wasn't hard. That was necessary. And he'll never make that mistake again."

I realized then that he was in total self-control, fully aware of the effect his words and demeanor had on his subordinates. He sought to give them the skills to become better soldiers and possibly save their lives.

Then he handed me an Uzi submachine gun and said, "Come on, let me teach you how to shoot this thing."

I fired my first weapon with, shall we say, mixed results. It wasn't the last time we brothers broke military regulations.

Returning to the US for my final year of high school, I applied to all the Ivy League colleges. Planning to study architecture, I explained that I could only begin my studies after three years of service in the Israeli military.

Though I graduated in the top 1 percent of my high school class, all the colleges refused to consider this irregular request except Yale, which took the unusual step of accepting me three years in advance.

Later, after I joined the army, I asked for another one-year extension because of my service as an officer in a special unit. Amazingly, Yale agreed. Then I asked for another one-year extension. Again they agreed. I wrote back in appreciation.

Yet after five years in the military, where I was exposed to cutting-edge technology, I realized that I wanted to attend a university with a clear technological orientation. With much trepidation I wrote Yale a deeply apologetic letter explaining that I had decided to attend the Massachusetts Institute of Technology, MIT. I remain grateful to Yale.

As the end of high school approached and my army service beckoned, I adopted a daily regimen of physical exercise—running, swimming and lifting weights. This helped prepare me for what was coming, but only to a point. As I would soon discover, my military service in a special forces unit required much greater physical exertion. At times this physical exertion would be coupled with extreme psychological duress, and no amount of training prepares you for that.

War clouds began to gather over Israel as my senior year came to a close. As in the 1956 Suez Crisis, in 1967 Egypt's dictator Gamal Abdel Nasser once again choked Israel from the south by closing the Strait of Tiran. He demanded that the United Nations remove its peacekeepers from the Sinai, flooded the peninsula with 100,000 soldiers and threatened to destroy Israel.

Israel's prime minister, Levi Eshkol, sent Foreign Minister Abba Eban to Washington. Eban asked America to live up to its promise to keep the strait open, a guarantee that it had given Israel in 1956 when it forced Ben Gurion to withdraw Israeli forces from the Sinai.

"What guarantee?" was effectively the Johnson administration's response to Eban's request. President Lyndon Johnson was weighed down by the Vietnam War. He was not interested in confronting either the Arab states or the Soviets who backed them.

Israel was on its own.

Grasping what was happening, I asked the school to be relieved of my final weeks of study in order to return to Israel as soon as possible. Earlier that year I had sent a request through one of my uncles to his acquaintance, former deputy defense minister Shimon Peres, to bring forward my enlistment date from November to August 1967. As the clouds of war gathered, I wanted to hasten my arrival even more.

My desire to bring forward my return to Israel was not only motivated by the mounting military crisis. I had a premonition that something bad would happen to Yoni.

My parents did not try to stop me. They merely asked, "Are you sure there will be a war?"

"Positive," I answered. "The Arabs will go through with it. Besides, I want to see Yoni before the war starts." This sealed the matter.

My American friends held a modest farewell party for me, which genuinely moved me.

6

THE SIX-DAY WAR

1967

I landed in Israel on June 1, 1967. Like the rest of the country, the airport was enveloped in darkness. The blackout was necessary since it was assumed that the fighting could break out at any moment. Egypt and Syria were joined by Jordan in a military pact. All three pledged to annihilate the Jewish state.

Many Israeli citizens were gripped with fear. Graveyards for mass burials were prepared in case of disaster. Twenty-two years after the Holocaust, would we now face another extermination?

This mood did not penetrate the army. Yoni, who had been released from military service six months earlier, was now mobilized into reserve duty. Days before the war, he expressed the army's confidence in a letter he wrote to my parents: "Here there is no fuss and no panic. . . . If anything does happen, we can't lose. Our men are just too good. . . . In the end we will win decisively."[1]

The army waited for the government to decide what to do in the face of the ever-tightening noose around Israel's neck. Who would fire the first shot?

In a letter to his girlfriend a few days before the war, Yoni joked about this. "We sit and wait. What are we waiting for? Well, it's like this: An Englishman, an American and an Israeli were captured by a tribe of cannibals in Africa. When they were already in the pot, each of them was allowed a last wish. The Englishman asked for a whiskey and a pipe and got them. The American asked for a steak and got it.

"The Israeli asked the chief to give him a good kick in the backside. At first the chief refused, but after a long argument he finally agreed. At once the Israeli pulled out a gun and shot all the cannibals.

"The American and Englishman asked him: 'If you had a gun all the time, why didn't you kill them sooner?'

" 'Are you crazy,' answered the Israeli, 'and have the UN call me the aggressor?' "[2]

After sleeping overnight in a darkened Jerusalem, I went to search for Yoni.

In wartime, Israel's army consists of virtually all the able-bodied men in the country who are called up for reserve duty. The problem was where to find my brother among them.

"Look in the orchards around Ramleh," I was told through the unofficial grapevine that instantly and mysteriously spreads classified information to people who need to know in Israel, and to them alone. "That's where you'll find Brigade 80."

Trouble was, there were an awful lot of orchards around Ramleh. The reserve paratroop brigade was bivouacked under leafy shade to hide from possible aerial reconnaissance. I walked into one of their groves along the road leading from Ramleh to Gedera. Several reservists were preparing coffee on a makeshift stove. They were in their early thirties at most, but to me they looked far too old for this. They should have been home with their families, I thought.

"Yoni?" one of them said, scratching his head. "Oh yeah, the young guy. Look in the next grove."

I wandered through the next cluster of citrus trees, but I didn't find him. Then, at the other end of a long row of trees, I saw him staring at me in utter disbelief. "Bibi, what are you doing here?" he asked, and broke into his broad grin as we ran toward each other.

Over coffee I asked him what he thought was going to happen.

"We'll win," he said simply. "We have no other choice."

In the days before the war, I joined my friends in filling sandbags to protect building entrances and windows. This proved necessary.

On the morning of June 5, I was awakened by a deafening noise outside the apartment I was renting in Jerusalem. I ran to the roof and watched in fascination as Jordanian shells exploded meters away from my building in the heart of the city. Jordan had not heeded Israel's warning to stay out of the fray. Most of the shells fell in open spaces, but a number slammed into residences, killing twenty civilians and wounding hundreds. The Knesset (parliament) building and the Israel Museum, housing the ancient Dead Sea Scrolls, were also targeted but were not hit.

The Six-Day War had broken out. In a surprise preemptive air strike on the first morning of the war, the Israeli Air Force (IAF) destroyed the air forces of Egypt, Syria and Jordan. The IDF burst through Egyptian defenses in the Sinai and swept all the way to the Suez Canal. Amid the Jordanian shelling of Jerusalem, Israel defeated the Jordanian army and captured the territories all the way to the Jordan River in the east.

During the last two days of the war, the Israeli army finished perhaps the toughest task of all—conquering the formidable Golan Heights, which for nineteen years had been used by the Syrians to shell and harass the Israeli villages below. By June 11, the war had ended with a stunning Israeli victory. In six days the IDF conquered the Sinai, Judea and Samaria, Gaza and the Golan. Most enthralling, it liberated the Old City of Jerusalem.

The eastern part of Jerusalem, including the Old City, had been conquered by the Jordanian army during Israel's 1948 War of Independence. The Jordanians destroyed the Jewish Quarter and expelled all its Jewish residents, including families who had been living there for centuries. Now, after nineteen years of Jordanian occupation, these people could come back to their homes, in fact the entire *People of Israel* could come back home.

Israelis visited the Temple Mount, where King Solomon had built the first Jewish Temple three thousand years earlier, and the nearby City of David, which Solomon's father, King David, built and designated as Israel's capital, a designation maintained in the hearts of the Jewish people for three millennia. Divided by walls and barbed wire for nineteen years, Jerusalem was now a city reunited.

I had spent the war in an underground shelter. Reports about Israel's amazing victory cascaded down on Jerusalem along with artillery shells.

Some youngsters played Russian roulette with enemy artillery and ran in Jerusalem's streets. A few were killed. Though I was an adventurous eighteen-year-old at the time, I thought that risking one's life for nothing was the height of folly.

Now at war's end I could finally exit the shelter. Standing in the radiant summer sun, I took in the magnitude of what had happened. We had broken the siege, we ensured our survival, we were triumphant. Israel had achieved a victory of Biblical proportions. Things would never be the same.

But for me there was little time to rejoice. I had received word that Yoni had been wounded in battle on the Golan Heights four hours before the end of the war.

As a reserve paratroop officer he had taken part in several decisive battles, including the battle at Um Katef, which broke through Egyptian defenses in the Sinai. Landing with helicopters behind Egyptian lines, the paratroop force to which Yoni belonged attacked the Egyptian fortifications from the rear, clearing the way for the rest of the Israeli army.

On June 7, two days into the war, Yoni scribbled a postcard to his girlfriend, Tutti: "That's it. A battle has ended. I am well and all in one piece. We left the expanses of sand strewn with the bodies of the dead, filled with fire and smoke. . . . Right now it's a bit hard [to smile]. When you smile something inside hurts. Tonight, and maybe tomorrow or the day after, we'll be shooting again, and again there will be dead and wounded. I'll be alright but I'm sorry for the others. . . . I long and love. Try to find Bibi and tell him everything's OK."[3]

Yoni was later transported to the northern front with other paratroopers for the assault on the Golan Heights. In the final thrust against the fortified Syrian outpost of Jelebina, he reached out to help a wounded fellow soldier. Syrian fire smashed into his elbow.

Bleeding heavily, he summoned all his strength and crawled under the crossfire in excruciating pain toward the Israeli lines. Reaching safety, he collapsed and fainted. He was hospitalized in Safed. There were no details about the seriousness of his condition.

Full of trepidation, I entered the orthopedic ward in Safed's Ziv Hospital. Yoni lay in the last bed on the left, surrounded by amputee soldiers. His limbs were whole but his elbow was shattered. He was told he would be handicapped for life and relieved from military duty in the reserves. I breathed a sigh of relief. Yoni would now be permanently out of danger, never to face the hell of war and the risk of early death again. My fearful premonition hadn't materialized after all.

But I wasn't that far off. Four days after the war, Yoni wrote my parents from his hospital bed. "For me, it's enough to be alive. And I don't say that ironically. When you see death face-to-face; when you know there is every chance you too may die; when you are wounded and alone in the midst of a scorched field, surrounded by mushrooms of smoke from exploding shells, with your arm shattered and burning with terrible pain; when you're bleeding and want water more than anything else—then life becomes more precious and craved-for than ever. You want to embrace it and go on with it, to escape from all the blood and death, to live, live, even without hands and feet, but breathing, thinking, feeling, seeing and taking in sensation."[4]

I stayed by Yoni's bedside in the hospital in Safed and cared for my wounded brother. When I returned to Jerusalem, I joined the multitudes streaming to the Western Wall, then still hemmed in by shabby dwellings. Standing next to Herod's massive foundation stones—the ramparts of the Second Jewish Temple—I felt the pulse of history. The Rock of Our Existence, I later called that sacred place.

I could now visit the grave of my paternal grandfather in the ancient cemetery on the Mount of Olives. During the Jordanian occupation, many of the graves had been desecrated, the headstones used for building material. My family was lucky. My grandfather's grave was intact.

In the two months following the war and before my enlistment date in the IDF, I crisscrossed the newly liberated lands, touching the waters of the Jordan, bathing in the salty waters of Qalya in the northern edge of the Dead Sea, eating dates in Jericho, visiting Bethlehem, Hebron, Shechem. Here was the Bible brought to life, the past locking hands with the future. We were back in the heart of our homeland!

After our resounding victory, there was much talk of "Now the Arabs will sue for peace." To me this sounded naïve. I did not believe that their outright rejection of the Jewish state would be swept away so quickly. It would take, I thought, many more victories and many more years.

The talk of concessions only discouraged the Arabs from compromising. Yoni expressed this view six years later, in 1973: "I want peace very much," he wrote. "I don't like to live by the sword, a life of killing and trying not to be killed."[5]

But he also wrote, "I see with sorrow how a part of our people still clings to unrealistic hopes for peace. Common sense tells them that the Arabs haven't abandoned their basic aim of destroying the state. But the self-delusion that has always plagued the Jews is at work again. They want to believe, so they believe. They want not to see, so they distort [reality]. It would be comic if it wasn't so tragic."[6]

Decades later I often shared Yoni's frustration. We are a people of hope. Our national anthem, Hatikva, means hope. Without hope we would never have been able to rise from the ashes of the Holocaust and reestablish the Jewish state. But as I told my fellow citizens time and again, you can't build peace on hope alone and you certainly can't build it on false hope.

Sooner or later, a false peace will crash on the rocks of Middle Eastern realities. The real foundation of peace in our area is hope that derives from strength, and the consequent realization by our neighbors that Israel is here to stay.

A few weeks before my enlistment I visited Yoni in Haifa, where he had been transferred to Rambam Hospital and was to be operated on again. He was confined to the orthopedic ward.

"C'mon," he suddenly said to me, "let's get out of here and eat some good hummus at the port."

"What about the staff?" I asked.

"That's easy," he said, and reached for a doctor's white tunic that was hanging on the wall. He quickly put it on, covering his bandaged elbow. The two of us, "Dr. Netanyahu" and his younger brother, walked confidently out of the hospital through two checkpoints. After devouring two plates of hummus with semi-grilled pita, our favorite, we made our way back to Yoni's room. As he returned the doctor's tunic to its place, a young nurse saw him. One smile at her and she let it go.

On August 2, 1967, I enlisted in the army at the induction center in the Tel Hashomer base, near Tel Aviv. Planning to follow in Yoni's footsteps, I volunteered for the paratroops. But there was time to kill until the army's selection process was completed.

Cleaning latrines and sweeping kitchen floors, we fresh recruits were tormented by *jobnik* (noncombat) corporals. On one occasion Yoni showed up to visit me wearing jeans and a military tunic with a lieutenant's insignia. His injured elbow was in a sling. When he heard a corporal lash out at us for no reason, he took him aside and said something to him that made the corporal slink away.

"What did you tell him?" I asked him.

"That rank isn't a license for abuse," he answered.

But rank did demand discipline. Awaiting placement in the army's various units, we fresh recruits were clustered in large tents. When the staff sergeant yelled, "Everyone on the parade ground in sixty seconds!" one of the recruits lying on a field cot and leisurely smoking a cigarette blurted nonchalantly, "And if not?" He was summarily taken away by military police. Years later as prime minister I would be reminded of this incident every time somebody suggested a course of action that didn't take natural limitations into account.

"This is guaranteed to work, Prime Minister."

"And if not?" I'd ask. But unlike that soldier on the cot, I wasn't about to be taken away. Instead I'd insist, "Give me another suggestion."

After a few more days of screening in the army's induction center, I was admitted to the paratroops. I was ready to pack my gear when I recognized a high school friend of Yoni's in a sergeant's uniform approaching me.

"Hey, Katzer," I said. "What are you doing here?"

"I'm recruiting," he replied.

"What for?"

"The Unit. Come with me."

"What unit?" I asked.

"Never mind, just come with me."

"But I already volunteered for the paratroops," I said.

"Don't worry about that, we'll take care of it."

I consulted Yoni about this. Though a proud veteran of the paratroops, itself an elite force, he was unequivocal about the offer to join the Unit.

"Go for it," he said.

That is how I was ushered into Sayeret Matkal, the special forces unit of the Israeli army.

The founder of Sayeret Matkal was the legendary Avraham Arnan, who in 1957 had braved opposition from the army's top command to establish the Unit, which he gradually turned into a specialized, almost scientific force. He encouraged the Unit commanders to come up with imaginative and sometime wildly unconventional solutions to operational problems. What was important were the *results*, not the way you achieved them.

Arnan based the Unit on two models. The first was Unit 101, an IDF commando group in the early 1950s commanded by Ariel Sharon which included stellar warriors such as Meir Har-Zion. Though Unit 101 operated for a mere five months in 1953, it perfected nighttime navigation and specialized in night raids behind enemy lines.

Arnan also consciously copied David Stirling, the famed commander of the British Special Air Service (SAS), whom he had met.[7] All of us at Sayeret Matkal read *The Phantom Major*, Virginia Cowles's biography of Stirling, which detailed his daring raids across Nazi lines in North Africa in which he and his men destroyed hundreds of German aircraft.[8]

Years later, following Yoni's death in 1976, I was in London seeking support for an international conference on terrorism I organized in his memory. Shimon Peres, the defense minister, had introduced me to Nicholas Elliott, former director of Britain's MI6 intelligence service. Elliott brought me to White's, a club in the St. James's district. A very tall gentleman walked in.

"This is David Stirling," Elliott said to me.

"Sir," I said, standing up, "we in Israel have read the book about you. We've learned a great deal from you."

Stirling nodded. From an earlier meeting with Arnan he probably knew of the Unit, one of several outfits around the world that were modeled after the SAS. The Unit's dining hall was decorated with a big banner of Stirling's motto, "Who Dares Wins," shrunken even further to two words in the terse Hebrew translation. Years later, when I was prime minister, Sayeret Matkal officers gave me a small desk souvenir after they completed a daring operation I had authorized. "Who Dares Wins," it says, with a pointed addition, "When the Boss dares to authorize."

After some tests and questioning for the Unit, I joined a dozen other recruits. Most came from *kibbutzim* and *moshavim* (cooperative farming villages). A few like me came from cities.

Though we were a handful selected from a very large pool, our membership in the Unit was far from guaranteed. We would have to complete one of the longest and most grueling military training courses before we would be entrusted with the Unit's covert missions. Roughly half of us would make it, and this after a winnowing selection process that eliminated a far bigger number of initial candidates.

At the time, new recruits to the Unit did their basic training with the paratroops before joining the Unit itself. From the heat of summer and into the cold of winter, basic training consisted of weapon training, forced marches, fire exercises and soggy pup tents. The training was so demanding that every few weeks our boots would need to be fitted with new crepe soles.

I was soon hospitalized with pneumonia. After hospital, I was sent to a military convalescence home in Haifa, but I escaped back to basic training. A soldier convalescing with me called it "the stupidest thing you can do," adding, "Enjoy this while you can."

Basic training was followed by a parachuting course. Parachute jumps were already outmoded by then and principally served as a test of character. Helicopters were a more efficient way of transporting troops and supplies. But ethos and prestige mandated that we jump out of planes, so we did.

I can't say I enjoyed the jumps. Exiting the old French Nord planes, we were thrown into a windy turbulence, followed by a quiet descent until we suddenly saw the ground rushing at us. Altogether, in jump school and later in the Unit, I parachuted only fifteen times.

On the fifteenth jump, during an exercise simulating an airborne raid on an enemy artillery battery, I landed on rocky ground in the Negev. My right knee, which had been operated on in the US when I was sixteen, swelled to the size of a football. I was put on a stretcher and my teammates carried me to the staging area near the target.

The pain in my knee was exacerbated by the endless wobbling of the stretcher from side to side as my fellow soldiers carried me shoulder-high on the uneven terrain to the staging area. I was sure I'd fall from the stretcher and hit the ground a dozen times. It's always better to carry a stretcher than to be carried on it. We completed the mission, but I never jumped again.

In those days after the Six-Day War we hankered for action. One of our commanders in basic training, a blond sergeant with a Romanian accent who had seen battle a few months earlier in the war, said quietly, "Don't wish for it. You'll get your chance soon enough."

After several months of basic training and jump school, we were given a weekend pass before the obligatory march to the Unit.

"Rest well," they told us. "And show up on Sunday. First bridge south of Haifa."

7

THE UNIT

1967–1968

O n a winter day in 1967 I went to the Haifa home of Ilan Shapira, whom I had befriended in basic training. Ilan came from a South African family, and we often conversed in English. Over the years I intermittently stayed in touch with his family after he was killed in the Yom Kippur War.

Ilan and I made our way to the gathering point. We were given Uzis and started the 120-kilometer march to the Unit. Soon we were overtaken by one of the worst winter storms in decades. We marched along the sea and then on the roadbed on which Israel's coastal highway was later paved.

Toward the end of the march I helped pull two of my teammates forward who grasped the back straps of my gear. After less than twenty-four hours we crossed a makeshift Bailey bridge over a tributary of the Yarkon River to enter the Unit in the Kfar Sirkin air base.

Our travails didn't end there. We were greeted by unbelievably rude officers who harangued us and pushed us around. Where was the Unit's famous informality and camaraderie that we had heard so much about? After an hour or so, our tormentors suddenly stopped shouting at us and howled in laughter. They were members of the team a year ahead of us pretending to be officers in the unit's time-honored reception party.

The next day, muscles sore but spirits reinvigorated, we were asked to come to a big hangar. We assumed we would be issued our personal weapons but no weapons were to be seen. Instead we were given a pocket-size notepad and a pen with a string to attach to our shirt pocket.

"This," the commander said, "is one of your most important weapons. Write down every task you are assigned to do, and don't tear off the page until every task is accomplished."

Half a century later, I haven't shaken that habit. Every day I still write down tomorrow's tasks and cross off what got done from yesterday's list. Following through on details is not a pedantic compulsion. I know of no other way to get things done. Most of the people I have known who achieve big goals follow up on small details.

The next stop that morning was a classroom. In walked the commander of the unit, Lieutenant Colonel Uzi Yairi. A few years later he would be killed in a hostage rescue mission at Tel Aviv's Savoy Hotel. Yairi went straight to the blackboard and drew a dot.

"This is each of you," he said.

Then he drew a circle around the dot. "The circle is your team. Whatever you say beyond your team belongs to the entire world. So learn to keep the secrets you'll be entrusted with. Don't share them with others. Not with other teams. Not with your girlfriends. Not with your family. Not with anyone."

Next were the ropes. They dangled from a metal frame six meters high. "Start climbing, hands only. Legs at a ninety-degree angle," we were ordered.

Within a few months we could climb many times without rest. Grappling the tough rope, the skin of our hands thickened like the rind of an orange and assumed the same color. In those days you could tell someone from the Unit just by looking at their hands.

The Unit's training was remorselessly tough but purposeful. It combined endurance with intelligence. Brain was valued more than brawn, although brawn also received a good chunk of the training and stragglers weren't tolerated.

Most of the first year was spent in the field, but when we would return to the base the living conditions were comfortable. Or at least I thought so. We gradually moved from tents to rooms and the food was tolerably good. The field training, mostly in land navigation, in which the Unit was unsurpassed, was interspersed with crash courses in demolitions, communications, paramedic training, weaponry, camouflage, desert driving, Arabic, captivity training and many other skills.

What struck me immediately about the Unit was its no-holds-barred approach to achieving results. Commanders encouraged their soldiers to make suggestions on how to better perform our tasks. Set the objective, then figure out the best way to get it done.

I could handle the forced marches and the physical challenges of training better than most of my colleagues. On one occasion this included a march in which we carried sixty-kilogram packs "to test our capacity to carry loads."

This was an uncharacteristic mistake of the Unit. Many of its soldiers, including me, would pay dearly in later years for such excess. From the age of thirty-two, I suffered from chronic back pain.

A few years after I was discharged, the Unit mandated back X-rays for all its recruits, lightened the loads and developed sleek aluminum packs to better carry them. But as a fit eighteen-year-old I felt completely at ease with any kind of physical challenge the Unit demanded, and then some.

When it came to land navigation, however, I suffered a distinct disadvantage. Most of my fellow soldiers came from kibbutzim and were already familiar with using maps. I immersed myself in this new discipline. You could never *overstudy* the navigation route and the terrain surrounding it. I devoted myself to this task with the perfectionism I learned from my father and with the advice I received from Yoni, who was now a student at Harvard University, married to his girlfriend Tuttie. He wrote me detailed instructions on navigation, with an emphatic conclusion:

"Remember . . . A soldier who doesn't know how to orient himself in the field has to rely on others. He's not independent! The things I'm now telling you—from experience—you must never forget."[1]

First we went through three months of daytime navigation. The beauty of the country mesmerized me. Starting in the low hills of Ramot Menashe, we climbed the mountains of the Upper Galilee, traversed the flat plains of the Negev, and roamed the hills of Judea and Samaria, often stopping in places with which I was familiar from the Bible.

One such week of navigation began near Kadesh Barnea, a spring in the Sinai desert that the Bible says was visited by Moses and the Children of Israel. We were to go east and cross the entire Negev. Unfortunately, we chose the hottest week in decades. The temperature soared at noon to close to 45 degrees centigrade (113 degrees Fahrenheit). Our instructions were clear: start marching after dawn, by 10 a.m. find shelter from the heat, wait in the shade until 4 p.m., and then resume marching until nightfall.

By 10 a.m. of the first day my navigation partner and I came to the dirt road that marked the old border between Egypt and Israel before the Six-Day War. There was no shade to be found in the barren expanse. The sweltering sun beat down on us. We were running out of water and running out of time.

Where to hide from the sun?

Metal carcasses of vehicles were strewn on the road. They had probably been destroyed in the war. The Bedouins had stripped them of everything of value, but there was enough shade beneath the metal frames for us to crawl under.

Yet when my partner and I crawled underneath, we were nearly fried alive. The heat radiating from the scorching metal was even hotter than the open sun. Now I was really worried. No trees, no shade, no protruding rocks—nothing to give us even a smattering of cover.

What to do? We were on a ridgeline. A steep wadi spiraled down from the old border road to lower ground. Descending, I saw an opening on the side of the wadi half a meter in diameter.

What luck! It led to a large underground cistern the Bedouins had carved into the rock to trap water from the sudden rain showers that fall in the mountains in the winter and culminate in dangerous torrents that sweep the desert.

These desert torrents can kill you, and over the years they have tragically claimed the lives of unsuspecting youngsters trapped in the rushing water's path. Navigating the desert in the Unit, we quickly learned that as soon as we saw clouds on the horizon we should climb to higher ground. But now we were in the driest summer in years and there was no such danger.

My partner and I crawled into the cistern. A pleasant coolness enveloped us. There was no water in the cave, only a mild dampness. We lay on a ledge that was used to collect the water, content with our unexpected salvation.

But then we heard a strange hissing sound. Something was moving underneath us. In fact, the whole place was moving. Once our eyes adjusted to the darkness, we saw that the rocky floor beneath us was completely covered with gigantic cockroaches.

The bugs soon covered our bodies and crawled on our faces. We pushed them aside in disgust, only to have the relentless creatures cover us again. But necessity overcame revulsion. The damp coolness was worth it.

Once we made our peace with this crawling carpet, we encountered another problem. After twenty minutes or so we were . . . cold! Freezing cold! The only way to overcome this was to crawl back out, warm ourselves in the sun for twenty minutes, and then roll back in.

We passed the time this way until the tapering afternoon sun enabled us to continue the march. A few hours later we arrived at the endpoint, where we would finally have unlimited water.

A small two-wheel trailer had been left there for us with twenty-liter water containers made of metal. Unfortunately, they were fastened tightly to the trailer by padlocked metal chains and there was no way to lift them up so we could drink the water. We could break the locks, but I thought of another solution. I unscrewed the barrel of my Uzi submachine gun and used the barrel as a metal straw with which we sucked up the water to our heart's content.

This was typical of what the Unit expected from us. Unforeseen problems require unforeseen solutions. Don't give in to a problem and don't complain. Solve it. Think outside the box and use whatever you have at your disposal to complete the mission.

In daytime summer navigation in the desert we sometimes got so thirsty and sun-beaten that we began to fantasize about anything cold or wet.

"Bibi, I'm dreaming of buckets of ice cream, all in different flavors. What are you dreaming of?" my partner told me one day as we panted our way up a desert cliff hundreds of meters high.

"Me?" I answered, catching my breath. "I'm dreaming of a swimming pool full of ice-cold lemonade. I'm drinking as I'm swimming."

But there were no pools of lemonade to be found. The only water we encountered was a rancid pool in a shaded crevice, boasting green fungus and dead frogs. We plunged naked into it and cooled our overheated bodies. Having exhausted the water in our canteens, we gave in to the temptation and drank from the brackish water, a mistake that resulted in a year of intermittent diarrhea.

After completing our daytime navigation training, we graduated to nighttime navigation. When I first witnessed a commander demonstrate nighttime navigation in the Unit, it seemed like magic. He led us in total darkness through dozens of kilometers in rugged territory, not once using a map or compass, occasionally glancing at the stars. (Those were the days before GPS navigation and computer simulations.) I would soon acquire the magician's craft.

Study the Torah day and night, our sages said. Topographical maps now became my Torah. At night I would march along the thirty-kilometer route I had memorized earlier that day in fifty-meter intervals. During the day we were supposed to sleep and then chart and memorize the next night's route. In the field, I found it hard to sleep in daylight. Awakened by the sun several hours before my teammates, I would devote myself to map study like the devoted yeshiva student brought to life in Hayim Nahman Bialik's poem "Ha-matmid."

During training, I leaned that extreme fatigue could be fatal. Once, after a week of nighttime navigation atop the Negev's steep Mount Arif, my teammate and I were so tired that we experienced hallucinations as we sleepwalked our way forward.

"Look, look!" I cried out to my teammate deliriously. "Can you see these small donkeys with monkeys on their back? Let's catch them and ride out the rest of the route."

"Yeah, I can see them," he answered. "But I'm too weak to chase them."

There were no donkeys and no monkeys. There was nothing around us but steep cliffs from which we would have fallen to a certain death if we gave chase to our fantasies. What was astonishing was that we had identical hallucinations. I discounted that as part of my delirium, but years later I read in a biography of David Stirling how he and two of his SAS soldiers also experienced unexplained identical hallucinations under extreme fatigue. The mystery remains.

Sometimes the hallucinations turned out to be real. I ended another of these weeklong night navigations at Villa Melchett, on the shore of the Sea of Galilee. The villa was built by a British-Jewish lord in the 1930s. Exhausted from crossing the steep mountains of the Galilee, my two partners and I sprawled on the villa's lawns and instantly fell asleep.

A few hours later we were woken up by a strange bustle around us. We instinctively reached for our weapons. Yet when we looked up, we saw a wondrous scene. Beautiful women in eighteenth-century dress, powdered and coiffured, were strolling around us. White-wigged waiters in period clothing were carrying trays stacked with delectable fruit.

We looked at each other in disbelief. Were we dreaming?

Then we saw a man with a megaphone shouting orders to a camera crew. We had fallen asleep in the middle of a film set that used Villa Melchett as a backdrop. The extras and actors had simply skirted around the three unshaven, unwashed soldiers lying snoring on the grass. Why wake sleeping dogs?

One of the tasks we were given as new recruits to the Unit was to observe the Suez Canal border-crossing point on behalf of senior team members who needed safe passage across the waterway to conduct secret missions in enemy territory. By night we would build a camouflaged position on the canal's Israeli bank; by day we would observe the opposing Egyptian bank from within that position.

Cooped up during the day, we would relieve ourselves into empty combat ration cans. At night we took turns using night scopes and sleeping on the open ground. Though it was bitterly cold, I never covered myself completely with the sleeping bag. My arms had to be free to reach for my weapon lying next to me in case we were attacked by enemy soldiers crossing to our side.

Old habits die hard. In fact, this one never died at all. Still today, I find it hard to sleep with blankets covering my arms and shoulders.

In one navigation in the Galilee, we learned a different lesson. Divided into two-man squads, we raced through the thirty-kilometer course. My partner and I completed the final stretch of the navigation route by crossing the Mount Carmel Forest.

We finished first, well ahead of the other squads. None of the others were in sight. We would bask in our triumph as we greeted them at the endpoint.

Suddenly my partner discovered that one of our topographical maps was missing. This violated a cardinal principle of not leaving anything behind in the field. After all, these navigation exercises were just practice runs for the day when we would secretly penetrate enemy territory. We had no choice but to retrace our steps to search for the map.

It was nowhere to seen. How would we ever find it? Standing in what I thought was our exit point from the dense forest, I took a reverse azimuth on my compass and started marching into the woods. This was as close as one can get to searching for a needle in a gigantic haystack. But then, incredible luck! There on the shaded forest floor was the missing map! We were the last squad to arrive at the endpoint, but we had left nothing behind.

Throughout this training period one message was ingrained in us again and again: don't fudge your tasks and don't compromise with results. When I became an officer I in turn instilled this same principle in my soldiers. Their lives and the fate of our missions would depend on it.

8

COMBAT

1968–1969

A few months into my time in the Unit, we were suddenly mobilized for a raid across the Jordan on the village of Karameh, from which the Palestine Liberation Organization (PLO) was launching raids into Israel. The mission was to dismantle this terrorist base by driving the terrorists out of the village. Our commander, Amiram Levin, issued Kalashnikov assault rifles to several of my teammates.

Fearing that I was going to be left out, I asked him, "Why am I not receiving a Kalashnikov?"

"Because you're taking a MAG," he said.

That made sense. The MAG machine gun was heavy and I was one of the bigger soldiers.

We crossed the Jordan River on the Allenby Bridge in a long file of armored personnel carriers and tanks and fanned to the south of Karameh. After an initial firefight most of the PLO fled. Their leader, Yasser Arafat, escaped from the northern side of the village on a motorcycle. Years later, when I met King Hussein of Jordan, I told him of my first visit to his country. There were many other visits I did not mention.

The PLO had been founded by Arafat, Ahmad Shukeiri, and their Palestinian cohorts to conquer and destroy Israel in 1964, three years before the Six-Day War in which Israel took control of Judea and Samaria (the West Bank) and Gaza. Their goal was never to "liberate" these territories, because these lands were in Arab hands when the PLO was established. The goal was and remains Israel's destruction.

Led by Arafat, the PLO totally rejected Israel's right to exist, inculcating its followers with a burning hatred of Israel, and spreading outlandish lies about Israel and Zionism.

After the defeat of the Arab armies in 1967, the PLO and affiliated terror groups like the Popular Front for the Liberation of Palestine (PFLP) swung into action. They sent terrorists across the Jordan River, hijacked an Israeli plane to Algeria, and shot at an Israeli plane parked at Zurich airport in Switzerland. When the war on terror gathered steam, our training in the Unit was constantly interrupted as we were called into action again and again. Many of our activities in that period focused on retaliating for terrorist attacks or foiling impending ones.

Sometimes this led to bizarre encounters. Returning one night from an operation in Jordan, my teammates and I ran into two PLO terrorists returning from an operation on *our* side of the border. A quick firefight ensued on the banks of the Jordan in which we killed one of the terrorists. The other succeeded in escaping to the Jordanian side.

The PLO's cover force then began to fire at us from the high ground across the river, while our cover force responded with mortar shells that initially missed their mark and fell near us. Luckily, no one was hurt. At daybreak I was ordered to bring the dead terrorist to a burial site, a task that required overcoming much queasiness given that half his head had been blown off.

A few months after the raid on Karameh, PLO terrorists based in Beirut, Lebanon, attacked an Israeli plane on a stopover in Athens. In retaliation, we were sent to Beirut Airport to blow up Lebanese planes. Our commander in this mission was the legendary Raful, Colonel Rafael Eitan, a strong, silent type who later became army chief of staff and served as minister of agriculture in my cabinet. Raful instructed us to wear red berets. This was the first and only time I went into combat wearing a beret, which I thought was absurdly theatrical.

As our helicopters hovered over Beirut Airport our excitement grew. We could see more than a dozen Lebanese airplanes on the tarmac. We landed in the airfield and made our way to our targets. I placed an explosive charge between the wheels and the fuselage of one of the planes. My fellow soldiers did the same with the other planes.

After ensuring that the planes were unoccupied, we set off the charges. Flying back to Israel, we could see the airport below us lit with enormous flames. It was like something out of a movie.

The raid on Beirut Airport instilled a false confidence in us. We had mastered nighttime navigation and our weapons. We had perfected the ability to march quickly and accurately to any destination. We felt we could do anything, carry out any operation, with no loss of life. Yet in more clearheaded moments, I knew better. I had already learned that the distance from triumph to tragedy was often only a few centimeters wide.

TRAGEDY CAME EARLY.

Early in my time in the Unit, I developed a close friendship with my teammate David Ben Hamo. Unlike most other teammates who came from kibbutzim, David was a city boy who came from a Moroccan family in Beer-Sheba. He was a brilliant student, and exceptionally modest and sensitive.

After he returned from Karameh, his mother asked him why he chose to volunteer for such a dangerous unit. He answered, "If every mother says this, who will fight for us?"

A few days after Karameh, during a training exercise, David and another gifted soldier from the adjoining team, Zohar Linik, were fatally wounded when a shell exploded in the mortar they were firing. David died in my arms on the way to Tel Hashomer Hospital. It is a moment that lives with me always. Some thirty years later I visited his family in Beer-Sheba. His mother, forever stricken with grief, had left his room exactly as it was on the day he died. When as prime minister I sent men into battle, I would always think of David's mother and the other mothers of Israel grieving for their fallen sons.

In early 1968, Egypt mounted a war of attrition against Israel along the Suez Canal. Egyptian forces carried out deadly commando raids on the Israeli side of the canal. Army command ordered the Unit to conduct a counter-raid on the Egyptian side. Shortly after nightfall we crossed the canal on three Zodiac rubber boats.

Naval commandos had earlier stretched a rope from the Israeli side of the canal to the Egyptian side. Using a roller on the rope, the commandos speedily and silently rolled our Zodiacs forward, reminding me of how workers long ago manually rolled small carts on railway tracks.

Unseen, we reached the other side and ambushed an Egyptian military truck. There was no joy seeing up close the agony of the enemy soldiers we cut down. But our troops, long yearning for a response to Egyptian attacks, were elated. So was the army's Southern Command. Do it again, they ordered the following day. Though I thought the intervening forty-eight hours might give the Egyptians time to anticipate our next move, I wasn't prepared for what ensued.

As we silently approached the Egyptian side of the canal on our second nighttime crossing, we were met with intense gunfire. Egyptian soldiers had dug foxholes every fifty meters along the bank. In the boat ahead of me, Haim Ben Yonah, the first among us to become an officer, was hit and fell into the water. Our cover force opened fire at the Egyptians from the Israeli side of the canal.

We were caught in the middle. As crossfire whizzed around us, I told my fellow soldiers that being in the water would be safer than staying in the boat as sitting ducks. Wearing a half-inflated life vest, I jumped into the warm waters of the Suez. I thought I would hold on to the rope running alongside the boat while the naval commando on the boat would roll the Zodiac back to the Israeli side of the canal.

I forgot the twenty kilograms of gunner's ammunition on my back. Combat fitted, the ammo pack was strapped so tightly that I couldn't free myself from it. I immediately began to sink.

Somehow I managed to kick my way back up to the surface, gulped for air, and began to sink again to even greater depths. My lungs were about to burst. Summoning my last reserves of will before succumbing to the panic of suffocation, I made one last, desperate effort to reach the surface and extended my hand upward.

Somebody grabbed it and pulled me up.

Exhausted, I was towed to our side of the canal amid the furious crossfire. As I lifted myself out of the water, a rocket-propelled grenade exploded a few meters next to me. It made absolutely no impression on me. I had survived an awful fate, death by drowning.

Over the years, a debate broke out as to who on that boat extended the hand that saved my life. I could never know because my head was underwater when this fateful act took place. Not wanting to be picky about it, I thanked everyone who claimed to be the one.

Fifty years later, I received a message sent to one of my team members, Michael Maimon, from Israel Nir, another team member from Kibbutz Elon, whom I had not seen for nearly half a century. (He had gone to the US to build nuclear plants.)

Nir wrote: "I was seated next to Bibi on the second boat when the shots were fired. We all jumped promptly into the Canal. Unfortunately, Bibi was carrying MAG ammunition on his back. He sank like a rock. Noticing that he was underwater and unable to float back up, I grabbed him and pulled him up enabling him to breathe. Others then helped me pull him into the boat." [1]

Many decades later, I offer a belated and much deserved thanks also to my fellow soldier Israel Nir.

Haim Ben Yonah, who fell in this operation, was a great loss. Literally head and shoulders taller than the rest of us, he was older and more experienced, a natural leader of men. There was no surprise when he was picked first among us to go to Officers' Training School.

At Kibbutz Yehiam, where Haim was buried, I met his mother, a Holocaust survivor. She told me that had Haim been born two years earlier he would have been thrown into the ovens in the Nazi death camps like a million and a half other Jewish children. At least, she said, my son died wearing the uniform of a Jewish soldier defending his people.

BEFORE HAIM'S DEATH and after I had spent little more than a year in the Unit, Uzi Yairi, the Unit's commander, summoned me to his modest office.

"Bibi, you're going to Officers' Training School." He wasn't asking.

I explained that since I planned to attend Yale University, I couldn't sign up for the additional two years required to become an officer in the Unit.

"You're going." Uzi was adamant.

"I'm not," I said, equally adamant. Uzi's face reddened.

"You have a weekend pass. If you're not back here on Sunday with a positive answer, I'll throw you out of the Unit."

This was a fate worse than death. I had no way out. Over the weekend in Jerusalem, I decided to consult Yoni.

Now married, he had completed his first year at Harvard. His elbow had been operated on twice in Israel after the war and a third time at Walter Reed Army Medical Center with only partial success. He knew it was unlikely that he could ever do reserve duty in the army again.

But as the war on terror grew, he decided that he simply could not stay in America while his friends were fighting in Israel. He enrolled in Hebrew University in Jerusalem, where he studied mathematics and philosophy.

He wrote to my father, who was then teaching at the University of Denver: "We must cling to our country with our fingernails and with all our strength. Only if we do so will Israel remain the State of the Jews. Only then will they not write in the history books that once indeed the Jews roused themselves to action and held on to their land for two decades, but then they were overwhelmed and once more became homeless wanderers. That is why I have to be here now."[2]

On leave from the army, I would often spend time with Yoni and Iddo. Iddo had not wished to stay in the US. He returned to Israel for high school studies, living with a family in Jerusalem. Growing in body and mind, our little brother soon towered over us, a lanky six foot two.

Despite his war wound, which prevented him from fully extending his arm, Yoni had remarkable stamina. Even though I was in excellent shape, I found it hard to keep up with him when the two of us ran in the Hebrew University stadium and up and down the hills of Jerusalem.

In America I had taken in Yoni's stories from the army. Now he took in mine. He wanted to know everything about the training in the Unit, the operations I took part in, and how I was doing. Within permissible limits, I shared this with him.

We also discussed history, philosophy, world politics and Israel's situation. I brazenly spewed forth my opinions, as yet untempered by experience or maturity. Since I hardly ever discussed such topics with my teammates in the Unit, Yoni was my outlet and sounding board. He listened patiently, often saying little.

What a shock it was for me to discover so many years later what he was thinking.

In 2018, in an annual commemoration of Yoni's fall at Entebbe, one of his university friends mentioned something that Yoni had said to him about me.

This friend later put it in writing: "In the fall of 1968 Yoni returned to Israel from his studies in Harvard. He came to live near me at the Kiryat Yovel neighborhood of Jerusalem. We met frequently, almost every day. He spoke about you a great deal with admiration and love. I've never seen such love of a brother to a younger brother, and that impression lingers fifty years later.

"Yoni also said a number of times, letting out a laugh intended to emphasize his words, that you will be Prime Minister. He did not explain his statement, and I asked for no explanation. Yoni saw in you things that no one else saw, that you too could not envision then."[3]

Pondering this today I cannot explain how Yoni could think that I would one day lead Israel. I was young and unformed, filled with a youthful certitude that is not always the best prescription for leadership.

Certainly it wasn't partisan politics that drove Yoni to make such a far-reaching assertion. Yoni and I had absolutely no interest in that. Though he decidedly belonged to the political right, Yoni wrote sympathetically of Labor prime ministers Levi Eshkol, who decided to bring the remains of Ze'ev Jabotinsky, the founder of Revisionist Zionism and a political opponent, to be buried in Israel, and Golda Meir.[4] Yoni was, as one of his left-leaning friends said after his death, a pragmatic nationalist.

Perhaps he was impressed by my tenacity when I discussed world events and recognized that much of the power of my arguments was due to the influence of Father's ideas. I'll never know, just as I won't know if any of these thoughts about me were in the back of his mind on that fateful day when I went to see him following Uzi's ultimatum to me. They were certainly not in mine. It would take close to another twenty years for me to even *consider* running for prime minister.

NOW IN JERUSALEM with Yoni and Iddo, I presented my dilemma to my older brother.

"What should I do," I asked him, distressed. "What should I tell Uzi?"
He thought for a long moment.

"Tell him I'll go in your place," he finally said. I was stunned.

"*You?*" I was flabbergasted. "You're *old* [he was all of twenty-three], you're married, and besides—you're an invalid." I also had my quiet reservations on the clannishness of the Unit's kibbutz soldiers. I had somehow managed to fit in there, but would Yoni?

Yoni waved all objections aside. For months he had been following the growing tensions surrounding Israel, and my own participation in the unfolding events: the raid on Karameh, the raid on Beirut Airport, action along the Suez Canal and more.

Moshe Dayan, the defense minister, had called on reserve officers to rejoin the army as regulars in the face of the war of attrition that we were now fighting.

Heeding that call, Yoni's mind was made up. He would not only enlist: he would join Sayeret Matkal, the vortex of action.

"But how can you expect Uzi Yairi to take a handicapped veteran like you to be a combat team leader?" I pushed back.

"Just tell him to pull my file," Yoni responded.

Overcoming my initial unease, I finally relented.

On Sunday morning, I walked into Yairi's office.

"So, have you decided?" Uzi pressed.

"I have," I said. "I'm not going, but my older brother is willing to take my place."

"Who's your brother?"

"Yoni. Ask about him. You'll see for yourself."

Yoni's file showed that he had graduated first in his class in Officers' Training School, along with superlatives showered on him by his superiors. Uzi accepted my proposal.

I was off the hook, but now the problem was how to get Yoni past the army's medical exam. A doctor who was a recent immigrant examined him. Not being fully versed in Hebrew, he apparently mistook the word *marpek* (elbow) for the word *perek* (joint), and for some reason he decided to check Yoni's right knee. He then nodded his approval.

That was it. Yoni was now in the Unit. He became a team leader and then served as a company commander in Sayeret Haruv, a unit in which he led several battles against PLO terrorists who infiltrated the Jordan River valley. Later he returned to the Unit as *maflag*, a commander responsible for the training of all junior teams. The round-the-clock demands on him took a toll on his marriage. He and his wife parted.

Yoni's entry as an officer in the Unit freed me to complete my military service in the normal time of three years and continue to university. But that's not what happened. The challenges to Israel's security were growing constantly, and with each passing month my confidence grew that I could successfully lead men in clandestine operations and in battle.

The Unit now had a new commander, Lieutenant Colonel Menachem Digli. He was tall and slim like Uzi, but unlike the intense Yairi he was charming and easygoing. He too brought up the offer that I go to Officers' Training School. This time I accepted. I deferred my Yale enrollment and passed the Officers' School entrance exams with top marks.

9

COMMANDER

1969–1972

Before I set out for Officers' Training School, Yoni was determined to give me some advice. He suggested we go to the hills near Migdal Zedek, a few miles from the Unit.

A centuries-old manor house built on the ruins of a Crusader castle, Migdal Zedek was the site of a World War I battle that pitted Turkish and German forces against the British Expeditionary Force that came from Egypt. Sitting on a rock outcropping, Yoni simulated a much smaller battle.

"See that hill over there? An enemy force has just opened fire on you. What do you do?" Yoni asked me.

"That's easy," I said. "I leave cover fire here to keep them pinned down, take the rest of my men into the wadi there, then emerge unseen and storm the enemy from the side."

"That's fine," Yoni said. "But you forgot something."

"What?" I asked.

"That the enemy also moves," he responded. "Don't assume he's static. While you're down in the wadi, he may be moving to lay a trap for you. So you've got to lift your head from time to time to see what your adversary is doing."

This was sound advice, equally useful in the military and later in politics.

Because I had gone through the Unit's tough training, the Officers'

Training School's physical challenges were disappointingly easy, though there was one moment which nearly culminated in tragedy. We were taken to the Kishon River near Haifa to get familiarized with naval matters. Sitting in the same type of Zodiac boats we had used in the Suez crossing, we were asked to jump into the water with full gear. One of my fellow cadets, Ruby Peled, said that he didn't know how to swim. A cadet from the naval commandos told him, "Don't worry. We're here!"

As soon as he jumped into the water, the weight of his gear began dragging him under. Ruby recalls that I jumped into the water and pulled him to safety, notwithstanding my own near drowning experience a few months earlier during the Suez firefight.[1]

Otherwise, I enjoyed the classes about strategy and tactics in Officers' School and I appreciated the military analysis of terrain, transport routes and topography, this time not for commando raids or clandestine operations, with which I was familiar, but for armored columns and large mechanized formations. Graduating with honors, I went on to another three months of Intelligence Officers' School (Sayeret Matkal formally belongs to the Intelligence Corps).

Now I was ready to receive the dozen members of my team. The route I chose for their 120-kilometer march to the Unit differed from the one I took two years earlier as a fresh recruit. Meeting them at Afula, in the Jezreel Valley, we marched south to the Valley of Dotan where Joseph was sold to slavery in Egypt by his brothers.

From there we cut westward to the Mediterranean Sea and then headed south until we reached the Unit. This long march was not as arduous as the previous one, and not only because the weather was better. When you lead, the going is always easier.

My soldiers did fine on the march. They now officially belonged to "Team Bibi," since teams in the Unit were named after their commander. They came from towns, villages and kibbutzim and formed a strong and lasting bond with each other. They still meet yearly a half century since that day in Afula, sometimes with their grandchildren. I join them when I can.

But upon receiving them I had one question: Could they carry the loads often required for the Unit's operations? Two teams were recruited to the Unit simultaneously. One was commanded by me, the other by a fellow officer named Yossi Kalmar.

By chance most of the bigger soldiers went to Yossi. Worried that this could be a disadvantage, I raised it with Yoni.

He looked up at me from a book he was reading.

"Bibi," he said, "it won't make any difference. They'll carry the loads. But more important, remember that there are no good soldiers and bad soldiers, only good officers and bad officers. Make sure you're the good kind and your soldiers will do everything you ask them to do."

He was right. I was a rigorous and serious officer, holding my men to exacting standards, at times perhaps too exacting. Every three months, I would shrink their number by letting team members go who I thought did not meet my requirements. Most of them did well in the other branches of the army.

I was heartbroken when two of them were later killed in the 1973 Yom Kippur War, one a helicopter pilot mutilated by a Syrian mob after he went down. Over the years I often wondered: Had I kept them with me, would they still be alive?

But after Yoni's death, I learned to put aside the "what-ifs." Obsessing over hypothetical courses of action that would have avoided tragedy is simply too painful and gets you nowhere. What if I had accepted Uzi Yairi's original request to attend Officers' Training School? What if I had resisted Yoni's pressure to replace me in the Unit? Would Yoni still be alive?

There was no end to this. I decided to stop delving in this and to no longer engage in what Americans call "relitigating" the past. Instead, I accepted the stark principle: Life has no replays.

I DID EVERYTHING in my power to avoid putting my soldiers at unnecessary risk, but on one occasion I haphazardly broke this rule. I took my soldiers on a hike down the open water channel that carries the spring water of Wadi Kelt to Jericho. The water channel hugs a cliff's edge. As long as we walked inside the channel, we were safe.

At a certain point the channel entered a crevasse and emerged on the other side through a hole too small to crawl through. We had to climb around it, suspended over the steep ravine below. If anyone slipped, they would fall and die. I was the first to go. My soldiers dutifully followed. Miraculously, no one fell that day.

Still, I could never forgive myself for this. I vowed never to repeat such a mistake and to stick to the old adage: a good commander achieves the mission with minimal or no sacrifice, a poor commander sacrifices many. To which I added, don't risk anyone on unnecessary missions or unnecessary wars. As Israel's prime minister, I always remembered this.

Though usually meticulous about my soldiers' safety, I was less careful about my own. I was given my own personal transport, a Jeep of World War II vintage. I would race this most unstable of vehicles on Israel's then-shaky roads.

Yoni repeatedly warned me that I was driving recklessly. To no avail. Coming out of Jerusalem one day, I overturned the Jeep. I lost consciousness and woke up on the asphalt. The Jeep was tottering on an embankment and almost fell to the abyss below. I sustained minor but painful injuries. Yoni was delighted when he visited me at Hadassah Hospital. "Now you'll definitely drive more carefully," he said.

The team I commanded soon achieved good standing. Avi Dichter, a member of a younger team who later became head of the Shin Bet security service and a minister of internal security in Ariel Sharon's government, described the differences in how our two teams conducted regular morning exercise in the Unit.

"At 6:30 we would start the day with a 1,500-meter run followed by three climbs up the ropes with arms only. But Team Bibi? They'd run *3,000* meters and climb the ropes *five* times,"[2] he said. My team won the Unit's sports contest.

After the Unit's teams were tested by the navy, mine was selected for a special joint mission with the naval commandos unit, known as Shayetet 13. Notwithstanding the intense rivalry between the two special units, I grew to appreciate the commandos as valiant and highly professional warriors.

Our joint mission required that we complete a course in military diving at Atlit, the naval commando base on the Mediterranean. It was dominated by the ruins of the last castle evacuated by the Crusaders when they left the Holy Land for good in 1291. In Israel, a land fought over for millennia, modern military bases often adjoin those of yesterday and modern battles often take place on ancient battlefields.

As I practiced diving each day in the bay overlooked by this once-magnificent castle, the question entered my mind: Would we too suffer the fate of the Crusaders, who after two centuries yielded the Holy Land to the Muslims?

This was a common hope among Israel's Arab enemies, but I was convinced we would do better. Unlike the Crusaders, we had been attached to our land for more than three millennia and overcame incredible odds to regain it. Yet the question of ensuring Israel's power and permanence lingered in my mind.

After a few weeks of underwater training, we wrongly thought we could match our naval commando instructors, only to discover there were many things we had yet to learn about the sea. Spearfishing in the bay of Atlit, we were suddenly swept by powerful currents that pulled us far out into the Mediterranean. There was no use resisting. Rising to the surface, we inflated our life jackets and lay on our backs. Might as well enjoy the ride, I thought. The current carried us in a long arc into the sea and then deposited us north of the castle.

On another occasion, diving in the Kishon port near Haifa, we were immersed in water that was contaminated with chemicals and engine oil. But we were soon faced with a more immediate problem, the absence of a magnetic field. We were put under a huge floating metal platform that rendered our compasses useless.

Diving in pairs in total darkness and connected to each other with a short rope, my partner and I soon went around in circles.

We began to deplete our oxygen supply, until we found a solution. Holding on to metal girders that supported the platform from below, we made our way out of that dark expanse. Though the joint mission with the naval commandos ultimately didn't materialize, I learned a valuable lesson: get out of dangerous traps as soon as you can.

The first mission I led as an officer reinforced this lesson. My team and I landed by helicopter at night in an Arab country. I checked that all my soldiers were crouched behind me and signaled to the helicopter pilot to take off. In the silence that followed, I peered through my binoculars to ensure that all was clear in the first leg of the route I had charted for our mission.

A stretch of low-hanging barbed wire two meters in front of me caught my eye. It had a metal plate attached to it. I moved closer. An ominous triangle was painted on both of its sides, the universal sign for "Beware Minefield." I told my men to freeze.

This was a "Houston, we have a problem" moment.

I radioed mission control.

"It seems," I said in code, "there's a fifty percent chance that we landed in a minefield."

This was a shocker. The intel guys should have discovered the mine-field by scanning time-series aerial photographs of the landing zone. How could they miss it?

"Are you sure there's a minefield there?" mission control asked.

"I'm sure," I replied. "But I don't know if I'm inside it or outside."

A long silence followed. I later learned that a heated argument broke out between Colonel Avraham Arnan, the legendary founder of the Unit who was now head of collection in Military Intelligence, and Major General David "Dado" Elazar, who was chief of operations at the time.[3] Against Dado's objections, Arnan insisted that the mission be called off immediately. The helicopter should be sent back to hover above and winch us up to safety one by one.

Dado asked me what I thought.

"Well, I see a wadi with boulders about a hundred and fifty meters away," I said. "We'll crawl on the ground to spread our weight so we don't detonate the mines." I explained that once we get to the boulders, we'll be fine. We'll either exit the field on the boulders, or we'll discover we weren't inside the field in the first place.

Dado agreed.

I lay flat and gently jabbed the ground in front of me at regular inter-vals with my commando knife. That was the only time in my military ser-vice that I used this knife, other than to puncture cans of army preserves. My men dutifully crawled behind, forming a human caterpillar.

Reaching the wadi, we got to our feet. We skipped from boulder to boulder until we reached a nearby road and saw that the minefield fence curved away from us. So we weren't inside it after all! Picking up our pace, we made up for lost time and completed our mission. We returned to Israel just before dawn.

As prime minister, I authorized many daring missions, but not all. Perspective changes when the dispatched becomes the dispatcher. I learned this first the hard way as a young team commander, tasked with carrying out one of the toughest physical missions the Israeli army has carried out.

Ehud Barak, then commander of the Unit, told Yossi Kalmar and me to prepare for a particularly demanding operation in which we would stay more than one night in Syrian territory. This operation would require a year of training and we would have to combine our two teams into one force.

"Who would be the commander?" I asked.

Barak answered that he would decide that when we were close to the mission date.

I could not accept that. Yossi Kalmar, the commander of the other team, was a truly fine officer. He was my roommate and my friend. But if I was to take charge of this combined force, I would need to train it as one team in my own way and according to my own standards. Kalmar would probably want to do the same.

Barak refused this demand. I said I accepted his decision, but he should accept mine as well. He should give Kalmar the command. I would leave the Unit to begin my university studies.

Over the weekend, Barak changed his mind. On Sunday, he told me that he decided that I would take charge of both teams after all. I went to see Kalmar before he left the Unit. It could not have been easy for him, but he was a perfect gentleman and accepted Barak's decision.

I began intensively training my enlarged team for the big operation in Syria. To prevent shepherds from discovering our daytime position, we studied the behavior of sheep herds in the Galilee and perfected techniques of daytime camouflage, first in a practice run on Mount Hermon and then inside Lebanon. My guides for these tasks were two Israeli legends.

The first was Salim Shoufi, a Druze from the Golan village of Majdal Shams, which was captured by Israel from Syria in the Six-Day War. The Druze were a Middle Eastern sect with a distinct religion whose members lived mostly in the mountains of Syria, Lebanon and the Galilee. Before the war, Salim had regularly crisscrossed the Israeli-Syrian border and given Israel valuable intelligence on the Syrian army.

My second guide was Israel's most famous warrior, Meir Har-Zion. Meir achieved fame in the 1950s in Ariel Sharon's 101 unit, which carried out Israel's first retaliatory raids into Arab territory.

When in the 1950s his sister Shoshana was murdered by members of an Arab tribe who came from Jordanian territory, Meir crossed the border with three friends and exacted revenge from the tribesmen. He later lived a solitary farmer's life on a cliff's edge, next to the aptly named crusader castle of Belvoir (Beautiful View), which overlooks the Jordan Valley. He named his farm *Ahuzat Shoshana*, Shoshana's Estate.

In his late thirties when I met him, Meir was gaunt and quiet. He suffered from battle wounds that inhibited some of his movements. Salim, then in his mid-forties, was equally quiet but heavyset. I suggested that they both dispense with joining us on the steep nocturnal climb on the Hermon slopes and meet us at the endpoint of the exercise. They insisted on coming along. And well they did, because I learned valuable tips from these masters of nighttime navigation and daytime camouflage.

"I see a sheep den," Salim would whisper to me in the dark.

"Where?" I'd ask, failing to find it with my binoculars in the dark night.

"Right there," he said, pointing.

Sure enough, we'd soon walk past a sheep den.

Before daylight we cleared the ground, built our daytime position with rocks and camouflaged it with bushes.

"This isn't good," Meir said, pointing to a lone rock we left a few meters away with its muddy side exposed. "A shepherd passing here will see that someone removed this rock from its original position. This will immediately arouse his suspicion and give your position away."

Up close I grew to admire these two men even more. In civilian life Salim owned a restaurant overlooking Birket Ram, a picturesque volcanic lake in the Golan where I would later often stop and visit.

"How's Yoni?" he would ask, having formed a close bond with the two of us over the years.

Though I had less contact with the reclusive Meir, three decades later he would support me when I resigned in protest over the 2005 unilateral withdrawal from Gaza by the government of his former commander, Ariel Sharon.

Going against his commander, whom he deeply respected, must have been excruciatingly difficult for Meir. It was difficult for me too. Sharon was one of Israel's greatest generals and had led the decisive crossing of the Suez Canal in the Yom Kippur War. But as prime minister, he had succumbed to pressures from the left when he made his decision to unilaterally withdraw from the Gaza Strip, uproot eight thousand Jews and destroy twenty-one Israeli communities in the process. His efforts to convince his followers that Israel's security would be served by these actions failed to convince Meir. Meir was as uncompromising in his convictions as he was uncompromising in his standards during our training on the Hermon.

The deepest impressions he made on me were not only his military perfectionism, which was unsurpassed, but the depth of his commitment to Israel and the unassuming manner in which he imparted his valuable experience to us young soldiers. He understood that the rebirth of Israel requires generations of fighters who will unreservedly defend our state, and are willing to sacrifice themselves if necessary.

"Don't come back if you don't complete the mission," he once told me.

MONTHS OF TRAINING went by in 1971 and winter approached. We were finally ready to launch the operation. Just then, Defense Minister Moshe Dayan decided to postpone the mission indefinitely. My soldiers were furious.

"Why is this old fogey hesitating? Doesn't he know we're good for it?" they carped.

Dayan, exceptionally brave in battle, who when he was the age of my soldiers had distinguished himself in many dangerous operations, knew well the difference between the responsibility of the dispatcher and the eagerness of the dispatched. I'm sure similar rantings were leveled at me on those occasions when as prime minister I declined to authorize missions for which dedicated soldiers had labored long and hard to prepare.

Two months later, Dayan changed his mind and gave us the green light for the mission. Eager to go, we now faced a new problem. We would have to carry heavy loads in the dead of winter, which in the Hermon and the Golan can be bitterly cold. If we wore extra clothing and these got wet, they would weigh us down even further.

As long as we kept moving, we would be warm. When we rested, we would be cold in any case because our clothes would be soaked with sweat from the physical exertion. We decided we could do without winter garb and set out in regular army fatigues.

Starting out at night from the army's fortified position on Mount Hermon, we descended what was later dubbed by my team Emek Bibi ("Bibi's Valley"). We made our way to our daytime hideaway inside Syria, a niche in the cliffs overlooking the Syrian Golan Heights that I had chosen from aerial photographs. It proved to be an ideal hiding place, comfortably shielding us from both the wind and the shepherds nearby.

After an uneventful day in the cliffs, we pressed ahead with our mission. The weather turned from soggy to wet and then to a veritable deluge. My men labored under their packs, which grew heavier with each successive downpour.

As commander, I carried only an Uzi, binoculars and a small radio. My job was to navigate to our designated target through the storm, which I did with precision, though I constantly had to wipe my face from the rainwater streaming down my eyes.

As we left the plateau of the Syrian Golan and began climbing our way back to Israel on the slopes of Mount Hermon, the temperature had plummeted. The downpour turned into a heavy blizzard. Deep snow covered the slopes, making our ascent back to Israeli territory more difficult than we had imagined. Our fatigues were soaked with sweat, rain and snow. They began to freeze. The cold was causing severe pain in our hands and feet. If anyone was silly enough to urinate while climbing, that extremity would freeze as well!

A painful weariness and a dullness of mind began to set in, typical of looming hypothermia.

Since helicopters could neither fly nor land in the blinding blizzard, aerial extraction was impossible. A ground extraction force led by Uzi Dayan, who would later join me in the Sabena rescue, teamed up with us.

But Uzi couldn't help either. Like the rest of us, his extraction team began to freeze, too.

In the numbness of the biting cold, the temptation to sit down was all but irresistible. I remembered what the experienced Salim had told me: "In the snow, if you sit down, you don't get up."

Just then, right before my eyes, one of the soldiers did just that. He was a member of a more senior team who was added to the mission to help carry the extra heavy loads. Powerfully built, he was the biggest man in the force. I relieved him of the pack he was carrying. He was too heavy to carry up the mountain and we were too weak to do so. We barely carried ourselves.

"Get up," I feebly said, more a mumble than a command.

He looked at me with glazed eyes and didn't respond. "Get up," I repeated, and slapped him on the face.

Again, no response.

I realized that if I didn't get him on his feet he would die there in a few hours.

Suddenly I thought of a solution. Each of us carried in our gear a "survival dose," an aluminum tube of caramelized milk. I would give mine to the soldier and the glucose would prop him up. In the horrific cold even the simplest moves became complicated, but somehow I managed to extract the tube from my gear and unscrew its plastic cover. Now all I had to do was turn the cover upside down and with its pointed tip puncture the aluminum coating at the top of the tube.

This was more than I could accomplish. My frozen fingers had bloated to the size of cucumbers and were totally useless. The plastic cover fell and disappeared in the snow. Now there was no way to get the glucose out of the tube.

I scolded myself. Are you going to let this man die here because you can't figure out a way to puncture this stupid tube? Think, goddammit, think! I had another flash. The Uzi submachine gun I was carrying had a forward sight with a sharp tip to pinpoint targets. I asked the soldier next to me to hold my Uzi as I furiously banged the top of the aluminum tube on the Uzi's tip. The aluminum gave way.

Luckily, the caramelized milk did not freeze. I squeezed the glucose into the soldier's mouth. He sprang to his feet like a defrosted Popeye.

Miraculously, we all made it to the Israeli bunker fortress at the top of the mountain.

No one died that day. No one lost fingers or toes to frostbite. General Mordechai "Motta" Gur, commander of the Northern Front, gave me and Uzi citations for outstanding command and expressed his appreciation to our soldiers for the successful completion of our mission. I still remember the soup I was given in the Hermon bunker as the best soup I ever had (and I've been to some fine restaurants since). But I didn't feel the soles of my feet for days.

THIS WOULDN'T BE my last encounter with Mount Hermon. A year later, in 1972, my team was chosen for a secret mission to the position the Syrians had been occupying at the peak of the Hermon range, a few kilometers away and a full one thousand meters higher than the Israeli position. The Syrians had vacated their site because of heavy snows.

I chuckled at the irony of fate. Nearly drowning in the Suez Canal, I was later chosen for a diving mission with the naval commandos. Nearly freezing to death on Mount Hermon, I was now chosen to scale the range's highest peak in deep snow.

But this time we were much better prepared. The Unit had sent men to Switzerland. They came back with the latest equipment and clothing to ensure warmth and mobility. In typical fashion, our technical unit designed aluminum snowshoes that they claimed were better and more durable than the Swiss ones.

"What chutzpah!" I scoffed. "The Swiss have been doing this for centuries." But amazingly, when we tried both sets of snowshoes, ours *were* better, at least for the task before us. Once again, we climbed the Hermon in the dead of winter, but this time I felt we weren't on the *Titanic* but on the *Queen Elizabeth 2*.

Our socks and gloves were warmed with chemical packets, our clothes with electrical batteries. We were connected to each other with a rope so no one would get lost or fall off a precipice. Special goggles shielded our eyes. Still, the blinding snow limited our vision. I solved this problem by studying the topography so minutely that I could tell where we were by the changing angle of my snowshoes.

My partner and deputy in leading this operation was Giora Zorea, the Unit's deputy commander, from Kibbutz Ma'agan Michael. The son of a respected former general, he had lost a brother, Jonathan, a pilot who was shot down in the Six-Day War. He would soon lose another brother, Yohanan, a tank officer who would fall in the Yom Kippur War.

Giora and I got to be friends and I often visited him on his kibbutz. Tall and athletic, he was a no-nonsense straight shooter. Rare for a Unit operation, we chatted all the way to the Syrian summit and back. In those swirling snowdrifts there was no chance of anyone overhearing or seeing us. Nonetheless, we spoke in hushed tones.

Back in Israeli territory, Giora suggested we drive to his nearby kibbutz to sleep instead of driving all the way to the Unit.

"Are you sure it's okay?" I asked.

"Sure," Giora said. "I'll drive. It's not that far away."

I dozed off and woke up in midair. The van had hit the curb and flew off the road. It landed deep in the mud of an embankment.

"Damn it," Giora uttered. "We busted the van. What will Shlomo Israeli say?" Shlomo Israeli was the Unit's famed logistics sergeant.

"Giora," I said, "just be glad we're alive."

BACK IN THE Unit after the accident with Giora, I continued to train my soldiers for more operations. Once, after simulating a five-day mission in enemy territory, we awaited extraction by helicopter in a wheat field north of Beer-Sheba. We were exhausted, having passed the week raiding by night and sleeping by day in camouflaged positions. Light planes had simulated dropping us supplies in enemy territory.

Lying on the ground and secretly observing an IDF military base I planned to penetrate later that night as part of the exercise, I suddenly felt a sharp pain in my neck. I had been bitten by a yellow scorpion. My pulse raced to 200 as the paralyzing poison spread to my face and chest.

Leaving the exercise, I rushed by car to Soroka Hospital in Beer-Sheba. Dusting off my fatigues and putting on a brave face as befitting an officer in Sayeret Matkal, I approached the pretty young nurse at the emergency ward.

"Yes, what's your problem?" she asked.

"I was bitten by a yellow scorpion."

"Is that all?" she said. "Just sit down. It will pass in a few hours."

It turned out that yellow scorpions can kill a small child, but to an eighty-kilogram adult they do nothing other than cause severe pain. Chastened, I rejoined my team.

The next night's raid proved more successful. Our task was to penetrate the Dahariya police fort, south of Hebron, and then "eliminate" the force inside it. The key part was to get in without being seen.

To avoid real casualties, the defenders were notified in advance that we were coming, making success that much harder. But by a series of ruses and decoys we were able to complete the penetration without being noticed.

By the end of this week of continual endurance, my fatigues were hardened and bleached by dried sweat. Yet when we reached the end of this great effort, the simulated extraction failed to materialize. The young helicopter pilot sent to extract us could not land because the rotors raised too much dust.

Yoni, as a senior commander in the Unit, had joined me to oversee the extraction exercise.

I looked at him in disbelief.

"You mean to tell me," I asked, "that in a real operation they'll leave us in enemy territory?"

"Wait," he said.

Half an hour later we again heard the familiar throbbing of rotors. The experienced squadron commander, Nehemia Dagan, landed the chopper in one try. Yoni and I went to see him in the cockpit.

"You didn't really think we'd leave you in enemy territory, did you?" he said, grinning.

By now Iddo had joined the Unit. Though he was less physically fit than Yoni and me, he showed great willpower in meeting the Unit's physical demands. He too was later asked to become an officer in the Unit, but he declined.

Yoni wrote to my parents in 1971 about his impression of our younger brother. "Iddo is a very good soldier. He has a good deal of psychological toughness which helps him a lot. I knew he had excellent qualities, but everyone always said, 'Iddo isn't like Yoni and Bibi.' This is true in a way.

It seems to me he is more mature and more critical than we were at his age. In all other matters he falls short of his brothers in nothing."[4]

Now we were three brothers in a unit of no more than a hundred fighters, a clear violation of military norms. The Unit's commanders did their best to separate us in dangerous missions. This was not always a simple task, as the effort to separate Yoni and me during the 1972 Sabena rescue would soon prove.

That rescue was celebrated in Israel. We sixteen soldiers were taken to meet the president, Zalman Shazar, and given other honors. Due to the Unit's secrecy, our identities were kept in the dark. But this did not apply to Ehud Barak, who made sure that leading journalists would write glowingly about him.

Down the years, Barak made much political hay of the Sabena rescue, repeatedly publicizing a photo of himself disembarking the plane in white overalls, not bothering to let people know that he didn't personally storm the plane. He was a bystander. His only role in storming the plane was standing on the tarmac and blowing a whistle.

Touted for years as Israel's most decorated soldier, Barak never bothered to emphasize another largely hidden fact: four of his decorations were given not for leadership under fire but for intelligence-gathering operations. Novel during his time, they were routine by the time I became a team commander in the Unit. The fifth was for overall command of the Unit.

Another Unit officer, Nehemia Cohen, who fell in the Six-Day War, received an equal number of decorations, including one given posthumously for courage under fire in the battle in which he died.[5] In fact, my fellow team officers and I carried out many intelligence missions of the kind Barak was decorated for.

But there was one marked change. Our reward for successfully completing the sort of intelligence missions that Barak had been so lauded for was not a decoration but a dinner in one of the Yemenite restaurants of Tel Aviv's Kerem Hateymanim neighborhood. With the passage of time, as such operations became so routine, even these rewards were dispensed with.

Following the Sabena rescue, I carried my wounded arm in a sling for a few weeks. Seeing this, one of my relatives, bewildered by the many operations I took part in, said, "I don't understand. Aren't there any other soldiers in this army?" There were, and many would soon pay a tragic price in lives lost during the Yom Kippur War. But between the Six-Day War in 1967 and the Yom Kippur War in 1973 the Israeli army carried out an unprecedented number of special ops in which Sayeret Matkal and a few other select units took a leading part.

These were exactly the five years of my military service. In 1972, my active-duty career was coming to an end. During those years I had nearly drowned in a firefight in the Suez Canal and nearly froze to death on the Syrian slopes of Mount Hermon. I was bitten by a scorpion south of Hebron and pierced by a bullet in the Sabena rescue. I had participated as a soldier and commander in clandestine operations across the enemy lines in all the countries that surrounded Israel, sometimes deep beyond our borders.

But I had come out alive, and no less important, so had my men.

BIBI IN COMBAT OPERATIONS
1967–1972*

LEBANON

BEIRUT AIRPORT ★ Beirut

Damascus ★

▲ Mt. Hermon

0 Miles 100

0 Kilometers 100

GOLAN SYRIA

COMBAT SITE

Haifa •

GALILEE

JORDAN RIVER

— Jordan River

SAMARIA

Tel Aviv • LOD AIRPORT KARAMEH

★ Amman

Jerusalem ★

GAZA JUDEA

Ber Sheba •

ISRAEL JORDAN

NEGEV

Mediterranean Sea

SUEZ CANAL

Suez •

Sinai Desert

Eilat • • Aqaba

EGYPT

SAUDI ARABIA

© 2022 Jeffrey L. Ward

* Map does not include missions that remain confidential

10

FAREWELL, LEBANON

1972

There was one final mission in front of me before I went back to civilian life, and it took place in Lebanon on the very day I was released from the army.

Two years earlier, IDF pilots had been shot down over Syria. The Syrian government refused to release them and they languished in jail. A swap was needed. Military intelligence had learned that Syrian intelligence officers who served on the Syrian General Staff would conduct observation tours along the Israel-Lebanon border. Like Syria, Lebanon was in a state of war with Israel and made its border with Israel available to senior Syrian officers. If captured, they would be excellent collateral, especially since high-ranking officers in the Syrian army came from well-connected families favored by the regime.

We set up an ambush in the eastern part of their tour, but the Syrian officers failed to show up. We set up a second ambush on the western side of the tour on a ridge close to the Mediterranean.

Entering Lebanon at night, I led my team to a position I had chosen, a bend in the road below the ridge where the Syrian officers would peer into Israel. Our task was to block the escape route for the Syrians and prevent the arrival of Lebanese reinforcements.

The main force, led by Ehud Barak, was to carry out the ambush farther uphill. Still farther uphill, another team that included Iddo would set up another blocking force to prevent the Syrians from escaping. I set up my camouflaged position fifty meters from the road and went to sleep. At 7 a.m. the sentry woke me up.

"Bibi, there's a tank coming our way!" he said.

A gun barrel appeared on the steep road climbing toward us. Soon we could see that it was attached not to a tank but to an armored vehicle. A Jeep with several armed Lebanese gendarmes followed in tow. Evidently this was the Lebanese forward force. Its commander chose to stop exactly at the bend in the road by which we were hiding.

The gendarmes parked on the side of the road, pulled out some folding chairs, and made coffee. The gun turret of the now-unmanned vehicle was pointed directly at us, but we had not been spotted in our camouflaged position. Fifty meters apart, we both waited for the same Syrian officers to come up the road.

While we lay silently hidden, a Lebanese shepherd passed us by without noticing a thing and headed in the direction of the main force. I alerted Ehud by radio but the shepherd discovered a wire leading to an explosive charge that Ehud's force had prepared for the ambush. The Unit officer closest to the shepherd pounced on him with two other soldiers, one of them Iddo. They pulled the shepherd into the awaiting ambush and told him to lie quietly beside them. Terrified, he did what he was told.

As the time approached for the Syrian officers' arrival, two of the gendarmes began to walk toward my position. I released the safety from my Kalashnikov.

"No one shoots until I shoot," I whispered to my men.

The Lebanese gendarmes came closer, chatting to one another. They were about thirty years old, and for some strange reason they were wearing military overcoats on a hot summer day. I could see the unshaven whiskers on their faces.

I prayed silently, "Please don't look sideways."

I assumed they were married and had children, and I knew that if they glanced at us I would have no choice but to shoot them and the rest of their force. That would scuttle the mission.

Luckily, they too passed by and didn't see us. I silently thanked Salim Shoufi and Meir Har-Zion once again. Their training had just saved *Lebanese* lives and enabled us to continue with the mission.

But I was now faced with a new problem. My men and I were sandwiched between the main Lebanese force with a gun turret pointing straight at us and the two Lebanese gendarmes who had now perched on the slope behind us. When Ehud's force would ambush the officers of the Syrian General Staff, the Lebanese gendarmes in front of and behind us would surely go to help the Syrians. It was up to me and my men to prevent them from doing so.

Dado Elazar, now the IDF's chief of staff, asked me what I thought. I said I could handle it. One of my soldiers would pin down the two gendarmes behind me, one would spray machine gun fire on the main Lebanese force, while I and two other soldiers would run in an arc and finish them off. Unlike in Yoni's simulated exercise in Migdal Zedek three years earlier, when he'd taught me about paying heed to shifts in enemy positions, I could *see* the enemy soldiers and knew they would be totally taken by surprise. After five years in one of the best fighting units in the world, I felt supremely confident in myself and my men.

But Dado did not want to spill too much blood or risk too many casualties in this operation. He instructed Ehud and me to stay hidden and do nothing. When the limousine with the Syrian officers came through, we let it visit the observation post on the ridgeline and return to Beirut. The gendarmes behind us rejoined their comrades, again without spotting us, and they all left the scene peacefully.

We stayed put and planned to leave Lebanon at night. But since Ehud's force had kept the shepherd with them, his sheep had made their way back to the village without him. His fellow villagers went to look for the missing shepherd and came upon Ehud's force.

There was no point in hiding anymore. The main force rose up, released the shepherd, and even chatted with the men from his village. Then they walked back to Israel without incident. My team and I did the same. Returning to the Tel Hashomer base, where I had been inducted five years earlier, I was released from military service.

At dawn, I lay in ambush in Lebanon. At dusk, I was a civilian.

The postscript to this episode came soon. The released shepherd and his comrades spilled the beans and described in detail what happened. The story appeared in a French newspaper. Amazingly, Syrian intelligence failed to pick it up and the Syrian officers continued their tours.

A few weeks later, another contingent of the Unit, this time led by

Yoni with Uzi Dayan as his deputy and including Iddo once again, crossed into Lebanon and set up another ambush. In this third attempt, Yoni had to enter a village and he got the job done. In a brief firefight he and his team seized five senior Syrian officers. A few months later they were exchanged for our imprisoned pilots. Yoni and his team were among those who welcomed the returning pilots in an air base in the north of Israel.

But by the time I heard this, I was back in the United States.

11

MIT

1972–1976

In July 1972 I arrived in Boston and prepared to enroll at MIT's School of Architecture. Having served five years in the military, I was much older than most of my classmates. I soon discovered I could make up for lost time. I took on an exorbitant workload, cramming four years of undergraduate courses into two. After brushing up on my math and physics, I dispensed with attending class in some courses and merely took the semester's final exam.

This required focus. I set a goal, slept little and studied a lot.

My girlfriend Miki and I had parted during my last year of military service, but we reunited in Boston in the summer of 1972. She had completed her undergraduate studies in chemistry at Hebrew University and was accepted as a doctoral student in chemistry at Brandeis University. We were soon married and lived together next to the Brandeis campus in Waltham, Massachusetts. I drove to MIT in Cambridge for school.

A year later, in the summer of 1973, on a brief leave from the army, Yoni joined me in Boston. We both enrolled in Harvard University's summer school, taking Professor Karl Deutsch's seminar on nationalism. I also took an MIT summer course in political science given by Professor Ithiel de Sola Pool, a descendant of the Spanish Jews my father studied and wrote about.

Yoni and I ran in the Greek-style Harvard Stadium, met other Israeli students and reveled in each other's company. We visited our parents in

Ithaca, New York, where my father had become head of the Department of Semitic Languages and Literatures at Cornell University. He was a devoted teacher, hardly ever missing a lecture.

Over the years I received many grateful letters from his American students, and I deeply regretted the fact that he never taught in Israel. Iddo, by then released after his three years of service in the Unit, was at Cornell, about to start his university studies there, when Yoni and I visited our parents. This would be the last time all five of us would be together.

Somehow, I sensed this and had someone photograph us. For years, I've been looking for this last photo of our entire family and have yet to find it.

Back at MIT, I continued my studies with full force. I studied architectural design for my major, but like all undergraduates at the university I also gained a basic familiarity with math, statistics, physics, rudimentary engineering and computers (then using punch cards).

Three things were seared in my mind from that period and would later play a role in my years as prime minister.

The first was the accelerating pace of technological change. When I went to take a math test, students crowded the entrance to the classroom trying to bar entry to one of the students because he had a "pocket" calculator (the size of a shoebox) while we were still using slide rules! The student was allowed in.

That simple event crystallized for me more than all the lectures I heard and all the books I read that technological advance was critical for achieving competitive advantage. In Boston in the 1970s you could clearly see the beginning of the digital revolution. MIT spawned companies in the ring roads that surrounded the city, a model similar to Stanford's Silicon Valley and one that I thought could be replicated in Israel. Companies producing computers and "word processors" were popping up everywhere, and cellular phones were in their early stages of development.

I also heard rumors that a certain building on MIT's campus housed people working for the CIA or something called the NSA. It began to dawn on me that what I was seeing in the Boston area was a winning combination that could launch a thousand technological ships: military intelligence, academia and business clustered together and working in tandem.

Of course, there was one critical component necessary for this model to work: free markets. That, too, began to crystalize in my mind. Technology and free markets were both prerequisites for economic growth. This became one of the fundamental principles that guided my thinking decades later when I set out to reform Israel's economy.

The second event that would leave an enduring impression on me took place in a course I took in statistics. One of the lectures was devoted to the mathematics of epidemics. The most important insight I gained from this course was not merely that epidemics start slowly and suddenly take off. It was that exponential growth is totally *counterintuitive*. Until the curve takes off, most people think that an epidemic will continue to grow incrementally.

This understanding proved invaluable to me fifty years later when I realized that I had to do everything in my power to quickly conclude a deal with Pfizer on vaccines, well before other governments did so. This enabled Israel to get out of the Covid crisis in early 2021 faster than any other country.

The third insight I gleaned at MIT came from that same statistics course. The lecturer asked us a baffling question: "How many Ping-Pong balls could fit in MIT's entrance hall? You have two minutes to reply."

The hall was a cathedral-like space with many nooks and crannies. How could we come up with an answer in 120 seconds? It turns out we could. Quickly estimating the volume of the hall and dividing it by a hypothetical cube made of several Ping-Pong balls, most of us got it right within a reasonable approximation and within 120 seconds!

Years later I would bring up this example in many government meetings. When I asked government officials to estimate how much time or money a certain project would require, the answer would invariably be "We need X weeks or Y months to give that answer." And just as invariably I would hurl the Ping-Pong balls example back at the bureaucrats.

"No, give me your best assessment now," I would say.

But I would be gracious enough to let them have more than two minutes. Most often, I'd request the answer by the end of the meeting or by the beginning of the next. Most of the time intelligent people can give intelligent estimates, and a lot quicker than they think.

Who knows how much money and time were saved for the state of Israel by an MIT lecturer's hypothetical question about Ping Pongs?

12

THE YOM KIPPUR WAR

1973

I didn't hear the news until late in the day on October 6, 1973. Egypt and Syria carried out a surprise attack on Israel on the holiest day of the Jewish year, the Day of Atonement. The Yom Kippur War had broken out.

The war was aimed at reversing the humiliating defeat of 1967 six years earlier and, if luck would hold, achieve a crushing defeat of Israel.

There was a great scramble as Israelis from all over North America tried to get onto the first planes bound for Israel. Along with several Israeli students from MIT who were all reserve officers, I raced to John F. Kennedy International Airport in New York City. Using my connections with Motta Gur, then military attaché in our embassy in Washington, I managed to get on the second plane. Coming from Cornell, Iddo was on the third.

But first I had to *get* to JFK. Shimon Ullman, who was studying artificial intelligence at MIT and later became a successful AI entrepreneur, was the driver. Hitting the curb a few miles before the airport, the car flew in the air.

Not again! I thought.

Shimon, a former air force pilot, somehow steered the vehicle back on the road. Dazed, we quipped that the hard part was behind us; now we only had to get through a war. The plane to Israel was packed with returning reservists. A good many of them would not be alive by the end of the month.

The government was initially at a loss as the war raged on two fronts, north from Syria and south from Egypt. Landing in Israel, I joined a makeshift force of the Unit that went down to the Sinai to guard our tank crews against attacks by Egyptian commandos. The Israeli tank crews were still stunned by the thousands of Egyptian antitank missiles that had taken a terrible toll on lives and machines.

From the Sinai, I was sent to the Syrian front, where I led a clandestine mission in Syrian territory. Our navigation route was photographed from the air a day earlier, showing dead Syrian soldiers who served as route markers for me at night on the way to our mission.

It later emerged that a day before the war, an Egyptian Mossad agent had warned Israel that a surprise attack was imminent.[1] Prime Minister Golda Meir and Defense Minister Dayan failed to act on this and other alarming intelligence warnings.

Not heeding Chief of Staff Elazar's urging, they refused to approve a preemptive strike even after it was fully understood that an attack on Israel was coming. Perhaps they feared being accused of precipitating a new Middle East war, believing that preemptive action would impede support from the United States.

Golda Meir should have known better. I always admired her, and I still believe that she is not fully appreciated for her varied contributions to Israel, including her warm embrace of Soviet Jews when she served as Israel's first ambassador to Moscow in the darkest days of the Cold War. But on the critical decision of preemption, Golda missed the mark.

Preemptive action is always a difficult decision for political leaders because they can never prove what would have happened if they hadn't preempted. Nevertheless, faced with a life-threatening challenge, Israel should always put its security first and when necessary—strike first. The alliance with the US will take care of itself. Most Americans, including their presidents, understand that when push comes to shove, Israel must do what is necessary to defend itself. Besides, everyone likes a winner and striking first usually gives you a big advantage.

This is why, despite objections by US administrations, most Americans ultimately supported Levi Eshkol's decision to preemptively strike the Arab air forces at the start of the Six-Day War and Prime Minister Menachem Begin's decision to destroy Saddam Hussein's nuclear plant in Iraq in 1981. Equally, many Americans have supported my decision to confront Iran's nuclear program and authorize repeated actions against it. Without such assertive policies and actions, Iran would have had a nuclear arsenal long ago.[2]

Of all people, Golda was in a perfect position to mitigate the political cost of preemption. With her perfect American English and her grandmotherly manner, she could have easily defended Israel's actions where it counts most—in American public opinion.

Yet, inexplicably, Golda, who had an excellent rapport with the American people and with President Richard Nixon, failed to act. With no preemptive strike by Israel, Syria and Egypt had an uninterrupted head start. After the initial gains by the Arab armies along the Suez Canal and the Golan, it was left to Israel's enlisted and reserve soldiers to turn the tide of battle. And turn it they did, with great courage and sacrifice.

Within three weeks the UN Security Council demanded a cease-fire. At war's end the Israeli army was at the gates of Damascus and Cairo. Given the multiple surprise attacks that Israel had sustained, this was an unprecedented military turnaround, achieved first and foremost by the heroic actions of Israel's rank and file. Regular soldiers and reservists put their lives on the line against the overwhelming Egyptian and Syrian onslaught.

Along the Suez, Israeli soldiers fought to the death against the Egyptian force that crossed the canal. In the Valley of Tears, in the Golan Heights, tank commanders like the decorated Avigdor Kahalani stood their ground against a vastly superior Syrian force of 1,200 tanks and 50,000 men in what was perhaps the greatest tank battle in Israel's history.

Commanders like Kahalani and Yanosh Ben Gal and enlisted men like Lieutenant Zvika Greengold, who received the Medal of Valor for single-handedly destroying scores of Syrian tanks, saved the day.

Yoni was also among those fighters on the Syrian front. He rushed there with a force from the Unit and offered his help to Raful, then a division commander on the Northern Front. Raful asked him to guard Israel's military headquarters on the Golan at Nafah, which had been nearly overrun by Syrian forces.

On the second day of the war, Yoni's force saw two Syrian helicopters land two kilometers north of Nafah and then take off again. Shai Avital, a young soldier in Yoni's force and later a commander of the Unit, described what happened.

"We spotted a landing of Syrian commandos near Nafah and were told that we were the last force to defend the place. We moved fast to that location. We stood on the road looking for the enemy when suddenly heavy fire was opened on us, killing one of our officers.

"The Syrians caught us in a position very convenient for them. They were behind cover while we were exposed. Somebody had to start giving clear orders or the situation would have been grim. There wasn't much firing after the first barrage. We were waiting for somebody to do something. I began to be frightened, very frightened.

"Then I saw a sight I'll remember all my life. Suddenly Yoni calmly stood up, as if nothing had happened. With hand movements he signaled to the men to get up. We were all lying down behind cover, and he began to go forward as if this were a fire exercise. He walked upright, giving orders right and left. I remember my thoughts as his soldier: Hell, if he can do it, so can I! I got up and started to fight."

An officer in this battle, who was later with Yoni at Entebbe, recalled:

"As soon as they opened fire on us, Yoni conducted a battle the likes of which I've not come across even in the books. I remember we stormed in two groups, Yoni's on one side and mine on the other. When I reached the top of the hill, I saw a crevice farther ahead where one or two Syrians were firing at us.

"Before I could move, Yoni had already taken his men and in a matter of seconds stormed their position. The picture I always remember is that of Yoni running ahead of eight men and destroying the enemy force. When I reached the crevice, I saw ten dead Syrian commandos. This was a classic example of leadership under fire with relatively small losses."

The battle ended with the annihilation of the entire Syrian commando force, which numbered some forty men. Yoni's force of some thirty men suffered two casualties.

Yoni never told me or Iddo the details of this battle, and we didn't ask. Only once did Iddo hear him remark offhandedly, "Poor Syrians. What rotten luck to run into the best fighting unit in the world." Without saying it to him, Iddo thought they had even worse luck. They ran into Yoni.

After blocking the Syrian assault on the Golan, the Israeli army went on the offensive. Yoni's force was attached to the attacking tank battalions for reconnaissance and protection. When the weary tank crews who had been fighting all day were in night encampments, Yoni's force protected them while wiping out enemy tank-hunters. On other nights Yoni reconnoitered behind the Syrian lines and ambushed Syrian supply lines.

After an Israeli tank assault on the dominant Syrian position of Tel Shams failed, Yoni heard over military radio that his friend Yossi Ben Hanan had been left seriously wounded in enemy territory. Ben Hanan was a celebrated tank commander and later a general in the army. A famous photo of him smiling in the Suez Canal while holding high a Kalashnikov rifle had appeared on the cover of *Life* magazine after Israel's victory in 1967.

If Yossi wouldn't be rescued quickly, the Syrians would soon either kill or capture him and his loyal tank driver, who had stayed with him. The area was covered by Syrian machine gun fire. Previous rescue attempts had failed.

Yoni went to Yanosh Ben Gal, the division commander, and volunteered to get Yossi out. Yanosh gave him the go-ahead. En route to the rescue, Yoni and his men met retreating Israeli soldiers who told them, "Don't go there. It's suicide."

They pressed on. When they got beneath Tel Shams in the dark, Yossi shouted to Yoni to go no farther for fear that he and his force would be cut down by Syrian fire.

"Shut up, Yossi," Yoni said. "I'm in command now."

He took the wounded tank commander and his driver back to Israeli lines. For this and his other actions in the war, Yoni was decorated with Israel's Medal of Valor in 1974. When years later a daughter was born to Yossi, he named her "Yoni."

At war's end, the Hermon mountain that had plagued me now plagued my two brothers.

An Israeli reservist force atop the Syrian summit sent distress signals that they were in danger of freezing and needed to be guided down the mountain. Yoni and an extraction force from the Unit, which included Iddo, flew to the Hermon in a helicopter. Because of the fog and the harsh weather conditions, the helicopter could not reach the summit.

Yoni set up a makeshift headquarters at the closest place he could find. He dispatched the extraction team to bring them down.

The team braved the harsh weather and the steep slopes. After a few hours of worsening conditions, the team leader reported that one of the soldiers, Shai Shaham from Kibbutz Kabri, was lagging behind. Suffering from hypothermia, his condition steadily deteriorated.

Yoni told the reservists at the summit to send a force to help carry the soldier to the top. As Shai shivered on the ground, only a kilometer from the summit, his fellow soldiers tried to warm him with their bodies. Nothing helped. The reservists came too late. The team leader reported to Yoni that Shai had died.

They left the body of their fallen comrade and wearily climbed to the top. When they reached the summit they found the rest of the reservists clustered in a nearby cave. The weather soon cleared and the helicopter brought them all down. Shai's body was later retrieved.

This tragedy confirmed to me the horrific cost my team and I were spared in our freezing climb up the Hermon during that terrible blizzard. In tests of survival, luck is often the essential companion to fortitude.

Throughout the war, I anxiously inquired about Yoni and Iddo. Hearing little or nothing about them, I assumed they were alive, and thankfully this was proven true. But the same couldn't be said of many of my childhood friends, fellow soldiers, and other acquaintances. One by one the names of the dead filtered in, at first in a nebulous cloud of rumors and then in a torrent of certainty. Israel lost 2,656 of its finest youth, with thousands more injured, some carrying their wounds for life.

The war ended with the Israeli army on the outskirts of Damascus in the north and 101 kilometers from Cairo in the south. Just three weeks earlier, Defense Minister Dayan warned that we were on the "verge of the destruction of the Third Temple." The remarkable turn-around was achieved by the bravery and sacrifice of the enlisted and reserve soldiers fighting to save the Jewish state and the future of the Jewish people. Going into battle, many felt that the Biblical dream of ages and the destiny of the Chosen People depended solely on their faith and courage.

*   *   *

IN THE SUMMER of 1974, I again returned to Israel from Boston, this time for a voluntary stint of reserve duty. Being a student abroad, I was exempt from this service, but I felt the need to contribute my part in the national effort. One weekend on leave from my reserve duty, I met Yoni in Iddo's book-laden apartment in the charming Ba'ka neighborhood of Jerusalem. After the war, Iddo decided to stay in Israel to study medicine. He was now married to Dafna, a law student at Hebrew University who shared our passionate Zionist values.

The three of us and Iddo's wife, Dafna, decided to go to a movie that evening. Yoni and I went to the ticket counter a few hours before to make sure we had tickets.

Wearing civilian clothes, we patiently stood in line waiting for our turn. Suddenly two young men jumped ahead of the line. The crowd yelled foul, but as the two bullies were big and strong, nobody did anything. Yoni and I looked at each other. We went up to the counter. Yoni, always committed to fairness, told the two to back off.

"I'm a war invalid," lied one of them (disabled soldiers don't need to stand in line).

Yoni rolled up his sleeve, showing the scar of his war wound. "Are you really?" he said, pushing the bully aside.

A brief scuffle followed between the four of us. The bullies left without getting their tickets.

"We'll be back with our entire gang and we'll get you guys!" they warned us.

Back in Iddo's apartment before the movie, Yoni, Iddo and I prepared contingencies. What if they did come back with reinforcements? We put our special forces training to use, a team of three, and devised a quick plan. Yoni and I would wear our army boots (to be able to kick better). Iddo would serve as a clandestine reserve force in the rear. Dafna and Ophir, the German shepherd dog that Dafna had raised, would stay behind in the parking lot just in case the goons decided to go for the car.

At the designated time, we went to the movie theater. The bad guys didn't show up.

Yet humorous as the story was, I remember that weekend in Iddo's apartment for a far more profound reason. It was then that I had one of the most memorable conversations of my life. Yoni and I spoke about the

Yom Kippur War. He didn't say a word about his exploits, the battles he had led or the decorations he received for rescuing Yossi Ben Hanan.

What he did say was a quiet rephrasing of what he had observed eight years earlier in one of his unforgettable letters to the family in Philadelphia, after his first battle in Es-Samu: "In battle, lions become rabbits."

"In war," he said to me, "reputations evaporate, only character holds."

He noted that he knew that he was among the few who kept their wits, who knew what to do in the face of mortal danger and who did it.

He didn't say this in self-aggrandizement but in a tone of sadness tinged with a genuine concern for Israel's future. I should have reassured him that a people producing heroes like him will overcome whatever challenges the future will throw at us. But stunned by his somber mood, I said nothing. This was the last time I saw him.

13

HASBARA

1973–1976

T he Yom Kippur War had a deep impact on all Israelis. The tragedy of losing friends as well as the understanding that Israel must
never again allow itself to be vulnerable weighed on me, as it did on many
others.

The trauma of losing so many soldiers and the mismanagement by
the government of the war's early stages also shattered what had been
until now the political invincibility of the Labor Party. Though Labor
still won the elections in 1974, the aftershock of the war heralded its
defeat in the polls by the Likud Party in 1977, under Menachem Begin's
leadership.

When I returned to Boston after the war, I barely slept for close to
a week. On a cold November day, I climbed the steps leading to MIT's
main building on Massachusetts Avenue in Cambridge to return to my
studies. Arab students were vociferously handing out anti-Israel leaflets. I
noticed a small group of Israeli students handing out *pro*-Israeli material.

I walked up and offered my help to one, a doctoral student in engineering named Uzi Landau. He would later become a Knesset member
for Likud and serve as transportation minister in one of my governments.

On that day on the steps of MIT, Uzi ushered me into the trenches
of the Hasbara[1] war, Israel's never-ending public relations battle against
slander and defamation. In Boston this battle involved volunteers from
the Israeli Student Organization, who worked in close cooperation with

Israel's deputy consul general in Boston, Colette Avital. A future member of Knesset for Labor, Colette often says she is responsible for launching my public career.

I was now sent by the student organization to give lectures defending Israel to anyone who would listen. Since I was the new kid on the block, I traveled to less-desirable locations. My first speaking engagement was at the Shabbat Breakfast Club at a synagogue in the town of Hull, thirty miles from Boston. The club consisted of ten elderly Jewish men who ate Shabbat breakfast at the back of the shul. The youngest was in his late seventies. I knocked on the door and went in. The members were busy eating and talking noisily.

"Abe, pass the butter."

"I already did, you *alte kaker*. You pass me the lox."

I cleared my throat, but this elicited no response.

"What about the potato salad?"

"There's no potato salad today."

"So pass the bagels."

I cleared my throat again.

"Who's that? Is that the kid from Boston?" someone asked.

I used that as my entry cue. Introducing myself, I started to go through the detailed presentation I had prepared on the Arab oil boycott which was choking America. My talk was constantly interrupted by "Hey, Mo, any more lox left?" or "Where's the cream cheese, anyone see the cream cheese?" but also an occasional "Let the boy speak!"

Such was my introduction to public speaking. I never had a tougher audience.

It took me a while to learn a simple rule: *You have to start with the bagels.*

Like all banal sayings, the one about connecting with your audience was true.

Passionate and didactic, I initially structured my speeches logically, but it was *my* logic and *my* structure. Over time I learned how to relate these to the experiences of my audience.

The more I studied the Middle East, the better I got at presenting my ideas. My fellow Israeli student at MIT Yossi Riemer and I took on research assistant positions at the local Jewish Federation. Together we produced a study showing that the Middle East was rife with internecine Arab conflicts and a deep hatred of the West.

What was clear was that the Arab radicals didn't hate the West because of Israel, *they hated Israel because of the West*. Israel represented the kind of open and liberal Western society they detested.

In those days these conclusions were downright heretical. Many Western intellectuals and diplomats believed that the Arab and Muslim world's hostility toward the US and Europe was solely rooted in American support for Israel. Once that support ceased, or Israel ceased to be, the anti-Western hostility would disappear.

Yossi and I did our modest part to help debunk this false proposition by coming up with a simple chart. We listed numerous violent attacks reported in various conflicts within the Arab world in a single month.[2] None had anything to do with Israel. How then could Israel be the cause? And anyway, why was the Middle East "conflict" always in the singular and not in the plural?

The region suffered from a surfeit of *conflicts*: Arabs against Arabs, Arabs against non-Arabs, Shiites against Sunnis, Islamic radicals against moderates, and nearly everyone against the West.

A far greater number of lives were being lost in these conflicts than in all the Arab-Israeli wars combined. Israel, Yossi and I said, was the only solid rock in these shifting and violent sands and the only reliable ally of the United States in the Middle East.

Pretty soon word got out in the Boston area that we had something new to say and a new way of saying it. Speaking invitations poured in.

This culminated three years later in a televised debate in Boston's Faneuil Hall organized by WGBH, Boston's PBS television channel. The subject was "Should the US support the establishment of a Palestinian state?" On the pro side was the veteran American diplomat George Ball and the Arab academic Fouad Ajami, who later wrote courageously about the ills of Arab extremism and became a defender of Israel as well as an admirer of my father. But in that debate, he and Ball squared off against me and Michael Dukakis, a member of the Massachusetts House of Representatives and later governor of Massachusetts and a presidential candidate. In those days I used the family name Nitay when in America—the pen name my father used to sign his many influential articles in the 1930s in support of Zionism—because it was easier for Americans to pronounce.

By now experience had tempered my manner. This helped because television favors cool over hot. Dukakis and I won the debate with a broad margin in an audience polled in liberal Boston.[3]

I didn't know it at the time, but my rise in Israel's Hasbara battles occurred against the wishes of Israel's top representative in Boston. In 2021, Colette Avital revealed the degree to which Israeli bureaucracy was politicized when she served at the Boston consulate. She recalled the instructions she received from her boss, the consul general. One day, she said, he showed her "two drawers with two sets of cards and said: 'The white cards list the people we are in contact with, the blue cards list the people who we were not allowed to be in contact with. One name on the blue cards was an architecture student named Benjamin Nitay.' "[4] To Colette's credit, she disregarded this instruction.

This incredible politicization of putting party above country at all times was not in my makeup. Even while at school, though I was coming from the right, I devoted vast amounts of my time to helping the Labor government of Yitzhak Rabin by defending his policies in my many speaking engagements. I did so because I believed it was important for my country.

AFTER THE TRAUMA of the Yom Kippur War, Israel was being pressed by Secretary of State Henry Kissinger to withdraw from the Suez Canal without receiving any significant concessions from Egypt. Resisting this pressure required the application of counterpressure. It was on this issue that I finally understood my father's great political insights, and it was here that he taught me principles of statesmanship that would guide me in future years.

Father was still teaching at Cornell University. Earlier, when he had been a professor at the University of Denver, he and Mother had invited their next-door neighbors, the Reverend John Wesley Rice and his wife Angelena over for dinner. They were accompanied by their young teenage daughter, Condoleezza, already a gifted pianist. Neither set of parents could possibly imagine that one day their children would meet on the world stage, Condoleezza as US national security advisor and later as secretary of state, and me as the prime minister of Israel.

Coming to Boston often in 1974, Father would occasionally meet our tight-knit band of Israeli students at MIT. In addition to Uzi Landau and Yossi Riemer, it would eventually include the Leventer brothers, Yoav and Oded; Shlomo Kalish, a fighter pilot who later became a Lubavitch follower and venture capitalist; and two other brothers, Zvika and Hanan Livneh, who both served with Yoni, Iddo, and me in the Unit. Zvika and Yoni were on the same team that raided Beirut in 1972 and eliminated PLO leaders plotting attacks on Israel. Both Livneh brothers were to tragically die of cancer at the age of fifty.

The members of our small Israeli community at MIT supported each other. We occasionally went skiing together on the icy New Hampshire slopes and regularly discussed current affairs, including with my father when he came to visit.

My conversations with Father were eye-opening. He put forward a stark proposition: in today's world, you can't defend a military victory without a political victory; you can't defend a political victory without a victory in public opinion; and you can't win public opinion without an appeal to justice. If your adversaries succeed in portraying your cause as unjust, they will gradually erode your position. It didn't matter if your cause was a genuinely moral one if you didn't present it as such. Some of the greatest aggressors in history portrayed themselves as just and their victims as unjust. This happened to Israel time and again. Israel kept winning on military battlefields and losing on political ones. Israel's clearly just war of self-defense in 1967 was portrayed by Arab propaganda as an aggressive war of conquest. They conveniently hid the fact that they laid a siege of death on the tiny Jewish state, choked its trade route to Asia and formed a tristate military pact that openly called for Israel's annihilation.

Arab propaganda systematically covered up the true root cause of the Israeli-Arab conflict—the persistent Arab refusal to recognize a Jewish state, whatever its borders. It covered up the fact that the PLO, the Palestine Liberation Organization, was established in 1964, three years before Israel's victory in the Six-Day War, during which Israel seized control of Judea, Samaria and Gaza.[5] Where exactly was the Palestine that the PLO sought to liberate before the Six-Day War in 1967? Judea, Samaria, the Golan and the Sinai were in *Arab hands* when the war broke out. There were no "occupied territories" to liberate when the PLO was established. Its goal was to annihilate Israel, pure and simple.

Retroactively erasing this simple historical fact in the minds of many in the West was a tremendous victory for Arab propaganda. It was a truly Orwellian inversion, achieved through what I later called the reversal of causality, turning the *results* of Arab aggression against Israel in 1967 into its *cause*.

This echoed a similar ploy used after Israel's War of Independence in 1948, when the Arab states turned one of the war's results, Arab refugees, into its cause. But there wasn't a single Arab refugee when six Arab armies set out to destroy fledgling Israel at its birth. In fact, the Arab-initiated war on Israel resulted in *two* refugee problems, not one—a great number of Jewish refugees were expelled from Arab countries after the war. After the War of Independence, Arab propaganda turned history on its head.

These and other fictions were used by the Arab world to mobilize international pressure on Israel to withdraw from the territories of Judea, Samaria, the Golan and the Sinai, which it took in legitimate wars of self-defense.

Arab propaganda was not limited to falsifying modern history. It sought to falsify *ancient* history as well, beginning with its appropriation of the term *Palestine*, a term whose complex history was deliberately obfuscated for political purposes.

The name Palestine is derived from the Philistines, a seafaring people from Crete who invaded the coast of present-day Israel around 1200 BCE, shortly after the Israelite conquest. The main Philistine dominions never extended much beyond the coastal strip between Gaza and today's Tel Aviv, and the Philistines disappeared as a people under the Babylonian conquest in the sixth century BCE. It was the Roman Empire, bent on destroying every vestige of Jewish attachment to their land after two successive Jewish rebellions, that invented the name *Palestina* to replace *Judea*, the original name of the country, with the intention of obliterating its historic Jewish identity.[6]

While the Roman name disappeared in the land itself shortly after the Muslim conquest in the seventh century CE, Christian cartographers kept it alive in their own lands and bequeathed it to the Allied negotiators at the 1917 Versailles Peace Conference and then to its inhabitants, who adopted it once the British took control following World War I.

Until the twentieth century, the name Palestine referred exclusively to the ancient land of the Jews, as did the names Judea, Judah, Zion and Israel. The Arabs who lived there were called Arabs, just as the Armenians, Turks, Druze and Circassians who migrated into Palestine were still called Armenians, Turks, Druze and Circassians. With the exception of the Jews, who called the land "Eretz Israel" (the Land of Israel) and viewed it as their national home, all of those groups considered themselves to be living in "Southern Syria," and never identified the land as a unique national homeland for themselves.

Paradoxically, under the British Mandate[7] between the two world wars, it was the *Jews* who often referred to themselves as Palestinians. As Golda Meir once said, "I am a Palestinian. From 1921 to 1948, I carried a Palestinian passport [issued by the British Mandate]. There was no such thing in this area as Jews, Arabs and Palestinians. There were Jews and Arabs."[8] Earlier, she had also said, "There was no Palestinian people considering itself as Palestinians."[9]

Thus, before the term *Palestine* was politicized, it was simply a synonym for the geographic area encompassing the Land of Israel, or Eretz Israel, and was used as such between the two world wars. While the Palestinians can argue that their national identity emerged in the first half of the twentieth century, the historical facts simply do not support the false claim that an Arab Palestinian national consciousness goes back earlier than that. It didn't.

In Boston after the Yom Kippur War, Father stressed that the campaign for public opinion and the fight against Arab propaganda had to be coupled with a systemic and direct appeal to leaders. Whereas a public campaign should center mainly on questions of justice, the appeal to leaders should center mainly on interests: Why is the position we are advocating in the interest of your country? What will be the benefit to the US for supporting our position and what will be the costs of opposing it? Bring the argument to leaders, my father said. If you can't get to them, get to those who can influence them, and no less important, to those who would oppose them.

After the Yom Kippur War, Israel was under heavy US pressure to withdraw from parts of the Sinai and the Golan. Father suggested that we approach Eugene Rostow, formerly President Johnson's undersecretary for political affairs. After the Six-Day War, Rostow had helped draft United Nations Security Council Resolution 242, which stipulated that in a peace settlement Israel would withdraw "from territories" to secure and recognized boundaries. Rostow and his colleagues deliberately used the phrase "*from* territories" rather than "*the* territories," to make it clear that Israel was not being asked to give up all of the land it had gained in self-defense and return to its immensely vulnerable pre–Six-Day War borders. Moreover, by insisting on "secure and recognized boundaries" they conditioned such a withdrawal on security and peace arrangements with Israel's neighbors.[10] Rostow was clearly a great supporter of Israel. We would try to convince him that the present American policy was endangering not only Israeli interests but American interests as well.

We went to Washington to see Rostow in 1974. Father argued that current US policy was weakening America's only reliable ally in the Middle East and therefore weakening America in the face of Soviet attempts to dominate the region. Rostow agreed and arranged meetings for us with Paul Nitze and Admiral Elmo "Bud" Zumwalt, two highly respected figures in the American defense establishment.

I mostly listened during these meetings, impressed by Father's cogent presentation. He combined civility and firmness, quickly painting with an artist's brush the strategic picture he wanted to convey. He listened patiently to questions and opposing views, answering them honestly and to the point.

It was then that I realized I was in the company of a master. Only then did I learn what my father had done in the United States during the 1940s, activities he never publicized. They were so startling that they bear some elaboration, especially since I later replicated some of them during Israel's battle against Iran's nuclear program.

14

FATHER

W ho shaped Father's thinking on Zionism?

First and foremost, Theodor Herzl.

The founder of political Zionism wrote about the impending destruction of European Jewry forty years before it happened. As Father wrote, "It was clear to Herzl that what awaited the Jewish People was extinction."

What is amazing about Father's analysis is that it was written three years *before* the advent of World War II and the Holocaust, by a young man of twenty-seven. After the Holocaust, it was often said that few, if any, foresaw its horrors. This is patently not true.

Even as a twenty-three-year-old, in 1933, my father was one of those remarkably perceptive people who sensed what was coming. That year, he wrote what appears in hindsight as an astonishing prophecy.

> Racial antisemitism is inciting a global war against the existence of the Jews, as a race that "poisons" human society. If racial antisemitism spreads, it will not only endanger Jewish rights but the existence of Jewish people everywhere.
>
> In the face of the *Holocaust* facing the Jewish people, our role is to repeatedly remind the entire world what Germany is inculcating to its own sons. We can only crush racial antisemitism if we prove that German racism is not directed at Jews alone. We must

convince others that Hitlerism's attack on the Jews of Germany is an attack on human society as a whole.[1]

Perhaps the history of the twentieth century and the fate of multitudes, including six million Jews, would have been different if more had paid heed to such warnings in time.

In addition to Herzl, the primary influence on my father's recognition of what was happening at a time when virtually all other Jewish leaders dismissed such warnings as "alarmist" and "panicky" was the Russian Jewish activist and founder of Revisionist Zionism, Ze'ev Jabotinsky. In Warsaw in 1938, on the Jewish fast day of Tisha B'av (marking the destruction of the Second Temple in Jerusalem by the Romans), he said to Poland's three million Jews, almost none of whom were to survive the war:

For three years I have been imploring you, Jews of Poland, the crown of world Jewry, appealing to you, warning you unceasingly that the catastrophe is nigh. My hair has turned white and I have grown old these years, for my heart is bleeding that you, dear brothers and sisters, do not see the volcano which will soon begin to spew forth its fires of destruction. I see a horrible vision. Time is growing short for you to be spared. I know you cannot see it, for you are troubled and confused by everyday concerns. . . . Listen to my words at this, the twelfth hour. For God's sake: let everyone save himself, so long as there is time to do so, for time is running short.

But Jabotinsky, like Herzl, also saw a glimmer of light in the darkness: the establishment of a Jewish state. Today more streets in Israel are named after Jabotinsky than after any other person, this in honor of a man who never assumed power, who died before the establishment of the state, and who in his lifetime and decades afterward was vilified like few others before him.

In addition to Herzl and Jabotinsky, Father was also influenced by Max Nordau, the late-nineteenth-century European writer whose seminal book, *Degeneration*, foresaw the coming decline of Europe. Nordau's conversion to Zionism came one day in the autumn in 1895 when his young friend Herzl called on him. Herzl's advocacy for the immediate establishment of a Jewish state, and the exodus of Jews to it, was perceived by most as utter folly. One of his friends, Jacob Schiff, suggested that he present his project to Nordau because in addition to being a writer Nordau happened to be a psychiatrist.

"Schiff says that I'm insane," Herzl said.

Nordau turned to his friend and said, "If you are mad, then I am mad as well. I'm behind you and you can count on me."[2]

Thus began a unique partnership between two of Europe's leading Jewish intellectuals, combining prophetic genius with pragmatic purpose. Together they gave birth to political Zionism, the movement that revolutionized modern Jewish history. Mount Zion in the heart of Jerusalem, and the name Zion itself, which was synonymous with our eternal capital, symbolized the reestablishment of a Jewish state in which the scattered Jewish people would reassemble and begin their national life anew.

After the horrors of the Holocaust, Father was seized by the urgency of forming a Jewish state. Like Herzl, he saw it as the indispensable instrument to ensuring Jewish survival. Yet he was also preoccupied with the question of how the Jewish state, once established, could continue to survive. In this he was greatly influenced by Jabotinsky's 1923 essay "The Iron Wall," which argued that Arab reconciliation with Zionism would occur only when the Jewish state became so strong that the Arabs would abandon any hope of destroying it.

This would require, of course, a strong Jewish army. In this, Father deeply valued the efforts of the Jewish commander Joseph Trumpeldor and the non-Jewish officer John Henry Patterson, who joined Jabotinsky in forming the Jewish Legion in World War I. Father also greatly admired Aaron Aaronsohn.

Aaronsohn was a brilliant scientist who in 1906, as a young man of thirty-three, discovered "the mother of wheat," emmer, believed to be the ancestor of all modern wheat plants. This discovery would eventually help feed millions.[3] In many ways Aaronsohn pioneered Israel's agricultural innovation that would later make it famous throughout the world.

But Aaronsohn also pioneered something else. In World War I, he created the first Jewish intelligence network in modern times, harking back to Joshua's spies 3,500 years earlier. Who could imagine that the intelligence-gathering base located in his experimental agriculture farm would serve as an inspiration to the Mossad and Israeli military intelligence, institutions that remain critical for Israel's security?

Prior to the war, the Ottoman Empire had ruled the Holy Land for four centuries. Aaronsohn was convinced that the Ottoman Turks would never willingly cede land to create an independent Jewish state. They would have to be driven out. When the Great War (World War I) broke out, pitting the Allied powers, including Britain, against the Central Powers, including Turkey, Aaronsohn secretly went to Cairo to meet British commander General Edmund Allenby's superb intelligence officer, Colonel Richard Meinertzhagen. With Meinertzhagen's blessing, Aaronsohn began operating a spy ring on the shores of the Mediterranean under the code name NILI, an abbreviation of a Biblical phrase referring to the eternity of Israel's destiny.[4] He and his thirty brave colleagues recruited from neighboring communities provided invaluable intelligence to the British, including the secret communication code used between the Germans and the Turks. The information Aaronsohn supplied helped change the course of the war.

Aaronsohn's efforts were deeply appreciated by the British. After the war, British intelligence official Baron William Ormsby-Gore said that NILI was "admittedly the most valuable nucleus of our intelligence in Palestine during the war." A secret letter thanking the NILI network acknowledged that Britain could not have won the war against Turkey without the aid of the NILI spies.[5]

Aaronsohn also had a decisive impact on the British officer and diplomat Sir Mark Sykes, one of the influential officials who helped draft the Balfour Declaration in 1917. The declaration proclaimed support for "the establishment in Palestine of a national home for the Jewish people."[6] Upon its completion, Sykes burst into the adjoining room and joyously proclaimed, "It's a boy!" Many know that Chaim Weizmann, who had lobbied effectively for the declaration, was in that room on that momentous day. Few know that so was Mark Sykes's friend, Aaron Aaronsohn.[7,8]

The gifted and eccentric Sykes was to die in the Spanish flu epidemic in 1919. That same year, Aaronsohn tragically died in a plane crash over the English Channel.

I have often thought of the extraordinary spirit of NILI's heroes, and especially of Aaron Aaronsohn. The outstanding American diplomat William Bullitt, who had met Aaronsohn during World War I, wrote this of him: "The Jewish race had many brilliant leaders but when Aaron died I believe it lost the man who, before all others, could kindle the hearts and minds of men of other nations to active sympathy. And not Zion alone will suffer for his loss."

"He was the greatest man I have ever known,"[9] Bullitt summed up. This, from a worldly statesman who was a senior trusted advisor to Presidents Woodrow Wilson and Franklin Roosevelt and who worked closely with Lloyd George, Winston Churchill and Charles de Gaulle.

Would our history have been different if this visionary man of action had not died young? Would he have achieved political prominence despite his utter inability to suffer fools? Would he have been able to use his towering intellect, his great influence over British and American officials and the IOUs he collected from the British military during World War I to break the blockade of Jewish immigration to Palestine from Europe imposed by Great Britain, which backtracked on the Balfour Declaration between the wars?

I can't dismiss the possibility. Some people *are* irreplaceable.

BY HIS TWENTIES, Father had already earned a name for himself as a prominent intellectual, producing a prodigious body of writing that made a deep impression on his readers. This reputation paved the way for his fateful meeting with Jabotinsky in London in 1939.

As the leader of Revisionist Zionism, Jabotinsky advocated for Jewish rights over all of our ancient homeland and a liberal economy. This was opposed by Socialist Zionism, led by David Ben Gurion, which was more inclined to a territorial compromise and preferred a socialist economy.

Father had been deeply influenced by Jabotinsky ever since he was a student in Hebrew University, when he read Jabotinsky's articles and saw him protesting against Britain's abandonment of the Balfour Declaration. At the age of twenty-four, Father founded and edited a daily newspaper, *Ha-Yarden* (The Jordan). Inspired by Jabotinsky, Father advanced through his newspapers the goals of establishing a Jewish national home, securing unrestricted Jewish immigration and achieving an independent

Jewish state. This necessitated repeated attacks on British policy, which by then actively opposed these goals. In response the British Mandate government shut down *Ha-Yarden* several times.

Jabotinsky had developed the "Theory of Public Pressure" in an article he wrote in the spring of 1929.[10] He posited that the most potent influence on democratic governments is the pressure of public opinion. It matters not, he argued, if a government is headed by the friendliest of leaders. If your opponents apply sufficient pressure on that government, it will eventually tilt against you. To balance this, you must sway public opinion to your side by an unceasing public campaign "like the constant drizzle on a green English lawn," he said.[11]

Jabotinsky wanted to appeal directly to British public opinion in order to press the British government to change its policies toward Zionism. Because of Arab pressure and a desire to adhere to its colonialist policies, Britain had become resolutely opposed to unrestricted Jewish immigration to Eretz Israel and the creation of a Jewish state. Pro-Zionist counterpressure was needed. And where to better apply it than in London? Jabotinsky based himself there.

In 1939 Father thought this was a mistake. He went to London to see Jabotinsky.

"I believe you should move your activities to the United States," Father said.

"Why?" Jabotinsky asked, intrigued by this frontal challenge from a man half his age.

"Because you should be in America," Father answered. "The United States is a rising power in the world and its policy on Zionism will be critical. It has a large Jewish community. Convince America, and it will force Britain to change its policies."[12]

Agreeing with Father's analysis, Jabotinsky assembled a delegation of Revisionist Zionists from several countries. Father came as a representative from Eretz Israel and raised significant amounts of money from wealthy supporters of Revisionist Zionism to fund the delegation's activities.

The group arrived in New York. At first they made no headway. The leaders of the American Jewish community were largely opposed to Zionism, as was President Roosevelt, who believed support for Zionism would place an undue burden on Britain's relationship with the Arab world.

In the face of the stagnant response to their efforts, Father suggested to Jabotinsky that they shift their initial focus toward the creation of a Jewish army to help the Allies fight the Nazis, an idea that Jabotinsky had been advocating since the beginning of the war. Giving the Jewish people a military force of its own after centuries of being largely defenseless was important in its own right, and would also help pave the way for eventual Jewish statehood. Jabotinsky agreed. The delegation convened a rally promoting this idea in Madison Square Garden. It drew thousands and was a resounding success. The path forward was opened.

Then, on August 3, 1940, at a Beitar Movement summer camp near New York, Jabotinsky died of a heart attack at the age of sixty. My father was one of his pallbearers. The shock and despondency of his many followers around the Jewish world are hard to describe. It was second only to that felt by multitudes of Jews after Herzl's early death in 1904. The shepherd was gone, the sheep scattered.

Father was equally forlorn, but he recovered and pressed on. A year and a half after Jabotinsky's death, the New Zionist Organization of America asked Father to succeed Jabotinsky as its head. From that position he made efforts to influence both public opinion and American leaders.

The public campaign included ads in leading newspapers attacking British anti-Zionism. Father solicited funds to finance these ads. They were pointed, sharp and powerful.[13] In the pre-television age this form of political advertising helped galvanize American public opinion for Zionism.

My father coupled this campaign with numerous meetings with journalists and newspaper editors, and with many rallies and public meetings. Some of these public gatherings were attended by Colonel John Henry Patterson, the British commander of the Jewish Legion in World War I, the first Jewish fighting force in close to two millennia. During that war, Jabotinsky had lobbied the British authorities to establish such a force. Patterson was chosen as its commander.

Patterson's Jewish soldiers performed admirably at Gallipoli and later in Palestine. His second-in-command was Joseph Trumpeldor, who had been a valiant Jewish officer in the Russian army and who lost an arm in the Russo-Japanese War of 1905.

"Trumpeldor," Patterson later said, "was the bravest man I ever saw."[14]

After his advance in the British army was blocked by his pro-Zionist sentiment, Patterson ended up in the United States, where he befriended my parents. Father and Patterson had great admiration for each other. When my parents had their firstborn son in New York in 1946, they named him Jonathan, the "Jon" in honor of Patterson and the "Nathan" in honor of my grandfather.

I grew up with a silver cup given by Patterson to Yoni on his *Brit* (circumcision). It says: "To my darling godson Jonathan from your God-father J. H. Patterson." On important family occasions, including my marriage and the Brit ceremonies of my two sons, we drank from this cup.

Thus, the commander of the first Jewish fighting force since the Bar Kokhba revolt two millennia earlier passed the cup to one of the future commanders in the army of the Jewish state. Patterson died in America in 1947 and asked in his will to be buried next to his brave Jewish soldiers. In 2016 we carried out his will. As prime minister I participated in a ceremony in which Patterson's remains were buried next to his men in Moshav Avichail, near the city of Netanya. His grandson and the descendants of his Jewish soldiers attended the ceremony.

DURING WORLD WAR II, Father's relentless public campaign in America for a Jewish state gathered momentum. But it still did not tip the balance of American policy. Roosevelt remained adamantly opposed to the creation of a Jewish state. Yet from the outset, Father did something virtually unprecedented in Zionist and Jewish circles at the time.

He went to the Republicans.

He did so not because of an innate identification with this or that party but because he believed that influencing Republican policy was the best way to influence *Democratic* policy. It's hard to describe how novel this approach was at the time. Then, nearly all American Jews were Democrats and shunned Republicans, an attitude reciprocated by the Republicans.

My father's entry to Republican circles was facilitated by the beautiful and intelligent congresswoman Clare Boothe Luce, wife of *Time* magazine publisher Henry Luce. A brilliant editor and writer in her own right, she was impressed by Father's unconventional arguments and the way they addressed American interests.

She introduced him to a host of Republican leaders, most notably Senate Minority Leader Robert Taft. My father presented to Taft the arguments of why it was in America's interest to support the creation of a Jewish state. In June 1944, the Republican Party in its national convention adopted a platform calling for unrestricted Jewish emigration to the Land of Israel and for the establishment of a Jewish state there. Roosevelt was furious, but just as Father had predicted, he was cornered. Within a few months the Democratic Party's national convention adopted the same resolution supporting the creation of a Jewish state.

Many believe that bipartisan American support for the establishment of Israel came only after President Harry Truman's recognition of Israel. In fact, the twin resolutions by Republicans and Democrats preceded this recognition by four years and in many ways facilitated it. And the main engine for this bipartisan support for a Jewish state was Father and his group at the New Zionist Organization of America. With relentless and focused activities, they achieved this remarkable breakthrough not by cowing to anti-Zionism but by standing up to it, and by appealing to the pro-Zionist sentiments cultivated earlier by American evangelicals.

My father was thus one of the de facto progenitors of America's bipartisan support for the state of Israel and the first to bring it into practical fruition. It was ironic that decades later I would be falsely accused of not appreciating the importance of American bipartisan support for Israel when in fact my own father had initiated it.

But he was not alone. Other people participated in the effort, most prominently the Irgun (armed Zionist organization) activist Peter Bergson and the journalist-playwright Ben Hecht. Unlike Father who concentrated on the demand for a Jewish state from the start, Bergson initially concentrated solely on urging America to save European Jews. He therefore studiously avoided criticizing Britain's anti-Zionist policies. It was only later that he and his group joined the demand for the creation of a Jewish state.

Much of Father's activities and those of Bergson and his Irgun group are described by the historian Rafael Medoff in his book *Militant Zionism in America*.[15] One reviewer summed up Medoff's findings: "Their genius lay in their ability to influence U.S. policy and [Medoff] credits them with three political achievements: 1) Assent by England, which needed American support, to a Jewish fighting force to join the Allied struggle against Hitler; 2) Roosevelt's creation of the War Refugee Board, his only meaningful response to Hitler's annihilation of the Jews; 3) Republican adoption in 1944 of a convention plank endorsing Palestine immigration and statehood, a move the Democrats felt obliged to imitate, thereby establishing an important precedent in American politics."[16]

Father never took credit for his immensely important historic contributions to the struggle to establish the Jewish state. A true idealist, he was content with the results of his efforts and didn't publicize his own role in achieving them. This placed him among the rare people in public life who actually achieve lasting change, and distinguished him from so many run-of-the-mill politicians who take credit for things they had nothing to do with. The result was that until recent years, the historical record of Zionism omitted Father's many contributions.

The concerted efforts of decades of Labor governments further minimized awareness of Father's influence, as well as that of nearly all who didn't share Labor's ideological views. This was particularly true regarding the role of the underground resistance organizations. The Haganah, associated with the Labor Party, was lionized in school curriculums and official ceremonies. The Irgun and the Lehi, associated with the Herut Party (later Likud), were hardly ever credited for their decisive role in ending British Mandatory rule, which paved the way for Israel's independence.

OVER THE YEARS I have often been falsely accused of intervening in American elections on behalf of Republicans, something I scrupulously avoided doing. That accusation was also leveled at Yitzhak Rabin when he served as Israel's ambassador to Washington during the Nixon years. Rabin's accuser was none other than the historian Arthur Schlesinger Jr., a speechwriter for President John F. Kennedy and an advisor to the Democratic Party.

Writing in the *New York Times* before the 1972 presidential elections, Schlesinger had slammed Rabin in a wild screed: "No foreign envoy since the unfortunate Sackville-West in 1888 has intervened so mindlessly in internal American politics."[17] Rabin protested that these accusations were baseless.

Like Rabin, I was motivated not by partisanship but by the questions of which policies would best serve Israel's interests at any given time. As a student active in Israel's public relations efforts in America and later as an Israeli diplomat in the US, the people I first approached to counter American pressure on Israel or to confront international terrorism were not Republicans but traditional Democrats like Eugene Rostow, Senators Henry Jackson, Daniel Inouye, and Daniel Patrick Moynihan and Congressman Tom Lantos. My approach was always based on *policy*, not *party*. I approached American administrations not as a Republican or as a Democrat but as an *Israeli*. Thus I later opposed President George H. W. Bush's political pressure on Israeli prime minister Yitzhak Shamir (so much so that Secretary of State James Baker temporarily sought to bar me from the State Department), President George W. Bush's pressure on Prime Minister Ariel Sharon's government during Operation Defensive Shield, and President Barack Obama's policies on the Iran nuclear agreement. On questions I believed crucial for Israel's security and future, I tried to recruit the support of leaders from both parties, and I contested presidents of both parties equally when I believed their policies endangered Israel.

In my official capacity as deputy chief of mission in Israel's embassy in Washington, I accompanied Shimon Peres, then leader of the Opposition in the Israeli Knesset, to his 1982 meeting with President Ronald Reagan when our ambassador Moshe Arens was on a visit to Israel. Peres, an activist in the Labor Party from a very young age, had been defense minister during the Entebbe rescue and now as leader of the Labor Party he was running for the post of prime minister. A year later, as acting ambassador, I met the Democratic candidate for president Walter Mondale at his request, alongside my meetings with President Reagan's top officials. Contrary to later falsifications, I maintained this evenhanded policy when I became leader of the Opposition myself and then prime minister, meeting time and again with opposing presidential candidates Bill Clinton and

Bob Dole and opposing candidates Mitt Romney and Barack Obama. I also met with hundreds of American lawmakers. Half were Democrats, half Republicans.

In this I emulated my father, who tried his hand with members of both parties. But Father didn't stop there. He wanted not only the politicians but also the professionals in the State Department, the Pentagon, and the White House to support a Jewish state, or at least not to block its creation. After World War II he felt it was necessary to directly influence the foreign policy bureaucracy. The State Department was vehemently opposed to the establishment of a Jewish state and blocked access of Zionist delegations to many key decision makers. Capitalizing on the connections he had built, Father was taken up the ladder from one official to the next, starting with Loy Henderson, head of the Near Eastern Affairs Bureau in the State Department.

Henderson was a noted Arabist and a staunch anti-Zionist. Yet hearing Father's presentation and powerful arguments on why supporting Zionism served vital American interests, in this case America's desire to block Soviet domination of the Middle East, he felt it was important that others in the State Department hear them too. He took Father right up to acting Secretary of State Dean Acheson, and from there to the head of the army, Dwight D. Eisenhower, who had led the historic victory over Nazi Germany.

Father's meeting with General Eisenhower took place in 1947. Eisenhower keenly listened to Father when he explained how a Jewish state would serve as an American bulwark against Soviet attempts to take over the Middle East. Father argued that a Jewish state would have the most powerful army in the region.

Eisenhower was incredulous.

"How's that possible?" he asked. "You have only six hundred thousand people."

"General," Father responded, "you've seen in two world wars how we Jews fight for others. Imagine what will happen when we fight for ourselves."[18]

Eisenhower was sufficiently impressed to have Father repeat his entire presentation to a full assembly of the army's general staff.

All this was carried out by a young man in his thirties who a decade earlier barely knew any English, who lacked any substantial organization or funds, and who had to overcome continual obstruction from the opponents of Zionism. My father succeeded because he understood how to generate political influence in America. He was the quintessential practitioner of Jabotinsky's formula: *Influence governments through public opinion, influence public opinion by appealing to justice, influence leaders by appealing to interests.*

In 1948 his work for Zionism was done. The Jewish state was established. Having spent nearly twenty years laboring as a writer, newspaper editor and emissary for the Zionist cause, he could now retire to private life and continue his historical research. Somehow during his Zionist activities in America he had managed to write a doctoral thesis on the philosophy of Don Isaac Abravanel, the great medieval leader of the Jews of Spain, later expanded into a book, *Don Isaac Abravanel*, which was warmly reviewed by *Commentary*.[19] Father and Mother took their son Jonathan back to Israel, where Father would devote his efforts to the study of history while earning a decent living for his family. These were the happy years of my Jerusalem childhood. With his involvement in political affairs behind him, my father edited the encyclopedia and carried out his historical research.

The one exception took place in 1956. After repeated terrorist attacks from the Egyptian-controlled Sinai Peninsula, Israel conquered the Sinai on November 5, 1956. Prime Minister Ben Gurion intended for Israel to stay there indefinitely. He was immediately challenged by a UN resolution on November 7, led by the United States and the Soviet Union, demanding Israel's withdrawal. The following day, Ben Gurion received an urgent telegram from President Eisenhower reiterating this demand. The next day, November 8, Ben Gurion announced that Israel would withdraw from the Sinai in stages.

Father asked to see the prime minister. Aware of his reputation, Ben Gurion agreed.[20] The meeting took place on November 16.

"You'll be faced with additional American pressure," my father told the prime minister, knowing that Ben Gurion intended to make border adjustments around the Gaza strip.

Father explained that the only way to block this American pressure was to send an Israeli delegation to America to begin a vigorous public opinion campaign in order to influence Congress and put counterpressure on the administration. The prime minister didn't follow Father's advice and eventually capitulated to all of Eisenhower's demands, including refraining from making any border adjustments. He got little in return aside from UN peacekeepers in the Sinai and an American promise to keep the Strait of Tiran open. As we've seen, that promise would be broken.

Ben Gurion was a decisive leader who had a historic role in the founding of the state and in steering it in its early years. He boldly passed the decision to form an independent state in 1948 in a narrow executive committee vote of 6 to 4. The "no" votes came from those who feared both an Arab onslaught and opposition in the United States. Ben Gurion's determination was eventually vindicated by the hard-won Israeli military victory in the War of Independence. Yet eight years later, Ben Gurion did not see what was coming, nor did he fully understand what to do about it.

Father related all this to me in Boston when we discussed the pressure that Kissinger was now placing on Prime Minister Rabin to withdraw from the Sinai, which had been captured again during the Six-Day War.

"Why don't we go to see Rabin?" I suggested.

"I don't know him," Father said.

I thought I could arrange the meeting. Rabin's daughter, Dalia, served as a secretary in the Unit and knew Yoni and me. Yoni was well known in military circles. I was wounded at the Sabena rescue. I was certain Rabin would receive a positive recommendation for meeting Father and me, and he did.

The meeting took place in Jerusalem, at the prime minister's residence on Balfour Street, in the summer of 1974.

Rabin was sitting in the living room, holding a glass of whiskey. He was direct and avoided small talk, yet there was a captivating shyness about him. He listened to my father's description of where the American pressure was bound to lead. We told him of our activities in the United States, including the meetings with Rostow and the defense-establishment leaders Nitze and Zumwalt. That got his attention. From his service as Israel's ambassador to Washington, he knew these were distinguished and influential men.

"You're doing all this at your own initiative and at your expense?" he marveled.

We nodded.

Interested in countering the American pressure on his government, Rabin asked me to get in touch with Ehud Avriel, then Israel's consul general in Chicago, a trusted Rabin man. We parted.

I met Avriel at Chicago's O'Hare Airport. He opened some doors for us in Washington, but again there was no focused government campaign to sway American policy. Like Ben Gurion, Rabin soon withdrew under American pressure from the Mitla and Gidi passes in the Sinai and from Quneitra in the Golan in return for very little.

I realized that absent a full-throttled government effort led by the prime minister, a public campaign in America was doomed to failure. My father could succeed in advancing Zionist causes in the pre-state years because there was no Israeli government at the time. He could argue that he represented the interests of the Jewish national movement as much as anyone. But after the advent of the state, dealing with an American administration required the personal involvement of the prime minister and his senior representatives. And if they weren't willing and able to communicate directly and effectively with the American people, they could face intolerable pressure from any American administration. These insights would later guide me in my relations with successive US administrations.

During the summer of 1974, in which I met Rabin and did my reserve duty, I also met Avraham Arnan, the founder of the Unit. He and Yoni had grown close and at one point Arnan lived in our vacant house on Haportzim Street. My meeting with Arnan took place in the scenic village of Ein Kerem, purportedly the birthplace of John the Baptist, next to an ancient spring.

"Bibi," he said, "I have a proposal for you. I'm going to establish a new special unit unlike anything we've had before, and I want you to set it up and be its first commander."

If he had approached me two years earlier upon my release from the army, I probably would have said yes. But in my two years in Boston, during meetings with Father and my Hasbara activities on behalf of Israel, I had been exposed to some basic truths. Israel could win wars on the military battlefield but lose them on the political one.

While I had no intention at that time to enter political life, I had lost the innocent enthusiasm that characterized my five years of military duty. I knew that by serving in the Unit and taking part in its special operations, I contributed in a significant way to Israel's security. I valued the courage, sacrifice and dedication of our soldiers and commanders in Israel's standing army. But even at the peak of my military service, when I was totally immersed in leading my men in challenging missions, I never saw myself pursuing a military career.

I respectfully declined Arnan's offer, regretting that I had to disappoint this most idealistic of patriots, who devoted his entire life to outstanding contributions to our security.

15

"ONE DAY IT WILL HELP YOUR COUNTRY"

1976–1978

Though I had no clear idea where this newfound understanding would take me, I knew I had to complete my education. Returning to Boston from my summer vacation in Israel, I began my second and final undergraduate year at MIT. My mother, who had earlier suggested that I study architecture, now suggested I apply to MIT's business school.

"If you're going to be an architect, you may as well know how to run your business," she said.

As usual, her pragmatism made sense. In our childhood, Mother predicted Yoni would be a writer, Iddo a pianist and I a painter. It didn't quite turn out that way, though through his posthumously published letters Yoni became his own biographer. Iddo became a doctor, an author and an award-winning playwright, his plays shown in New York off Broadway and elsewhere in America, Israel, Italy, Russia and other countries. Though I am fairly adept at drawing, I didn't live up to my mother's forecast. But I did follow her advice and applied to MIT's Sloan School of Management. I was accepted.

It was there that I befriended some fellow Israeli students, including the Leventer brothers. Wanting to broaden our education beyond essential business concepts, we lobbied the Sloan School for two courses designed especially for us, one in philosophy and the other in entrepreneurship. Amazingly, the school consented. Philosophy wasn't exactly a staple on MIT's menu, and while a course in entrepreneurship is commonplace today, it was highly unusual in those days. Yoav and Oded Leventer were the sons of an industrialist entrepreneur father. They knew that without entrepreneurship and innovation, businesses go nowhere. I would greatly benefit from that insight.

Professor William Bottiglia taught us philosophy and Arnie Amstutz, a businessman, taught us entrepreneurship. Each week Amstutz brought a different entrepreneur who would describe the development of a new business idea. The most memorable was twenty-six-year-old Raymond Kurzweil. Working out of a proverbial garage, he showed us his Kurzweil Reading Machine for the Blind. This was an early application of artificial intelligence that analyzed the structure of printed letters, assembled them into words, and then read them out in a robotic monotone. Kurzweil correctly predicted that an opposite transformation from voice to text would also take place. He later became a prophet of the synergy between human and machine intelligence.[1]

The information revolution was taking place before our eyes, and a good portion of it was being rapidly developed by the technology companies around Boston. Having graduated with a master's degree from the Sloan School in 1976, and having two more years to kill until Miki completed her doctorate in chemistry and we would return to Israel, I considered applying for a job with one of these high-tech firms. Finally, at Yoav Leventer's suggestion, I decided to apply instead to the prestigious Boston Consulting Group.

To this day, I'm not sure why they accepted me. Since I had no business background, it may have been the recruiting interview that tipped the scales.

"Your client has a widget factory. His competitor also has a widget factory. Since the competitor is not publicly traded there's no data on his production. How do you get that information?"

Coming out of the Unit, that was right up my alley.

"Well," I said, "I'd measure the output of the competitor's smokestacks and compare it to the output of our client's." This went on for an hour or so. I was accepted. It was a fortuitous turn of events.

BCG assembled graduates from Harvard, MIT, Stanford and other elite schools. One of them was Mitt Romney, though since I was a fresh recruit and he was already a manager and a rising star, our paths crossed only years later when I became prime minister and he was the governor of Massachusetts.

BCG paid its consultants handsomely and sent them on missions (called "cases"). A typical case would involve systematically studying a firm's position in the three C's (cost, competitors, customers), then taking a month to analyze the data and put them into relevant graphs, and another month to frame recommendations and present them concisely in a series of coherent slides.

In later years, recalling the brevity and conciseness of these presentations, I railed in vain against the plethora of irrelevant data and fuzzy recommendations piled into government slide presentations. In sheer exasperation, I would often stop the presenter and turn off the slides.

"What are you trying to say? Tell me in one sentence," I'd shoot off under the triple influence of Father, the Unit and the Boston Consulting Group.

"Prime Minister," came the usual reply, "it's more complicated than that."

"I know it's more complicated. But try anyway," I would insist.

For many government bureaucrats and military personnel used to covering themselves with multiple and conflicting recommendations, this was cruel and unusual punishment. But it was a valuable habit I learned at BCG. Unlike governments, private companies would not pay for fuzzy presentations that didn't advance defined goals and did not add value.

Ensuring clarity and simplicity is a tough intellectual challenge, which I seldom delegated to others. Whether presenting economic facts as finance minister or exposing Iran's secret nuclear program as prime minister,[2] I would personally prepare the presentations and go to the heart of the matter. With rare exceptions, I followed a simple rule: say something clear or say nothing at all.

Knowing my penchant for clarity and brevity, representatives of the Teachers Union once lobbied me for increased funding while I was in office. They displayed a slide containing the word "input" with an arrow pointing to the word "output."

"Actually," I said, "it's the other way around. Output determines input."

First determine the desired results, then decide how much you're willing to spend to get them. This was of course anathema in the public sector, where virtually all the discussion focuses on how much is given to a particular project and not on its results.

On my first day at BCG, its founder and chairman, the brilliant Bruce Henderson, called me to his office. Then in his seventies, Henderson was a tall and eccentric southerner who had revolutionized the world of strategic consulting with his novel ideas. He had worked in aircraft production in World War II and witnessed the experience curve at work. The more aircraft parts a firm produced, the lower the cost of producing the next part.

But Henderson went further. Competitive advantage, he said, was gained by increasing the firm's share of the market. Market share reflected the cumulative experience that firms had gained in driving down the cost of producing and selling their products and services. If firms continually lower the price of their products and services while they lower their cost, they shut competitors out of the market. As the markets stabilize, the dominant firm left standing becomes what Bruce called a "cash cow," producing the funds to develop promising new products in growth markets. This so-called BCG matrix analysis and other ingenious concepts, initially dismissed by many, proved immensely powerful and made BCG an "elite unit" in the consulting world.

When I walked into his office, Henderson asked me to shut the door.

"I know you'll go back to your country," he said, "so learn what you can here. One day it will help your country."

I had no idea what he was talking about, but he turned out to be absolutely right. At BCG I got a preliminary understanding of how *firms* achieve competitive advantage. This would prove instrumental to me in steering Israel's economic policies toward free markets that would enable not only Israeli companies to do so, but also give our *nation* a competitive advantage against others. For some reason, Henderson developed an interest in me, because in another meeting he gave me Anthony Cave Brown's book *Bodyguard of Lies*. The book describes Churchill's efforts to guard intelligence secrets in World War II, chief among them the cracking of the Enigma code. Those lessons too proved relevant in later years when I became prime minister.

I was at BCG just long enough to pick up these valuable insights. But my work there was cut short by an event that forever changed my life.

16

AGONY

1976

The days leading up to July 4, 1976, were filled with anticipation. For me and many others, the American Bicentennial celebrated the birth of liberty in the modern world. Tall ships sailed into Boston Harbor. Families were planning their long weekends. Picnics abounded.

It would have been a glorious day for us Israeli students at MIT, too, but it was marred by the news we had received earlier in the week of the hijacking of an Air France plane. The plane had taken off from Tel Aviv, destined for Paris, until the hijackers diverted it to Entebbe, the main airport of Uganda. The news reports said that negotiations had begun between Israel's government and Ugandan dictator Idi Amin to secure the release of the hostages.

Then, on the morning of July 4, breaking news swept the entire world. An Israeli force had carried out a daring rescue mission in Uganda, liberated the hostages and was flying them back to Israel. The report added that "one officer was killed."

My elation over the rescue was abruptly cut short. Why did they say "officer"? Normally they would say "soldier."

I took an atlas from my bookshelf and calculated the distance from Israel to Uganda: 3,550 kilometers. A rescue that far away would require three to five Hercules planes, with between 150 and 200 soldiers on board. At least a quarter would be officers who would demand to be on such a mission. What were the odds? 1:50. There have been worse odds before, I told myself. But I couldn't relax. I was certain that it was Yoni and the Unit under his command who carried out the rescue. The question kept gnawing at me. Why did they say "officer"? Was this "officer" in a special role?

I called Iddo in Jerusalem.

"Is Yoni back?" I asked.

"Not yet," Iddo responded. "They'll let me know when they land."

Iddo told me he felt something wasn't right. As the hours passed, my anxiety grew.

I called Iddo again. Again, the same response. I tried to calm myself but could not.

Finally, several hours later, the phone rang.

"It's Iddo," I said to Miki, "to tell me Yoni is dead."

I picked up the phone. Iddo was on the line.

"Bibi," he said quietly, "Yoni has been killed."

The silence that followed was indescribable in its agony on both sides of the line. In that moment of utter shock, I could only think of my parents.

"I'll go to Abba and Imma," I said to Iddo, my voice choking. "They shouldn't hear this on the news."

Iddo agreed.

For seven tortured hours, Zvika and Ruthie Livneh drove Miki and me from Boston to Ithaca, a Via Dolorosa of unspeakable pain. When we got to Ithaca, I walked alone on the path leading to my parents' modest home near Cornell.

As I got closer, I saw my father through the big front window. He was pacing back and forth, deep in thought, his hands clasped behind his back.

Suddenly he turned and saw me.

"Bibi." He smiled in surprise, but when he saw my face, he instantly understood. He let out a terrible cry like a wounded animal.

I heard my mother scream.

If there was a moment in my life worse than hearing about Yoni's death, it was telling my parents about it. I felt like a man on a rack whose limbs are torn from him one by one.

How could I go on living?

Somehow we found the strength to get to JFK and board a plane to

Israel. On the long flight home, we wept silently in our seats as our hearts burst.

I tried to gather strength from the courage of my parents, who bore their grief with incredible dignity. I felt I owed it to them and to Yoni not to break down. Supporting myself, I supported them.

The funeral on Mount Herzl was packed with the leaders of Israel and many of Yoni's fellow soldiers. Shimon Peres, the defense minister, gave an unforgettable eulogy:

> Jonathan was an exemplary commander. With his boldness of spirit, he overcame his enemies. With his wisdom, he won the hearts of his comrades. Danger did not deter him and triumphs did not swell his heart. Of himself he demanded much, while to the army he gave the sharpness of his intellect, his competence in action and his skill in combat.
>
> In the university he studied philosophy. In the army he taught self-sacrifice. To his soldiers he gave his human warmth. In battle he imbued them with coolness of judgment.
>
> This young man was among those who commanded an operation that was flawless. But to our deep sorrow, this operation entailed a sacrifice of incomparable pain—the first among the storming party, the first to fall. By virtue of the few the many were saved, and by virtue of the one who fell a nation bent under a heavy burden rose again to its full height.
>
> And of him, of them, one may say in the words of David:

> *They were swifter than eagles,*
> *They were stronger than lions. . . .*
> *O Jonathan, thou wast slain in thine high places.*
> *I am distressed for thee, my brother Jonathan. . . .*

> The distance in space between Entebbe and Jerusalem has shortened the distance in time between Jonathan, the son of Saul, and Jonathan, the son of Benzion.
>
> The same heroism in the man. The same lamentation in the heart of the people.[1]

On July 8, 1976, two days after this remarkable eulogy and in the nadir of grief, Father sent Peres a letter.

> Though the depth of pain in which I am immersed in this hour still prevents me from finding the appropriate words to express my feelings and thoughts, I could not delay for even one more day the expression of my appreciation and profound gratitude for your extraordinary eulogy for Yoni.
>
> In your words was the inspired spirit that always guided the finest of our leaders. You captured the feelings of the entire nation and of freedom-loving people everywhere. You summoned words to express the unsurpassed courage of our army, and you captured in bold and powerful strokes the unforgettable and wondrous character of our beloved Yoni, who is now beloved by our entire people. In your speech, you erected his memorial. It will forever be a part of our nation's paean, inspiring future generations of heroes.[2]

Even when Peres and I faced each other decades later from opposite sides of the political divide, I could never forget the appreciation my father had expressed in that letter. Political disputes could never remove the underlying sense of sympathy and warmth I always felt toward Shimon.

We sat *Shiva* at Iddo and Dafna's house in Jerusalem's Ba'ka neighborhood. Prime Minister Rabin, Opposition Leader Menachem Begin, Chief of Staff Motta Gur and thousands of others came to offer their condolences.

As the crowd ebbed and flowed, my parents, Iddo and I kept up appearances. The nights were fitful and sleepless. I lost my sense of taste. I did not know *if* I would live, or *how* I would live. I drowned in sorrow.

But in the course of the *Shiva* something happened that was akin to the hand that had rescued me years before from that other drowning.

A young woman of thirty showed up. She had married a friend of Yoni's who had passed away years before. She had known Yoni when they were both seventeen. He was never her boyfriend or lover, and Yoni was not yet famous. Yet thirteen years later she brought to us letters Yoni had written her husband as a teenager.

At the request of the journalist Uri Dan, we had given a few quotes from the letters Yoni sent our family, which he incorporated into an article about Yoni published in the newspaper *Maariv*. A competing newspaper asked to publish in full any letters we'd give them. The few we gave were received with tremendous enthusiasm. The editor of *Maariv*, an old acquaintance of my father's, then asked if there were more letters. When he heard we were thinking of publishing them as a book, he offered to do so through the paper's publishing house.

We agreed. Over several months Mother and Father and Iddo, with help from me, collected hundreds of Yoni's letters. They formed a record of his life from the age of seventeen, when he was a homesick Israeli youth in America, to a few days before his fall in Entebbe.

When *Yoni's Letters* appeared in Hebrew, the first edition sold out in days. It has since become a source of inspiration for generations of Israeli youth and Israeli soldiers. For more than forty years it has never been out of print.

The famous writer Herman Wouk, a friend of Yossi Ben Hanan, the stranded tank commander whom Yoni had rescued at Tel Shams, wrote a foreword to the English edition.

"The reader holds in his hands a remarkable work of literature, possibly one of the great documents of our time," Wouk wrote. "Like Anne Frank's diary, it is a fortuitous, not a deliberately created, work of art. These are all random jottings, hasty unselfconscious scrawls. They comprise a true and brilliant portrait of a hero, the only wholly convincing one that I know of in a contemporary literature of anti-heroes. The lands of the free will need such men until the day when the last tyrannies that spawn the terrorists are faced down. Yoni inspires and ennobles us, and he gives us hope. That is the best art can do."[3]

Yoni expressed his soul in his letters and described his life and thoughts with the terse prose of a natural and powerful writer, at times rising to the poetic. Given that many of these letters were written by candlelight in pup tents or in the field after a grueling day, this was all the more remarkable.

The book was published in English under the title *Self-Portrait of a Hero: The Letters of Jonathan Netanyahu*. The *New York Times* wrote that the book was "a convincing portrayal of a talented, sensitive man who knew that good is no match for evil without the power to physically defend itself."[4] The *Boston Globe* wrote that "Yoni's unpretentious accounts of his accomplishments, simply written and thus more grand, make him the convincing hero he was and make us wish that more like him were among us."[5] *Military Review* said it was "a magnificent testament to the hero of Entebbe, containing a leadership credo of unmatchable quality."[6] I relate this not only to encourage others to read Yoni's letters and discover for themselves who Yoni was; I bring this up because in many ways these letters saved me.

The act of publishing Yoni's letters in Hebrew and English was more than therapy. We were erecting an enduring monument for Yoni, one chiseled by his own words. As the American writer George Will wrote, "Jonathan was not only Achilles, he now is, through his letters, his own Homer."[7]

But Yoni's letters could not cover Entebbe. In the *Shiva* we learned some of what happened. Years later Iddo filled in the gaps. He meticulously interviewed many people, including most of the soldiers in Yoni's assault force. He then proceeded to write the definitive work on the Unit's role in Entebbe, called *Yoni's Last Battle*, and later published another book with detailed excerpts of interviews with mission participants, called *Sayeret Matkal at Entebbe*.[8]

In his rigor and unrelenting honesty, Iddo brought not only his experience as a soldier, his skill as a writer and the diagnostic discipline that would accompany his practice as a doctor of radiology. There was something else.

He reminded me of Father.

17

ENTEBBE

July 4, 1976

On June 27, 1976, an Air France plane flying from Israel to Paris with 248 passengers on board was hijacked by Arab terrorists after a stopover in Athens. Remembering the Sabena rescue, the hijackers steered clear of Israel, turning instead to Africa. They landed at Entebbe Airport in Uganda on Monday, June 28.

The four hijackers, two Germans and two Arabs, were met there by several Palestinian terrorists. The hostages were taken to the airport's Old Terminal building, which had been decommissioned. There they were held captive by the terrorists, aided by the Ugandan army. At that time, Uganda was ruled by the brutal dictator Idi Amin, who was in cahoots with the terrorists.

From the safety of Entebbe the hijackers demanded the release of more than fifty terrorists, most of whom were imprisoned in Israel, along with a few in other countries. The deadline for their release was set for Thursday afternoon, July 1. If Israel refused to meet their demands, the terrorists threatened, they would start executing the hostages. They separated the Israeli passport holders and non-Israelis they believed to be Jews from those they believed to be non-Jews. On Wednesday they began releasing the non-Jewish hostages, who were flown to Paris, keeping all the Israeli and other Jewish passengers at Entebbe. The plane's brave non-Jewish pilot, Michel Bacos, and his crew refused to leave and stayed with their passengers, leaving a total of 106 passengers and crew remaining hostage.

This selection of Jews to be murdered at Entebbe evoked horrible memories of the selection of Jews to be murdered in the Nazi death camps only thirty years earlier. One of the hostages, Dr. Yitzhak Hirsch, had survived the Birkenau concentration camp, adjacent to Auschwitz. His entire family was murdered there. "The kidnapper shouted in German, typical of the language I used to hear at the camp. It took me back 30 years. Horrible screams," Hirsch later recalled.[1]

Thursday morning, with the deadline fast approaching, Israel officially agreed to meet the demands of the terrorists. In response, the terrorists extended the deadline to Sunday, July 4, at noon.

Late Tuesday and into Wednesday, Israeli army strategists had been discussing the possibility of rescuing the hostages. At first those discussions led nowhere. With the release of the non-Jewish hostages, however, Israel gained the possibility of acquiring crucial intelligence about the Old Terminal at Entebbe, which increased the chances of preparing an operational plan. Thus, on Wednesday night, while Yoni was supervising an operation in the Sinai, he was asked to come as soon as possible up north to the IDF main headquarters in Tel Aviv in the event that new intelligence could enable a rescue mission.

At that time, the main plan being proposed was parachuting soldiers and rubber boats onto Lake Victoria. In the trial run the boats capsized. That, along with concerns that Lake Victoria was infested with crocodiles, nixed the plan.

By Thursday evening in Tel Aviv, Yoni received the formal order to prepare the Unit for a possible raid on the airport.

The overall mission was to be commanded by Chief Infantry and Paratroop Officer Brigadier General Dan Shomron. Under his command would be paratroopers who would join the Unit force on the first plane, light the runways for the other planes and seize the New Terminal. There would also be a Golani Brigade force on a different plane—which would help bring the freed hostages aboard the waiting aircraft—plus a medical team. The Unit under Yoni's direct command was tasked with the heart of the mission: storming the Old Terminal, killing the terrorists and the Ugandan soldiers aiding them, liberating the hostages and destroying the nearby MiG aircraft so that they could not give chase during the force's return flight. Shomron and his command group would initially position themselves in the New Terminal. Yoni would lead the Unit to the Old Terminal.

At around 10 p.m., Yoni gathered a few of the officers in the Unit at his office. After several hours of brainstorming, they had formed their basic plan of action for the Unit's assault.

The IDF's overall plan called for the Unit's force of some sixty men— plus a paratroop force of nearly eighty men—to be flown to Entebbe in three C-130 transport Hercules planes. A fourth plane would carry the Golani force and the medical teams. The second plane would land seven minutes after the first to give Yoni and his men time to storm the Old Terminal. The other planes would then land in rapid succession.

Yoni detailed the Unit's role. Once the first plane landed, thirty-three of the Unit's men would proceed in a Mercedes and two Land Rover Jeeps to the Old Terminal. They would wear the uniforms and berets of Ugandan soldiers. The Mercedes would be made to look like Idi Amin's presidential car and the Jeeps like those used by the Ugandan army.

It was hoped that the Ugandan guards surrounding the building would assume that this was a Ugandan force, possibly the very one that accompanied Amin on his occasional visits to the hostages, thus raising no suspicions. Ideally, the guards might even wave the vehicles through. But should the guards try to check the vehicles and their passengers, the Israeli force would take them out.

After getting past the guards, the force would continue to the Old Terminal, get out of the vehicles and quickly reach their assigned entrances. Several squads were allocated to the two main halls on the ground floor where the hostages were thought to be held. This would be the most dangerous part of the mission. The halls had large glass windows through which the terrorists could see the storming party and fire at them before they would have a chance to enter the building and eliminate the terror- ists.

Other squads were assigned to clear the remaining parts of the ground floor of terrorists and Ugandan soldiers and the top floor of additional Ugandan troops. A small team would give cover fire against any shooting from the roof and the control tower. Yoni and his command team would position themselves outside the main entrance to direct the flow of sol- diers to the different locations. If something went wrong, they too would storm the building. All this would be accomplished by the thirty-three Unit fighters led by Yoni.

A second Unit force of some thirty men led by Yoni's former deputy, Shaul Mofaz, would land in the second and third planes. Driving four armored personnel carriers, they would quickly cordon off the Old Terminal from a possible attack by the Ugandan army. Besides the large Ugandan force believed to be stationed in the Old Terminal, there was a Ugandan regimental air force base some two hundred meters away and a Presidential Guard on a nearby hilltop. Mofaz's force was to destroy the MiG fighter planes parked near the Old Terminal to prevent the Ugandans from shooting down the C-130 transport planes once they had the hostages and were heading back to Israel.

After midnight, Yoni broke from the small-group planning session and briefed other officers on the raid, telling them to prepare accordingly.

"Yoni was very tired," Muki Betser, who would serve as Yoni's second-in-command during the operation, later recalled. "You could see it by looking at him. Actually, we were all tired. At a certain point I suggested that we stop and get some sleep. Yoni agreed, and the small planning team went to sleep. It turned out later that Yoni remained alone at his office and continued to work on the plan. When he presented it to us at 7 a.m. the next morning after sleeping at most an hour or two, I saw how much further he had developed it. There were many points that we hadn't considered which Yoni had thought through to the end. He now presented the plan complete, perfect, down to the last detail."[2]

As more intelligence came in, Yoni changed a few details. On Friday, he briefed the soldiers and the officers about the full plan, supervised some of the rehearsals, held a meeting with the commander of the C-130 transport squadron and his officers and went several times for meetings and briefings to the IDF headquarters in Tel Aviv.

His most important meeting there was with Defense Minister Shimon Peres. Peres was grappling with a crucial question: Should he recommend to Prime Minister Rabin to launch the rescue operation? He consulted Israel's legendary war hero, former chief of staff Moshe Dayan, now a civilian.

Dayan told Peres to trust Air Force Commander Benny Peled and Unit Commander Yoni.[3]

But Peres wanted to hear from Yoni directly. "He presented the plan to me in detail," recalled Peres, "and I liked it very much. The two of us sat alone. . . . My impression was one of precision and imagination . . . and complete self-confidence . . . which no doubt influenced me. We had a problem with lack of intelligence but Yoni said, 'Do you know of any operation that wasn't carried out half blind?' "[4]

That night, with Chief of Staff Motta Gur looking on, the Unit and the various supporting forces conducted a mock-up exercise on a full-scale model. "We practiced according to the plan," says Muki. "We placed two soldiers who acted as guards on the runway. They ordered us to stop. We did, and Yoni 'shot' them with a silencer. We then continued toward the terminal." Muki later elaborated: "During the preparations for the raid, Yoni foresaw a situation in which we would encounter two Ugandan guards . . . and our response in such a case was to take out the two guards with silencers."

After taking out the guards, speed would be essential. The goal was to reach the entrances before the terrorists realized what was happening and started spraying the hostages with automatic fire.

Following the exercise, Gur met with the various commanders and asked for their opinion about the chances of success. He spent the longest time with Yoni.

"It was understood by all of us that the words of one man will determine whether we get the go-ahead," said Mofaz, who would himself one day serve as the IDF's chief of staff and Israel's defense minister. "We all waited to hear what Yoni had to say. The responsibility on his shoulders was huge."

"Yoni told Motta he had every reason to believe that if the hostages were still there the Unit could pull it off," recalled Muki. "The bottom line was, 'It can be done.' I saw Motta's reaction, and I'm convinced that Yoni's words gave him the required confidence to go get the go-ahead from the cabinet."

Following his discussion with Yoni, Dan Shomron and the other officers, Motta said that he had reached a decision in favor of the operation. He would recommend to Prime Minister Rabin and Defense Minister Peres to authorize the mission.

A few hours later, Yoni went home for a brief nap. Early the next morning, Saturday, July 3, he said good-bye to his girlfriend Bruria (Yoni and Tuttie had divorced four years earlier). Returning to the Unit, he held one last inspection of the men and conducted an hour-long tactical briefing with the officers, followed by more briefings at Ben Gurion Airport.

Before departing the Unit, during a brief break, Yoni told his driver: "Listen, Yisrael, I'm going to salute the flag. Once in his life a guy's got to salute the flag." Standing alone before the flag in front of his office, without the ceremony or protocol customary in the Israeli army, Yoni saluted the flag for a long moment.

At noon four planes (and a fifth spare plane) took off for Sharm el-Sheikh, at the southern tip of the Sinai Peninsula. There they would await word as to whether the government had given them the go-ahead to continue to Entebbe.

After landing at Sharm, the men gathered to hear Yoni's final briefing. "Remember," Yoni emphasized. "We will be by far the best fighters in that airfield." He told them this was a mission they could do and must do.

"This final briefing by Yoni was superb. It was focused, concise and exactly foresaw the events as they were to occur," wrote, forty years later, Amir Ofer, the first to enter the hostage hall during the battle. "I was especially impressed by his ability to disregard his own personal danger and to brief us as if he were a staff officer staying behind, not someone who would lead such a small isolated force in battle, carrying out an extremely complex mission in a far-away hostile land."[5] "It was a speech I'll never forget," said Alex Davidi, a member of the Unit. "He gave us confidence that we could do it. His leadership and his ability to affect us were simply above and beyond anything."

The soldiers needed this encouragement. They were about to do something truly extraordinary. In case they failed and had to scatter in Uganda, they were given "escape maps" copied from an atlas. These maps showed Uganda in the center and Kenya to the east. Everybody understood what it meant should they have to use them.

The cabinet meeting lingered on and on. Prime Minister Rabin and the ministers agonized over the decision of whether to launch the operation. Yet if the raid was to be carried out, the planes would have to take off from Sharm immediately. The hostages were to be executed the next day at noon. It would take the planes eight hours to reach Entebbe, flying low over the Red Sea to avoid radar detection by either Egypt or Saudi Arabia before making a hard turn southwest toward Uganda. The optimal time to land was considered to be midnight. This meant the government's final decision would have to be made and delivered *during* the flight to Entebbe. If the cabinet did not approve the operation, the planes would turn around midway and head back to Israel.

The lead plane was crowded. It carried Yoni's assault party with its three vehicles, as well as the paratroop force whose main mission was to seize the airport's New Terminal.

Yoni and Muki sat down with Amos Goren, a soldier of the Unit who had been added at the last moment to the assault force, replacing a soldier who had become ill on the flight to Sharm. On the back of an airsickness bag Yoni sketched the outline of the terminal, the assault routes, the various entrances and the task of each squad, including the squad Amos had joined.

"While Yoni was explaining all this to me," said Amos, "we were informed that the government had given us the green light to carry on to Entebbe, that we were going to do it. . . . He explained to me my role, as though we were going to perform an exercise."

With some five hours left until they reached Entebbe, Yoni sat in the Mercedes reading a book. After a while, not having slept for several nights, he went to a cot in the cockpit behind the Hercules pilot, Captain Joshua "Shiki" Shani, and fell into a deep sleep. Shani was amazed. "Where does this calmness of his come from? Soon he's going into battle, and he sleeps as if nothing is happening!" Shani later said. "I saw Yoni's handsome face in slumber. . . . Even before that, he looked to me like Judah the Maccabee."[6]

A half hour before landing, he was woken up. Once his men were geared up and sitting in their places, Yoni moved among them, speaking to each in turn.

"There was this reddish light, and I remember that we saw his face," related Shlomo Reisman, one of the soldiers. "He wasn't wearing his beret or his ammo vest and he didn't carry his weapon. . . . He spoke to the men, smiled at us, said a few words of encouragement to each one. It was as though he were leaving us, as though he knew what was going to hap-

OPERATION JONATHAN: ROUTE TAKEN FROM ISRAEL TO ENTEBBE

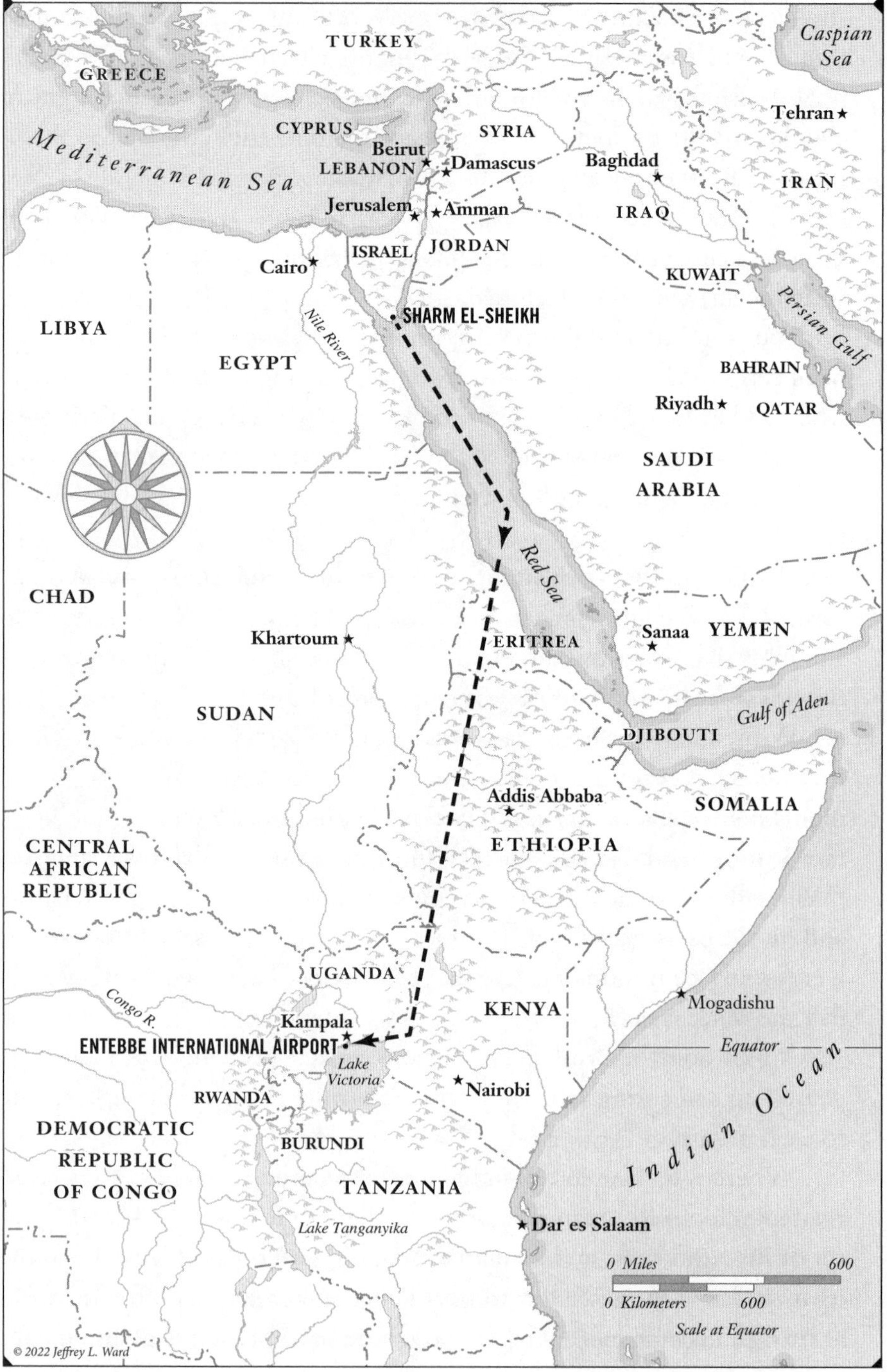

pen to him. He didn't issue any orders but just tried to instill confidence in us. I remember that he shook hands with [Pinchas] Bukhris, the youngest soldier in the force. . . . He acted more like a friend. . . . I sensed he felt that from here on everything, or at least nearly everything, depended on us. Yoni had seen a lot of combat, and quite a few of the soldiers there had seen none at all, or a lot less than he had. And I remember him going by, joking a little, exchanging a few words, easing the men's tension before battle."

With lights off, the plane landed at Entebbe. The back door opened and the Mercedes limousine rolled out. Yoni and the driver sat in the front, three soldiers sat in the middle, and four more soldiers sat in the back. The Mercedes, bearing Idi Amin's presidential flag, was followed by two Land Rovers packed with armed soldiers.

As they approached the Old Terminal, two Ugandan guards appeared from the dark and shouted "Halt!" One pointed his rifle at them and cocked it. This was standard procedure in Uganda; the men were prepared.

The car slowly approached the guard. When the guard was in range, Yoni and the officer behind him, Giora Zussman, shot him with pistols fitted with silencers. The guard reeled back, wounded, but did not fall.

It was then that loud shots were heard. The shots may have come from one of these two Ugandan guards, some say. Others in the Mercedes thought the shots came from the Jeeps, while some of those in the Jeeps thought it came from the Mercedes. Whatever the source, once the loud shots were heard, the men in the Land Rovers fired at the two Ugandan guards, killing both.

Fearing that the element of surprise was lost, Yoni ordered the drivers to get to the control tower as fast as possible. Luckily, the terrorists did not comprehend the significance of the shots fired two hundred meters away. The force got out of their vehicles and walked silently toward the corner of the Old Terminal building, where the hostages were being held. As soon as they rounded the corner they would be exposed, in front of the glass windows.

Muki, who was in the lead as planned, broke the silence by opening fire. He then suddenly stopped when he reached the corner of the building and continued firing his weapon from there. The storming party halted behind him. "The men didn't understand what was going on, why Muki had stopped," said Amos. "The men stopped behind him. Yoni shouted to run forward."

"He kept shouting 'Forward, Betser,' calling Muki by his last name," recalled Alex Davidi.

Yoni knew that in a few seconds the terrorists, realizing an assault was under way, would begin to kill the hostages. As long as Muki was standing against the wall and firing his weapon, the rest of the force could not pass him; otherwise they would be cut down by his bullets. Yoni saw that Muki wasn't responding to his commands. The moment Muki stopped shooting, Yoni took the lead. "I remembered him running forward," said Amos. "He passed Muki, who had stopped. He was the first man to come out of the corner of the building."

Now past the corner, Yoni pulled the rest of the men behind him. They were now running in front of the glass entrances, exposed to the terrorists inside. There were bursts of gunfire. Someone shouted that Yoni was hit. The men pressed on, following Yoni's orders to tend to the wounded only after the hostages were freed.

Amir Ofer had run past Yoni to the second entrance. One of the German terrorists shot at him through the glass door and missed. Amir returned fire and killed him on the spot. Entering the terminal, he discovered that he was the first soldier inside. His commander, Amnon Peled, followed right behind him. Entering the room, Amnon saw two terrorists, a man and a woman, crouching and aiming their Kalashnikovs at Amir. He fired and killed them both. Muki and Amos entered next. Amos scanned the room, looking for more terrorists. "First I saw Amnon," he said. "Then I looked to my left and saw the two terrorists who had been shot. I saw the fully lit room with all the hostages lying on the floor. From the left, a terrorist suddenly leaped, holding a weapon. I shot him. The first bullet went through his Kalashnikov and entered his chest. I shot three more bullets and finished him off."

With that, the four terrorists who were inside the main hall and posed the most immediate threat to the hostages were eliminated. Other Unit soldiers rushed in to other parts of the Terminal, killing three other terrorists and some Ugandan troops. The rest of the Ugandan soldiers fled.

The dazed hostages were liberated. They were rushed by the Unit's soldiers to the transport planes for the flight back to Israel.

Yoni was lying on the tarmac. He was still alive but rapidly losing blood. He had been hit in his arm and in his chest.

"At the end of the fighting," said the Unit's doctor, "somebody came to help me place him on a stretcher. It was then that some consciousness returned to him. . . . He was perhaps roused by a soldierly instinct. There was great deal of shooting toward the control tower, which made a lot of noise, and he tried to get up."

Yoni was transferred by Jeep to the evacuation plane, which had taxied close to the Old Terminal. A team of doctors desperately tried to resuscitate him, to no avail. The commander who led the charge of one of the most daring and successful rescue missions in history had fallen. Yoni was gone.

Forty years later, Amir Ofer summed up Yoni's role in the Entebbe rescue operation: "Yoni performed on the highest possible level in this mission. Throughout the preparations, he led the process, briefed the men, took upon his own shoulders the responsibility of telling the higher-ups (as well as the officers below him) 'We can do this,' when all around him there were not one nor two who weren't sure of it. The briefing he gave us at Sharm was a masterpiece—the best pre-operational briefing I have ever heard. His instructions there later guided me when I lost contact with my commander.

"His performance during the ground operation was superb. He made the right decision to shoot the Ugandan guard; the right decision to accelerate the vehicles; the right decision to get off slightly before the planned point; and he grasped [the grave meaning of] Muki's halt and gave the right orders to solve the problem. In terms of its consequences, this was possibly the most important and dramatic moment in the history of the IDF. The lives of the hostages were at stake, and they had just a few seconds left in the hourglass. . . . The consequences of failure there were much beyond the loss of the hostages and soldiers. . . . It is impossible to gauge the political damage to Israel and the damage to the IDF's deterrence had we failed. Countering this, there was only a small force which was numerically inferior by far [to the Ugandan army nearby], which was meant to solve the problem through the element of surprise and qualitative superiority; and Yoni—upon whose shoulders and his alone lay this awful responsibility under the most extreme stress one can imagine—was at that very moment focused, purposeful, reading the situation clearly and responding exactly as was needed. A true commander."[7]

LOADED WITH THE hostages and Yoni's body, the evacuation plane took off from Entebbe. Of the 106 hostages, three were hit by gunfire and would die of their wounds. The rest were unscathed. However, a day later, seventy-five-year-old hostage Dora Bloch, who had previously been taken to a hospital in Kampala due to severe illness, was mercilessly executed.

Among the paratroop force sent to secure the New Terminal, one brave soldier, Surin Hershko, was shot by a Ugandan policeman as he climbed an external staircase. He was paralyzed for life.

The returning planes landed at Nairobi, the capital of Kenya. That country had earlier agreed to let the Israeli planes refuel on their way back to Israel.

"On our plane there was endless chatter," recalled Shlomo Reisman. "Everyone was telling what happened to them. It seemed that everything was going great, that we had succeeded. Then someone came in and said that Yoni had died. All at once, everyone fell silent. . . . We were hit hard, and each of us withdrew into himself."

"I saw Yoni's body lying in the plane, wrapped in one of those awful aluminum blankets the doctors use," said Matan Vilnai, the head of the paratroop contingent in the raid. "I saw the hostages completely stunned, shadows of men. What hit me then was a kind of feeling that for a military man was totally illogical. I thought to myself that if Yoni was dead then the whole thing wasn't worth it."

When the planes left Kenya a short time later, no report had yet arrived in Israel of any dead among the force. "When the last plane took off from Nairobi," said Motta Gur's secretary, "there was a wave of rejoicing at the Kirya headquarters. The Chief of Staff's driver brought in a few bottles of champagne and everyone celebrated. After they left, Motta Gur and his aide Hagai Regev stayed alone. I went to the kitchen to make some coffee. Suddenly the other secretaries rushed in. They grabbed me and said: 'Yoni was killed.' I dropped everything and went to the Chief of Staff's office. I opened the door of the room I'd left two minutes before, which had been full of rejoicing over our success. I saw the Chief of Staff sitting, face fallen, terribly sad. Hagai was crushed. In one minute, all the joy had been erased. . . . It was as though nothing else mattered. Everything took on a different meaning."

Gur went to Peres's office, where the defense minister had lain down to rest. Peres recounted the moment in his diary. "At four in the morning Motta Gur came into my office and I could tell he was very upset. 'Shimon, Yoni's gone. A bullet hit him in the heart. . . .' This is the first time in this whole crazy week that I could not hold back the tears."[8]

The planes carrying the soldiers landed in Israel in the morning at the Tel Nof air base. Rabin and Peres were there to greet them. So too was Yoni's commander in the Golan Heights during the Yom Kippur War, Brigadier General Yanosh Ben Gal. A hero of that war and one of the most courageous and respected commanders in the Israeli army, Yanosh had said that Yoni, ten years younger than him and of junior rank, was the first officer he met whom he looked up to. He was devastated by the news of Yoni's death.

"How could you have let this happen!" he said in anguish to the Unit's officers.

When Muki came out of the plane, Peres turned to him and asked, "How was Yoni killed?"

"He went first, he fell first," Muki answered.[9]

18

TERRORISM

1976–1980

Many bereaved families find some consolation by commemorating a fallen son. Our family was no different. But in addition to immersing ourselves in collecting and publishing Yoni's letters, we were soon engulfed by another pursuit. Though Yoni had died in the war on terror, he never thought this battle was merely a military conflict. He saw it also as a political and moral struggle between civilization and barbarism. I now devoted myself to this battle.

The 1970s marked the beginning of a wave of international terrorism that swept the Western world and continues to this day. The terrorists cast aside all civilized norms put in place after World War II. Noncombatants were fair game and no one was exempt from their murderous assaults. Like wild beasts prowling the world's cities, airways and waterways, the terrorists bombed innocent bystanders in Western capitals, hijacked aircraft, commandeered ships and even tried to assassinate the pope.

Many of these attacks were carried out by Palestinian terrorists. They blew up three aircraft in the Jordanian desert in 1970, attacked Israeli planes in Switzerland and Cyprus and hijacked a Sabena airplane to Tel Aviv and an Air France plane to Entebbe. They hijacked the cruise ship *Achille Lauro* and threw a wheelchaired passenger, Leon Klinghoffer, overboard. My parents almost took that very cruise ship a year before.

The terrorists landed on the Tel Aviv coast and took hostages in the Savoy Hotel (where Uzi Yairi was killed while rescuing them). They massacred Israeli schoolchildren in the town of Maalot in the Upper Galilee and murdered eleven members of Israel's Olympic team in Munich in 1972.

Though after Sabena and Entebbe, terrorists worldwide understood that governments could act decisively against the taking of hostages on hijacked planes, they emulated other forms of Palestinian terrorism and invented new types of attacks. German terrorists bombed a nightclub in Berlin, Italian terrorists kidnapped and murdered the Italian prime minister Aldo Moro, Japanese terrorists released sarin poison gas in Tokyo's subway, French terrorists set off bombs in Paris, Basque terrorists kidnapped and killed innocents in Madrid and Irish terrorists bombed London and Margaret Thatcher's Conservative Party conference in Brighton, England.

While the actual physical carnage of these violent attacks was limited compared to all-out military conflicts, the fear they generated was often greater. It seemed that no one was safe. Busloads of children could be blown up—and were. Entire planes could be blown out of the sky—and were, as in the downing of a Pan Am flight over Lockerbie, Scotland. What would happen if terrorists got their hands on far more lethal weapons than the ones they currently had access to?

Apologists justified the terrorists' acts of wanton murder by arguing that "one man's terrorist is another man's freedom fighter." If the terrorists' case was just, they argued, the means they chose to advance them were also just. After all, wasn't terrorism the inevitable response of the oppressed against their more powerful oppressors? Weren't those desperate young people in Milan, Beirut and Bonn merely responding to a host of social and political ills? These ills were the "root causes" of terrorism, went the argument. Correct the ills by addressing the terrorists' grievances and the problem would go away. If, instead, governments tried to respond with force, they would only drive the terrorists to become more desperate and make matters worse. Endlessly repeated by Western intellectuals and the media, these claims assumed the cachet of self-evident truth.

Perhaps unsurprisingly, in the face of such attitudes the response of Western democracies to the growing international terrorist threat was weak and confused. Some countries sought to cut separate deals with terrorists. A few fought back, as in the German storming of a hijacked German aircraft in Mogadishu, Somalia, in 1977, following the example of Entebbe. But most responses were flaccid and pusillanimous. As a result, terrorism continued to grow.

Since terrorism had become international, it had to be fought internationally. What was clearly needed was a coherent and united response—moral, political, and military—to defeat the scourge. Yet the West lacked a common policy of defense or offense against a force that was relentlessly attacking them. The first place to effect a change was in the most decisive battleground, that of ideas. Could terrorism be defined, or was it merely dependent on the eye of the beholder? Was it a response to societal and political ills or was it, as I believed, an expression of a totalitarian mind-set that was simply assuming a new form? What and who were the forces behind these varied attacks? Were there common threads linking them to each other? What were the terrorists' weak points? Could they be effectively fought?

These were the questions my father and I discussed after Yoni's fall at Entebbe. Entebbe had been a turning point in the battle against international terrorism. Israel had overcome German and Palestinian terrorists sheltered by the ruthless dictator of an African country. It did so with the help of another African country, Kenya, which let Israel's Hercules planes refuel on its territory on the way back from Entebbe to Israel.

Could we use the fame of the Entebbe rescue to launch a worldwide conceptual change in the battle of the democracies against terrorism?

That is exactly what we decided to do. It was not pie in the sky. I had already seen firsthand the power of my father's lucidity and clairvoyance. I knew that his potent ideas could serve as a fulcrum to move the world.

But it was still a long shot. We needed to form an organization to disseminate a new approach to fighting terrorism in Western public opinion and among the key leaders of democracies. My father suggested that we convene an international conference on terrorism in Jerusalem on July 4, 1979, the third anniversary of the Entebbe rescue. We would challenge the arguments for legitimizing terrorism one by one and propose a totally new approach to fighting international terror.

Although, or perhaps *because*, I knew that the practical task of accomplishing such a plan would fall on me, I was tempted by this mission. It would be a worthy continuation of Yoni's legacy, and it would carry the battle in which he fought and died to bigger and more decisive battlefields.

Though I had fought terrorists myself in the military and had a deep appreciation for Israel's military ingenuity and courage in this war, I knew that what we set out to do had not yet been done—to harness the will and resolve of the free world to unite politically against international terrorism. Could we really achieve this? My father was twenty-nine years old when he went to see Jabotinsky in London. I was now roughly the same age. He had relied mostly on the sharpness of his intellect and the boldness of his vision. I had his wisdom to guide me and Yoni's legacy—which was considerably more. Even if I didn't succeed, at least I would fail in the service of a great and noble cause. I decided to try.

Consulting my family, we established the Jonathan Institute in 1977 to advocate for a new Western policy toward international terrorism. My father organized a strong and distinguished board of directors. It included Justice Meir Shamgar (later chief justice of Israel) and Eliyahu Lankin, a respected Jerusalem lawyer who had been the commander of the *Altalena*, the ship carrying much-needed ammunition and weapons from Europe for the beleaguered and outarmed Jewish army during Israel's War of Independence. Off the shore of Tel Aviv, Ben Gurion ordered soldiers commanded by Yitzhak Rabin to fire at the ship, which soon sank, taking its precious cargo with it. Sixteen were killed by bullets and in the water; many others were wounded. Ben Gurion's defenders claimed that he feared that those weapons would be used by an independent militia in an insurrection against the newly formed government, but the evidence points to the contrary.

Avraham Stavsky, one of those falsely accused in the Arlosoroff trial, was cut down by a hail of bullets and died. Menachem Begin, commander of the Irgun, who had a strong sense of history shaped by the recent Holocaust he had escaped, was on the ship. He stopped the Irgun from retaliating against their Jewish brethren, saying the immortal words "There will be no civil war."[1]

Lankin was one of the gentlest people I ever met. He spoke about the *Altalena* tragedy with profound pain, still disbelieving that Jews could act this way toward other Jews.

Another member of the board was Professor Ezra Zohar, who years earlier as the IDF's chief medical officer achieved fame by eliminating the rationing of water in training, saving the lives of many soldiers who would have otherwise died of dehydration. He later wrote a scathing critique of Israel's socialist bureaucracy titled *In the Grip of the Regime*, which influenced me greatly.[2]

The board asked me to be the institute's executive director. I asked for and received a leave of absence of several months from BCG to set up the organization. Bruce Henderson kindly agreed to continue paying my salary while I was on leave, and I myself took no wages from the institute. I then resumed my work at BCG for another year, though my true focus was now elsewhere. Altogether I was at BCG from 1976 to 1978.

MY FIRST TASK for the Jonathan Institute was to raise funds, which I did mostly in the United States. Yoni's story had gained worldwide fame, and fame opened doors. Opening pockets was another matter. But within a few months, with some help from my father, I had raised enough to launch the institute's first project, the Jerusalem Conference on International Terrorism.

I did not always succeed in fund-raising. At first I was deeply disappointed when I failed. Couldn't the people I approached understand that we were determined to change the Western world's policy on terrorism, and weren't just trying to commemorate a fallen brother and son? Well, no, most of them didn't. And why should they? I was young and clearly driven by a sense of mission, but who could take seriously such an ambitious goal? Out of respect for Yoni, a few did help. And as I would discover, if I was patient enough to discuss the issues seriously, many would open not only their wallets but their hearts and minds as well.

The first to do so was the kind and thoughtful Jake Feldman, a wealthy Jewish industrialist from Texas, to whom I was introduced by Defense Minister Shimon Peres. Feldman immediately signed a check for $100,000, a tremendous sum in the 1970s. Then in his seventies, Feldman told me how his grandfather, an impoverished Jewish immigrant, came to Texas in the nineteenth century. Starting from the center of a frontier town, he would walk to its outskirts until he could not see the last house.

Great-grandfather Abraham Marcus, circa 1880.

Grandparents Nathan and Sarah Mileikowsky-Netanyahu, circa 1910.

Grandparents Benjamin and Mollie Segal at the time of their wedding, Minneapolis, 1887.

Parents Cela Segal and Benzion Netanyahu in their twenties, circa 1935.

Cela and Benzion with their eldest son, Yoni, New York, 1948.

"The original Bibi," cousin Binyamin Ronn, one of Israel's first air force pilots, whose nickname was passed on to Benjamin Netanyahu, Israeli Air Force base, 1949.

Benzion and Cela with Bibi (left) and Yoni, Jerusalem, 1952.

Bibi at three, Yoni at six, Jerusalem, 1952.

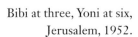

Editor in chief of the *Encyclopedia Hebraica* Benzion Netanyahu with an assistant, Jerusalem, circa 1956.

Bibi at twelve, Iddo at nine, Yoni at fifteen, family home, Jerusalem, 1961.

The proud mother and her three sons, Yoni at nineteen, Bibi at sixteen, Iddo at thirteen, Savyon, 1965.

On the varsity soccer team in the suburbs of Philadelphia, from Cheltenham High School yearbook, 1966.

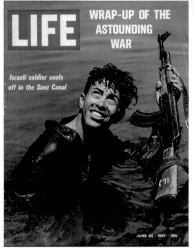

LEFT: Lieutenant Yoni Netanyahu, Independence Day march in Jerusalem, 1966. RIGHT: Tank commander Yossi Ben Hanan, whom Yoni would later rescue during the 1973 Yom Kippur War, on the cover of *Life* magazine after Israel's victory in the Six-Day War, Suez Canal, 1967.

"After seeing death face-to-face, life becomes even more precious." Yoni, wounded in battle on the Golan Heights during the Six-Day War, 1967.

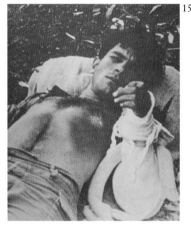

Commanders of Unit 101, forerunner of the Paratroopers Brigade and the Sayeret Matkal: (from left, top row) Meir Har Zion, Ariel Sharon, Moshe Dayan, Danny Mat; (front row, right) Rafael "Raful" Eitan, 1953.

17

Colonel Avraham Arnan, founder and first commander of Sayeret Matkal (the Unit), 1950s.

18

Bibi in an annual ten-kilometer run circling Mount Tabor, Galilee, 1969.

19

Bibi (first on right) and fellow soldiers graduating from Officers' Training School, Mitzpe Ramon, 1969.

20

"Who dares wins." Roll call in the Unit: (from right, front row) Yossi Kalmar, Bibi, Uzi Dayan, 1970.

21

Training Team Bibi in house-to-house combat: (left) Arik Gerstel (later Bibi's wing member during the Sabena rescue), and Bibi, Golan Heights, 1970.

22

Training with the naval commandos, Atlit naval base, 1971.

23

Jeep navigation exercise with Team Bibi, Negev desert, 1971.

24

With members of Team Bibi overlooking the Lebanese border, 1971.

Yoni and Bibi in the Unit, 1971.

Team Bibi before an operation in Syria: Bibi (far right, standing), Salim Shoufi (fourth from right, back row), 1971.

Receiving a citation from President Zalman Shazar after the Sabena rescue, with Bibi's arm in a sling from a gunshot wound, President's House, Jerusalem, 1972.

"This time with proper winter gear." Training for a mission on Mount Hermon, 1971.

29

Yoni in a moment of rest on Mount Hermon during the Yom Kippur War, 1973.

30

31

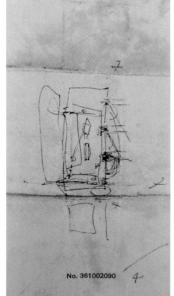

Last known photo of Yoni, taken three weeks before Entebbe while he guided Nobel Prize–winning economist Thomas Schelling on a tour of the Golan Heights, 1976.

Airsickness bag with the attack diagram that Yoni sketched for late-joining soldier Amos Goren on the flight to Entebbe, 1976.

32

Old Terminal, Entebbe Airport, 1976.

Back in Israel from Entebbe, unloading the Mercedes used by Yoni and his team to deceive Ugandan airport guards, 1976.

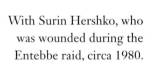

At Yoni's funeral: (from upper left) Iddo, Benzion, Bibi, Prime Minister Yitzhak Rabin; (lower left, with sunglasses) Minister of Foreign Affairs Yigal Allon, Mt. Herzl, Jerusalem, 1976.

With Surin Hershko, who was wounded during the Entebbe raid, circa 1980.

36

"Modern Moses." Theodor Herzl, founding father of Zionism, Basel, Switzerland, 1897.

37

38

Eighth Zionist Congress: (numbers added to identify attendees), grandfather Nathan Mileikowsky-Netanyahu (no. 5, front row center), future first president of Israel Chaim Weizmann (no. 18, second row center), future leader of Revisionist Zionism Ze'ev Jabotinsky (no. 54, fourth row, fourth from left), The Hague, Netherlands, 1907.

Colonel John Henry Patterson, commander of the Jewish Legion during World War I, godfather of Yoni, circa 1917.

"He was the greatest man I have ever known." Aaron Aaronsohn, Zionist leader, scientist, spymaster, circa 1916.

Ze'ev Jabotinsky, leader of Revisionist Zionism and spiritual leader of the future Likud Party, 1930s.

David Ben Gurion, leader of the Labor Party and Israel's first prime minister, 1950s.

Menachem Begin, leader of the Likud Party and Israel's sixth prime minister, 1970s.

Meeting with President Ronald Reagan at the White House: (far side of table, from left) Israeli ambassador to the US Moshe Arens, Israeli president Yitzhak Navon, Deputy Chief of Mission to the Israeli Embassy Benjamin Netanyahu; (near side of table, from right) Vice President George H. W. Bush, President Reagan, Secretary of State George Shultz, 1983.

Chatting with President Reagan and Israeli prime minister Yitzhak Shamir at the White House, 1983.

"Check your fanaticism at the door." First speech to the General Assembly of the United Nations as Israel's ambassador to the UN, New York, 1984.

Meeting with the Lubavitcher Rebbe, Rabbi Menachem Mendel Schneerson, New York, 1984.

47

At the UN, holding the war crimes file of former UN secretary-general
Kurt Waldheim, 1985.

48

Cela and Benzion, Jerusalem, mid-1980s.

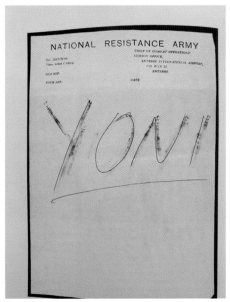

Sign held by a Ugandan soldier
greeting Iddo, Bibi and daughter Noa
on a visit to Entebbe Airport, 1989.

Iddo with a Ugandan official and soldier, Entebbe Airport, 1989.

Prime Minister Yitzhak Shamir
and his deputy minister at the
Madrid Peace Conference, 1991.

With wife Sara and son Yair,
Jerusalem, 1994.

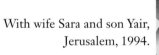

Campaigning for prime minister, Jerusalem,
1996.

He would then stake out a claim for the lots in that area and those properties naturally accrued in value as the town expanded.

This story was very much on my mind when as finance minister in 2003 and again as prime minister in 2009 I authorized massive investments in Israel's roads and railroads in order to enable Israeli families to break out beyond "the last houses" of the country's center. Once people could get out of the congested core of Tel Aviv, they would live in and invest in communities along the fast roads we would build.

Railroads and fast highways, I believed, would help create a social and economic revolution by finally turning hitherto dormant and backward "development towns" into thriving communities. That's exactly what happened in Kiryat Gat, Or Akiva and dozens of other towns in Israel after my government revolutionized Israel's transportation infrastructure in the years between 2010 and 2020. And the genesis of that revolution for me was Jake Feldman's recollections in Dallas a quarter of a century earlier. Armed with generous contributions from Feldman and others, I felt confident enough to proceed to organize the Jerusalem Conference. The first job was to hone the conference's message.

Quite by chance, I met in Boston Peter Lubin, a brilliant student at Harvard. An exceptionally talented writer singled out as such by the great Vladimir Nabokov, Peter lived an intellectual émigré's life in the heart of Cambridge. His father-in-law, Robert Fitzgerald, had written one of the classic translations of Homer, and his entire family was steeped in literature and refined culture. Most important, Peter and I shared a common approach to the battle against terrorism, seeing it not only as a military battle but as a civilizational one.

The terrorists assaulted the basic foundations of the laws of war, obliterating the distinction between combatants and noncombatants. By habituating people to the idea that their supposedly just causes justified mass murder, the terrorists neutered man's sense of sin. My father went a step further. It was not only that the terrorists' goals did not justify the murderous means they chose, he said. It was that their choice of means revealed what their true aims were, and these certainly were not freedom and human rights. Those who trample human rights into dust by deliberately blowing up buses full of children or crushing a baby's skull do not create democracies. They have a totalitarian mind-set that recognizes no limits to power. When they actually gain power they inevitably create not democracies but fearful dictatorships that continue to terrorize their subjects. *The choice of means reveals what the true aims are.* This fundamental truth is revealed over and over again, from the Khmer Rouge in Cambodia to the Taliban in Afghanistan to Hamas in Gaza.

At my request, Peter crystallized these ideas in a brief booklet that we sent to those we invited to the conference. His writing was powerful and original. To sharpen mine, he gave me Strunk and White's immortal book, *The Elements of Style*, and said, "When you get better at following these style rules, you can break them occasionally." No sounder advice could be given on the subject.

But where to begin? Whom should we invite first? Peter was unequivocal. "Before you go to the politicians, go to the intellectuals." The first person he suggested we see was the noted English writer and historian Paul Johnson. For years he had been the editor of the *New Statesman*, one of Britain's most influential political and cultural magazines. I went to see him in his charming seventeenth-century London home. His flaming red hair mirrored his fiery disposition. Yes, he would gladly come to the conference. He thought that terrorism could be fought and defeated, but that such a victory would require laser-sharp intellectual clarity. I knew he and Father would hit it off immediately at the conference.

Like others who had begun their intellectual careers on the left, Johnson gravitated to a conservative position in the 1970s. He was intimately familiar with leftist intellectual icons like Frantz Fanon, who gave intellectual legitimacy to the risible philosophical arguments put forth by the terrorists. Such apologists and sympathizers supported the terrorists because they invariably attacked the liberal Western societies that they themselves abhorred. After Johnson, I went to see Norman Podhoretz, the influential editor of *Commentary* magazine, who had undergone a similar intellectual journey in America, and Bayard Rustin, the famed Black civil rights leader who lambasted the argument that terrorists were fighting for human rights.

Pulitzer Prize–winning columnist George Will was next. He said right away that he would come. The noted scholar of Soviet Russia

Richard Pipes also agreed to attend. He would present the philosophical roots of the Soviet Union's support for and practice of terrorism, a theme echoed by Vladimir Bukovsky, the great Russian dissident who exposed the Soviet Union's use of psychiatric wards against political dissidents. Recently exchanged for a Russian spy, Bukovsky would be a powerful voice in distinguishing genuine freedom fighters from bogus ones.

Not all the writers and scholars I approached could come, but I enjoyed meeting with them nonetheless. In Rome I met the famed Italian writer Luigi Barzini, who described to me the terror tactics used by Italian fascists and their precursors, which he had detailed in his book *The Italians*. In London I met the great scholar of the Arab world Elie Kedourie. Most of those whom I approached, like the British scholar Brian Crozier, did promise to attend, as did Professor Annie Kriegel from Paris, who would speak to the appeal terrorism held for Western European intellectuals. To deal with the specter of nuclear terrorism, my father invited Professor Edward Teller, the father of the hydrogen bomb. Suffering from bad health, Teller agreed to send us his remarks.

We also invited Professor Thomas Schelling from Harvard, the distinguished political economist and Nobel Prize winner who wrote *Strategies of Conflict*, which Yoni and I had both read. An Israeli doctoral student of Schelling's from Harvard, Michael Handel, who had befriended Yoni when he was at Harvard's summer school, suggested that Yoni take Schelling to the Golan when Schelling visited Israel in June 1976. Three weeks before Entebbe, Yoni gave Schelling a private tour of the Golan that lasted a full sixteen hours.

Schelling was clearly influenced by Yoni's arguments. A few days later in a lecture in Jerusalem on the "Termination of Wars," Schelling said, "If I were a Syrian, I would realize there is no chance whatsoever of stabilizing the Middle East situation without territorial concessions, however much I might hesitate to give up the Golan to Israel. No one can guarantee that making such a concession would bring about a political settlement, but it is vital that a Syrian dove should appear who could rise to such an act of courage and self-sacrifice without which wars cannot be terminated."[3]

In other words, Schelling reversed the equation. It wasn't Israel that had to make territorial concessions for peace. It was *Syria*. Yoni had convinced him that if Israel didn't hold on to the Golan, peace would be unsustainable. Schelling agreed to come to the conference immediately.

To deal with the response of European states to terrorism, I was helped by Shimon Peres, then leader of the Opposition in the Knesset. Peres introduced me to a host of present and former European political leaders, ranging from France's Jacques Soustelle, to a former head of the North Atlantic Treaty Organization (NATO), to socialist and conservative political leaders from Germany, the Netherlands, Italy, Ireland and Britain. It was critical for us to present as broad a political spectrum as possible. Following this principle, we invited Prime Minister Menachem Begin and Shimon Peres himself to open the conference. We also invited former heads of Israeli intelligence and leading scholars of the Arab world to describe the role of Arab states in sponsoring terrorism, and the PLO's role as a proxy for them.

But which political leaders to invite from the United States and how to reach them? My first choice was the much-venerated Democratic senator Henry "Scoop" Jackson of Washington, the stalwart champion of human rights whose Jackson–Vanik Amendment insisted on Jewish emigration from the Soviet Union. My second invitee was George H. W. Bush, who served as head of the CIA and was much talked about as a candidate for the upcoming presidential election. Also invited were Senator John Danforth of Missouri and Congressman Jack Kemp of New York.

But how do we get to these people? Here Father had a brain wave. He went to see Axel Springer, the powerful and avidly pro-Israel German publisher. Standing next to my father in his office in West Berlin, Springer pointed to the Berlin Wall below and said: "Here is where freedom ends. Your son died for freedom. You are fighting for freedom. I will help you." With Springer's connections we opened many doors, including many of those I already mentioned. Altogether we had secured promises from some fifty distinguished participants from eight countries. They would make an extraordinarily powerful gathering. If they came. As the opening date of the conference approached, July 2, 1979, my father grew anxious.

"Are you sure all these people will come to Jerusalem?" he asked me. "Would the international press come? Would there be sufficient public attendance?"

I calmed him down.

"Father," I said, "when you were not much older than me you had met the leaders of America, you met Eisenhower. I am merely following in your footsteps. You needn't worry. They'll come, and the conference will be a great success."

IT WAS.

For three days the sessions rolled forward with eloquent presentations by fifty noted speakers. The conference constituted a political, intellectual and moral assault on international terrorism the likes of which had not been seen before.

It advanced three fundamental insights. The first was to define terrorism as "the deliberate assault on the innocent to inspire fear in order to gain political ends." One could substitute "ideological" for "political," and "noncombatants" or "civilians" for the "innocent," but the idea was clear. Terrorism is not the unintentional killing and wounding of civilians that accompanies every war, but deliberate, systematic and politically motivated attacks on civilians. Terrorism was a form of warfare but constituted a clear war crime. It was not defined by the ends that the terrorists professed to be pursuing, but by the means they used.

The second insight was the understanding that *international* terrorism was not carried out by frustrated individuals or ragtag groups but rather by organized states. Before the conference, Peter Lubin and I had asked conference participants to address "state-sponsored terrorism," a term that was vehemently challenged by some of the journalists attending the conference. In hindsight it is obvious that Arab states like Libya and Syria were sponsoring Arab terrorism and that Soviet Bloc countries were sponsoring European terror groups. But it wasn't obvious then. In fact, this idea was strongly contested by many journalists, so much so that the *Wall Street Journal* correspondent reporting from the conference wrote that "a considerable number in the press covering the conference were much annoyed."[4] We had to fight long and hard to seed this pivotal idea of state-sponsored terrorism, and for it to gain acceptance.

Conference participants helped by giving compelling evidence of the support given by Arab states and the Soviet Union to the plethora of terrorist organizations attacking Western democracies. They offered them shelter, weapons, money, training and, very often, instructions. The Soviets concentrated on destabilizing Western Europe, Arab states on destabilizing just about everyone else. We didn't argue that the Soviets and Arab states were in coordination with each other. Sometimes they were and sometimes they were not. Our argument was simple: without the support of sovereign states, the whole structure of international terrorism would collapse. Terrorism was thus a conveniently deniable and criminal proxy war used by Arab and Soviet state sponsors to wage war against their enemies.

The third insight of the conference derived from the second. Since international terrorism was a weapon of totalitarian and dictatorial regimes against democracies, democracies should unite in applying military, political and economic sanctions against those states, and not just against the terrorist organizations that serve them.

The effect of the conference was profound. Journalists from America, Europe, South America and Asia gave it considerable coverage. The ideas we put forward began to percolate in the policies and public discourse of many nations.

But perhaps the most potent effect of the Jerusalem Conference was the way it coherently assaulted the moral pretensions of the terrorists and their supporters. This was magnificently expressed by Paul Johnson in his thunderous speech, "The Seven Deadly Sins of Terrorism."

Among these sins, Johnson listed the Promotion of Totalitarianism ("Terrorism actively, systemically and necessarily assists the spread of the totalitarian state"); the Exploitation of Freedom ("Terrorism exploits the apparatus of freedom in liberal societies and thereby endangers it"); and the Enervation of Democracy ("The deadliest sin of terrorism is that it saps the will of a civilized society to defend itself").[5]

A practicing Catholic, he nonetheless gave a scathing critique of Pope John Paul II for meeting Yasser Arafat, condemning the meeting between "His Holiness and His Depravity."[6]

I took no public role in these proceedings but, behind the scenes, made sure the conference ran smoothly. In the months afterward, I edited and published the proceedings in a book titled *International Terrorism: Challenge and Response*. I added my own short summary:

The recent fantastic growth in international terror, the enhanced prestige of terrorists and even the specter of international sponsored terrorist states, are the direct result of the state support extended to terror movements. The current threat promises to become intolerable when terrorists gain access to weapons of mass destruction, or when they gain control of whole peoples and governments establishing themselves in de facto terrorist states.[7]

My work with the Jonathan Institute was done for now. With the conference, a global antiterror campaign had been launched and the conceptual seeds of both defining and fighting international terrorism had been planted.

My only regret was that I hadn't taken my father's advice to invite Ronald Reagan, at the time a distant presidential candidate.

"Reagan," I said, "he's an actor."

"He's a man of conviction," Father answered. "Invite him."

As usual, Father knew best. But having already invited Bush, I thought that inviting two presidential candidates was too much, fully justifying the cliché about youth's triumph over wisdom. It would take another Jonathan Institute conference and another five years for the full force of our ideas to reach Reagan. Had I listened to Father, we might have shortened the process by a few years.

At any rate, I could now return to my private life.

19

BUSINESS

1980-1982

In 1978, before the conference was held, I had ended my work at BCG, Miki had completed her doctorate, and we'd had a daughter, Noa. Then, in 1979, Miki and I divorced. Miki was a wonderful mother to Noa and we both had her best interest at heart. Miki went on to become the general director of Israel's Ministry of the Environment and a member of Israel's Atomic Energy Advisory Board. Divorce always scars children, but Noa has gone on to enjoy a fulfilling family life with her husband, Daniel, and their five delightful children. They follow an observant Jewish life and live in an Orthodox neighborhood of Jerusalem. Noa worked for several years for the Joint Distribution Committee, helping acclimate African refugees and others in Israel.

After our divorce, Miki and Noa moved to Jerusalem, and I needed a job, preferably in Jerusalem, so I could be close to Noa. I did not want to earn a living from an organization formed in Yoni's memory and looked for a new opportunity.

But the city was almost exclusively a government town at the time, largely devoid of industry and high-tech firms. Both were then in their infancy in Israel and were centered mostly on Tel Aviv. One of the few significant private businesses in Jerusalem was Israel's leading industrial manufacturer and marketer of furniture, RIM Industries. It was established by the Eisen family, who came from Panama. I applied for the role of marketing director at RIM and got it.

I devoted myself totally to the job. To save money I lived in a garage converted to a spartan one-room apartment in the rural community of Motza, adjoining Jerusalem. Aside from motivating a sales force and directing advertising, my main contribution to the company was to apply some of the concepts I had learned at BCG. I used the company's existing scale advantage in manufacturing to drive down marketing costs and gain market share. Israel had high inflation at the time but I still tried to drive prices down, which in an inflationary environment usually means raising them more slowly than the competition. My only foray into technology was to insist on what in 1980 was a bizarre idea in Israeli retail: that each of the company's two hundred salespeople would have sales targets and daily computerized performance reports broken down by product sales data (which I closely correlated with advertising). The company's market share soared, as did its profits.

During my time at RIM I married Fleur Cates, whom I had met in Boston. Her father's Jewish family had escaped Nazi Germany and had settled in London. British born, a graduate of Cambridge University and Harvard Business School, she too had worked at BCG. Fleur came to Israel, worked for Scitex, an early Israeli high-tech company, but soon returned to the United States to work for BCG's competitor Bain & Company.

After my first year at RIM, I told its chief executive officer, Rolando Eisen, that I too was going to Boston. Fleur had spent a year in Israel and I would now spend a year in Boston. Rolando surprised me with an unexpected offer.

"Why don't you spend half of every month here and half of every month in Boston?" he suggested.

"But I wouldn't be able to work for you there," I answered.

Rolando said that if I spent two weeks a month in Israel, that was good enough for him. He would even increase my pay. I accepted. In Boston I went to the Harvard Business School library and read dozens of books on marketing, direct mail, advertising, business management and the like. Back in Israel, I would test the most innovative ideas, adopt the ones that worked and discard the ones that didn't.

Then, in early 1982, I got a phone call from Moshe Arens, at the time chairman of the Knesset's Defense and Foreign Relations Committee. Arens had been a seventeen-year-old member of Jabotinsky's Beitar movement in New York when my father was on his Zionist mission in America during World War II. Arens recalled how he accompanied my father to his rallies and even bought him a shirt at one time. Later, after graduating from the California Institute of Technology with a degree in aeronautical engineering, Arens immigrated to Israel. On the day of his marriage to his wife, Muriel, he bumped into my father in Jerusalem and invited him to his wedding.

I had first met Arens myself in 1974 when I came to see Rabin with Father about helping Israel's public relations battle in the US. Arens was already a Knesset member at the time and understood immediately what we were trying to do to counter American pressure.

As I was leaving I asked him, "Do you know my brother Yoni?" He said he didn't.

Walking out the door, I said, "You should. He'll be important one day."

Now, eight years later, Arens had been chosen by Prime Minister Begin to become Israel's ambassador to the US. In his austere living room in one of the few modest homes in the wealthy community of Savyon, he told me that he expected that we would soon have to act against the PLO terrorist enclave in Lebanon.

Arens knew what he was talking about. He received detailed intelligence reports not only about the many attacks the PLO had carried out against Israel from Lebanon, but also about the many attacks they *planned* to carry out. Sooner or later, we would have to act against the organization. This would necessarily produce a negative reaction in America and he was looking for someone to help him fight the battle for American public opinion when all hell broke loose.

Arens had attended the Jerusalem Conference on International Terrorism and spoke of its worldwide impact. Learning that I had organized it, he decided to call me. Would I be willing to become his deputy in Israel's Washington, DC, embassy?

I thought quickly. Arens respected Father and as a youngster accompanied him in his public activity in America. He was a student of Jabotinsky. For the first time, the state of Israel would have an ambassador in Washington who understood how the battle for American public opinion should be waged. I liked Arens. He was a straight shooter. What he told me about the impending confrontation in Lebanon made sense. I could do good for the country, and I would work under a person I respected and trusted.

"Why not?" I answered. "Let's do it."

20

DIPLOMAT

1982-1984

On June 6, 1982, a full-scale war with Lebanon erupted, just as Arens predicted. Several days earlier, Palestinian terrorists had tried to assassinate Israel's ambassador to the United Kingdom, Shlomo Argov. Paralyzed for life, Argov lived, but Israel had had enough.

After years of incessant terrorist attacks from Lebanon, Israel sent its army to South Lebanon—the area that the PLO had taken over and turned into an anti-Israel terrorist ministate. The IDF reached as far as Beirut and laid siege to the PLO's leadership there. Yasser Arafat and the entire PLO command were forced to leave for Tunisia. The main fighting abated after three months and the bulk of the Israeli force returned home, but there were periodic Palestinian attacks on the Israeli soldiers remaining in the country.

In the weeks before the war broke out, I had visited the Foreign Ministry, then housed in kibbutz-like shacks at the entrance to Jerusalem. Its professional diplomats briefed me on the cast of characters I would meet in the US State Department. Since I had already covered much of this ground in my earlier activities on behalf of the Rabin government and the Jonathan Institute, I knew the briefings were on the mark. But one thing was always missing. There was much talk about this and that personality, but there was no talk—zero—about how to affect public opinion, the true force that could influence, for better or worse, American policy toward Israel.

Now, knowing Arens's plan, I kept all that to myself. As soon as the war broke out, the negative press coverage began wreaking havoc on Israel's position. It caused even a sympathetic president like Reagan to halt sales of F-16 fighter jets to Israel in an effort to rein in our forces.

My introduction to the foreign service was met with public opprobrium. A senior columnist wrote against the outrage of appointing a "novice political appointee" to such a sensitive post as the deputy chief of mission in Washington, and a "furniture salesman" at that! This was the first press attack directed against me. It was a little bigger than a postage stamp, but not by much. It preoccupied me for days. This would change.

Arens stuck to his guns and pushed my appointment through. Before I left for Washington, I wanted to see our forces near Beirut firsthand. Crossing the border into Lebanon, I was reminded of my last day in the army ten years earlier, when I crossed the border in the other direction.

I circled the mountains overlooking Beirut by car, saw the awe-inspiring cedars of Lebanon mentioned in the Bible (King Solomon imported them to build his Temple), and met some Lebanese Christian leaders allied with Israel. Then I made my way to Washington. When I got there, I discovered a full-scale firestorm. It was even worse than I expected.

Israel was being massively criticized in the American press, its invasion of Lebanon excoriated. The terrorist attacks that prompted the invasion in the first place were ignored by the international media in favor of covering the physical damage caused by the IDF. Lebanese civilian casualties were dramatized nightly on television.

Arens was doing a heroic job, appearing frequently on American channels to explain Israel's actions. He was precise and logical, and he aroused respect. He developed a close rapport with President Reagan, and especially with Secretary of State George Shultz.

This mitigated the pressure somewhat but there was still much to do. Before I could join the fray, however, I had to deal with a wage strike. On one of my first days on the job, the Foreign Ministry union had ordered all foreign service employees not to show up for work in any of Israel's embassies around the world. Arens was exempt from this but I was not. I couldn't believe it. Israel was engaged in a full-scale diplomatic and media war, and I was told to sit on the sidelines! There was no way I would abide this. Saying I came to serve my country and not the union, I was the only member of the foreign service worldwide to break the union's directive and show up for work. In retaliation, the union ordered my car and driver to be withdrawn for the strike's duration. I walked.

Arens had assembled a first-class embassy team to deal with the Reagan administration, Congress, the Treasury and the Pentagon. The embassy spokesman was the able Nachman Shai, who later served as the IDF spokesman during the Gulf War.

Soon a peculiar problem arose. Prime Minister Menachem Begin was coming to Washington and only a limited number of embassy staff could accompany him and Arens to the Oval Office. As Arens's deputy I outranked the others. I was amused as each expressed in his turn why it was important for Israel that he attend. To solve the problem of the missing extra space, I volunteered to stay out. A stunned silence ensued.

Later, outside Arens's office, one of the staff members pulled me aside and said, "Bibi, if you keep this up you won't get very far." I didn't go. Arens appreciated that.

I took on anything he asked me to do, from organizing who would sit in which limousine to drafting letters. But the main effort was to brief journalists, convince Jewish groups to support Israel's position, meet senators and members of Congress and grapple with State Department officials.

The pressure on Israel was mounting. Defense Secretary Caspar Weinberger was highly critical of Israel, probably identifying with the Arabist leanings of the foreign policy establishment that viewed Israel as a burden on the US.

In August, President Reagan was outraged when he saw a photo of a little Lebanese girl with her arms blown off by an alleged Israeli strike. I looked at the photo. Something was wrong. It wasn't clear that she had lost her arms. I asked the Foreign Ministry in Israel to ask military intelligence to check into this.

They came back with a startling answer. The girl was okay. She hadn't lost her arms, and she was wounded not by an Israeli attack but by a PLO attack. We put this out in the press to mitigate the damage and presented it to the White House.[1]

Still, as the crisis continued to simmer in Lebanon even after the

PLO was expelled from Beirut and the main fighting abated, the traditional Arabists in the State Department persuaded Reagan, who was pro-Israel by nature, to put forward his own plan for peace in the Middle East. He did so in a speech on September 1, 1982. Undersecretary of State Lawrence Eagleburger called me to his office and said, "You'd better put your seat belt on."

The Reagan Plan was nothing more than a rehashing of the Rogers Plan of 1969 and other similar recipes, addressing the "root cause" of the conflict. Essentially they all said the same thing. Israel was to freeze settlements for years, adopt the principle of "territory for peace" and enable the Palestinians to form a self-governing authority that would later develop into a full-fledged sovereign state in association with Jordan. No part of Judea and Samaria (the West Bank) was to be designated as part of sovereign Israel, leaving Israel with indefensible borders.

I told Eagleburger that Prime Minister Begin would never agree to this. The inherent problem in our conflict with the Arabs wasn't the absence of a *Palestinian* state, but the presence of a *Jewish* one, I said. The persistent Arab refusal to recognize the right of the Jewish people to a state of their own is what had been driving this conflict since the beginning of the twentieth century. Not only did the Reagan Plan not address this critical issue. By putting the onus of the continuation of the conflict on Israel, it encouraged the Palestinians and other Arabs to continue to reject the very idea of a Jewish state, thus pushing the possibility of an enduring peace ever further away.

Begin did indeed reject the Reagan Plan, calling it the "saddest day" of his life "since becoming Prime Minister."[2]

Begin, the first prime minister from the right, had broken the mold. With exceptional oratory that evoked Jewish history, fidelity to the Land of Israel and defense of Jewish rights, he had captured the imagination of millions in Israel who like him were considered outcasts by the left-dominated establishment. Dignified, garbed in suits, he was anything but the typical Israeli *sabra* (native-born Israeli). As leader of the Irgun he had commanded the underground revolt against British rule in what became Israel, and in 1981 he had ordered the bombing of Saddam Hussein's nuclear reactor to protect his country. Yet it was Begin who had also made the first historic peace agreement between Israel and an Arab nation, signing a treaty in 1979 for which he and Egyptian president Anwar Sadat had been jointly awarded the Nobel Prize.

The Reagan Plan would wither on the vine, taking its place among similar American and European efforts that have, time and again, attempted and failed to break the logjam of the Arab-Israeli conflict.

THE MOST CHALLENGING moment in the Lebanon War came on September 16, 1982, when members of the Phalangists, a Lebanese Christian militia, massacred possibly hundreds of Palestinians at the Sabra and Shatila refugee camps near Beirut. Israel and its defense minister, Ariel Sharon, were accused of masterminding this savagery. Sharon had supported and armed the Phalangists who were aligned with Israel, but he certainly did not instruct them to carry out this or any other massacre.

But this slander about a supposed Israeli-led atrocity had spread like wildfire around the world, riling Prime Minister Begin.

At the height of the press attacks on Israel a few days after the Sabra and Shatila massacre, Begin called me at the embassy.

"Mr. Netanyahu," he said, "please take pen and paper and write down what I say."

He then proceeded to dictate an ad that he asked me to place in the *New York Times*, the *Washington Post* and elsewhere. Titled "Blood Libel," it sought to counter the lies that blamed Israel for the massacre. IDF soldiers in fact were not involved in any way in this tragedy.

I did as he asked, changing a word here and there.

But the storm continued to rage, including in Israel. Massive crowds demonstrated in Tel Aviv, accusing Sharon of being a "murderer" and "the Butcher of Beirut." The protesters called for Israel, which was maintaining a security belt in South Lebanon, to withdraw from the country completely. Under pressure, Begin set up a Commission of Inquiry, headed by a Supreme Court judge, to investigate whether Israel had any involvement in the massacre at Sabra and Shatila.

While the commission was investigating, we at the embassy had to do battle on several fronts: pushing back on follow-up attempts by the Reagan administration and others to impose unacceptable terms on Israel, while defending our actions in Lebanon. In this effort there was a clear division of labor. Arens handled national television and the major papers and I handled secondary media outside the Washington Beltway.

Newspapers back then still wielded a powerful influence over public opinion, especially their editorial and op-ed pages. I looked up the fifty top newspapers in the United States. Our ten consulates covered the areas in which they were published and distributed. If each consulate submitted an op-ed article to their local papers every few months, we could produce a critical mass of op-eds to influence the senators, members of Congress and other decision makers who read those pages.

I set up a small cottage industry in the embassy to prepare and distribute the op-eds. Sharply crafted by writers I recruited, they were signed by Israel's consuls. I allowed the consuls to insert changes to suit their particular audiences. If they submitted good op-eds on their own, I encouraged that, too. Soon we blanketed the key opinion markets of the United States with a steady stream of pro-Israeli op-eds debunking the vilifications leveled against us. Nothing on this scale had been done in America since my father published his ads during World War II.

We started hearing the arguments and ideas we were seeding in print on television. When others repeat your ideas as their own, you are getting traction.

In February 1983, the commission submitted its report, which was immediately released to the public. It found that Israel had not had any involvement in the massacre at Sabra and Shatila. But the commission added a kicker: although Ariel Sharon had not been directly involved, and had not foreseen the massacre, he *should* have foreseen it. For this omission, the commission said, he should be removed from office.

I thought this was preposterous and dangerous. You cannot expect leaders to foresee every possibility and punish them for not doing so. This hinders decision making, hampers risk taking and induces a "protocol" mentality, whereby decision makers cover their rear ends by endlessly explaining why they should do nothing. Iddo wrote a damning article in an Israeli newspaper against the commission's conclusions and recommendations.[3] He was among the very few who stood up in Sharon's defense.

There was massive public pressure from the left to have Sharon, then a champion of the right, removed from office. Begin eventually capitulated and named Arens as Sharon's replacement as defense minister. Roughly a year after my arrival in Washington, in May 1983, Arens left for Israel. I was to stay on as acting ambassador for six months until the new ambassador, Meir Rosenne, a respected expert in international law, came to Washington.

Before the appointment of Rosenne, Arens had tried, unsuccessfully, to have me appointed ambassador. He told Minister of Foreign Affairs Yitzhak Shamir that I would continue to wage the battle for public opinion in the US, and that this was the most important job of an ambassador today.

Shamir was tough as nails. He would become prime minister in 1986 and was committed to the Land of Israel with the same iron intensity that guided him during his days in the pre-state Lehi underground and later in the Mossad. Short on words, he did not personally lead the international Hasbara wars in Israel's defense but preferred to delegate this task to others, principally to Arens and later to me.

But in those days, Shamir had little interest in what Arens was talking about. He told Arens that at thirty-three, I was too young and inexperienced, and that the Foreign Ministry specialists all agreed that a "professional diplomat" was what was needed in Washington. The irony is that they said this to Arens, a champion of the private sector and a totally independent thinker, who was the quintessential antithesis of this very recommendation.

THE SIX MONTHS before Meir Rosenne arrived to take over as ambassador were long, but they launched my public career.

During this time, the embassy received a request for Israel's acting ambassador to appear opposite an Arab ambassador on ABC's *Nightline*, a nightly news program at 11 p.m. hosted by the veteran journalist Ted Koppel. These were the days before round-the-clock television news, and *Nightline*, established after the takeover of the US embassy in Tehran in 1979, had created a new kind of platform to reach a broad audience and discuss global issues in depth.

I went to the ABC studios on K Street in Washington, sensing that this could be an important opportunity in my efforts to sway public opinion on behalf of Israel. It would be my first appearance in a significant television forum since my debate on Boston's local PBS station six years earlier. In the intervening time I had acquired a great deal of experience.

Nightline was a televised political boxing arena, Koppel a fair and professional referee. The Arab ambassador and I slugged it out for fifteen or twenty minutes. I don't remember the exact topic, probably "Terrorism," "Israel's Aggression," "American Middle East Policy," "The Palestinians," or any of the other usual suspects.

At the end of the program I felt I had been a bit stiff, rigidly sticking to prepared lines, but when I walked out of the studio, the American camera crews smiled at me with their thumbs up. That was a good sign.

Soon Koppel invited me to more nightly matchups. I let myself be looser in my responses, often in off-the-cuff rebuffs, though I was always aware I was representing the state of Israel and my words had to be measured to suit government policy.

Since I usually agreed with these policies, this didn't present much difficulty. I found that if I *believed* in what I said, and presented my arguments forcefully and thoughtfully, I could get my message through effectively.

Evidently Koppel's audience thought the same. As happens to anyone appearing frequently on television, people began to recognize me on the street, in shops and in restaurants. I was now asked to appear on all the other networks—on morning shows, nightly news, weekend shows. While Israel was an interesting subject, I had pivoted the discussion to one of much greater interest to the American public: how America should fight the terrorism that was now threatening and killing Americans.

I tried to speak my mind, speak my heart, and above all speak plainly. I avoided jargon assiduously. In addition to *The Elements of Style*, Peter Lubin had also given me Stanislav Andreski's hilarious book, *Social Science as Sorcery*, and after I read his indictment of "pretentious nebulous verbosity," I could never look a "paradigm" in the eye or garble a sentence with "parameters" and other such imprecise patter again.

If I occasionally used one of these expressions, I now offer a belated apology. Throughout my public career I fought a resolute war against jargon used by government officials—with only partial success. I could usually control what came out of my mouth and out of my office, but generally not much more than that.

I was becoming known inside and outside the Beltway. Since my arrival in the city I had been making the rounds, befriending a host of influential people. Over lunch, Len Garment, Nixon's former advisor, gave me wise counsel: "Take your time, listen carefully, and you'll be all right." I had been to see Lane Kirkland, the respected chairman of the AFL-CIO, whom I had previously met at the Jerusalem Conference. He was highly influential among Democrats and Republicans alike. Various Washington intellectuals and journalists were also friends, including the Pulitzer Prize–winning writer Charles Krauthammer, the *New York Times* columnist William Safire and the famed television anchor David Brinkley.

Brinkley invited me for lunch to meet his friend Frank Sinatra, who was a lifelong supporter of Israel. I found him down-to-earth, without any inflated sense of self-importance. Brinkley asked me to explain to Sinatra the situation in the Middle East, which I did. He understood instinctively Israel's need to defend itself against terrorist aggression from Lebanon, which reminded him of facing up to bullies in his early years in Hoboken, New Jersey. I was very much taken by his unassuming manner, his broad grin and his famously blue eyes. This pattern repeated itself from time to time as I was asked by others to brief their friends and acquaintances.

Even more so after my *Nightline* appearance, Fleur and I were invited to the homes of Washington's leading media figures, including the *Washington Post*'s publisher Katharine Graham and her daughter, Lally Weymouth, political leaders from both parties and prominent officials in the administration. But just as I felt I had turned a corner and was ready to charge forward, the new Israeli ambassador arrived to take Moshe Arens's place.

I was now in a bind. Meir Rosenne, an expert in international law, was among the best of the traditional diplomatic core. He could speak well with his counterparts in the State Department, but like most of his colleagues in Israel's diplomatic service, his style was not geared to the TV age. In the American media you are given one chance to make a first impression. If you don't perform well, you will rarely be invited again.

It must have been hard on Rosenne. Having assumed the top spot in Israel's foreign service, he now found as his deputy someone who was publicly overshadowing him. I treaded carefully, out of respect for the man. Besides, who needed an intramural fight? Rosenne and I both understood this and kept a respectful distance from one another.

As the eighth anniversary of Entebbe approached, I asked and received permission from the Foreign Ministry to convene the Jonathan Institute's Second Conference on International Terrorism on July 4, 1984. It would be in Washington, instead of Jerusalem. The institute would pay the conference costs, but I would be allowed to use embassy staff to help in this public relations effort on behalf of Israel.

This time the going was infinitely easier. When I began organizing the first conference, I was an unknown twenty-eight-year-old carried forward largely by Yoni's fame and guided by my father. Now I was known in my own right, and I had built connections with leading members of America's political, intellectual and media elites. The ideas initially presented in 1979 in Jerusalem about state-sponsored terrorism and the moral bankruptcy of the terrorist cause had taken root. It was now possible, I thought, not only to amplify these ideas but to focus on the question of *how to win the war* against terror.

David Bar Ilan, a world-class Israeli pianist and a gifted writer whom I had befriended in New York, joined Peter Lubin in helping me organize the conference. He later edited the *Jerusalem Post* and wrote biting and witty columns exposing the falsehoods and distortions of the Israeli press.

In addition to Paul Johnson, Norman Podhoretz and George Will, I invited reporter and author Bob Woodward, of Watergate fame. I also invited Republican senator Paul Laxalt and Democratic senator Daniel Patrick Moynihan, a former US ambassador to the United Nations. Two world-renowned scholars of the Arab world, Bernard Lewis and Elie Kedourie—who had not been able to attend the first conference but agreed to come to the second—discussed the roots of Arab terror. Jeane Kirkpatrick and leading scholars of communism discussed its Soviet and totalitarian roots. William Webster, the head of the FBI, spoke about fighting terrorism in the United States. Moshe Arens and Yitzhak Rabin spoke of the need to confront terrorism internationally. But the most important statement came from Secretary of State George Shultz, whom I had met several times before.

After repeatedly calling on television for an active policy that would include diplomatic, economic and military sanctions against terrorist states, I was heartened when Shultz told me that he was deeply interested in the ideas I was championing. He had been particularly shaken by the October 23, 1983, suicide bombings of the US Marine barracks in Beirut, which killed 241 marines. This attack had spurred me to systematically shift the focus of the public debate on terrorism to threats faced not only by Israelis, but also by Americans. It had also shifted American sympathy from Lebanon to Israel, lessening the political pressure on the IDF to curtail its activities in Lebanon.

At one point during that terrible year in which the Beirut bombings occurred, Shultz called me into his office and told me that he was extremely concerned about the spread of terrorism.

"These terrorists aren't human beings," he said. "They're animals."[4]

He made it clear that he was determined to effect a change in America's antiterror policy from one of passive defense to a more active one. He wanted to take the battle against the terrorists to their bases abroad and to the countries supporting them, "even if there are some who are opposed to this." (He meant primarily Defense Secretary Caspar Weinberger, who was hesitant about using America's armed forces against terrorist targets.)

Shultz suggested we hold a series of meetings in which we would work to define what the United States could do in conjunction with other countries of the free world to uproot the terrorist scourge. He readily agreed to speak at the second Jonathan Institute conference.

There, on July 4, 1984, eight years after the Entebbe rescue, Shultz made the following statement to the gathered diplomats and journalists:

> Many countries have joined the ranks of what we might call the "League of Terror" as full-fledged sponsors and supporters of indiscriminate, and not so indiscriminate, murder.
>
> Terrorists and those who support them have definite goals. Terrorist violence is the means of attaining those goals.
>
> Can we as a country, can the community of free nations, stand in a purely defensive posture and absorb the blows dealt by terrorists? I think not. From a practical standpoint, a purely passive defense does not provide enough of a deterrent to terrorism and *the states that sponsor it*. It is time to think long, hard, and seriously

about more active means of defense—defense through appropriate preventive or *preemptive* actions against terrorist groups before they strike.[5]

Everyone understood that a Rubicon had been crossed. Here was an architect of US policy saying that the US should not merely respond to specific terrorist attacks but pivot to preemptive action. And he aimed his comments at the state sponsors of terrorism.

Like the Jerusalem Conference before it, the Washington Conference had immense consequences. But whereas the Jerusalem Conference was primarily an assault on the intellectual foundations of terrorism, the Washington Conference was designed to directly influence American policy on fighting terror in concrete ways.

As before, I edited the conference proceedings in a book, titled *Terrorism: How the West Can Win*. I was encouraged to do so by Roger Straus of the prestigious publishing house Farrar, Straus & Giroux. Unlike the previous book, in which I had written brief introductions to each chapter and edited the essays of others, this time I wrote a lengthy essay myself about how I believed the democracies of the world could defeat international terror. I ended the book with the following words:

> Terrorism is a phenomenon that tries to evoke one feeling: fear. The one virtue most necessary to defeat terrorism is the antithesis of fear—courage. Courage, said the Romans, is not the only virtue, but it is the single virtue without which all the other virtues are meaningless. Confusion and vacillation facilitated the rise of terrorism, clarity and courage will ensure its defeat.[6]

Publishing this book had two important consequences. First, it spread the ideas of the conference far and wide, thanks in part to a long feature in *Time* magazine, at the time perhaps the most influential weekly in the world.[7]

The second consequence was the direct impact it had on a key decision maker: Ronald Reagan.

As Shultz wrote me about two years after the conference, on May 2, 1986: "This morning on the long flight from Washington to Bali [en route to a G7 Summit] I noticed the President reading your book. Several times during the flight he came to the place where I was sitting and commented on various passages in the book which he read aloud to us. . . . He gave me his copy, telling me I have to read the book, adding: 'I want it back.' "[8]

What began as my father's idea after Yoni's fall at Entebbe culminated less than a decade later in a new and far more aggressive American-led approach to combating global terrorism.

Under Reagan and Shultz's leadership, the United States imposed diplomatic and economic sanctions against terrorist states including Libya, Syria and Iran. The US fought with determination to apprehend the PLO gunman who murdered the wheelchaired American Leon Klinghoffer on the *Achille Lauro* cruise ship in October 1985, intercepting the terrorists' escape plane in midair over the Mediterranean and forcing it to land at a NATO base in Sicily, where the hijackers were arrested by Italian police.

Above all, Reagan and Shultz sent a powerful message to terrorists the world over when, in April 1986, together with Margaret Thatcher's Britain, they bombed Libya in a raid in which dictator Mu'ammar Qaddafi himself nearly lost his life. After the Libyan bombing a Kuwaiti newspaper blamed this shift in American policy on my influence. I couldn't have been prouder to take the blame.

These successes encouraged the Reagan administration to work for an overall change in the Western stance toward terrorism. On May 7, 1986, the United States called a summit of Western leaders in Tokyo, in which sweeping resolutions were adopted calling for an aggressive Western defense against international terrorism. In 1987, Congress passed the firmest antiterrorist legislation yet, ordering the closure of all PLO offices in the United States.

After twenty years in which international terrorism under the leadership of the PLO had enjoyed virtually unrestricted freedom of action, the West had finally begun to grasp the principle that the terrorist organizations and their state sponsors should no longer be able to escape punishment for their deeds.

*	*	*

OF COURSE, THE West's battle against terrorism was not without its setbacks. Toward the end of its term, the Reagan administration sought a "dialogue" with the PLO and considered recognizing it as a legitimate political body. The "root cause" theory occasionally rears its head even among the most sober leaders and thinkers. Another setback came with a revelation in November 1986.

While the United States had been stepping up its war against terrorism, some in the Reagan White House had been simultaneously negotiating with Iranian-controlled terrorists in Lebanon for the release of American hostages in Iranian custody. The agreed-upon price was shipments of American weapons to the Iranian regime. Shultz was outraged. In his memoir, he wrote: "Every principle that the President praised in Netanyahu's book on terrorism had been dealt a terrible blow by what has been done."⁹ Fortunately, Shultz's tenacious campaign to steer the United States away from its dealings with Iran paid off. Within a matter of weeks, he was able to reassert control over Middle East policy, and the American government returned to the course he had set with President Reagan.

But despite these and other setbacks, the Reagan-Shultz antiterror policy of the 1980s was an overall success. International terrorism was dealt a stunning blow. Its state backers were laid bare, its perpetrators unmasked. There were sharp political, economic and military actions delivered by the West against terrorism's chief sponsors that caused them to rescind their support and rein the terrorists in. And the destruction of the PLO base in Lebanon during the Lebanon War deprived terrorists from many countries of their most useful staging ground for terrorist operations against the democracies. The Soviet-Arab terrorist axis was on the verge of extinction, as was the Soviet Union itself. The West's airlines, cities and citizens seemed to be safe once again. After nearly twenty years of continual savagery, international terrorism and the threat posed by terrorist states appeared to be collapsing into the dust.

BUT DID IT? Years before 9/11, I could see clouds on the horizon with the advent of radical Islam. I believed then, as I do now, that the greatest danger terrorism posed was the emergence of Islamic terrorist states that could dispatch fanatics to the West. Worse, they could acquire nuclear weapons and the means to deliver them. With such weapons of mass death, they could graduate from terrorizing their own citizens and their neighbors to terrorizing the *entire world*.

"By far the most disconcerting prospect," I wrote in 1985, "would be the acquisition of weapons of mass destruction by the principal terrorist states of the Middle East—Iran, Libya and Syria."[10]

Years later all three terrorist regimes would attempt to develop nuclear weapons. Under the threat of American military intervention, Libya gave it up. After an Israeli air strike on its nuclear reactor in Deir Ezzor with US political support, Syria stopped. Iran continued.

21

AMBASSADOR

1984–1988

By the time of the Washington Conference, I had changed jobs. At Arens's recommendation, Shamir had brought forth my candidacy for Israel's ambassadorship to the United Nations after the formation of the unity government in September 1984. Peres was prime minister, Shamir foreign minister, Rabin defense minister and Arens minister without portfolio, permitting him to attend cabinet meetings without overseeing a specific government department. After two years Peres and Shamir would switch jobs. In the polarized world of Israeli parliamentary politics, neither Labor nor Likud could form a government on its own. The solution was to combine forces and rotate the role of prime minister after two years. But would this two-headed government approve my appointment to the UN?

Unlike the previous attempt to appoint me as ambassador to the US, there were practically no objections to my appointment as UN ambassador. The only reservation came from a minister who asked, "But who can get into Bibi's shoes in Washington?"[1] This from a Labor minister!

Peres approved me despite knowing, of course, that I belonged to the right side of the political spectrum. Though we would later become political rivals, we always kept open channels between us.

Underneath it all I always remembered with deep gratitude the way he treated my family and me after Yoni's death. Shimon was always kind and generous to us in word and deed.

The end of my service at the embassy and beginning of my time at the UN completed a series of two-year stints. After five years in the army, I spent two years receiving my undergraduate degree at MIT, two years receiving my business degree at the Sloan School, two years at BCG (with time off to set up the Jonathan Institute), two years as the institute's executive director and two years as deputy chief of mission in Israel's embassy in Washington.

Each of those life and career changes was prompted by recommendations from others: service in the Unit by the active recruitment of Yoni's friend; studying architecture at MIT and attending its business school by the suggestions of my mother; applying for a job at BCG by Yoav Leventer's recommendation; serving as Arens's deputy in Washington by his request. I had taken all these decisions with an attitude of "What the hell, let's give it a try and see what happens." But this was something new. I had *wanted* this position. I believed that the United Nations could provide a global stage to advance Israel's position in the world.

I recalled the unforgettable 1975 speech of Haim Herzog, Israel's ambassador to the UN, as he tore apart the resolution equating Zionism with racism. I remembered the strong speeches of another Israeli ambassador, Joseph Tekoah, and the powerful words of Daniel Patrick Moynihan and Jeane Kirkpatrick, who as American ambassadors to the United Nations unfailingly defended not only the United States but Israel as well. This kind of offensive and unapologetic attitude was the one I needed to replicate. It not only fitted me well; it was, I knew, the only thing that would work.

FLEUR AND I set up house at 1010 Fifth Avenue, the official residence of Israel's United Nations ambassador. A few floors below lived Arthur Ochs "Punch" Sulzberger, publisher of the *New York Times*, whom I befriended. But our closest friends were neither journalists nor politicians but the Zises brothers, Jay and Sig, two enterprising New Yorkers in the finance business who lived down the block. There were other good friends, including the Zamir family, who had come from Iran.

For exercise, I would walk the forty blocks from the Israeli consulate housing the UN mission on Forty-Second Street to the residence on Eighty-Second Street and Fifth Avenue. People often stopped me on the street—having recognized me from my appearances on television— nearly always to express their support. The American Secret Service assigned bodyguards to me but had to change the agents to younger ones because of these brisk walks. I devised ways to rapidly walk nonstop by going westward on the cross streets when meeting a red light. In typical Unit fashion I sought to lower the time of each march.

One of the first meetings I had when I came to serve in the United Nations was with Henry Kissinger. He invited me to lunch at New York's posh Four Seasons Hotel. Aware of charges that he had held back the supply of weapons to Israel during the Yom Kippur War, Henry told me that he was committed to Israel's security and future. We met several times during my stay in New York and in the years after that. I found his advice practical and his historical observations illuminating.

I never told Henry the joke he may have heard from others. So here it is. On one of his visits to Jerusalem, Kissinger visits the city's Biblical Zoo. He achieves a miracle: a lion and a lamb cohabit in the same cage. The world press is astounded.

"Dr. Kissinger," the journalists clamor, "how did you achieve this amazing result?"

"It's very simple," says Henry. "You take a cage, you take a lion, and you put in a new lamb every day."

Years before I met him, Kissinger had said, "In public life you draw on the intellectual capital you accumulate before you enter it." I did my best to continually replenish my capital. While in office I continued to read—a lot.

Though addicted to history books and political biographies—I have now read so many books about Churchill, whom I much admire, that I immediately discard any that aren't written in a novel and gripping way— I also often explored other subjects according to whatever work I was doing at the time. Thus when I was at BCG and RIM Industries, and then again later when I became finance minister, I read books on economics and technology; when I sought to turn Israel into a cyber power, I read books on cybernetics, and so on. Books have to say something substantive—and say it well. Good books are my escape from drudgery; good works on history illuminate the present as much as the past.

My most memorable meeting in my first months at the United Nations was not with a fellow diplomat but with a great rabbi. Shortly after I came to the UN, my secretary told me that Shmarya Harel, a former soldier of mine, was outside the office asking to see me. He hailed from a kibbutz in the Negev. When he walked into my office, I didn't recognize him. Fully bearded, he wore the black dress of a Chasid, an ultra-Orthodox Jew.

"Bibi," he said, "it's me, Shmarya."

I learned that he had traveled the world, worked odd jobs, and finally found inner peace in the Lubavitch movement. He invited me to come to the movement's celebration of Simhat Torah, the marking of the conclusion of the annual cycle of Torah readings and the beginning of a new cycle. It would be held next to the rabbi's residence at 770 Eastern Parkway in Brooklyn.

The Lubavitcher Rebbe, Rabbi Menachem Mendel Schneerson, was a brilliant student of mathematics, physics and philosophy at the University of Berlin, of mechanics and electrical engineering at the ESTP (School for Major Projects) in Paris, and had audited mathematics at the Sorbonne before becoming a leading rabbinic authority. His Lubavitch movement was a worldwide endeavor to embrace all Jews and rekindle in them a love of Judaism and the Jewish people.

When Shmarya and I arrived, the Rebbe's meeting hall was packed with thousands of Chasidim. Singing and dancing on the bleachers and on the floor, they formed heaving hills and valleys of the faithful. The Rebbe was on a small stage at one end of the hall with his back to them. He was swaying back and forth, reading the Torah.

"Go to the Rebbe *now*," Shmarya said.

"But he's reading," I said.

"Go now!"

Not knowing the customs, I did as he asked. I climbed the stage and carefully approached the sage from behind.

He took no notice of me.

I gently tapped his shoulder.

"Rebbe," I said in English, "I came to see you."

"Just to see?" he responded, looking at me across his shoulder with his laser blue eyes. "Not to talk?"

We started to talk in Hebrew, his in a strong Ashkenazi accent. The cacophony of song and merriment around us was deafening. Yet the Rebbe's message came through load and clear.

"You are going to the House of Lies," he said, referring to the United Nations.

"Remember," he continued, "that even in a hall of total darkness, if you light just one candle, its precious light will be seen far and wide. You will light that candle of truth for the People of Israel!"

We spoke for ten minutes, then twenty, then thirty. The Rebbe spoke about the Jewish people, the Land of Israel, and the Torah. Minute by minute the Chasidim grew more and more impatient, and I began to hear a growl rising from the crowd. I was keeping their beloved Rebbe from them.

Finally, after a full forty minutes, our conversation ended. The Rebbe turned to the Chasidim and led them in song, which became a roar. Then he went down from the podium to the center of the hall where he and his brother-in-law, both in their eighties, danced with the Torah Scrolls. As I saw these two elderly rabbis holding the Torah and circling each other I felt it was our ancient Jewish heritage that was dancing in that pale light. I was moved beyond words.

During my subsequent years of service in the UN, the Rebbe regularly sent me messages of encouragement and support through several of his followers who became close friends. After my maiden speech at the UN in 1984, he sent me a message that said, "You gave us much *nachas* [satisfaction] from your first speech. God willing you will continue on this path!"[2]

THAT FIRST UN speech of mine was directed at the General Assembly. Every year Israel's credentials were challenged by a resolution that sought to expel it from the United Nations, usually initiated by Arab states or Iran. My speech would be devoted to rebuffing this effort.

At the time, I was reading a book on Greek history. I was struck by the example of the ostracon, with which I was already somewhat familiar. This was the technique by which factions in the Athenian assembly would expel an undesirable opponent. I focused my speech on that, and it would turn out to reflect what I tried to do in many of my other speeches in the United Nations. Be concise, avoid jargon, forget diplomatic niceties, refer to broader interests, make one main point:

> I expected that on first speaking to this body I would be doing so in defense of my country. I did not expect to be compelled to defend the United Nations itself.
>
> The attempt we have just witnessed to deny Israel its credentials was not merely one more attack on Israel. It was an attempt on the very life of this body.
>
> Whatever its faults at least the United Nations offered a meeting place for all the nations of the world. Destroy the principle of universality and you deal a mortal blow to the United Nations.
>
> This same principle guided the ancestor and model of all modern parliaments, the ancient democracy of Athens. But the first seeds of its subsequent downfall were sown when one faction of Athenians, determined to expel a blameless adversary, introduced the ostracon, the ballot of expulsion. Over the years the method proved irresistibly tempting. First one member was expelled, then another, and then another. The widespread adoption of the ostracon so undercut the prestige and popular support of the Athenian assembly that it was to vitiate fatally its moral, and thus its political, authority.
>
> Remove the pillar of universality and this glass tower [too] may come crashing down.
>
> All of us here have a choice to make. We can continue to tolerate efforts to turn this body into a parody of itself, degenerating to the likes of the farcical "parliaments" that solemnly meet in Damascus, Tripoli and Tehran, whose representatives here have been the moving spirits behind today's exercise.
>
> Or we can say to them: *Gentlemen, check your fanaticism at the door!* Those who enter this house must be prepared to live by its rules and above all by the fundamental principle of universality.

From that point on many usually stony-faced delegates would often come to listen to my speeches, occasionally allowing themselves a quick smile or screwing up their faces, depending on the country they represented.

I befriended many delegates at the UN, some from countries with which Israel had no relations. In 1988 I joined Shamir when he met Soviet foreign minister Andrei Gromyko and, in an early Chinese effort to develop diplomatic relations with Israel, I also met the Chinese ambassador.

But it was my media appearances that reverberated most. In the media capital of the world, I regularly met with the editorial boards of the major newspapers and the major television networks, on whose programs I appeared innumerable times. I wrote op-eds for the *New York Times*, the *Wall Street Journal* and the *Washington Post*.

In 1985, I flew to CNN headquarters in Atlanta. As an all-news television channel, the Cable News Network was still novel five years after its founding. "Headquarters" is stretching it a bit. CNN was then based in a modest Howard Johnson's–like structure. I could see it had potential and began to appear on its programs regularly.

A few years later I accompanied visionary CNN founder Ted Turner on his visit to Israel, flying over the country in a helicopter. Like many others on their first visit, he was surprised how small it was, and he spoke at length about the need to continually expand its water supply (something my governments did later with massive desalinization).

In the mid-1990s, when Fox News began broadcasting, I appeared there frequently as well, recognizing its impact on public opinion. Its trailblazing owner, Rupert Murdoch, became a close friend to both me and Israel. He was always a staunch and unflinching supporter of Israel and viewed it, as I did, as the foundation stone of the free world in the Middle East. Israel has not had a better friend.

In all my media appearances I stressed the need to resolutely fight terrorism and not give in to terrorist demands. In May 1985, the Israeli press reported that the government led by Prime Minister Peres was planning a large prisoner exchange with the Popular Front for the Liberation of Palestine (PFLP). Israel would release more than one thousand terrorists in exchange for several Israeli citizens held hostage by the terrorist leader Ahmed Jibril.

This flew in the face of everything I was advocating in America and all the positions put forward in the two international conferences of the Jonathan Institute.

Going out on a limb with a slim hope of changing Shamir's mind, I booked an interview for myself on a morning news program on Israel radio. I knew the government ministers would be listening on their way to the cabinet meeting where a final decision would be made. Before going on the program, I called my key staff at the UN into my office.

"I'm going to criticize the impending government decision," I said, "and I'm prepared to leave the job. All of you who were appointed by me—you should prepare to leave as well."

Peres was furious about the interview and said I should be reprimanded. Shamir said nothing. But Peres was right. You can't represent a government and simultaneously take a public position opposed to that government. In my forty years in government and in parliament, I did such a thing only one more time, years later when I voted against my party knowing that I could be removed from the Likud list.

Though Peres did reprimand me, I was allowed to keep my position at the UN. Still, I had been prepared to bite the bullet. I mention this because as I would discover, some Knesset members and ministers not only like to have their cake and eat it too, they actually *demand* to have both. I didn't. I was prepared to pay the political price for my convictions if that's what the Likud voters or my superiors in government decided.

The next month, another case arose about which I had strong convictions, and which showed the strength of the growing cooperation between Israel and the United States when it came to fighting terrorism.

In June 1985, a TWA airliner from Cairo to San Diego was hijacked by Arab gunmen and diverted to Beirut. The passengers were held as hostages. In order to sharpen their demand for the release of terrorists jailed in Kuwait and Lebanese Shiites being held by Israel, the gunmen murdered an American passenger in cold blood and threw his body onto the tarmac. Fearing that American troops would storm the plane, the terrorists scattered the hostages among safe houses in various parts of Beirut, in effect eliminating the option of an Entebbe-style rescue.

At the start of the crisis, a special communications channel was established between Shultz, Prime Minister Peres and Foreign Minister Shamir.

As Israel's ambassador to the United Nations, sensitive messages concerning the crisis were often passed back and forth through my office. Shultz's assistant Charlie Hill called me daily to brief the Israeli government on developments and to consult with us as to how the United States should proceed.

Reagan and Shultz had been leading American policy in the right direction. From the first, I insisted that the key to escaping from the trap would be an unequivocal American refusal to give in to the demands of the terrorists. But when the hostages were dispersed throughout Beirut, the terrorists threatened to begin killing them immediately if their demands were not met. The day this ultimatum was issued, Hill called me to ask what I thought the American response should be.

"Issue a counterthreat," I told him. "Make it clear to the terrorists that if they so much as touch a hair on any of the hostages' heads, you won't rest until every last one of them has been hunted down and wiped out."

Hill said he would pass the message to Shultz. Days later, he called back to say that they had acted on this recommendation and that the results had been positive.

Over the following days, the Americans were unrelenting. The terrorists eventually tempered their demands, and the tension began to subside. Eventually, a face-saving compromise was arranged whereby the hostages were released.[3]

EARLY IN 1986, I learned of a rumor that Kurt Waldheim, a former United Nations secretary-general and a candidate for Austria's presidency, had a file as a Nazi war criminal—in the United Nations no less! There were always whispers about Waldheim's past but a UN file was something new.

"Do you have such a file?" I asked the United Nations Secretariat.

"We don't know," came the answer.

"Why not?" I asked.

"Because we're not allowed to open the archives."

During World War II, Churchill had established a tribunal of the sixteen Allied governments (some in exile) to document Nazi war crimes for future prosecution. The tribunal's findings were handed over to the United Nations when it was established. The files were stored in one of the UN buildings in New York.

I asked once more to see them.

"You can't," a UN official explained. "When the archives were deposited in the United Nations, it was agreed they will be opened only with the unanimous consent of all sixteen countries."

"What the . . ." I muttered, outraged.

In the face of such obstinacy I set out on a yearlong public and diplomatic campaign to convince these sixteen governments to give their consent. In this I was greatly helped by Edgar Bronfman Sr. and Israel Singer of the World Jewish Congress.

It was like peeling a diplomatic onion. One layer led to another, and then to another, until at last all the countries had agreed. We had opened the padlock.

When I walked into the unlocked storeroom, I saw rows and rows of cardboard boxes containing yellowing files. Picking up a box marked with the letter *W*, I started going file by file. Sure enough, there was a file marked WALDHEIM KURT. It detailed acts of wanton murder that this Austrian Nazi officer's unit carried out in the war.

Declassified documents later showed that the CIA had been aware of some details of Waldheim's wartime past since 1945. They didn't publish the information and Waldheim was able to assume the august post of United Nations secretary-general, in which he was warmly welcomed around the world.

In a UN press conference I exposed his war crimes for all to see, and things changed. Though Waldheim still won the Austrian presidency, his name was forever tarnished and he became persona non grata, shunned by the US and by nearly every other nation outside the Arab world.

No less important, the archives provided a wealth of hitherto undocumented information on many other crimes.

FROM YEAR TO year during my tenure at the United Nations, the issue of Soviet Jewry acquired growing importance. Jewish dissidents were openly challenging the Soviet regime. They spoke out against the Soviet ban on Jewish religious teachings, the study of Hebrew and Zionism, and above all the denial of the right of Jews to emigrate to Israel.

In a speech at the UN Human Rights Committee, I noted that in most countries border fences are set up to keep illegal migrants from *coming in*, but in the Soviet Union they were set up to prevent Soviet citizens from *getting out*. For Soviet Jews, the Soviet Union was one vast prison. The most important pressure tool to date was the US Jackson–Vanik Amendment, passed in 1974, which had conditioned grain sales to Russia on allowing Jews freedom to emigrate. Yet by 1984 the number of Soviet Jews released was still minuscule—less than a thousand. How to bust the Soviet gates open and set millions free?

In the initial stages of the struggle, the brunt of applying political pressure on the Soviet Union was carried out by various American Jewish organizations, including the Coalition to Free Soviet Jews and the National Conference on Soviet Jewry in the World Jewish Congress. Mobilizing volunteers to canvass Congress, the administration and the press, they did a heroic job in generating public awareness to the plight of their Jewish brothers and sisters behind the Iron Curtain. I participated in rallies they organized, including one early effort in 1985 in front of the Soviet embassy to the UN, when I joined Ambassador Jeane Kirkpatrick, Senator Daniel Patrick Moynihan, New York City mayor Ed Koch, and Jewish leaders in demanding the release of Soviet Jews. This was before Israel fully joined the fray, and my participation was prompted more by my own initiative than by directives from Israel.[4]

I looked for additional forms of pressure that could be applied to the Soviet Union. In the United Nations I observed Soviet representatives at close hand and noticed something peculiar. Every time President Reagan's Strategic Defense Initiative (SDI), or "Star Wars," was mentioned they flew into a fit. They would constantly raise the subject unprompted, assailing it as "destabilizing" and "threatening world peace." Evidently the possibility that American defensive missiles would intercept incoming Soviet nuclear missiles worried them a great deal. Understandable, since such an American advantage would nullify Soviet parity with the US.

Israel was to later deploy a homegrown version of this technology with amazing success. Its Iron Dome defenses have intercepted thousands of incoming missiles, a bullet hitting a bullet in the sky!

But this technology, as with the technology needed for Star Wars, was still many years away: from my time in the Washington embassy, I knew that the American project was far from viability. So why are the Soviets so panicky? I wondered. They probably assumed that the US was more advanced than it actually was. I also believe that they thought they could no longer compete with American technology in any sphere.

I could see that the Soviet representatives at the United Nations were well aware of the dysfunctional state of the Soviet economy. If Star Wars came to fruition, their technological and financial inferiority would be exposed. The psychological and military shield of invincibility of the Soviet system would be threatened. President Reagan appeared resolute. He called the Soviet Union the "Evil Empire," and though the American press disparaged this characterization, it resonated with the American public.

I thought this was an incredible opening. If we intensified the anti-Soviet human rights campaign in America, the Soviets would seek ways to mitigate their image as the Evil Empire, thereby lessening the American impetus for investing in the fantastically expensive Star Wars program. And what cheaper way for the Soviet Union to achieve this mitigation than by letting hundreds of thousands of Soviet Jews emigrate to Israel? These Jews were branded as "disloyal" to the Soviet Union anyway, an inherently "foreign" element. I believed Jabotinsky's principle of applying the pressure of public opinion on democratic governments could now be equally applied to the Soviet regime to change its policies.

To encourage the Soviets, I made sure through circuitous routes that the Soviet mission in the United Nations was aware of this calculus. In every possible contact with American leaders and opinion makers, I sought to link Soviet-American strategic talks to Soviet goodwill gestures toward Soviet Jews. I then started to seed the number 400,000 at every opportunity, making it known this should be the *minimum* number of Jews released, in short order.

I recruited the Jewish organizations fighting for Soviet Jewry to drive home this demand. We also put forward the demand to immediately release leading dissidents. This, I believed, was the cheapest of all concessions the Soviets could make. I was confident that with a bit more pressure they would cave.

When Avital Sharansky, wife of the imprisoned activist Natan Sharansky, came to see me accompanied by Avi Maoz, I told her that I was sure this would work. I suggested she should continue her indefatigable meetings with American leaders while we would carry the fight to the general public. Avital agreed, but not everyone did.

When Yelena Bonner, the iconic dissident Andrei Sakharov's Jewish wife, came to New York, she said to me, "The Soviets will never release Sakharov. He will die a prisoner."

"I don't think so," I said. "In fact, I think they'll release him soon."

I told her of my strategy.

"You don't know the Soviet Union," she said.

Sharansky was released in February 1986, Sakharov from house arrest in December 1986. Though not a Jew, Sakharov was an inspiration for the Jewish dissident movement in the Soviet Union. After him, many prominent Jewish dissidents were released as well. The doors of the Soviet prison were cracking. Soon they would be flung wide open.

Still, there were those who didn't understand the forces at work. Many Israeli leaders were wary of seeking to apply American pressure on the Soviet Union (why get into the middle of the fray? they were thinking). They didn't understand the opportunity Star Wars presented. In the 1988 Knesset elections, when I ran for the Likud list, I debated the Labor minister and my former commander Motta Gur. He argued that he could consider holding on to Judea and Samaria if we had massive immigration of Jews from the Soviet Union. Presumably he thought that would affect the demographic balance in Israel's favor. I countered that such a migration was around the corner and described the reasons for this.

"You Revisionists always indulge in pipe dreams," Gur said, dismissing my assessment.

But this wasn't a pipe dream at all.

Soviet Jews would be released because the Soviet empire was in tatters. That was certainly my view, one that I had developed over the previous decade through telling conversations.

In 1979, at the first Jonathan Institute conference in Jerusalem, I had spoken with the great Soviet dissident Vladimir Bukovsky. "Benjamin," he had said, "please understand, the Soviet regime is desperate. Everything is rotten inside. Nothing works. It's one big rotten core held together by the façade of invincibility provided by nuclear ICBMs parading in Red Square." He predicted that within a decade the Soviet Union as we knew it would collapse. He was right on the mark.

In 1984, I had another conversation that had underscored this point to me. Herb Okun, the deputy US ambassador to the UN, had come to his post after serving as US ambassador to communist East Germany.

"What's it like there, Herb?" I had asked him.

"Oh, nothing much," Herb answered. "They live in dilapidated housing, drive funny little Trabants, drink vodka all day while watching eight hours of West German television."

"What!" I asked in disbelief. "What did you just say?"

"They watch eight hours of West German television every day and then drink themselves to sleep," he repeated.

"You mean to tell me that watching eight hours a day of West German television doesn't have any effect on them?" I asked incredulously.

"None that I can see," Okun answered.

"Herb," I said, "that can't be. It's just a question of time until the cracks will appear."

The conversation made me recall an engineering course I took at MIT. We loaded a small model bridge with steadily increasing loads and photographed the process. The bridge held fine, until it suddenly collapsed. Yet upon closer examination of the film we could see tiny cracks propagating in the structure well before the fall.

Five years later, in 1989, when I had left the UN and become deputy foreign minister, I participated in a seminar on East Germany organized by the Foreign Ministry staff. They explained that a "young reformist leadership" was emerging in a new East Germany. A noted university professor specializing in Germany explained in a weighty expert's tone that East and West Germany would coexist as two separate entities for decades to come.[5]

Many of my colleagues nodded in agreement. I begged to differ. Remembering my conversations with Herb, I believed that East Germany would soon collapse. It did, a few months later.

This wasn't the only time that I commented on what happens to people manipulated by state media as they become steadily exposed to information provided by free media. On September 4, 2010, during an interview with Anat Berko for her doctoral thesis on suicide bombers, I spoke about the effect social media will have on the Arab world.

"Arab society," I said, "is coming in touch with information networks that are steadily opening up. This phenomenon will have a snowball effect, and its power will grow beyond the power of mosques and regimes. The information revolution is a global typhoon that will destabilize societies, governments and cultures. It cascades by itself. Israel is quite ready for it, but it will threaten Arab regimes."[6]

Three months later, on December 17, 2010, a Tunisian street vendor named Mohamed Bouazizi set himself on fire and unleashed a conflagration in Arab social media that led to the so-called Arab Spring, whose convulsions are still with us today. Throughout the Middle East the battle still rages between the forces of medievalism and modernity. For the moment, the best we can hope for is that the latter will be led by enlightened rulers. Liberal democracy as enjoyed in the West is still a distant dream.

IN 1988, THE impending collapse of the Soviet Union accelerated the historic release of Soviet Jewry. Starting in 1989–90, the Soviets released hundreds of thousands and ultimately more than a million Soviet Jews whose arrival in Israel changed the course of Israel's history. It all began with the efforts to achieve the freedom of leading Jewish dissidents, including Natan Sharansky.

Sharansky later described how in his captivity he drew inspiration from the Entebbe rescue. He cut out a photo of Yoni from a newspaper and placed it on the wall above his bed. "During my nine years in prison each time I saw an airplane in the sky I thought of Entebbe," Sharansky said. "Each time I knew that an Israeli airplane would come to take me home."[7]

He was right about our unswerving commitment to achieve his release and that of Soviet Jewry. Sharansky later acknowledged the important contribution of the Star Wars campaign to achieving that goal. But once achieved, a new problem arose. Where should they go?

When Soviet Jews began to be released in significant number, Shamir, now prime minister, resolutely insisted that they should first come to Is-

rael. After all, repatriating them in their historic homeland was the rationale presented to the Soviets to obtain their release.

Once in Israel, they could freely choose to either stay in the country
or emigrate to the United States. But getting them to Israel first would at
least give us the opportunity to fulfill one of the founding missions of the
Jewish state, the ingathering of the exiles in the Promised Land.

Jewish opinion was split on this issue. George Shultz's opinion was
not. A champion of human rights, he insisted that Soviet Jews should
make the choice of their final destination while still in Russia.

Shamir asked Arens and me to help convince Jewish leaders, and
especially Shultz, who held me in high regard, to change their minds.
Shultz finally did. Shamir, a champion of the Jewish homeland, prevailed.
He is seldom given credit for his persistence, which delivered to Israel a
massive infusion of immigrants.

The many Soviet Jews who chose to stay in Israel soon participated
in every realm of Israeli life, becoming leading academics, scientists, technologists, athletes, musicians, writers and artists, and helped secure Israel's demographic and economic future. And Ariel Sharon, then housing
minister, deserves credit for the massive logistic operation that he led to
build housing for hundreds of thousands of immigrants, a huge number
relative to the population at the time.

AS WORD OF my activities in the United Nations spread, invitations
to speak to Jewish and non-Jewish audiences poured in from across the
United States and from abroad. I visited Australia, Brazil and Argentina,
Colombia and Peru, as well as many European countries. I received private dinner invitations from such celebrities as Princess Margaret, Jac-
queline Kennedy Onassis and other well-known figures.

I tried to accommodate as many of the invitations as I could, with one
proviso. I would not dress up in a tuxedo.

"I am not a penguin," I protested to my staff.

Costume changes simply demanded too much time. And I usually
spoke off the cuff, only preparing notes when time permitted.

Several books and articles have been written about my "secrets" of
effective communication. I was interviewed for none of them. Rumor

had it that I had undergone months of intensive training in the US that prepared me for my television appearances. In fact, the only "training" I received was two forty-five-minute sessions toward the end of my service at the UN with Lilyan Wilder, an experienced communications coach, at her initiative. She called and asked to see me years after my reputation was already established as an effective communicator.

"I've been watching tapes of your appearances," Lilyan said. "Unlike my other clients, I have nothing to teach you."

"So why did you ask to see me?" I asked.

"Just to reinforce what you already know," Lilyan said. "Your strength comes from speaking with conviction. Make your point succinctly and early on, and stick to it. Everything else is less important."

She showed me a few tapes: in some I did this; in others I didn't. That was that. Not a word about hand gestures, camera angles, lighting, or anything on the supposed key to it all—body language.

The only tip I ever got on that subject came years later when on a visit to France I met the famed actor Sean Connery, whom I instantly liked for his down-to-earth manner.

"Just sit up straight," Connery said.

Given that I have a tendency to lean forward and sideways in seated interviews, that was a valuable suggestion, though one I sometimes still fail to follow.

AS MY TERM ended, Fleur and I decided to part. She would stay in the US, while I would return to Israel. I speak sparingly of the end of my first two marriages. Anyone who has gone through such things knows they are never easy.

Fleur became a successful business consultant and continued her wholehearted support for Israel. The fact that we parted amicably and that she and Miki have both fended off repeated attempts by Israeli journalists to bad-mouth our relationships says much about their character and integrity.

After four years in the United Nations, I had to decide what to do next.

Entering political life was now clearly a viable option. Israeli politicians and political activists frequently visited the UN. The Likud Party members among them asked me if I planned to join the party by running for its Knesset list in 1988. Most asked this hoping I would say yes, a few hoping I would not. Sure enough, the latter soon advanced an offer that I become head of the Jewish Agency, the body that assists Israel's government in dealing with Jewish communities worldwide.

"Think about it," they said. "You can take Herzl's place as the leader of the Jewish people."

I politely answered that the Jewish Agency was established decades before there was a Jewish state as the provisional government of the Jewish people. But once Israel was established, the Agency's importance was greatly diminished. With all the respect I had for the Agency, the fate of the Jewish people would be determined in the state of Israel, not in the Diaspora.

I decided to go back to Israel and try my luck as a candidate on the Likud list for the Israeli legislature and Israel's supreme governing body, the Knesset.

BEFORE I DID so, I had one more stop. I went to see the Lubavitcher Rebbe. It had been more than four years since our first meeting, and I came to say good-bye. He was not happy with my decision and tried to dissuade me, while lamenting the situation in Israel.

"There are no good tidings from Israel," the Rebbe said. "Action is key and there is no action, but maybe you can influence from here the leadership there."

"I intend to return to Israel and to try to influence things there," I answered.

The Rebbe insisted, "There is still much to influence here at the United Nations.... You know there is a Jewish *mitzvah* [injunction] to influence the gentiles. This is your job to do."

I dodged this diplomatically.

"I haven't forgotten our first meeting," I said, "and I have acted as the Rebbe said, standing proud and strong. Yet I have been here for years."

Evidently this length of service didn't impress the Rebbe. "You can stay here until the arrival of the Messiah," he said.

But I stood my ground. Thanking the Rebbe for all his encouragement, I said I hoped to see him soon.

"I am still in the beginning of my journey, and you too are in the beginning of yours," he said.

And then the Rebbe told me something that stayed with me ever since.

"You will have to struggle with 119 [there are 120 Knesset members]," he said, and then he added, "Surely you will not be impressed by this, because God is on your side."[8]

One hundred and nineteen?! I thought. I wouldn't have even a single ally? Surely he must be exaggerating.

A few weeks later, in response to my farewell note, he sent me a warm letter addressed to "the much-vaunted public servant, engaged especially in defending the Land and People of Israel at the United Nations."

The Rebbe expressed his wish that "your ascent [Aliyah] to Israel will be an ascent in every sense of the word and may you continue to use your talents and opportunities for this noble end."[9]

This gave me hope. I might find some allies after all.

22

POLITICS

1988–1993

Back in Israel, I booked a television interview on an influential political program. I announced my plans to enter political life by seeking a place on the Likud Knesset list. Israel needed to be strong domestically and strong on the world stage, and I felt I could contribute to both goals.

The next day I realized that I had set off a depth charge. The leading newspaper ran a big cartoon titled "A Star Is Born." It showed three small chicks in a bird's nest and a gigantic chick that had just been hatched. The three small chicks were affixed with the names of three rising Likud politicians, Dan Meridor, Ehud Olmert and Roni Milo, known as the Princes. They all had Shamir's ear and vied with each other as to who would lead the Likud one day. My name was affixed to the gigantic chick.

The Princes weren't the only ones who felt threatened. Yossi Sarid, a leader of the left, wrote that I would soon discover that Israel is not America and that I would be a brief and passing phenomenon. Sarid made common cause with my opponents from Likud, explaining that I was "shallow," a "sound-bite man," "all show—no substance," "soon to evaporate."[1]

They relied on the overwhelming concentration of left-leaning journalists in Israel's press, still largely unchanged today after thirty years, to drive this message home to the public.

In Israel's first decades, the country's press was fairly balanced. Although the ruling Labor Party controlled the monopolistic state radio (it is said that Prime Minister Ben Gurion actually dictated news headlines), the three major dailies represented a broad spectrum of news and opinion from right to left.

This began to change with the introduction of the single-channel state television in 1966. Television gradually overtook the newspapers as the main source of information and entertainment for the public.

State TV was largely a closed shop dominated by the left. It was a main breeding ground for media personnel who would percolate into the two state-regulated commercial channels that were later launched. Legislation made it exceptionally difficult to introduce any additional broadcasters and effectively impossible to launch competing news channels.

While it is common that the mainstream media is dominated by the left in most Western democracies, these countries also have alternative media, such as cable news and talk radio, that reach large segments of the population. Israel has none of that. Most Israelis get their news from just two left-leaning nightly news channels. This monopolistic stranglehold on information and opinion has only recently begun to loosen with the spread of social media that enables other voices to be heard.

Though there have always been a sprinkling of right-leaning journalists, most of the newscasters, editors and program producers hail from the left. Especially since the historic election of 1977, when Likud elevated Begin to prime minister, the dominant media oligarchy has sought to maintain their power through legislative barriers to entry into television and radio. They see it as their mission to pull public opinion to the left.

Thus, when a left-leaning government wins an election, they celebrate. When a Likud government wins, they can hardly hide their chagrin.

Many in the leftist media elite flatly reject the democratic choice of Israeli voters. Nearly half a century after Likud's first victory, they still viewed it as a usurpation of their natural and privileged monopoly on power.

Nothing expresses this better than a 2022 interview with Haim Yavin marking forty-five years since the 1977 Likud election win. Yavin, who from 1968 to 2008 was the prime-time news anchor on Israel's state television channel and is often called Israel's Walter Cronkite, said this:

YAVIN: Mapai [Labor] ruled for many years, the Likud came, turned things on their head, caused a revolution, and *grabbed* power. There is no better term for it. They *grabbed* power.

INTERVIEWER: They didn't grab power. They got into office in a democratic election.

YAVIN: True, but I call it *grabbed*. Why? Because the Labor Party and their many supporters did not accept, and until today *do not* accept, the 1977 upheaval—the *revolution*.[2]

Winning elections time and again, I would become the object of an obsessive campaign that escalated as the press failed to block my many victories in democratic elections and my successive tenures as prime minister. The media monopoly's antipathy would ultimately become my most potent opponent, acting effectively as the main opposition party.

THE MINUTE I returned to Israel and ran for the 1988 Likud Knesset list, the favorable coverage I had received from Israeli media while at the UN changed. The media echoed the attacks of my political opponents, including the charge that I was "shallow"—an empty suit.

My frequent and substantive public appearances soon rendered this particular charge ineffective and a new line of attack was put forward. Now I was not really a true Israeli but an "American import," since I had spent "more than half my life" in America.[3] Technically, this was almost accurate. I was thirty-eight years old and I had spent altogether eighteen years in the United States.

Of course, my detractors neglected to mention that those years were composed of six years as a minor when I accompanied my parents, four years of university studies common to many Israelis, two years at BCG and another six years devoted to diplomatic service in which I defended Israel on the world stage.

What an irony! My great-grandfather had been one of the few Jews to immigrate to the Holy Land in the nineteenth century from America, my mother had been born in Petach Tikva in 1912, my father came to

Jaffa in 1920, my two brothers and I served in Sayeret Matkal, in whose battles Yoni died and I was wounded, and I may have been the first and perhaps the only person *in history* to give up his American citizenship twice. I first gave it up when I enlisted in the IDF in 1967. A subsequent US Supreme Court decision ruled that American citizenship cannot be annulled because of conscription in a foreign army. My US citizenship was thus restored, but I volunteered to give it up again on the eve of my departure to serve as an Israeli diplomat in Washington. Yet the Israeli press echoed the spin hatched by my political foes that I was not "Israeli enough."

The "American" canard would finally come crashing down eight years later in an incident that occurred after I was elected prime minister. The Jerusalem subsidiary of the *Haaretz* newspaper published a shocking exposé. I was not merely an American.

I was actually a CIA agent named John Sullivan.[4]

This grew out of a special investigation of my "secret past" conducted by the Labor Party during the elections. Finding my Social Security number in the US, they discovered it belonged to an American by the name of John Sullivan. Since he was nowhere to be found, he must be a CIA fabrication, they reasoned. The exposé was written by "celebrated editors and investigative reporters" (Israel's leftist journalists often lavishly praise one another). Had Israel elected a CIA plant as its prime minister?

A Labor politician took to the Knesset podium and confronted me with the question, "Who are you, John Sullivan?"[5]

The farce lingered for a few more months, until an enterprising Israeli journalist, one of the few not in the leftist choir, tracked down John Sullivan. He was a retired postman in Vermont. It turns out that in a mishap that occurs rarely, the US Social Security Administration had "parked" our two names in the same number.

Needless to say, the Israeli press barely covered this revelation. My career in the CIA ended abruptly and silently.

All politics is cruel; Israeli politics is crueler than most. This is natural. No politician should be exempt from scrutiny and criticism, but what gradually was leveled against me was a systematic campaign of lies. The theme of the attack constantly changed. "Shallow" gave way to "American," which gave way to "CIA agent," which gave way to "liar."

The technique was always the same. First, blow up a press story with a dubious allegation, and then when the allegation is punctured ignore the facts. *Something* is bound to stick eventually.

The "liar" campaign had two seminal milestones that were used to buttress the credibility of many lesser claims. The first occurred right after the John Sullivan fiasco. In September 1996, three months after I became prime minister, I gave an order to open an exit door at the Western Wall tunnel to facilitate the movement of tourists visiting the site.

I did so only after being encouraged by the Shin Bet (Israeli Security Agency) chief, Ami Ayalon, who assured me that there was no significant risk involved. Events immediately proved him wrong. Yasser Arafat falsely claimed that I was digging a tunnel to undermine the sacred Al-Aqsa Mosque and exhorted his followers to "save" this holy site. Severe fighting broke out between his forces and our soldiers, claiming lives on both sides. In the aftermath of this violent outbreak, I was asked if I had consulted the Shin Bet chief before opening the tunnels. I said I had and that Ayalon encouraged me to do so. But then Ayalon, who later sought to lead the Labor Party, denied that he had encouraged me to open the tunnel.

The press had a field day. I was portrayed as a liar. Twenty years later, in an interview in 2016, Israel Hasson, who headed Shin Bet Central Command in charge of Jerusalem during the tunnel incident, said of his former boss, "Ayalon did not tell the truth about the opening of the tunnel. He recommended to Netanyahu to open the tunnel."[6]

Transcripts from a conversation Ayalon had with me two weeks before the opening and published twenty years confirmed this.

"There is no problem," Ayalon said. "We need to hurry. I've been saying for a long time that we need to do this [opening]."[7]

Another fictitious story about my supposed lack of credibility occurred in 2006 after I gave an interview to the newspaper *Yedioth Ahronoth*. I recollected strolling with my mother down Ein Gedi Street and seeing soldiers training in the Allenby Camp, a military facility left to us by the departing British army.

The paper inaccurately quoted me saying I had seen "British" soldiers in the Allenby Camp and, since I was born after they had left the country, that clearly was not possible.

At my insistence, the newspaper later published an exceedingly brief correction that presented the facts: "A reexamination of the interview transcript reveals that Netanyahu indeed spoke of 'soldiers' who trained in *British facilities*. He did not say 'British soldiers' or 'British policemen.' "[8]

They had the tape of the interview in their possession all the while, but the elapsed time enabled the canard to spread that I had "lied again."

Even today, long after the facts have come out, these two lingering lies about me are offered as "definitive" proof that I don't tell the truth.

AS THE VOTE for the 1988 Likud Knesset list approached, I met with as many of the 2,500 Likud Central Committee members as I could. They were the ones who would choose the Knesset list in the upcoming elections. A special place was reserved in the Central Committee for the Founders Group, the elder statesmen of the party, many of whom had been valiant fighters in the Irgun and Lehi underground. All were followers of Begin and Jabotinsky. One of their leaders, Avraham Appel, took me under his wing.

I genuinely enjoyed meeting these old-timers in their weekly Friday gatherings in the "Avivit Café," a coffee shop in a Tel Aviv gas station. They were unalloyed gold, almost entirely devoid of the usual intrigues of rivalry and jealously that generally accompany politics.

I reached out to other groups as well. They too appreciated my service in the United Nations but many of their members were deeply enmeshed in internal Likud battles. The party was then divided into political camps: the Shamir-Arens camp, the David Levy camp, the Ariel Sharon camp and the Moshe Katsav camp. All wanted to lead the party.

Though I belonged to the dominant Shamir-Arens camp, I maintained cordial relations with Sharon, Levy, Katsav and their followers. Running for the Knesset at the age of thirty-eight, I remembered the winning principle I discovered when I ran for class president at the age of twelve: be nice to everyone. I assembled a dedicated band of Likud activists from around the country who volunteered to help get me elected. The fact that the Founders vehemently supported me also helped. Though they too were identified with the Shamir-Arens bloc, they were highly respected for their genuine dedication to the party's ideals.

The vote for the Likud Knesset list took place in June 1988 at Herzliya Country Club. I campaigned right up to the last minute, changing shirts frequently in the blazing heat. The Central Committee members would rank the 104 candidates competing for the Knesset from one to fifty. Not all fifty would ultimately make the Knesset: If the Likud won forty seats in the general elections (out of the 120 seats total in the Knesset), for example, the first forty on the list would get into the Knesset, and if the election result was lower the cutoff point would shift accordingly. The expectation was that Likud would win thirty-five seats.

I finished first, Moshe Katsav came in second, and Benny Begin, the former prime minister's son, came in third. Given the sharp competition between them, Arens, Levy and Sharon came in lower.

This, however, was only the first round—a "beauty contest." The second and more decisive voting round would take place a week later, and have the same Central Committee members vote again. This time, candidates who had made the top forty in the first round had to submit their candidacy for a specific place on the list.

Neglecting the advice of more seasoned political supporters, I targeted the fifth place on the Likud list of an expected slate of thirty-five, after Arens, Sharon, Levy and Katsav, but before other senior members of Likud. The voting strategy for this second ranking was so complicated that it almost required game-theory knowledge. I'll spare the reader the arcane details. Suffice to say that I narrowly won the fifth place by six votes, but well ahead of the young Princes vying for future leadership of the party.

Undoubtedly egged on by the Princes, who viewed me as someone attempting to upstage them in a bid for cabinet seats, Shamir promptly announced that irrespective of our high standing, Begin and I would not serve as head ministers if he formed the next government, though we could be deputies. In retrospect I can appreciate his sensitivity to my thrashing of the party's traditional pecking order.

Likud won the most seats of any party in the Knesset general elections in 1988, enabling Shamir to form a government with other right-wing parties. Arens was appointed minister of foreign affairs. He asked me to join him as his deputy minister. I gladly agreed to work with my old boss from Washington. I was now back in the dilapidated shacks of the Foreign Ministry, doing odd jobs for Arens and plying the political fields of Likud.

AS I WOULD learn firsthand over the next four years, being a deputy minister is never a plum job. In Israel's political system, the head ministers are legally required to sign off personally on just about everything their deputies do, and nearly all deputy ministers complain about the lack of clear responsibilities and instruction. Still, I found ways to fill up my time. Here's one example of my schedule in September 1990:

> Lunch in London (with British Deputy Foreign Minister)
> Dinner in Paris (with French Deputy Foreign Minister)
> Breakfast in Boston (at MIT)
> Lunch in New York (with Jewish Organizations)

And this was in forty-eight hours!

Evidently the deputy ministers I met were in a similar bind, because they all readily agreed to meet me.

So, for the most part, my time as deputy minister of foreign affairs was unremarkable, a "must do" rite of passage for a future ministerial position.

There were however two events of note that occurred: one in the Gulf War, the other during the Madrid Peace Conference.

In August 1990, Iraqi president Saddam Hussein invaded Kuwait. When the US dispatched its forces to expel him, Saddam fired forty-one rockets into Israel. Fearing a chemical attack, the government instructed Israelis to stay in rooms sealed with plastic sheets and wear gas masks.

During the war, I appeared dozens of times on American and Western television channels. On one such occasion, the siren alerting us to go into shelters was sounded. Rather than stopping the interview, I suggested to the CNN reporter that we continue it wearing gas masks.

"This is the darnedest way to conduct an interview," I said.[9]

This unusual television moment received much international attention, as did another CNN interview in which I displayed a large map of the Middle East. I "walked" through the Arab countries from Morocco to the Indian Ocean with the open palms of my hands. Then I covered Israel with my thumb.[10]

For many used to seeing the map of Israel alone on a full screen, a great Israeli Goliath "oppressing" the small Palestinian David, this demonstration came as a shock. It was Israel that was David. This was the best way I could think of to convey that the Arab world was hundreds of times the size of Israel.

These interviews may have been seen by some unlikely viewers. When visiting Japan that year, singer Perry Como was asked by the Japanese government how to improve Japan's image in the United States. He suggested they hire my services.[11]

Before the Gulf War, as American and coalition forces were organizing to throw Saddam's forces out of Kuwait, Arens had reassumed the post of defense minister and David Levy had taken over as minister of foreign affairs. Arens now urged Shamir to send our forces to Iraq to take out Saddam's rocket launchers that were firing Scud missiles into Israel. How could we sit back when Saddam was rocketing our cities?

Shamir resisted. He decided to heed the American request to stay our fire because the Americans were already engaged. They were concerned that an Israeli attack might unravel the international coalition they had assembled. I believed this fear was exaggerated and I thought that not retaliating for rocket attacks against us would weaken our deterrence against future attacks. Despite this, I ultimately came to the conclusion that Shamir made the right call.

Unlike what later happened with Iran's nuclear program, the US in this case was *not* sitting on the sidelines in the hope that diplomacy or goodwill would somehow stop Saddam. It invaded Iraq in January 1991 and was systematically destroying the Iraqi armed forces. I was sure they would soon neutralize the Iraqi elements in western Iraq that were launching rockets on Israel.

It wasn't that Israel wasn't up for the fight. We were more than willing to do our share. But why send our forces when others were willing and able to do the job in keeping with their own national interests, especially when they asked us not to join the effort?

*   *   *

WITH SADDAM BEATEN, and the US feeling empowered by what they thought was their newfound prestige and power in the Middle East, the American diplomatic corps became set on bringing Israel, Syria, Jordan and the Palestinians to the peace table. The US sought to fashion a New Middle East by resolving the Israeli-Palestinian conflict and settling our conflict with Syria as well.

Since Israel refused direct talks with the PLO so long as it advocated Israel's destruction, the architects of the Madrid Conference concocted a circuitous formula by which Palestinians who were not formal PLO members would be incorporated into a joint Jordanian-Palestinian delegation (though everyone knew that the PLO called the shots in this delegation). Shamir asked me to join the Israeli delegation as the coordinator of our public relations efforts in the conference. Though I was technically working under Foreign Minister David Levy as deputy, I was mostly reporting directly to Shamir. Levy, feeling sidelined by Shamir, did not go to Madrid.

As the diplomats are fond of saying when they have little else to say, the importance of the Madrid Conference was the fact that it convened. If anyone expected that sitting around a common table with all the world to see would temper the proceedings, they were soon proven wrong. As expected, everyone played to the gallery, *their* gallery. The speeches were largely wooden and flat. The conference concluded with a decision to continue bilateral talks between the delegations in Washington, some of which I later attended. They didn't get very far either.

During the Madrid Conference I sat poker-faced in the row behind the Israeli delegation as hailstones of jargon swept through the conference hall. At an intermission, Prime Minister Shamir approached me from behind and put his hand on my shoulder. A photo of this produced another political depth charge. Publicized in the Israeli press, this picture was widely interpreted by the cognoscenti as a sure indication that Shamir was tapping me as his successor. In fact, he was doing nothing of the sort.

In Madrid, Palestinian spokeswoman Hanan Ashrawi and I also sparred it out in endless television appearances that were broadcast around the world. She was a worthy opponent.

Thirty years later, she resigned from her position in the Palestinian

Authority, explaining that "it's not a question of peace. It's a question of democratization. It's a question of good governance." Complaining that there had been no Palestinian elections for more than fifteen years, she vowed, "I won't be a part of it anymore."[12] The Palestinian Authority was a morally bankrupt tyranny, but at the time she spoke passionately of its sincere desire to advance peace, as opposed to Israel, represented by me, which obstructed peace.

Emerging from these predictable televised jousting matches, I thought I could do something different. I arranged an Israeli press conference for all the Arab journalists covering the conference. This was thoroughly unconventional at the time. Most of the journalists came, and I let them fire questions at me. One by one they leveled the usual vilifications, and one by one I rebuffed them with factual counterarguments. But I tried to do so in a noncombative way.

Having met several Arab diplomats in the United Nations, I was shocked to discover a simple truth: *They didn't know even the most rudimentary facts about the history of our conflict or of our historic attachment to the contested land*. For decades they had absorbed the lies of Arab propaganda and believed them to be true.

The fact that this propaganda was taken for truth was typically explained away by American diplomats as deriving from different *narratives*, another piece of jargon used to denote that each side's arguments are relative and beyond any objective examination of the facts.

Competing "narratives" have been very much present in the Knesset, too. In a late-night debate in 2013, an Arab Knesset member was debating a Likud member about who preceded whom in what is now Israel. The historical facts are not that difficult to establish, since the Jews appeared in what became the Land of Israel roughly 3,500 years ago and the Arab conquest of this land occurred some two thousand years later, in the seventh century CE.

The Arab member of the Knesset summed up his speech with a sharp, double-edged barb: "We were here before you, and we will be here after you."

At two in the morning I had had enough. I asked to use the prime minister's prerogative to speak and gave my shortest speech in the Knesset:

"To the Knesset member who just spoke, I say this: The first thing you said didn't happen, and the second never will." [13]

The house broke up in laughter.

I COULD HAVE reminded the Arab Knesset member of other historical facts once known to many schoolchildren but which have since been forgotten—or distorted by anti-Israel propaganda.

The history of the Jewish people spans almost four millennia. The first thousand years or so are covered in the Bible, and are attested to by archaeology and the historical records of other, contemporaneous peoples.

As the centuries progress, the mists of time and the myths gradually evaporate and the unfolding events come into sharp historical focus.

Reading the Bible from second grade on, I could easily imagine Abraham and Sarah on their long trek from Ur of the Chaldeans to the land of Canaan almost four thousand years ago. Abraham envisions one God, unseen but present everywhere. He buys a burial cave in Hebron and bequeaths the new land to his progeny.

The descendants of Abraham's grandson Jacob are enslaved in Egypt for centuries, until Moses takes them out of bondage. He leads them for forty years in the wilderness to the Promised Land, giving the Children of Israel the Ten Commandments and a moral code that would change the world.

The indomitable Joshua conquers the land, wily David establishes his kingdom in Jerusalem, and wise Solomon builds his Temple there, only to have his sons split the realm into two.

The northern kingdom, Israel, is destroyed, its ten tribes lost to history. The southern kingdom, Judea, is conquered and Solomon's Temple is destroyed by the Babylonians, by whose rivers the exiled Judeans weep as they remember Zion. They rejoice when in 537 BCE they are reinstated in their homeland by Cyrus of Persia, who lets them rebuild their destroyed Temple.

The Persian rulers are replaced by Alexander the Great, one of whose heirs seeks to eradicate the Jewish religion. This sparks a rebellion led by the brave Maccabees, and the independent Jewish state they establish lasts for eighty years.

It is overtaken by the rising power Rome which initially rules through proxies, the most notable of whom is Herod the Great. Herod refurbishes the Jerusalem Temple as one of the great wonders of the ancient world.

In its bustling courtyard a Jewish rabbi from the Galilee, Jesus of Nazareth, overturns the tables of the money changers, setting off a chain of events culminating in his eventual crucifixion and the beginning of the Judeo-Christian tradition.

When the Jews rebel against Roman rule, Rome destroys Jerusalem and Herod's Temple in 70 CE. Masada, the last rebel stronghold, falls three years later. Despite the devastation, sixty-two years later the Jews rebel again under the fearless Bar Kokhba, only to be crushed even more brutally. The Roman emperor Hadrian bars the Jews from Jerusalem and renames the country Palestina, after the Grecian Philistines, who have long disappeared.

Unlike them, the Jews do not disappear. Under Roman rule they flourish in the coastal plain and in the Galilee in cities like Yavneh, Bnei Brak, Safed, Tiberias and Zippori. Denied a central temple, they build hundreds of smaller temples, called synagogues. They communicate with the great Jewish centers of learning in Babylon, Yemen and others that soon spread in the eastern Mediterranean and other parts of the world.

Contrary to the common belief that the Jewish presence in the Land of Israel is ended by the Romans, the country remains primarily Jewish. In 212, the Roman emperor Caracalla bestows Roman citizenship on the Jews because they are considered "a people with their own country."[14]

The Jews of Palestine are granted considerable autonomy by Rome and later by its successor, Byzantium. Over the next three centuries in the Land of Israel, great rabbis compile the Mishna, Gemara and the Jerusalem Talmud, interpretations of the Torah that guide social conduct and religious worship. Despite centuries of Roman and Byzantine domination, the Jews continue to yearn for independence, rebelling unsuccessfully against Rome once again in 351.

Incredibly, in 614 the Jews of Israel are still fighting for their freedom. They raise an army that joins the Persians in seizing Jerusalem and ousting the Byzantines from Palestine. In the siege of Tyre alone, the Jews deploy more than twenty thousand fighters.[15]

But in 636 a historical turning point occurs that tragically affects the Jewish people's presence in their homeland. The Arabs burst into the land from the Arabian Peninsula, having earlier destroyed the Jewish communities there. The rule of the Byzantines had been harsh for the Jews, but it is under the Arabs that they are finally reduced to an insignificant minority.

Though small numbers of Jews continue to live in the Land of Israel throughout the centuries, it is during the first two centuries of Arab rule that the Jewish people cease to be a national force of any consequence in their own land.

Jewish emigration from the Land of Israel is prompted by several factors, including the economic allure of Jewish communities in the eastern Mediterranean. But it is conclusively finalized by one other phenomenon that had never occurred before in Jewish history. Unlike previous conquerors, the Arabs pour in a steady stream of colonists, often military battalions and their families, to Arabize the land. Expropriating Jewish property, houses and labor, the Arabs succeed over the next two centuries to achieve what the might of Rome had not: the final uprooting of the Jewish farmer from his soil.[16]

Thus it is not the Jews who usurp the land from the Arabs, but the Arabs who usurp the land from the Jews.

Anti-Israel propaganda paints it backward. The truth is simple:

The Jews are the original natives, the Arabs the colonialists.

Arab colonial rule leaves the country in ruin. For the next one thousand years, Arab rulers are replaced by the Crusaders, who are in turn ousted by the Muslims led by Saladin. They are supplanted by the Mamluks, who are booted out by the Ottomans, until they too are evicted four centuries later by the British in World War I.

Throughout these long centuries, no people claim the land as their distinct homeland except the Jews. Alone they cherish Jerusalem as their eternal capital, proclaiming on each Jewish New Year "next year in Jerusalem." Dispersed for centuries, suffering unparalleled persecution in their rootless sojourn among the nations, the Jews never lose hope of returning to the Promised Land. Individual Jews continue to return throughout the ages, joining the tiny Jewish communities that never left.

But the land is barren, sparsely populated and undeveloped. Visiting the Holy Land in 1867, Mark Twain echoes many contemporary travelers when he says, "A desolation is here that not even imagination can grace with the pomp of life and action . . . the desolate and unlovely land is hopeless, dreary and heartbroken."[17]

A century later, Arab propaganda depicts things differently. It describes Palestine in the nineteenth century as a lush land teeming with a flourishing Arab population.

"The Jewish invasion began in 1881," says Arafat at an infamous United Nations speech in 1974. "Palestine was then a verdant area."[18]

It wasn't.

Visiting the Holy Land in 1881, the famous British visitor Arthur Penrhyn Stanley reaffirms Twain's observation fourteen years earlier: "In Judea, it is hardly an exaggeration to say that for miles and miles there was no appearance of life or habitation."[19]

In the second half of the nineteenth century, Jewish immigration brings the fallow land back to life. The Jews build farms, plant orange groves, erect factories. This induces immigration of Arabs from neighboring countries who join the indigenous Arab population. From 1860 on, the majority of Jerusalem's inhabitants are Jewish.

Even so, by the turn of the twentieth century the total population in the Holy Land doesn't exceed four hundred thousand, less than 4 percent of the present population. As the visiting German Kaiser notes in 1898, "There is room here for everyone."[20]

With the advent of Zionism, the Jewish national movement, the call goes out to establish a full-fledged modern Jewish state in the Jewish ancestral homeland. This call receives added moral weight after the Jews help the British oust the Ottomans in 1917, as reflected in the Balfour Declaration, which pledges that Britain favors "the establishment in Palestine of a national home for the Jewish people."[21]

Under Arab pressure between the two world wars, the British renege on this promise and block the Promised Land to Jewish emigration, trapping millions of Jews in Europe who are doomed to perish in the Holocaust.

In 1947, the UN resolves to partition the land into a Jewish state and an Arab state. The Jews agree, the Arabs refuse. Five Arab armies set out to destroy the newly declared Jewish state. Outnumbered, outgunned and with enormous sacrifice, the Jews win. The Jewish state of Israel is reestablished in the Jewish ancestral homeland.

Failing to destroy it time and again, Israel's enemies now seek to delegitimize its existence with an outrageous attempt to wipe out history. No, the Arabs were not here before us. No, the Philistines were not Palestinians. No, the Romans did not end the Jewish presence in the Holy Land. The Arabs conquered the land and greatly contributed to the dispossession of the Jews following thousands of years of Jewish habitation.

Now, with unparalleled chutzpah, anti-Israel propagandists claim that the one people who clung to this land for more than three thousand years has no right to live there in its own sovereign state. That's why at 2 a.m. in the Knesset I simply said, "Enough is enough."

NO MATTER THE truth of ancient and modern history, the outright distortions continued to abound in the Arab world as well as in the West.

In an inversion of reality, the Jews were blamed for attacking the Arabs, whereas the opposite transpired. At the Madrid Peace Conference I was facing journalists who were essentially superspreaders of these myths.

Speaking to them, I remembered the bagels lesson from my first speech. Though I responded to every allegation, my real goal was to win the respect of Arab journalists and to seed doubt about their demonic characterization of Israel. I engaged each of their questions personally and as respectfully as I could. I tried not to fall back on hackneyed formulations and I occasionally surprised them with new information.

I relate this not because the ground shook that day. It didn't. But here and there a small crack did appear. Years later, in the events that led to the Abraham Accords, one of my Arab interlocutors remarked that he remembered favorably this press conference in Madrid.

Although the conference achieved little, my work in Madrid was well received in Israel. The press covered most of it. When Shamir and other ministers praised my activities in a government meeting, I realized that I could not stay for long in the Foreign Ministry under David Levy. The arrangement was clearly unsustainable. With Arens's help I was moved to the post of deputy minister in the Prime Minister's Office to avoid political friction.

THOUGH MY TIME as deputy foreign minister had not been noteworthy absent the Gulf War and the Madrid Peace Conference, there were some other memorable episodes. In a United Nations conference in Geneva, Switzerland, I took the measure of Yasser Arafat and debunked his conspiratorial lie.

A founding member of the PLO, Arafat, who had actually been born in Cairo, assumed prominence because of his abject refusal to accept Israel's existence. He led the battle against Israel from adjacent states and was expelled first from Jordan in 1970 and then from Lebanon in 1982. The fact that Arafat was a godfather of modern terrorism—among the first to deploy airline hijackings and systemic suicide bombings—did not prevent the United Nations from lionizing him. He was supposedly cut from heroic anticolonialist cloth, while in reality he imposed a dark and backward tyranny on his people in his quest to exterminate the Jewish state.

A great showman and a notorious liar, Arafat made no attempt to hide his militancy. Standing at the UN podium, he wore a military uniform and brandished a pistol while spewing antisemitic poison.

In Geneva, Arafat showed a recently minted Israeli memorial coin that, according to him, displayed "a secret map" revealing Israel's true "expansion plans," which included annexing Turkey, Iraq and a good chunk of the Middle East. I countered the next day that the "secret map" that Arafat presented was the outline of a pottery fragment we had recently unearthed. It was several thousand years old, and it wasn't a map but a piece of an archaeological relic.

So much for that fib.[22]

There was also one experience I had early on during those deputy foreign minister years that deeply moved me. In 1989, I asked to visit Entebbe. Since we had no formal diplomatic relations with Uganda at the time, the Mossad arranged the visit. I asked my twelve-year-old daughter, Noa, and Iddo to join me.

As we flew from Nairobi to Entebbe, our excitement and trepidation grew. Excitement because for years Iddo and I had studied the layout of the airfield and knew it by heart. Trepidation because we would finally visit the place where we lost our brother. Flying over the Entebbe airfield, we could clearly identify the runway, the New Terminal, and the Old Terminal, where Yoni fell.

When we disembarked next to the New Terminal, we were met by a Ugandan soldier who held a sheet of paper with one word handwritten on it: "Yoni."

We asked to be driven to the Old Terminal. The driver didn't quite know how to get there. We directed him through the connection between the two runways. Passing by the airport's New Terminal, we saw an external staircase.

"This is where Surin was hit," we noted. The extraordinarily brave Surin, a man of inspiring courage and nobility, had become a lifelong friend and came regularly to commemorate Yoni at his graveside.

As we approached the Old Terminal, I was surprised by the size of the control tower. Up close it was much bigger and more commanding than it appeared in the photos. It was still riddled with bullet holes from Yoni's last battle.

Iddo and I retraced Yoni's steps. Here is where he and his men shot the guard, here is where the force stopped, here is where Yoni led them out of that corner and saved the day, and here is where Yoni fell. We stood silent for a long moment at that spot.

I have since visited Entebbe twice more. My second visit was in 2001, when President Yoweri Museveni invited my wife Sara and me and our sons, Yair and Avner, to a ceremony commemorating the twenty-fifth anniversary of the rescue. Iddo was unable to come, but his wife Dafna and his son Yoav joined us.

The Ugandan troops conducted a moving ceremony that they perform for fallen comrades. A metal plaque was also affixed to the control tower commemorating the rescue. It lists the names of the Israelis who lost their lives in the raid.

After the ceremony, I remarked to President Museveni how unusual this was. After all, Yoni's force were foreign soldiers who attacked Uganda and killed Ugandan troops.

"Benjamin," he said, "you must understand. The raid on Entebbe was not only a blow to international terrorism. It was also a blow to Amin. This was the first time that his image was shattered. He murdered hundreds of thousands of our people. We were fighting him and hid in the jungle. When we heard of this raid we knew for the first time that we could defeat him."

My parents never joined me on my visits to Entebbe. I don't regret that, and I understood their decision. How much pain would they have endured?

After I entered politics, I tried to visit them as often as I could in our family home on Haportzim Street. My mother was an active woman to the end of her days, tending to the house, meeting with friends and family, and helping Father with his scholarly work. Sometimes she would take a break and sit on the big couch in the living room, overlooking the entrance hall. She would have a faraway look in her eyes.

"Imma, what are you thinking about?" I asked her one day.

"I'm thinking of my Yoni'le," she answered, using the diminutive form of Yoni's name that she called him as a child.

She paused and then added, "I have only good memories."

AS 1992 APPROACHED, the Likud Party appeared invincible and seemed destined to win the next elections in Israel. But like the weather, political fortunes can change quickly.

Three things happened that derailed the expected result. The first was the ubiquitous infighting between the Likud's rival factions. The second was a knifing incident in which a Palestinian terrorist killed a young Israeli girl on the Bat Yam beachfront, near Tel Aviv. The third was the emergence of a strong Labor leader, Yitzhak Rabin.

Peres rescinded his candidacy for prime minister to make way for the more popular Rabin, his archrival in the Labor Party. Thus, while the Likud fractured, Labor showed a veneer of unity. Rabin promised that he would not take the country to the left and that he would crush "the wave of terrorism that was sweeping the country."[23] None of that would be borne out in the years to come.

Our warnings that Labor's agenda, even under the respected Rabin, would bring about *real* waves of terror were derisively dismissed by Labor politicians and by most of the press that supported them. The Likud was tired and corrupt, they said, and it should make way for new blood.

Labor's campaign included a successful slogan, "Down with Corruption!" Even though Shamir was as straightlaced as you could find, by dint of constant repetition this false characterization of corruption stuck. I was to encounter the power of false characterizations myself yet again years later.

As the election campaign approached, I faced another personnel dilemma. I had come to the conclusion that Israel's political system was dysfunctional, especially as regards the economy. It would not enable even a reform-minded prime minister to enact necessary market improvements, since various interest groups could always muster a few Knesset members to bring down such a prime minister at any time. The solution, I believed, was to have Israel's citizens directly elect the prime minister and free him from the risks of a no-confidence vote in the Knesset.

Rabin shared this view. I met him several times to advance a bill for direct elections that would be grandfathered to a future date. Nine other Likud members said they would join. But then we hit a snag. Shamir and all the senior Likud members were against direct elections of the prime minister, probably fearing Rabin's popularity. Other Knesset members feared the reform would deprive them of the power to bring down a prime minister.

The all-powerful Likud Central Committee met a few weeks before the scheduled voting on the bill. They warned that any Knesset member who voted for the bill would be wiped off the Likud list. The nine quickly evaporated.

All eyes were on me.

I truly believed that without this political reform, Israel's economy would suffer stagnation for decades. Labor members of Knesset taunted me, saying they would eat their hats if I voted for the bill. But I did. To make matters worse, mine was the deciding vote. This was one of the very few times that I voted against my party. In a parliamentary system with narrow majorities, this is an extreme act.

My political life was now on the line. I had three weeks to save it before the Central Committee voted for the Knesset list. I decided on a simple triage: concentrate on the undecided. That left about a thousand people to see and reach in twenty days. I met as many as I could, individually and in groups. When the votes were counted, I came in second after Moshe Katsav. I more than survived.

YET WHILE I was doing well, my party wasn't. We lost the elections of 1992 in a resounding defeat. Rabin quickly formed a Labor-led government. My fellow Knesset members and Likud ministers were dejected. I was less so. Electoral defeat, personal or collective, is hard, but it's not *that* hard. It helps if you remember that you escaped death several times and faced immeasurably greater personal tragedies.

I expected Arens to announce that he would compete with Rabin for the country's leadership and run for prime minister for Likud in the next election. Naturally I intended to support him wholeheartedly. But Arens surprised us. He announced that he was resigning from the Knesset. Shamir resigned as well.

It was only after it was clear that neither Shamir nor Arens would continue to lead the party that I threw my hat in the ring. In 1993, I announced that I would run for party leader and head of the Opposition. If I won I would face Rabin in the 1996 election as Likud's candidate for prime minister.

23

NATHAN

Only in retrospect can I see that my entrance into political life was in many ways predestined by the legacy I inherited from my paternal grandfather, Rabbi Nathan Mileikowsky, who changed his name to Netanyahu after arriving in the Holy Land.

Nathan was born in the village of Krevo in Belarus in 1879, my grandmother Sarah in the village of Shadova in nearby Lithuania in 1885. The Jewish community in Vilnius, the capital of Lithuania, was known as Jerusalem d'Lita to emphasize its concentration of eminent rabbis, scholars and intellectuals. Later it was almost entirely destroyed by the Nazis. My family escaped this fate by a decision made by my grandfather Nathan.

The son of a farmer, he was marked from childhood as precociously talented. Sent at the age of ten to Yeshiva and at eighteen to the famed Yeshiva of Volozhin, whose alumni included the great poet Bialik, he became an early disciple of Zionism. At twenty years of age he started giving impassioned speeches to Jewish communities throughout Europe to encourage Jews to pack their belongings and go to their ancestral homeland, the Land of Israel.

Nathan's influence was so great that he became one of the most sought-after speakers in the Jewish world, spreading the message of Zionism in hundreds of Jewish communities in Poland, Eastern Europe, Britain and the United States. He even reached Siberia.

When he died prematurely of typhus in 1935 at the age of fifty-five, the newspaper *Haaretz* published a glowing obituary titled "Dreamer and Fighter." It included a description by an American Jewish journalist, B. Gitlin, who had accompanied Nathan in his appearances in Poland.

"One cannot imagine the power of his influence," wrote Gitlin. "It was hard to find a hall big enough to contain the great crowds that would come to hear him speak. People broke doors and windows and fought ushers in order to hear the famous orator. Eventually it was necessary to stop these assemblies in order to stop these outbursts."[1]

Haaretz notes that these speaking tours were often spiced with adventure:

> In one of the assemblies someone pointed a rifle at him. The crowd became frantic. He calmed them down and calmly continued his speech. Nathan was then arrested. In Galicia he was accused of fomenting rebellion against the government and he crossed the border in a winter wagon during a nightly storm. He worked in the most dangerous conditions, but when he left Poland 12 years later in 1920 he knew that Zionism in Poland had been implanted in the hearts of the Jewish masses and that he had a great role in achieving this. His name was famous in the farthest corners of Polish Jewry.[2]

Haaretz cites similar ecstatic reactions from American Jewish audiences during Nathan's appearances in the United States in the 1920s and early '30s, where "he gave 700 speeches in 270 days" on behalf of Zionism[3] before tens, and possibly hundreds, of thousands of people. Up to the late 1960s, I was still approached by people who, learning that I was Nathan's grandson, told me that they immigrated to Israel after hearing my grandfather speak.

Nathan's passion for Zionism was aroused by the modern Moses of our people, Theodor Herzl. The imperative for a national salvation for Jews was driven home to Nathan in 1905 in an incident that nearly cost him his life. Standing in a railway station in the city of Homel in Belarus with his younger brother Yehuda, the two were easily identified by their dress as Jews by a gang of antisemitic hooligans.

"Yids!" they roared and ran toward them.

"Run, Yehuda, run!" Nathan cried.

Seeking to save his younger brother by giving him time to escape, he faced the onslaught of the hoodlums. They clubbed him with metal rods and left him for dead. He later described his thoughts as he lay in the snow and mud by the railroad tracks before losing consciousness: "What a disgrace! Is this what has become of the descendants of the Maccabees? If I live, I will take my family and go to the Land of Israel where we will rebuild our life as a free and proud nation."

It would take him fifteen years to do that. In the interim he gave speeches on behalf of Zionism around the world and assumed the post of headmaster of Jewish studies in the prestigious Jewish Gymnasium (high school) in Warsaw, Poland. There his eldest son, Benzion, my father, was born in 1910. He was followed by eight more siblings, seven brothers and one sister.

My grandmother took both the earlier absence of children and the later abundance of progeny in stride. She was a highly intelligent and devout woman who read the Bible each day. In her later years she lived with the family of her only daughter, my aunt Miri. In large family gatherings my many cousins, her adoring grandchildren, would congregate around her.

"Eat, children eat," she would encourage us.

"And what about you, Grandma?" we would ask.

"Don't worry about me, children," she would invariably reply. "I ate in my childhood."

When she died in 1970, I was heartbroken that I was unable to attend her funeral because I was engaged in a Unit mission. She was buried next to Nathan in the ancient cemetery on the slopes of the Mount of Olives, overlooking the Temple Mount in Jerusalem. Yoni and Iddo came from the army and personally covered her grave. Other cousins joined in, leaving the caretakers who normally do this task standing quietly aside.

At home in Warsaw, Nathan and Sarah made a point of only speaking a renascent Hebrew with their children, brought back to everyday usage only a few decades earlier after being used almost exclusively for liturgical purposes for centuries on end. This linguistic revival has no parallel in the annals of nations. It was led by the likes of Professor Klausner and most prominently by the trailblazing linguist Eliezer Ben Yehuda, whose great-grandson was one of my classmates in Jerusalem.

The rebirth of the Jewish people was accomplished by simultaneous political, cultural and linguistic revolutions that occurred in a remarkably short time.

But what the Jewish people lacked and needed most was a state of their own, and this was blocked by the Ottoman refusal at the start of the twentieth century to even grant free Jewish immigration to what is now Israel. Through his speeches and other means, Nathan sought ways to advance the goals of Zionism.

The German ambassador to Warsaw during World War I must have gotten a whiff of this. Impressed by Nathan's extraordinary impact on Jewish audiences, the German authorities made Nathan an offer early on in the war. Germany would secretly ferret Nathan in a submarine to the United States (just as they smuggled Lenin to Russia in a railway car in 1917). Once in America, Nathan was to sway the American Jewish community not merely toward Zionism but also against tsarist Russia—which Germany was fighting in the war. In doing so, the Germans hoped the US would have more reason to stay out of the fight against them, so as not to help Russia.

In return, the Germans promised, Germany would use its influence to change the policies of its ally Turkey toward the creation of a Jewish state. For additional incentive the offer included a vast sum of money for Nathan. Nathan did not respond to the money offer. Instead he insisted on ironclad guarantees that his Zionist demands would be fulfilled. In response, the Germans upped the cash offer.

"The Kaiser said that he tried to influence the Turkish Sultan," wrote *Haaretz*, "but the Sultan refused."[4]

So did Nathan.

I suspect that even if the Germans had agreed to his terms, Nathan's lack of belief in the certainty of the deal and his basic reluctance to help Germany against the Allies would have scuttled the proposal.[5]

On August 15, 1915, the German army marched into Warsaw. Nathan's family lived in a grand European semicircular apartment building. As five-year-old Benzion and his younger brother watched from a window above the courtyard, German troops were ransacking the shops on the street. Benzion saw his father approach the German commanding officer.

"You belong to a nation that produced Goethe and Schiller. How can you allow this barbarism to go on?!" he reproached him.

The German officer, by all appearances a highly educated man, was startled. Here was a Jewish rabbi berating an officer of an all-powerful army. Incredibly, he apologized to my grandfather and reined in his troops.

Nathan did not identify with any of the political parties in the Jewish world of the day. He was a disciple of Herzl and not of one of the political offshoots that sought to realize his great vision.

Yet to his chagrin, on one occasion Nathan had to enter the political fray and challenge no less than his idol Herzl himself! When in 1903 Herzl had seen that he could not break the Turkish stranglehold on the creation of a Jewish state, he was willing to consider a British offer for Jewish autonomy in British-held Uganda. Herzl foresaw the impending doom of European Jewry before anyone else did. He saw Uganda as a temporary safe haven, a "night station," he called it, in which the Jewish people could save themselves from extermination and from which they could later advance to Palestine.

Herzl's clairvoyance about the Holocaust almost forty years before its occurrence was nothing short of prophetic. But he could not organize sufficient support for the implementation of the Uganda plan.

Perhaps in retrospect one can appreciate Herzl's rationalist view that a haven, any haven, was needed to save millions of European Jews. But the Jewish people's attachment to the Land of Israel was more powerful, and only its force could ultimately harness the Jewish masses to concerted political action.

When Ze'ev Jabotinsky voted against Uganda, he admitted that he did not know why. It was "one of those 'simple' things which counterbalance thousands of arguments."[6]

Nathan was more explicit in explaining why as a young man he resolutely opposed and finally helped defeat the Uganda plan at the Zionist Congress of 1905. Twenty-five years later, after the relationship between Britain and the Zionists had soured, my father asked Nathan if the opposition to Uganda had been influenced by the belief that the project was impractical and that the British would not see it through. He clearly remembered his father's reply.

"On the contrary," Nathan said. "We believed that the British would be faithful to their word. In those days England enjoyed a great reputation among the Jews. But it was precisely because we believed that the project *could* be carried out that we were all the more opposed to it. For so many centuries the Jewish people had made so many sacrifices for this land, had shed their blood for it, had prayed for a thousand years to return to it, had tied their most intimate hopes to its revival—we considered it inconceivable that we would now betray the generations of Jews, who had fought and died for this end. It would have rendered the whole of Jewish history meaningless. We *had* to oppose it."[7]

Even before the Uganda plan was officially shelved, Herzl swore renewed allegiance to Jerusalem, vowing to the Zionist Congress in the ancient Hebrew prayer, "If I forget thee Jerusalem, may my right hand lose its cunning."

I've often thought about Herzl's dilemma. More than anyone else, and *before* almost anyone else, he saw the approaching catastrophe of annihilation. He understood this when as a young journalist for the Viennese newspaper *Neue Freie Presse*, stationed in Paris, he covered the infamous Dreyfus trial. Alfred Dreyfus, a French Jewish officer, was falsely accused of treason and sentenced to harsh imprisonment on Devil's Island. Though Dreyfus would later be exonerated after Herzl's death, Herzl reached an inescapable conclusion: If such blatant antisemitism can happen in Paris, the apex of Western civilization, it can happen *anywhere*, with unimaginably tragic consequences.

As twenty-seven-year-old Father wrote about Herzl in 1937:

Herzl knew that even if it were possible to conceive of rescue operations whose implementation requires hundreds of years, world Jewry did not have those hundreds of years at its disposal. He heard the thunder rumbling from a gathering storm of Jew hatred coming closer and closer. *It was clear to him that the Middle Ages would be revisited upon the Jews in all the states of Europe*, and he repeated this observation time and again.

Herzl wrote that "the stone is rolling down the mountain slope," and he knew where it would stop, "at the bottom, the absolute bottom! Will there be devastation? Will there be confiscation? Will they expel us? Will they murder us? *I anticipate all of these things and more.*"[8]

This flew in the face of the leading voices in the Jewish world who argued that the Jews would eventually be accepted in European society or that establishing global socialism or communism—systems in which religious and national identity would in theory fade away—would solve the "Jewish Problem."

Herzl believed that antisemitism was too ingrained for either course to work. Instead he proposed that the Jewish people establish their own independent state, to which all Jews could come if they chose to do so.

He was the first to offer a concrete plan for such a state, one that included political and financial institutions such as Bank Leumi, which serves the Jewish people to this day. In his book *Altneuland* (Old New Land), he presented a detailed vision of a modern technological and scientific Jewish nation.

"The Maccabees will rise again," he wrote in 1896, at the start of his campaign for Zionism. "The Jews who wish for a state will have it. We shall live at last as free men on our own soil. The world will be freed by our liberty, enriched by our wealth, magnified by our greatness. And whatever we accomplish there for our own welfare will powerfully benefit all of humanity."[9]

In August 1897, following the First Zionist Congress, which he convened in Basel, Switzerland, Herzl wrote in his diary, "*In Basel I founded the Jewish state*. If I say this aloud today, I will be met with widespread laughter. But perhaps in five years, certainly in fifty, everyone will recognize this."[10]

He was the first Jewish statesman in modern times who worked solely for the Jewish people. To the Jewish and non-Jewish masses, he conducted a forceful public opinion campaign. To the heads of state, he appealed on the basis of their national interests.

Initially, Herzl found greater receptiveness among non-Jews than among many of his own people. He succeeded in obtaining an audience with Kaiser Wilhelm II of Germany. To the Kaiser he described Zionism as a plan that would not only divert the energy of some of Germany's young radicals, whom he knew the Kaiser was interested in ridding from his realm, but create a Jewish protectorate allied with Germany at the crossroads of the Middle East. By October 1898, only a year after Zionism had made its debut at the First Zionist Congress, he had met with the Kaiser three times.

Appealing again to self-interest, Herzl was able to secure an audience with the Ottoman sultan, in Constantinople in May 1901. Invoking the story of Androcles, who removed the incapacitating thorn from the lion's paw, Herzl told the bankrupt sultan, "His Majesty is the lion, perhaps I am Androcles, and perhaps there is a thorn that needs pulling out. The thorn, as I see it, is your public debt."[11]

Herzl proposed to remove the thorn with the help of the great Jewish financiers. He would soon be disappointed. Unlike the Jews of Russia and Eastern Europe, most of the great Jewish financiers in the West did not embrace Zionism. They subscribed to the assimilationist worldview and believed in the prominence of European liberalism. Undeterred, Herzl pressed on.

Having been unsuccessful in his attempts to open the gates of the Holy Land to Zionism, and fearing the fate of European Jewry in the face of rising antisemitism, Herzl proposed the establishment of a temporary Jewish haven in Uganda.

Had I been around when such a prophet proposed the Uganda plan, what would I have done? On the one hand, a possible escape from the inferno of Europe might have saved millions of Jewish lives. On the other, Uganda could have turned out to be a dead end where the Jewish people would be stuck in a land not their own.

Herzl said that after liberating the Jews he would turn to the liberation of the Black people of Africa.

"Think of the hair-raising horrors of the slave trade," one of his characters says in *Altneuland*. "Human beings, because their skin is black, are stolen, carried off and sold. . . . Now that I have lived to see the restoration of the Jews I should like to pave the way for the restoration of the Negroes."[12]

Almost a century later, Israel's rescue of Ethiopian Jews showed Zionism to be the only movement in history to transport Blacks out of Africa not to enslave them but to liberate them. This of course did not prevent the UN from surreally and outrageously labeling the color-blind Zionist movement as "racist."

Even though the Uganda plan was meant to provide only a temporary safe haven, it would have probably also pitted the Jewish people against the local population in a country to which we had no historical claim or attachment. The Land of Israel was the only country to which we were attached for thousands of years and to which Jews returned over the centuries.

I would have sided with Nathan.

In 1904, Herzl died at the age of forty-four, a giant of history. In the eight short years between 1896 and 1904 he changed the course of Jewish destiny by giving his people a practical plan and practical organizations to achieve national salvation after two millennia of unrelenting massacres, exiles and pogroms. His followers carried on his vision, and fifty years after he made his prediction that this is how long it might take for a Jewish state to come into being, the United Nations voted to create it. A few months later, Israel was established.

FOUR YEARS AFTER Herzl's death, twenty-nine-year-old Nathan was one of the fifty delegates to the Eighth Zionist Congress meeting in The Hague, Netherlands.

A photograph of the delegates shows him seated among the great leaders of the modern Jewish revival, including Chaim Weizmann, later the first president of Israel, Jabotinsky and many others whose names today adorn streets and boulevards in Israel. This photograph records an event that is as close as one can get to the Israeli equivalent of the *Mayflower*.

In 1920, at the age of forty, Nathan made good on his vow and brought his expanding family to Israel. After four years in Safed in the Galilee, they moved to Jerusalem, where my father went to university, met my mother, and became politically involved in Jabotinsky's movement. But not Nathan. He retained cordial relations with Jabotinsky and his colleagues in the adamantly nationalist Revisionist Zionism on the right, but was also viewed favorably by Ben Gurion and other leaders of Socialist Zionism on the left.

The so-called Arlosoroff Affair forced him to abandon his neutrality. On June 16, 1933, the socialist leader Haim Arlosoroff was murdered at night on the beach in Tel Aviv. The next day, Labor spokesmen falsely accused the Revisionists of committing the murder. Father had met two of the accused earlier that day in Zion Square in Jerusalem. He knew that his friend Abba Ahimeir, one of the accused, was a man above reproach and he also knew that it was physically impossible for him and the other accused to have committed the crime.

He went to see his father to convince him that this accusation was a politically motivated "blood libel" of the left against the right.

At Benzion's urging, Nathan examined the facts of the case. Convinced that the charges were trumped up, he went to see Chief Rabbi Abraham Isaac Kook, who was universally respected by secular and Orthodox Jews alike. He implored the great rabbi to speak out against the "witch hunt trial." When the chief rabbi came out against the "great injustice," the die was cast. Public opinion shifted in favor of the defendants. After initially being found guilty, they were later acquitted by a higher British court.

A little over a year later, in 1935, Nathan died of typhus. Many in the Jewish community mourned him. Chief Rabbi Kook eulogized him in a speech that described his inner turmoil, obliquely referring to the Arlossoroff trial.

"I saw the suffering of his soul in the face of events that he considered alien and trampling the sanctity of our people,"[13] wrote the revered rabbi. Nathan's heart had been torn when he saw the injustice of brothers defaming their innocent kin.

When Prime Minister Begin instructed me to tackle what he called the "blood libel" against Israel on the Sabra and Shatila incident while I was serving at the Israeli embassy in Washington, he knew that as Benzion Netanyahu's son I would be familiar with the Arlosoroff Affair, which he was clearly referencing.

He later set up a special commission on the Arlosoroff Affair to further clear up the fake charges against the Zionist right, despite the fact that a full half a century had passed and that a British court had acquitted the falsely accused.

Begin understood the lingering effect of fake charges used to smear an entire political camp. Unfortunately over the years, partisan venom was used to smear others on the right. It would escalate in the 1990s to scandalous proportions when I would be falsely accused of fomenting Rabin's assassination.

24

LEADER OF THE OPPOSITION

1993–1996

Upon my entry to Israeli politics I would encounter a partisan venom hauntingly similar to what my grandfather fought against more than half a century earlier.

When Father learned that I intended to enter the fray and run for prime minister as leader of the Opposition, he was far from enthusiastic.

"Do you think you can really win?" he asked.

"I believe I can, Father," I said.

"Perhaps you will," he responded. "But if you do, the left won't let you stay. They will do anything and everything to bring you down."

I knew he was harking back to the Arlosoroff Affair. But surely times have changed, I thought.

Brushing aside Father's gloomy warning, I plunged ahead. The wellsprings of my motivation were deep. Drawing on the values I received from my grandparents, my parents and my brother and from their absolute commitment to the ideal of the Jewish state, I saw my entry into public leadership as a continuation of my family's legacy.

It also coincided with the expansion of my own immediate family. In 1988 as deputy foreign minister I flew from the United States back to Israel. On a stopover in Amsterdam's Schiphol Airport I went to buy some gouda cheese. So did my future wife, Sara. To fund her university studies in psychology she was working as a flight attendant on El Al, Israel's national carrier, but on this flight she was "deadweight" aircrew, not on duty.

Meeting at the airport's shop, it appeared we both liked the same type of cheese and, as it turned out, many other things as well. Taking her telephone number, I called her a day after we landed in Israel. My first question was, "How old are you?"

"Thirty," she answered.

I breathed a sigh of relief. She looked at least a decade younger than her actual age.

I discovered that in her military service she was assigned to do psychological tests for elite units, including my own.

"Lucky for me you came nine years after me. I'm not sure what grade you'd have given me," I said.

She laughed. I was also delighted to hear that her political views were similar to mine. She always brought to them added sensitivity and deep compassion. A gifted master's degree student of psychology at Hebrew University in Jerusalem, she was reprimanded by her lecturer when she objected in class to his description of Israel's political climate in the 1980s as rife with fascism. The professor called her in and said, "You have a brilliant future as a psychologist ahead of you. Don't ruin it by voicing these opinions."

She stuck to her convictions and graduated with distinction.

I asked my friend David Bar Ilan, who was living in Jerusalem at the time, to invite us both to dinner so he could give me his impression of Sara. Sara politely declined the invitation, saying that she had to accompany her father for checkups in the hospital.

"That's a good sign," said David. "She's got her priorities right."

ON ONE OF our early dates we toured the ruins of Gamla, in the Golan. It was a particularly hot day and Sara effortlessly climbed the steep slopes. We bathed in the Sea of Galilee to cool off. I asked Sara if she was okay, and she said she was. Of course, it was I who ended up with sunstroke. So much for macho bravado.

I visited her parents' modest home in Kiryat Tivon, near Haifa, which reminded me of the home I grew up in. A scholarly father, a practical mother who kept the family together, and gifted brothers (in Sara's case a mathematician, a high-tech entrepreneur and a philosopher).

I was intrigued by the fact that from Sara's room I could see the ruins of the Sanhedrin court, the famed Jewish Judicial Council uncovered after two millennia. We walked up to it and then went to the equestrian statue of Alexander Zeid, the mythic fighter who eighty years earlier had created on these hills the first Jewish self-defense organization. It was there, two years later, that I proposed to Sara.

Our son Yair was born in 1991, our son Avner three years later. Thus with a young family—and often lending a hand changing diapers—I set out to challenge Rabin's government.

But before I did so, I prepared myself. I asked Father what he thought was the prerequisite quality for somebody taking on that job.

"What do *you* think?" he said.

"A clear vision of where you want to lead the country, a strong commitment to that vision, and sufficient flexibility in navigating toward achieving it," I answered confidently.

To my surprise, Father waved all that aside.

"You need that for any leadership position. A university president, a head of a company or a military commander would all give the same answer."

Now I was intrigued.

"So, Abba, what do *you* think is uniquely required to be PM?" I pressed.

He paused and then uttered one word that astonished me.

"Education," he said. "A broad and deep education. Otherwise you'll be at the mercy of your clerks."

A quarter of a century later, I watched an episode of *The Crown*, a favorite show of Sara's. Feeling inadequately informed about world affairs in discussions with experienced civil servants before an upcoming visit by President Eisenhower, the young Queen Elizabeth decides to broaden her education by hiring an esteemed tutor from Cambridge University.

"They're far more intelligent than I am. In any confrontation, they'd outdebate me, outthink me, and outmaneuver me," Elizabeth's character says in the dramatized episode.

"You were drilled for years in the finer points of our Constitution. You know it better than me, better than all of us. You have the only education that matters," replies a fictitious Professor Hogg.[1]

Despite its literary license, I was floored by this segment. It makes a point similar to the one made by my father. But there was one big difference. A constitutional monarch may get away with a good education in constitutional law alone, but the prime minister of Israel cannot. A person holding that office needs more.

Over the years, I recounted the story of my father's response many times. He was right, of course. Without a basic understanding of economics, military affairs, technology and science, a prime minister is rendered helpless before the "experts."

But there was one discipline that supersedes them all. When the veteran American journalist Dan Rather visited me in 2018, he brought along his grandson, a young student at Dartmouth College. The young man asked me point-blank what I thought was the most important subject to study for a political career.

"There are actually three," I said. "History, history, and more history."

To this day, devouring works of history gives me both a pleasurable escape and a necessary map and compass to chart the course of Israel among the nations. How can you know where to go if you don't even know how you got here?

HISTORY TAUGHT ME that political fortunes could often change swiftly by a combination of external events and purposeful effort. But how could I direct meaningful change after a resounding defeat for my party in the 1992 elections? Our defeat had left Likud in shambles. As often happens in these circumstances, despair joined recrimination.

Labor was seen as invincible. Rabin was a popular leader with solid security credentials. His promise not to veer too far to the left with territorial concessions reassured many. He promised that he, and he alone, would "navigate" the government's course.

He did not know that as he was uttering those words, Shimon Peres and some of his young associates had begun secret contacts with the PLO. These secret contacts would soon lead to the Oslo Accords, which would implant Yasser Arafat and his cohorts around Jerusalem and in the hills above Tel Aviv.

I didn't know this either. My first task was to win the Likud leadership. To do that I would have to break the deadly competition between the various camps and, I believed, enact countrywide primaries open to all Likud registered voters. I envisioned 250,000 voters who would choose the party's leadership and the Knesset list instead of the 2,500 Central Committee members—an increase by a factor of 100! In general, the larger the voting body, the better the results.

Here I hit a brick wall. The party seniors—Levy, Sharon and Katzav—opposed primaries. So did many in the Central Committee who knew their power would be diluted if primaries were enacted. How do you get the cat to give up the cream?

By the pressure of public opinion, of course.

In fairness, it must be said that a significant number of Central Committee members were by then open to this change. They realized it was needed if the Likud was to regain power. Primaries in which hundreds of thousands of registered Likud members voted were the only way to open up the Likud to new blood supported by the grass roots.

Beyond the usual rallies and meetings with party members, I embarked on a project that eventually tilted the balance toward holding primaries. With an expanding group of dedicated Likud supporters whom I embraced and admired, I recruited volunteers throughout the country and asked them to man hundreds of stands in which people could register to become voting members of Likud. Volunteers enthusiastically staffed these "Register for Likud" posts in shopping malls, sports arenas and other places of public congregation. They had my picture on the stands, to make sure those who were canvassed knew that I was behind the campaign.

Within a few months, the number of Likud's registered voters swelled by 100 percent, to a quarter of a million, just as I had hoped. Public enthusiasm on the right at the sight of this infusion of so many new voters helped me overcome opposition within the party to primaries. The Central Committee voted for them and scheduled the elections for March 24, 1993. Levy, Katsav and Benny Begin signed up for the race. I won by a comfortable margin. My request to enact primaries for the Knesset members as well was also approved.

My direct connection to Likud voters became the enduring basis of my political power. If my fate had been left to the politicians, I would never have become prime minister or stayed in power.

Yet after becoming party leader I could have been more magnanimous in victory. While I did not bear down on veterans like Sharon and Levy, I did not give them the special deference they deserved as senior members of the party. Nor did I consult sufficiently often with tribal elders Shamir and Arens. Being retired from political life, they could have offered wise advice. It wasn't coldheartedness on my part. I was simply a young man in a hurry.

WHILE I WAS engaged in *politics*, I did not neglect *policy*. During my campaign for the Likud leadership, I began writing the book *A Place Among the Nations*, an exposition of the rise of Zionism, with detailed rebuttals of the various attacks against Israel. I also laid out a vision of "a durable peace," which was the name the publishers gave the book in subsequent editions. Though I relied in no small measure on my speeches at the UN and elsewhere to write it, the work also involved considerable research, carried out by Yoram Hazony.

Writing the book consumed me. On a good day, writing forces you to distill ideas, to order them logically and to breathe life into them with unexpected language. For me there is no more satisfying intellectual exercise.

But it also requires time. That's why I could never write any of my books when I was in executive positions like prime minister or finance minister. *A Place Among the Nations*[2] came out in 1993, shortly after news of the impending Oslo Accords broke out. In those days before the international mainstream media went totally off the reservation on anything related to Likud or me, the book received many complimentary reviews abroad.

Usually polemical books like the one I wrote receive harsh scrutiny and unrelenting criticism from political opponents. An array of fact-checkers roam its pages looking for easy targets to devour. A straggling factual error here, a clumsy formulation there. There was no such criticism by the English-language reviewers of the book and not a single fact was challenged.

But when the book was published in Hebrew, the response from the Israeli press was . . . no response! They simply ignored it, seldom challenging my arguments which debunked their positions head-on.

This was at once heartening and disappointing. Heartening because it showed that I and those who helped me research the book did our work diligently, disappointing because intellectual and ideological battle helps disseminate ideas. What was the moral basis of Zionism? Did we take another people's land or did we reclaim land that was taken away from us? How could peace be achieved with our neighbors? Would it be realized with far-reaching concessions or with minimal or no concessions? And which security arrangements would maintain our power of deterrence?

This ideological battle wasn't theoretical. It was as concrete as you can get. Soon after Rabin's entry into office, it focused on the Golan Heights. Rabin's government was being encouraged by the Clinton administration to cut a deal with Hafez Assad, the Syrian dictator, in which Israel would cede the entire Golan to Syria.

American administrations, fed for decades on the theory of territorial concessions, could hardly think any other way. Only withdrawal from "the occupied territories" could lead to peace. But they could be flexible in the *choice* of territories that Israel should first withdraw from.

Since Rabin was aware of the strategic importance of Judea and Samaria, he figured: Why not start with a withdrawal from the Golan Heights? After all, it was thought, Syria was a major player in the Middle East. If Israel struck a peace deal with Damascus, surely this would open a path to peace with the Palestinians. The price of the peace was a full Israeli descent from the strategic heights of the Golan.

It never occurred to those advocating this position that, as Yoni had explained to Professor Thomas Schelling, if Israel went down from the Heights, it would become so vulnerable that it would *invite* a Syrian attack and the peace would collapse.

The possibility of political change in the Arab states that would make Israel's situation even more precarious never occurred to them either. This in fact happened when parts of Syria were taken over by Islamists during the civil war, in Egypt with the Muslim Brotherhood takeover, and in Gaza with Hamas's seizure of power.

The advocates of total withdrawal were in effect saying that to "make peace" you must create the conditions that could make war a lot more likely. Unlike the 1979 peace with Egypt, which left the vast Sinai Peninsula (twice the size of Israel) as a demilitarized buffer zone between Egypt and Israel, the Golan Heights had no strategic depth. It was all of twelve kilometers wide on average.

But, rising three hundred meters above the Israeli Sea of Galilee, it had strategic *height*. If Israel gave up that height advantage, the Syrian army could simply march to the shores of the Galilee below, at once threatening Israel's key water reservoir and being in a position to invade the northern part of Israel with no topographical obstacle standing in its way.

Little interest was given to the nature of the brutal Syrian regime and the possibility that it would use this strategic advantage to improve its starting position for a future war. The prevalent view was that the mere *act* of signing a peace agreement would ensure the durability of that peace, a peculiar conception given that many wars often start from the violation of existing peace treaties.

The Munich Peace Agreement of 1938 is perhaps the most famous example. To achieve peace with Hitler, British prime minister Neville Chamberlain acquiesced to Hitler's demand to give him the Sudeten Mountains in Czechoslovakia. Once Hitler got possession of those strategic heights, he tore up the peace treaty and marched into Prague without even firing a shot.

In *A Place Among the Nations*, I drew a distinction between two kinds of peace: that between democracies and that between democracies and dictatorships. With few exceptions, democracies tend toward peace. You don't get reelected if you continually start wars and send your sons and daughters to die on foreign battlefields. Dictatorships, on the other hand, *get* to power by practicing aggression against their own people. So what will prevent them from practicing aggression against their neighbors?

The answer is . . . nothing, except the force of deterrence. Peace with a dictatorship, or at least nonbelligerence with it, is achieved not by debilitating concessions but by powerful deterrence—not by *weakness* but by *strength*.

The dictatorship that I was most concerned with was actually not Syria but Iran. On February 19, 1993, I published an article titled "The Great Danger."

"The greatest danger to Israel's existence is not found in the Arab countries, but in Iran,"[3] I wrote.

I consistently argued that we must take action to prevent Iran from realizing its nuclear ambitions.

All these arguments, based on history and common sense, were dismissed by the foreign policy elites in both Israel and Washington. The election of Rabin was seen as an opportunity to break the logjam and make a historic peace, beginning with Syria.

But first one obstacle had to be removed. The Ford administration had given Israel a commitment that the Golan Heights would effectively remain in Israel's hands. President Clinton's secretary of state, Warren Christopher, was dispatched to Israel to change that.

Christopher devised a new secret agreement by which the US would receive from Israel "a deposit"—an advanced promise to cede the Golan Heights in exchange for a future peace deal. This was required because Hafez Assad, the Syrian dictator, insisted on first receiving such an Israeli commitment before he would even consider moving forward with any political negotiations with Israel. As would later become evident, Assad actually had no intention of making a formal peace, but the Rabin government nonetheless agreed to a full withdrawal from the Heights in exchange for a peace agreement.

I thought this was a grave mistake. I believed Israel should retain the high ground of the Golan in any future deal. From this position we could easily reach Damascus, only twenty kilometers away, if Syria violated the peace.

News of some kind of negotiation regarding the Golan had trickled out to the public. Though none of the details about the "deposit" were known, people understood that the Golan was up for grabs. This flatly contradicted Rabin's pre-election promises. On June 10, 1992, thirteen days before the upcoming elections, he had said in a rally marking twenty-five years of Israeli settlement on the Golan: "It's inconceivable that even in times of peace we would descend from the Golan Heights."[4]

Now, after the elections, he was secretly negotiating to do just that.

I held the same position before and after the elections. In September 1992 I stressed in a press interview: "The first condition for peace between Israel and any Arab country is denying the Arab side a war option.

For a genuine and stable peace the Prime Minister must demand from the Syrians to give up the Golan Heights."[5]

Rabin's government continued to deny that any practical plans to withdraw from the Golan were being hatched, let alone negotiated, while in fact they were engaged in negotiations to do so. A popular protest movement, including former Labor supporters, began to challenge the idea of ceding the Golan.

One day in 1995 I received a phone call from a government official who wanted to meet me discreetly. We met secretly at my apartment. My interlocutor was a respected professional and a member of the government's negotiating team with Syria.

"I know I'm taking a big personal risk," he told me, "but I feel I can't be part of this deception any longer. I'm giving you this document. Do with it whatever you want."

"You know," I told him, "there'll be an investigation once it comes out. Are you prepared to take that risk?"

"Yes, I am," he said quietly. "I thought about it long and hard. My conscience tells me that this is what I must do. I can't lend a hand to this deception."

He gave me the text of the briefing points to the IDF chief of staff in preparation for a meeting with his Syrian counterpart. It showed that Israel had caved in on three security conditions that Rabin had said he would insist on maintaining: the strategic Mount Hermon would no longer be in Israeli hands; Syria's army would not be reduced; and buffer zones would be established that would be symmetrical on both sides of the future border. This meant that the IDF would be pushed back from the Syrian border into tiny Israel the same distance that the Syrian army would be pushed back into much larger Syria.

In a Knesset debate I revealed the document.[6]

All hell broke loose. The government's response was self-contradictory. It both denied the contents of the document and accused me of jeopardizing Israel's security by revealing it. I replied that Israel's security was being jeopardized by the government's planned concessions and not by their revelation, which actually served Israel's security.

Earlier I had led other activities to galvanize the Golan protests. I convened the Likud Party's convention on the Golan to underscore our refusal to leave the Heights. I met regularly with the Golan Regional Council and coordinated public activities with its members. All this, alongside Syria's obstinacy not to give even the mildest of concessions, eventually halted the deal. By 1996, the Golan was saved, for the moment at least.

BY THEN THE government's attention was focused elsewhere.

Rabin had found out years before that shortly after the swearing-in of his government in 1992, Shimon Peres's assistant Yossi Beilin was engaged in secret negotiations with PLO representatives in Norway's capital, Oslo. When Rabin learned about this, a few weeks after the Oslo meetings had happened, he wrote an irate letter to Peres. He complained that these negotiations would scuttle the chance for progress with the Palestinian delegation that had attended the Madrid Peace Conference and was still periodically meeting its Israeli counterpart in Washington.

He argued that Peres was swapping negotiations with the relatively moderate Palestinians who came to Madrid for those with the most extreme element in Palestinian society, the PLO leadership living in exile in Tunis after they had been kicked out of Beirut during the First Lebanon War in 1982.

Nonetheless, Rabin agreed to sign the Oslo peace agreement with Arafat. The signing ceremony took place on September 13, 1993, in a grand event hosted by President Clinton on the White House lawn. It enabled the creation of a Palestinian Authority in Judea and Samaria, effectively emplacing the PLO leadership on the high ground adjacent to major Israeli population centers.

The Oslo agreement was approved by the Knesset by a hair-thin margin of one vote, that of a Knesset member who later achieved lasting notoriety by selling his vote for a deputy minister's Mitsubishi.

The Oslo agreement, actually a series of agreements interchangeably referred to as the Oslo Accords, was meant to give the Palestinians a gradually expanding autonomous authority. It was widely understood that this agreement would ultimately evolve into a full-fledged state. Would this lead to peace?

On May 10, 1994, a few months after signing the Oslo Accords, Arafat spoke candidly in Johannesburg, South Africa.

"In my eyes," he said, "this agreement has no more value than the one signed by the Prophet Muhammad with the Kureish Tribe."[7]

Muslim audiences immediately understood what he meant. The Kureish were a formidable Jewish tribe in Arabia. Unable to defeat them, Muhammad signed a peace deal with them. Once his force was strong enough, he abandoned the deal and destroyed the Jewish tribe.

Most of the time, Palestinian officials were more careful to adhere to the advice of senior Palestinian leader Faisal Husseini, who said at Birzeit University on November 22, 1995: "Everything you hear and see today is for tactical and strategic reasons."[8] But at times, Palestinian officials would break the camouflage, making statements that clearly indicated their intentions of claiming all of Israel and destroying its people, like "The lights that shine over Gaza and Jericho will also reach the Negev and the Galilee."[9] Or "We must remember that the main enemy of the Palestinian people, now and forever, is Israel."[10] Or "We are returning to Palestine, and we are passing from the small Jihad to the great Jihad."[11]

Arafat himself sometimes spoke even more candidly. On January 30, 1996, he said in a closed meeting to forty Arab diplomats in Stockholm's Grand Hotel, "We intend to destroy Israel and to establish a pure Palestinian state. . . . We will make the life of the Jews miserable and take everything from them. . . . I don't need any Jews."[12]

In a radio address on the Voice of Palestine on November 11, 1995, he said, "The struggle will continue until *all* of Palestine is liberated."

Lest anyone had doubts that by "all of Palestine" he meant not only Judea and Samaria and Gaza but all of Israel, he had proclaimed two months earlier, on September 7, 1995, "O Gaza, your sons are returning. O Lod, O Haifa, O Jerusalem, you are returning, you are returning," in Arabic to a Palestinian audience.

True to his deceptive character, he was careful not to mention places like Haifa and Lod, which were well within pre-1967 Israel and ostensibly not in the PLO's plan for a state, when he spoke before Western audiences.

On September 13, 1993, the day he signed the Oslo Accords, Arafat used more oblique language in explaining to a Palestinian audience that the agreement was nothing more than the PLO's "Phased Plan." This plan, calling for the destruction of Israel in stages, had been adopted by the PLO in 1964 and was well familiar to Palestinians.

The unchanging and thinly disguised PLO strategy of destroying Israel in stages completely contradicted Oslo's ostensible message of peace and reconciliation. So did the post-Oslo flood of official Palestinian exhortations dehumanizing Jews as pigs and teaching schoolchildren to glorify Palestinian suicide bombers.

As usual, little of this entered the international discourse or caused governments to rethink the much-vaunted Oslo Accords. There was supposedly a honeymoon between the PLO and Israel under Prime Minister Rabin; Arafat and Rabin were jointly awarded the Nobel Peace Prize in 1994 "for their efforts to create peace in the Middle East." It was inconceivable that the prizewinning Arafat could be swindling the entire world.

Of course, anybody with a sober view of the facts could see that this was precisely what was happening. But what Yoni had written years earlier about some in Israel was now true of many in the international community: "They want to believe, so they believe. They want not to see, so they distort."[13]

The international community, led by the United States and the Rabin government, enthusiastically pressed for the implementation of Oslo, regardless of the PLO's violations of the spirit and letter of Oslo and its ongoing incitement for the extermination of Israel.

Oslo was to proceed in stages. First Jericho and Gaza were ceded to Palestinian control and weapons were given to the Palestinian security forces, again flatly contradicting Rabin's election promise to "get Gaza out of Tel Aviv."

In a Knesset debate on May 11, 1994, I addressed Rabin.

"You just put Gaza in every part of Israel," I said. "And don't tell the residents of [nearby] Kiryat Gat and Ashkelon that the PLO's Fatah [their governing party] will protect them from Hamas Katyusha rockets."[14]

Eight days later, in a Knesset committee, Rabin dismissed my warnings.

"These are familiar horror stories," he said. "They promised us Katyusha rockets from Gaza. . . . There wasn't and there won't be any Katyushas. You hear all this talk because the Likud is deathly afraid of peace."[15]

Middle East pundits, like most pundits, seldom bother to review their past political prognostications. But in this case it is clear who got it right

and who got it wrong. As I predicted, the PLO's Fatah did not stand up
to Hamas and indeed often joined it in terrorist attacks. In 1994, shortly
after Arafat was brought to Gaza from Tunis, an unprecedented wave of
Palestinian suicide bombings against Israel began.

After Israel's withdrawal from Gaza, Fatah caved to Hamas, which
has since used the territory to launch more than ten thousand rockets
into Kiryat Gat, Ashkelon, Beer-Sheba, Tel Aviv, Jerusalem and many
other parts of Israel.

The situation in the Palestinian-controlled areas of Judea and Samaria was hardly better. Arafat was ensconced there in 1995. His PLO
forces systematically violated his commitments under Oslo to fight and
jail terrorists. Sometimes they made a show of jailing them, only to soon
release them in what was called a "revolving door" policy. Often they simply colluded with them. As a result, terrorist attacks multiplied, especially
suicide bombings.

In successive waves of Palestinian terror attacks in 1995–1996 and
later in 1999–2002, more than a thousand Israelis would die in terrorist
attacks. The Israelis murdered after the Oslo Accords were referred to by
Rabin and the left as "sacrifices for peace," a ghoulish phrase revealing
moral and political obtuseness.

PLO rule did not do wonders for the Palestinian people, either. Opponents and critics were intimidated, silenced, jailed, and in some instances killed. Arafat oversaw a kleptocracy that siphoned considerable
sums from foreign aid to private pockets. Corruption prevented many
entrepreneurial Palestinians from transforming the Palestinian economy
to a free market.

Despite our differences on the Golan and Oslo, I did support Rabin
wholeheartedly on the peace treaty he made with Jordan in 1995. It involved modest territorial concessions and formalized a de facto peace
that had already existed for decades between Israel and the Hashemite
Kingdom.

Still, to get Likud approval for the peace with Jordan I had to convene a formal meeting in which I explained that though our historical
attachment to the East Bank of the Jordan will forever stay in our hearts,
we should relinquish practical claims to this land. This was no small matter for the Likud elders, my staunchest supporters, who fought for Jabo-

tinsky's slogan, "Both banks of the Jordan are ours." This was actually the promise given to the Zionist movement by the international community at the 1920 San Remo Conference. I explained that since the eastern side of the Jordan River is populated by four million Arabs, realizing this generational aspiration was not going to happen. The Likud backed me.

The national concurrence on the peace with Jordan was an exception. As in the case of the Golan, the protest movement against the Oslo Accords gathered steam. It manifested itself in hundreds of rallies, some bringing together hundreds of thousands of people. As in all public rallies of the right, the press minimized the number of participants, just as it inflated it when the rallies came from the left.

When in one protest rally I heard the word "traitor" leveled at Rabin, however, I was thunderstruck and came out forcefully against it.

"No, he is not a traitor," I told the crowd.

"He's mistaken, and we will correct his mistakes when we form the government. But remember: we are all brothers, and we all share the same destiny.

"We're dealing with political adversaries, not enemies." [16]

Rabin was an Israeli patriot. Though we differed on Oslo, we shared many positions, such as on the incipient danger of a nuclear Iran and on the need for defensible borders facing a potential eastern front.

But his decision to implant Arafat and the PLO, who never truly acquiesced to the Jewish state, near Israel's major population centers was doomed to failure. Instead of bringing peace it brought terror.

The cascading terrorist attacks emanating from PLO-controlled areas did not cease for a moment. This blunted the effect on public opinion of the White House signing ceremony of the Oslo Accords, in which Rabin was clearly seen uncomfortably shaking Arafat's hand. Equally, Palestinian terrorism cast a dark shadow over the august ceremony in Sweden, where Rabin, Arafat and Peres were given the Nobel Peace Prize.

The Peace Prize was greatly devalued when, after Oslo, the archjihadist recipient of the prize, Arafat, steadfastly continued to foster terrorism. In my long tenure as prime minister I could never be tempted with a Nobel Prize to do things that I thought would endanger Israel.

Posterity is a better judge of historic achievement than politically correct committees meeting in Scandinavia.

In the years following Oslo, the evident collapse of security after a sham peace deal gave me a distinct advantage over Rabin in the polls. A February 2, 1995, poll on Israel's Channel 2 pitting me against Rabin in a direct vote for prime minister gave me 52 percent to Rabin's 39.[17] A Tel Aviv University poll six weeks later increased that margin to 60 percent versus 40.[18]

Two months earlier, in January 1995, the *Washington Post* had reported that the Clinton administration was mobilizing to help Rabin win the upcoming election.[19] Rabin, the paper explained, was the administration's great hope to reach "peace in the Middle East."

With Clinton's help the gap between Rabin and me narrowed, but he still faced an uphill battle. Given the mounting public challenge to his policies and popularity, Rabin and Peres decided to rally their own supporters in a mass gathering of their own.

Bringing together an impressive crowd in Tel Aviv's central square on November 4, 1995, Rabin joined Peres in singing "A Song for Peace," the anthem of the left. Leaving the rally, he was shot twice by Yigal Amir, a twenty-five-year-old religious fanatic. Rabin died shortly afterward in nearby Ichilov Hospital.

THE ENTIRE COUNTRY, the entire world, went into shock.

So did I.

Receiving the news in the small apartment Sara and I rented in Jerusalem, I experienced a genuine shudder of horror and grief.

How could anyone commit this madness?

Rabin was a hero of Israel. As a young officer in Israel's War of Independence, he led the force that opened the road to beleaguered Jerusalem. As chief of staff, he prepared and led the army for the great victory in the Six-Day War. As prime minister, he bore the ultimate responsibility to launch the daring rescue at Entebbe.

Whatever our political disagreements, I never forgot all this. I remembered my first meeting with him and Father some twenty years earlier and his visit to our *Shiva* after Yoni's death. Many other meetings we had fleeted through my mind.

This was a tragedy of historic proportions. It was not so because it "killed peace." It didn't, as the bombs exploding around us following the Oslo Accords clearly showed.

It was horrendous because a leader of Israel had been murdered by one of our own. This had not happened for two millennia, since the internecine battles between Jewish sects fighting each other on the walls of Jerusalem while the Romans besieged the city in 70 CE.

Begin himself understood this, as he demonstrated in 1948 when he stopped an armed response by the Irgun to the sinking of their ship *Altalena*, in which sixteen of their members had been slain. Begin's decision averted a potentially disastrous civil war.

The days after Rabin's assassination were packed with emotion. Many world leaders came to his funeral. President Clinton gave a moving eulogy. Official and unofficial ceremonies were held in Rabin's memory. In all these gatherings the religious right and I were implicitly or explicitly blamed for Rabin's murder.

My repeated calls to my supporters before the fateful assassination to view Rabin as a misguided political adversary who will be replaced in elections were tossed aside.

My antagonists in the press and on the political left constantly accused me of being an "Enemy of Peace" and an "Inciter of Political Violence." These outrageous and false claims were endlessly repeated and accepted as uncontestable truth by the elites in Israel and abroad.

They were given an added boost by a nighttime demonstration against the Oslo Accords in Jerusalem's Zion Square. With several of the protest leaders I stood on a porch and addressed the crowd before us. *At least fifty meters away*, deep in the crowd, a young man stood holding a regular 8½-by-11-inch sheet of printer paper. It showed Rabin in a Nazi uniform. Live Israeli television cameras focused in on the page, making it appear that everyone in the rally could see this reprehensible rendering of Rabin.

Of course, I didn't. Draw something on an 8½-by-11-inch sheet and see if you can see *anything* five meters away. You can't.

This didn't matter to my detractors, nor did the fact that it later turned out that the sign had been distributed by a Shin Bet agent named Avishai Raviv tasked with the mission of provoking the religious right to political extremism with precisely such antics in order to enable the security service to identify potential troublemakers.

In a completely incoherent inversion, I was accused of fomenting incitement against the prime minister with a mini-poster I could not even see, which had been produced by an arm of the Prime Minister's Office. In a late-night Knesset debate shortly after the rally, I condemned the use of the Nazi uniform and again explained that we were dealing with political adversaries and not with enemies or traitors.

Most books about me have been written by left-leaning journalists, who repeated the canard that I led the "extreme right-wing incitement against Rabin" or did nothing about it.

But there are some notable exceptions. One typically hostile biographer atypically wrote, "The charge that [Netanyahu] led the incitement has become accepted truth. But at no point did Netanyahu use the vocabulary of the far right against Rabin and his ministers. He didn't join in the chorus calling for 'Oslo criminals' to be put on trial for treason. He confronted those who were chanting 'Rabin the traitor,' admonishing them, 'He's not a traitor, [but] he's making a big mistake.' "[20]

After Rabin's tragic assassination, Joseph "Tommy" Lapid, a respected journalist who later served as a minister of justice and was the father of left-of-center politician Yair Lapid, went further. Debating a left-wing minister, he said, "There are those on the left who for political profit are making cynical use of Rabin's murder by denouncing the Likud for political gain.

"Netanyahu consistently condemned the violence and incitement. Why are you making political capital from the assassination?"[21]

In the months following the assassination, any criticism of Oslo was henceforth deemed "incitement" and an attempt to kill "Rabin's legacy." Never mind that this "legacy" morphed into fantasy. For all my disagreement with Rabin, he was not what the left made him out to be. In his last speech to the Knesset, delivered a month before his assassination, Rabin spoke against a full-fledged Palestinian state. He specifically said that in a final peace settlement, the "Palestinian entity," as he called it, would be *less than a state.* He insisted that Israel would maintain large settlement blocs in Judea and Samaria and in Gush Katif, in the Gaza district. He declared that Israel would maintain control of the Jordan Valley "in the broadest meaning of that term" as Israel's security border in the east. All this meant that under Rabin's plan, Israel would keep full control over

sizable parts of Judea and Samaria. Rabin also made clear that all of Jerusalem and its settled environs would remain under Israeli sovereignty.

"First and foremost," he said in his final Knesset speech, his plan
called for a "united Jerusalem, which will include both Ma'ale Adumim
and Givat Ze'ev, as the capital of Israel under Israeli sovereignty."[22]

This is far removed from the story that the supporters of Oslo try
to tell. They argue that had Rabin lived, he would have facilitated the
creation of a full-fledged Palestinian state with unrestricted sovereignty,
encompassing nearly all of Judea and Samaria, with half of Jerusalem as
its capital. This is simply not true. In many respects, Rabin's vision did not
conform to leftist tenets. Though the glorifiers of Oslo will never admit
it, at the time of his death Rabin's positions were closer to mine than to
theirs.

They also conveniently forget that the rosy reality of peace they envisioned did not blow up *after* Rabin's assassination. It blew up *before* it,
with waves of Palestinian suicide bombings emanating from areas that
Israel had handed over.

To give a terrorist organization committed to Israel's destruction
control of areas enveloping Israel's cities could produce no other result.

The Oslo fantasy that peace was at hand but was nipped in the bud by
a national tragedy is just that—a fantasy. Oslo in its original conception
had collapsed well before the assassination.

A quarter of a century later, most Israelis understand this. But in the
aftermath of the assassination, all honest appraisals of Oslo were cast
aside and furious blame was directed at anyone who had dared criticize it.

What happened then was an inversion of democratic norms. The action of one murderous criminal was used to delegitimize an entire sector
of the public. In a democracy, you can argue and debate as much as you
want, but you can't cross the line into violence or the threat of violence.
If you do, your action is illegitimate and derails democracy itself. Equally
obvious, an attempt to silence an entire citizenry because of the actions
of one murderous individual is not in keeping with how a healthy democracy functions.

The mourning for Rabin, which initially had cut across political lines,
was now being used as a political weapon against his opponents. Many
opponents of Oslo felt they were being accused of complicity in Rabin's

murder. This blanket condemnation alienated a huge part of the Israeli public and was to have monumental consequences shortly.

Naturally, Shimon Peres was chosen by the Labor Party and the Knesset to replace Rabin. Unnaturally, Peres decided not to hold snap elections immediately but to wait six months. Shimon always believed he lost the 1981 elections to Menachem Begin because Begin bombed Iraq's nuclear reactor shortly before the elections.

Incredibly, to the end of his days Shimon told me and others that this action was a mistake that was driven purely by political consideration. In a peculiar way it was. Begin later said that he ordered the bombing because he was convinced that if Peres became prime minister he would never give the order to destroy the reactor, even though Saddam was fast developing a capacity to perpetrate another genocide against millions of Jews.

Now Shimon committed another spectacular blunder, this time in the political field. Some speculated that he postponed the elections against me because he didn't want to get elected on "Rabin's coattails." Besides, the polls gave him a huge advantage of some 35 percent over me. What could possibly happen in a few months?

A lot, actually.

For one, the incessant campaign blaming the right for Rabin's murder created a boomerang effect and motivated people to vote against those hurling these false charges. For another, I recovered my bearings and began to organize our election campaign. The real question before the voters was who would stand up to the pressures to relinquish Israel's security and prevent the establishment of an armed Palestinian state on the outskirts of Tel Aviv. I brought in Arthur Finkelstein, a sharp-witted American campaign consultant. He was hopeful from the start. We met for the first time in a restaurant in Jaffa.

"I like what I see," he said.

"What do you see?" I asked.

"You," he said. "You walked into the restaurant and no one was indifferent. I work for politicians that nobody would give a rat's ass for. They'd walk into a room like this and no one would even turn their heads to see them."

"Okay, Arthur," I said, "that's a nice come-on. Now tell me how we win this election."

Arthur had no-nonsense Bronx street smarts. He combined an eye for reading polls with knife-edge ruthlessness. He laid out several campaign rules that were new to me and to everyone else in Israel. First, dilute your positive and negative messages to a few simple slogans. In our case it was "Netanyahu for a secure peace," contrasted with "Peres will divide Jerusalem."

Arthur's second rule was to keep politicians away from professional jobs such as polling, messaging and advertising.

His third rule was to have your professionals prepare a television advertising campaign that repeats your messages ad nauseam, "until it comes out of their ears."

These and other Arthurisms were later adopted by most political campaigns in Israel. Arthur himself was later employed by other politicians. But our initial work together had the excitement of novelty and freshness.

As the polls began to narrow in the months leading to the elections, the Clinton administration grew increasingly worried that I would win.

Bill Clinton and I had a civil relationship. I had first met him, as well as Hillary, before the 1992 elections in a visit to Washington in the Madison Hotel. They had asked that I "brief them both" on the situation in the Middle East. I made a mental note of the "both." (I don't think I'll detract anything from their interest in the region by saying that they were probably curious to hear my briefing because of my standing with Jewish and non-Jewish Americans.)

I saw Clinton again during the signing of the peace treaty with Jordan in Israel's Arava Valley in 1995. That year, I also sent him my third book on terrorism, *Fighting Terrorism*, and he sent me back a cordial letter. Notwithstanding his civility, I knew his administration would do anything to defeat me.

In fact they did. Totally committed to the idea of a fully independent Palestine, they were not aware that Rabin himself had been opposed to such a state.

Clinton sent his number one campaign strategist, James Carville, his pollster Stan Greenberg and his top team of experts to Israel to help tip the scales in Peres's favor.

Special envoy Dennis Ross would later say, "We did everything we could to help Peres," and Clinton's national security advisor, Sandy

Berger, would also later admit, "If there was ever a time that we tried to influence an Israeli election, it was Peres vs. Netanyahu."[23]

Normally such an outrageous and systemic interference in another democracy's elections would elicit outcries of protest from the press in America and Israel alike. No such protests were heard. Totally supportive of Peres, the press in both Israel and the United States was silent.

Though the odds were stacked against us, we weren't fazed.

"About Carville," Arthur said, "we can beat him."

Clinton and Peres organized an international peace conference in Sharm el-Sheikh a few weeks before the elections. Peres, Clinton, President Hosni Mubarak of Egypt, King Hussein of Jordan, and Arafat all showed up and danced the dance. Yet a few months earlier, soon after Peres was installed without an election as replacement prime minister following Rabin's assassination, King Hussein had sent me a message through his brother Crown Prince Hassan, asking: Would I meet Hassan secretly in London?

In a London flat the crown prince and I hit it off immediately. I liked Hassan. Straightforward, with a humorous streak, he didn't even attempt to hide his concern about a Peres victory. Though they wouldn't admit it publicly, he and many Jordanian officials I met over the years were concerned that an armed Palestinian state could destroy the Hashemite regime and take over Jordan.

Since suicide bombers kept exploding themselves in their midst, few Israeli voters were swayed by the grand convocation for peace in Sharm el-Sheikh. Yet while the gap between Peres and me had shrunk, it was still a substantial 10 percent difference. Everything was up to the television debate scheduled a few days before the elections. Arthur crossed his fingers that Peres would agree to do it. He did.

We tried a quick simulation with some of the Likud Knesset members playing Peres, but I felt it didn't do the job. I took a suite at Jerusalem's King David Hotel and spent the three days prior to the debate locked inside it with Arthur and Sara. We ran through all the possible questions and then some. The debate would be held with the two candidates not standing behind podiums but sitting down behind two opposing desks. I prepared notes, which I would spread on the desk before me. When the hour approached, I kissed Sara good-bye and shook Arthur's hand.

I knew this was make-or-break.

Going into the television studio, I disregarded the hostility of the journalists assembled there. Peres was an experienced and highly respected political leader. I was a novice. They were there to see the kill, and I was the prey.

The debate began.

I was focused and obeyed the eleventh commandment, "Thou shalt stay on message." Peres was not at his best. I suspect he was disgruntled at being forced to deal with a television challenge from an upstart like me. He must have remembered our first meeting some twenty years earlier, when I was twenty-seven years old and he was already defense minister.

When asked by the moderator if he had any question to ask me, he said dismissively, "I have nothing to say to him."

I knew then that I had won the debate. Arthur was pleased. The elections were two days away and the outcome of the debate could help decide the race.

"If we had another two days, the rollout effect of the debate would give us a clear victory. This will be close," he said.

On election night we took some rooms in the Hilton hotel in Tel Aviv. Tensions were high as 10 p.m. neared, when voting would close and exit polls would be announced.

At 10 p.m. sharp, exit polls were announced. They all indicated that Peres had won. A big groan of disappointment arose from my supporters. So we didn't pull it off after all.

I called Arthur.

"What do you think?" I asked.

"I'm looking at the numbers. I figure this could turn, but on a dime," he answered.

I hadn't slept for several nights and I took a nap. At two o'clock in the morning I heard shouting from the adjacent room. I had taken the lead. It stayed that way till the end of the counting. I defeated Peres 50.5 percent to 49.5 percent.

At forty-six, almost twenty years after Yoni's fall at Entebbe, I became prime minister of Israel.

PART II

HIGHLANDS

25

PRIME MINISTER

1996–1999

Among the first to call and congratulate me on my election victory was President Clinton.

"Bibi, I've got to hand it to you." He chuckled. "We did everything we could to bring you down, but you beat us fair and square."

Quintessential Bill, I thought. He wasn't telling me something I didn't know, but here was the president of the United States admitting without batting an eyelash to a brazen intervention in another country's elections. Clinton's frankness was refreshingly politically incorrect. You could see how the famous Clinton charm carried him through a myriad of minefields. I let it go and said I looked forward to working with him.

When the news of my victory broke through to the American media, the White House briefed reporters that Clinton was disappointed but would carry on with the pursuit of peace. After all, wasn't the historic peace agreement between Egypt and Israel made by a Likud prime minister?[1]

Practical as ever, Clinton invited me to the White House a mere three weeks after the election. During the election campaign I had of course strongly criticized the Oslo agreements. This created an obvious dilemma for me. On the one hand, governments are guided by the continuity of international agreements. On the other, this agreement was seriously flawed and compromised Israel's security.

I resolved the issue by saying that despite my grave reservations, I would honor the agreements under two conditions: *Palestinian reciprocity and Israeli security*.

As Oslo was to be carried out in stages, I would proceed to the next stage, known as the Hebron Agreement, only if the Palestinians kept their side of the bargain, foremost on matters relating to security. I insisted that the Palestinians live up to their pledge to rein in terrorism and to jail Hamas terrorists. If they did their part, I would do mine.

"If they'll give, they'll get" was the way I put it, along with a corollary: "If they won't give, they won't get."[2]

With the exception of the hard right who wanted me to tear up the Oslo agreement outright, most right-of-center and centrist opinion agreed with my policy. Israelis were tired of voluntarily ceding things to the Palestinians and receiving terror in return.

I explained all this to Clinton when we met in the White House. He asked me if I would honor the Hebron Agreement. I said that under the twin principles of reciprocity and security I would.

Shimon Peres had signed the Hebron Agreement, which promised that Israel would vacate our troops from the Arab neighborhoods of the city of Hebron. Israel would retain its troops in Hebron's ancient Jewish Quarter and in the Cave of the Patriarchs, where the Fathers and Mothers of the Jewish nation were buried—Abraham, Isaac and Jacob, alongside Sarah, Rebecca and Leah.

It was left to me to carry out this agreement, a highly emotional challenge given that Hebron was the oldest Jewish settlement, dating back some 3,500 years. Moreover, nearly all its Jewish residents had been murdered or expelled in a massacre in 1929. Their descendants were among those who renewed Hebron's Jewish Quarter after Israel gained control over the city in the 1967 Six-Day War.

In Washington, Clinton received me cordially. Sara and I brought five-year-old Yair and eighteen-month-old Avner with us. We did not want to leave them for a full week without their parents.

Clinton kindly put us up at the presidential guest quarters, Blair House, the first of eleven such stays during my fifteen years as prime minister. By the time of my last visit there in 2020, our children had matured and so had some of the original staff, who reminisced with us about our first visit twenty-four years earlier.

Clinton was always kind to my family. We brought Yair and Avner with us to Washington one other time during the Clinton presidency. On that visit, Sara was en route to an event at a Jewish school in Washington.

"Ma'am," the American Secret Service agent attached to her suddenly said, "the president is inviting you and the boys to the Oval Office."

"But I have a scheduled event at the school," Sara said.

"Ma'am, when the president of the United States invites you, I think you should go," the agent advised her.

Sara quickly turned around, picked up the boys and went to the White House. Clinton was a very gracious host. When Yair saw a multicolored baton on the president's desk, he asked Clinton, "What's that stick?"

"That's an African chief's baton," the president answered.

"What's a chief?" asked Yair.

"That's like your father," Clinton explained.

The nearly two-year-old Avner didn't remain idle. He threw the Oval Office sofa pillows on the floor and jumped up and down on them.

"Just like my two-year-old nephew," Clinton laughed.

Back during our first visit to Washington, Vice President Al Gore held a big reception for us, attended mostly by leaders of the American Jewish community.

"Bibi," Gore announced to the guests, "I've done some research on you. I found that on your high school soccer team you played left forward," he said, eliciting a burst of laughter.

"That's right, Al," I retorted, "but I always kicked to the right!"

More laughter.

While I was briefing congressional leaders, Clinton invited Sara to a tour of the Oval Office. Throughout his meetings with me he appeared cordial and friendly. I later learned that he took offense at some of the things I said or the way I said them at our joint public appearances. He felt I wasn't deferential enough.

"Who's the f-ing leader of the free world?" he is said to have complained to his aides.

I certainly didn't want to offend the president and in retrospect I wouldn't change the substance of anything I said. But I may have overreacted in my tone to the White House campaign of political pressure that preceded and accompanied the visit.

Clinton wanted me to continue on two political tracks, the Palestinian and the Syrian one, and to make far-reaching concessions in both. His staff briefed the Israeli press, saying, "We will not put the negotiations with Syria on ice."[3]

I countered that Syria would have to first dismantle the headquarters of the myriad terrorist organizations housed in Damascus, just as the PLO would have to fight and jail Hamas terrorists, cancel its Covenant, which called for Israel's destruction, and stop their terrible antisemitic indoctrination of Palestinian schoolchildren, who today are still being taught to seek our annihilation.

This last point, which exposes a major reason the Palestinian-Israeli conflict lingers, is seldom covered by the media or discussed by Western elites.

My political and security demands of the Palestinian side were in the spirit of the Oslo Accords but not what my American hosts wanted to hear, so they simply chose not to address them. Instead they preferred to focus on the expectation that I should meet Arafat as soon as possible "to iron things out."

I left the White House knowing that I was dealing with a US administration totally in the grip of the Palestinian Centrality Theory. It held that Palestinian grievances were the heart of "the Middle East conflict," ignoring the conflicts in the Middle East that had nothing to do with Israel. White House officials simply refused to believe that Palestinian violations of Oslo were rooted in a refusal to genuinely recognize Israel, arguing instead that Palestinian grievances were rooted in the expansion of Israeli settlements, just as they believed that Syrian antagonism to Israel was rooted in our presence on the Golan.

The overriding axiom was that the Palestinians would not make peace unless we withdrew from Judea and Samaria and Gaza and that Syria would not make peace unless we withdrew from the Golan. The conclusion of this line of thinking was not complicated: get Israel to withdraw from all these territories and you'll have peace.

But all this flew in the face of the facts. Palestinian and Syrian grievances against Israel were not rooted in Israel's holding on to this or that territory. That's why they attacked us from the Golan, Judea and Samaria, and Gaza when those areas *were* in their hands. Their grievances were directed against Israel's very existence, in *any* territory.

The inability of America's diplomats to see this simple truth remains astonishing. But to face it they would have to chuck the sacred "territory for peace" equation.

That formula could work with Egypt because President Anwar Sadat didn't seek our destruction, but it couldn't work with the Palestinians because they did. That the Palestinians were able to pull the wool so easily over the eyes of American officials was no small achievement for Palestinian spokespersons like Hanan Ashrawi and Saeb Erekat. They put a human face on the Palestinian annihilationist goal and persuaded the world that all that was necessary to advance peace were Israeli territorial withdrawals.

In this they received enormous help from the Israeli left and the Israeli media. If Israelis agreed with this claim, why shouldn't the rest of the world?

You didn't need to be a genius to understand that as long as the Palestinians and others clung to an ideology hell-bent on destroying Israel, Israeli withdrawals wouldn't advance peace. Rather, they advanced terror and war because the territories we vacated were taken over by forces committed to our destruction who used it launch attacks against Israel.

None of these simple facts had registered with generations of foreign service specialists. Now it was the turn of a new slate of Clintonite aides, mostly Jewish, to take on what US envoy Aaron Miller called "a mission" to bring about a historic peace.[4] They didn't let the facts get in their way.

The reason withdrawals didn't produce peace, they argued, was not that the underlying Palestinian goal was to eliminate Israel but that there hadn't been *enough* withdrawals. This led to their second inescapable conclusion. To get more withdrawals they needed to overcome the real "obstacle to peace," namely, me.

American policy was therefore geared to place maximum pressure on me to withdraw from territory or to remove me from office, something they had failed to do in the recent elections but would seek to do again next time around.

Surprisingly, this line of thinking didn't change even after I left office. A succession of Israeli leaders who came after me—Ehud Barak, Ariel

Sharon and Ehud Olmert—offered the Palestinians and Syria unimaginable and dangerous concessions, even more than Rabin and Peres had offered before me. They all failed to get peace.

Even then, the messianic diplomats in Washington still didn't get it. They didn't understand that the PLO, the so-called moderate faction in the Palestinian camp, would not abandon its goal of destroying Israel. It sought to first reduce Israel to indefensible boundaries by using American and international pressure. Once that was achieved, the ultimate goal—wiping out the Jewish state altogether—would be that much closer.

These "moderates" were challenged by the "extremists," led by Hamas, who believed that this two-stage approach and the diplomacy that went with it were unnecessary altogether. Terror alone would do the job. They were encouraged in this view when they saw that Israel continued to implement the Oslo agreements without demanding a full stop to terrorist attacks. In the years after the Oslo Accords were signed, they concluded that terrorism paid off.

One of the key goals in my first term as prime minister was to change the Palestinian perception that "terrorism pays" to "terrorism doesn't pay." I did this by insisting on security and reciprocity. I was open to measured concessions that didn't endanger Israel's security, but I insisted that these would not come about as a result of terrorism.

The American negotiators' most fundamental misperception of the region was that Israel was the *problem* in the Middle East. It was the *solution*. Its advanced technological society could help modernize the entire Arab world, if only Arab leaders deigned to recognize its right to exist and the security conditions that guaranteed that existence.

For too many years these Arab leaders waited for the Palestinians to make peace with Israel. This was a futile wait. The rejectionist Palestinian tail wagged the Arab world into political paralysis.

The Palestinians were not interested in having a state of their own *next* to Israel. They were interested in having a state of their own *instead* of Israel. That's why, when the 1947 UN Partition Resolution offered to create a Jewish state and a Palestinian state, the Palestinians rejected the state offered to them—while we accepted the one offered to us.

Time and again, the Palestinians galvanized the Arab world to try to annihilate the Jewish state, and their leadership never really gave up on that goal. But in successive wars, as Israel defeated one Arab state after another, some of the Arab governments began to make separate peace agreements with Israel. First Egypt in 1979 and then Jordan in 1994 made formal peace agreements with Israel, while other Arab countries developed informal ties with it.

This led me to a far-reaching conclusion. The road to a broader Middle East peace between Israel and the Arab world did not go *through* the Palestinian seat of government in Ramallah. It went *around* it.

As far back as the 1990s, I understood that if we wanted a broader peace, we would have to go directly to the Arab capitals. As long as we kept going down the rabbit hole of seeking to first remove the Palestinian veto on peace, we would never get there. Palestinian politics are hopelessly mired in their extremist fantasy of annihilation. And there is always a Palestinian faction to out-Hamas Hamas.

To Clinton and his associates this was heresy, merely excuses and obstacles that I was piling onto the road to peace. Incredibly, as we will see, this view persisted in some quarters even after my government, working with the Trump administration, achieved four historic peace agreements with four Arab countries—the United Arab Emirates, Bahrain, Morocco and Sudan.

It is a mystery to me how otherwise perfectly intelligent people could fall into the trap of buying the bogus Palestinian narrative. They persisted on refusing to recognize that the real cause of the "Palestinian Problem" was . . . the Palestinians themselves! Their refusal to accept a Jewish state was the heart of the conflict.

I dwell at length on this here because from my first visit to Washington, the combined effort of successive American administrations and my opponents on the Israeli left branded me, a prime minister who would later make peace with four Arab states, as the sworn enemy of peace.

On the final day of my first official visit to Washington, I sat alone late at night in the exquisite Blair House library. I looked up at busts of Franklin, Washington, Hamilton, Jefferson and Lincoln on their pedestals. Whoever had selected those busts had gotten it right. I thought long and hard about my own strategy for securing Israel's future in the face of the challenges before me.

I would have to chart a course with an American administration that was at loggerheads with my beliefs, agreeing with American proposals that did not jeopardize Israel's security and resisting them when I thought they would. All the while, I would emphasize that it was our historical right and not only our might that justified our claim to the Land of Israel.

I would seek to build Israel's economic, military and diplomatic power to ensure its future and to achieve a genuine peace with those in the Arab world who actually *wanted* peace. Given the volatility of Middle Eastern politics, it would always need to be a peace built on Israeli strength and deterrence.

MY CRITICAL VIEW of American policy in the Middle East should not obscure my broader and enormous appreciation for America's role in the world.

It was the great misfortune of the Jewish people and all of humanity that the United States was not the leading world power in the first half of the twentieth century. Conversely, it was our great fortune that in the second half of the twentieth century the United States emerged as the greatest power on earth.

Not accidentally, the first half century was marked by Western weakness, culminating in tragedies including the unimaginable Holocaust, while the second half was marked by American strength in defense of freedom, including the triumphant rise of the Jewish state.

America was the guardian of liberty worldwide. As a nation founded on the idea of a new promised land, it had a natural affinity for the rebirth of the Jewish nation in the original Promised Land. Israel was seen by most Americans as a plucky and valiant democracy in the heart of the Middle East, sharing the same values with Americans and willing to fight for them.

Gradually, and especially after Israel's stunning victory in the Six-Day War, America showered Israel with vital military assistance and gave it political backing in international forums. American entrepreneurs were the first to recognize Israel's vast technological potential and to invest in it.

In response, Israelis across the board were unabashedly grateful and unabashedly pro-American, even when the tide of fashionable international opinion turned against the United States during the Vietnam War.

Like Israeli prime minister Golda Meir, who also spent formative years in the United States, I never lost my admiration and deep affection for America and its people. The differences of opinion I had with American presidents on Middle East policy were like arguments within a family, and family is irreplaceable.

This is why I always viewed America as Israel's indispensable ally and why I took pride that as Israel's power grew, it increasingly became an invaluable ally of the United States.

I devoted my first speech before Congress to amplifying this message. The Republican-controlled House of Representatives invited me to address a joint session of Congress on July 10, 1996, and I was received warmly on both sides of the aisle.

The speech I gave, titled "The Three Pillars of Peace," stressed the importance of security and reciprocity in strengthening peace and countering terrorism, the need to foster democratic values to counter the spread of Middle Eastern radicalism, and the urgency of stopping Iran from developing nuclear weapons.[5]

To block the flow of deadly technology to Iran, I would soon meet with Chinese president Jiang Zemin and Russian president Boris Yeltsin. I repeated to them what I said that day before the US Congress: "The most dangerous regime is Iran, that has wed a cruel despotism to a fanatic militancy. If this regime were to acquire nuclear weapons, this could presage catastrophic consequences, not only for my own country and the Middle East, but for all mankind."

The international community, I said, must isolate such regimes and prevent them from acquiring weapons of mass destruction.

In my speech to Congress I also touched on another theme I believed was crucial for Israel's future—reforming its economy. Israel could not build its military power without becoming economically independent. This would necessitate a complete overhaul of the semi-socialist economic policies that had governed the country for decades. Another decade would pass before this vision of a true free market economy would be fully realized.

Achieving economic independence for Israel would also require gradually freeing Israel from dependence on American economic aid, which in my eyes had become a form of welfare.

"Israel has reached childhood's end, and it has matured enough to begin approaching a state of self-reliance," I said.

Against the advice of most of my economic advisors, I committed in my speech before Congress to eliminate over a ten-year period the annual $1.2 billion of American civilian *financial* assistance to Israel. Israel would retain the $2.2 billion annual *military* assistance that served Israeli and American strategic interests in the Middle East.

Since 76 percent of the funds given to Israel were earmarked to purchase American-made products, the US investment in Israel's security was also an indirect investment in American industry.

Critics grumbled that I had "tossed away a fortune for public relations." Not so. Unlike military aid, I viewed US financial aid as politically unsustainable and economically unwarranted.

Israel was no longer America's poor relative, and many in Congress were beginning to question allocating such a vast sum to an ally that was clearly not impoverished. Could this "welfare allotment" be preventing Israel from enacting long-needed reforms for trimming government fat?

Many in Congress thought so, and I agreed. My public commitment to end this assistance sealed the matter. By 2007, a phased ten-year drawdown of US financial aid was completed with no damage to the Israeli economy. On the contrary, many economists later saw that this move contributed to the country's economic development.

Returning to Israel, I was hailed as a "magician" by the right. I had gone into the lion's den in Washington and somehow emerged unscathed. I had not veered from my campaign pledges or from the policy of reciprocity.

But these were early days. For now, I had to concentrate on getting the government I had just formed to govern. Yet I made time for one memorable and inspiring meeting. It was immediately followed by a great tragedy.

ON FEBRUARY 3, 1997, Sara and I visited the Vatican. Once past the imposing Swiss Guards, we were guided to a long corridor. There at the far end waiting to greet us was Pope John Paul II. As we approached the pontiff, I could see his eyes brighten when he saw Sara.

"Polska," he said to her. "You look like a Polish girl."

"My father was born in Poland," Sara replied with a smile.

The pope took a genuine interest in us. Holding both our hands, he said movingly, "You are so young, yet you are the leaders of the Jewish people."

Speaking of the deep affinity of Christianity and Judaism, he said warmly: "You are our elder brothers."

Though he was already bent with early signs of age, Pope John Paul stood tall. I could not fail to be impressed with his charisma and conviction, his passion for freedom and human dignity, the twinkle in his eye.

With him, as later with Pope Benedict XVI whom I met on a visit to Israel, and Pope Francis, whom I met in the Vatican, I discussed Judeo-Christian relations. All three pontiffs were strong supporters of the rapprochement between Jews and Christians that had evolved in the last century. The three were also familiar with Father's book on the Spanish Inquisition, which took a fresh and nuanced historical view of the role of the church during that turbulent episode of history.

I invited Pope John Paul II to visit Israel. In Jerusalem in 2000, he left this note in the Western Wall: "We are deeply saddened by the behavior of those who in the course of history have caused these children of yours to suffer and, asking your forgiveness, we wish to commit ourselves to genuine brotherhood with the people of the Covenant."

Returning to Israel from the Vatican, I resumed business as usual the next day. As I conducted a cabinet meeting, my military secretary rushed in and interrupted the proceedings.

"Prime Minister," he said, "there's been a terrible accident. Two of our helicopters collided in midair near the Lebanese border. They crashed to the ground with dozens of soldiers inside."

I was stunned. The room went completely silent.

"How high were they?" I asked, hoping beyond hope.

"High, sir."

Seventy-three soldiers and airmen lost their lives that day in Israel's worst aerial disaster. I declared three days of national mourning and lowered the flags to half-mast. I requested ministers and Knesset members from my own party and across the aisle to attend the funerals. My heart, the entire nation's heart, went out to the families whose lives would never be the same again.

26

FIRST REFORMS

1996–1999

My very first reform as prime minister involved a bread-and-butter issue—literally.

When I entered the cabinet room for the new government's first meeting, I was astonished to see that the cabinet table was laden with a sumptuous breakfast: omelets, cheese, various breads, tomatoes, cucumbers, jams, butter, and cakes and cookies galore.

The cabinet ministers were already busy munching away, passing dishes to one another. It reminded me of the Shabbat Breakfast Club in the synagogue in Hull, Massachusetts.

"What's all this?" I asked the cabinet secretary in disbelief.

"Prime Minister, it's been like this for several years now," he answered.

"No longer," I said.

The following week, when the ministers arrived to the weekly government meeting, they found a more modest spread in the foyer. Anyone who wanted to eat could do so—there.

A quarter of a century later, that culinary reform has not been rolled back.

Of course, I soon had more substantial challenges on my plate. When I assumed office, Israel's economy was still largely semi-socialist and state controlled, dominated by a small number of powerful monopolies. Foreign currency was regulated and Israel trailed nearly all Western European countries in gross domestic product (GDP) per capita.

I was committed to changing this.

One of my initial reforms was to keep a campaign pledge to reduce the number of ministers, akin to US government secretaries, to eighteen.

I believed eighteen ministers was already an inflated number for running a small country—in fact, any country—and I stuck to that number throughout my three years in office.

This decision turned out to be penny smart and pound foolish. In Israel's tiny parliament of only 120 members, one or two disgruntled Knesset members can often bring down the government. I learned that limiting the number of ministers, even if it cohered with my message of thrift and good sense, was a totally untenable position and couldn't be sustained by future governments, including my own. There is a need to give cabinet seats to as many Knesset members as possible in order to ensure the coalition's stability in Israel's political system. In my later governments, additional ministers cost millions but saved *billions* in budget negotiations. The solid majority they brought with their appointment helped pass structural economic reforms that would not otherwise have been possible.

The second reform I pursued was privatization. Israel's government owned or controlled an enormous array of economic assets, often in wasteful monopoly arrangements that punished consumers with high prices and poor service. While almost everyone agreed that many government firms should be privatized, nobody did anything about it. Typically, a minister would agree that another minister's companies should be sold, as long as those under his own jurisdiction were not.

From the ministers' point of view this made eminent sense. Government companies are ripe plums ready for plunder. They offer reserved seats on the board of directors for political cronies who would then work to advance the ministers' political future. Prying these companies loose from government control would require a great deal of persistence, which I had in abundance.

By the end of my first term as prime minister, the total assets we privatized reached $4.5 billion, well exceeding the value of all privatized assets in the previous forty-eight years of Israel's existence. This included the privatization of Bank Hapoalim, the flagship of the Labor Party and the symbol of the old statist policies. It marked a watershed moment in Israel's shift to a market economy.

"Privatizing Bank Hapoalim in Israel is like opening McDonald's in Red Square," one of my colleagues quipped.

In my efforts to explain my economic policies, I often referred to the many successful Israelis who made it abroad.

"How come," I said, "we have amazingly successful Jews outside the country and very few inside? Could it be that we in Israel got all the lemons of the Jewish people and the Diaspora got all the able ones? Well, no, we know that's not true. Because when the 'lemons' leave Israel, they do very well outside. So it's not the people, it's the *system* we have here, and we've got to change it."

By far the most important reform I enacted in my first term as prime minister was to liberate Israel's rigid foreign currency controls. In 1998 Israel still resembled many third-world countries with regards to currency. Israelis could not take more than $7,000 out of the country without special authorization from Israel's central bank, the Bank of Israel. Returning from abroad, they had to redeposit and register all foreign currency they held inside the country.

This made even the simplest international economic transaction bureaucratic hell. A friend described how he had to get special authorization from the Bank of Israel to pay with dollars for a subscription to *Newsweek*.

Many now forget that these absurdities persisted well into the 1990s, when the world's economy was fast becoming a globally connected community. As goods, funds and services were transferred around the world at the touch of a button, Israel was being sidelined by its obsolete foreign currency restrictions.

Many Israeli firms were themselves developing the latest internet technologies for transferring and safeguarding these financial transactions for the citizens of other countries to use—but not their own.

As a believer in markets, my natural inclination was to do away with these obsolete restrictions. Some steps for currency liberalization had been made before me, but many more were needed. They involved first loosening the security belt kept by the government around foreign currency exchange rates, which were meant to keep the shekel within a prescribed range of other currencies. If the shekel got too high, the Bank of Israel would sell off dollar reserves; if it got too low, it would buy them.

Doing away with this arrangement was repeatedly urged by Professor

Jacob Frenkel, then governor of the Bank of Israel, but was vehemently opposed by the finance minister I appointed, Dan Meridor. He and many others in the financial bureaucracy argued that without government support the shekel would be greatly devalued.

These fears couldn't be ruled out entirely. But I came down on Frenkel's side, as a first step in my larger plan of eliminating foreign currency restrictions altogether. This decision was one of the factors that led to Meridor's resignation.

I appointed Professor Yaakov Ne'eman, one of Israel's leading business lawyers, to replace him as finance minister. It was the first time in Israel's history that a nonpolitician headed a major government department.

Ne'eman and Frenkel now joined forces to urge me to complete the lifting of all foreign currency controls in one dramatic act. Several prime ministers since Israel's founding had been urged to do this, but no one had dared because of the risk involved.

"This could bring about a currency collapse like the one that tumbled the Mexican peso," economic experts warned me, referring to the Mexican government's decision in December 1994 to lift currency controls.

"A mountain of foreign reserves would move out of the country and the shekel would become worthless," they added.

I listened to these warnings attentively, but I was convinced Israel could simply not proceed toward the year 2000 without freeing its currency.

Do you believe in free markets or don't you? I asked myself. Well, if you do, then get on with it.

I decided to risk it.

In February 1997, I began foreign currency liberalization. On May 14, 1998, on Israel's fiftieth Independence Day, I lifted nearly all restrictions.

At first nothing happened. I breathed a sigh of relief. But then money did begin to move in big amounts. Except that it moved *into* the country, not *out* of it. As foreign markets appreciated the liberalizing policy we initiated, the shekel's value stabilized.

Thus in one historic decision, my government brought to an end five decades of misery for millions of Israelis. They would no longer have to hide dollars under mattresses or be limited in making international bank transactions. They lived in a free country, and they were now allowed to do with their money whatever they saw fit.

The shekel was now a free-floating currency and could be traded anywhere in the world. For the first time since the founding of the state, Israelis were able to take their money out of the country as they pleased.

As it turned out, this move helped Israel weather future economic storms. Many Israeli companies now branched out to foreign markets, thereby building sufficient market and financial muscle to withstand downturns, such as the Intifada from 2000 to 2003 and the NASDAQ tumble in 2002.

In 2004, I removed the last minor vestige of these controls. Israel had become fully integrated into the first-world economy.

I followed a simple rule: *Whenever possible, remove barriers to trade. Money, trade and investments generally flow to the freer economies and away from the more controlled ones.*

So do customers, as competition drives down cost.

This was evident when we introduced competition in fixed-line international telephone calls soon after I got into office. In *one week* the cost of calling abroad went down by 80 percent, and it has stayed down since. Widespread usage followed and it was more equitable. Now people from the poorer neighborhoods or development towns could easily call their Israeli relatives and friends in Los Angeles or New York. Anytime objections to privatization were raised by the unions or their academic apologists, I would bring up the beneficial examples of privatized cell phones and international calls to fend off their arguments.

We achieved similar results by introducing competition in public transportation, enabling private bus lines to compete with Egged, the mammoth publicly subsidized bus cooperative that reigned supreme for half a century. Passengers paid considerably less on the privatized lines and enjoyed better service.

I now focused on quickly increasing the number of high-tech-trained engineers and technicians in Israel's colleges and universities. The high-tech sector's growth potential in Israel would be inhibited not by financial capital but by human capital, for the simple reason that Israel's state-controlled universities were not producing enough scientists, mathematicians and engineers. Absent an overall market reform in higher education, only government intervention could change the situation.

All Israeli universities received substantial government subsidies and were governed by a steering committee composed of the heads of the universities and the education minister. I convened the steering committee and asked Elisha Yanai, chairman of Motorola Israel, to present a program for the rapid increase in the number of Israel's engineering graduates. Then I spoke.

"Gentlemen," I said, "I have no desire to interfere in any way with academic freedom. I come from an academic family and I have the utmost respect for the study of humanities. But if in the present state of the world economy, the government's money can be used to fund either the study of seventeenth-century Tibetan poetry or microelectronics, then we must put it in microelectronics."

The university presidents agreed. We initiated a program that ended up increasing the number of science and mathematics graduates by 50 percent in six years, including graduates from private colleges whose accreditation my government expedited.

Many of these graduates had served in the intelligence and technological units of the IDF. They were used to solving problems quickly, often encouraged to cut red tape by improvising and innovating.

While Israel's competitors were playing technological chess, Israeli entrepreneurs were playing technological *speed chess*. With this attitude they were able to successfully carve specialized niches in the global technological market. All this meant that Israel could potentially create great economic wealth.

The crème de la crème of this technological corps was the military's Talpiot (hilltop) program, which culled a few dozen of the best and brightest recruits of each year's intake, trained them, and sent them on "think missions" in military intelligence, the Mossad, and other branches of Israel's security and scientific agencies. My cousin Benjie Machnes (another Benjamin), a former IAF pilot, was one of the founders of Talpiot.

I understood the entrepreneurial promise of the program and supported its expansion. But I also knew that the full realization of Israel's technological potential would depend on a much broader economic transformation that still lay in the future. As with bus lines, reforms would have to be introduced again and again across the economy in a full-fledged economic revolution.

On the face of it, the economic numbers were beginning to look good. Foreign investments had reached approximately $25 billion during my term, the number of new high-tech start-up companies had reached close to a thousand per year, and the deficit had been whipped into shape, dropping from $6.6 billion in 1996, when I entered office, to $2.3 billion in 1998. Foreign exchange reserves climbed to unprecedented levels, from $8.8 billion in mid-1996 to $22.7 billion at the end of 1998.

But despite the numbers, the economy had not yet undergone the structural revolution I had in mind. That would require my total attention, and I could not give it because for the rest of my term I would be preoccupied with fending off political pressure from the Clinton administration.

I realized that a free market revolution would require something else: *passion*—total unswerving passion by the finance minister, backed by the prime minister, to effect radical change. I realized then that if I was re-elected prime minister, I might have to personally take on the role of finance minister as well. I kept these thoughts to myself.

INITIATING THE DRAMATIC liberation of Israel from a controlled economy to a free market economy was one of two great changes in Israel's global standing that I initiated in my first term. The second was to begin to expand our international contacts beyond the traditional sphere of the United States and Western Europe, a revolution that would be completed in my subsequent terms as prime minister.

Nothing could replace our indispensable alliance with the United States, a partnership rooted in common civilizational values. But this did not mean that the United States should be our *only* ally. Thus, in my first term, I sought to warm ties between Israel and two other global powers, China and Russia.

After receiving American approval, Israel had agreed to provide the avionics to a Russian AWACS plane (an aircraft with enhanced radar) that would be sold to China and India. The US subsequently changed its mind and we had no choice but to abort the project. I visited Russian president Boris Yeltsin in Moscow in 1998. The first part of my meeting with him was devoted to this subject. The second was devoted mainly to the need for Russia to *not* supply Iran with nuclear or missile technology.

Yeltsin was friendly and, on that day, sober. But he was without energy. I could see that he already viewed Russia as a waning power.

Nothing demonstrated this decline more vividly than the government guest facility where our delegation was housed. A relic from the communist era, it had a huge old 1950s refrigerator, totally empty except for a jar of caviar and a bottle of vodka (which I don't drink).

Since I suffer from a bad back, courtesy of my military service in the Unit, my advance team had requested a hard mattress. If none was available, my team was instructed to ask for a board to put under the mattress. The mattress is the first, and most of the time the *only* thing, I check when I am given a hotel room.

I sat on the mattress. It was rock-solid.

I lay on the bed.

"This is by far the hardest bed I've ever laid on," I said to Sara.

Too hard, in fact. Lifting the bedsheets, I discovered why. The Russian chambermaids had put the board *above* the mattress and covered it with a bedsheet.

I relate this not to mock Russia. It underscores a widespread feeling of humiliation that I sensed in Moscow. The opening up of Russia from Mikhail Gorbachev to Yeltsin revealed that Russia had fallen hopelessly behind the West. This was a sentiment the next leader of Russia, Vladimir Putin, would be determined to change.

My visit to Beijing was friendly. China's leader, Jiang Zemin, received me warmly. He was genuinely interested in learning about the Jewish people and Israel, which were already held in high regard in China thanks to our contributions to Chinese agriculture. Jiang Zemin expressed to me his great admiration for the legacy of the Jewish people, who produced such geniuses as Albert Einstein.

"The Jewish people and the Chinese people are two of the oldest civilizations on earth," he said, "dating back four thousand and five thousand years, respectively."

I agreed, adding India to the list.

"But there are one or two differences between us," I said. "For instance, how many Chinese are there?"

"One point two billion," replied Jiang Zemin.

"How many Indians are there?" I pressed on.

"About one billion."

"Now how many Jews are there?" I queried.

No answer.

"There are about twelve million Jews in the world," I said.

Several Chinese jaws dropped in the room. This number of people could be contained in a large suburb of Beijing.

"Mr. President," I said, "since the Jews have been around for thousands of years, that is a remarkably low number. Two thousand years ago the Jews constituted ten percent of the population of the Roman Empire. Today there should have been two hundred million Jews."

"What happened?" asked the Chinese president.

"Many things happened," I replied. "But they all boil down to one big thing. You, the Chinese, kept China; the Indians kept India; but we the Jews lost our land and were dispersed to the four corners of the earth. From this sprang all our calamities, culminating in our greatest catastrophe, the Nazi Holocaust in the twentieth century. This is why for the last two thousand years we have been trying to retrieve our homeland and re-create our independent state there."

I was trying to impress upon the Chinese leadership the importance of refraining from supplying Iran with nuclear weapons technology. That would jeopardize not merely the modern state of Israel but an ancient and admired civilization.

Jiang Zemin assured me that China was not selling such technology to Iran, something I verified just in case.[1]

These were early days in our relations with both China and Russia. The full force of Israel's technological capabilities was not yet perceived by these governments, because it had not yet been realized in Israel itself. It would be fully unlocked only after dozens of far-reaching free market reforms I would enact five years later as finance minister would have their effect. Yet a few glimmers could already be seen in the late 1990s.

I emphasized these capabilities on visits to two other Asian countries,

Japan and South Korea. There, too, and especially in Japan, Israel's technological potential beckoned.

On the way back from one of my visits to Asia, I was invited by the leader of Azerbaijan, Heydar Aliyev, to stop in Baku. I sent a reply that we could only do so at one in the morning.

"I don't mind," Aliyev responded. "We'll have an early breakfast and you will see the sun rise over the Caspian Sea."

In a Soviet-era guesthouse on the shores of the Caspian, Aliyev gave us a twelve-course breakfast, saluting "Sara Hanum" (Madame Sara) before each new dish. When the sun rose over the sea, we completed the feast by going out to the terrace. For Israelis used to seeing the sun set over the Mediterranean to the west, seeing the sun rise over a body of water to the east was an unusual sight.

And a welcome one, after the longest breakfast in our lives.

Twenty-five years later I visited Azerbaijan again. I stood with Heydar's son and heir, Ilham Aliyev, on the terrace of a glistering modern guest home built next to the old one. By then the relations between our countries, as between Israel and so many others, had undergone a complete transformation. Azerbaijan borders Iran. Having Israel as a friend didn't hurt. Tiny Israel was now ranked among the dozen most powerful countries in the world. The formula was simple. Power attracts, weakness repels.

How we achieved this transformation is not always understood. It was part of a deliberate strategy that from day one was central to my agenda.

THOUGH THE FULL rise of Israel on the world stage would be seen only after my tenure as finance minister and my subsequent terms as prime minister, we received an early message of appreciation for Israel's strength from an unexpected source.

In early January 1998, Saddam Hussein placed limitations on UN inspectors charged with monitoring a possible revival of Iraq's nuclear program. Tensions flared between the US and Iraq, raising fears that Saddam would target Israel once again in retaliation for an American military action. I directed the military to make defensive and offensive preparations for such a contingency.

In late January, Russia's deputy foreign minister came to see me with a message from the Iraqi dictator.

"Saddam asked me to convey to you that he has no plans to attack Israel," he said.

I passed back a pointed response:

"Tell him that's very wise of him."

NOTWITHSTANDING SADDAM, DURING my first term two great issues competed for my attention: American pressures for dangerous Israeli concessions and the rise of Iran. To these were added a succession of endless crises, some real and some manufactured by a largely hostile Israeli press.

27

SARA

From the moment I assumed office, the Israeli press was unrelenting in its criticism of me. This got worse as they realized I wasn't going to kowtow to their misperceived interpretation of Rabin's legacy and create the Palestinian Wonderland that in their minds would bring instant peace. I continued to insist on reciprocity and security and resisted pressures from the Americans for withdrawals that would endanger Israel.

Having been wrongly accused of shattering Rabin's legacy and the hope for peace, I was held responsible for deepening the despair of Oslo's staunch supporters and adding to the suffering of Rabin's family. This justified any attack on me, including attacks on *my* family.

Though we were a young couple with two beautiful little boys, and I was the first prime minister to have such a young family, and though Sara at thirty-six was the youngest wife of any Israeli prime minister, the press began to rip us to pieces.

The Israeli journalists' bias against us got so bad that even people overseas began to joke about it. Evangelical Christians, strong supporters of Israel and me, quipped that if I walked on water on the Sea of Galilee, the Israeli press would run banner headlines the next day saying "Netanyahu Can't Swim!"

As the prime minister's wife, Sara, who had completed her MA thesis in child psychology in 1996, put her career on hold. She diligently made the rounds of various charitable organizations, receiving virtually no attention or accolades in the press for her philanthropic work—nor for her many visits to bereaved families, with whom she formed a genuine bond. Her empathy for the suffering of others and her role as a doting mother and a daughter with absolute dedication to her parents were never mentioned or appreciated.

Instead, the press would latch on to some disgruntled former employees who left the residence or were fired. Sara's good deeds were simply non news, well hidden from the public. She sustained an endless campaign of character assassination.

Over time this became a burgeoning industry of defamation and lies, orchestrated and organized by leading Israeli press outlets and a few law firms specializing in preparing legal suits against Sara.

Ex-employees would be given fawning interviews and were patted on the back as long as they were useful. They were often provided free legal representation by leftist lawyers. Some members of our household staff were deliberately recruited while still working in the prime minister's residence.

The vilifications and falsehoods would not abate even years later, when Sara took a day job as an expert child psychologist for the Jerusalem municipality. The only prime minister's wife to hold a day job of any kind, and not a ceremonial post often designed for many prime minister's wives, she would go three days a week to Orthodox schools to help children and their families sort out problems, often dealing with broken families and children with emotional difficulties. Within that cloistered community of parents and children she was adored and sought after, "Sara the psychologist," an angel of comfort and good sense. She wore the obligatory long dress and covered her elbows, brought sandwiches from home and stood in line for the water cooler and coffee.

"She was," wrote one of her supervisors, a venerated senior psychologist, "a very effective, professional, and dedicated psychologist. She was respectful and humble. I was shocked to read the inaccurate and undeserved press attacks against her."[1]

This vicious onslaught went on for more than twenty years!

Returning home from work or a philanthropic event or from her work with children, Sara would turn on the television to learn of the latest Sara "scandal," as a new fabricated "affair" would cascade over our heads.

Eventually, with the rise of social media, many people caught on to the charade of press deception and concealment and began to appreciate her true character, her compassion, her unbelievable courage and her fortitude in the face of decades of disparagement and lies, something few if any public spouses had been subjected to for so long.

People began saying they *admired* Sara for being so strong. They appreciated her devotion to family, to schoolchildren, to lone soldiers, to Holocaust survivors and to bereaved families. Many testimonials about her genuine caring for people began to surface on social media.

One example will suffice, precisely because it was avoided by the press for years. Had Sara come from the left she would have received endless acclaim for it. Visiting a hospital, Sara befriended Mika, a gifted ten-year-old girl with cancer. For the next ten years she celebrated birthdays with Mika, got to know her parents and gave gave them comfort and advice. Mika would often come to the prime minister's residence and to Independence Day celebrations as Sara's special guest.

In 2018, Vladimir Putin invited me to Moscow. Since this coincided with the World Cup soccer semifinals, which were then being held there, Sara and I were invited to attend a match and were told we could bring two guests. The question arose: Should we would take our boys (Avner is a big soccer aficionado), or perhaps our staff members, who coveted the much-desired seats?

"Neither," Sara said. "We're taking Mika and another child with cancer who loves soccer."

Mika was unbelievably excited. So was Alon, a thirteen-year-old boy who had received a heart transplant in Croatia, as we would be attending the semifinals game between Croatia and England. He had also undergone chemotherapy and transplants in Israel and was confined to a wheelchair, with oxygen support. I rolled him up the ramp to the stadium and together with Sara and Mika we made our way to the VIP box.

When Croatia won, Alon was so ecstatic that he jumped out of his wheelchair, hands in the air, cheering with joy. Sara brought Alon and Mika to meet the president of Croatia, who was seated in the same box as us. They were given Croatian team scarves.

Alon thanked Sara and me. He wrote that we gave him a gift that made him feel even better than his wonderful medical team did. "When I was with them in the stadium, I felt they cared for me like Mom and Dad. I got to fly in the Prime Minister's plane and to ride in his car, to meet world leaders and to see one of the greatest matches ever. These were the happiest moments of my life."[2]

Alon died a few months later. Sara and I wept with his family.

Journalists hardly wrote a word when Sara later led an Israeli foreign ministry delegation to bring aid to an earthquake-stricken region in Guatemala, the first such visit by a wife of an Israeli prime minister. Sara and the delegation brought vital medicine for children who drank contaminated water and an Israeli contribution for a new village named in gratitude "New Jerusalem." She was escorted by Guatemala's president, received extensive live television coverage and was greeted with the warmest affection and respect. She came back to Israel to an ever-growing campaign of calumny.

Yet the steadily increasing appreciation for Sara's humanity and courage couldn't help but emerge. As the years passed, one of Sara's qualities that people began to notice was her ability to judge character. She could smell a phony a mile away. The public appreciation of this ability grew when, as she predicted, certain politicians turned out to be crassly opportunistic instead of idealistic, as they had pretended, and betrayed the voters' trust.

"Sara was right all along" was a common refrain that went viral on the internet in later years.

My young wife who was mercilessly attacked early on later evolved into a figure many Israelis admired, respected, and loved. They saw through the transparent smear campaigns, the bogus police investigations, the false charges that would escalate in subsequent years and the double standard applied to other political spouses. Many had had enough. Each new attack boomeranged and reaffirmed the view that Sara was the victim of an unending witch hunt intended to get at me.

This line of attack was directed not only at my wife but also at our eldest son Yair.

Early on in my first term as prime minister, Sara took on a Dutch nanny to help with our two little boys. Soon the nanny and Yair were satirized on a prominent television puppet show, which broke long-standing rules against the abuse of children in the media. Yair spent a week hiding under a desk in his kindergarten. When the nongovernmental "Association for the Protection of Children" was approached to intervene, its director tersely said, "Netanyahu's child does not deserve protection."[3]

Such a breaking of basic norms was grotesque. To make matters worse, Yair was subjected to an endless stream of abuse from other children. "Your father murdered Rabin," they would say.

Little wonder that when we were hounded by the press and chased by hostile paparazzi, Yair would take cover and shout at them, "Go away!"

I winced at the toll my service as prime minister was taking on my wife and son. The relentless attacks on them were and remain dagger thrusts to my heart. I had chosen to enter the fray to become prime minister, and they were the innocent sufferers of that decision.

But there were some exceptions. One Sunday morning in a cabinet meeting in 1998, I was handed a note. Four-year-old Avner had disappeared from his kindergarten. He was nowhere to be seen. I stopped the meeting. The police were immediately informed and began a massive search. Sara was beside herself. So was I. A quick check established the known facts. Avner's kindergarten teacher had told the children to come into the classroom to eat fruit.

"But I don't like fruit," a headstrong Avner responded.

Staying in the yard, he saw the gate open as a mother took her child home. Avner's security guard was elsewhere, patrolling the perimeter of the kindergarten. Avner walked out the open gate carrying his backpack, looking for Yakov, the driver who was to take him home a few hours later.

Not finding Yakov, Avner continued his search. He made his way down a spiraling road that served a nearby parking lot. Luckily no cars were on it, because they likely would not have seen the toddler as they took the sharp turns of the ramp. When Avner got to the bottom, he was about to exit onto the main road connecting Jerusalem and Tel Aviv.

But a toll booth with parking attendants stood in his way.

"Where are you going, little boy?" they asked him.

"I'm looking for Yakov," he said.

"Who is Yakov?"

"Yakov is Yakov," he answered.

"Who is your mother?" they asked.

"Imma," Avner answered.

"And who is your father?"

"Bibi."

The parking attendants went into brief shock. Brushing aside the momentary fear that they might be accused of kidnapping the prime minister's son, they immediately informed the authorities.

Sara and I breathed more than a sigh of relief as we embraced our son. For once, so did most of the Israeli press.

28

KING HUSSEIN

King Hussein invited Sara and me to a secret weekend rendezvous with him at his estate outside London. As we were flying to London we were informed that the king was hospitalized. We returned to Israel.

Hussein recovered soon after and the trip was rescheduled. Flying again to London incognito in a Mossad-chartered plane, Sara and I were brought to Hussein's stylish home outside the city. His staff prepared a kosher Friday night dinner, and the following morning Hussein and I met for the first time.

We hit it off. I assured him that I viewed the survival of the Hashemite Kingdom of Jordan as a vital Israeli interest and that, if necessary, we would intervene militarily to prevent its downfall.

Israel had threatened to do this once before, in September 1970, when it seemed that Jordan was about to be overrun by the PLO and invaded by Syria. The PLO had earlier flooded the country and begun staging terrorist attacks against Israel from Jordanian territory across the Jordan River, prompting the raid on Karameh that I participated in and many other battles. When Syria then threatened to intervene on behalf of the PLO, Israel reinforced its forces in the Golan, warning Syria to stay put. It did.

But Hussein had had enough. The blowing up of three international aircraft by the PFLP in the Jordan desert was the last straw. Declaring

martial law on September 16, 1970, he unleashed his army on the PLO
and killed thousands of Palestinians. From September 17 to 27, his forces
were deployed in Palestinian-controlled areas in what became known as
Black September, nearly triggering a regional war involving Syria, Iraq,
and Israel.

Under Hussein's ruthless attacks, many Palestinians sought to cross
the Jordan River into Israel for safety, voting with their feet on how they
truly viewed the "cruel and inhumane" Israelis facing them. The PLO
terrorists and their leaders escaped to Beirut, where they established a
new base of terrorist operations against Israel, until the IDF drove them
out in the First Lebanon War.

Though thwarted, the PLO's designs on Jordan lingered. Some 70
percent of Jordan's population are Palestinians, yet the ruling Hashem-
ites, originating in Saudi Arabia, relied on Jordan's Bedouin tribes to rule
the country. I believed that if Hussein were toppled, Jordan, with its long
border with Israel, would become a base for the establishment of a hostile
Palestinian state, which could then be used as a staging ground to launch
an all-out war to destroy Israel.

I addressed this common threat head-on with Hussein, and also
sought to allay any suspicions he might have had that I harbored any
ideas about "solving the Palestinian Problem" by making Jordan the Palestinian state. I told Hussein flat out that I had ruled this out when as the
Likud Opposition leader I supported the peace treaty Rabin had signed
with Jordan.

After lunch, Hussein brought Prince Hamzah, his fourth son and his
first by his American-born fourth wife, Queen Noor, to meet us. I got
the clear impression that he was grooming the boy for future succession.
But like Hussein's brother, Crown Prince Hassan, Hamzah would later
be pushed aside for the crown in favor of Hussein's older son, Abdullah. At any rate, that balmy weekend in London with the king was the
beginning of a comfortable relationship that served both our countries'
interests.

Then on March 13, 1997, an unforeseen tragedy occurred in the so-
called Island of Peace, a strip of territory on the banks of the Jordan
River. Under the Israel-Jordan peace treaty, Israeli farmers continued to
cultivate this parcel of land, which was guarded by Jordanian soldiers. Is-

raeli schoolchildren would take field trips to see peace in the making. On one of these field trips, a deranged Jordanian soldier gunned down seven Israeli schoolgirls from the Israeli town of Bet Shemesh.

Hussein called me and asked to come with me to see their families. On March 16, the king publicly apologized for the horror. We went together to pay our respects to each of the grieving families sitting *Shiva* in their homes.

Visibly moved, Hussein stood by me and said to their parents, "Your daughter is like my daughter. Your loss is my loss." The king knelt before them, his eyes moist with tears.

He touched my heart and the hearts of all Israelis. This contrasted dramatically with Palestinian celebrations after every cruel terrorist incident, and the Palestinian leaders' reflexive reaction to either commend the action or at most issue an inane statement "condemning violence from all sides." Hussein's humane response to the tragedy strengthened the relationship between Israel and Jordan even further.

In 1997, beset by Hamas terrorist attacks that murdered twenty Israelis,[1] I decided to strike back at the terrorist organization's leadership that had orchestrated these attacks from abroad. Targeting terrorist leaders was one of the most effective means of deterring and preventing future attacks.[2] This method of fighting terrorism had been adopted by successive governments before mine.

At my request the Mossad produced a list of several Hamas terrorist chiefs. The most consequential among them appeared to be Khaled Mashal, a rising figure in Hamas who pushed for increasing the terror campaign against Israel. For operational reasons he was not accessible in any of the "easy" countries, places where our agents would enjoy relatively easy access and also where there would be fewer complications if anything went wrong. The Mossad finally recommended Jordan, which enjoyed the first advantage but not the second. This made the importance of an efficient "in-and-out" plan paramount.

The method chosen to target Mashal was a fast-acting chemical agent. Nonchalantly tapped on the back of his neck, he would be mortally ill within hours. The source of the illness would not be immediately, if ever, understood, thereby achieving the removal of a dangerous terrorist leader without eliciting calls for vengeful retaliation. The attack on

Mashal would be carried out in Jordan's capital, Amman. I asked about the getaway plan and was assured that it would work.

Then everything went wrong.

The Mossad agents intercepted Mashal as he approached an office building in Amman and applied the chemical to the back of his neck. But it was anything but nonchalant. Mashal's security guards understood something was wrong and gave chase to the agents, who were apprehended by Jordanian police two blocks away. As Mashal was taken to the hospital in rapidly deteriorating health, what exactly had transpired was still unclear to Jordanian authorities.

I was informed of this calamity at Mossad headquarters by the intelligence agency's head, Danny Yatom. Appointed by Peres, Danny had been an officer in the Unit and had served as Rabin's military secretary. Though we were on opposite sides of the political divide and Danny would later serve as a Labor member of Knesset, we maintained the code of honor of Unit veterans, in those days still unbroken by political polarization.

"We've had an operational failure," he said straightforwardly.

After briefly discussing our options, I instructed him to fly immediately to Amman, thirty minutes away by helicopter, to brief King Hussein. No doubt, I knew, Hussein would be terribly upset. As Danny was about to leave, I stopped him near the elevator.

"Danny, haven't you forgotten something?"

"What?" he said.

"The antidote."

Though Israeli scientists had developed an antidote to the chemical agent, it had not yet been tried. But letting the Jordanians administer it was my only way to begin to sort out an otherwise impossible situation. If Mashal died in Amman, the crisis would spiral out of control. I needed to achieve three things—bring the Mossad agents back to Israel, save Mashal, and resolve the crisis with Jordan's monarch.

KING HUSSEIN JUSTLY felt abandoned and betrayed. Couldn't we have chosen a different venue for this operation than Jordan? he fumed. And if he released the Mossad agents, wouldn't he be accused of collaborating with Israel?

Extricating ourselves from this royal mess would require careful maneuvering, but it would be immeasurably more complicated if Mashal died. Danny Yatom had an Israeli specialist guide the Jordanian doctors in applying the antidote.

There followed a long and bizarre night in which the prime minister of Israel, the head of the Mossad, and the heads of Israel's other security agencies received hourly reports on the terrorist chief Mashal's progress. He teetered from death to life and finally, toward morning, we were told that the antidote had worked.

Step one completed.

Though suffering from a fever and flu, I kept my cool and focus during the long hours it took to get Mashal the antidote.[3] Yet I should have realized from the start that Jordan was an ill-advised location for such an operation. Better to be wise in avoiding pitfalls rather than clever in extricating from them.

On to step two. To pacify the frustrated King Hussein, I asked Efraim Halevy, a Mossad official who had an exceptionally close relationship with the monarch, to help with the negotiations. Over the coming days Halevy suggested a swap. We would release the ailing Hamas spiritual leader Sheikh Yassin from an Israeli jail to Gaza and in return Jordan would release the Mossad agents.

This release was further warranted, I was told, because Sheikh Yassin was in such bad health that if he died in an Israeli prison we would be accused of killing him, possibly inciting a backlash. Most of the heads of Israel's security agencies recommended his release. We would unload Yassin, get the Mossad men back, and let Hussein take the credit with the Palestinians for negotiating this outcome.

I authorized the deal. The swap was made on October 7, 1997, our agents were freed, and Yassin was released to his home in Gaza. Relations with Jordan eventually were restored to normalcy. Yassin didn't die of illness but did die seven years later, in 2004, during an Israeli air strike targeting Hamas leaders ordered by Ariel Sharon in response to an outburst of Hamas terror.

I knew I would face criticism for the deal but I remembered the lesson from my first clandestine operation: *When you're in a minefield, get out as soon as possible.* Make the necessary decisions, end the crisis, and face the music. It is bound to fade.

But it didn't fade that quickly. A cover story about me in the *Economist* was titled "Israel's Serial Bungler." It described the Mashal affair and criticized me for it. Though Mashal was an appropriate target and though the Mossad recommended Jordan as a venue, I should have nixed such an operation in a friendly country.

The *Economist*, usually a prescient magazine, predicted that I would be a total failure. The magazine was so slanted against my leadership that when I later led Israel's free market revolution, which served as a guide for many of the world's economies, they barely mentioned this great Israeli success. In the few instances they did, they edited me out of the picture. Like so many others in the British intelligentsia, they too had bought the Palestinian Centrality Theory hook, line, and sinker.

THOUGH RELATIONS WITH Jordan improved steadily, I noticed that after another meeting I had with the king they began to sour again for a seemingly inexplicable reason. I soon learned why.

My chronic lower-back pain, due to my youthful excesses in the Unit, often forces me to sit cross-legged during long meetings to ease the strain. This is simply not done in Arab society. You do not point the sole of your shoe at your interlocutor. Not being mindful of this, I did just that in my meeting with Hussein, who felt insulted. I sent an apology. We decided to patch things up in another secret meeting.

In 1998 we met again in Britain, this time on my way back from a visit to the United States. The meeting took place in another house that King Hussein owned in London where he and Queen Noor were staying at the time.

For some reason Noor did not know that Sara would be there as well. The queen came downstairs after a shower with wet hair, wearing jeans and a T-shirt. Things got off to a bad start when Noor said to Sara:

"You Israelis came to Palestine after the Holocaust and took the Palestinians' land."

"It's not their land," Sara answered. "It's been our land for over three thousand years."

I was never prouder of my wife.

King Hussein and I skirted this minefield and moved on. The relationship between Jordan and Israel cruised along comfortably.

29

FIRST SKIRMISH

1996

My first term in office did not lack other crises, which had begun almost immediately after I took office.

On September 23, 1996, some two months after I returned from my first visit to Washington, I decided to open the Western Wall tunnel. I was encouraged to do so by Jerusalem's new mayor, Ehud Olmert, and by Ami Ayalon, head of the Shin Bet security service.

The tunnel was built by the Maccabees 2,200 years ago and ran along the rampart later built by King Herod to buttress the Temple Mount. Since it was wide enough for only one person to pass at a time, tourists would come to its end and turn around to make their way back to the entrance before another group of visitors could enter. If I opened an exit at the tunnel's end, this would allow continuous flow in one direction and double the tourist traffic. This increased flow would also give a boost of new business to Palestinian shops along the Via Dolorosa, where the tunnel would open up.

With this improvement, a great number of pilgrims would be able to more easily visit the Western Wall, retrace the footsteps of Jesus through the stations of the cross on the Via Dolorosa, and visit the Church of the Holy Sepulchre. In one fell swoop they could tour the cradle of the Judeo-Christian heritage.

All that was required was to create an opening the size of a door at the northern end of the tunnel, which is what I now authorized.

At first nothing happened. Early the morning after I authorized the plan, I left for a meeting with French president Jacques Chirac in Paris and a late afternoon meeting with German chancellor Helmut Kohl in Bonn. Unlike Chirac, who was combative and unfriendly, Kohl was extremely friendly. A year earlier, when I was still leader of the Opposition, he had taken the unusual step of inviting me to Bonn. He had invited Sara and five-year-old Yair to come as well. In true Prussian fashion his staff had a timetable for Yair.

"Sara, you've got to see this," I said when I saw Yair's schedule. "Nine-oh-five at chocolate factory. Nine-oh-nine tasting of chocolate sample!"

Talk about a clash of cultures. But Kohl was anything but confrontational. A towering figure, he put his arm on my shoulder and said, "Young man, when you get to be PM don't worry about Europe. I'll take care of Europe for you." And he did.

But this current visit, after opening the tunnel, would be cut short. When I landed in Paris I received the first reports of Palestinian unrest and rioting. Arafat falsely claimed that I was tunneling under the Al-Aqsa Mosque to try to collapse it, and other such nonsense.

This wasn't the first time and far from the last that the Palestinians would try to spark a holy war with lies about the Temple Mount. They not only lie about the holiest site in Judaism; they try to erase historical facts by destroying archaeological artifacts that prove the existence of the Jewish temples.

In 1999, in the course of construction in the area on the Mount referred to as Solomon's Stables, the Waqf Islamic custodians were caught red-handed attempting to dispose of Temple-era artifacts found in truckloads of earth that they irresponsibly removed from perhaps the most sensitive archaeological site in the world.

My government put a stop to that with the help of private foundations that painstakingly went through the rubble and preserved many precious findings.

By the time I got to Bonn, the outrageous lies that we were tunneling under the Al-Aqsa Mosque had sparked a mini-war. Palestinian police were shooting at Israeli soldiers with whom they had gone on joint patrols only a few hours earlier.

I apologized to Kohl and said I had to return to Israel immediately.

The helicopter that had brought me was still spinning its rotors as I made my way back.

I landed at Ben Gurion Airport and asked my staff to arrange a phone call with Arafat. On the way back to Jerusalem I had already instructed the military to advance our tanks forward to face Palestinian positions.

In my office I picked up the phone and spoke to Arafat.

"Mr. Chairman," I said, always deferential in using this formal title, "we are in a time of crisis, so I will be brief and to the point. You have thirty minutes to call off your forces and effect a complete cease-fire. If you don't, I will send in our tanks and destroy your regime."

Silence.

A moment later, Arafat responded, "I understand."

The conversation ended.

Exactly thirty minutes later all fighting stopped.

Seventeen Israeli soldiers and some eighty Palestinian policemen died in the mini Tunnel War. In the aftermath, Palestinian terrorist attacks against Israel largely ceased. Arafat realized that my reciprocity policy was not limited to political affairs but extended to terrorism and violence as well. In the face of violence, we would respond with full force.

Quiet was restored.

President Clinton quickly resumed pressing for a meeting between Arafat and me. Since I had committed in the elections to respect existing international agreements, subject to Palestinian reciprocity, I agreed to the meeting. We met on October 7, 1997, at the Erez Crossing between Gaza and Israel. As I expected, Arafat was shrewd and calculating, though I was surprised at his tendency to lurch into non sequiturs until his staff brought him back to earth.

More often, his negotiation style was tactical. This included his fits of rage. While they were ineffective on me and my chief negotiator, Yitzhak "Itzik" Molcho, he tried them nonetheless. At one point, seemingly offended by something said by Shaul Mofaz, now chief of IDF operations, Arafat got up dramatically.

"This is Arafat you are speaking to!" he exclaimed and threatened to walk out. But at our urging he quickly sat down again.

I would soon counter that with a walkout threat of my own when Arafat wanted to discuss Jerusalem. Now it was the Palestinians' turn to calm me down. This was a predictable game, and predictably we delegated further discussion to our chief negotiators, Molcho on the Israeli side and Nabil Abu Rudeineh and Saeb Erekat on the Palestinian side.

An expert in negotiation, Itzik Molcho was a seasoned and much-respected Jerusalem lawyer. His ability to get on with people masked an inner toughness. I knew him from my teens, when he dated and later married my second cousin Shlomit. I trusted his judgment, his professionalism, and his discretion. The Molcho family came from a distinguished line of Sephardi Jews expelled from Spain in 1492. I often poked fun at Itzik, telling him he was a "Hidalgo," one of the aristocratic courtiers of the Spanish kings my father wrote about.

He proved immensely helpful in my negotiations with Palestinians, Jordanians, Americans, and later with Emiratis and Saudis. Molcho even developed a cordial relationship with Arafat. Months after the Tunnel War subsided, Molcho turned to the Palestinian leader.

"Mr. Chairman," he said, "what made you say that we were undermining the Al-Aqsa Mosque?"

"Don't you know that this is the place where Al Buraq [the prophet Muhammad's mythic horse] ascended to heaven?" Arafat replied.

"But Mr. Chairman," Molcho protested, "the door was opened in a tunnel hundreds of meters away from the Al-Aqsa Mosque. Al Buraq couldn't have ascended to heaven from inside the tunnel."

"Well, maybe he moved aside a few meters," Arafat said, literally side-stepping that one.

In my ongoing talks with the Palestinians I stressed my clear demand that the Palestinian side do whatever was necessary to prevent terrorist attacks against Israel. If it did not, I would consider using not only military force but economic measures as well that could cripple the PLO regime.

Arafat apparently got the message, because the number of Palestinian suicide bombers dropped precipitously. My policy had brought terror to its lowest level in the decade following the signing of the Oslo Accords, *three* fatal suicide bombings in the three years from 1996 to 1999, compared to *ten* such bombings in the three years that preceded my tenure and *103* in the equivalent period that followed it.[1]

A different way to illustrate the same result was given by a usually unfriendly but honest journalist in September 2001: "Yitzhak Rabin's second term as Prime Minister lasted 39.5 months and during this time 178 Israelis were killed in Israel and in the territories, an average of 4–5 a month. Peres served as Prime Minister 7.5 months and his monthly average was roughly 9. Ehud Barak served some 20 months and during his term 3 Israelis were killed each month. Benjamin Netanyahu was the most sparing in this regard. He served as Prime Minister for more than 36 months during which on average 1 Israeli was killed per month."[2]

Having begun to stabilize the security situation, I now turned my attention to the Hebron Agreement. Honoring it was the only *specific* commitment I had given during the election campaign. The right was upset that I didn't break my election promises, but this was the mandate I had received from the voters.

After improving the security clauses in the agreement, I carried out Israel's part of the deal in January 1997. I was accused by some in the settler community of abandoning one of our most cherished historical sites. I didn't. A quarter of a century later, Hebron's Jewish Quarter and the Cave of the Patriarchs are still firmly in Israel's hands. The nearby community of Kiryat Arba has doubled in size.

I made a mental note of the arrangement we made in Hebron. No one was uprooted from their homes, and separate access and security provisions were made for Israelis and Palestinians, which would stand the test of time. This example would help in formulating the Trump peace plan I would work on more than twenty years later.

After the Hebron Agreement there was the briefest of honeymoons with the Clinton administration. Clinton sent me a letter commending me for my "courage" for making a tough decision. He sent Arafat a similar letter. I thought that was peculiar since the only courage Arafat displayed was the courage to receive the Palestinian neighborhoods we had transferred to his control. But this was clearly as good as it was going to get.

"Netanyahu and Arafat are both allies of the United States," the White House briefed Israeli reporters.[3]

This was incredible. The democratically elected leader of the staunchest ally of the US and the leader of a terrorist organization that had murdered hundreds of Americans were put on equal footing. But such was the diplomatic mind-set of Washington in those days.

The administration suffered from double-barreled myopia. First, it refused to see that the core of our conflict with the Palestinians was the persistent Palestinian refusal to recognize a Jewish state in any boundary. Second, it refused to really internalize that Israel's government was dependent on a parliamentary system in which the prime minister could be toppled at any moment by the slimmest of majorities.

The US administration constantly sought to advance its misplaced messianic quest for a magical peace via "courageous" acts on the part of Israel's leaders, even if these acts meant political suicide. Would American presidents consider taking "courageous actions," such as, to use a historical example, far-reaching concessions to the Soviet Union if Congress could remove them from office *the next day*? Of course not.

Yet this didn't prevent American presidents and their envoys from attempting to tutor Israeli prime ministers, especially me, about the need for "courage" and "leadership." I was being lectured about courage from people who had neither risked their own lives in war nor their political lives. When such "leadership" wasn't forthcoming from me, this was proof of a clear failure of character by a politician guided solely by cynical and personal interests.

The conflict between national necessity and political survival is as old as democracy itself, but it didn't apply here. What stood in the way of the concessions I was pressed to make was simply my belief that they would greatly endanger Israel. So why make them? This too has eluded many American pundits. They might have noted that when I *did* believe certain measures were vital for Israel's future, I didn't hesitate to take them.

This was the case with my deciding vote for direct elections of the prime minister and with the politically suicidal economic reforms I later enacted as finance minister. Faced with decisions vital for Israel's future, I allowed no consideration of personal expediency to stand in my way.

Right after the implementation of the Hebron Agreement, Clinton invited me to the White House to celebrate the deal. His aides believed that I had been tamed and could now be led to the corral of settlement freezes and significant withdrawals on both the Palestinian and Syrian fronts.

Our honeymoon was cut short by my decision to build Jerusalem's Har Homa neighborhood. I made that decision because of Palestinian designs on our capital. From nearby Bethlehem there was a steady encroachment of illegal Palestinian housing that sought to penetrate Jerusalem from the south and connect with the city's Palestinian neighborhoods in the north.

I decided to put a stop to that by authorizing construction work on a barren hill facing Bethlehem. Rabin had also laid out plans for Har Homa's construction, but he hadn't given the final go-ahead.

I did.

Har Homa was in the municipal boundaries of Jerusalem drawn right after the Six-Day War. Israel never accepted any formal limitation on building neighborhoods within these boundaries, including under the Oslo Accords. Nonetheless, the decision to build Har Homa was met with severe Palestinian and international censure. Arafat demanded that I rescind the authorization. I did not.

As usual, loud protests ensued. The British foreign minister, Jack Straw, visiting Israel, literally joined hands with the Palestinian leader Faisal Husseini in a Palestinian march condemning the Har Homa project. He was supposed to have dinner with me that evening. I promptly canceled it.

For me, I said, that was the last straw.

The protests eventually died down; the Palestinian southern thrust into Jerusalem was blunted. Today Har Homa has forty thousand residents, a small city within a city.

For the Clinton administration, the fact that a Likud prime minister carried out the extraordinarily difficult and risky Hebron Agreement was, if not small potatoes, no more than a side dish. The fact that I dared build a new Jewish neighborhood in our capital? Now, that was a real outrage.

Clinton was furious. In truth it must be said that Har Homa also got Arafat off the hook. He was seldom challenged for not stopping incitement and various other Palestinian violations of the Oslo agreement. He could now say that the lack of progress in the negotiations was due to this project and the Israeli "aggression" it supposedly represented. The US administration constantly briefed the press against me in an attempt to pressure me to make concessions to Arafat. This would be the main subject of my next visit to the United States.

Landing in Washington in late January 1998, I prepared for my next round of discussions with the president. My first meeting was with the

Reverend Jerry Falwell, the evangelical leader and one of Israel's staunch-est supporters. With other Christian organizations, he assembled a packed house in DC's Mayflower Hotel that gave me a rousing welcome.

Evangelical support for the restoration of the Jews in the Holy Land has deep roots, stretching back to the Christian pilgrims who visited it over the last two millennia.

In the nineteenth century, British, American and European clergy-men started agitating for the return of the Jews to the Land of Israel.[4] Christian Zionists even preceded Jewish Zionists and were quick to sup-port their cause. In 1904, one of Herzl's closest associates, the Anglican priest William Hechler, was the only person who was allowed to join Herzl's family around his deathbed. It was to him that Herzl whispered his parting words to his followers: "Give my regards to all of them and tell them that I gave my heart's blood to my people."[5]

Evangelical agitation for the ingathering of the exiles and the Jewish restoration in the Holy Land became politically forceful in America in the closing decades of the nineteenth century. William Blackstone, a self-ordained evangelical minister and close associate of Dwight Moody, *the* evangelist leader of the day, drafted the Blackstone Memorial—a petition asking President Benjamin Harrison to use his influence on behalf of the Jewish people. He called on the president to persuade European leaders to prevail upon the Ottoman sultan to open the province of Palestine for Jewish settlement and the creation of a Jewish national home.[6]

"Why not give Palestine back to them [the Jews] again? According to God's distribution of nations it is their home, an inalienable possession from which they were expelled by force. . . .

"Why shall not the powers which under the treaty of Berlin in 1878 gave Bulgaria to the Bulgarians and Servia to the Servians [sic] now give Palestine back to the Jews? These provinces, as well as Roumania, Mon-tenegro, and Greece, were wrested from the Turks and given to their natural owners. Does not Palestine as rightfully belong to the Jews?"[7]

Among the 431 prominent Americans who signed the petition were John D. Rockefeller, J. P. Morgan, future president William McKinley, Chief Justice Melville Fuller and many congressmen.

Although the Blackstone Memorial did not have an immediate impact on President Harrison, it is considered the first draft of America's proposed response to the active debate at the time, known broadly as the Jewish question, about what civil and national status Jews should have. Years later, in 1916, Blackstone presented a revised version of his petition to President Woodrow Wilson and saw the principles he'd argued for enshrined in American law in 1922 under the Lodge-Fish Resolution that called for "the establishment in Palestine of a national home for the Jewish People."[8]

In the closing decades of the twentieth century, evangelicals furthered their status as Israel's most ardent backers. To evangelicals, the establishment of the Jewish state was the miraculous realization of Biblical prophecy.

In places as far afield as Scandinavia, Africa, Polynesia, Brazil and Korea they established bastions of support for Israel. But it was the powerful American evangelical community that exerted the most significant influence.

They believed in the unity of Jerusalem, supported the Jewish communities in Judea and Samaria and raised funds to help the needy in Israel. Gradually the traditional suspicion of Israelis toward Christian proselytizing gave way to a warm, appreciative attitude. The evangelicals were not out to convert Israel's Jews to Christianity but they were unabashedly seeking to convert many governments to more supportive attitudes to Israel.

Rabin was the first prime minister to recognize the budding influence of evangelicals; Begin and Shamir appointed special liaisons to the evangelical community; I embraced evangelicals openly and wholeheartedly. I appreciated the unstinting support of evangelical leaders such as Pat Robertson, Jerry Falwell, Robert Jeffress and Mike Evans. My Dutch friend Jan Willem van der Hoeven established the International Christian Embassy in Jerusalem. Pastor John Hagee established Christians United for Israel, a potent and extremely influential organization that worked tirelessly to promote Israel's cause in America and elsewhere.

When evangelicals visited Israel, I was impressed with their familiarity with the Scriptures and ancient Biblical sites. They in turn were surprised at my familiarity with the Gospels and Christian history, which I gleaned from reading Klausner and other writers. I was moved by their spiritual devotion to Judeo-Christian tenets, and the depth of feeling they experienced as they followed the footsteps of Jesus from the Sea of Galilee to the Temple Mount in Jerusalem.

I visited Christian churches of all denominations throughout Israel, engaging in historical and theological discussions with their devoted and usually thoughtful clergy.

Walking one day in 2001 with my family in the Valley of the Cross, next to my home in Jerusalem, I knocked on the door of its fifth-century Greek Orthodox monastery. A young Greek priest kindly showed us about, the first time I had entered the imposing structure since I played as a child in the fields outside its massive walls. We were deeply saddened a few months later to learn that this young priest was murdered by terrorists on the outskirts of Jerusalem.

My alliance with Christian believers was thus both emotional and conceptual. The initial opposition to this alliance from Orthodox Jews had dissipated and was replaced by antireligious leftists who sometimes paradoxically evoked religious arguments. Didn't I know that the evangelicals plan to convert all the Jews to Christianity at the End of Days?

Confronted with this assertion, I fell back on Rabin's response: "We'll argue about that when we get there."

Now, in 1998, faced with Clinton's pressure campaign, I turned to Israel's evangelical allies for help.

They gave it generously.

Clinton was decidedly unhappy with my ability to rally their support, especially when I met evangelical leaders before I met him in Washington in 1998, and he told me as much. He undoubtedly understood Falwell's proclamation to me that "we stand with Israel!" as a pledge to counter the president's pressure on me. But just then the news began to break about an affair the president purportedly had with one of his female interns. A few mean tongues wagged that the Jewish Monica Lewinsky was a Mossad agent I had planted to embarrass the president. It wasn't even a bad joke.

My official meeting with Clinton dealt mostly with the Palestinians, but I raised the issue of Iran and the efforts being made in Congress to pass sanctions on Russian companies supplying Iran with ballistic missile technology.

Clinton suggested a more intimate evening meeting at the residence floor in the White House.

In an attempt to address my concerns about Israel's security in any future peace agreement, we discussed the possibility of an Israeli-American defense treaty. I was willing to consider this under the condition that Israel would retain complete freedom of action to defend itself against any threat. The possibility of such a treaty presented many challenges, including the question of whether Israeli soldiers would be required to fight for American interests in other parts of the world, whether the US would have military bases in Israel, and many other complex issues.

We didn't get very far in exploring them. Clinton would periodically exit the room and come back a few minutes later. I assumed he was dealing with the Lewinsky crisis. I didn't say a word about it, but I kept my comments short to enable him to close the meeting as soon as he chose. I greatly appreciated the fact that he put a brave face on it all, maintaining his focus in our discussions. We called it an early night.

The next day the Lewinsky affair exploded. Washington could talk of nothing else. That pretty much wrapped up our visit.

I asked my staff to prepare material on a possible US-Israel defense treaty, but we never really got back to it. In the coming months Clinton was naturally consumed with extricating himself from the Lewinsky affair.

30

WYE RIVER

1998

The furor created by the Lewinsky affair in no way lessened the Clinton administration's frustration with the lack of progress on their cherished quest for peace. In fact that frustration may have even increased.

In late 1998, I visited the United States again for the annual meeting of the Jewish Federations of North America, to be held in Indianapolis. The president refused to see me, so I skipped Washington and went straight to Indianapolis. From there I flew to Los Angeles, where my friend the Hollywood producer Merv Adelson gathered stars like Kirk Douglas to stand by Israel and express their support in various ways.

In an earlier visit to Los Angeles when I was deputy foreign minister, Merv had organized a pro-Israel banquet and placed the actor Gregory Peck next to Sara. Peck told her that his mother always wanted him to be a doctor or a lawyer. He would later tell his mother, "You see, I am all that you wanted me to be. As an actor I can be a doctor, a lawyer and so many other things."

These were days when Hollywood was still unabashedly sympathetic to Israel. But my visit was overshadowed by "the meeting that never was," since Clinton and I were in Los Angeles at the same time. Israeli reporters gleefully pointed out that the closest I got to Clinton was when our planes were parked next to each other at Los Angeles International Airport.

Around the time of my visit to the US, I received a message from

Ronald Lauder, Estée Lauder's son who later became head of the World
Jewish Congress. I had befriended him in New York during my tenure as
Israel's ambassador to the UN. Lauder told me that a Lebanese intermediary on behalf of Syria's dictator, Hafez Assad, had approached him with
an entreaty to begin secret negotiations with Syria. Would I be prepared
to send him discreetly to Damascus as my unofficial envoy?

I said yes, provided that he kept the US out of it.

Lauder went back and forth several times between my office in Jerusalem and Assad's office in Damascus. He amused Assad with his New
York brand of Jewish humor. In turn Assad passed on the message that he
was prepared to make peace with Israel in exchange for a full withdrawal
from the Golan.

When Lauder came back with my demand that we stay on top of the
Heights, Assad brushed this off.

"Syria has a decrepit army while Israel is a superpower. What do they
have to worry about?" he said.

This hardly convinced me. After to'ing and fro'ing, and after several
more of Lauder's visits, I finally got Assad to agree to a potential arrangement in which Israel would stay atop the Golan Heights. The border
between Israel and Syria would be *on* the Golan and not below it on the
shore of the Sea of Galilee. Israel would retain the high ground and be in
easy striking distance of Damascus if the peace broke down.

To this day I am not sure why Assad was negotiating secretly with
me. He too was under heavy American pressure to negotiate a deal with
Israel. He may have gotten wind of one of my first acts after I was elected
prime minister, when I insisted that Secretary of State Warren Christopher cancel Rabin's "deposit" for a full Israeli withdrawal from the Golan
and recognize the importance of the territory to Israel.

I asked Secretary Christopher to write me a letter affirming that the
Golan was critical to Israel's security, and he did. Although at the administration's request I kept the Christopher letter discreet, it was a major
diplomatic achievement that Assad may have learned about through his
own channels.

I suspect he was loath to negotiate through the US, which he dis-
trusted. Perhaps he thought that if I could stand up to the Americans on
the Golan, there was no reason to negotiate through them. He might

have thought, "Let's see what I can get from Israel on my own. They are the ones who make the decisions anyway." But as he would soon find out, it wouldn't be easy to get anything at all.

My own interest in holding these negotiations was to seek a tolerable alternative to the relentless American pressure for far-reaching concessions on the Palestinian front, concessions that would effectively reduce Israel to a twelve-kilometer-wide strip along the Mediterranean with our backs to the sea. If I could achieve a responsible deal with Syria with minimal Israeli withdrawals and maximum security, I might earn just enough political capital to withstand American pressure for irresponsible and dangerous withdrawals in Judea and Samaria and Gaza.

That's why I kept the US in the dark about these negotiations. Though I assumed US intelligence was aware of their existence, I shared nothing with Clinton's emissaries.

The deal with Syria never came through. Assad presented its outline to the new chief of staff of the Syrian army. A high-ranking Druze in Syria, he felt he had to be more Syrian than the Syrians.

"How can we accept such a surrender?" he fumed at his boss.

Since Syria's chief of staff refused to accept my precondition that Israel stay on the Golan, Assad nixed the deal. I stopped all further negotiations.

The deal with Syria aborted, I now had to face American pressures again on the Palestinian front. The White House, the State Department and the president himself periodically issued statements saying that Israeli settlements were "an obstacle to peace." Despite my repeated protests, they barely said a word about the constant Palestinian violations of the Oslo Accords and the unceasing incitement by official Palestinian agencies that regularly called on Palestinians to annihilate Israel and kill Jews wherever possible.

Such statements flooded the press, the schools and virtually every other institution controlled by the Palestinian Authority. Arafat's government named public squares and government buildings after terrorist killers who murdered Jews, the greater the number of Jewish victims the greater the honor.

Apparently in the American view this was *not* an obstacle to peace. Neither was the revolving-door policy that Arafat adopted to jail Hamas and other terrorists and then quickly release them.

All this passed by the Clinton administration with barely a whimper. Getting it to say *anything* negative about the Palestinian Authority was like extracting a stubborn tooth from an uncooperative mouth. The overwhelming balance of US statements laid the blame for the lack of progress for peace at Israel's doorstep and with me personally. Arafat was nearly always given a free pass.

I was expected to give territory to a leader of a terrorist organization that openly called for Israel's destruction, that serially released Hamas and other terrorists from jail, and that inculcated Palestinian children with the "glory" of bombing Jews to smithereens!

Most Israelis shared with me a totally different idea of peace and a genuine yearning for bringing an end to our conflict with the Palestinians. But the blinders over the eyes of American policy makers kept them from seeing this.

In fairness to the Americans, how could I expect them to be more Israeli than some leading Israelis? The Israeli press constantly accused me of complicity in Rabin's assassination and of torpedoing a peace agreement that was right around the corner. Leah Rabin, the prime minister's widow, welcomed Arafat to her home and called him a hero of peace.

Clinton sent a host of envoys to the Middle East, including Philip Habib, George Mitchell, Dennis Ross, Martin Indyk and Aaron Miller, as well as Edward Djerejian for Syria. The less combative Warren Christopher was soon replaced as secretary of state by Madeleine Albright, who was expected to take a tougher line with me. During that long and difficult year of 1998 and its aftermath, we met several times in Jerusalem, Washington and London.

Albright later said in her memoirs that negotiating with me was a form of "torture." I take that as a compliment. I was defending the Jewish state. I knew the Jewish people would never have another chance for national revival. There is a limit to the number of miracles that fate can apportion to a people and the Jewish people have received more miracles than most.

If taking a tough stance to ensure my country's survival meant that I would become the target of endless political and character smears from the Israeli press, the political left and successive US administrations, then so be it, I felt.

Sometimes, however, I did lose patience in the face of these ad hominem attacks. Before one meeting in London with Albright, the British press, clearly briefed by American officials, published dramatic headlines such as "Countdown to Peace," announcing that the future of "peace in the Middle East" rested on the outcome of my discussion with the US secretary of state. As usual, the subtext was that it was up to me, and me alone, to make the necessary concessions for peace to materialize.

When the meeting began in a London hotel, Albright gave me an ultimatum to accept some unacceptable aspect of the negotiations with the Palestinians.

"You have two hours to give me an answer," she told me. "If you don't, I'll go down to the press corps in the lobby and tell them who is responsible for blocking peace."

I was furious.

"Madam Secretary," I said, "I don't need two hours. I don't need even two minutes. Let's end this meeting right now and we'll both go down to the world press. You tell them whatever you want. I'll tell them that as the prime minister of Israel I will not endanger over three thousand years of the Jewish people's struggle for a place among the nations by capitulating to conditions that would endanger the one and only Jewish state."

We didn't go down to the lobby.

This meeting in London was part of my endless jousting with the Clinton administration. Getting the "breakthrough for peace" and the Nobel Prize that went along with it were among the American officials' highest goals. They tried peace with Syria and failed. They tried peace with the Palestinians and failed. They *had* to get a breakthrough. If that meant trampling on me, this posed no problem for them.

The US upped the pressure. I reached out to Jewish and evangelical groups to make my case, knowing their support for Israel would apply counterpressure. I met with congressional leaders on both sides of the aisle and explained my position. But the pressure was still on. The fact that my policy of reciprocity almost completely stopped the waves of Palestinian suicide bombings paradoxically enabled the Clinton team to renew their efforts to resume the negotiations begun at Oslo.

Oslo stipulated a road map by which Israel would redesignate some territory in Judea and Samaria from category C (fully controlled by Israel) to category B (partly controlled by the Palestinians). Some territory was also to be redesignated as category A (fully controlled by the Palestinians). Before this redesignation would take place, I demanded that the Palestinian Authority first formally renounce the Palestinian Covenant calling for Israel's destruction and that the redesignated territories be reduced to a minimum. The change in designation would occur in several tranches but only if the Palestinians would first fulfill specific security conditions.

All this was to be negotiated in a summit at the Wye River plantation in Maryland on October 23, 1998, where Clinton, Arafat, and I would meet to try to seal the deal. Several months of secret preparations were conducted between Itzik Molcho, Dennis Ross and the Palestinian official Abu Allah prior to that meeting. Clinton brought there the ailing King Hussein from a US hospital where he was being treated for cancer. Hussein made an impassioned plea for peace, directed at me. While I disagreed with his analysis, I was genuinely moved by the fact that he made the journey from his sickbed to be there.

I told him of my son Yair's concern for his health. In one of our meetings two years earlier, Hussein had crossed the bay to Eilat from nearby Aqaba and visited me in the Orchid Hotel, where Sara, Yair and I were staying. Seven-year-old Yair opened the door and was startled to see the king dressed informally.

"Are you a real king?" he asked in Hebrew.

"Yes, I am," answered Hussein after we translated the question.

"So where's your crown and royal wand?" Yair persisted.

"He's a king even if he doesn't wear the crown," I said.

This meeting left a deep impression on Yair. When he learned of Hussein's illness, he cried and asked:

"Is the good king very sick? Will he get well?"

Yair decided to make a painting for the king of an extraterrestrial being that came to earth with a magic cure. He dedicated it to King Hussein with the words "get well soon."

I sent the painting by diplomatic channels to Hussein but it reached Amman and not the Mayo Clinic where the king was being treated. Now in Wye he asked Sara, who accompanied me, to send him a copy. Luckily, we had a copy that we framed and sent to the clinic.

The king sent Yair a thank-you card in which he told him how deeply moved he was by the painting, which I was told he kept by his bedside.

I BROUGHT WITH me to Wye Ariel Sharon, then minister of infrastructure, seeking to facilitate as wide a consensus in the government as possible for any decision I might make. The Settlers Council of Judea, Samaria, and Gaza sent a delegation to Wye to stiffen my resistance to American pressure. Since they were barred from entering the compound grounds, I went outside to see them.

"I'm doing my best," I told them.

That hardly satisfied them.

Wye had the usual crises associated with such summits. At one point when the American team failed to provide certain guarantees promised to us, I ordered my delegation to pack their bags. Though the US side later scoffed at this "tactic," at the time they took it seriously enough to restore the guarantees. It was no bluff—I would have walked.

One of Arafat's demands was that I release Palestinian prisoners jailed for complicity in terrorist attacks and activities. I said I could consider releasing a few if Egyptian president Hosni Mubarak simultaneously released some Israeli citizens unjustly jailed in Egypt on fake espionage charges. When I called Mubarak directly from Wye, he refused. I explained to Clinton that given Mubarak's refusal I could not meet this Palestinian demand. Furthermore, I told Arafat that he had dangerous killers roaming around in the Palestinian Authority and that he needed to deal with them by any means necessary. Clinton blew a fuse and walked out in a storm, accusing me of not rising to the historic occasion.

In the strained silence that followed, Secretary Albright scolded me as if I were a schoolchild.

"Now see what you've done! You've upset the president of the United States!"

It was London all over again.

Controlling my emotions better this time, I explained that no offense was intended. The issue wasn't anyone's personal feelings: for me it was Israel's security and its future, and on this I would not compromise.

Seeing the impasse, I suggested that Arafat and I meet alone. I asked him to write down the three most important issues for him and I would do the same for myself. His number one issue was the redesignation of territory. My number one issue was security, followed by Israeli control of the strategic Jordan Valley. We finally agreed on the tranches and the security conditions that went along with them. Altogether they amounted to 13 percent of Judea and Samaria, but only 3 percent would be passed to full Palestinian control.

Clinton was delighted. Earlier he had promised that if the deal went through, he would release the jailed Israeli spy Jonathan Pollard, who had by then served fifteen years in an American prison. Israel had ceased all spying activities in the US after his capture in 1985.

The day Pollard was arrested, I had accompanied Rabin to a New York restaurant. He was then defense minister, on a visit to the US; I was UN ambassador. Word came in that an American citizen had tried to receive asylum in our Washington embassy. The embassy refused his request and he was apprehended by the police. It was the first time I heard of Pollard and his story. I could not make out if Rabin had any prior inkling of it.

I thought spying *in* America, even if not *against* America, was the height of folly. The responsibility for this mistake lay squarely with the government of Israel. Previous governments wavered on openly assuming that responsibility. When I later became prime minister I did not. I said Pollard was working on behalf of a misguided arm of Israeli intelligence. His thirty-year prison sentence was much longer than those meted out to Soviet spies who had actually spied against America and damaged US security. I told Clinton that releasing him would put this sorry affair to rest and would be a humanitarian act that would buy him much goodwill from the Israeli public.

Clinton agreed to release Pollard in the days leading up to Wye. This was designed to be an added incentive for me to do the deal. Now, in the concluding hours of the conference, as the final communiqué was being drafted, he asked to see me.

"Bibi," he said, "I'm sorry to drop this on you. But I can't release Pollard. I'm getting enormous pushback from the Pentagon and the CIA. George Tenet [the CIA director] threatened to resign. I just can't do it."

I was stunned.

Here was the president of the United States, whose officials constantly berated me for not having the courage to make difficult decisions that involved the security of my country and that could topple my government, backing away from a solemn commitment because of a bureaucratic hurdle that in no way threatened his presidency.

I retired to my room. Should I break off the deal? I wondered. I strongly considered it, principally because the integrity of the US side seemed to me to be in serious doubt.

But in the end I decided not to do so. Wye was a minimalist deal. Israel didn't relinquish any substantial amount of territory or any areas of strategic or historic importance. I doubted I could get better terms, and the pressure on Israel for much bigger concessions would follow if a deal wasn't made here.

I gritted my teeth and went through with it. On October 23, 1998, I signed the agreement.[1]

Pollard would remain in jail for the next two decades. Throughout my tenures as prime minister, I worked incessantly to release him and bring him to Israel. Despite my efforts, we had to await the completion of his prolonged sentence. Ron Dermer, whom I later appointed ambassador to Washington, kept regular contact with him.

On December 29, 2020, I greeted Pollard in Israel as he disembarked from a plane with his cancer-stricken wife, Esther, who died less than a year later. They kissed the ground. We embraced.

Returning to Israel from Wye, I faced a political firestorm. Though the agreement passed the Knesset on November 17 by a vote of 75–19, the religious parties to the right of Likud threatened a no-confidence vote to remove me as head of state. Labor, which had promised a parliamentary "safety net" against a no-confidence vote if I signed the Wye agreement, promptly reneged on their offer. They supported the Wye agreement and then still worked to topple my government. Seeing that the government was about to fall, I dissolved the Knesset on December 21 and called for early elections. Labor's Ehud Barak would be my opponent for prime minister.

In the course of the election campaign I visited Rabbi Avraham Shapira, the head of the Merkaz Harav Yeshiva, which carries on the tradition of the venerated Rabbi Kook, who had eulogized my grandfather Nathan.

I went to see Rabbi Shapira because his was the flagship yeshiva of the religious right which was fraying my coalition.

The rabbi received me with a question. "When I was a child in Jerusalem I heard your grandfather Rabbi Nathan speak with such passion about the sanctity of the Land of Israel. What would your grandfather say about Wye?" he asked.

"I don't know," I answered. "He died in 1935, well before I was born." That didn't faze him.

"So ask your father what Rabbi Nathan would have said," he replied. Checkmate.

I went to see Father and told him of this conversation.

"What should I tell him Grandfather would have said?" I asked.

Father thought for a moment. Although he was against the Wye agreement, Father understood the consequences of the government's collapse.

"Tell the rabbi that your grandfather was a very smart man," he answered, "and he would have said that it is better to sacrifice three percent of the land than to lose one hundred percent of it, which is what will happen if Barak wins the election."

But the soundness of Father's advice eluded the right.

We also had a problem with the center of the electorate. Things were too good. Terrorism had been stopped, so the security issue which normally favors Likud was not relevant at the moment. In 1996, 67 percent of voters had listed security as their number one issue. By 1999, that had dropped to 40 percent. I was a victim of my success.

But the main problem was a loss of cohesiveness on the right. That opened the electorate up to an effective campaign by Barak's party, whose name he changed from Labor to One Israel.

In a careless moment during the campaign, Barak said that if he had been born a Palestinian he too would have joined a terrorist organization. When I went after that statement, Barak countered with a vitriolic personal attack.

"Bibi," he pronounced, "Yoni would be ashamed of you."

This, I thought, was as low as you could get. But no, Barak would later go even lower.

Barak presented himself as another Rabin, a security-minded ex-general who would effectively pursue peace but not veer too much to the left. The Oslo agreement, he said, "was perforated with more holes than Swiss cheese."[2] What he didn't say was that he would do away with most of the remaining cheese and leave Israel with an even more perforated agreement.

Barak set up a string of questionable NGOs that added tens of millions of dollars to the One Israel campaign. These were only nominally investigated. The party's heavily funded ad campaign, guided by Clinton's closest advisors, James Carville, Stan Greenberg and David Shrum, attacked the Likud on wasteful spending on settlements that left an old woman unattended in a hospital corridor in Nahariya. A new One Israel government, their slick campaign promised, would correct this.

Once again the US president was putting his thumb on the scale of an Israeli election.

My government had brought down terror, restored security, introduced the checks and balances of reciprocity to runaway political negotiations with the Palestinians and introduced several unprecedented economic reforms.

Yet a good portion of the public took the improved security situation for granted. The desire for a quick fix for a final peace agreement with the Palestinians was still at its height, at odds with my gradual approach of step-by-step agreements stressing security and reciprocity. This tipped the scales. I knew as much and told my consultant Arthur Finkelstein three months before the election that I was destined to lose.

"It's just a matter of exiting gracefully," I said.

Ehud Barak defeated me by 56 percent to 44 percent, with the victory margin provided by the Israeli Arab voters, who preferred him 95 percent to 5 percent over me. The Jewish vote was almost evenly divided. Barak immediately negated his campaign promise by moving to the left.

Shortly after the exit polls were announced, I announced my resignation from the Likud Party leadership and from the Knesset. Ariel Sharon was soon elected as Likud Party chairman and leader of the Opposition.

In his usual cheery way, Clinton called me shortly after my resignation announcement.

"You'll be back," he said.

Sara agreed. I doubted it.

I was fifty years old. As far as I was concerned, my political life was behind me.

DESPITE HIS CONTINUED efforts to get me out of office, it was impossible to dislike Bill Clinton personally. Even in the toughest encounters, he maintained an even keel and a glint in his eye that disarmed you. A natural and gifted politician, he was less guided by ideology than by the desire to solve problems by finding a middle ground.

It was this search for the center that had guided his economic and social policies when he passed the North American Free Trade Agreement (NAFTA) in December 1993 and the sweeping welfare reforms that put him at odds with the left wing of the Democratic Party. In my conversations with him I was impressed by his mastery of these and other economic issues.

He was also naturally sympathetic to Israel. In his speech to the Knesset in 1994, he recalled the words of his ailing pastor who accompanied him on his first trip to Israel. "If you abandon Israel, God will never forgive you."

However, in his eyes and those of his staff this often meant "saving Israel from itself," since time and again Israeli voters apparently didn't know what was good for them. (This prompted one of my colleagues to wryly comment, "After all, what do we know? We just live here.") And if saving Israel required intervening in Israel's electoral campaign, so be it.

Clinton twice sent his personal political advisors to help Peres and Barak in the Israeli elections against me, openly admitting the first effort to me when it failed and openly celebrating the second when it succeeded. The irony was that I was falsely accused of interfering in the US elections by the very people who intervened in mine.

Clinton was genuinely smitten with Rabin, whom he looked up to. His oration at Rabin's funeral and his words "Shalom, chaver" ("Farewell, friend") were genuinely moving.

He undoubtedly absorbed the libelous venom directed at me as being responsible for derailing the much-vaunted Oslo agreements that he celebrated on the White House lawn with Arafat, Rabin and Peres. That these agreements effectively collapsed well before Rabin's assassination and my premiership, when Arafat instigated a campaign of murderous suicide bombings against Israel, was lost on him.

If only Israel would make more concessions, Clinton believed, the Palestinians would make their peace with us. He visited Israel after the Wye River conference in December 1998, went to Gaza and spoke passionately to the Palestinian National Council, believing his emotional appeal would win their hearts. When I failed to deliver the far-reaching concessions that he thought were necessary for a final peace settlement, he put all his chips on Barak and helped him defeat me.

Soon after Barak's victory, Clinton invited him to a gala dinner at the White House. They embraced ecstatically before the cameras. A guest swears he heard them say, "We did it." Everyone present shared in the jubilation. They believed peace was at hand.

Not long after, the two met at Camp David and agreed on their next move. Clinton had little more than a year left in office. He was determined to make history. The stage was set for the grand spectacle at a Camp David summit for the historic Israeli-Palestinian peace.

In June 2000, a towering Clinton embraced the shoulders of Arafat and Barak as he ushered them into the rustic cabins of Camp David.

What followed was a fiasco for all the world to see. Barak offered sweeping concessions, including 92 percent of Judea and Samaria and a Palestinian state with part of Jerusalem as its capital.

Arafat turned him down.

He could no more make a final peace settlement with Israel than he could fly to the moon. After all, the entire Palestinian national movement, which he had led for decades, was premised on having Israel disappear.

How this obvious fact could have eluded both Clinton and Barak is nothing short of incredible. Blinded by the search for political glory, and perhaps a Nobel Peace Prize, Clinton and Barak dove deep into the rabbit hole of the Palestinian peace narrative and discovered there was nothing there. Barak later disingenuously offered the explanation that his real goal had been to "smoke out" Arafat and expose his real policies.

Yeah, right.

Clinton at least frankly admitted his disappointment. Since the proverbial obstacle to peace (me) was gone, he genuinely expected to achieve a historic agreement, and when that failed to materialize he implicitly placed the blame on Arafat.

But even then his explanation for the failure was tactical. The president and his peace team simply couldn't bring themselves to admit that their quest for the Holy Peace Grail was based on a false premise. It wasn't Israeli rejectionism and the absence of a Palestinian state that prevented an Israeli-Palestinian peace. It was *Palestinian* rejectionism and the existence of a Jewish state.

Following the failure at Camp David, Arafat intensified the terror campaign against Israel. The godfather of modern terrorism believed Israel would cave under the pressure. Yet even in the midst of murderous Palestinian terror attacks, Barak and Clinton wouldn't let the facts get in their way.

Before Clinton left office, he and Barak threw one last Hail Mary pass. Meeting on December 19, 2000, during the presidential transition period, Barak's representatives agreed with Clinton to arrange another meeting between a Palestinian and an Israeli delegation in Taba, Egypt, on January 21. Since this would be just one day after George W. Bush's inauguration as the new president, no American representatives attended.

In Taba, Barak upped his Camp David ante by offering another 4 percent in territorial concessions, increasing the territory Israel would cede to a Palestinian state from 92 percent of Judea and Samaria to 96 percent. He was even willing to give the Palestinians a foothold on the Temple Mount.[3]

Arafat still refused.

He intensified his terror campaign even more. Barak's coalition collapsed and he was booted out of office on March 7, 2001, earning him the distinction of being the shortest-serving prime minister in Israel's history at the time.

Clinton was well meaning without being mean. The signature foreign policy achievement he sought was beyond his reach and he never truly grasped the real cause of his failure. The assumption that the Palestinians would make peace with Israel for the right price neglected to take into account the inherent clash between their national movement and the existence of a Jewish state altogether.

31

WILDERNESS

1999–2002

On election night at Tel Aviv's Hilton hotel I had prepared my concession speech in advance, along with the resignation paragraph which I shared only with Sara. When I delivered it, many in the crowd began to groan. Some wept. I thanked them for their support and went off into the sunset.

Sara and I owned an apartment on Jerusalem's Gaza Street and Sara's tiny apartment in Givatayim and pretty much nothing else. One journalist gleefully noted that "as Arafat exits Gaza, Netanyahu enters it."

At 11 a.m. on October 20, 1999, the police knocked on the door of our Gaza Street apartment. The press had been alerted in advance. Camera crews were arrayed in rows in front of the entrance. It was later said that the female police officer in charge had had her hair done early in the morning for the occasion.

"This is a court order for a search in your apartment," she told us.

"Can you come back later and be done before the children return from school?" Sara replied.

"Nope, it has to be done right now. Please step aside."

Sara held them off until our lawyer arrived.

The police proceeded to comb the apartment, stacked with as-yet-unpacked boxes from our three years' stay in the prime minister's residence.

A few days earlier, a leading newspaper had published a fake story that we had taken valuable official gifts given to the prime minister that belonged to the state. On this flimsiest of canards, the police were now subjecting us to a humiliating publicized search. They combed every part of the apartment, emptying cupboards and bookcases. Nothing was spared.

They found nothing, except an enameled box in my study.

"What's that?" they asked.

"It's a box," I said.

"I know it's a box," the officer said, "but what does it contain? Jewelry?"

I said, "If you really want to know, it contains *rahat lokum* [Turkish delight] that was brought to me by an envoy from one of his visits to Damascus."

"So where is the *lokum*?"

"I ate it."

This may sound comical now, but at the time it wasn't. A sense of violation and indignity welled up inside us. Somehow I kept my cool and so did Sara, though I could tell she was seething.

Hoping to find troves of cash, the police opened a safe in one of the rooms, only to find a souvenir revolver given to me by King Hussein. They took some handwritten notes and letters that Sara had written. They found nothing else. And that was that.

They left in a burst of spectacular headlines about the "hordes of precious gifts" discovered in the apartment that would now serve as the basis for a full criminal investigation. This investigation would last one whole year, with all our arrivals for interrogations at police headquarters televised.

It seemed that the press and their collaborators in the legal bureaucracy were committed to making sure that my exit from politics was not temporary but permanent. This was an early lesson for me in the dishonesty of the investigators and their symbiotic relationship with the press.

The "Gifts Affair," as it came to be called, was the by-product of the "Mover's Affair." A mover who had previously worked for Sara and me privately also transported our belongings out of the prime minister's residence. He submitted an inflated bill to the government that I allegedly endorsed. The press went wild with accusations that this inflated bill was a ruse by which I covered my previous private moving costs. It wasn't. I had paid him his due but I refused to have the Prime Minister's Office pay his inflated bill.

This accusation didn't hold since several people were present in the Prime Minister's Office when I was shown the inflated bill he had submitted and said, "Don't pay him even one shekel." We later learned that on an earlier occasion he submitted a similarly inflated bill to a leading bank, which also refused to pay him.

Squeezed by the police about his inflated billing, the mover told them that in transporting our belongings from the residence he saw that some of the boxes contained official government gifts. This allegation was leaked to the press with transparently coordinated criminal and search investigations that promptly followed and formed the ongoing Gifts Affair.

Over the course of hundreds of hours of police interrogations in the coming months, Sara and I were grilled on every lead, every video clip, every scrap of paper that might possibly prove that we had escaped with valuable government-owned loot.

No treasures were found, for the simple reason that we didn't take any. Nearly all official gifts were listed, categorized and kept in the basement of the Prime Minister's Office. Others were stored in a government warehouse and were not in our possession. The few that were in our possession were allowed by regulations because they cost less than one hundred dollars and included such things as straw hats from Panama and wooden shields given to us by visiting African leaders.

This was all kept from the public by press and police alike. Instead, the press constantly explained that the police were busy digging and that new revelations were forthcoming.

Going into my first police interrogation, I remembered the POW training I received in the Unit. Sayeret Matkal fighters, IAF pilots and naval commandos undergo a special weeklong course to be prepared in the event of capture.

Cardinal rule number one: Stay alive! This rule was enshrined after an Israeli soldier, Uri Ilan, captured by the Syrians during a 1956 intelligence operation, committed suicide rather than reveal the secret mission he was on. We were instructed in various techniques on how to outwit our captors. Cardinal rule number two: If tortured, hold out for as long as possible to let your fellow soldiers escape back to Israeli lines. But again, don't sacrifice your life.

During the POW training exercise, my team was "captured" during a grueling stretcher march, in which we carried a "wounded" soldier on a stretcher for miles on end. Blindfolded with shackled hands, we were thrown into a dungeon and made to sleep on the floor next to buckets of urine. One by one, we were summoned to endless interrogations.

I figured, this is just an exercise, what can they do to me? Kill me?

But it wasn't going to be that simple.

"Think you're smart, don't you?" my interrogator bellowed at me. "Put your blindfold on. Now, I ask you again, what is your unit?"

"Benjamin Netanyahu, serial number 2030233," I answered again, divulging the minimal allowed information. Suddenly I felt a sharp kick with a pointed shoe above my knee. The pain was excruciating.

"I ask you again," I heard him say. "What is your unit?"

Same answer.

Another kick. Then another, and another. Nearly fainting, I held my ground. After ten kicks, the interrogator stopped.

"You can go now."

I lay in my cell, kneading my thigh in a futile effort to make the pain go away. Ultimately I stuck to my script and passed the test.

Twenty-five years later, as prime minister, I had attended a rally of Likud supporters in the town of Pardes Hana. The room was crowded and the guests clamored to come and shake my hand. I noticed one guest who rather than approach me receded into the shadows. But I caught a glimpse of his face.

"Hey, I know you," I said.

He came into full view. Sure enough, it was my sharp-footed interrogator.

"It's okay," I said. "You did what you had to."

We didn't share our secret with the assembled crowd.

Now, in my police interrogation, I remembered my POW training. My interrogators might not kill me but they could kill my public reputation. They would do everything in their power to undermine me.

Was there anything I could do in the face of this Kafkaesque absurdity?

It's a psychological game, I said to myself. Think! I was told to sit down behind a small desk, with four intense interrogators facing me. They started firing questions at me.

Suddenly I got to my feet. I would answer their questions standing upright, strolling about, looking *down* at them.

"You can't do that, sir," they said.

"Why not? Where does it say I can't?" I answered.

And so it went.

In one of the simultaneous interrogations of Sara and me (as though we were a crime family), we were each shown a film of a ceremony we attended in the Diamond Merchants Center. Sara is seen receiving a pin given to her by the daughter of the head of the Diamond Merchants Association.

"Where is that pin?" they asked her.

"I have no idea," Sara responded. "But it was just a ceremonial pin."

"Do you mean to tell us that the daughter of the Diamond Merchants Association gave the wife of the Israeli prime minister a worthless pin?"

"That's exactly what I'm telling you," Sara said.

"You know it was gold and diamonds. Admit it!" the investigator insisted.

Back in our apartment, a thought popped into my mind.

"Sara," I said, "can you find this goddamn pin?"

"I don't know. I'll look for it," she said.

Amazingly, she found the association pin amid all the boxes in the disheveled apartment.

It was made of aluminum.

I promptly had my lawyer bring in an expert appraiser, an Orthodox Jew from Tel Aviv's diamond district. He examined the pin with a jeweler's magnifying glass.

"So how much is it worth?" I asked.

"Oh, I'd say about 5.95 shekels [a little over a dollar]," he said. "I'll give you an official appraisal for it."

During my next interrogation, I said, "Before you start, I owe you something. You wanted to know about the pin. Here's the pin and here is an official appraisal of its worth."

The interrogators tried to keep a poker face.

Another item the police had interrogated us about was a handwritten note Sara had written to her secretary after our official visit to Beijing.

"Please thank our embassy in Beijing for the Banana Bird," the note said.

"Where is the Banana Bird?" they asked. "What is it made of? Gold? Jewels? Diamonds? Where did you hide it?"

"I have no idea what you're talking about," Sara said.

"But we have the note in your own handwriting," said the chief investigator.

"Can I see the note?" Sara asked.

"Here it is!" said the interrogator triumphantly.

Sara took one look at the note and burst out in laughter.

The police had misinterpreted Sara's handwriting, reading "Banana Bird" instead of "Banana Bread." When we were in the official guesthouse in Beijing, we liked the fried bananas sprinkled with bread crumbs. Seeing this, one of the embassy staff gave Sara two packets of banana bread crumbs to take home. Sara made a note to her secretary to thank the embassy staff for the kind gesture.

Back home, Sara found the two packets of Chinese "Banana Bread" toppings, still in their original wrappings. Another set of police jaws dropped when I showed the interrogators the packets in our next interrogation.

I suspect that the rank-and-file interrogators were beginning to feel uncomfortable, but they were egged on by their superiors. The gifts farce was unraveling, but it would take another few months for it to end.

When it did, the press of course covered none of the details of its comical collapse. The gifts case may have been closed, but a "cloud of impropriety was left hanging over the questionable practices of the former prime minister and his acquisitive wife" was the line the journalists put forward.

In fact, the exact opposite was true. The ramrod-straight state comptroller, former Supreme Court justice Eliezer Goldberg, wrote in his 2001 report that the first prime minister to fully list, register and deposit gifts to government possession in an orderly fashion was . . . me.[1]

*　　　*　　　*

BY THE TIME of the "Gifts Affair," I was familiar with being subjected to this kind of witch hunt. In my first term as prime minister I was interrogated in my office in the so-called Baron-Hebron Affair.

It was claimed that I intended to appoint as attorney general Ronnie Baron, a Jerusalem lawyer, in order to please his friend Aryeh Deri, the leader of the religious Shas Party, who was under investigation. In exchange, Deri would vote for the Hebron deal.

This was outlandish. I had no intention to appoint Baron. My candidate was an eminent conservative lawyer, Dan Avi-Yitzhak. A few days before the cabinet meeting in which I would announce his appointment, I asked Tzachi Hanegbi, the justice minister, to inform the state prosecutor of my choice. Hanegbi came back and said that Avi-Yitzhak was himself under investigation for some dealings with a Polish bank (he was later cleared of all charges). As this was an ongoing investigation, I could not inform Avi-Yitzhak of the circumstances that led to his removal as a candidate for attorney general.

It was then and only then that I called Baron to take on the job. I was willing to do so after receiving a warm recommendation from the justice minister, who had clerked at Baron's office. I made a cardinal mistake, however, in not telling Avi-Yitzhak that I was dropping him from the job. A mere three days before the scheduled cabinet meeting, he heard about it in a leaked news story. Not knowing of his own circumstances, he must have been perplexed.

The "Hebron-Baron" concoction was the main, though not the only, false theory that floated in the air as to why I decided to appoint Baron. And it was passed on to an otherwise reputable journalist, Ayala Hasson, who "broke" the story.

The press went wild. "Netanyahu is tampering with Israel's democracy," "Netanyahu is destroying our justice system," blared the headlines, capped by "The gravest scandal in the history of Israeli democracy." The all-powerful news editor of one of Israel's two television channels said that this was "a case cast in concrete" that would end my political career.

I took on Amnon Goldenberg as my lawyer. Highly respected and experienced, he heard me out and said, "This is nothing."

"They'll shut the case because your first defense witness will be the state prosecutor," he explained. "She'll have to testify that you intended to appoint Avi-Yitzhak and not Baron, and that it was she who nixed your first choice. How could you have made a deal on Hebron in exchange for appointing Baron when you clearly didn't intend to appoint him? So leave it alone, it will pass."

I breathed a sigh of relief.

"Oh, except for one thing," he said.

What now? I thought.

"Don't meet alone with any of those involved in the case, or they'll nail you for witness tampering."

For the next three months, I would have a third party always present in my meetings with the justice minister and others. Predictably, the case was closed, but the leftist press pressured the attorney general, who closed the case, to include an accompanying "public report" that inexplicably included some vague reference to "questionable practices" by the prime minister. This was widely believed to be an attempt to pacify the left. What these "questionable practices" were was left unspecified, but this was the first fake cloud to appear on my legal horizon, to be followed by many, many more.

Having earlier survived "Hebron-Baron," I now survived the "Gifts Affair." I shrugged away the absurdity of it all.

IN THIS HORRIBLE year of police investigations, my parents kept a stiff upper lip. Though they said they had expected these sorts of absurdities all along, I knew they carried an inner pain over them. Yet when I saw them periodically, they were always strong and supportive.

On vacation with Sara and the boys on the shore of the Sea of Galilee in 1999, I received an urgent phone call from Daphna, Iddo's wife.

"Bibi," she said, "Cela's had a stroke. Come quickly."

My heart beating, I raced to Hadassah Hospital in Jerusalem. Mother was recovering. She suffered no cognitive damage and was her usual vibrant self. But she was incapacitated in her right leg and would have to undergo physical therapy. I visited her almost daily. Within a week the entire staff of the therapeutic ward, nurses and doctors alike, were enchanted by her.

"Your mother is unbelievable," said the head nurse to me. "She's like one of us. She's always smiling and she's such a warm person."

This was vintage Cela. It was hard to find someone who didn't like her. From week to week her condition improved. But five weeks after the stroke, she had another, which caused her to lose consciousness. She never woke up.

Father, Iddo and I, along with Sara and Daphna, took turns at her bedside. The doctors explained that there was no hope. When she was put on a respirator, some of the doctors said there was no point continuing. But we couldn't accept this. We would do anything to keep Mother alive. All of us surrounded her. She slowly waned away, until the monitors showed a horrible flat line. We all wept.

"Imma, my Imma," I cried through the tears. I owed so much to this extraordinary woman who gave me life and nurtured me through times of turbulence and happiness alike.

When Yoni died and whenever I attended funerals of fellow soldiers, I thought this was a perversion of nature. Parents should not bury their children. I was sure that when my parents died I would take it in stride as an inevitable reality. It would be all right. But Mother died and it wasn't all right.

I mourn for her to this day.

Father was deeply bereaved. He had relied so much on her. How would he live without her? On her gravestone, ninety-year-old Benzion inscribed a tribute of love in haunting Hebrew that defies translation. Without doing justice to the powerful rhythmic words, here is the substance of his epitaph. He described Mother as:

The crown of her family and the rock of its accomplishments.
    Her grace and beauty, her wisdom and sincerity, captured the hearts of all who knew her.
    Her courage and love of country inspired her sons.
    With nobility of spirit she bore her sorrow at the fall of her son Jonathan, a hero of Israel.
    Virtuous and wondrous was she to the end of her days.

The funeral, held on February 2, 2000, at a cemetery overlooking the entrance to Jerusalem, attracted thousands. People from all walks of life, including hordes of yeshiva students, crowded the cemetery. Some knew my mother, many others had only heard of her, and still more had heard of my father.

But there was one additional explanation for this massive turnout. Innumerable people identified with my family and me and wanted to express their support in the midst of what they considered a political witch hunt. Many who came to console us said as much when they visited the overflowing *Shiva* in our home on HaPotsim Street.

RISING FROM THE *Shiva*, I had to get my financial house in order. Here I was, an Israeli prime minister accused of impropriety and corruption, when in truth I could barely scrounge a living to feed my young family. After nearly twenty years in public life, I received an after-tax monthly pension of eight hundred dollars. I needed to find a way to earn money.

My friend the Hollywood producer Merv Adelson put me in touch with Harry Rhoads's Washington Speakers Bureau. Speaking engagements for political leaders out of office were practically unheard-of in Israel at the time, but this was a booming business in America.

My first speaking engagement was at a speaking marathon held in a Tampa, Florida, ice hockey rink. Thousands of people paid to hear a long line of speakers go one after the other. They expressed their approval or disapproval by their applause, and the organizers thus had an indication of whom to invite next time. A speaker who didn't get the audience's approval was finished.

This was the Hull Shabbat Breakfast Club on steroids!

I seldom prepared for a speech more than I prepared for the one in Tampa. My family's livelihood depended on it.

"This is it," I said to Sara, who came with me. "In exactly twenty minutes we'll know if we sink or swim."

"You'll be great," she encouraged me.

"We'll know that if I get them on their feet."

Half an hour later the place came crashing down with a prolonged standing ovation. Sara stood next to me with tears in her eyes. I kissed her and smiled.

"We'll be fine," I said.

In this pre-smartphone era, people lined up to shake my hand and get autographs. I willingly obliged. After all, it was their hard-earned money that was paying my fee, and I owed them every bit of respect.

Soon the speaking invitations started pouring in. I traveled the United States and visited the continent between the two coasts. In a speaking engagement in Nashville, Tennessee, Sara said we should go to the Grand Ole Opry.

"But I don't like country music that much," I protested.

"We can't visit Nashville without going to the Grand Ole Opry," she insisted.

At the end we were the last to leave the performance. I was totally captivated by the artistry, the emotions and the music. This was replicated years later when Sara and I were invited to a Russian ballet on a visit to Moscow when I was foreign minister. When I said, "I hate ballet," Sara came back with the same argument.

"You can't be in Moscow and not go to a ballet."

"Okay," I said, "but remember Shia Glazer?"

Glazer was a famous Israeli soccer icon of the 1950s. Before the Israeli team lost by a respectable 2–1 score to the mighty Russians in a home game, they played their first game in Moscow, where they attended the obligatory Bolshoi performance. A few minutes into the dazzling pirouettes and aerial spirals, Glazer walked out.

"Why are you leaving, Shia?" his teammates asked him.

"I got the point," he answered.

I found this hilarious. Sara was unimpressed.

"Bibi, you're not walking out of that ballet! No way! You can't do this to our Russian hosts."

"Okay, Sara," I said in resignation. "I'll recede into the shadow of the box and sleep while you enjoy yourself."

Once in the box, I positioned my chair so that I could not be seen by anyone else and began to doze off. But within a few minutes I awoke. Before I knew it I was absolutely enthralled by the rendition of *Swan Lake*, totally lost in its beauty. We met the dancers backstage and complimented them.

In both Nashville and Moscow, as happened earlier in Washington, where as a soccer aficionado I grudgingly attended my first American football game between the Washington Redskins and the Miami Dolphins, I was on my feet cheering wildly at the end.

Though I also spoke in places as far afield as Europe, Mexico and Australia, most of my speaking engagements were in the US. In many of the visits I was accompanied by Spencer Partrich, an American whom I met in 1999 at a dinner held by a mutual friend, Professor Eliezer Rachmilevitch.

Spencer came from a poor Jewish family in Detroit, had studied law and became a highly successful businessman of prefabricated homes. We became instant close friends. I fully trusted his judgment and wisdom. Spencer combined street smarts with worldly sophistication. And he had a rollicking sense of humor. Sometimes we would break down laughing at some absurdity we both identified. I delighted in his company.

While the speaking engagements poured in, I was also made an offer by Zvi Marom, the founder of an Israeli company that produced switch-routers for internet infrastructure, to work as a door opener for companies abroad.

I liked Marom immediately. He was irreverent and independent. We forged an easy friendship, which is just as well because we traveled together to digital trade shows in Helsinki and Geneva, and to facilities such as the gigantic CERN particle accelerator in Switzerland, where the British scientist Tim Berners-Lee was working when he connected several computers in one of the pioneering efforts that developed the internet.

In these and other sorties I learned firsthand about the emerging digital economy. I could see the endless possibilities for the betterment of people's lives offered by the digital revolution, and a better understanding of how various governments, industries and companies were seizing the future.

In early 2000, the tech markets reached stratospheric heights. People believed a new physics was emerging, an internet economy supposedly free of the forces of economic gravity, devoid of the fundamental need to earn more than you spend. In one gathering of a venture capital group I attended in Sun Valley, Idaho, the guest speaker titled his talk "Toward the NASDAQ 30,000." The NASDAQ had reached 5,048 on March 10, 2000. But instead of going to 30,000, it would drop to 1,114 on October 9, 2002.

Investment and merger fever gripped the world. With unlimited appetites, paying enormous prices and showing little or no concern for future earnings, tech companies were gobbling each other up.

In Israel this meant a huge infusion of foreign investment. One Israeli company, Chromatis, was bought for \$4.8 billion by Lucent. Investors were feverishly driving up the American NASDAQ, the British AIM and the other tech stock markets. Israel's economic growth rate jumped up to 6.4 percent in 2000. A new world of fabulous prosperity was at hand.

I kept my skepticism mostly to myself, declining what seemed to me outlandish business propositions and judging that the markets could not sustain their present heights for long. Many companies were wildly over-valued and could never justify their current price with future earnings.

"It's the tulip bubble all over again," I said to a friend on a visit to Belgium in February 2000, referring to the infamous boom and bust of the market in tulip bulbs some four hundred years ago in nearby Amsterdam.

Thankfully, I avoided the pitfalls of the market, continued to increase my income and kept my family well cared for financially.

As the global and Israeli economy tanked, Sara and I were able to buy a weekend home in Caesarea, which we could now afford. Close to the magnificent historic port on the Mediterranean built by King Herod, it would serve as our family's retreat, a place where we could unwind, swim in the pool or bathe in the sea. Herod, one of antiquity's great builders, definitely knew how to relax, though he seldom did.

Life outside politics was good. During my first tenure as prime minister I would go with Sara to the boys' parent-teacher meetings. But now that I had more time to give to my family, I sometimes took part as an accompanying parent on class trips. On one such occasion I accompanied eight-year-old Avner on his class trip to the sand dunes near the Mediterranean city of Ashdod.

Like little gazelles, the children climbed to the top of a particularly steep dune. I followed suit. When I got to the top, one girl said to Avner, "Your father really climbs well for his age."

"Why, how old do you think I am?" I asked the girl.

"I don't know, old," she said. "Maybe thirty."

I should do this more often, I thought.

AFTER I LEFT office, I happily stayed away from politics. The only clouds on our horizon were the unceasing police investigations, but we learned to live with them.

Other clouds soon gathered over Israel. With Barak in office, Arafat ratcheted up his terror campaign. Barak's response was to offer more concessions, which in turn merely resulted in more terror. Caesarea's restaurants emptied. Tourism in the country had dwindled to a trickle. "Please come back," Israelis would implore me on the street.

I had no intention of doing so. In one of my rare public interviews, I said I was speaking as a "concerned citizen" in the face of the weakness that Israel's government showed. But the calls for my return were getting stronger. I dodged these requests, saying I couldn't do it. Israeli law required the prime minister to be a Knesset member, and I had resigned from the Knesset.

"Never mind that," said my supporters in the Knesset. "We'll enact a special Bibi Law, enabling a nonmember of the Knesset to be prime minister."

Despite my protests, they passed the bill. "Now that we passed the Bibi Law, you've *got* to come back," my Knesset colleagues pressed.

Barak's poll numbers had plummeted to record lows; mine were soaring. Opinion polls showed me beating him 70 to 30 percent. Pressed into a corner, I said that I would consider reentry into political life only if the Knesset dissolved itself.

The Knesset had been elected along with Barak in 1999 and was considerably to the left of what would have been the case after new elections now. I could not enact the policies I wanted with such a slim coalition. What was the point of returning to the Prime Minister's Office if I couldn't get anything done?

I knew the chances that the Knesset members would agree to put themselves up for election were close to nil, but I insisted just the same. In the odd chance they would acquiesce to my demand, I would have no choice but to go back into office, but then at least I could get things done.

Yet there was another reason I insisted on these impossible terms. *I didn't actually want to go back.*

For the first time in my adult life, I was enjoying freedom. Sara and I could be with our boys. We could tour the world. We could *live*. I was not ready to jump back into the swamp.

Of course, no one believed me. The political class and the press were certain that I was just being coy. They assumed that with the "Bibi Law" passed, I would throw my hat in the ring and run in direct elections for the post of prime minister the minute Barak's government fell.

And fall it did, with amazing speed. Having failed to get a deal with Arafat after offering unbelievable Israeli concessions, having failed similarly with Syria, and having brought the country to a standstill in the face of multiple terror attacks, Barak lost his majority and his premiership came crashing down in a resounding resignation on December 9, 2000.

The press frenzy was wild.

Would I stick to my pledge of running for prime minister only if the Knesset dissolved itself? Labor Knesset members said they would eat their hats if I didn't run.

I never bothered to check their diet, but a large sigh of relief was heard in Sharon's camp when I announced I would not run. Though nominally the head of the party, Sharon would have had to move aside if I had decided otherwise, because all the polls showed I would beat him handily in the Likud primaries. His supporters couldn't believe I let go of the reins of power that easily.

Yet while you can perhaps reenter political life anytime, this doesn't mean that you'll be reinstalled in power. When I finally did decide to go back into politics less than two years later it would take me another eight years to regain the premiership.

Sharon easily defeated Barak and became Israel's prime minister on March 7, 2001.

IN THE STITCH of time before the end of the elections and the formation of the new government, Sara and I visited the Moscow branch of Chabad, the international organization of the Lubavitcher Rebbe's followers. The new president of Russia, Vladimir Putin, who had been elected in 2000, attended the event. Putin adopted a particularly friendly attitude to Russia's Jewish community. It was said that as a teenager he was befriended in St. Petersburg by a Jewish family and taught judo by one of its members. As the religious ceremony ended, Putin approached Sara.

"May I borrow your husband for fifteen minutes?" he asked.

"Sure," she said, later asking me, "How could I refuse?"

We went to a side room and spoke for four hours. When we emerged from the meeting, everyone had left except the Israeli ambassador to Moscow, who kept Sara company. She took it in stride.

Clearly, something unusual had happened. I had already forfeited my opportunity to return to power. It was late at night. A perfunctory meeting of fifteen minutes with a former Israeli prime minister would have sufficed.

Yet Putin invested hours in our meeting. He couldn't possibly have known that eight years later I would return to power and that we would meet every few months and talk on the phone every few weeks.

What did we talk about in those four hours? Russia, Israel, America, the world and Putin's positive attitude toward the Russian Jewish community. But it wasn't the things we said; it was *how* we said them. From the first moment, I took the measure of the man. Putin was smart and shrewd and totally committed to restoring Russia's standing as a great power. It wasn't that I had any illusions about the Russian leader, knowing as I did how power was amassed and kept in Russia. Yet it was precisely because of my assessment that I was dealing with someone who couldn't be toyed with that I decided to be straightforward with him.

I couldn't know it at the time, but this meeting in a Moscow synagogue would later prove important for Israel's security in its battle against Iran's attempts to implant itself militarily in Syria.

32

CITIZEN AGAINST TERROR

2001-2002

I came back from Moscow to a country besieged with continual terrorist attacks. In the face of a rising tide of Palestinian suicide bombings, Sharon's popularity was quickly slipping.

Arafat's terror campaign, the so-called Second Intifada, had started in the lead-up to the failed September 2000 Israeli-Palestinian summit at Camp David. It accelerated afterward with Barak's dangerous offer of further concessions, and the violence continued under Sharon. For some reason, initially, he barely responded to the violence.

"Restraint is a component of power," he said.

No, it wasn't, not in the face of exploding buses, restaurants, discothèques and hotels. The clamor for my return resumed.

Sharon finally acted in 2002, after a particularly vicious Palestinian terror attack on Passover night in a Netanya hotel murdered thirty Israelis and injured 140. The attack capped off the bloody month of March of that year, in which more than 135 Israelis were murdered by Palestinian terrorists.

Sharon sent the army into the refugee camps in Shechem (Nablus) and Jenin, two Palestinian-controlled cities where Palestinian terrorists were based, and then to other cities.

The army wisely didn't move in the streets where they could be mowed down but instead broke down and went through the walls of adjoining houses, a technique perfected by the Irgun more than half a century earlier in the battle for Jaffa.

The international uproar was deafening. On April 6, a few days into the operation, George W. Bush, now America's president, issued a stiff warning to Sharon to "immediately" stop the fighting.

Two days later he reiterated his warning: "I meant what I said to the Israeli Prime Minister. I expect there to be withdrawal without delay. I repeat: I meant what I said."[1] The White House spokesman briefed that "immediately" meant "right now, today."

No stronger message could come from Washington. I called Sharon.

"Arik, I think I can help you," I said.

"How?" he asked. I could hear the suspicion in his voice. He never could quite make me out.

"I'll go to Washington and speak to Congress and the press. But I'll only do so with your approval," I answered.

Sharon agreed. In his dire situation, what did he have to lose?

I took Ron Dermer with me. A recent immigrant to Israel from America, he had been the strategist for several years for Natan Sharansky's Russian immigrant party, Yisrael BaAliyah. Sharansky had sent him to me before the 1999 elections with the polling data of Israel's Russian immigrants. He told me I was going to lose.

"I know that," I said.

"So what will you do?" he asked.

"Lose," I said.

After this brief initial meeting, we met again a year later and began to form the closest of working and personal bonds. Ron was a graduate of the Wharton School and Oxford University. He had a deep and broad education. He understood America and American politics as few people did. And though he read Jabotinsky, he didn't need to. He already understood the Theory of Public Pressure.

A tall, dark-haired former quarterback and point guard, Ron was the shrewdest of straight shooters. Such a combination is rare. Often those who are very shrewd are not the most direct and honest, but I could always rely on Ron's word and trust the integrity of his advice.

Motivated by undiluted Zionism, Ron is a Jewish patriot. However, with all his shrewdness, he had what at times I found to be an innocent naïveté that could not fathom some of the Machiavellian machinations of Israeli politics. Though I tend to be highly focused on the tasks at hand, I allowed myself to engage in philosophical and historical discussions with Ron, which were always pleasant diversions.

Arriving in Washington, we organized a meeting in Congress with dozens of senators from both parties. On April 10, 2002, two days after President Bush reiterated his unequivocal demand for Israel to immediately stop its antiterror operation, I addressed the assembled senators.

"I am concerned," I said, "that when it comes to terror directed against Israel, the moral and strategic clarity that is so crucial for victory over terror is being twisted beyond recognition.

"I am concerned that the imperative of defeating terror everywhere is being ignored when the main engine of Palestinian terror is allowed to remain intact.

"I am concerned that the state of Israel, that has for decades bravely manned the front lines against terror, is being pressed to back down just when it is on the verge of uprooting Palestinian terror."

Now I took a direct shot at the US administration.

"My concern deepened when, incredibly, Israel was asked to stop fighting terror and return to the negotiating table with a regime that is committed to the destruction of the Jewish state and openly embraces terror."

In a question-and-answer session with the senators I called for an immediate change in US policy and a cessation of the pressure directed at Israel.

This was followed by some two dozen television and radio interviews given during twenty-four hours. Since some of these interviews were pretaped, I appeared on four or five programs simultaneously.

The message hit home.

The next day the Bush administration was already briefing reporters that Israel had a right to defend itself and to complete the sweeping up of terrorist strongholds in Palestinian-controlled areas.

I thought it necessary to reinforce this point with larger audiences. Mass rallies were arranged in both Washington and London, where I would be the keynote speaker.

On April 15, 2002, only a week after my speech to the senators, the rally was held in Washington to show solidarity with Israel. Braving the blistering heat in America's capital, more than 150,000 people turned out to make the event the largest pro-Israel rally in the history of the United States.

I focused my remarks squarely on a point that I had only briefly addressed in previous speeches—the root cause of terrorism. I deliberately referenced Martin Luther King Jr., a great supporter of Zionism.

Do not be fooled by the apologists of terror. They tell us that the way to end terror is to appease it, to give in to its demands because, they tell us, the root cause of terrorism is the deprivation of national and civic rights.

If that were the case, then in the thousands of conflicts and struggles for national and civil rights in modern times we would have seen countless instances of terrorism. But we did not.

Mahatma Gandhi did not use terrorism in fighting for the independence of India. The peoples of Eastern Europe did not resort to terrorism to bring down the Berlin Wall. And Martin Luther King did not resort to terrorism in fighting for equal rights for all Americans. Speaking in this city, in this very place four decades ago, he preached a creed that was the very *opposite* of terrorism.

Why did all these people pursue their cause without resorting to terror?

Because they believed in the sanctity of each human life. Because they were committed to the ideals of liberty. Because they championed the values of democracy. Because they were *democrats*, not *totalitarians*.

The root cause of terrorism is totalitarianism, a tyranny that systematically brainwashes the minds of its subjects to suspend all moral constraints for the sake of a twisted cause. Those who *fight* as terrorists *rule* as terrorists, setting up the darkest dictatorships whether in Iraq, Iran, Afghanistan or Arafatistan.

To the anti-Semites of the world, we send a message of defiance: The Jewish people are not afraid. We will roll back the savage assaults against us and courageously stand up to our enemies.

Friends of Israel, stand tall and stand proud. We will win this war, secure our state and preserve our liberty. In defending the Jewish state, all of you here today, Jews and non-Jews alike, are defending the cause of liberty, a cause that has once again made America, Israel and all defenders of freedom the last, best hope on earth.[2]

On May 6, three weeks after the rally in Washington, some fifty thousand members of Anglo-Jewry gathered together in London's Trafalgar Square to express their solidarity with Israel. As was the case in America, the event would become the largest pro-Israel rally in British history.

In London I felt compelled to contrast the actions of Palestinian terrorists against Israel with the methods employed by the Jewish underground fighters in Israel's struggle for independence from British rule half a century ago, methods that many in Britain falsely label today as terrorism.

In hundreds of actions by the Jewish underground movements before Israel's War of Independence, only a handful involved civilian casualties. In *thousands* of actions by Palestinian organizations, a handful *didn't* involve civilians. Unlike the Jewish underground, the Palestinian terror organizations systematically targeted noncombatants and gloried in the civilian deaths they caused.

"The question now is not whether Israel will fight—for we have no choice but to fight—but whether Israel will have to fight alone. Will the free nations of the world support a beleaguered democracy, or will they succumb to the sophistry of the apologists of terror?

"The people of Britain," I said in London, "knew that the road to peace with Germany did not go through Hitler nor around Hitler, but over Hitler. His Nazi regime had to be dismantled if there were to be any hope for peace. Likewise, the people of Israel know that the path toward peace with the Palestinians does not go through Arafat nor around Arafat, but over Arafat. Yasser Arafat was, is, and will always be a terrorist. His regime has got to be dismantled if there is to be any genuine peace."

This wasn't theoretical. During Israel's military operation, Israel intelligence found damning documents showing that Arafat had personally orchestrated many of the terrorist attacks and suicide bombings that preceded Israel's action.

"With a murderous and fraudulent regime such as Arafat's," I said, "it is impossible to make peace. Only with a new Palestinian leadership that abandons terror and the goal of destroying Israel can we negotiate a genuine peace for which we all yearn, pray and dream."[3]

Three months after calling for Israel to withdraw immediately from Palestinian cities, President Bush was calling "on the Palestinian people to elect new leaders, leaders not compromised by terror."[4]

My public activity, combined with the activity of many others, had helped turn the tide. The Theory of Public Pressure proved itself once again. I returned to Israel and to private life.

HAVING SMASHED THE strongholds of Hamas fighters in Shechem, Jenin, Bethlehem, and other Palestinian cities, and having apprehended PLO hit men there as well, the Israeli army now resumed overall military responsibility for preventing terror from Palestinian enclaves. This policy successfully reduced terror until Sharon's unilateral and disastrous withdrawal from Gaza three years later.

But in the aftermath of Operation Defensive Shield, as the military operation against Hamas was called, terror subsided and Sharon's popularity soared. He consolidated his grip on power and on the Likud. Though I had helped him, he always viewed me as breathing over his shoulder.

Periodically I would visit him in the prime minister's residence on Balfour Street.

On one such visit I said, "Arik, there is a much bigger threat to Israel than the Palestinians, and it's Iran. You've got to focus the national effort on preventing Iran from getting nuclear weapons."

He agreed it was a worthwhile goal, but when I outlined the necessary military and political steps to achieve this, I could see he had no intention of doing the things I recommended. He simply wasn't there.

In desperation, I played my final card, one I had discussed earlier with Ron Dermer.

"If you do this," I said, "I will give you a written pledge that I will not enter the political arena and I will support you as prime minister for as long as you choose to stay."

That didn't do the trick either. The old warrior was immovable. I was truly worried. Through government back channels I was getting reports on how Iran was moving forward with its nuclear program, yet here was a government completely preoccupied with the Palestinians.

To be fair, they too were beset by a Bush administration that was taking its own turn in "bringing peace to the Middle East," buying again into the seemingly perpetual Palestinian Centrality Theory, though somewhat less intensely than their predecessors.

EARLIER, OF COURSE, President George W. Bush and the entire world were seized with the tragedy of 9/11. When the news broke, videos showed Palestinians dancing with joy on rooftops in Gaza and Ramallah. Israel grieved. That day, September 11, 2001, I was sitting in my office with the Egyptian chargé d'affaires. Egypt's president Mubarak, with whom I had friendly relations, had sent the chargé with a personal message to me to do what I could to advance peace with the Palestinians, including Hamas.

As we spoke, my secretary rushed into the room with the news of the first plane crashing into the World Trade Center.

"It looks to me like a terrorist attack," I said.

"Do you really think so?" asked the Egyptian diplomat.

A few minutes later came the second plane and that closed the matter.

"Please tell your president," I said, "that the world has just changed and that he and the rest of the Arab leaders have to stand squarely against terrorism everywhere. You can't cut separate deals with these animals, and that includes Hamas. If they get their way they will kill you all."

The chargé turned pale. He wrote down every word and left. A few years later, as an Egyptian envoy in Iraq, he would be murdered by Islamic terrorists. I was told he was beheaded.

The aftermath of 9/11 was the first time I regretted not having taken the prime minister's post. From that position I would have had a fighting chance to influence the United States to go after Iran's nuclear program.

As things stood, I would have to make do with other means. Nine days after the attack, on September 20, I was invited to a committee of the US Congress to speak about the unfolding events.

I recounted my 1995 warning, which was in response to the 1993 terrorist attack in the parking garage of the World Trade Center, that Islamic terrorists would eventually seek to bring down the towers altogether. "Well, they did not use a nuclear bomb," I said now. "They used two 150-ton fully fueled jetliners to wipe out the twin towers. But does anyone doubt that given the chance, they will throw atom bombs at America and its allies?

"On September 11, we received a wake-up call from hell. Now the question is simple: Do we rally to defeat this evil while there is still time, or do we press a collective snooze button and go back to business as usual?

"The time for action is now.

"Today the terrorists have the will to destroy us, but they do not have the power. There is no doubt that we have the power to crush them. Now we must also show that we have the will to do just that. Once any part of the terror network acquired nuclear weapons, this equation will fundamentally change, and with it the course of human affairs. This is the historical imperative that now confronts us all."[5]

A few weeks after September 11, I met privately with US defense secretary Donald Rumsfeld. It was clear the US would go to war with Iraq. By that time I had learned that Israel could neither confirm nor rule out the possibility that Saddam was pursuing the development of nuclear weapons. But my main focus was elsewhere. I asked Rumsfeld about Iran. When he spoke of the complexity of forming a broad coalition against terrorist states like Iran, I said that the mission must determine the coalition and not the other way around. Rumsfeld agreed.[6]

In other informal conversations with friends in the administration, I was more direct, urging them to use the impending victory over Saddam to give Iran an ultimatum: *Dismantle your nuclear program or you will suffer the same fate*. I thought this would be the most sensible benefit of the war. Knocking out Saddam was a worthy goal, but not leveraging his defeat to achieve this larger goal was a wasted strategic opportunity.

In a hostile *New Yorker* article published years later on the neoconservatives who ran American policy on Iraq, I was criticized as being "worse than all of them" because I advocated dealing not only with Iraq but with Iran as well.[7] This was true, but unfortunately my advice was not taken. The Bush administration was content with its lightning-fast victory over

Saddam. Blocking Iran's nuclear weapons ambitions was the last thing on the mind of American policy makers at the time.

The Iranian regime, fearing that the US would still carry the fight to them, halted for a short time its nuclear program. But after a year or so, when the Iranians realized there was no direct American military threat, they resumed the nuclear program under a thinly disguised "civilian research" program. We got tangible and incriminating proof of this ploy in 2017 when I authorized the Mossad operation that captured Iran's secret nuclear archive and brought it to Israel.

In the last thirty years, the *only* time that Iran completely halted its nuclear program was in that one year following the Gulf War when the regime was concerned that the US would act against it militarily. Absent a credible threat of military action, Iran continued its nuclear program.

It became increasingly clear to me that it would require Israeli strength and resolution to halt Iran's march to the bomb.

33

THE VISION

2002

When did I decide to return to politics?

Though I wasn't at all sure I would return following my defeat in the 1999 elections, even in my resignation speech I left the door open.

"I am taking a leave of absence," I said, carving a phrase that would be later used by several politicians who were put in similar situations.

That a return was possible was not in doubt. My prominence in Israeli politics was undiminished. Even after Sharon, then in his mid-seventies, assumed control of the government and the party, I was clearly the heir apparent.

But what to come back *for*? Power by itself didn't interest me. Without a clear purpose it is ultimately futile. My entry into public life and service in the corridors of power were always directed to clearly defined goals: to mobilize the free world to do battle against international terrorism, to defend Israel against political and military threats, to begin reforming its economy, and to bolster understanding of the justice of our cause and our rights in our ancestral homeland.

But now as a private citizen I had time to think. All these various strands of thought and action had a common thread. They were meant to assure Israel's future. There is no longevity guarantee in the life of nations. The Jewish people had overcome incredible odds in reestablishing the Jewish state, but that state was still beleaguered by forces that sought its destruction. The chief force seeking our annihilation was no longer the Arab world but the Islamic Republic of Iran. Its quest to arm itself with nuclear weapons would threaten not only Israel but the entire world.

How could a small nation withstand such an assault and continue to thrive?

It would need to become stronger, I believed, much stronger. Strength would enable us to forge alliances, which in turn would be force multipliers. All nations need alliances, including superpowers. So much more so a small country beset by innumerable challenges.

As I pondered these questions, a clear plan crystallized in my mind. The key to ensuring Israel's future in the twenty-first century was to make *a quantum leap in Israel's power.*

I believed there was a clear path to achieving this multiplication of power, one that would catapult Israel to the front line of the world's states.

In my second meeting with Ron Dermer in May 2000, I laid out this vision.

"What is the first prerequisite of national power?" I asked.

"Military power," he answered.

"Correct," I said. "But fighter jets, tanks, drones, submarines and intelligence cost a lot of money. We can't build military power without first building economic power, and the key to that is free markets and advanced technology. The combination of military and economic power will give us diplomatic power. Many countries in the world, including Arab countries, will be interested in forging ties with us when we become world leaders in civilian technology and military intelligence. If we combine all this with our ability to influence US policy through public opinion, we'll quickly climb the ladder of nations. We will walk among the giants."

That, in a nutshell, was my vision. While each source of power augmented the other, this vision had one clear foundation—economic power.

This was a complete reversal of the received wisdom about securing Israel's future prevalent among the elites in Israel and the West. They believed that power would come from peace. I believed that peace would come from power.

The more I thought about the imperative of building Israel's power among the nations, the more I believed this was both necessary and feasible. I also knew it would necessitate my return to politics to lead this change.

No one else espoused this doctrine with such fervor or had the capability to carry it out. I would have to claw my way back up what the nineteenth-century British statesman Benjamin Disraeli famously called the "greasy pole" of politics. Success was far from certain.

"How long did it take Rabin to return to the Prime Minister's Office?" I asked Ron.

"Fifteen years," he said.

"Right," I responded. "It could be a long schlep, and nothing is guaranteed."

But at least I now had a coherent purpose that could justify the endless struggles and sacrifices that political life demands.

Was I up to it? Not right away, as my refusal to simply walk into the Prime Minister's Office after Barak's collapse clearly proved. But after two years of enjoying freedom as a private citizen, I thought about it more and more. Politics ought to provide a life of purpose, and I had a purpose—two in fact: to elevate Israel's power and thus contribute to securing its future, and to address the threat of a nuclear Iran that would endanger my country and the entire world.

I had rested and I had traveled, circumnavigating the globe with Sara and our two boys. In Paris we took them to Euro Disney, in New York to Broadway's *Lion King*, in Los Angeles to Disneyland.

In Sydney we climbed the Sydney Harbour Bridge, followed by climbing the extraordinary Uluru, or Ayers Rock, the wondrous sandstone rock in the heart of the Australian continent. Ten-year-old Yair showed remarkable grit when he joined me in climbing its only accessible ridge, holding on for dear life by gripping the metal chains along the steep slope. He was saved by an accompanying Israeli security guard from being blown of the escarpment by a strong wind. I could have killed myself. Had I forgotten—with my own child—my vow never to risk lives and limbs unnecessarily?

Perhaps this sense of guilt is what led me to confront a passenger on our flight back home through Bangkok, Thailand.

Avner was crying after a spoon he was holding hit his eye when the plane hit turbulence.

"Madam," the irate passenger lashed out at Sara, "can't you shut him up?"

"He's just a little boy," she protested. "Don't you have children of your own?"

"I have boys, too, and they don't behave like that. Just shut him up!"

That was that.

I walked up to the passenger and clenched him by the lapels of his fashionable leisure jacket.

"Listen, that's my son and he's been hurt. Now you shut the . . . up."

The passenger went into shock. He had recognized me earlier and had even sent me a note of appreciation at the beginning of the flight. That's not how political leaders are supposed to act, he must have thought. But it is how *I* acted.

We heard no more complaints during the rest of the flight.

When it came to physically protecting my family, I was always ferociously unyielding as though possessed by some primal instinct. I had in fact surrounded the pool in our home in Caesarea with the ugliest metal fence imaginable to keep our boys safe until they learned how to swim.

On other trips we went to Positano in Italy and to Monte Carlo on the French Riviera with my good friend Meir Habib. Born in France to Zionist Jewish parents who hailed from Tunisia, Meir was educated in Israel's Technion and became a successful businessman. He later became a member of the French parliament and was a gallant fighter for Jewish and Israeli causes. But in those carefree days, unburdened by public responsibility, we enjoyed our holidays with our wives and young children.

These were delightful diversions, but they were just that, *diversions.* Was I really built for a life of leisure at the age of fifty-two? Probably not, and certainly not after I had developed my vision for Israel.

I decided to plunge back into politics. On November 6, 2002, Sharon appointed me as foreign minister, with the understanding that I would run for Likud's leadership in the party primaries leading up to the 2003 elections. We both knew that I would very likely lose, as polls clearly showed this would happen, and I promised to loyally support him and campaign for him if that was the result.

I ran not because I thought I would win, but from a longer-term calculation of shoring up my base. By setting myself up as Sharon's only challenger I was also establishing the fact that I was his natural successor, just as he had been mine. Receiving a respectable 40 percent of the vote and the second place on the Likud list, I was satisfied that that goal had been achieved.

As I had promised, I now supported Sharon and campaigned for him in the elections. In the election rallies he attended, Sharon spoke of the great team of young and experienced political leaders he had running with him.

"Bibi, too, Bibi, too!" the crowd shouted. Sharon at first pretended he didn't hear them, and when the chorus got too loud, he disparagingly sniffed, "Yeah, Bibi, too, Bibi, too."

"You reap what you sow" and a hundred other clichés raced through my mind as I heard this. I had handed Sharon power on a silver platter and in return got brazen ingratitude.

But as usual, one voice dominated all the others in my brain. Grin and bear it and just get on with it, I told myself.

Which is exactly what I did.

34

CRISIS

2003

Ariel Sharon easily won the elections. Then he offered me the position of finance minister.

That was a shocker.

No one wanted to get close to the Finance Ministry because in 2003 Israel was in its deepest financial crisis in decades. Given the challenge of taking over a godawful mess, I had some serious thinking to do before I gave an answer.

The terror attacks of the second Palestinian Intifada and the dot-com collapse had taken their toll. Growth had been negative for two years in a row, unemployment soared, and the average personal wage dropped by a staggering 6 percent in 2002. Foreign investment was fast drying up.

Israel's central bank governor, Dr. David Klein, warned of the impending collapse of a large bank, which could bring down the entire banking system. The savings of millions of citizens were in jeopardy. Israelis were rapidly losing their jobs, their livelihoods, and their living standards.

The previous government had tried various means to halt the hemorrhaging, but none of the remedies seemed to work. It introduced tax reform, but its major provisions extended well into the future and did not produce the desired growth to reduce the ballooning deficit.

As a result of high budget deficits, Israel's central bank also raised the prime interest rate to above 11 percent, thereby choking small and middle-sized businesses, which were collapsing in droves. Cafés, restaurants and shopping malls emptied of customers, and many long-standing institutions shut down.

Jerusalem's famed Fink's restaurant, open continuously since 1932, finally closed its doors. Its owner, the son-in-law of the founder, lamented: "We survived the War of Independence, the austerity program in the 1950s, the 1966 recession, even the terrible slump of the Yom Kippur War and the oil embargo. But this is too much. We just can't hold on anymore."

Less urgent than the collapse of small businesses but no less troublesome in the long term were the pensions of hundreds of thousands of workers who had vested their hopes for a secure retirement in the Histadrut, or General Federation of Labor.

The Histadrut's older pension funds were in actuarial bankruptcy. This meant that although the pensioners had paper commitments to have their pensions paid in due course, there was no financial basis for these commitments. The pensions were effectively diluted, if not worthless.

Some of these funds had in fact already collapsed and were kept afloat by periodic cash injections from the government.

But whereas these financial obligations could break Israel's economy in the future, there were other, more pressing burdens that the government was already finding hard to carry. Chief among them was Israel's lavish social welfare system, which could not be sustained for long, since for a third consecutive year Israel was unable to raise money in the international financial markets.

"Don't ask us for credit," I later learned some international bankers wisely advised Finance Ministry officials. "That way the word won't go out that we've refused your request."

The Sharon government's only recourse was to try to raise money from the Israeli public. To do so, it had to offer higher and higher rates on its long-term bonds, paying an astronomical 11 percent on a ten-year note (compared to 4.5 percent in the US at the time).

In the corridors of government, officials began to whisper about shutting down government and municipal offices a few days a week, and about the possible collapse of Israel's welfare payments. These payments, a staple in the lives of many Israelis, would have to be cut even more radically, or possibly eliminated altogether.

Nir Gilad, head of the Finance Ministry's General Accounting Office during this period, later revealed in a press interview the magnitude of the crisis engulfing the nation when Sharon made me the offer to take charge of the economy.

"In June 2002 the state of Israel faced bankruptcy. We all understood that the situation resembles what happened in South Korea and the Philippines—a dramatic drop in the value of the local currency," he said. "The public didn't know this because it was a secret matter. The discussions between the Prime Minister, the Finance Minister and the Central Bank Governor were kept secret. We didn't want anyone to know about it."[1]

Though I, too, did not know of these secret discussions, I could plainly see that the government was making great efforts to curb spending. But though necessary to prevent the collapse of the economy, a cut in spending by itself would not produce economic growth. And without such growth the economy would continue deteriorating.

In the midst of this economic collapse, Sharon's surprising offer to me to take the Finance Ministry was immediately judged by all as a political masterstroke. If I was harebrained enough to take the job, the pundits said, I would most likely fail, thereby removing from the scene Sharon's main rival for the future leadership of the country. And if by some twist of fate I succeeded, I would save Sharon's government and allow him to take the credit.

Sharon was shrewd and witty, with a biting sense of humor that he often used to belittle his rivals. Long ostracized by the left, he would later relish his political rehabilitation in fashionable circles after his 2005 decision to withdraw from Gaza. I suspect that deep down he never felt truly comfortable in their embrace and constantly needed to maintain his bona fides with them.

An astute judge of character, he figured that as his finance minister I would be genuinely absorbed in reforming the Israeli economy and not engaged in political ploys against him. Likely assuming that I would either save the economy or hang myself politically, he would let me implement the most antipopulist economic measures in Israel's history if I chose to do so. Politically this could be suicidal for me.

"Fight to stay on as foreign minister, or take on another ministry, any ministry," friends and advisors said. "But don't take Finance. That way you won't jeopardize your chances to return one day to the post of prime minister."

A wise politician calculating the odds would not take the job. Most likely its holder would go down with the economy. Any attempt to stop the downward slide would require even harsher measures than those already taken, and these could seriously hurt my popularity with my constituents.

Many fateful decisions in my life were resolved in short bursts of self-examination. This was no different, especially as I had only a few hours to decide. If I became finance minister I would severely jeopardize my chances to return to the post of prime minister. But *why* did I want to return to the office of prime minister in the first place? To transform and modernize the Israeli economy and fight Iran's efforts to develop nuclear weapons. If I could try to achieve the first goal, was the attempt not worthwhile?

If Israeli politics is crueler than most, it's also more fickle. Unexpected upheavals abound. Who can tell what the future has in store? Why not seize this opportunity to refashion the economy, an opportunity made possible precisely because of the depth of the crisis we were in?

I decided to accept Sharon's offer.

35

FAT MAN, THIN MAN

2003–2005

In 2005, the Nobel laureate Milton Friedman wrote this about Israel's economic malaise:

> Israel is a nation with great economic potential, yet it is a clear case of arrested economic development. Israel's human capital and geographical location at the heart of the Middle East should have naturally produced a thriving and prosperous economy.
>
> Israel can be the Hong Kong of the Middle East but that potential has been blocked for decades.
>
> What held it back? Far reaching and rigid government intervention in the economy, socialist policies embraced by the government and unnecessary state ownership of critical means of production.
>
> Israel can change all this by adopting broad free market policies.
>
> Fortunately, Finance Minister Benjamin Netanyahu, who specialized in economic issues, understands the problem and is willing to use his political capital to bring a solution.

This was easier said than done. In 2003, it required persuading not only my government colleagues but also the public at large that we needed a radical shift to free markets.

As finance minister I often began meetings with members of the public with a query: "Who's the richest person in the world?"

"Bill Gates" was the immediate response. In 2003, the founder of Microsoft topped every major list of individual wealth.

"Okay, who was the richest person in the world twenty years ago?"

One of the older members in the audience usually got it right.

"The Sultan of Brunei."

"That's right," I would respond. "The Sultan of Brunei sits on a small sea of oil. Twenty years ago he was the perennial number one on the list of the world's richest persons. Bill Gates overtook him because conceptual products are more valuable than raw materials. Products of the mind can make you a lot richer than oil."

The audience would nod in agreement.

"Now, which country produces the most conceptual products relative to population size?"

"Israel!" the audience would respond in unison.

"So one final question."

Now the audience was taut with expectation.

"If we're so smart, how come we ain't rich!?"

How was it possible that in 2003, Israel, one of the world's most technologically gifted countries, was stuck in the middle rungs of the global economic ladder as a "developing economy," with a GDP per capita of only $17,000? Israel was blessed with creative, talented citizens who possessed a natural entrepreneurial spirit. Israeli military intelligence had developed generations of gifted knowledge workers. Israel spent more on R&D relative to GDP than any other country on earth.

So indeed, how come we weren't rich?

To me, the answer was clear.

Israel *had* become rich, but in the wrong ways: rich in bureaucracy, rich in welfare, rich in taxes, rich in unions and rich in monopolies. Yet it was poor in the most precious of commodities: freedom, the freedom to initiate and profit from economic enterprise and the fruits of one's labor.

In the land of the Bible, the economic race went not to the swift, but to those with better political connections. Hard work was not rewarded; strikes were. The unions holding the economic chokepoints of the country in the seaports and airports, in the banks and in the electricity and water monopolies went on strike with astonishing frequency, paralyzing the economy and winning enormous pay raises to boot.

Seeking to help the poor, successive governments doled out welfare indiscriminately. The number of people receiving guaranteed income from welfare went through the roof between 1990 and 2002, growing fifteen times faster than the population. To pay for these expenditures, heavy taxes were levied upon workers and businesses, further depressing economic activity.

Most of the Israeli economy was hopelessly mired in this antiquated semi-socialist bog, arresting the flow of market forces and blocking enterprise.

Israel's technological prowess was no cure for these ills. Technology, science, and education by themselves do not make you wealthy. Otherwise, Soviet Russia would have been among the world's richest countries. Free markets are the indispensable component for wealth creation.

Put another way: Technology without free markets does not produce wealth. Free markets without technology do. But technology *and* free markets are an unbeatable combination.

This is where I intended to take Israel.

In democracies, significant economic reforms never reach fruition without leaders who are willing to spill their own political blood. This is so because economic reforms nearly always involve taking on powerful opponents: unions, welfare lobbies, big business, resistant bureaucrats and rival politicians. Most political leaders prefer not to plunge into these shark-infested waters.

Even if they dare to *begin* reforms, they seldom see them through because they quickly encounter strikes, demonstrations, violent protests, negative ad campaigns and press vilification. Worse, they could be thrown out of office, their careers ended.

Achieving a free market revolution in Israel's economy would require enormous inputs of *vision, power and will*. Absent any one of these components, no significant reforms can take place.

But in Israel in 2003, all three essential conditions for change were present.

First, I had a clear *economic vision* of where I wanted to steer the country. Thirty years of education, experience and reflection, including my time at BCG, had honed that vision to a detailed plan guided by market principles.

Second, I had sufficient *political power* to carry out my vision. There was an absolute majority of 61 seats in the Knesset supporting my policy, made up of the Likud with 40 seats, Tommy Lapid's pro-market Shinui Party with 15 seats and Avigdor Lieberman's Russian immigrant party, Yisrael Beiteinu, with 6 seats.

Lieberman, an immigrant from Moldova, began his political career as my personal assistant and was then appointed by me to be the Likud party manager and later director general of the Prime Minister's Office. He subsequently formed Yisrael Beiteinu, a party of his own aligned with the right, catering mostly to the older generation of Russian immigrants.

I was confident I could deal with any recalcitrant populists in the Knesset coalition by my strong position in the Likud and by my tacit pact with Sharon. He would run foreign and defense policy on Likud principles; I would run the economy on market principles.

Third, I had abundant *political will*. Totally determined to achieve Israel's free market revolution, I was willing to risk my political future for it.

I studied the experiences of other nations. I could see how global changes in economic power were changing history. The Soviet Union had lost its preeminence as a global superpower because it failed to adjust to market principles. China was fast taking its place because it did. The same dynamic was evident in Singapore and Ireland, small countries that fifteen years earlier had per capita incomes lower than Israel's, but by implementing far-reaching market reforms had surged ahead of us and had even overtaken Britain and Japan, becoming significant actors in the global economic sphere.

Lee Kuan Yew, the father of modern Singapore, put it best when he explained why his country had chosen the path to a market economy: "Communism collapsed and the mixed economy failed. What else is left?"[1]

There was no reason, I thought, why Israel with its superb human capital couldn't join the ranks of such rich countries.

The key was implementing free market reforms that would unleash their enormous abilities and energies. Within fifteen years, I believed, Israel could join the list of the twenty countries with the highest per capita income and living standards. Ultimately, during my subsequent tenures as prime minister this goal would be achieved.

But as Israel's new finance minister in 2003, I knew I had to move with great speed to start the revolution. The opponents of reform regroup very quickly, and reformers must use whatever window of opportunity they have before that happens. The market reforms I had started as prime minister had been completely halted under the subsequent governments led by the two former generals, Barak and Sharon. Neither had introduced any significant economic reforms. I knew that to achieve my goals, I needed to have at least two uninterrupted years to carry out several bursts of concentrated market reforms. Otherwise the economy would sputter and the plane would fail to take off.

Moving into the dilapidated quarters of the Finance Ministry, I remembered the wise words of a British management consultant. Visiting Israel in 1980, he gave a lecture to an audience consisting mostly of young executives, many of whom, like me, had served as officers in the army.

"You have been given command of new recruits and your mission is to conquer the enemy's command post," he began. "What is the first thing you do?"

The answers came quickly: "Reconnoiter and collect intelligence"; "Develop a plan of attack"; "Leave sufficient covering fire and approach from the flank"; "Wait for nightfall to begin movement."

The lecturer let his audience members exhaust themselves and then said simply, "You're all wrong. The first thing you should do is pitch your tent, pick your officers, and then order the ordnance sergeant to equip your men with gear and weapons. The second thing you must do is drill your soldiers. You say 'march left,' they march left. 'March right,' they march right. Only after you have staffed, equipped and trained your force can you go out to face the enemy."

Some twenty years later, I could only take this sensible piece of advice so far. To pitch my tent, I invited to my office Rachel Barnoon, a friend of the family and a well-known interior decorator.

"It's all yours," I said. "Do anything you want with the place. One thing, though, you can't spend a single shekel."

Exasperated, she moved a few pictures on the wall and pleaded, "At least let me fix that ugly hole in the carpet."

"Absolutely not," I replied.

That hole in the carpet would prove invaluable against other government ministers in budget negotiations. How could these ministers recently housed in plush new offices make exorbitant demands on the country's purse? After all, weren't we in the Finance Ministry walking on tattered rugs? The creaking and ancient seating arrangements in my office served a similar purpose. The couches actually lasted through three budgets, until they literally collapsed under the strain of old age.

Now for the staff. Certainly I would have preferred to take the time to carefully choose my key personnel for the battle ahead. But at the same time I knew that the urgency of Israel's economic crisis would simply not allow me to staff first, act later. I therefore decided to build my team as I went along.

The Finance Ministry had many of the best and brightest minds in government already, and I made sure that key available positions were filled by people who shared my reformist zeal. I kept Ori Yogev as budget director, recruited Yossi Bachar from the banking sector—at forty-eight, the oldest of the group, besides myself—to be general manager, and brought in Yaron Zalicha as comptroller general. Aside from being young, dedicated and experienced, nearly all had one common feature in their resumes: they had worked in the private sector, and consequently knew what running a business entailed.

Professor Stanley Fischer, who had served as vice chairman of the International Monetary Fund and whom I later got Sharon to appoint as Israel's central bank governor, said of this group that it was the finest team he had seen anywhere.

My staff and I went to work feverishly, putting in eighteen- to twenty-hour days and barely catching any sleep. Within three weeks we presented an economic plan to the government. Three months later we passed it in the Knesset, the most revolutionary free market program in Israel's history. It included dramatic government budget cuts; unprecedented wage, welfare, and tax reductions; investments in infrastructure; raising of the retirement age and privatization of government companies.

To help pass this program through the Knesset, I unabashedly used the carrot of US loan guarantees to Israel that the American government had discussed with Sharon in his previous term as prime minister. It was withholding these loans until Israel adopted an economic reform plan to rescue its economy.

US officials sensibly argued that they did not want to throw good money after bad. Granting the loan guarantees depended on Israel's reaching economic milestones, to which I was only too happy to agree.

My interest in these loans was more political than economic. I believed we wouldn't really need them if we implemented my program, but in this I was virtually alone. On the other hand, because everyone else did believe we needed them, I could use the terms for receiving the loans as leverage for my reforms. Besides, cheap credit is never something to sneer at.

These American loan guarantees thus provided a double whammy. They placed a constraint on the Knesset's spendthrift ways while providing extra oxygen for the Israeli economy in the form of cheaper and readily available American credit. At first, the US team led by John Taylor, deputy secretary of the Treasury, carefully examined our semiannual performance, but in time their scrutiny waned. Almost without exception, we regularly exceeded our targets and we added ambitious reforms to our list of things to do.

Because of the crisis, most foreign investors had ditched our country and didn't see a reason to return. A handful of potential European investors was all I could muster for an audience in my first months as finance minister. I told them that despite the dot-com collapse and the Intifada violence, the Israeli economy would rebound because of the massive economic reforms I planned to enact.

Fifteen minutes into my presentation, I could see the look in their eyes change as they began to believe that I was serious.

"So, Finance Minister, tell us what you think we should invest in," they said.

"I'm not an investment broker but I'll give you one tip," I replied.

Now they were listening carefully.

"Invest in a parking lot in Tel Aviv," I said. "Invest in *anything*! Because *everything* in Israel will go up."

I'm not sure they took my advice, but if any of them did they would not have regretted it.

While preparing my economic plan, I knew that the actual recovery would begin not when the markets would believe my *intentions*, but when they had sufficient proof of my *ability* to carry them out. Getting something quickly enacted was therefore vital.

I kept looking for one basic image, one defining story or vignette, that would clarify to the public what we were about to do. But how to concisely explain that the purpose of the recovery plan was not merely to rescue Israel from the present crisis but also to address the country's inherent lack of competitiveness, which prevented us from keeping pace with other countries?

Israelis had not grown up in a culture of competing lemonade stands. Our one shared experience was service in the army.

In a nationally televised live news conference in which I presented my policy, I described Israel's economic malady with a story from my first day in basic training. The company commander ordered us to line up in a straight row on the parade ground for what was called the elephant race. I was first in line.

"Netanyahu," he said, "put the man to your right on your shoulders. Every other soldier do the same."

I had to put a medium-sized soldier on my shoulders. To my right, a small soldier had one of the biggest men in the unit straddled on his shoulders, while a big soldier carried one of the smaller men on his back.

When the commander blew the whistle, I could barely move forward. The small soldier to my right collapsed after two steps. The big man shot off like a cannon and won the race.

All economies, I said, were engaged in a similar race. In each, the public sector, "the Fat Man," straddles the shoulders of the private sector, "the Thin Man." The private sector creates most of the added value in economies and is the engine of job creation and economic growth. It carries the public sector on its back and pays for it.

In London I had once heard a tour guide express this truth in unembellished Cockney. He pointed to the City of London, the seat of business, and then to Westminster, the seat of government.

"Here's where they make it, there's where they spend it," he said.

If the public sector gets too big, the private sector will slow down or collapse under its excess weight. A bloated public sector, Big Government, will demand higher taxes and higher interest rates to sustain it and these too will place an additional burden on the private sector.

In 2003, Israel's public sector had reached well over 50 percent of GDP, among the highest in the developed world, an unbearable weight on the shoulders of a shrinking private sector. Taxes were sky-high and government and union monopolies stifled competition. The Israeli economy was facing imminent collapse.

The path to economic recovery was clear: *Reduce the public sector, strengthen the private sector and remove barriers to competition.*

The Fat Man, Thin Man image soon became the stuff of heated debate. Taxi drivers discussed it with passengers, stand-up comedians used it in their routines and the government unions rejected it.

The unions devoted most of their efforts to scuttling the first part of my plan, which was to put the public sector on a strict diet. Not surprisingly, the public sector had no interest in seeing their pay cut. After all, they protested, government workers were paid less than private sector workers.

Actually, they were not.

In Israel, workers in the private and public sectors had for years been paid roughly equally, an ominous sign. But while public sector wages had actually kept their value in the previous two years, private sector wages had dropped by 8 percent as businesses shrank or collapsed, laying off tens of thousands of workers. Worse, during one of Israel's greatest economic catastrophes the public sector had actually *added* people to its payroll.

Individually, public sector workers were not getting huge pay. Most, in fact, were paid modest wages, and many of them did fine work in important fields such as health, education and the nation's security. But over time the public rolls had expanded beyond Israel's capabilities, adding too many workers to government. This expansion punished the better workers, who could not get the pay they deserved because of the need to pay a bloated workforce.

My solution to this problem was not to undertake massive firing in the public sector. I believed annual attrition in hiring was a better way. That meant not hiring people for the many jobs vacated each year by retiring government workers. I also passed a law capping government expenses, thus effectively ensuring that the rolls of the annually departing retirees would not be refilled.

I tackled the unions directly, requesting they take on a significant pay cut worth roughly $1 billion. This was a great sacrifice, but I promised to restore present pay levels by 2005, at the end of two years, since I estimated correctly that the economy would recover by then. I also passed in the government a decision to cut the pay of ministers and Knesset members by 17 percent.

Despite this leadership by example, the unions would have none of it. Never before, they said, had any public unions taken wage cuts.

Wage *freeze*, yes; wage *cuts*, never!

They threatened a general strike.

I knew that without such a cut in the public payroll I could not bring down taxes, without lower taxes there would be no growth, and without growth there would be no recovery. A battle with the Histadrut labor federation appeared inevitable. We were heading for a prolonged general strike, one that could paralyze the economy for weeks, perhaps months.

But here Ori Yogev, the soft-spoken but hard-nosed Office of Management and Budget director, came up with a brilliant yet simple suggestion: If a general strike was an inevitable price to be paid for one reform, why not consider passing several reforms simultaneously? This way we would *maximize the number of reforms per strike!*

Yogev was tireless in arguing for a strategy of simultaneous rather than sequential market reforms. I would often tease him in our staff meetings.

"So, Ori," I would say, "are there any fields you haven't burned yet?"

I liked his can-do attitude, which perfectly matched the revolutionary spirit I wanted to impart to our reforms.

From other countries' experiences, such as New Zealand's economic transformation under Finance Minister Roger Douglas, I was aware of another important principle: *If you carry out several market reforms simultaneously, the cumulative growth effect is bigger than the sum of their individual parts.*

Each reform supports the other by removing barriers to competition, increasing productivity and sending a powerful message to the markets to increase investments.

I decided to risk a prolonged general strike and pass several big reforms at once.

The biggest reform adamantly opposed by the unions involved the Histadrut's pension funds. For years these funds had served as the playground for Histadrut and Labor politicians. There was talk of questionable practices and mismanagement that had wreaked havoc with pensioners' savings.

Israel's pension system, like that of all developed nations, was gradually losing its financial base because of the surge in life expectancy. This was a positive result of the dramatic improvements in medicine and is one of the true blessings of the modern age. But it tore apart the statistical foundations on which pension systems are based.

The original idea was that many young working people would support fewer older people in their nonworking old age. When America started its Social Security program in 1935, most retirees would begin collecting benefits at sixty-five and life expectancy was only sixty-three. But now, close to a century later, average life expectancy in both the US and Israel was in the mid-seventies.

While life spans had steadily increased, the retirement age had barely changed. In Israel it was sixty-five for men, sixty for women. Instead of the neat age pyramid (envisioned by Otto von Bismarck, the German chancellor who pioneered pension schemes in the late nineteenth century), many governments now faced a reverse pyramid, with more elderly people at the top and fewer and fewer young people at the bottom. As a result, less and less money was saved to support pensions.

All governments know about this time bomb waiting to explode. But few have the guts to do anything about it, preferring to push the problem into the future.

Alas, the future has one unfortunate quality. Sooner than you think, it becomes the present.

In Israel as elsewhere, the actuarial imbalance in the pension system meant eventual financial disaster. The funds committed to pensioners were several hundred billion shekels. There was no way this would be paid out without major pension reform. This crisis was a long way off and did not require urgent action. Which is precisely why I decided to tackle it.

I knew that by taking on pension reform, a long-term problem, I would signal to savvy markets that I was committed to making fundamental structural changes in Israel's economy.

I focused on two efforts: gradually raising the retirement age from sixty-five to sixty-seven for men and from sixty to sixty-four for women, and rescuing and rehabilitating the massive unions' pension funds.

I told the unions they would no longer manage their failing pension funds. The Finance Ministry would appoint professional managers to run these older funds and privatize the management of the newer funds in open bids in the marketplace.

The government would commit $20 billion spread over forty-five years to save the pensions. We would sharply reduce the amount of fixed-rate designated bonds the pension funds had been receiving from the government, which had hitherto absolved them of the need to invest in the country. They would now have to invest in infrastructure projects such as roads, railways and waterworks as well as the stock market and corporate bonds.

In the developed world, pension funds account for a significant part of the bond and stock markets, in the United States as much as 50 percent. In Israel, by contrast, there was almost no bond market except government bonds and a very thin stock market. In my eyes, pension reform was less part of Israel's immediate problem as much as it was part of the *immediate solution*. In one fell swoop this reform would save future pensions, create a bond market and strengthen the stock market.

But before all this could happen, we had a huge battle in front of us.

The massive pension fund reform elicited howls of protests from the unions. They had a hard enough time swallowing the huge cut in government workers' pay, but they simply could not stomach the pension reform. They insisted that such a reform be negotiated with them.

Reaching no agreement with the unions, I decided to force the issue by legislating the reform. Immediately after I submitted the pension legislation to the Knesset, the unions announced a general strike on April 29, 2003. The country would be paralyzed for months, but I didn't back off.

To his credit, Prime Minister Sharon backed me fully and did not flinch. Facing a brick wall of government resolve, the reform bill was passed and the unions ended the strike on May 18. Israel thus became one of the few countries in the world that had begun to successfully tackle its pension problem.

The pension reform produced three huge benefits. First, deprived of their guaranteed-income government bonds, the pension funds began investing in Israel's infrastructure, providing a much-needed source of capital for the physical development of the country.

Second, the emergence of a private corporate bond market hitherto unheard-of in Israel created additional capital.

Third, seeking to take advantage of pre-reform pension benefits that were about to disappear, many government workers chose early retirement. This reduced the government payroll by an astonishing 6 percent in 2004, the largest reduction of government workers in Israel's history. In fact, there had never been *any* reduction in the public payroll until then.

MY GOAL WAS ambitious—to limit the annual growth of government spending to 1 percent.

Since Israel's population grew annually at about 2 percent, over several years this budget limitation would dramatically lessen the load on the shoulders of the Thin Man, encouraging growth. It would also drastically lower Israel's mammoth debt, the numerator in the debt-to-GDP ratio that investors use to measure how indebted a country is.

As part of this reform, we stopped pegging the huge expenditures on welfare allowances to wage hikes but pegged them instead to inflation, breaking a long-standing automatic escalator of government spending.

The other escalator of uncontrollable spending was runaway legislation by Knesset members. In Israel's parliamentary system, individual Knesset members could submit their own personal legislation for pet projects to benefit their constituents, which could require vast sums of the public's money. We put a stop to that by legislating a limit to the cost of private bills. This reform was one of the many tools successfully used by coalition whip Gideon Sa'ar to impose an iron discipline on the coalition that helped pass the government's budgets and reforms.

I enacted a complementary scissors movement: cutting spending while cutting taxes. Having done the former, I now focused on the latter.

The previous government had passed a tax reform program that was to be implemented gradually until 2009. Although I had many reservations about specific provisions in the program, I decided not to tamper with it for fear of getting bogged down in prolonged legislation. Instead, I compressed the time for the completion of the program by three years, to 2006, sending a clear message to the market that taxes would come down, and fast.

We did, however, also eliminate the excessive marginal personal tax rate of 65 percent, enacted by the previous government, correcting a monumental blunder that forced many high earners to either cheat, leave the country or turn themselves into corporations.

I took this even further and announced that if tax revenues exceeded expectations, we would lower tax rates again.

This last step was met with incredulity.

I explained that reducing Israel's high tax *rates* would actually increase tax *revenues*.

How could cutting taxes produce *more* tax revenues? My critics ridiculed my statement. Tax cuts, they argued, would reduce tax revenues and increase the deficit, thereby further shortchanging vital government services. "Haven't you heard of the Laffer curve?" I asked my detractors in the Knesset Finance Committee.

"Lauffer?" they asked derisively. "Who's this Lauffer?"

"It's Laffer, and for your information there are non-Jewish economists," I shot back.

While there was debate in certain situations over the applicability of the curve popularized by economist Arthur Laffer to show that cutting tax rates can result in increased total revenue, I had no doubt that it would work in grossly overtaxed Israel.

I believed that putting more money in the hands of consumers and businesses would be a strong growth engine for the economy.

Yet many Israelis had been taught to believe that growth engines were primarily government-funded projects, especially in infrastructure. I explained that roads and railways were important and that they could also be financed by private capital, but the biggest drivers of growth were increases in competition, productivity and investments brought about by market reforms.

"And what will further fuel economic growth?" I asked in exasperation. "Lower taxes, lower taxes, and still lower taxes!"

It is hard today to reconstruct the dismissive reaction my drive to lower taxes encountered. It was as if there weren't plenty of examples showing that countries with lower tax rates experienced more rapid growth. This is especially true in the global economy, where investors, consumers and workers can transition with relative ease to lower-tax economies. A country like Israel, at the higher end of the tax spectrum, really had no choice but to cut tax rates.

My campaign to lower taxes also met stiff opposition from an unexpected source: the Finance Ministry's legal arm.

"Finance Minister, you can't lower taxes because we won't be able to defend you," the government lawyers said.

"Defend me where?" I asked.

"In the courts."

"Why, has anyone taken me to court?"

"Not yet, but they will. The social lobby will argue that lowering taxes favors the rich and discriminates against the poor."

"This is hogwash," I said. "Lowering taxes will grow the economy, increase tax revenues and enable giving more benefits to the truly needy."

I could see that I wasn't getting through. In my frustration I said, "Fine. Don't defend me, I'll do it myself. And I'll bring with me several Nobel Prize–winning economists to argue my case."

That did it. Nothing more in this vein was said, and I was not taken to court.

In my first year as finance minister we slashed the top personal income tax rate from a whopping 60 percent to 49 percent and cut the corporate tax from 36 percent to 30 percent, and later to 24 percent. We reduced the VAT (value-added tax) and eliminated custom and sales taxes.

We also enacted special personal income tax cuts for the lower tier of taxpayers to equalize income distribution and spur consumption. Finally, we introduced lower and simplified investment taxes to attract Israeli and foreign investors.

With lower tax rates, Israel's economy began growing rapidly, and much of the criticism over lowering taxes subsided. The more we lowered tax rates the lower the debt-to-GDP ratio fell, from 102 percent in 2003 to 89 percent in the first half of 2006. A decade later, thanks to robust growth and the spending caps we put in place, it had dropped to 60 percent.

By 2008, for the first time in anyone's memory, the Fat Man and the Thin Man weighed the same.

36

"DON'T READ THE PRESS"

2003-2005

Most political discussions of economic policy focus on a subject of secondary importance—the budget. Budgets divide the pie; they don't enlarge it. Properly managed, they ensure that a government's spending is in line with its revenues.

This is necessary but insufficient to ensure growth in national income, just as balancing one's checkbook doesn't ensure that one's personal income will grow. You can't live on ballooning bank overdrafts for very long, whether you are an individual or a government. As Abraham Lincoln said, "You cannot keep out of trouble by spending more than you earn." Sooner or later, someone has to pay.

Balancing your accounts doesn't make you rich. It just keeps you from going deeper into debt or reaching bankruptcy. To get more money, an individual must work more or get better pay for his or her work.

The same is true of an economy. To grow, it must get more people to work and have them engage in more productive jobs.

But for this to happen, businesses must be able to compete and expand. Increasing competition in the economy was therefore a major focus of my economic plan. I once again used the Fat Man, Thin Man analogy to punctuate this point.

Having filled the Thin Man's lungs with oxygen by lowering his taxes and making credit available to him, and having put the Fat Man on his

shoulders on a strict diet, nothing could stop the fit Thin Man from racing ahead. Right? Wrong.

In Israel, when companies tried to run forward, they hit a ditch of
overregulation. When they crossed the ditch, they hit a fence. When they
crossed the fence, they hit a wall. These were bureaucratic barriers to
competition, and we needed to remove many of them to enable Israeli
companies to race forward and compete effectively.

The most immediate barrier to effective competition were the seaports. Israel remained one of the few countries whose seaports were
closed to competition. Nominally controlled by the state, they were in
reality governed and mismanaged by powerful labor unions. The lion's
share of Israel's GDP passed through them, giving the unions enormous
power to paralyze the economy every time their demands were not met.

The results were endless strikes during the 1990s, a decade in which
Israel became the world record holder in strike days per worker, four
times more than second-place Italy.[1]

These disruptions forced many manufacturers to leave the country
and drove away investors. Inefficiency in the seaports cost each family
in Israel hundreds of dollars a year in higher prices on a wide variety of
products.

The port reform we advanced was aimed to change this. In 2004, following a year of negotiations, legislation and strikes, we reached a historic
agreement with the Histadrut labor federation. The obsolete Ports Authority was dissolved and separate competing government port companies were established. These were to be gradually privatized, Eilat's port
within five years, Ashdod's and Haifa's within fifteen years.

Though it would end up taking twenty years to implement and was
not always fully realized, the port reform nonetheless ended a stagnation of nearly sixty years, launching thousands of ships and millions of
containers.

But before it passed the Knesset it met stiff resistance from the
unions. The ports were shut down for months as a result of strikes, causing great damage to the economy.

The unions' Achilles' heel was their exorbitant pay. I was unrelenting
in targeting it. Some stevedores received triple the average wage, skilled
labor got more. When the union attacked me for quashing "workers'

rights," I retorted that they were the ones who were choking millions of citizens, driving their fellow workers out of jobs and being paid a fortune to boot.

Information about union excesses soon started to flow into my office from irate citizens. I learned that a particularly well-connected dockworker in Ashdod was being paid a handsome monthly wage for running a maritime museum that didn't exist. Another drove a Jaguar and a BMW, all on a dockworker's salary.

In the rough-and-tumble world of Israeli politics, I was given the chance to land a knockout punch. I dubbed the battle to reform the ports the "Battle of the Jaguar."

This image stuck, shifting public opinion further into our corner. Once the public was strongly behind us, the unions could not sustain a strike for very long. Union members encountered criticism from family members, neighbors and everyone else, and their morale began to erode.

Still, it took a full year from the time it was presented to the government to pass the port reform in the Knesset. During this long year, my staff and I would periodically meet with Histadrut chief Amir Peretz and his staff for protracted negotiation sessions. Typically, Peretz would begin with a personal diatribe against me that would last ten to fifteen minutes. I retained my composure and stuck to the issues, though some members of my staff seethed with anger and passed me notes to return fire.

I saw no point in that. I was interested in results.

As I later discovered, the Histadrut campaign against me began to draw blood only when it shifted its focus from union pay to welfare allowances. The representatives of the highest-paid workers in Israel, whose frequent strikes threw thousands into unemployment, presented themselves as champions of the downtrodden, while vilifying leaders whose policies helped create hundreds of thousands of new jobs as enemies of the workingman.

One of these long nightly sessions with the unions ended at 2 a.m. in the Kfar Maccabiah hotel, near Tel Aviv. Everyone was exhausted.

I looked across the table at the dozen union chiefs sitting opposite me.

"You are all here because you are leaders. I respect your abilities and your rise to positions of leadership. But I have to tell you something in the spirit of candor that should exist between people who respect each other."

They all looked at me.

"It's over," I said. "The days when this table can shut down the country are over. Things will never go back to where they were before."

A stony silence ensued.

In fact, they did shut down the country several times afterward, but even so, I was right. The era of the big strikes was coming to an end because the passage of port reform communicated above all else a newfound resolve to confront the unions' monopolistic power.

Ports were one of the most important cogs in the union strike machine, and that cog was now largely undermined. As part of the agreement on port reform, the unions promised not to strike for the next five years. The creation of competing companies created new incentives for each port to compete for more work, rather than join forces to strangle the economy for more pay. Indeed, following the port reform the number of workers actually *rose* to handle the increased traffic through the ports.

It is hard in retrospect to understand how monopolistic arrangements are tolerated for so long. Reforms have a ratchet-like quality. Once a reform kicks in, as in liberalizing foreign currency and the ports, people quickly forget what life was like before.

For a leader who risks his career to get such reforms passed this can be bad news, because people don't necessarily value the subsequent benefits. But in a deep sense this forgetfulness is good, because once people get used to freedom they seldom want to go back. Government may not always go forward with new reforms, but they seldom go backward and undo reforms that have been passed.

Sometimes, what I considered to be conventional measures to end strikes were seen as strange and out of place by others. In the strike against pension reform, the union shut down many government services, from issuing passports to collecting garbage.

"Fine," I said, "delete the strike days from their pay."

My staff did a double take.

"We'll have to refund the deleted amount when the strike is over," they said.

"Why?" I asked.

"Because we always have," came the reply.

"Not anymore," I said. "There is a cost to strikes, and they will pay it."

To my amazement, I learned that all previous strike days had been paid for by the government. But I was determined to no longer play by the old rules.

On another occasion, the customs workers in the national airports struck, threatening to bring air traffic to a standstill. Passengers clogged the air terminals, unable to enter the country.

I told Eitan Robb, the customs and tax head, to throw the arrival gates open. He did, and for a few hours passengers entered Israel without customs control. The strike ended almost as quickly as it began.

To some this may be reminiscent of President Reagan's response to the air traffic controllers' strike in 1981. But because of the breadth of union control of Israel's economy and the long duration of our confrontations, it resembled more Margaret Thatcher's pitched battles with the all-powerful coal miners' union.

On a visit to London I was asked by a journalist, "Who was more impressive in economic reform, Thatcher or Reagan?"

"Thatcher," I said.

"Why?" he asked.

"Because from its very beginning America was built right."

The journalist said that if that was the criterion, then I had a much tougher job than Thatcher. Unlike Israel, Britain was never truly socialist.

ON APRIL 8, 2013, Margaret Thatcher passed away. Queen Elizabeth decided to honor her with a state funeral at St. Paul's Cathedral. Winston Churchill was the only other prime minister who had been accorded such an honor. Given the queen's purportedly strained relationship with Thatcher, it was a gracious acknowledgment of Thatcher's importance in postwar Britain.

I attended, along with other heads of state and prime ministers.

Sara and I were given the honor of sitting in the front row, facing the coffin. As usual, the British were unsurpassed in ceremony.

"Listen to the hymns," I whispered to Sara. "Jerusalem and Hebrew themes appear over and over."

Later, in a reception with the family, Thatcher's daughter, Carol, approached me.

"My mother really admired what you did for Israel against tremendous opposition," she said.

"I had a good example to learn from," I answered.

I recounted my last encounter with Thatcher. In 2005, when I was finance minister, Sara and I were passing through Britain and the former prime minister invited us for lunch at the Goring hotel.

I had met her before, sitting next to her at a dinner when she visited the Knesset in 1998 after she had left office. I always admired her tenacity and conviction.

After a long list of speakers, which included Senator Joe Biden, she rose to speak.

"I have never lost an election and this is because I can read a crowd. This crowd is hungry. As a woman and mother, I say, 'Serve dinner!' "

Everyone cheered.

When I lost the premiership in 1999, she wrote me a one-sentence letter: "I am sorry you lost."

When I saw her in London in 2005, she was terribly frail, her health and concentration in obvious decline. Nonetheless, she went out of her way to make sure that Sara and I, and the members of my staff, were properly served.

She also gave me a useful piece of advice: "Don't read the press. I never did."

She then recounted in detail her experience with the coal miners' unions.

Before the tenure of the "Iron Lady," it was believed that democratic governments in the postwar era could not take on the most powerful unions. Thatcher's willingness to confront Britain's coal miners and their fiery leader Arthur Scargill broke this mold. It earned her lasting antipathy from many but it also proved to many governments, and to me, that powerful unions were not invincible.

"You see," she said, "they had to know we were serious. We stockpiled coal in electricity plants in advance of the strikes, and we explained to the British public that they were being victimized by the unions."

Did she understand the global impact this confrontation would ultimately have?

"Oh yes. We were the first to do this. I mean Ronnie's fight with the
air controllers was minor in comparison," she said, referring to Reagan's
decision to fire striking air traffic controllers in 1981.

Then she paused to reflect about Reagan, whose moving funeral she
had attended a few months earlier.

"Ronnie was a good man. He had all the right ideas," she said.

Her eyes grew misty, and then she added quickly, "Not very good
with numbers, though."

My wife and I said good-bye to this remarkable woman who had
saved Britain from economic decline and who is still maligned by those
who can't forgive her for breaking the pipe dream of the unionized welfare state.

IN ISRAEL, MY willingness to risk my career for what I thought was
right and the backing I received from Sharon sent a powerful message of
resistance to the unions. In their frustration, they intensified their campaign against me, calling me the enemy of the workers.

I was not. I was the enemy of monopolies and a friend of the workers,
and if the monopolies were union committees that stifled competition,
paralyzed the country and sent thousands out of work, I would fight them
without hesitation.

I viewed the lack of competition in the Israeli economy not merely
as a chronic problem but as an *opportunity for growth*. Privatizing government companies and breaking up monopolies are some of the reforms
that create an unstoppable growth engine when rapidly enacted. Since
government companies often *were* monopolies, we needed not only to sell
them off but also to break up their privileged position in the marketplace,
giving their competitors a fair chance.

With few exceptions, state-controlled companies were a drain on the
economy, requiring regular injections of taxpayer money to keep them
afloat. Typically they had an inflated workforce, inflated management and
inflated salaries. Almost invariably, their productivity was low and they

blocked productivity gains in other sectors of the economy by frequent strikes and poor service.

During my first tenure as prime minister, my government had privatized more government-held assets than all previous governments combined. Now we introduced an additional competitor into the cellular phone market to compete with the government telecom monopoly, Bezeq. Before we did so, only a fraction of Israelis used cell phones, paying a lot and getting poor service in return.

With increased competition, cell phone use exploded to more than 7 million users, averaging one per citizen. Meanwhile, user cost went down while service quality went up.

Almost overnight, a phone service that under a government monopoly was limited to the few well-to-do became a staple of every Israeli, including low-income earners. And while Bezeq reduced its workforce, the number of people employed in the telecommunications sector shot up dramatically.

As finance minister, I was determined to do even more in privatization. I was fortunate in having Eyal Gabbay in charge of privatization, a young but experienced professional who had worked in my office when I was prime minister and then in the private sector. Now in the Finance Ministry I decided that before we tackled whales like the banks, we would begin with small fish.

"We need a quick success," I said to Gabbay and Ori Yogev. "What do you suggest?"

"How about El Al?" came the answer.

El Al, Israel's national airline, was an internationally known brand but its financial performance was choppy, reflecting all the ills of state-owned companies. Selling it would send a positive message to the markets. Previous attempts to privatize the airline floundered in the face of union opposition, religious parties that objected to the airline's flying on the Jewish Sabbath, and the Defense Ministry, which objected on grounds of national security.

I made it clear to the unions that strikes would not stop me. We got the consent of the religious parties and found satisfactory ways to ensure civilian flights during wartime.

El Al was sold within months of my becoming finance minister.

Within weeks its share price doubled. Israel was still in deep economic crisis, but investors around the world took notice. There were those who believed enough in Israel's economic future to buy its national airline.

Once the unions internalized my absolute determination, privatization proceeded more smoothly. The unions were left to haggle only over money, usually the financial arrangements for the workers who would be laid off. My policy was to be generous with these workers. It was both humane and saved the taxpayers billions in the long run.

After we withstood the initial national strikes and the political conflicts with the unions, my relations with them underwent a steady improvement. Union leaders gradually understood that Israel had entered a new era of a market economy and that this required a more responsible and cooperative attitude on their part, which I welcomed and appreciated. In later years when I would resume the post of prime minister, we would usually settle problems in a productive dialogue at a round table, sometimes literally, on the patio at the Balfour residence. The bitter enmity was gone and was often replaced with friendship.

I led the privatization of other government-owned companies, including the ZIM shipping line and Bezeq—we had earlier introduced competitors in the cell phone market but now privatized the company itself. Between 2003 and 2005 we privatized $3.9 billion of government assets, nearly three times the amount privatized in the preceding fifty-five years.

Perhaps the most significant government assets to be sold off were the three banks that dominated nearly all banking activities in Israel. As prime minister I had privatized Bank Hapoalim. Now as finance minister I sold off Israel Discount Bank and set in place the machinery to sell off Bank Leumi.

All three banks had been nationalized after a bank share scandal in 1983 in which the government stepped in to save the banks from collapse. Successive committees had urged that the banks be returned to private ownership.

This sell-off was a crucial component in reforming Israel's capital markets. Before the reforms, Bank Hapoalim and Bank Leumi had effectively controlled over two-thirds of all savings, offering low interest rates for savers and depriving many Israelis of a solid financial future. Savings were channeled by these banks to finance spending by the government, the labor unions and cronies, preventing productive investments that could generate growth.

The concentration of bank power, and the widespread cross-ownership of Israeli industries by a small number of wealthy families, produced an extraordinary distortion: Roughly two-thirds of loans went to just 1 percent of borrowers![2] Alongside heavy government borrowing, small business owners and entrepreneurs were effectively deprived of credit and an opportunity to grow.

I was determined to change that.

As soon as I took over the Finance Ministry in 2003, I asked Dr. Yossi Bachar, the director general of the Finance Ministry, to lead this reform through. It took me a full year to recruit him from the private banking sector.

"If you do only one thing in your life," I added, "it should be this—a major capital market reform. I'll affix your name to it."

"Leave everything aside," I told him. "Appoint three deputies to do the day-to-day administration of the Finance Ministry. But get this reform done. Without it, Israel will have no functioning capital markets and no significant growth. With it, we'll be winners."

With perseverance and considerable diplomatic skills, Bachar did exactly what I asked of him. So did I. By the time he tragically died of cancer fifteen years later, the reform he led was universally known as the Bachar Reform. The final stages of privatizing Bank Leumi occurred under my watch as prime minister in 2018.

Not surprisingly, our approach to bank reform was initially met by stiff opposition from the bank triopoly, which fought to protect its powerful and privileged position. Fortunately, several dedicated allies helped me fight the public battle, including Daniel Doron, an indefatigable free market intellectual, and Professor Marshall Sarnat, the country's foremost banking expert. They mobilized students and a few reform-minded journalists to bolster support for the capital market reform, which included privatizing the banks and the Histadrut funds, as well as enacting new pension management rules.

Perhaps my most consequential reform alongside foreign currency liberalization, the capital market reform quickly produced three benefits.

First, by denying the pension funds privileged bonds, the reform forced the funds to provide much-needed capital to *private businesses*, creating competition for the two large banks that hitherto cornered the market.

Second, the reform removed from the banks the provident and mutual funds that dominated private saving, giving *households* cheaper financing and better returns on their savings.

Third, *foreign banks* could also issue government bonds, further breaking the bank monopoly.

Because of its complexity, the Bachar Bill took longer to pass than any of the other economic reforms I led. To complete it, I had to stay in the government longer than I intended, absorbing criticism for not resigning during the lead-up to the 2005 withdrawal from Gaza. But it was worth it.

Goods can't move without open ports, cars can't travel without fast roads, and most businesses can't grow without affordable credit. We now paved a credit superhighway for growth.

This fit my gospel: *Reduce the Fat Man, strengthen the Thin Man and remove the ditches and fences in his way.*

"*THIS* IS SOCIAL JUSTICE!"

2003–2005

All my market reforms were anathema to the self-described "social justice" lobby, which accused me of "piggish capitalism," enriching the rich and impoverishing the poor.

I argued the opposite: it was free market reforms that had lifted a billion people out of poverty in Asia, while the policies of the social lobby, guided by a distorted interpretation of social justice, kept hundreds of millions of people impoverished in unreformed countries.

What is social justice, anyway?

The Hebrew prophets Isaiah and Amos said social justice meant charitably helping the weakest members of society: the poor, the aged, the sick, the handicapped, the orphaned, the widowed.

Some two thousand years later, the greatest Jewish thinker of the Middle Ages, Maimonides, had a somewhat more complicated approach.

Social justice, he believed, was a series of activities to help others. He ranked these on the rungs of a ladder, reserving the lowest rung for giving handouts, the middle rung for providing loans, and the top rung for helping people get jobs. Maimonides believed that the greatest help one could render others is to help them stand on their own feet.

So who was right, the prophets or Maimonides? As in the well-known joke about a rabbi's response when asked to adjudicate between two potentially conflicting claimants, the answer is: they're both right.

The key to sorting out the possible tension between these two conceptions of social justice is to understand that they deal with two different groups of people: those who can work and those who cannot. Those who can work should go to work. Those who cannot should be helped. This is not only good morality; it is good economics.

In fact, the *only way* that you can help those who can't help themselves is to get the able-bodied to work and then tax them modestly. I emphasize the word *modestly* because, as we have seen, if you overtax you often end up with less and not more money to help the needy.

In Israel this distinction between the two populations had been gradually eroded. For decades, the proportion of people living on welfare and government-guaranteed income rose steadily. By 2002, only 54 percent of the adult population participated in the workforce, the lowest participation rate in the developed world (the average for the thirty-eight member countries of the Organisation for Economic Co-operation and Development [OECD], which Israel was not a part of, was 70 percent).[1]

Entire segments of the population, especially the ultra-Orthodox and Muslim Arab communities, were severely underrepresented in the job market. They and others were supported by an elaborate system of welfare payments that grew year by year, keeping able-bodied adults out of the job market and placing an enormous strain on those who did work.

Indiscriminate welfare spending had ballooned to $10 billion a year by 2002, making it the second-largest item in the government budget, trailing only interest payments. Assorted welfare organizations and NGOs lobbied to increase this welfare spending further. I knew these organizations would be gunning for me with a vengeance, but I also knew that without reforming welfare I couldn't put the country back on track.

The first big welfare issue I tackled was child allowances. Nearly all countries have them, but in Israel the government doled them out in a peculiar fashion. The more children a family had, the bigger the allowance for each additional child became. The child allowance for each of the first two children was $35, for the next child it grew to $75 and after the fifth child it was roughly $200 for each successive one.

This created a built-in incentive for large families, especially among Israel's ultra-Orthodox and Muslim citizens. By having more and more children, they could live off child allowances. Underrepresented in the job market, they were overrepresented in the welfare and poverty rolls.

The distorted child allowance scheme threatened to eventually collapse Israel's economy.

We had to act.

The reform I introduced in 2003 lowered child allowances to the level of the first child and gave families a few years to adjust and enter the job market. I received enormous criticism for it, but it helped secure Israel's economic future.

Change was quick. Many Haredim (ultra-Orthodox) and Arab citizens joined the workforce, exited poverty and became part of the Israeli success story. After the reforms were enacted, overall participation rates in the job market grew dramatically, from 54 percent in 2003 to 64 percent in 2018.[2] After trailing the OECD average for years in job participation rate, Israel was rapidly catching up with the rest of the developed world.

The reform had unintended demographic consequences as well. In 1996, Arab births in Israel exceeded Jewish births by 2 to 1. By 2018, Jewish birth rates exceeded Arab birth rates for the first time.

As expected, inequality initially grew and reached its peak in 2006. But once the transition to jobs was under way, inequality steadily dropped and reached its second-lowest point in twenty years in 2018.

There was in fact no conflict between free markets and social justice. The first made the second possible.

The tax revenues of a growing capitalist economy rained down like manna from heaven. Israel could now fund social services neglected for many years. This enabled the increase of old-age benefits, help for the handicapped, and many other social benefits.

Perhaps the most dramatic confrontation over welfare cuts involved the case of single mothers (actually single parents, though single fathers caring for children were rare). Israel's welfare establishment rightly wanted to assist single parents who cared for their children without the help of a spouse. But over time, the welfare benefits allotted to them expanded to the point at which a single parent of two, working part-time at twelve hours a week, was bringing in more take-home pay than the average Israeli.

This was wrong. I thought that we should help single parents by giving them more modest pay boosts and by subsidizing day care for children and transportation cost to work. But I did not give parents an incentive not to work. We therefore proposed giving single parents the subsidized amount they were earning for the first twelve hours provided they worked an additional twelve hours. We would establish a special fund to help especially distressed cases.

This may have appeared easy on paper, but asking people accustomed to government handouts to take jobs is exceedingly hard. The single-parent reform sparked a nationwide protest.

It began when a single mother of two named Vicki Knafo set out on a four-day march in July 2003 from her home in the Negev to the Finance Ministry in Jerusalem. She vowed to camp outside my office until I canceled the reform.

The press had a field day. Each day they reported on Vicki's advance, and told the stories of other single mothers who had joined her by marching to Jerusalem from other parts of Israel. One woman was photographed pushing her grown son in a wheelchair claiming she would make the journey on foot all the way to Jerusalem. She made the three-day march from the Galilee to Jerusalem in three hours, but the press didn't bother to examine such miracles.

By the time Vicki reached Jerusalem, she was waving a large Israeli flag, Joan of Arc style. She pitched a tent outside the Finance Ministry, with the help and evident delight of the Histadrut and social welfare lobby organizations.

Soon others joined her, and a tent compound was erected where anyone with a beef against the government's policies would come and protest. Sometimes the loudspeakers outside the Finance Ministry were so disruptive we could not conduct meetings inside.

In a quiet moment on a Friday afternoon when the press was not present, I went over to see Vicki. Sitting on the sidewalk curb, we agreed to meet again and formally discuss the single mothers welfare reform. I found her pleasant, intelligent and surprisingly composed for someone who had sudden fame thrust upon her.

When we met a few days later, however, she put forward a clear demand. To discuss the reform with her, I must first rescind it.

She argued that I could not ask single parents to work more because there were no jobs available. I knew that was wrong. Between 2001 and 2003, the government had removed some seventy thousand illegal foreign workers from the country; there were jobs on the market.

"But there are no jobs in development towns like Mitzpeh Ramon," she argued.

"Fine," I said, "we'll pay for transportation costs to Beer-Sheba."

"But there are only menial jobs there," she said.

"What is menial?" I asked.

Didn't Russian immigrant professors who came to Israel in the early 1990s sweep floors for a while? Didn't physicists and geologists take on all types of jobs involving manual labor? Any job honestly undertaken confers respect on the person performing it.

This value, so powerfully embedded in Israeli society in the 1950s and 1960s, had been almost completely eroded. For many Israelis, jobs were to be provided by the government, and they had better be good jobs.

In our second meeting, Vicki demanded that I defer the single-parent reform for one year until the economic situation improved. I knew that if at this early stage I gave in, my whole economic program would collapse.

Everybody in Israel waited to see if I would back off. Tackling powerful dockworkers was one thing. Tackling powerless single mothers was another. But an impromptu comment came to my aid.

A journalist asked me what I thought of Vicki's four-day march.

"Anyone who can march two hundred kilometers can get a job," I blurted out.

This hit home and took much of the wind out of the protest's sails. I would make some changes to the single-parent reform, but I would not rescind or postpone it.

The demand for government-provided jobs wasn't limited to blue-collar workers. Shortly after I became finance minister, I attended a rooftop parlor meeting with some fifty people in a well-to-do suburb of Tel Aviv.

A middle-aged man asked me pointedly, "What can you tell my son? He's a laid-off high-tech engineer. He hasn't worked for months."

"I can tell him that our policy will bring back growth, and the first sector to recover would be the high-tech sector, so your son could recover his job," I said.

"That's baloney," the father lashed out. "What can you tell him *now*?"

I looked at his son, a strapping young man in his late twenties.

"You want to know what I say to your son?" I repeated his question.

"Yes, I do."

"Okay, here it is," I said, looking at the young man. "Get a job! Sweep floors, wait on tables, start a delivery service. Get a job! Any job! But don't come to me!"

This was met with silence. The audience was in shock. Then some broke into applause, while others protested.

"But there are no jobs." (Yes, there were.)

"But you can't expect a high-tech engineer to take on menial labor." (Yes, I can.)

The saying "there's no free lunch" always resonated literally for me. In high school I washed dishes in the school cafeteria in exchange for my lunch. In my university years I took on odd jobs, as did Sara, who cleaned offices for three years and later became a flight attendant to finance her university studies in psychology.

GETTING PEOPLE TO start working was difficult enough; getting them to a place of work or bringing jobs closer to them was even more so. In the depth of a great economic crisis, I decided to invest massively in Israel's transportation infrastructure to connect the country's periphery with its center.

For years Israel lacked an adequate transportation system. Worn-down roads and few railways turned one of the smallest countries in the world into one of its most congested. The economic plan we introduced in 2003 and would later expand greatly developed the nation's infrastructure, first in transportation but also in fields such as energy and water.

We put out bids for the construction of highways, signed financing agreements for a light railway in Jerusalem, launched the Carmel Tunnels to create a ring road around Haifa and extend the Trans-Israel Highway northward, published tenders for a light railway in Tel Aviv and launched a multiyear plan for developing a network of national railways to connect every town and city exceeding fifty thousand inhabitants, tripling the investment in rail transportation.

We launched two new desalination plants on the Mediterranean coast. This was an important step in the desalination revolution I would complete when I would return to office as prime minister, giving the dry country of Israel water independence for the first time in its history.

We also launched an initiative to give Israel crucially needed energy independence. Within one year we nearly completed a sea pipeline for natural gas and began work on a land pipeline.

Since these projects would take years to complete, there were no ribbons to cut and immediate political benefits to gain.

It was all about the long term.

These projects would change the face of the country physically, economically and socially. Connecting a small country like Israel with rapid transport was a revolutionary economic and social reform. It encouraged people and businesses to move to the periphery and enabled residents of the periphery to work in the center of the country, narrowing gaps between the Tel Aviv megalopolis and the rest of the country.

This was the only way we could finally turn the *development* towns in the Negev and the Galilee into *developed* towns.

NOT EVERYONE APPRECIATED my policies. In 2006 I was confronted by a delegate from Venezuela to the Zionist Congress in Jerusalem.

"Have you no heart?" he protested. "Was your economic policy more important than giving old people their allowances or adding lifesaving drugs to the medicine basket?"

There was no way I would take this lying down.

"I became finance minister in mid-2003," I said. "The budget had already been set by the previous government. How much money did they allocate to increasing the medicine basket?"

Silence.

"Zero. How much more did we add a few months later in the 2004 budget?"

Silence.

"Ten million dollars." Growth had begun.

"And the year after that?"

Silence.

"Ninety million." More growth.

"By 2006 the sum reached one hundred and fifty million. So you can talk about compassion from here to eternity, but you can't fund it on an empty coffer. We made the economy grow and filled up the coffer. *This* is compassion! *This* is social justice!"

Applause.

"Wait, I'm not finished. Who cut four percent from the old-age allowances?"

Murmurs in the audience. "The previous government."

"Right," I replied. "But with growth we restored two-thirds of the cut in 2005, and all of it was restored by 2006. Plus we helped the truly poor whose allowances weren't cut at all."

Accused of "piggish capitalism," it was in fact our policy that got people out of poverty by inducing growth, creating jobs and generating tax revenues to help those who couldn't help themselves. This enabled us to give more medicine, greater day care subsidies, increased old-age allowances and other social benefits.

Undoubtedly, applying tough welfare cuts more gradually would have made political sense for me, but it would have seriously jeopardized our effort to save the economy in the short time we had to do so. It was painful medicine for many Israelis but necessary to save the patient.

Still, the power of false labels oft repeated should not be underestimated. Forced to admit the social and economic advantages of free markets, a social lobby participant in one of Israel's economic conferences drew a distinction between compassionate and heartless leaders.

"There are capitalists like Ronald Reagan, Margaret Thatcher, and Netanyahu and there are compassionate capitalists like Bill Clinton and Tony Blair," he pontificated.[3]

Really?

President Clinton boldly went against his union supporters when he signed the North American Free Trade Agreement, and against his Democratic base when he slashed America's welfare rolls by half, something even Reagan never dared do.

For his part, Blair came to power as British prime minister in 1997 only after removing from the Labor Party constitution its infamous Clause Four, which called for the nationalization of all major industries. Once in power, Blair did not reverse any of Thatcher's groundbreaking labor reforms, thereby pitting himself against his own party's labor union constituency.

These are some of the reasons why the United States produced millions of jobs in the 1990s while Europe did not, and why Britain after Thatcher continued for years to stand head and shoulders above other major European economies.

The real distinction was not between leaders who were compassionate and those who were not, but between those who mouthed empty slogans about caring for the poor and those who were willing to translate their compassion into productive, job-creating market reforms that give an opportunity for a better life to all.

WITH THE EXCEPTION of four years between 2005 and 2009, I steered the economy for two decades, first as finance minister and later as prime minister, enabling me to ensure the continuity of my free market policies.

Before we enacted the economic reforms in 2003, there were 56 multinational corporations with R&D centers in Israel. Less than twenty years later, in 2021, that number reached 400. For many of these companies their center in Israel is their prime R&D facility outside their home base. For some it's the biggest.

While Israel's GDP had contracted by 1.3 percent in 2002, three years later it was growing by more than 5 percent a year. Israel's growth rate ranked at the bottom of the OECD countries in 2002. Within three years, Israel was one of the fastest-growing countries in the industrialized world. This continued over the next two decades.

In 1999, Israel's GDP ranked 50th in the world. By 2020 it jumped twenty places to 30th place. GDP per capita made an equally extraordinary leap, from 34th place in 2009 to 19th in the world in 2019, outstripping Britain, France, Japan, Italy, and Spain.[4]

Most important, this growth was shared across all income levels. Inequality was dramatically reduced, principally because of the massive entry into the job market of previously unemployed people.

In 2012, to increase competition and lower prices I launched a groundbreaking reform to reduce the concentration of dominant firms in the economy by flattening "pyramid structures." Majority shareholders of holding companies could no longer indirectly control firms in which they held minority shares and were forced to sell them. Still more reforms were needed to further whittle down monopolies and increase competition. Some of these reforms were passed in subsequent years, but the last batch, which I had included in the 2021 budget proposal, was not fully implemented because my government fell that year.

Like many other democracies, Israel suffered from a chronic lack of execution of government decisions. While the major free market reforms were carried out, many other more minor decisions were not. This is typical of governments and large organizations—they make thousands of decisions that are not always followed up.

To change that, in 2015 I adopted a mechanism proposed by Eli Gruner, the director general of the Prime Minister's Office at the time, to monitor the status of all government decisions. Within five years the percentage of decisions carried out more than doubled.[5]

This rise of Israel's economy was a critical component of my vision for securing Israel's power in the face of the one country seeking our destruction, Iran. A powerful economy gave us the means to develop and acquire the most sophisticated weapons on earth, compensating for our small size. By contrast, totalitarian Iran had a closed economy whose growth was further stunted by the US-led economic sanctions that we pushed for from 2010 on.

By 2020 the GDP of Israel, with fewer than 10 million people, exceeded that of Iran, with 80 million.[6] While Iran's GDP would soon be boosted by removal of sanctions and skyrocketing oil prices, Iran's economy, unlike Israel's, did not undergo any of the structural changes that would assure stable and long-term growth. This would prove to be an indispensable component in providing Israel the means to fight Iran's nuclear weapons program.

Today all these results are taken for granted. Yet at the outset, the plan to overhaul Israel's economy was met with widespread criticism and skepticism. Various attacks on the plan appeared every few weeks, only to vanish almost as quickly when data released by Israel's central bank and the Central Bureau of Statistics refuted them. These attacks would then

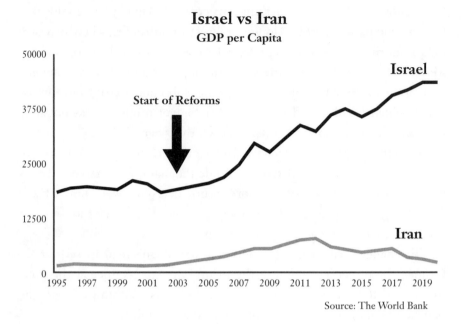

Israel vs Iran
GDP per Capita

Start of Reforms

Israel

Iran

Source: The World Bank

be replaced by new outlandish claims, which would then also be refuted by new data.

First the critics said the plan would not bring growth. When growth came, they charged that it was "jobless" growth. When jobs were created by the bushel, the critics claimed they were part-time jobs. When the recovery turned part-time jobs into full-time jobs, they claimed wages were falling. When it became clear that wages were rapidly rising, they grudgingly conceded that the economic plan was a success but argued that the spectacular growth of Israel's GDP was in reality driven by growth in our export markets. But that argument fell too when it turned out that our principal export markets in Western Europe were hardly growing at all.

A large part of the growth derived not so much from gaining market share abroad but from the revival of domestic consumption, spurred by tax reductions and economic reform.

A year after we passed the final reforms in 2005, the economic supplement of the otherwise generally hostile newspaper *Haaretz* published this summary of my tenure as finance minister.

The Israeli economy is today enjoying the results of the steps taken by Benjamin Netanyahu in 2003 in the depth of the Israeli recession.

For a country swept into a war that struck its cities, damaged personal security and entailed compensation in the billions, this stability is virtually miraculous. For better or worse, Netanyahu assumed the status of a leader, certain of his strategy and willing to fight for it to the utmost, even to the point of paying a heavy price in loss of popularity.[7]

When I agreed to take on the finance minister post, ten-year-old Yair was agitated. He thought there was no point.

"Abba," he said anxiously, "look at New York's skyline and look at Tel Aviv's. They have skyscrapers. We have nothing. We'll never be like them."

"Don't worry, Yair," I said. "Your father will become finance minister and you'll soon see skyscrapers here, too."

"You're just saying that. It will never happen," he insisted.

"We'll see, won't we," I said.

Twenty years later, Tel Aviv's forest of high-rise office and apartment buildings is visual proof of the force of the free market revolution we put in place.

Yet this watershed transformation of Israel was nearly aborted by an unforeseen political development during my tenure as finance minister. Luckily this event occurred after I had already put in place many structural changes in the Israeli economy. But by forcing me into a head-on confrontation with Ariel Sharon it nearly scuttled the indispensable capital markets reform.

I did everything in my power to prevent that from happening.

38

A CLASH OF HEAD AND HEART

2005

As finance minister, I was resolved to focus on the economic revolution I had envisioned. As far as I was concerned, this revolution wasn't a "nice to have" but a "must have" component in the transformation of Israel's global position. The historic opportunity to radically change Israel's economy and thereby dramatically upgrade its standing in the world was *now*, and I needed uninterrupted focus on it. But the single-mindedness of my attention on economic matters was constantly under siege. I was forever walking in a minefield in which political matters would force me to resign from my post as finance minister.

The first challenge came from the Bush administration, which insisted in June 2003 that Israel adopt a "Road Map for Peace," including Israeli withdrawals from key territories.

I drafted a list of fourteen "reservations" to the peace plan that would mitigate most of the risks for Israel, and, seeking to keep the economic engines roaring, I told Sharon that if the cabinet approved all fourteen, I would abstain from the cabinet vote on the Road Map rather than vote against it. I joked that I hoped that my Fourteen Points would be more successful than Woodrow Wilson's program for world peace under that same name.

I assumed, correctly, that nothing would come out of this new round of negotiations with the Palestinians, so there was no point in creating a crisis that could scuttle my economic reforms by coming out strongly against it.

But then something happened that I could not overlook.

On December 18, 2003, six months after I had passed my economic recovery plan in the Knesset, Sharon surprised the nation by announcing his plan to unilaterally withdraw from the Gaza Strip. His stated rationale was that Israel should rid itself of controlling this sizable Palestinian population, and would do so while giving up minimal territory. He argued that Israel's security would actually be enhanced and that if a single rocket was fired at us, Israel would retaliate massively with full international backing.

Gaza had no special hold on the public's imagination. Many Israelis would have been delighted to get rid of it. Sharon's move was aligned with this sentiment, even though it completely contradicted his campaign pledge a few months earlier never to uproot any of the Jewish communities built in the Gaza Strip during the previous four decades.

Since Sharon vowed never to test this proposition, his startling about-face in so short a time immediately aroused speculation. As Sharon was under criminal investigations for receiving illegal contributions from friendly benefactors, this led some on the right to coin a phrase, "The deeper the investigations, the deeper the withdrawal." They assumed Sharon's move fit what would prove to be a pattern: prime minister is investigated for some alleged wrongdoings, real or fabricated, prime minister veers to the left and offers territorial withdrawals, prime minister receives protection from the leftist press and the bureaucratic elites.

This had happened with Ehud Barak, who, while being investigated for illegal campaign funding, offered Arafat and Assad the shop in complete contrast to his campaign pledges. The pattern would hold with Prime Minister Ehud Olmert as well.

If Sharon's withdrawal announcement was based on a plan to extricate himself from his legal problems by veering sharply to the left, it worked. He was lauded as an Israeli Charles de Gaulle, who took France out of Algeria. They conveniently forgot that Algeria, unlike Gaza, was *hundreds of miles* away from France and not hundreds of *meters*. (The Algerians also did not seek the destruction of France.)

The left saw Sharon's withdrawal from Gaza as the first step to a full withdrawal from Judea and Samaria, especially since he let out that he was also considering withdrawing from four settlements in Northern Samaria as part of the Gaza Disengagement Plan.

My immediate thought after hearing his intention was, Who will take over Gaza if we leave? What does Israel get out of this?

"For every step we take," I said in response to this move, "we should get something in return," echoing the reciprocity policy I espoused as prime minister.

This made absolutely no impression on anyone. We were in a political earthquake. The ground had shifted, and here I was talking about the outdated concepts of reciprocity and security when we were being led to a rosy future by a resolute leader.

Two weeks later, Sharon formally announced his plan to vacate a total of twenty-five communities—twenty-one Israeli communities in the Gaza Strip and four in Northern Samaria.[1] Two weeks after that, he invited me to a meeting to try to mollify me.

"When Israel withdraws unilaterally," I said, "we know what Israel *gives*, but what does Israel *get*?"

Specifically I raised the troubling likelihood that Hamas would take over the areas we vacated and use them to attack Israel.

Sharon waved that aside. "We'll respond forcefully to the very first missile," he said.

"Once you establish the principle that you withdraw to escape terrorism, terrorism will chase you," I countered.

I was in a terrible quandary. On the one hand, I was convinced that unilateral withdrawals would lead to the creation of a Hamas terrorist enclave that would eventually endanger all of Israel. On the other, I knew that given the public mood and the incredible mobilization of the press, Sharon was guaranteed the votes to carry out his plan, even if I resigned from the government and opposed him.

From purely personal considerations, the thing to do was to resign. I could not be part of a government that would endanger Israel's security so irresponsibly.

Yet there was another side to this. If I left the position of finance minister prematurely, Israel's economic revolution would stop dead in its tracks, perhaps never to be resumed.

I decided to adopt a strategy of staying on as finance minister for as long as I could, delaying my resignation to the last possible moment. At the same time I would try to delay the Gaza Disengagement Plan from within the government by leading an effort to minimize its scale and maximize the security arrangements we would get in return. Simultaneously, I would push like mad to get dozens of structural economic reforms passed to change Israel's economy from a semi-socialist to a capitalist one.

I knew that my stay in the government was on borrowed time, and that the window of opportunity to transform Israel's economy was closing fast.

"I'll decide my position after I see the final elements of the plan, including what we would get in return," I told Sharon.

Though I didn't say it then, the things I thought Israel might get included American opposition to the Palestinian so-called "Right of Return" and American recognition of our strategic interests in Judea and Samaria, land that was the backbone of Israel's security and at the heart of our history.

Meeting the American diplomatic delegation of Nicholas Burns, Stephen Hadley and Elliott Abrams on March 14, 2004, two weeks after my conversation with Sharon, I raised my concerns and emphasized the need for reciprocity. They wanted to see me because of my prominence in the Likud and my clear disagreement with the disengagement plan.

"The disengagement plan is problematic," I said. "I still don't see in it the answer for Israel's security. Mohammed Deif, Hamas's leading terrorist, said a few days ago, 'If Israel withdraws from Gaza without getting anything in return, this will be a victory for the Palestinian resistance.' We therefore must ensure that Israel comes out of Gaza a winner and not a loser."

I knew by then that the chances this would happen were slim. But I persisted in deploying delaying tactics, figuring if Israel got something in the process, so much the better. A week after meeting the American delegation, in a speech before the Federation of Israeli Chambers of Commerce in Tel Aviv, I said, "The move has begun, but there should be no disengagement without appropriate reciprocal arrangements."

I spelled out three minimal conditions. First, Israel must control the

borders of Gaza, including all land, air and sea passes, to prevent terrorists from elsewhere in the world flooding the place.

Second, the security fence around Judea and Samaria needed to be
completed before any withdrawal.

Third, Israel must receive international and American backing for
unrestricted action against terror from Gaza.

My insistence on completing the security fence was grounded in two
reasons. First, I truly believed the fence was critical for the security of all
Israelis, since it would block terrorist access to Israel's cities and towns.
Even partially built, it had already proved a tremendously effective security measure in reducing suicide bombings. Second, completing the fence
would require *time*, and who knew what would happen with time?

I then added a fourth condition: "Formal and public American opposition to the so-called Palestinian Right of Return, which is tantamount
to the destruction of Israel."

Israeli acceptance of the Palestinian demand that Israel be flooded
with second- and third-generation descendants of Palestinian refugees
was widely understood by most Israelis as suicidal. It was also unjust. The
original Palestinian refugee problem came about as a result of the Arab
attempt to annihilate Israel at its birth. Having failed to vanquish Israel
militarily, the Arab states and the Palestinians sought to vanquish Israel
demographically.

Furthermore, the Arab attack on the embryonic Jewish state created
two refugee problems, not one. The Arab states promptly expelled an
equal number of *Jewish* refugees, roughly 800,000, who had lived in Arab
lands.

With less than 1 percent of Arab territory, Israel successfully absorbed
most of these Jewish refugees from Arab lands and integrated them as full
and equal citizens, even though they nearly doubled Israel's Jewish population at the time.

By contrast, despite their vast territories and cornucopia of oil riches,
the Arab states absorbed few of their Palestinian brothers, denying citizenship to them and their descendants, and thus for decades leaving them
in perpetual refugee status, to be used as political battering rams against
Israel.

I said publicly that the various conditions I had outlined comprised a single package, and without it I would not support disengagement. As I put it, the Israeli public didn't want us "to emerge from the disengagement as *friars* [suckers, the worst sin in Israeli folklore], receiving terror in exchange for withdrawals."

These arguments resonated with the public. Sharon correspondingly changed course, and, a month later, on April 15, 2004, President Bush sent him a formal letter opposing the Palestinian demand for the right of return and any resettlement of refugees in Israel. He also stated that Israel's final borders would not correspond to the vulnerable pre-1967 borders. Bush added that the US opposed political negotiations with the Palestinians and the establishment of a Palestinian state as long as the terror organizations in Palestinian-controlled areas weren't dismantled and the autocratic Palestinian Authority failed to enact meaningful internal reforms for democratization.

This was progress, and I said so. But alone, it wouldn't be enough for me to justify postponing my resignation for another eleven months, which is how much time was left before the next budget would be passed, my only opportunity to push through the last crucial batch of my economic reforms.

How could I stay on as finance minister to complete these essential reforms and stave off the disengagement that would force me to resign from the cabinet?

In many ways Sharon and I were walking the same tightrope. He sought to uproot the Jewish communities next to Gaza slowly and incrementally, and I sought to stay in the government as long as I could in order to finish passing my economic plan.

What followed was a turbulent year in which we played cat and mouse. Sharon agreed to my demand to hold a Likud referendum on the unilateral withdrawal. When he did so, the internal Likud polls showed he would win with a comfortable majority. But I and others soon changed that. We campaigned in rally after rally with Likud registered voters and steadily shifted opinion to oppose the plan.

Losing 60.5 percent to 39.5 percent, Sharon immediately said the results didn't oblige the government. I said he had no mandate from the public and when he sought one from our party he lost decisively.

Sharon couldn't have cared less for these democratic quibbles and neither did the press. Most of journalists stayed mum in the face of this obvious trampling of democratic norms.

The rejection of the Likud referendum caused a revolt in the party. A rebel Likud faction emerged in the Knesset. I didn't believe my resignation would stop the disengagement, but I knew it would definitely stop the economic revolution critical for Israel's future. If I had believed my resignation would have stopped the disengagement, I probably would have resigned. Since the actual vote on disengagement was put off, I had time to consider my options.

This was a classic clash of head and heart. My heart was with the opponents of the withdrawal. My head told me that my resignation would not stop the withdrawal but would stop my reforms.

I resisted the call by the opponents of disengagement to resign. Sharon in the meantime advanced an interim bill in the Knesset on October 20, 2004, to prepare for compensating Israelis slated for eviction. This would require specific legislation and several months of preparation. The Knesset resolution specifically stated that "this is not a resolution to evict Israeli communities."

Tzipi Livni, a Likud Knesset member and now a full partner of Sharon, explained this point to the Knesset.

"We will go back and convene the government *before any actual eviction takes place*," she said, clearly meaning to address my concerns. An actual decision to begin eviction would force my resignation, something Sharon also wanted to forestall for as long as possible.

The interim bill was clearly meant to provide me a ladder to climb down from instant resignation. Since the final decisions on the eviction and disengagement were left pending, I could hang on and try to get to March 2005, when I would pass the budget, and from there hang on for a few more months to pass the crucial capital market reforms. Nonetheless I was under public pressure to vote against this nonbinding bill.

Under Knesset custom, if a minister votes against a government bill, the prime minister can and often does fire the minister. It was clear that Sharon would have no option but to do so in my case.

To howls of derision, I voted for the interim bill. Headlines such as "Netanyahu Folds," "How Have the Mighty Fallen," and so on filled the newspapers. My opponents rejoiced; my supporters were dejected. I explained to them that when the final decision on eviction and disengagement came to the government, I would vote against it.

Though this is exactly what I ended up doing, the false claim endlessly repeated by opponents from left and right that I voted for the disengagement persists till this day.

Again, I kept a stiff upper lip and focused on passing my economic program.

On January 13, having succeeded to persuade the rebel faction in Likud to support my economic plan, I passed the initial legislation stages of my budget in the Knesset. Three weeks later, a nonbinding vote relating to settlement eviction was brought before the government that allowed for logistical preparations to get under way for the possible eventual eviction. (The eviction itself would require another separate vote.)

In the cabinet, unlike in the Knesset, differences of opinion are the norm and ministers don't risk being fired by the prime minister for voting against the government on bills.

I voted with the opposition against the eviction bill in the cabinet. I was one month away from the final passing of the budget bill. It passed along with vital tax reductions on March 29. But I was still months away from my most ambitious goal, the sweeping capital market reform that came to be known as the Bachar Bill.

Yossi Bachar needed more time to finish the job. Try as I may, the Knesset wouldn't let me fit the passage of his reform into a comprehensive reform bill passed simultaneously with the budget, as I had done with so many other reforms. It was too important and the Knesset wanted to discuss it separately.

"I need more time," Yossi told me.

"How much more?" I asked, knowing that my time in the government was running out.

"I think by July it would be ready," he answered.

July! How the devil would I hold out until July? But if I resigned before it was passed, the reform would not go through.

"Okay, Yossi, step on it" was all I could say.

The timeline meant that I could not escape one final humiliation. On July 20, the Knesset voted at the request of the Likud opponents of disengagement to delay the disengagement. Though Sharon had a solid majority against the delay, he warned that any minister voting for this bill in the Knesset would be instantly fired.

"Any minister" meant me. He knew my commitment to pass the Bachar Bill and he was flexing his muscles.

I dodged this by not showing up for the vote. Again, there were howls of derision from the press; again, gritted teeth from me.

While neither the press nor many of my supporters appreciated the seminal importance of my staying on as finance minister to see the capital markets reform through, there was one notable exception.

Milton Friedman, a Nobel Prize–winning economist and one of the most important economic thinkers of the twentieth century, understood its importance perfectly. On July 16, a week and a half before the Knesset finance committee voted on the Bachar Bill, he wrote the committee chairman, Yaakov Litzman, a letter in which he strongly urged passing the bill and praised my economic reforms.[2]

The public intellectual Daniel Doron, a lifelong advocate of free markets and an associate of Friedman's, wrote of the latter's support for my policies: "Friedman wrote to then Finance Minister Benjamin Netanyahu warmly supporting his several reform plans and congratulating him on his courage. He was especially supportive of the financial market reforms in which ICSEP [Doron's institute] participated. 'Your proposed reforms are excellent. If you can get these adopted you will have achieved a miracle,' he wrote."[3]

We achieved the miracle.

The Bachar Bill liberalized the capital markets by breaking the bank duopoly and creating new sources of credit in the economy. On July 25, the Knesset approved the capital markets reforms, which alone would do much to revitalize Israel's economy with much-needed capital.

Twelve days later, Sharon convened the government for the final vote on disengagement. Once approved, there was no going back. Eight thousand people would be evicted from their homes and Gaza would be handed over to the Palestinians, and to eventual Hamas control.

Time had run out.

After voting against disengagement, I handed Sharon a letter of resignation.

It was factual and firm. I reminded Sharon:

We resolved that we would make the final decision of eviction based on developments on the ground. To my regret, the government is ignoring reality. Just as I warned, Hamas is growing even stronger. Terror continues, mortar and rocket fire on the communities adjoining Gaza continues, and the terrorists proclaim that they will fire the rockets that expelled us from Gaza until the "final liberation of all of Palestine."

Just as I warned in 1993 that the Oslo agreements will bring terror attacks from Judaea and Samaria and rocket attacks from Gaza, I am equally convinced today that the disengagement will bring a growth in terrorism and not its decline.

What do we get for uprooting families and children, homes and graves? We will get an Islamist terrorist base.[4]

I further explained that I had stayed in the government despite my growing concerns over the disengagement in order to complete Israel's economic revolution. If I had resigned earlier, the game-changing capital market and tax reduction reforms would not have passed and my protest wouldn't have stopped the withdrawal.

I ended with a direct appeal to Sharon to maintain the vital economic gains we achieved for the country. "When I took on the post of Finance Minister two and a half years ago, Israel's economy was on the verge of collapse. Today it is a healthy economy, growing and prosperous. If the economic policy I have led will not be changed, this growth will continue and it will reach every part of our people."

I knew that no new reforms would be enacted, but I hoped that at least the ones passed would not be rolled back.

I then announced my resignation as finance minister and from the government.

In a press conference that evening, I went further, saying, "Once you form an Islamist base in Gaza, the rockets from Gaza will reach Ashkelon and Ashdod."

In fact, my so-called doomsday warnings were understated. Hamas would soon fire thousands of rockets at many Israeli cities beyond Ashkelon and Ashdod, including Tel Aviv and Jerusalem.

Eight days after my resignation, on August 15, the eviction of eight thousand Israelis in the Gush Katif communities and Northern Samaria began.

Sharon razed all the Jewish communities that had been built there over the past forty years. Houses, community centers, synagogues, businesses, farms—all were bulldozed. Even cemeteries were disinterred.

Heartbreaking scenes of settlers clinging to a remaining wall or roof were given short shrift on Israeli television. These settlers were "standing in the way of history." The press, the legal establishment, and academia all made common cause to move "history" along.

Legal and civil impediments regarding individual rights that would normally stand in the way of such sweeping action somehow magically disappeared. Buses carrying demonstrators to protest on the Gaza border were stopped, and protesters, including children, were arrested on the flimsiest of charges. All this was part of the crucial first step of carrying out the grand design of "territory for peace."

The plan's supporters were ecstatic, saying, "Today Gaza, tomorrow the West Bank and the next day, peace!"

Sharon was flying high.

Lauded by the Israeli press, he decided to capitalize on his popularity. Splitting from the Likud on November 21, he formed his own party, Kadima.

While the democratically run Likud had rejected his policy in a referendum he had pledged to respect before holding it and losing, he would now have his own party and Knesset members who would be totally beholden and obedient to him.

The day he announced the formation of Kadima, the Knesset was dissolved and new elections were called. Kadima received a whopping forty-two seats in the polls. The truncated Likud was tanking. I called a primary for Likud leadership before the election.

Though I won, I received only 44 percent of the vote, an indication of the dissatisfaction felt by the rank and file in the face of the harsh economic measures I enacted as finance minister and the fact that I stayed in the government as long as I did.

Sharon was still beset by legal problems involving questionable campaign contributions. As these problems mounted, leading TV commentators stepped in to defend him. It was one thing to start investigations to corral him into withdrawals. It was quite another to actually bring him down when more withdrawals were in sight. The left had a "right-wing" bulldozer advancing their agenda. They would protect him at any cost.

Incredibly, one commentator spelled this out. Sharon was too valuable to be brought down, even if he committed legal wrongdoings. "He should be protected like an *etrog*," the precious ceremonial citrus fruit that is carefully wrapped during Sukkot, the Feast of the Tabernacle. "He is the only one who can do this withdrawal."[5]

Others in the press chimed in, minimizing the charges against Sharon and lashing out at the few renegades in the Justice Ministry who insisted on continuing his investigation.

This extraordinary press largesse in the face of illegal contributions contrasted dramatically with the attitude of leading journalists and bureaucrats who later sought to bring me down on every conceivable trumped-up charge once they realized I wouldn't do "a Sharon" for them.

More than a decade later, when I was subjected, yet again, to trumped-up investigations, the leading commentator on the left who invented the *etrog* policy spelled things out clearly for me. If I had formed a national unity government with the left, ostensibly to make territorial concessions, "Sharon's *etrogization* would be nothing compared to the protection that would be offered *to Netanyahu*."[6]

Yet while protected, Sharon wasn't immune to failing health. On January 4, 2006, six weeks into the election campaign, he suffered a stroke that left him comatose, a state in which he remained until his death eight years later.

Ehud Olmert, then minister of industry, trade and labor, immediately took his place as acting prime minister. He did this by virtue of having been named stand-in premier, a position I had asked Sharon to give me when I took on the role of finance minister. Olmert got it as compensation for not receiving the finance minister portfolio (which he may not have wanted in the first place).

It was more than a title. The stand-in premier automatically assumed the prime minister job if the PM became incapacitated. Olmert was one of the Likud princes and a former Jerusalem mayor. Though an able, sharp-tongued politician and glad-hander, he had never made it to the heart of the Likud faithful. They felt he was too political and too calculating, and that he really didn't stand for the things they stood for. He had been relegated to the thirty-second slot on the Likud list in 2003. Now, by a stroke of . . . well, a stroke, he was catapulted to the post of prime minister.

Olmert quickly assumed control of the government and the Kadima party, which he would lead into the next election. Since the full effect of the Gaza withdrawal had yet to sink in, Kadima won the next election on March 28, 2006, on the stricken Sharon's coattails, though it lost a considerable number of Knesset seats.

The Likud Party, under my leadership, was pummeled.

39

"THIS *IS* YOUR LIFE!"

2005–2009

The election defeat of 2006 was overwhelming, the worst in my career. Likud had shrunk to twelve seats, a mere 10 percent of the Knesset. Even that was achieved by a hair's breadth.

During the actual counting, the twelfth seat hung in the balance between Avigdor Lieberman's Yisrael Beiteinu Party and the Likud. Lieberman competed with me on the right. Both Lieberman and I had eleven confirmed seats. If the twelfth seat went to him, he would be the leader of the Opposition and I would be almost entirely sidelined. Finally, the late-arriving soldiers' vote gave me this meager but crucial prize.

Count your blessings, I told myself. I made my way to Likud election headquarters. It was practically empty. I gave a stiff-upper-lip speech, but as far as everyone was concerned—the public, the political class and most of all the press—I was finished.

Coming back from campaign headquarters, I said as much to Sara: "This time it looks like it's really the end. Maybe I should simply resign and we'll get on with our lives."

It was at this crucial moment that she stood like a rock.

"Bibi, *this is your life*. The country needs you," she said. "And if you think of leaving, the last thing you should do is leave in such a humiliating defeat. Start amassing small victories. As you get stronger, you can decide what to do."

I followed her advice.

Likud may have shrunk to twelve seats, but they were *my* seats, given by voters who continued to believe in me despite the party split, the terrible press and the national zeitgeist that said, "We got out of Gaza and everything turned out all right." This widely held view would change in time.

For the time being, I sought small victories. I convened the Likud's shrunken faction every week and began parliamentary guerrilla warfare. The governing coalition was diverse and there were many exploitable cracks in it. Despite our small numbers, we began to deftly maneuver in the Knesset and actually won a substantial number of votes on bills we submitted, and blocked many bills by the government. We were alive and kicking.

The other thing I did was *listen*. The faction was tiny. Each person counted even more. In our weekly meetings, held in one of the smaller rooms of the Knesset, I let every one of the Likud Knesset members speak their mind. I didn't *pretend* to listen. I *listened*. I followed every word, asking questions when I wanted clarifications, and seeking and usually getting decisions by consensus.

However small a political party, and however united in purpose, it still had as in any human group its jealousies and ambitions.

"Don't you know why he said this?" a Knesset member would often point out to me after our weekly faction meeting, referring to some comment by one of his colleagues. "He's speaking from a position."

"Don't we all?" I would answer. "But if you hear a dozen people speaking from different positions, you're bound to get it right."

I really believed that. Experience taught me that most of the time you can figure out the optimal choice among the options presented. It's the option you didn't consider at all that will get you. Hearing out all faction members reduces that risk. It also communicates respect, which is something all politicians crave.

I had similar regular meetings with Likud mayors. Of the sixty or so mayors who identified with Likud before the elections, only a dozen or so remained loyal after. My meetings with them shored them up and provided me with valuable insights into the public pulse.

Little by little, Likud began to gather public support. But it would not be an easy job to challenge Olmert, who enjoyed overwhelming backing from the left and from the press.

Their support for Olmert and opposition to me remained unflinching even after Hamas took over Gaza in 2007. Hamas henchmen kneecapped Fatah policemen, threw them to their deaths from six-story buildings, and established Hamastan. This was followed by rocket and other terrorist attacks from Gaza, which, cleared of Israeli forces, was fast becoming an independent terrorist enclave.

Meanwhile, Olmert befriended President George W. Bush and began crafting with his administration the magical Israeli-Palestinian peace that had eluded all his predecessors.

Yasser Arafat had died at the end of 2004, and his loyal suit-wearing deputy, Mahmoud Abbas, also known as Abu Mazen, took over. Intelligent and calculating, Abbas had little of Arafat's charisma. But coming from the older generation of PLO leaders, his ascendancy kept the peace inside the organization and prevented a bloody war for succession among the younger claimants to the PLO leadership. Olmert went out of his way to court Abbas. He invited him to the prime minister's residence in Jerusalem several times, taking pains to be photographed with his arm around Abbas's shoulder.

Like Ehud Barak before him, Olmert was determined to carve his name into historic marble by forging a seemingly impossible peace. After all, wasn't the only thing that stood in the way of such a peace the timidity of Israeli leaders?

Since he too bought the Palestinian Centrality Theory and failed to understand that the Palestinian national movement was not interested in a political settlement over territories but rather in policide, Olmert and his team kept upping the territorial price they were willing to pay. Seeing this, the Palestinian Authority kept asking for more.

If we just gave a little more, Olmert and his colleagues thought, the Palestinians would finally agree to sign a peace deal. What would happen to that deal and how a truncated Israel could defend itself in its wake didn't overly concern the Israeli negotiators and their American interlocutors.

Olmert received rave reviews from Washington and from the Israeli press. Here, finally, was a prime minister who would lead us into the Promised Land by boldly giving up pieces *of* the Promised Land.

While Olmert was negotiating with the Palestinians and the Americans, he and I held the monthly security briefings between the prime minister and the leader of the Opposition. In one of them I put forward a proposition regarding Iran.

"Ehud," I said, "we disagree on the Palestinians but we should have no disagreement on Iran."

This was true, but only up to a point. Just as with Sharon before him, we disagreed on the importance of thwarting Iran's nuclear ambitions. For me, it was our highest priority.

But I had a specific idea in mind, so I didn't harp on this difference. Instead I said, "Iran needs investments. I believe we can start a divestment campaign against Iran."

"How?" he asked.

"By appealing to the investment funds of each of the fifty states in America," I said. Repeating what I had said to Sharon before going to speak to Congress in 2002 on Israel's behalf, I added, "I would only do so with your approval."

Olmert agreed. There was no harm in it, he probably thought, and if it would keep the Opposition leader preoccupied with his pet obsession, Iran, all the better.

I proceeded to meet state governors, beginning with Mitt Romney in Massachusetts, and state legislators far and wide. Within a few months, twenty state funds had disinvested from Iran. This was the beginning of the economic sanctions that would ultimately gather force and cripple Iran's economy. Those sanctions, along with the fear that as prime minister I would later authorize a military action against their nuclear installations, led to Iran's decision to enter talks with the US about limiting its nuclear program.

Unfortunately, the US would later give up its clear advantage in these talks and agree to a deal that enabled Iran to continue pursuing its nuclear program under the mantle of an international agreement.

After having success at the state level, I sought in early 2007 to move to a federal disinvestment bill in Washington. To give the initiative added moral weight, I sponsored a bill in the Knesset to commit Israeli companies not to deal directly or indirectly with Iran.[1] It passed in 2008, the only bill that I personally sponsored in all my years as a Knesset member.

Though charges against Olmert for receiving cash envelopes and a long line of other corruption-related accusations were beginning to surface in 2008, his hold on power seemed unshakable. The press continued to give him cover. As long as he kept offering generous territorial concessions to the Palestinians, he would be protected.

Olmert's standing was buttressed by an important development. In one of our security briefings, he shared with me intelligence that showed Syria was building an atomic reactor in Deir Ezzor, in eastern Syria, with the help of the North Koreans. Olmert had asked the US to destroy it. The US refused but said it would support an Israeli strike. Olmert told me that he planned to do it. I said I would wholeheartedly support such a strike.

I soon learned that a debate had arisen inside the government about whether to bomb the reactor from the air or send the Unit to destroy it from the ground. I told Olmert that I supported an aerial strike, seeing no point in risking the Unit soldiers when a few aircraft could do the job with relatively little risk.

On September 7, 2007, the news broke that Israeli aircraft had destroyed Syria's nuclear reactor. Officially Israel stayed mum, but everyone knew the truth. In a television interview a few days after the raid, I was asked if I knew about it and blurted out carelessly that I did. In fifty years of public life I hadn't made many such lapses in my public career. This was one of them.

The press immediately went berserk. "Netanyahu compromised a national secret," "He had to show that he was part of Olmert's success," and so on.

The truth was, it was an honest slip of the tongue meant to express my appreciation for the one important positive thing the prime minister did during his term and that I wholeheartedly supported.

"ALWAYS EXPECT THE unexpected," Margret Thatcher advised me in our meeting in London in 2003. The unexpected in 2006 came in the form of the brutal and unprovoked July 12 slaying of three Israeli soldiers and the abduction of two others by Hezbollah on the Lebanese-Israeli border.

No Israeli leader, like leaders in any democracy, wants to appear weak. Olmert prided himself on being decisive. He would now prove himself a decisive military leader. Perhaps too decisive.

Lacking any real military experience (his brief military service was as a reporter for the army magazine), he acted before completing a thought-out plan with clear goals. He may have believed that his actions would buy him political capital to carry out his plans concerning the Palestinians.

Whatever the case, within forty-eight hours he launched a military operation against Hezbollah in Lebanon, declaring as his first goal "the return of our soldiers," a clearly unachievable mission in the span of a few days' fighting.

The few days expanded to the full-fledged Second Lebanon War, which lasted five weeks. Hezbollah attacked the north of Israel with nearly four thousand rockets, killing forty-four civilians and destroying many homes. One hundred twenty-one soldiers were also killed in the war. Lacking a clearly defined mission from the political leaders and clear achievable goals, the army's campaign was meandering and indecisive.

The government needed something, *anything*, to justify an end to the fighting. UN Resolution 1701 was drawn up, stipulating that Hezbollah was not to deploy in South Lebanon or place any armaments there. This arrangement would be monitored and enforced by the United Nations Interim Force in Lebanon, or UNIFIL.

Although this UN resolution was useless from the start and was never implemented by even an iota, at the time it served as a face-saver for the government when it agreed to a cease-fire. The Israeli press hailed this as a "tremendous achievement." Yet the missing soldiers were still missing, Israel's cities had been pummeled, and many young lives had been lost.

One of them was twenty-two-year-old Michael Levin. I spoke to his grieving parents in Philadelphia. Inspired by Yoni's letters, Michael made Aliyah, joined the paratroops, and fell in Lebanon. His family later established the Lone Soldier Foundation to help thousands of immigrant soldiers without a family in Israel. Their stories are moving distillations of the Zionist spirit.

During the war I refrained from criticizing the government and offered it unstinting support. After the war, I voiced my criticism of the way it was fought. My criticism was mild compared to the opposition that welled up in many segments of the public, including reserve soldiers who felt abandoned by incompetent political leaders.

Absent a political directive, the military had run in circles in Lebanon, accruing unnecessary casualties in the process. The war was clearly mismanaged and civilian defense was in shambles. Olmert's numbers collapsed. His public support fell to 6 percent.

His legal problems began to resurface, and now that he was political roadkill his press protection was removed. He would have to resign and be replaced by a new champion of peace capable of leading the left's agenda.

This would be Tzipi Livni, his foreign minister, who enthusiastically embraced the negotiations with the Palestinians. Sensing that his time in office and his political capital were running out, Olmert offered Mahmoud Abbas the wildest concessions yet, including Palestinian control of the Temple Mount. Abbas was immovable, demanding even more. No deal was made and Olmert was forced by his fellow coalition members, in particular Ehud Barak, his defense minister at the time, to announce that he would resign after the upcoming elections.

He would stay as a caretaker prime minister until a new government was formed. Livni was given the opportunity to form a new government but she failed. New elections were called.

I went into those elections with a potential coalition at the ready. By now, Likud had recovered considerably. But I still had to ensure that a potential Likud-led coalition would get at least 61 seats, a majority in the 120-member body.

My strategy was *not* to campaign aggressively against potential coalition partners so as to maintain a "bloc" of support that would ensure victory. The election results gave Likud 27 seats to Kadima's 28. But the Likud-led "bloc" garnered 65 seats, a clear and decisive win. Within a few weeks I formed a government. Nine years after I left the Prime Minister's Office, I retook the reins of power.

These nine years weren't wasted. During the first three, I ensured my family's livelihood. During the next three, I led a free market revolution of the Israeli economy. In the final three, I began a disinvestment campaign against Iran.

I was sixty years old, tempered by experience. I had come back from political oblivion. Though lacking the innocent enthusiasm of entering office for the first time, I was armed with a much clearer mission: I could now proceed to try to fully realize my plan to turn Israel into a power among the nations.

But as in my first tenure as prime minister, I would also have to deal with a new American administration at odds with my vision, headed by a young and energetic new president, Barack Obama.

PART III

SUMMIT

40

"NOT ONE BRICK!"

2009–2010

Entering the Prime Minister's Office for the second time in 2009 after a ten-year hiatus, I noticed a marked change in my own conduct. Though the pace was still hectic, I was considerably less frantic.

I use the word "frantic" because an undeniable frenzy of activities accompanied me in all my posts. I am an incurable workaholic, a voracious reader, an indulgent eater. All that was fine until I got to the top office.

The prime minister's schedule is carved up in measured slices. In my first term these were exceedingly thin. Aside from weekly cabinet meetings, Knesset sessions and routine meetings with the chiefs of security, my schedule was taken up by constant demands for meeting with bureaucrats, politicians, journalists and others.

A decade later I spaced out my time better, eliminating many meetings with "nudniks" (busybodies). I gave myself more opportunities to meet ministers and Knesset members. With the passing of years I became more tolerant of human foibles. I spent more "think time" with key staff members and others who could challenge conventional thinking—and me.

I also spent more time with my family on weekends in our new Caesaria home. We walked on the Mediterranean shore. In other moments I enjoyed solitude. Well, with a small army of special agents in tow.

Another somewhat less dramatic change was in my attitude toward the hostile press. In my first term as prime minister my attention on vital tasks was often thrown out of kilter by the need to respond to attacks and constant queries from the media. I attended to every slight and denied every falsehood. My press officer was soon dubbed "the denier."

My sensitivity had evolved. When I entered political life as deputy chief of mission in Washington, the first press attack against me was barely bigger than a postal stamp. It troubled me for days.

At sixty, ten years older than when I ended my first term as prime minister, I was considerably calmer and less personally consumed with what the media wrote or said about me. Gradually my focus shifted from taking personal offense to a utilitarian approach. How much political damage did a particular political attack cause? Deal with it, but don't dwell on it. Move on. Though the attacks had now gotten to the size of a double spread in the paper, I could shrug them off within a few hours.

I suspect that actually made things worse. Many of the left-leaning journalists sensed that unlike many politicians on the right, I felt neither intimidation nor subservience in dealing with their criticism. And that's putting it mildly.

Still, it would take a few more years to fully develop the "Bibi hide" that enabled me to later sustain press attacks of unprecedented intensity and duration. The thick skin I acquired was no different from the calloused hands I developed from climbing ropes in the Unit. If you climb enough political ropes, you can develop a degree of resilience that most people find hard to fathom.

But there was one exception. The attacks on Sara and the boys always drew blood and hurt like hell. I could never truly reconcile myself to the suffering they endured from press attacks unlike any other family in Israel ever had to sustain. Yet it was Sara and the boys who looked past the attacks and always supported me in addressing the greatest challenge I faced when I returned to the Prime Minister's Office—rolling back the threat to Israel's security from Palestinian terror and the threat to its very existence from Iran.

Meeting this challenge would involve working with a new administration in Washington.

*   *   *

I FIRST MET Barack Obama in March 2007. He was a senator from Illinois running for president of the United States. I was the Opposition leader running for prime minister of Israel.

I was leaving Washington, where I had spoken at the annual conference of the American Israel Public Affairs Committee (AIPAC), and he was returning to Washington from the campaign trail. The only place where our schedules meshed was Reagan National Airport. We met at a superintendent's office. I came with Sara and three aides, he with only one. Five minutes into the meeting, impressed by Obama's intellect and charisma, I thought that could soon change. Obama struck me as highly focused, gracious and an attentive listener.

Sara agreed. "He's going to win the Democratic nomination," she told me soon after. Few believed that at the time.

During the meeting, after I had made my case for backing individual state divestments from Iran with federal legislation, he told me he would look into proposing such a federal divestment bill in the Senate, which he did a few days later.

We took the other's measure. Each of us was deeply rooted in opposite sides of the political divide. Obama's economic and foreign policy resembled those of a typical social democrat. I was an economic conservative and a foreign policy hawk. We were both what the pundits call conviction politicians. He believed in the primacy of soft power. I believed in the primacy of hard power, especially in the Middle East.

Of course, I assumed that we would not see eye to eye on the Palestinian issue, just as I had not seen eye to eye with his predecessors. But all this was secondary in my mind to Obama's willingness to increase pressure on Iran, the most important issue for me.

In most democracies, leaders seldom ascend to power without a strong streak of pragmatism. Was Obama a pragmatist? I certainly hoped so. Despite clear ideological differences, he came across that way, so much so that coming out of the meeting at the airport I told Ron Dermer half-wishfully, "I can work with that guy."

I said this despite the facts that were brought before me about Obama's mind-set, especially his tendency to view the world through an anticolonialist prism. I felt sure Obama wasn't familiar with the historical record that showed that if any "colonialism" was involved in the case of

Israel, it was the colonialism practiced centuries earlier by invading Arabs against the natives of the land they displaced, the Jews.

Another worrisome sign was Obama's choice of the staff members he brought on over the course of his campaign, many of them veterans of the Clinton administration who were hostile to me and to my policies.

The aide Obama would come to rely on the most for his advice on Israel was his chief of staff, Rahm Emanuel, who had served as Clinton's chief political advisor. He was a fiery opponent of the right in Israel despite, or perhaps because of, the fact that his father had been a member of the Irgun in 1948. Like many others, he too viewed the core of the conflict in the Middle East as the absence of a Palestinian state, and the core of that problem was the settlements.

Never mind that some "settlers" had returned after the Six-Day War to communities from which they and their fathers had been kicked out of by Arabs years earlier, as in Gush Etzion, where the Jewish residents were either massacred or expelled in Israel's War of Independence in 1948, or in Hebron, where a centuries-old Jewish community was destroyed in a ruthless massacre in 1929.

Yet another troubling sign were Obama's reservations, as expressed during his Senate campaign of 2004, concerning the security fence that the Sharon government had built in the early 2000s. Built more or less on the 1967 border, its purpose was to help protect Israel from the wave of Palestinian suicide bombers who, lacking any physical barrier, infiltrated the country from the Palestinian centers in Judea and Samaria. These terrorists claimed the lives of more than one thousand Israeli civilians during the Second Intifada, between 2000 and 2005.[1]

Though some on the right initially opposed the construction of the security fence because they feared it would demarcate a future political border, I unequivocally supported its construction from the outset. Saving innocent lives was the highest priority.

As a ten-year-old, Yair had befriended at school a beautiful girl named Gallila, who was an Ethiopian immigrant. One day Gallila failed to come to class. A Palestinian suicide terrorist had exploded the bus she took to school, blowing her and other innocent passengers to smithereens. Like his classmates, Yair was deeply shaken by this. I tried to comfort him, and I knew that the erection of the fence would help prevent many more such tragedies. It did. In fact the security fence and accompanying security measures worked—dramatically bringing down the number of terrorist attacks.

The security barrier was presented by the Palestinian Authority and its chorus of Israel haters as an "apartheid wall."

This is utterly false.

First, the barrier is not a wall. Ninety-five percent of it is a fence that could be easily removed once the threat of terror ceases.

Second, it doesn't keep peaceful Palestinians out. Some fifty passages enable more than 150,000 Palestinian workers to cross daily into Israel's cities to earn a living and help the Palestinian economy.

THOSE FALSELY ACCUSING Israel of apartheid, especially radicals on US college campuses, deliberately ignore the fact that it is the Palestinian Authority that openly and unabashedly practices apartheid.

It will not allow even one Jew to live in a future "Judenfrei" (Jew-free) Palestinian state. Scandalously, the Palestinian Authority makes it a crime punishable by death to sell property to Jews and has carried out scores of extrajudicial executions of Palestinians accused of doing so.

By contrast, Israel's Arab citizens can go anywhere they want, live anywhere they want, buy whatever properties they want and live their lives with the same freedoms enjoyed by the rest of the population.

Israel is the only country in the Middle East where all citizens have equal rights, whether they are Jewish, Muslim, Christian or Druze. Like all members of Israel's population, Arab citizens can rise to the top of their professions of choice.

Arabs have the same opportunities as the rest of the population in all sectors, becoming doctors, lawyers, judges, titans of Israel's high-tech industry, government ministers and Supreme Court justices.

The one right that is afforded only to Jews is that of automatic immigration. After centuries of persecution and expulsions, the one and only Jewish state was founded as a haven for Jews anywhere in the world and as such it bestows citizenship upon immigrants of Jewish descent. Still, there is a process in place for non-Jews wishing to become Israeli citizens.

While Israel respects the rights of gays, women and minorities, the

Palestinian Authority in Judea and Samaria and Hamas in Gaza are rabidly anti-gay, subjugate women and oppress minorities.

Not a word of this appears in the outrageous claims against democratic Israel hurled by the apologists for the racist Palestinian regimes and other such regimes across the region, like Iran and Syria.

Contrary to anti-Israel lies, Palestinians are not governed by Israel, but by themselves. In 2005, the Jewish state entirely evacuated the Gaza Strip, turning over the territory to Palestinian governance. There is no Israeli presence inside Gaza. Palestinians in this coastal enclave are exclusively ruled by Hamas, a murderous group dedicated to Israel's destruction. The Palestinian Authority governs the Palestinians living in Judea and Samaria.

In both Hamas-controlled Gaza and in the Palestinian-controlled areas in Judea and Samaria, many Palestinians wish they had the civil rights enjoyed by Israel's Arab citizens. The areas not governed by the Palestinian Authority are considered "disputed territories" to be negotiated in a final peace settlement between the Palestinians and Israel. Yet the Palestinians have rejected every Israeli offer of a permanent peace agreement, since that would involve recognizing the Jewish state, and lately they won't even come to the negotiating table.

Israel's critics also ignore how the Palestinian Authority has desecrated Jewish and Christian holy sites and has attempted to stop Jews from praying at religious sites located on Palestinian-controlled territory. Palestinians have repeatedly ransacked and desecrated Joseph's Tomb, and have attacked Jews worshipping at the Western Wall.

During an Israeli antiterror raid in 2002 at the height of the Second Intifada, Fatah's militias infamously holed up inside the Church of the Nativity in Bethlehem, believed to be the birthplace of Jesus. They left one of Christianity's most sacred sites in shambles.

In Bethlehem, the Palestinian Authority enables Islamic gangs to intimidate Christian residents and confiscate Christian property. After the Palestinian Authority took over Bethlehem as part of the Oslo Accords, Christians were forced to flee in droves, with the Christian population of the once Christian-majority city drastically declining to about 13 percent.

The attempt to smear color-blind Israel as racist is ludicrous. Israelis comprise people who came from a hundred lands, including Black Jews from Ethiopia and Black Hebrews from America. All enjoy equal rights.

Israel also leads much of the world in sending emergency relief to crisis-stricken countries regardless of race, ethnicity or religion. It has deployed emergency search-and-rescue teams, erected field hospitals, or offered humanitarian aid in Armenia, Turkey, Rwanda, Sudan, Malawi, Democratic Republic of the Congo, Chad, Haiti, Nepal, Mexico, the Philippines, Japan, Ukraine, Sierra Leone, Liberia, Guinea, Sri Lanka, India, El Salvador and Guatemala. Israel even offered to send a team to Iran after a severe earthquake. Few countries can match this humanitarian record.

None of this is ever mentioned by the anti-Zionists who defame Israel on American and European campuses.

The apartheid libel against Israel is an inversion of reality, a deliberate attempt to smear the Jewish state with vicious lies while exonerating and even lionizing its racist and terrorist enemies.

The "apartheid wall" canard was thus part of a larger slanderous campaign of preposterous lies aimed at delegitimizing the Jewish state.

Yet when Obama was running for the US Senate in 2004 he criticized Israel's security barrier, prompting the progressive Jewish organization J Street, which often sided with Israel's worst critics even on such matters as Hamas and Iran, to laud his opposition as nothing short of "remarkable."[2] It was.

Doubts about Obama's attitude toward Israel were compounded by two other incidents. In February 2008, during the Democratic primaries, Obama addressed leaders of Cleveland's Jewish community who were known to be staunchly Zionist in their political leanings.

"I think," he said, "there is a strain within the pro-Israel community that says unless you adopt an unwavering pro-Likud approach to Israel that you're anti-Israel, and that can't be the measure of our friendship with Israel."

That was a clear alarm bell.

During nearly thirty years in public life I studiously avoided any reference to America's two political parties, except in the context of highlighting the bipartisan support for the Israeli-American alliance. I certainly avoided taking a swipe at any one of them.

This was not done, and yet Obama just did it.

Perhaps he tried to balance this impression four months later in his address to AIPAC. He vowed that "Jerusalem will remain the capital of Israel, and it must remain undivided,"[3] and received a rapturous response from the audience. This was immediately met with virulent Palestinian protests. A day later, Obama began walking back his statement, and four weeks later, on July 10, 2008, in a CNN interview, he said: "The truth is that this was an example where we had some poor phrasing in the speech. And we immediately tried to correct the interpretation that was given."[4]

In response, his rival for the presidency, Senator John McCain, pledged that if elected he would move the US embassy to Jerusalem.[5]

I took account of all this. Despite the warning signs that continued to accrue after our positive meeting at Reagan Airport, our policy differences, and the antipathy toward me of much of his staff, I wondered, Is the notion that Obama and I can work together a hopeless fantasy? Not necessarily, I thought.

In my first term as prime minister I had formed productive and friendly relations with social democratic leaders in Europe such as Prime Minister Romano Prodi of Italy and Britain's Labor prime minister, Tony Blair, as I would later form with other social democratic leaders such as President François Hollande of France and Prime Minister Alexis Tsipras of Greece, who named one of his sons Ernesto, after the Marxist revolutionary Ernesto "Che" Guevara.

I could form these friendships because we shared common interests and with goodwill could concentrate on areas of common ground rather than on ideological differences. I hoped to forge this type of pragmatic partnership with Obama as well.

As the US elections neared, Obama made a second trip to Israel, possibly to assuage concerns regarding his attitude toward the Jewish state. In July 2008, visiting the town of Sderot, which had recently experienced massive rocketing by Hamas, he said: "I feel for these girls as if they were my own daughters."

As I prepared with Ron Dermer for a meeting with Obama at the King David Hotel, we discussed the best approach to take. I was still Opposition leader, but hopeful that my return to prime minister was imminent.

"Here's what I plan to do," I said. "I'll say, 'We come from opposite sides of the political spectrum but we're both pragmatists. If we both get elected, I'm sure we'll find practical ways to work together.' "

First Obama and I met with our staff present, then he asked to remain alone with me.

Before I could say anything, he literally took the words out of my mouth.

"Look, Bibi," he began, "you come from the right, I come from the left. But I'm a pragmatist and so are you, so there's no reason we can't work together."

"I couldn't have said it better myself," I said, much relieved.

Of course, this hypothesis would be tested only if we both did, in fact, get elected.

The US election night coincided with one of the frequent trips Sara and I made to the Galilee. I had fallen in love with that enchanted region when as a soldier I hiked up and down its beautiful mountains and rolling hills, an Israeli Tuscany dotted with Biblical and Roman-era sites.

That day we were staying in the Scots Hotel in Tiberias, a converted Scottish missionary hospital. Two of Sara's older brothers had been born there half a century earlier. Luckily, they were spared the rats that prowled the wards in those early years of the state and tragically devoured the limbs of a newborn baby. None of these horrific memories lingered in the refurbished premises of the hotel overlooking the Sea of Galilee.

We had a glorious day. We visited the Roman baths in nearby Hamat Gader. We dined in our favorite restaurant, Decks, perched on the water of the historic lake. Before going to sleep I said to Sara, "By the time we wake up, Obama will be elected president."

It wasn't exactly a tough call. He had the energy, the momentum, and the tremendous enthusiasm of a good portion of the American public yearning for the change he had promised. You could always sense certain victory as clearly as you could smell certain defeat.

Sure enough, we woke up early to the Democratic victory celebrations in the US.

On January 21, 2009, Obama's first day in office, he phoned four Middle Eastern leaders: President Mubarak of Egypt, King Abdullah of Jordan, Prime Minister Olmert of Israel, and Palestinian Authority chairman Mahmoud Abbas.

Abbas's spokesman, Nabil Abu Rudeineh, quoted Obama as saying, "This is my first phone call to a foreign leader and I'm making it only hours after I took office."[6]

This was a clear indication of Obama's intention of focusing his foreign policy on the Middle East, and if Rudeineh was right, Obama was giving early and important symbolic preference to the Palestinians.

"It won't be easy," I said to Sara.

"You'll manage," she said. "But first *you* have to get elected."

The Likud, having recovered from its disastrous twelve seats in the 2006 elections, was polling well above thirty seats during the 2009 campaign, and I believed I could match Kadima, which was under Tzipi Livni's leadership.

Livni was a lawyer whom I had appointed in my first term to supervise privatization. She later became a Likud member of Knesset, then joined Sharon when they split off to establish Kadima. Though her parents were prominent Irgun members, she veered sharply to the left in advocating a Palestinian state. The coalition I had built to prevent Livni from forming a government *before* the elections was the key to enabling me to form a government *after* the elections. But I first had to sustain the Likud numbers in the polls.

Here I encountered the deadly paradox that I had to overcome in each of the next four elections. The more my supporters believed I was going to win, the fewer votes I would get. Confident of my victory, Likud supporters would either stay home or splinter their vote among other right-wing parties.

As election day approached, Likud was dropping in the polls. In the final days of the campaign, when the race between Livni and me tightened and voters on the right understood I might lose, my numbers rebounded.

The final vote tally was Kadima 28, Likud 27. But since I had 65 members of the Knesset's 120 members in my bloc, Shimon Peres, who recently had become Israel's president, had no choice but to give me the mandate to form the next government.

In Israel, as in most parliamentary democracies, the president is a largely symbolic role. Their main political duty is to decide to whom they give the mandate to form a government, and in that, too, they have limited leeway.

I decided to give Kadima a chance to join my government. Over dinner at Livni's home with her husband and Sara, I discussed the possibility of a national unity government and offered Kadima generous terms and portfolios. I did so because I thought I would need the broadest possible support to confront Iran's nuclear program.

After dispensing with the small talk, Livni and I sat down to discuss possible common policies. She made it clear that she regarded stopping Iran from getting nuclear weapons as secondary to the Palestinian issue.

At first I thought I hadn't heard her right. She repeated her position. I was flabbergasted. My stance was that the Palestinian issue had been around for nearly a century and might take many more decades to resolve. But there might not *be* an Israel to resolve it if Iran got its hands on atomic bombs.

At least she is honest, I thought. But there was no point in continuing the talks.

I next turned to Labor, led by Ehud Barak. Barak said he shared my concerns over Iran and agreed with me that stopping its nuclear ambitions was our top priority. I proceeded to include Labor and its thirteen seats in my government and appointed Barak as defense minister.

As promised during the election campaign, I included in the government Benny Begin, Dan Meridor and Moshe "Boogie" Yaalon, a former chief of staff in the IDF, and formed a kitchen cabinet of eight, which included them. This body would have to contend with the dual challenges of Iran and the pressure I expected from Obama on the Palestinian issue.

In late February, while I was forming the government, I received a delegation of Senate and House members headed by an old friend, the thoughtful senator from Connecticut Joe Lieberman. He and I had first met twenty-five years earlier when he was Connecticut attorney general and I was ambassador to the UN.

"For the first time in my lifetime," I told my American visitors, "Arab leaders are thinking strategically."

I used that word sparingly. Like *philosophy*, *strategy* is a term that has become so devoid of meaning as to include anything, as in "my strategy for choosing cheesecakes" or "my philosophy of haircuts." Yet I used the term here in its original meaning: Arab leaders, for the first time I could remember, were prioritizing threats and putting Iran at the top of their list.

This type of thinking had never been the norm. During World War II, many Arab leaders supported Hitler who, had he won the war, would have enslaved the Arabs, or worse. After the war, most lined up with the Soviets who had equal disregard and contempt for them.

But now Arab leaders increasingly understood that they faced an all-encompassing Iranian threat, and this had led them to reconsider their relations with Israel. These changing Arab attitudes were not yet fully apparent to the public and it would take several more years for them to come out in the open.

Preparing for my first meeting with Obama as president, I naturally wanted to concentrate on the Iranian threat and the opportunity it created for a broader Arab-Israeli peace. He, I was sure, would want to concentrate on the Palestinians. Little did I know to what extent.

ON MAY 19, 2009, I met Obama in the Oval Office. We began in a small forum, moved to an expanded one, and finally remained one-on-one. The meetings dealt with two subjects: Iran and the Palestinians.

Obama stated his commitment to prevent Iran from developing nuclear weapons. I responded by saying that I hoped these efforts would succeed, but that Israel reserved the right to "defend itself by itself." This phrasing implied that Israel should be able to act militarily against Iran on its own and would not seek American approval to do so. Obama, to my pleasant surprise, said that he agreed with that principle.

But when we moved to the Palestinian issue, Obama took the gloves off. With staff present, he made it clear that the US would not tolerate further stalling or obstructions in the peace process, leaving no doubt which party he thought was responsible for such things.

When we then were alone for a four-eyes meeting in the Oval Office, he was even more blunt.

"Bibi," he said, "I meant what I said. I expect you to immediately freeze all construction in the areas beyond the 1967 borders. Not one brick!"

"Barack," I said, "half of Jerusalem's residents live beyond those lines.

That alone includes almost two hundred thousand people. Do you expect us to stop building in neighborhoods like Gilo? These are integral parts of Jerusalem, like Georgetown is part of Washington."

"That's exactly what I mean," he said. "Not one brick, anywhere. Gilo, too."

This was clearly premeditated shock-and-awe.

Gilo was a thriving Jerusalem neighborhood of thirty thousand residents a few hundred meters from the long-bygone pre-1967 border. After close to half a century of urban growth, Gilo formed an uninterrupted continuum with the rest of Jerusalem and was a five-minute drive from the Knesset. Obama was effectively trying to reverse history.

Evidently Obama and his staff wanted to stun me into submission by making clear that the rules had changed. Whatever pressures past American presidents had placed on Israeli prime ministers, these would pale in comparison to the ones that would be applied to me. No more Mr. Nice Guy.

I told Obama that I would not build new settlements, something I had already decided on in Israel, and that I would take down illegal outposts not authorized by the government, something we did periodically. But I refused to commit to freezing construction *within* the settlements or in Jerusalem.

"You can't freeze life," I said. "People get married, they have children, they raise families. They need a roof above their heads."

Not only did I not believe that the freeze would advance peace, I believed it would produce the exact opposite effect. When the Palestinians saw this pressure for unilateral Israeli concessions while they were asked to give nothing, they would harden their positions. This was the opposite of the policy of reciprocity that I had introduced in my first term as prime minister. Instead of "give and receive," Obama was advocating "give and give more."

I tried to focus on the positive.

"Israel," I said to the president, "is willing to begin unconditional peace talks with the Palestinians immediately."

This didn't satisfy Obama either. He wanted concrete Israeli concessions on the settlements to put in his pocket and take to the Palestinians, believing that this would entice them to the negotiating table.

Like the rest of his administration, he also believed that this would prevent the supposed Israeli takeover of Judea and Samaria, even though the built-up area of the existing Jewish communities—the "settlements"—comprised less than 2% of the territory, mostly concentrated in three urban blocks around Tel Aviv and Jerusalem that Presidents Clinton and Bush openly assumed would always remain part of Israel. One year's construction in all the Jewish settlements put together added a minuscule amount to the total footprint.

Judea and Samaria was largely barren territory, disputed between Israelis and Palestinians. If Obama was so concerned with a few tiny outlying Jewish communities outside the blocks, he could have suggested a variety of creative ways to deal with them without effectively seeking to make life impossible for their residents or undermining natural growth in neighborhoods that under any final peace agreement would remain under Israeli sovereignty.

Geographically, Obama was making an Everest out of an anthill.

I was later told that Obama had given Mahmoud Abbas a secret commitment to establish a full-fledged Palestinian state before he left office. His chief of staff, the intense Rahm Emanuel, may have hinted at this possibility when he said in 2009 that in four years there will be a Palestinian state, notably adding that "it didn't matter who would be prime minister then."[7]

I could only hope that Emanuel wasn't signaling here that Obama would continue Clinton's practice of intervening in Israel's electoral process.

My response to Obama in the Oval Office that his draconian demands were both morally wrong and counterproductive, that the Palestinian-Israeli conflict was rooted in the Palestinian refusal to accept a Jewish state and not in the settlements, that choking off a quarter of a million people was neither just nor feasible—all this fell on deaf ears.

Obama reiterated his demand. To drive the point home, he said one last thing as we stood in the doorway to leave the Oval Office.

"You know, people often underestimate me. But I come from Chicago, where I had to deal with tough opponents." He then said something out of character that shocked me deeply.

The message was unmistakable. It was meant to intimidate me. The fact that the American president delivered such an offensive message in our first official meeting was highly disturbing. The prime minister of Israel was being treated as a minor thug in the neighborhood. It was this sense that the elected leader of a proud four-thousand-year-old nation was being mistreated and disrespected that got me back on my feet.

"Mr. President," I said slowly, "I'm sure that you mean what you said. But I am the prime minister of Israel and I'll do whatever I need to do to defend my country."

I felt dejected, and it must have shown on my face. When we came out of the Oval Office, Ron Dermer came up to me and asked, "What went wrong?"

"I'll tell you later," I said.

It was only on the flight back to Israel that I called him to the kitchenette at the front of the cabin, which was cleared of aircrew, and told him of the blistering exchange. He was startled too.

"Don't tell anyone," I said. "The only ones I shared this with besides you are Sara and Isaac Molcho when we were outside the Blair House. Let's keep it that way."

IN OUR MEETING at the White House Obama pushed for a two-state solution. I said that the terminology was less important than the substance, and the most important substantive issue for me in any political settlement was that security responsibility would remain in Israel's hands. This meant that Israel's security forces would have free access to pursue terrorists inside these territories and keep the area demilitarized from foreign forces and lethal weapons.

Without such powers it would be just a matter of time before Judea and Samaria became a launching pad for deadly attacks that could paralyze the country and wreak havoc on its citizens. Israel's Ben Gurion International Airport, for example, is within spitting distance of Palestinian villages overlooking it.

This was a clear point of contention, because the Palestinians argued that leaving security in Israel's hands would detract from their sovereignty. Yes, it would, and I made no effort to deny it.

I believed that the Palestinians should have all the powers required to govern themselves but no power to threaten Israel. If this meant they got a "state-minus," an "autonomy-plus," or whatever else they chose to call their political entity, so be it. I was not going to put my country's existence in danger. But at that first White House meeting, Obama didn't dwell on this point. The settlement freeze was the only thing that truly interested him.

The hard line continued later that evening in a dour State Department dinner with Secretary of State Hillary Clinton. True to script, she repeated the "Not one brick" demand and spelled it out to the press with all the anti-Bibi trimmings.

Was there any light moment in this inhospitable day? Actually there was. During a respite between verbal jousts, I asked Obama how his daughters were faring in the White House. Yair and Avner, I said, were finding it hard to adjust to the public scrutiny, now that they were older.

Obama's eyes lit up with genuine warmth. "Actually, my girls are doing just fine," he said.

"I'm glad to hear that," I responded, not adding that I was sure the American press treated his daughters more kindly than the Israeli press treated my boys.

I had finished the day with a head-on collision with the president of the United States. I left Washington, some of the press reported, "agreeing to disagree" on the Palestinian issue.

41

"LOTS OF DAYLIGHT"

2009

P resident Obama and I would also disagree on Iran.
Obama had made normalizing relations with Iran a top priority even before he assumed the presidency.[1] In a 2007 Democratic debate he said he believed the US should negotiate with Iran, prompting swift criticism from then-candidate Hillary Clinton.[2]

Shortly after he was inaugurated, on March 20, 2009, he sent an unprecedented conciliatory video message to the leadership and people of Iran on the Persian New Year. A year later he would add to that annual message, "Together with the international community, the US recognizes your right to the peaceful use of nuclear energy."[3]

He didn't question why energy-laden Iran needed to develop nuclear energy in the first place or why it hid key nuclear facilities in underground bunkers.

Still, in 2009 the full extent of the shift in American policy was not yet apparent to the public. When I left Washington, everyone understood that the new administration was much tougher on settlements than the previous administration but they had not yet realized that it was much softer on Iran.

Gradually all this would become clear. Two weeks later, on June 4 in Cairo, Obama proclaimed that he wanted to open a new chapter in the relationship between America and the Muslim world. His new priorities were made clear by his choice of destinations for his first foreign trip as president. He went to the Middle East, but did not visit Israel. He did, however, devote a sizable part of his Cairo speech to Israel and the Palestinians, each receiving an equal portion of his time. He implied that Israel's establishment was a product of the Holocaust, neglecting the thousands of years of attachment of the Jewish people to their homeland.

In what was a particularly jarring symmetry, Obama juxtaposed the suffering of the Jewish people during the Holocaust with the suffering of the Palestinians. This attempt to create a symmetry of suffering was outlandish. During a century of conflict, twenty-five thousand Palestinians died in battles and terrorist attacks against Jews, compared to six million Jews murdered in the Nazi genocide in four years.

Needless to say, the Palestine-Israel segment of the speech was topped off with Obama's banner issue: "Settlement construction must stop."

Iran was barely slapped on the wrist, the language used toward it almost gentle. He appeared to sympathize with Iran's charges against Israel's purported nuclear capabilities and suggested that adherence to the 1963 Nuclear Non-Proliferation Treaty would protect the world against nuclear proliferation.

"I understand," he said, "those who protest that some countries have weapons that others do not. No single nation should pick and choose which nation holds nuclear weapons," he declared, seemingly implying that a nuclear Netherlands posed the same threat as the ayatollahs with nuclear weapons.

"And that's why I strongly reaffirmed America's commitment to seek a world in which no nations hold nuclear weapons," Obama continued. "And any nation—including Iran—should have the right to access peaceful nuclear power if it complies with its responsibilities under the [1963] Nuclear Non-Proliferation Treaty."[4]

Never mind that Iraq, Syria, Libya and Iran all developed their nuclear weapons programs despite the fact that they were signatories to the NPT, as was North Korea for seventeen years until it decided to withdraw from the treaty.

Iraq and Syria were stopped by Israeli military action, Libya by the threat of American military action. North Korea, unthreatened, developed an atomic arsenal. If the world was relying on Iran's signature on the NPT, we were all in deep trouble.

Undoubtedly Arab leaders took note of all this. An American president soft on Iran and tough on America's ally Israel didn't bode well for them either. Iran was their enemy, too, and if that's how America treats Israel, its closest ally in the Middle East, they must have wondered what would be in store for them.

I was deeply troubled. True, I had policy disputes with other presidents, but here was one who clearly lacked the same intensity of feeling and sympathy toward Israel shared by most of his predecessors.

While they had all criticized Israel's settlement policy, I sensed that Obama was much more ideologically and personally vested in his criticism. He was totally committed to a Palestinian state, minimizing the consequences for Israel's security. He was absolutely determined to achieve a freeze on new construction in the settlements. His soft line on Iran also departed from the policy of his predecessors and augured badly for any potential squeeze on the Islamic Republic.

Five weeks after the Cairo speech, in July 2009, Obama met with a group of concerned American Jewish leaders in the Oval Office.

Malcolm Hoenlein, the executive vice chairman of the Conference of Presidents of Major American Jewish Organizations and an old friend, spoke up.

"If you want Israel to take risks, then its leaders must know that the United States is right next to them," he told the president.

Obama begged to differ.

"Look at the past eight years," he said. "During those eight years, there was no space between us and Israel, and what did we get from that? When there is no daylight, Israel just sits on the sidelines, and that erodes our credibility with the Arab states."[5]

This flatly contradicted many formal American statements about the closeness of the American-Israeli alliance. "Seems like Obama wants a lot of daylight between us," I told Ron Dermer.

Exchanges like the one Obama had with Jewish leaders in the White House made it clear to me that I was heading into an inevitable confrontation with Israel's most important ally. How would Israel navigate these white-water rapids for four years, I wondered, while avoiding a plunge to the bottom of a waterfall?

I decided on an approach that would help us avoid it for as long as possible. My first goal would be to persuade Obama to take a tougher stance on Iran. The second would be to show an Israeli willingness to achieve a political solution with the Palestinians. If they showed goodwill, we would begin negotiations. If they didn't, I would do my best to expose their intransigence before the American public and the rest of the world.

I had no illusion this would be easy. No matter what I said, no matter what conciliatory gestures I made, the Obama juggernaut would try to steamroll me to a Palestinian state more or less on the 1967 lines.

But it was the *public* in Israel and America that I wanted to reach. I would focus my vision of peace on a simple demand: that the Palestinians recognize the Jewish state. This was the core of the conflict and I intended to drill down on it.

Rather than "walking away from peace," as I was constantly being accused of doing by the administration's briefers, I would walk straight into it. I would give a major speech on my vision for an Israeli-Palestinian peace.

IN THE DAYS before the speech, I consulted with my Likud and coalition colleagues. I explained that given the new administration in Washington, we had to pursue a dual track: engaging in political negotiations with the Palestinians while pushing for a tougher American policy on Iran. Most agreed, though reluctantly.

I was drawing on the political capital I had earned, but I knew this was a finite resource. I had just won an election and I had a broad government, but time would gnaw at that too.

I called Vice President Joe Biden and gave him a heads-up on my speech. On one of my visits to Washington he had invited me to the official vice president's residence at the US Naval Observatory.

"You don't have too many friends here, buddy," Biden said. "I'm the one friend you do have. So call me when you need to."

I knew this was a genuine offer, and one that I presumed was coordinated with the White House as a useful back channel in time of need, though Obama's staff would probably have phrased it differently.

I chose Bar-Ilan University, a religious school, as the venue for my speech. In a brief opening I stated that the greatest danger to the world was the marriage of nuclear weapons with a radical Islamic ideology. I expressed my appreciation for the remarkable entrepreneurship of the Gulf States and Israel's desire to see a widespread regional peace.

I then expressed our willingness to begin talks with the Palestinians without preconditions. A successful *conclusion* to these negotiations, I said, would require two elements. The first was "a public, genuine and binding Palestinian recognition of Israel as the nation-state of the Jewish people." The second was security. The Palestinian areas would have to be demilitarized, with solid security arrangements for Israel.

"We don't want Qassam rockets on Petach Tikva nor Grad rockets on Tel Aviv and Ben Gurion Airport," I said. "The Palestinians will not be able to import such weapons, raise an army, close the airspace, or make treaties with hostile states or organizations."

Then came the clincher. In exchange for Palestinian agreement to these two basic requirements, *recognition* and *security*, Israel would agree on "the framework of a future peace agreement to a solution of a demilitarized Palestinian state alongside the Jewish state."

Repeatedly over the years, before and after the speech, I made it clear that Israel would retain security control on the ground and in the air over the entire area west of the Jordan River, including the Palestinian-controlled areas, causing some to argue that I hadn't offered the Palestinians unrestricted sovereignty over their domain. This was true, but I didn't spell out this point in my speech so as not to give the Palestinians an easy way out.

Even so, Hamas and the PLO both rejected the speech outright. The Obama administration initially said it was an "important step." Reactions in Israel from both left and right were more muted than I had expected. The left was reluctant to shed my image as an enemy of peace, while the right believed that the Palestinians would never recognize the Jewish state anyway.

Did I believe the Bar-Ilan speech would stop Obama's pressure? Not for a moment. Yet the speech, once given, did give me something to push back with against Washington's Palestinian steamroller. It also provided a conceptual framework for a much more detailed and workable vision of an Israeli-Palestinian peace that I would advance a decade later with President Trump's administration.

It took only a few days after the Bar-Ilan speech for administration spokespersons to change their positive tone. Faced with Palestinian rejectionism of the framework, the administration reached the wrong conclusion again: if the Palestinians won't embrace Israel's overture, let's put even more pressure on Israel. They began to bad-mouth me as a pusillanimous enemy of peace while hailing the Palestinian leadership as champions of peace.

Obama wisely left this unpleasant task to his subordinates. His public conduct with me was nearly always correct. He would consistently reiterate his commitment to Israel's security and the unshakable alliance between Israel and the United States. Yet Obama and his staff advanced two concepts that directly contradicted Israel's security.

The first, that Israel's security would be served by creating a Palestinian state, was shared by previous US administrations, though Obama pursued it with greater fervor. And as usual, the fact that such a Palestinian state would be a springboard to forces openly sworn to Israel's destruction and would reduce the Jewish state to indefensible boundaries was not considered a problem.

Obama's second concept was new and in many ways revolutionary. His vision of a new Middle East was based on a Pax Americana-Irana. The Islamic Republic of Iran was the rising power in the region, as he saw it. It was the neighborhood bully, sending its terrorist goons to every part of the Middle East and threatening everyone. True to his experience as a community organizer in Chicago's neighborhoods, Obama would seek out the bully, cut a deal with him, and thereby pacify the neighborhood.

The fact that this bully was an overbearing Islamist regime may have added to the attraction of this vision. After all, Obama was seeking not only to restructure the Middle East but to establish a new relationship with the entire Muslim world. Two big birds with one stone.[6]

The problem with this vision was that Iran wasn't playing ball. It didn't want to pacify the Middle East, it wanted to conquer it, as it would later show by dispatching its commanders and proxies to Iraq, Yemen, Lebanon and Syria, including at times full-time units of its military. Nor did it want reconciliation with the United States.

Iran wanted to develop nuclear weapons with which it could destroy the "Small Satan" Israel, threaten the "Great Satan" America and export the Shiite Islamic Revolution to the rest of the world. Pacifying Iran meant strengthening Iran.

Obama repeatedly vowed to prevent Iran from getting nuclear weapons, but as I would later discover, his actual policies would be to contain rather than to prevent an Iranian nuclear arsenal.

This accommodating attitude manifested itself during Iran's Green Revolution, just a few days after Obama's Cairo speech.

Iran had just conducted elections on June 12. The regime preselected the candidates allowed to run and disqualified many. But even that wasn't enough. It *still* rigged the results. The sitting president, Mahmoud Ahmadinejad, was declared victorious by a wide margin. The opposition, led by Mir Hossein Mousavi, cried foul and accused the regime of flagrant voter fraud. Our own intelligence showed that millions of votes were stolen. On June 13, Mousavi supporters turned out en masse in the streets to protest.

The opposition protests were the largest in Iran since the 1979 revolution.[7] It was clearly grassroots in nature as protests erupted simultaneously in many parts of the country despite the fact that the protest's leaders were quickly picked off by the regime and incarcerated, or "disappeared."

Iran's storm troopers, the Basij, beat and gunned down civilian protesters on city streets. Some of the scenes were particularly heartwrenching.

The picture of Neda, a young Iranian woman who bled to death on the sidewalk, reverberated around the world, much as the pictures of the Tunisian food vendor who burned himself alive would reverberate worldwide two years later. But unlike its response to images in Tunisia and later in Cairo, which sparked the Arab Spring and led to powerful and repeated condemnations of Arab governments from Washington, the White House response here was tepid.

On June 15, Obama said, "It is up to Iranians to make decisions about who Iran's leaders will be," adding that "we respect Iranian sovereignty and want to avoid the United States being the issue inside of Iran."[8]

In a June 23 press conference, he "condemned" the unjust actions,[9] but as one news report noted, "he downplayed the prospect of real change, saying the candidates whom hundreds of thousands of Iranians were risking their lives to support did not represent fundamental change."[10] "The world is watching and inspired by their participation, regardless of the ultimate outcome of the election"[11] was the most he could say.

The administration later tried to justify its lack of a strong response as wise statecraft, but nobody in the region bought it. It signaled a desire to cut a deal with Iran no matter the cost.

Though I didn't know it at the time, secret contacts between Tehran and Washington had already begun. They would later develop into full-scale clandestine negotiations in Oman, which we discovered through our own intelligence sources.

The fact that Obama avoided taking a tough stance against mass murder in Iran's streets and hid the negotiations with Iran from America's close ally, Israel, spoke volumes about where he was tilting.

I realized that a credible military threat against Iran's nuclear program would not come from the US. It would have to come from us. In an interview with the *Atlantic*, I said as much: "If America doesn't stop Iran's nuclear program we'll have to do it ourselves."

As soon as I entered office in 2009, I had directed the IDF and the Mossad to upgrade our preparations for such a contingency.

On July 9, meeting US secretary of defense Robert Gates, who was visiting Israel, I raised two points. Before getting to Iran, I surfaced the need to begin a process of normalization with the Arab states via a seemingly small step.

"Can you persuade the Saudis to enable civilian planes from and to Israel to fly over Saudi airspace?" I asked Gates. "This would cut our travel time to India by a full three hours."

My push for this "passage to India" stemmed from my belief that India would be one of the most important economic and political partners for Israel in the coming years. Equally, I thought that if I seeded the idea of overflights over the Arab states as an interim normalization step, it would eventually take root.

Gates didn't think the Saudis would do anything to normalize relations until we reached an agreement with the Palestinians.

"Anyway," he said, "the Saudis won't go first. They'll only follow others."

It took me another eight years to crack the overflights, but the Saudis did ultimately go first in allowing flights to and from Israel over their territory. This was achieved in 2018, well before the Abraham Accords peace agreements with other Arab nations were signed, and involved a great deal of secret diplomacy that I personally led. It also laid the groundwork for the announcement of Saudi Arabia opening its airspace to even more flights in 2022.

The second point I raised, moving on to Iran, was the need to prevent Iran from crossing a critical threshold of uranium enrichment by confronting them with a credible *military option* coupled with *crippling sanctions*.

Gates responded that the US reserved its military response to possible Iranian missile attacks on American bases and forces in the region.

"Besides," he said, "all the experts tell us that an American strike on Iran's nuclear facilities would unite the Iranian public behind the regime. Can all the experts be wrong?"

"Yes," I said, "all the experts can be wrong. They often are. Most Iranians hate this tyranny. They just tried to rebel against it. They'll cheer when you deliver a knockout punch to the regime. It would be a tremendous psychological blow to the mullahs' image of invincibility!"

I related to Gates what President Museveni of Uganda told me of the psychological effect of the raid in Entebbe, that before the raid Ugandans had "believed Idi Amin was invincible" and after it they knew they could "bring him down."

"You have the power to achieve the same result with the Iranian regime," I said to Gates. "You are Gulliver."

"Maybe so," said one of the generals accompanying Gates. "But there are a lot of Lilliputians on Capitol Hill."

Gates argued that the delaying effects of any Israeli military action against Iran's nuclear capabilities would be short-lived. I noted that the same thing was said of Israel's strike on Saddam Hussein's Osirak reactor, referring to our successful 1981 operation against a nuclear facility that never resumed operation. Gates countered that an Israeli strike would result in a full-scale war. Whether it would or not, I was willing to sustain a conventional war with Iran in order to avoid a war with a nuclear-armed Iran.

The policy of wielding an American military club against Iran's nuclear facilities while applying crippling sanctions would gain ground in Washington in the following years. It would be given greater impetus by the American concern that Israel under my leadership would attack Iran's nuclear facilities. Developing an American military option was meant to put me at ease while driving Iran to the negotiating table.

The administration flooded Israel with envoys and visitors. Some, like Defense Secretary Gates, discussed Iran with me. Others, like special Middle East envoy George Mitchell, discussed the Palestinians. In one of our numerous discussions, Mitchell said that East Jerusalem was the biggest issue for the Palestinians.

"Jerusalem," I responded, not for the last time, "is not a settlement. It's our ancient capital, seat of the Temple Mount, the holiest place for our people."

I pushed back forcefully against the demand that we freeze construction anywhere in our capital.

"Would anyone accept this in Washington, London or Paris?"

These twin issues, Iran and the Palestinians, were the focus of my upcoming annual visit to New York in September 2009, where I would meet Obama and address the UN General Assembly. As usual Obama pushed for a settlement freeze. As usual I pushed on Iran. We agreed to work together to see if we could advance negotiations with the Palestinians. Obama conducted a ceremonial meeting with Mahmoud Abbas and me at the UN in which we all declared our intentions to resume negotiations.

In the General Assembly, I went straight at Iran's President Ahmadinejad, a systemic Holocaust denier who had said a few days earlier from the UN podium that "the Holocaust was a lie fabricated by the Zionists." Few outside Iran knew that the regime held, every year, an official conference in Tehran of Holocaust denial.

I held in my hand the protocols of the notorious Wannsee Conference, in which Nazi officials planned the Final Solution.

"Is this a lie?" I asked.

I then produced the original building plans of the Auschwitz concentration camp, signed by Hitler's deputy Heinrich Himmler, which had been given to me during a recent visit I made to Berlin by the Axel Springer media group, which was proudly and unabashedly pro-Israel.

"Is this a lie, too?" I asked.

I commended the delegates who walked out of Ahmadinejad's speech and I attacked the delegates who stayed. How could they not call him out on his monstrous lie, one designed to facilitate a new Holocaust, this time to exterminate the six million Jews of Israel?

"Have you no shame? Have you no decency?" I railed at them.

Rare for a conservative Israeli leader at the UN, I received sustained applause at the end of the speech. But the annual Holocaust denial festival continues in Iran to this day.

OBAMA WAGED A relentless campaign against the possibility of an independent Israeli attack on Iran's nuclear facility. "An Israeli attack would endanger US military aid to Israel," an administration spokesman briefed the UPA news agency on April 24, 2009.[12]

However difficult it was to get the United States to adopt in any measure my approach of dual military and economic pressure on Iran, I had to try. That effort was continually hobbled by the Obama administration's focus on the settlements. After decades of conditioning, US and world public opinion was on his side. Rahm Emanuel linked America's ability to block Iran's nuclear progress to progress on the Palestinian track. It was clear: there was no way for the United States to make any progress on the Iranian issue without addressing the Palestinian issue.

Obama posited that a year's settlement freeze would bring the Palestinians to the negotiating table. I doubted it. If I was right it would partly smoke them out. In any case I knew I needed to buy time to further develop our military capabilities for a potential action against Iran. This meant absorbing blows on the Palestinian front.

It was time for hard decisions. I conferred with my colleagues in my kitchen cabinet. "We'll have to consider a freeze," I said simply.

Some embraced this. Others were unhappy about it but understood the need. We had endless discussions about the possible scope of the freeze.

Would it include all the settlements or just those outside the large urban blocks? What would be the duration of the freeze? How could we legally pass such a decision? What would be the compensation for contractors and families who were already financially committed to construction projects?

I would explain all these complications to Obama on my next visit to the White House on November 9, 2009.

In my prior discussions with Obama at the White House I had stressed that the freeze would not include Jerusalem. But this was papered over. Obama left it vague whether he agreed with my clearly stated position. Whether he did or not, building would continue as usual in our capital.

As it was, the freeze would be horrendously difficult politically. I discussed with the administration possible compensating normalization measures from the Arab states to cushion the blow. None were forthcoming. I said to Obama that I would need a few weeks to pass a decision. A full year's freeze was not possible but I thought I could manage ten months.

We ended the visit with a joint statement that we had a "positive meeting." Yet just a few days later, on November 19, Obama issued a statement from his visit to China that the nine hundred units that we authorized in Jerusalem's Gilo neighborhood "complicated our efforts to achieve peace." I gritted my teeth but stood my ground.

On November 25, two weeks after the Oval Office meeting, I passed a decision in the government for a ten-month freeze. Construction already in progress would continue. Everything else would be brought to a halt.

The decision was met with strong criticism from members of Likud and the settler community. "Netanyahu opened the floodgates to the eviction of Jews from their homeland," they cried. "The freeze would be followed by another freeze, and then another," they worried.

Not for the last time, I absorbed a blow on the domestic front for the sake of what I considered were more important goals on another, namely to lessen international opposition to possible action against Iran, with an eye on protecting Israel's future.

DURING THIS DIFFICULT time, I had some moments of joy. Avner at fifteen decided to compete in the National Bible Contest, which is like America's Scripps National Spelling Bee on steroids. The contest is held every Israeli Independence Day and is televised nationally. Competitors need to know the entire Bible inside out. Teenagers typically prepare for years and usually compete when they are seventeen or eighteen.

Avner's grandfather Shmuel, Sara's father, then ninety-four, was a venerated student of the Bible. Israel's first prime minister, David Ben Gurion, had invited him to his Bible study group. Sara's older brother Matanya won first place in the national youth Bible contest at ten years of age, an incredible feat, and was awarded the prize by Ben Gurion himself. Her second brother Hagi placed fourth in the national contest. Her third brother Amatzia placed third in the international contest.

Most winning competitors came from religious schools, but Avner came from a secular school, and he had only three months to prepare. As the competition began, Sara and I sat in the auditorium alongside other anxious parents. Our excitement knew no bounds when Avner won the national championship. He then placed third in the international competition, whose sixteen finalists were winnowed from twelve thousand candidates from around the world. Avner placed third behind two older contestants because he didn't know the answer to the question prepared for the prime minister to ask the contestants, an annual tradition.

Sara and I winced. So did many in the audience and at home who were rooting for Avner. He took it in stride. At least, I thought, that couldn't happen in a Koran test in Syria or Iran, because there the children of leaders would be fed the right question in advance.

After the contest, the moderator Dr. Avshalom Kor asked Avner why he entered the competition at the early age of fifteen.

"I knew I needed a few more years to prepare to be international champion, but I wanted grandfather Shmuel to still be with us to see me compete," he said.

Avner's performance and beguiling personality shot the ratings of the televised contest from about 2 percent to 15 percent. People adored him.

Sara and I, Shmuel and my one-hundred-year-old father couldn't have been more proud.

42

THE BATTLE FOR JERUSALEM

2010

As the freeze progressed, the Palestinians did not negotiate. Abbas found endless excuses not to come to the table. Why should he? He had the US continuing to press Israel, whereas in direct negotiations he would have to address my demands to recognize the Jewish state and make compromises on central issues such as security and refugees.

What's more, he could always rely on the periodic conflagrations between Israel and the United States.

He didn't have to wait long.

The crisis came during a visit by Vice President Biden in March 2010. A left-wing member of the Meretz party who as a member of Jerusalem's municipal council sat on a local zoning committee deliberately pushed through a decision to advance the planning of 1,600 apartments in Jerusalem's Ramat Shlomo neighborhood precisely on the day Biden and I met.

Ramat Shlomo was an integral part of Jerusalem, a few meters away from the old pre-1967 borders that had been completely erased by Jerusalem's urban development in the last half century. Still, given the American sensitivity to any howl from the Palestinians on construction anywhere in Jerusalem beyond the 1967 lines, the left-wing municipal official knew that the announcement of such an authorization during the vice president's visit would be seen as a deliberate provocation.

Before the authorization made the news, Biden and I had a working lunch. He offered me a piece of advice given to him by his father.

"Son," said Biden Sr., "don't get crucified on a small cross."

Problem was, I thought, there were a lot of middle-sized crosses out there. And one was erected that afternoon.

The housing announcement came as a complete surprise to me, and I believed the only reason for such an action was to sow discord between Obama and me. It worked. It produced a public uproar from the Palestinians, the left, the international community and, most important, the United States. Biden himself issued a statement saying that this announcement "undermines the trust we need right now and runs counter to the constructive discussions that I've had here in Israel."[1]

Over the phone, Biden and I put together a task force to stamp out the fire, consisting of Ron Dermer, US Middle East representative Dan Shapiro and Israel's ambassador to the US, Michael Oren. After hours of work they agreed on a statement I would issue later that night expressing regret for the timing of the announcement and explaining that this was merely a stage in the planning process. The authorized buildings would not be completed for at least two years.

While this statement was being worked out, Biden came with his wife Jill for a late dinner. We discussed his life, the tragedy he had to overcome with the loss of his first wife and daughter, the challenges he had faced raising his two sons, the support he received from Jill. It was a wonderful evening and a good ending to our meetings.

The following morning, Biden gave a speech at Tel Aviv University emphasizing the importance of the Israeli-American alliance. On his way to the airport to fly back to the US, he phoned me and said that there had been a lot of pushback from Washington on the announcement, but that he was glad we were able to put the matter to bed.

"Thanks for getting my chestnuts out of the fire," he said.

The storm was behind us.

Or so I thought.

The White House thought otherwise. The next day it escalated the Ramat Shlomo incident into a full-blown international crisis. Did they really believe that I had deliberately chosen to embarrass the vice president of the United States? Did they not know that the prime minister of Israel didn't involve himself in zoning in Jerusalem any more than the president of the US involved himself in zoning in Washington, DC?

More likely they seized on a deliberate provocation in a local planning committee in Jerusalem to manufacture unprecedented pressure on me to freeze construction in Jerusalem.

The next day, Hillary Clinton harangued me on the phone for forty-two minutes, mostly reading from a scripted text. "The announcement was a personal insult to the president," she admonished me. This was followed by a CNN interview in which she said that "the prime minister's decision calls into question his commitment to the US-Israel relationship."[2]

This was preposterous. Because of a few apartments in Israel's capital, the Obama administration said I was putting the entire historic Israeli-American alliance into question. If this was genuine outrage, it reflected the tendency of the administration to judge any point of contention with me in the worst possible light.

In an interview right after the Ramat Shlomo housing incident, David Axelrod, senior advisor to the president, was asked by a leading CNN journalist if Israel was an asset or a liability for the US in the Middle East. He dodged the question.

I sent Hillary a letter apologizing for the timing of the announcement and said that I would create a mechanism to monitor the timing of future ones. But I resolutely refused to commit to a freeze in Jerusalem. In fact, I pointed out, I was merely following the policies of all Israeli governments that since 1967 had authorized building throughout the city's municipal boundaries.

In an AIPAC annual conference in Washington on March 22, 2010, I pushed back powerfully against any concessions in Jerusalem.

"Jerusalem is not a settlement," I said. "Jerusalem is our capital!" The crowd went wild.

A day later I met with Obama in the Oval Office. "Bibi," he said to me, "that was a red-meat speech."

Indeed it was, but I felt it was necessary. Obama, who days earlier had passed his health care reform over much opposition, remained determined to get a freeze in Jerusalem. The Palestinian Authority kept moving the goalposts in explaining why they would not come to the negotiations and Obama kept moving his goalposts with them.

First they said they wouldn't come without a commitment to a two-state solution. They got the Bar-Ilan speech but panned it. Then they said they wouldn't come without a settlement freeze. They got a freeze but still didn't come. Now they said they needed a freeze in Jerusalem too.

I didn't budge. Obama asked me to join him in the White House's Roosevelt Room, where our staffs were waiting. Itzik Molcho, Ron Dermer and Michael Oren were with me. I was startled to hear the president say, "I have an assignment for you," as if we were his employees or students in a class and not the representatives of a sovereign nation. "The assignment" was to find, within a few hours, a solution to the Jerusalem logjam that would facilitate a resumption of negotiations.

As his aides explained to Dermer, the deadline was needed in order to present a positive outcome before the press reported a major crisis between Israel and America. Obama left the room.

I stayed with Molcho, Dermer and Oren in a final effort to find a way out of the crisis. We were fed sandwiches and cookies. Denis McDonough, the president's aide, continued to hammer away at Dermer that the news shows were beckoning and we still hadn't come up with any new ideas.

Finally, I had had enough. I left the team in the White House and made my way back to my hotel. I instructed Molcho and Dermer to hold their ground.

Much was made of the fact that I was shown out of a side door. In his memoir *A Promised Land*, Obama blamed me for leaking the details of our meetings and conversations that afternoon. I didn't. He also described as "fiction" the explanation that the housing announcement during Biden's visit was a product of a "misunderstanding," implying that I was the cause. Actually it wasn't a misunderstanding. A quick fact check by the White House would have easily established that it was a Jerusalem leftist's provocation meant to sow discord between Obama and me.

Back in Israel, I asked Dermer, who was spending Passover with his wife and three young boys in Miami, to return to Israel. Upon getting off the plane, he came directly to see me.

"We've been pummeled long enough. It's time to fight back," I said.

"What do you have in mind?" he asked.

"The first thing is to get a full-page ad in the leading American papers backing our policy on Jerusalem. That will start the ball rolling."

"What do you want me to do?" Ron asked.

"Muster all the pro-Israeli forces you can in the Jewish community, the evangelicals and the public at large."

Ron went back to the airport after being in Israel for all of six hours to rejoin his family and to reach out to the pro-Israel community in the US.

I called Elie Wiesel, the respected author, Nobel laureate and Holocaust survivor. I first got to know him when I was active in Hasbara at MIT and he was teaching at Boston University.

He was a powerful voice for Jewish remembrance and for fighting antisemitism.

"Elie," I said, "Israel and Jerusalem need you."

Wiesel was wedged between a rock and a hard place. He and Obama were close friends. The president had received him warmly in the White House. Elie was universally respected across the Jewish community and beyond, and he scrupulously avoided partisan politics in the US or Israel.

I spoke openly of his dilemma.

"I know how difficult this must be for you," I said. "I wouldn't approach you if the stakes weren't so high. Our hold on Jerusalem, our ancient capital, is being challenged. Your voice can make a difference."

"Are you sure?" he demurred.

"I'm absolutely sure," I responded.

A few days later a full-page ad appeared in the *Wall Street Journal*, the *Washington Post*, the *International Herald Tribune* and the *New York Times* titled "For Jerusalem." It was a direct appeal to Obama to stop the pressure on Jerusalem. It was signed by Elie Wiesel.

This was followed by statements from many supporters of Israel in America, including in Congress. Unlike the settlements, a united Jerusalem was an issue broadly supported by the American public. I knew Obama understood this and I assumed he would not want a full-scale public battle over an issue where I held the advantage. That assumption proved correct. The pressure subsided. We heard less and less on Jerusalem. The calls for freezing construction there eventually evaporated.

43

FIREFIGHTERS

2010

W hile the ten-month settlement freeze was testing the proposition that Mahmoud Abbas would come to the negotiating table, I still had a country to run.

My primary domestic focus was to extricate Israel from the economic chaos that gripped the entire world starting in 2008. Americans had been borrowing like mad without having the money to pay back, leading to the 2008 housing crisis. The laws of economic gravity dictated that this was unsustainable. The bubble had burst for everyone, but some economies fared better than others.

Israel's more conservative banks had borrowed less, so we were in better shape than many other economies that had joined the spending spree. With Finance Minister Yuval Steinitz I looked deeper into it. We concluded that the best thing to do was to follow a conservative and measured policy. This was the direct opposite of what nearly every Western nation did. While they spent trillions bailing out failed companies, we did nothing of the sort. We would not bail out failures. We passed a two-year budget signaling stability and lack of panic. We gave modest loan guarantees, effectively telling companies not to use the crisis to borrow irresponsibly. We increased the deficit by a modest one percent. Unlike the 2002 dot-com crisis, which hit many of Israel's high-tech firms hard, this economic downturn was short-term and largely skipped over our economy.

Our policies did the job and prevented the Israeli economy from drowning into an unnecessary ocean of debt.

Israel came out of the crisis faster than most other economies. In parallel I advanced, with Angel Gurría, the sympathetic director general of the OECD, Israel's entry into that association of advanced economies. In May 28, 2010, I went to the OECD's annual meeting in Paris.

I opened the speech with a variation of a Groucho Marx joke: "I wouldn't join a club that would accept me as a member unless it was the OECD."

After the laughter died down I presented Israel's economic figures and our high-tech prowess.

"Can Israel still be considered an emerging market?" I asked. "We have already emerged!"

I argued that it was in the interest of the OECD to have one of the world's most advanced technological economies as a member.

My reasons for wanting to join the OECD were twofold. First, I wanted global recognition that Israel was a developed economy. That would upgrade our credit rating and increase foreign investments. Second, I wanted to use the OECD's multi-country database as a mirror that I could hold before my ministers showing the best practices they should pursue in areas such as regulation, education, and digital information.

I put joining the OECD and passing a two-year budget as primary goals for Yuval Steinitz upon appointing him as finance minister when I took office in 2009. He achieved both goals within a year. We quickly passed a two-year budget, the first developed economy ever to do so. Ministers would now have a planning and operating horizon of a year and a half between one budget to the next, instead of a few months. Then, on September 7, 2010, Israel was admitted as a full member to the OECD. Three days later, S&P raised Israel's credit rating.

THE BIGGEST THREAT that concerned me was still Iran. While advancing our own military option against Iran's nuclear capability, I was keenly aware of Iran's plans to buy formidable S-300 antiaircraft missile batteries from Russia, which would make the Israeli Air Force's mission a lot more difficult in the event that we chose to strike.

On September 7, 2009, I had flown to Moscow for a clandestine meeting with Vladimir Putin. He received me in his private residence in a suburb of Moscow, the first of many such visits. In these meetings we would discuss how to increase our bilateral cooperation in trade, technology, agriculture and tourism. I often expressed my genuine appreciation for the incomparable sacrifices the Russian people and the Red Army made in defeating the Nazis.

But with rare exceptions, the main topic in our meetings was Iran.

"I know that you intend to supply Iran with S-300s," I had said in this first meeting. "Can you delay the supply?"

Putin said that Russia was bound by a contract and that Iran had already made a down payment.

While I was away, Israeli journalists inquired as to my whereabouts. The prime minister's spokesman said that I was reviewing a military exercise. When the news leaked out that I was in Moscow, a great furor arose, offering further "proof" that I was a congenital liar, as if the prime minister was obliged to share such sensitive information with the press.

I shrugged this off.

My next visits to Moscow were all public. On February 16, 2010, I met Putin again, this time in the Kremlin. Again the focus was on Iran and the S-300s, a subject I returned to in each subsequent visit.

The shipment ended up being delayed for a full seven years.

At the end of my second visit to Moscow, Sara and I visited Café Pushkin, following our time-honored practice of taking a few hours for ourselves at the end of foreign trips before returning to Israel.

It was late at night and we were the last customers on the restaurant's second floor.

An aide came to my table.

"Sir, the prime minister of Greece, George Papandreou, is downstairs. He asks if he could see you."

"Of course," I said.

Papandreou, who was also visiting Putin, came over with his foreign minister. Greece was undergoing a terrible economic crisis and he wanted to know what I had done to achieve Israel's "economic miracle," as he called it. We discussed this at length and I agreed to put him in touch with former officials from the Finance Ministry who had worked with me on our reforms.

I seized the opportunity to raise another subject.

"Prime Minister," I asked, "how is it possible that we meet here for the first time in a restaurant in Moscow? Israel and Greece are both Western democracies in the East Mediterranean. For decades we were separated by Greece's one-sided support of the Palestinians. What did you get out of it? Nothing."

Without mentioning Turkey's enmity toward both our countries, I said, "We have many common interests. It's time to build a true alliance between us."

Papandreou agreed enthusiastically. A few months later he visited Israel and shortly after that I visited Greece.

My visit helped encourage hundreds of thousands of Israeli tourists to prefer Greece over Turkey, a trend that would become a veritable tsunami after a May 2010 clash with Turkish militants on the Turkish ship *Mavi Marmara* who were seeking to get past the military blockade around Hamas-controlled Gaza. The ensuing bloody confrontation with Israeli naval commandos soured our relations with Turkey for more than a decade. In the interim we developed defense and commercial ties with Greece, and later expanded our cooperation to include Cyprus. We advanced plans for an underwater pipeline from Israel and Cyprus through Greece that would supply Israeli and Cypriot gas to Europe.

On my first official visit to Greece, Papandreou took me to the island of Poros. During lunch in a restaurant overlooking a beautiful bay, I noticed massive flames that began consuming a forest on the other side of it. Papandreou briefly glanced at the flames and continued eating.

I was stupefied. If it had been up to me I would have been turning the country upside down in an effort to put out the fire.

"George," I asked as politely as I could, "don't you want to do something about this fire?"

"Oh, don't worry, the planes will soon put it out," he answered.

Within minutes a squadron of yellow Bombardier planes flew in. Dipping into the bay, they deposited sea water on the flames. Within half an hour the fire was put out.

I asked my military secretary to place an order for a few of these planes. Before they could arrive, a massive fire broke out in the Mount Carmel Forest some months later, on December 2, 2010. Carried by strong dry winds, the blaze was unstoppable. Twenty-meter-high flames skipped from treetop to treetop. The fire destroyed much of the picturesque communities of Ein Hod and Bet Oren and reached the outer houses of Haifa, Tirat Ha Carmel and the Druze village of Daliyat el-Carmel.

Tragically, a bus full of prison personnel took a wrong turn and was trapped in the inferno. All its passengers were burned alive, as were several brave firefighters, including sixteen-year-old firefighting volunteer Elad Ribben.

Seeing the blaze on television in my Jerusalem residence, I quickly flew by helicopter to the Carmel. The firefighters were hopelessly outmatched. Nothing in their arsenal stood a chance against this force of nature. The fire came after a long dry spell and no rain was in sight. The only way to stamp out the fire was with specially equipped airplanes and helicopters—and we had none.

Remembering Poros, I instructed the National Security Council to set up a phone marathon to some thirty heads of state within flying radius. I had to get firefighting planes to Israel before the fire could burn the whole of the Mount Carmel Forest and then spread to other parts of the country.

The president of Cyprus, whom I had visited a few months earlier, sent Cyprus's only plane. Papandreou dispatched four of his yellow Bombardiers; they reached Israel by morning. Other planes and helicopters came from Russia, Italy, Spain, Switzerland, the Netherlands, and many other countries, even one from Turkey. Egypt and the Palestinian Authority sent firefighters. I valued the symbolic effort and said so.

Within twenty-four hours we had some thirty planes circling the skies of northern Israel, a veritable flying Tower of Babel. The IAF set up a special ground command and placed an Israeli pilot next to each foreign pilot to ensure communication and to avoid inflight collisions. The scene reminded me of aerial combat footage from World War I, with brave pilots diving over clouds of smoke to deposit their loads.

But there was a catch. The planes couldn't fly at night. Strong winds would carry the still-burning embers and start fresh fires in the dry timber. To be on the safe side, we needed more extinguishing power.

My military secretary Yohanan Locker, a brigadier general in the IAF and an F-16 navigator, approached me.

"Prime Minister, I found a monster plane. It's called a supertanker."

"Show me," I said.

"It's right here on the internet," Locker said. "A Colorado company says it can get it to any part of the world within twenty-four hours. It costs two million dollars."

"So get it," I said.

"I can't," Locker responded. "The Finance Ministry says I have to put it to bid."

I went wild. My shouting must have been so loud that they heard it in the nearby Finance Ministry.

Within a little more than twenty-four hours the supertanker was flying over the skies of Israel, covering the remaining flames with a red carpet of fire-extinguishing chemicals.

A few days later, the fire was finally put out. I thanked the foreign aircrews, our pilots and our firefighting crews. We visited the wounded in the hospital. One of them was a brave firefighter named Danny Khayat, the son of Motti and Batsheva Khayat. Batsheva was one of my father-in-law Shmuel Ben Artzi's devoted students. Like many others, she said that the years she had spent with Shmuel in her youth had changed her life and infused it with purpose.

Sara tended Danny's bed with Batsheva and arranged a donation for artificial skin implants. Horribly burned, Danny didn't survive. Joined in grief, our families remain tightly knit to this day.

We also tried to comfort the Ribben family. Elad, the teenage volunteer firefighter who perished, was the long-awaited only child of his elderly parents. A promising student who dreamed of being a pilot, he volunteered to help fight fires. I couldn't alleviate their grief, but I could do one thing.

I called in Yohanan Locker. "Yohanan," I said, "you have one mission. Build a firefighting squadron in three months. We'll call it the Elad Squadron."

Immensely capable, disciplined, focused on results and with a no-nonsense approach, Locker went to work. Three months later, on the dot, with the Ribbens attending, we inaugurated the Elad Squadron of twelve firefighting planes. Two more planes were later added. Over the next several years the squadron put out hundreds of wildfires, including one that almost burned down Yad Vashem, Israel's famed Holocaust memorial museum, embedded in the Jerusalem Forest.

While many praised me for the quick action during the Carmel fire, others demanded an official inquiry on the tragic loss of forty-four lives in the first hours of the blaze. Since the bus that claimed so many had taken a wrong turn into the fire, there was not much to investigate. But the clamor continued, egged on by the ever-hostile press.

This coincided with a state comptroller's report on the sorry state of Israel's firefighting equipment, which supposedly contributed to the tragedy. The author of that report was a state comptroller fond of publicity. His much-heralded report explained that the fire department needed better training, new uniforms, new fire engines and so on.

None of these recommendations would have helped put out the Mount Carmel Forest fire, or any fire in dense forest or on vast unpaved tracts of land. Regular megafires in California, Australia, Russia and Canada proved this conclusively.

With time-honored bureaucratic blindness, the two-hundred-page report neglected to mention the two words that made the *only* difference.

Firefighting planes.

AFTER HIS SUPERB building of the firefighting squadron in just ninety days, Locker took on another mission.

"Prime Minister," he said, "the coffee in your office stinks. I'm going to get the Prime Minister's Office to pay for a Nespresso machine."

It took him a full six months to get the approval through the absurd bureaucracy. But Locker's dogged determination finally broke through.

We raised two cups of fine espresso to celebrate his success.

44

MARMARA

2010

In September 1998, I was visited by Mesut Yilmaz, the prime minister of Turkey, with which Israel enjoyed close relations at the time. After dinner in the prime minister's residence, we had coffee in the living room.

"I have a favor to ask," I said. "The Topkapi Palace Museum in Istanbul has an ancient stone tablet that records an event described in the Bible. I would like the state of Israel to purchase it from you."

Two thousand seven hundred years ago the Judean king Hezekiah, anticipating an Assyrian siege on Jerusalem, dug a subterranean water channel under David's City, right next to the Temple Mount. Two teams of diggers some five hundred meters apart excavated the rock from opposing sides of the mountain. In the nineteenth century several archaeological efforts, probing the tunnel in stages, discovered the tablet placed by the two teams at the point where they met. Written in Biblical Hebrew, it says: "When three cubits were left to cut . . . the voice of a man . . . called to his counterpart. . . . And on the day of the tunnel [being finished] the stonecutters struck each man towards his counterpart, ax against ax, and water flowed from the source to the pool. . . ."

This was priceless, the Bible speaking to us in real time. Since the Ottomans ruled Jerusalem at the time, the tablet ended up in Istanbul.

"We have thousands of items from the Ottoman period in our museums," I said. "Pick any one you want and we'll trade."

"I'm sorry, my friend. I can't do that," he said.

"Then take *all* the Ottoman artifacts," I suggested.

"I can't do that either," he said.

"Then name your price," I persisted.

Again he refused my offer.

Yilmaz explained that there was a growing Islamist constituency in Turkey competing for power with the pro-Western constituency. He could not be the Turkish prime minister accused of giving Israel a stone tablet written in Hebrew that would be prominently displayed in Jerusalem, unequivocally proving it was a Jewish and not a Muslim city thousands of years ago.

"We're going to have a problem with Turkey," I said to Sara after Yilmaz and his wife left. A big problem, as it later turned out, when the Islamist Recep Tayyip Erdogan came to power on March 14, 2003.

Still, I set a goal of retrieving this precious inscription. Though it hasn't been done yet, I am confident it will eventually be achieved.

TWELVE YEARS LATER, in late May 2010, I visited Canada. I had earlier met its new Conservative prime minister, Stephen Harper, in New York in the UN General Assembly. Harper was an unabashed supporter of Israel. When I met him I liked him instantly. He was smart, highly educated and clear thinking. And he refused to bow to the winds of political fashion.

"Can I ask you a personal question, Stephen?" I said when we met in New York.

"Sure."

"Usually when someone is so tenaciously supportive of Israel, there's something in his personal background beyond ideology and politics."

"You're right," Harper said. He told me of his father, who after completing his military service became an accountant with one of the dominant business firms in Toronto.

"Harper," his father was told by his powerful bosses, "you have a brilliant future with us. Just follow the rules and stay away from those people."

When Harper's father understood that "those people" meant Canadian Jews, he left the firm. Sharing the same economic and political views,

I naturally looked forward to spending some time with Harper on my official visit to Canada.

But that was not to be.

On my first evening in Ottawa, I received word that a crisis had occurred. Israeli soldiers boarding the Turkish civilian passenger ship *Mavi Marmara* were attacked by Turkish militants wielding iron bars and clubs. In defending themselves, they killed nine rioters.

The *Marmara* was headed to Gaza to break our naval blockade, put in place in 2007 to prevent the smuggling in of the heavy weapons and rockets that Hamas periodically launched at Israel's cities. These weapons could only be delivered from the sea, given that the land passages to Gaza were inspected by Israel and Egypt. Our rationale for these inspections was security and nothing else.

When I reentered the Prime Minister's Office in 2009, I found a dizzying array of restrictions on imports to Gaza, including pasta. Well before the *Marmara* affair I found these limitations ridiculous and eliminated the lot. The Palestinians could import by land anything they wanted, except weapons and certain dual-use materials that could be used for weapon production or fortifications. Everything else, such as food, toys and clothes, was theirs for the asking.

I did the same thing in the Palestinian areas in Judea and Samaria. Shortly after taking office in 2009, I removed nearly half the roadblocks and checkpoints to help facilitate commerce and Palestinian economic growth, which I believed contributed to stability and peace.

The worldwide propaganda campaign describing Gaza as being "starved" by Israel ignored these uncomfortable facts. It launched a stream of small-boat flotillas carrying mostly European leftists and assorted anarchists who supported Hamas's demands to break the blockade in the name of "human rights."

Needless to say, these anti-Israel activists never dreamed of demanding that *Hamas* observe human rights by stopping the execution of political rivals, the persecution of gays and the subjugation of Palestinian women, let alone the deliberate targeting of Israeli civilians.

Up until my visit to Canada, we successfully intercepted all these boats at sea and peacefully returned their passengers to their home countries. But the *Mavi Marmara* was different. It was bigger, a lot bigger, and it was organized by the Islamist Turkish group IHH, which described itself as "a humanitarian group" but was anything but that. It was closely associated with Turkey's ruler, Recep Erdogan.

Before I left Israel, we had prepared provisional plans to intercept the ship, using heliborne commandos who would descend armed with rubber bullets and spray paint. I instructed our forces to carry video equipment to record the actual events.

Now in Canada, on May 30, 2010, I was woken up in the middle of the night.

"Prime Minister," said the caller, "there's been a botch-up. Our forces met resistance from Turkish militants armed with iron bars and knives. One of them grabbed a weapon from one of the commandos. Our guys barely extricated themselves, and they killed nine Turks in the process."

I called my staff.

"Pack up. We're going back to Israel." I apologized to Harper and asked our embassy in Washington to apologize to President Obama, whom I had hoped to see briefly after my visit to Canada. I would call him from the plane.

That turned out to be mission impossible. The plane I was flying was dilapidated and lacked proper means of communication. So much so that in one of our repeatedly interrupted calls, Obama quipped, "Bibi, why don't you guys buy a new plane and I'll pay for the communication gear."

When we finally were able to talk, it was far from amusing. The conversation occurred on a secure call in a hangar while on a refueling stopover in Toronto. I asked Ron Dermer to join me.

The UN Security Council was rushing to judgment. They were about to issue a presidential statement directed against Israel and calling for an investigation of the incident, just hours after it took place and well before any reliable information reached it. The IDF video showing the IHH attack on our forces made no impression on them.

I urged Obama to ask the Security Council members to wait until the facts were established. If they didn't agree, I asked him to veto the resolution.

Obama said he couldn't apply the veto.

"If I do that, America will be isolated," said the president.

I looked at Ron. We were both thinking the same thing. When a heavy fog descended over the English Channel, cutting off Britain from Europe, Churchill declared, "The continent is isolated."

Now we heard the leader of the greatest superpower the world has ever known expressing the reverse sentiment. The US had traditionally vetoed outrageous UN resolutions against Israel and was seldom concerned that it would be "isolated" as a result. It shielded Israel from UN excesses not only because they were patently absurd, but also because it believed that those taking potshots at Israel were also attacking America.

Now that American shield was removed as a result of Obama's concern over America's international legitimacy. He didn't see the US as taking a leading position and having the other nations follow. Rather, he felt that America should "lead from behind."

I decided on two courses of action. The first was to establish our own independent inquiry, led by former Supreme Court justice Jacob Turkel and staffed by respected Israeli legal scholars and notable figures from abroad, including the Irish Nobel Peace Prize laureate David Trimble and the former Canadian military judge advocate general Ken Watkin.

The committee's three-hundred-page report exonerated Israel and helped defuse some of the slander. It found that the actions of the Israeli Navy in the raid and Israel's naval blockade of Gaza were both legal under international law,[1] and accused the "IHH activists" of having armed themselves and conducting hostilities "in an organized manner."[2]

My second course of action was to speak confidentially to Ban Ki-moon, the secretary-general of the United Nations. Meeting in his office at UN headquarters in New York, he sought to reassure me.

"Prime Minister," he said, "I ask you to trust me. I will appoint a person of impartial integrity to lead our inquiry."

"When it comes to Israel at the UN, that will be a refreshing first," I answered.

I raised the recently issued Goldstone Report, a product of the highly biased and misnamed UN Human Rights Council, 70 percent of whose resolutions were directed against Israel.[3] That report had accused Israel of war crimes for defending itself against the targeting of civilians by Hamas rockets fired from Gaza.

"This is not the Human Rights Council," Ban Ki-moon said. "I will personally choose the commission head and you will not be disappointed with my choice."

He was true to his word. He appointed the former prime minister of New Zealand, Geoffrey Palmer, who also served as a minister of justice, to head up the commission.

The Palmer Report surprised many. Mostly fair and accurate, it too backed the legality of Israel's right to blockade Gaza and argued that it used force for self-defense. But it also added that this force was excessive and that the lives lost were "unacceptable."

For a UN commission, that was as good as we could get. The Palmer Report went a long way to bury the *Mavi Marmara* affair. But we were not out of the woods yet. International law enabled the Turkish government and Turkish citizens to get warrants of arrest for our soldiers and commanders in many countries.

To resolve that, I had to cut a financial remuneration deal with Erdogan. This was achieved a few years later, with the help of President Obama, at the time a close friend of the Turkish president.

45

THE LECTURE

2011

Throughout 2010 I had continued to develop a credible Israeli military option against Iran's nuclear facilities and to muster political support for it in the inner cabinet.

I knew that in order to carry out such a mission, I would also have to improve the political climate for Israel internationally. In particular, I would have to ease my strained relations with Obama. The best way to do that was to show the Americans that I was willing to move ahead on a political track, either with the Palestinians or with the Syrians.

I decided I would propose to Obama to discard the "freezes"—two months remained out of the ten months total—and other assorted preconditions for negotiations. I was prepared to come at his invitation to a Camp David summit with the Palestinian leadership, or alternatively with the Syrian leadership, and see if we could move directly to a final agreement with either one. If Mahmoud Abbas refused, we could try Bashar Assad.

These suggestions weren't prompted by a Pollyannaish belief that, this time, either the Palestinians or the Syrians were ready to make a genuine peace with us. The chances that such a high-pressure summit would crack their inherent opposition to the Jewish state's right to exist weren't high.

But if that miracle did take place and either party ended a century of hostility toward Zionism, I would be there ready to reciprocate. And if they didn't, perhaps even Obama would see the true obstacle to the peace he craved so much. Either outcome, I thought, would give me the sufficient diplomatic capital and operational time to prepare a strategic strike against Iran's nuclear facilities. Wary of leaks, I shared my proposal with only two people on my team: Ron Dermer and my military secretary, Yohanan Locker.

On July 6, 2010, I met Obama in the White House and asked to spend time one-on-one.

"In the two months left for the freeze," I said to the president, "I doubt Abu Mazen [Abbas] will come to the table. I suggest a one-shot peace summit without preconditions at your invitation, with a Syrian summit as a backup plan."

Obama liked the idea. He suggested a preliminary summit in Washington to "break the ice" between Abbas and me. I agreed. In the public statement at the end of our meeting I said, "Mr. President, the distance between Jerusalem and Ramallah is a fifteen-minute drive, and if we want to advance to peace we need to move to direct negotiations."

Obama said we had an "excellent discussion," and added that "I believe that Prime Minister Netanyahu wants peace. I think he's willing to take risks for peace."

It was the first and only time Obama let me out of the penalty box.

Little noticed but extremely impressive was how at the end of this visit Obama recited a carefully worded agreed-upon text, entirely from memory. Because we had attached great importance to each word, we had asked that Obama read out the statement from a podium. His staff declined but assured us that Obama would deliver the statement exactly as drafted.

While seated in the Oval Office, he did just that, perfectly. Here's what he said:

> Finally, we discussed issues that arose out of the nuclear non-proliferation conference. I reiterated to the prime minister that there is no change in US policy when it comes to these issues. We strongly believe that given its size, its history, the region it's in and the threats that are leveled against it, Israel has unique security requirements. It's got to be able to respond to threats or

any combination of threats in the region. That's why we remain unwavering in our commitment to Israel's security. The United States will never ask Israel to take any steps that would undermine its security interests.

It was the best meeting I had with Obama.

Two months later, Obama invited Abbas, President Mubarak, King Abdullah and me to Washington for a ceremonial meeting meant to launch the direct talks between us. This was followed by a summit a few days later in Sharm el-Sheikh and direct talks in Jerusalem shortly afterward.

The US prepared a press event with Hillary Clinton, Abbas and me. I had planned to speak from a prepared text in Hebrew but sitting there, I realized that I needed to speak in English in order to communicate my message to the entire world. For some reason it wasn't clear to my staff that this event would require me to make a detailed statement in English. Thrust into the meeting, I sat beside Hillary, who read out her prepared statement. I saw my Hebrew text prepared for a later meeting with the Israeli press. Left with no choice, I simultaneously translated it into English. I don't know if anyone could tell I was reading, but I'm sure no one could tell I was translating.

Sitting next to me, Hillary kept looking at the Hebrew text and then at me. The secretary of state might have thought that on handling text, Obama and I shared certain characteristics.

Washington was meant to break the ice but it was only partially successful. Abbas was cordial but highly circumspect. In Sharm el-Sheikh a few days later, with Hillary, King Abdullah and President Mubarak looking on, the summit caravan continued, again with no concrete results.

I had not been in Sharm for many decades and told President Mubarak that I was delighted to see the development of its hotels and resorts. Forty years earlier, Yoni and I, along with the rest of the Unit, made our way to its then-virgin beaches all the way from Eilat, riding captured Russian ZiL trucks on the unpaved coast and inland wadis. We dived in the enchanting underwater cliffs of Ras Mohamed, taking in the exquisite colors of the fish swirling around us.

"Hell," I said to my staff, pointing to the sea, "I'd much rather be diving out there than be cooped up in here."

A few days after the talks in Sharm, I met with Abbas and Hillary in the prime minister's residence in Jerusalem. A big public debate broke out about whether I should display the Palestinian Authority flag, as was customary with all foreign visitors. Despite the criticism, I decided to do so. The most important thing for me in this meeting was the substance rather than the symbolism.

I had already made clear that in any final settlement Israel would control security. But if the Palestinians wished to call their political entity with abridged sovereign powers a state, with flag and all, so be it.

Abbas had been to the Balfour Street residence several times before in chummy meetings with Olmert. Despite Olmert's largesse in offering irresponsible and far-reaching concessions, Abbas never bit. Receiving him cordially, I invited him and Hillary to my study.

I said, "We have a dispute on territory, powers and rights. In any case, I want to state clearly from the outset that a withdrawal to the 1967 borders is out of the question and that in any conceivable peace settlement, Israel would have to retain control of the Jordan Valley."

"Why do you insist on the Jordan Valley?" Abbas asked.

"Because in the Middle East anything could happen and this protects Israel from the east," I said.

I avoided saying that he and the Palestinian Authority could be toppled overnight and any territory we vacated would be taken over by radical Islamists aligned with Iran.

"What could possibly happen?" Abbas asked, discounting my concern.

"A lot," I said.

Three months later the Arab Spring would break out.

After the summits in Washington, Sharm and Jerusalem, Obama and Hillary must have concluded that my proposal for a Camp David summit was not realistic. Abbas now insisted that he needed an extension of the freeze to "see if I could be trusted as a genuine peace negotiator" before he could rejoin the talks.

The ten-month freeze was to end on September 26. The US shifted gears and now pressed Israel for a sixty-day extension.[1] A few days later in the Knesset I said that I would consider such an extension if the Palestinian Authority would recognize Israel as the homeland of the Jewish people. The Palestinians immediately rejected that proposal, so I didn't agree to the freeze extension.

Nonetheless, behind the scenes I explored with the Americans another possible compensation for an extension in the form of an additional squadron of F-35 fighter planes. These could advance our capabilities against Iran. At the annual conference of the Jewish Federations of North America held in New Orleans on November 8, I reiterated that "Iran's nuclear program must be stopped."[2]

Soon after, at the Regency hotel in New York, my staff and I carried out secret discussions with Hillary and her staff about the possible F-35 deal. In the end Obama decided that it wasn't worth it. The US would be accused of "bribing" Israel and he may have realized by then that even with an extension, Abbas wouldn't budge.

The Palestinian issue was left in abeyance.

The Arab Spring protests broke out in December 2010, first in Tunisia, then in Algeria, Jordan, Yemen, Oman, Libya and, most powerfully, in Egypt and Syria. The outbreak in Syria put an end to any possibility of a deal with that country, since you can't negotiate with a regime that has lost control over its own territory. The outbreak in Egypt's Tahrir Square occurred while I was having lunch with German chancellor Angela Merkel, who was visiting Jerusalem.

"Do you think this is serious?" she asked me.

"I think it's very serious," I answered. "I think it may precede a takeover by the Islamists."

While helping to supply Israel with much-needed submarines, Merkel never wavered from the European orthodoxy about the centrality of the Palestinian issue and the settlements.

I hoped that the massive political earthquake of the Arab Spring would open her eyes and those of other European leaders to the inherent instability of the Middle East and end their obsession with the establishment of a Palestinian state at all cost. Israel had nothing to do with this historic convulsion. In fact it was now the only piece of solid ground in the volcanic Middle East. More than Merkel, of course, I hoped that this would be the conclusion that Obama reached as well.

It wasn't.

Energized by the turbulent Arab Spring, Obama quickly issued demands for Mubarak to resign, something he never demanded of Iran's regime during Iran's massive protests. I cautioned Washington that Mubarak's demise could Islamicize Egypt.

A few weeks later, Mubarak did resign, leaving Egypt to be led by a temporary government. It would later be replaced by Mohamed Morsi, an Islamist associated with the Muslim Brotherhood, in what I viewed as a catastrophic development for Israel.

I met Mubarak several times in Cairo and Sharm el-Sheikh and liked him. He was far from the monstrous dictator depicted in the world press when he was brought down. Though he was by no means a benevolent ruler, he lacked the ruthlessness and tyrannical discipline of the Iranian regime which enabled it to stay in power. He was congenial and candid with me, expressing a continued commitment to the Israeli-Egyptian peace.

He lacked the reformer's zeal which could have elevated Egypt's scanty GDP per capita to robust prosperity for his people. I spoke to him many times of the enormous promise of converting the cold peace between Israel and Egypt to a warm economic peace, the kind we later developed with the Emirates and Bahrain.

"But we're growing at four percent a year," Mubarak protested.

"Mr. President," I answered, "with market reforms you could grow at twice that rate for a decade. And we can help you do it."

I drew a blank.

Unlike the dynamic and innovative Gulf economies, Egypt's economy was straightjacketed by endemic bureaucracy and corruption.

When I lost the elections in 1999, Mubarak invited Sara and me for a cruise on the Nile and a visit to the iconic rock-cut temple of Pharaoh Ramesses II in Abu Simbel. That's one invitation I regret not taking.

After Mubarak's fall, Obama resumed the pressure for Israeli withdrawals and the establishment of a Palestinian state. By now many in Israel understood that such a state would be taken over by the Islamist tsunami sweeping through most of the Arab world.

This fear was compounded by Abbas's sudden turn to Hamas, with whom he signed a reconciliation agreement in May 2011, likely out of fear of losing control to the rising Islamist tide. I sent a message to the US: How do you expect us to negotiate peace with someone united with a movement openly committed to our destruction?

Abbas then published an op-ed in the *New York Times* on May 16 that was breathtaking in its historical revision. Rather than tell the truth about the Palestinian rejection of the 1948 Partition Resolution and the launch of a war against Israel by five Arab armies, he lied that it was Israel that attacked the Arabs in 1948, and not the other way around. This met nearly universal condemnation in Israel but made little impression on the Obama administration.

Still, I did not give up hope that with the help of the Arab Spring I could convince Obama to put aside, at least for a while, his Palestinian obsession.

In late May 2011 I had a Washington trip planned. It would start with a scheduled meeting with Obama. A few days later, I would give a speech to AIPAC, and the day after that, a speech to a joint meeting of Congress. I planned a gracious speech at the Oval Office that would leave the door open for a political process with the Palestinians. But on the eve of my departure for the US, the White House informed Dermer that Obama would give a speech the next day in the State Department calling for a Palestinian state on the "'67 lines with swaps," a departure from the US position of the previous forty-four years.

I called Hillary immediately.

"Why are you forcing us into a confrontation?" I asked.

I got no clear answer. In the midst of Islamist revolutions throughout the Middle East and Abbas's embrace of Hamas after repeatedly refusing to enter peace talks despite a ten-month settlement freeze, the US was not only not backing away from its failed Palestinian policy—it was moving deeper into it!

I was absolutely furious. This was not merely bad policy; it was bad faith. On the plane bound for the US, I prepared a four-minute statement that I would give in the Oval Office in front of television cameras.

Ron Dermer and the Prime Minister's Office spokesman Mark Regev helped me draft the statement. Regev was an excellent professional diplomat whom I had pilfered from the Foreign Ministry. Born in Australia, he looked and spoke like the perfect English gentleman that he was. He had a way with words and he had a way with me. Whenever I planned to cross the line of brazen impropriety he would subtly try to nudge me back.

"Prime Minister," he would say, "I know what you're trying to say but can we phrase it somewhat differently?"

I often joked with him that he was like the lead conniving civil servant in the British television show *Yes, Prime Minister* but without the malice.

When we arrived at Blair House, Ambassador Michael Oren suggested a few more changes to temper my statement. Dermer, Oren and Regev worried that I wouldn't remember the text and suggested I prepare cards with a few bullet points.

"No cards, no paper, nothing. This is one that I'll remember word for word," I said.

I rehearsed the statement several times but the only time I got it right was in the Oval Office.

After Obama's initial words, I delivered in measured tones but in no uncertain terms a frontal rejection of "Palestinian demands" for a return to the 1967 lines. I did not mention that Obama endorsed each of these demands.

"It's not going to happen," I said to the president and to the world. "A peace based on illusion will crash on the rocks of Middle Eastern realities. For there to be peace, the Palestinians will have to recognize some basic realities."

First, I said, we can't go back to the 1967 borders. Second, Israel can't negotiate with a government backed by Hamas. Third, the Palestinian refugee problem will have to be resolved in a Palestinian state but not in the Jewish state.

"The ancient nation of Israel has been around for almost four thousand years," I continued. "We've experienced struggle and suffering like no other people. We've gone through expulsions, pogroms, massacres and the murder of millions. But I can say that even at the nadir of the valley of death, we never lost hope and the dream of reestablishing a sovereign state in our ancient homeland, the Land of Israel.

"And now it falls on my shoulders as the prime minister of Israel at a time of extraordinary instability and uncertainty in the Middle East to work with you to fashion a peace that will ensure Israel's security and will not jeopardize its survival. Mr. President, history will not give the Jewish people another chance."

Obama remained aloof but his staff was furious. Rahm Emanuel was no longer chief of staff but William Daley, who took over, was standing behind Dermer and squeezed his shoulder.

"Does your boss always lecture people in their office?" he whispered angrily to Ron.

"Only when they kick his country in their teeth," Ron replied.

My Oval Office remarks were given on Friday, May 20, and the following Monday I met with Vice President Biden in the Roosevelt Room of the White House.

"We're a proud country," he said sternly. "And no one, but no one, has the right to humiliate the president of the United States."

I explained that no humiliation was intended. I had merely clarified the elements critical for Israel's survival.

"To you, Joe, it's an important matter," I said. "To us it's a matter of life and death."

Biden lightened up.

"That reminds me of the story of the chicken and the pig," he said. "The chicken suggested to the pig that they please the farmer by preparing a breakfast of bacon and eggs for him. The pig objects, saying to the chicken, 'For you it's a contribution, for me it's a lifetime commitment.' "

Our delegation burst out laughing.

Notwithstanding his frustration with my "lecture," Obama pulled back somewhat on his 1967 borders formula after my speech, saying that any final peace settlement between Israel and the Palestinians would have to take into account "developments on the ground," a clear nod that the Jewish settlement blocs would stay in place in his envisioned plan.

When I spoke to AIPAC I said, "Israel is not what's *wrong* in the Middle East, Israel is what's *right* in the Middle East."

I repeated this theme the next day in my second speech to a joint meeting of Congress.

"Mr. Vice President," I began, addressing Biden, who was sitting behind me, "do you remember when the two of us were the new kids on the block?" referring to our early days in Washington.

"In Judea and Samaria," I said, "the Jewish people are not foreign occupiers. We are not the British in India. We are not the Belgians in the Congo. This is the land of our forefathers."

Israel is prepared to negotiate peace, I explained, "but it will not negotiate with a Palestinian government backed by the Palestinian version of Al Qaeda. I say to President Abbas: Tear up your pact with Hamas. If Abbas says, 'I will accept a Jewish state,' those six words will change history."

In the middle of the speech, an anti-Israel Code Pink protester began heckling from the gallery.

"You can't do that in Gaza, can you?" I said to tumultuous applause from both sides of the aisle. All in all, the speech received *twenty* standing ovations.[3]

It reverberated well in Israel, too. My speeches in Congress, as well as at the UN, were carried live on Israel's three television channels without interruption. These were the only times that the Israeli public could hear me without the interruptions of commentators and reporters; this was especially true for interviews, where I could often barely complete a sentence.

Perhaps this was another reason why my speeches in major international forums instilled such great pride among my supporters. Coming back to Israel from Washington, I was greeted as a hero, the "magician" again. But as soon as one front subsided, another broke out.

46

"WE'LL GET YOU OUT OF THERE, YONI"

2011

In 2011, housing costs were rising rapidly in Israel. A few years earlier the Olmert government had constricted building in the high-demand center of the country, hoping to disperse young couples to the less dense periphery. This was folly of the first order. As a rule, governments should tamper as little as possible with markets.

The center of the country was still where the jobs were. How did the government expect people to move back and forth to the periphery when there was no fast transportation grid to do that?

In the five years after I left the Finance Ministry, investment in fast transport to the periphery had been completely halted. The result was that young families didn't move to the periphery, and housing costs in the greater Tel Aviv area skyrocketed. In the summer of 2011, this sparked what came to be known as the "Rothschild protests," named for Tel Aviv's swank Rothschild Boulevard, where protesters set up makeshift tents.

Some commentators remarked that this was akin to the children of Manhattan's elites protesting that there was no affordable housing on Fifth Avenue. This was true, though geographically the housing crisis extended well beyond Tel Aviv.

The protest movement began to grow, soon accompanied by other demonstrations against the cost of day care and food prices. Though the protests had hit on real issues, they were commandeered by the left from the start.

Nearly all its leaders and spokespersons were left-wing. Two later became members of the Knesset in the Labor Party. A Channel 12 mobile phone tracking outfit found that nearly 80 percent of the protesters came from the top 20 percent income earners in the population.

The so-called social protest was anything but a protest of the disenfranchised. Rather, it was the protest of the well-to-do who wanted their children to be able to live next to them in the most affluent parts of the country, and who coupled this demand with legitimate complaints about other soaring prices.

But they were also united by something else. They were protesting against . . . me. How could it be that Netanyahu came back from the dead, that he's been running the country again for the last three years with no end in sight?

Hundreds of thousands crowded the streets of Tel Aviv. The Rothschild protests became the in-thing to do among the smart set. Two fashionable young women were overheard talking:

"Rina, are you coming to the protest on Saturday night?"

"No, I can't. We're in London this weekend but we'll make the next one."

The media desperately tried to find Likud and religious voters to put in front of the cameras, but as the protest became more and more overtly politicized, this proved almost impossible. Even so, the challenge was not to be easily dismissed. The affluent left was mobilized against me, and for once it was armed with real issues.

How long would the government last under these conditions? Labor had already split up a few months earlier, Barak staying in my coalition with four other members of the Knesset. The media mobilization was absolute. Over time, the combined onslaught of media-supported mass protests could erode my ability to govern.

There was little I could do to affect the cost of housing in the short term. In 2010, I canceled Olmert's limitation on building in the center of the country. A year earlier in 2009, I had authorized a whopping $10 billion infrastructure plan to build fast roads and rail to the periphery.

I also opened up land development, increasing private ownership of land by 50 percent, from 8 percent to 13 percent of Israel's landmass. In Israel 92 percent of the land had been publicly owned, due to its founding socialist ethos and the small size of the country, made even smaller by large tracts of land allocated to the military.

But these measures would take years to have an effect.

What to do now?

In the Bar-Ilan speech, I had decided to move *into* the storm, not *away* from it. I did the same now. I called in Professor Manuel Trajtenberg, an economist appointed by Olmert to the Council of Economic Advisors. I had worked with him well, even though he was decidedly on the left. He had a well-deserved reputation as a solid professional and no one would think that he was my lackey.

He wasn't.

"Manuel," I said, "I want you to head a committee that hears the public and gives the government recommendations for practical action."

"Why me?" Trajtenberg asked.

"You're respected and no one will think you're doing my bidding. I give you my word that I'll carry out no less than ninety percent of your recommendations and possibly one hundred percent. The reason I can say that is because I know you're a serious economist and not a populist. I trust your judgment."

It took several more meetings until Trajtenberg agreed. He set up the committee into working teams that addressed a variety of areas, heard representatives of the public, contractors and consumer organizations, and issued a thoughtful report. I implemented almost all his recommendations, including increased day care allotments for young couples and expanded subsidized housing for students.

The protests gradually subsided.

Some commentators ludicrously compared the economic protests in Israel to the Arab Spring protests sweeping North Africa and the Middle East. As thousands were being slaughtered in Syria and elsewhere, this rang hollow.

Still, the Arab Spring did hit our fences. Literally. The civil war in Syria next door—which included an ISIS insurgency challenging the Assad regime—threatened to spill over the border fence into Israel. Millions were uprooted from their homes. Unlike Europe, tiny Israel couldn't absorb hundreds of thousands of refugees and continue to survive as a

Jewish state. I gave strict orders to the IDF in January 2010 to prevent entry into our territory.

At the same time, I instructed the military to build a field hospital on our side of the Syrian-Israeli border. Israeli doctors, many of them Arabs and Druze, treated civilian victims of the Syrian carnage, some horribly mutated with lost limbs.

I visited them. They could not believe that the Israeli prime minister and Israeli medical teams were tending to them.

"They lied to us all these years," one father of a maimed child told me. "They said you Israelis were devils. But you are the only angels in this hell."

We took many of the wounded to Israeli hospitals, with one big proviso: we could not have them photographed. If their pictures were seen in Syria they would be executed when they returned to their homes.

When jihadists and Hezbollah operatives tried to open a new front across our border with Syria in the Golan, the threat of terrorist attacks and infiltration into Israel grew. We countered this by repeatedly striking their bases and their commanders. We also built a robust border fence along the entire Golan border similar to the one we built in the Sinai, completed in 2013.

The Arab Spring hit us from the south as well. As the protests in Cairo gathered steam, we vacated our embassy there except for a small staff. On September 9, 2011, I was woken up by an urgent phone call.

Thousands of protesters had gathered around the building where our embassy was lodged on the tenth floor. Armed with knives, clubs and iron bars, they threatened to enter the building, storm the embassy and murder the Israelis inside.

I rushed to the Foreign Office situation room, joining the head of Shin Bet, Yoram Cohen, and Yohanan Locker. The protesters had broken the outer fence and were about to penetrate the building. It was just a matter of time before they reached the embassy floor. I made contact with the Israelis inside the embassy and spoke to the man in charge.

"What's your name?" I asked.

"Yoni," he answered.

I was stunned.

A flurry of thoughts raced through my brain. Once again, in Africa, Israelis needed to be rescued from death. But now it wasn't Yoni who would rescue them but Yoni who needed rescue. I had to find a way to get him and his colleagues out in time.

"Prime Minister," Yoni said, "we're in the inner room. If they break through the outer door we placed furniture as barricades to delay them. We've got some Uzis—we'll fight to the end."

"Yoni," I said, "hang in there. We'll get you out of there."

I had no idea how I would do that.

I called Obama and asked for his help with the Egyptian government, but the ruling hierarchy appeared to have collapsed. Fearing a repetition of Mubarak's fate, General Mohamed Tantawi, now the nominal head of the government, had backed away and was not really in charge.

Through the security cameras we could see the rioters enter the building.

Yoram Cohen was on the phone with the local commander of the Egyptian security forces, trying unsuccessfully to get him to act and disperse the rioters from the building.

"Tell him," I said, "that Israeli helicopters are en route to Cairo right now."

This was a ruse. I had sent two helicopters to Cairo's airport to pick up the families of the Israeli staff. But I wanted the Egyptian security forces to believe that an Israeli commando unit would land on top of the building and carry out a rescue in the heart of Cairo, an unacceptable embarrassment for them.

At Cohen's urging and direction, the Egyptian security forces went into action. They entered the building. The rioters were about to smash through the outer doors of the embassy office. They were stopped in the nick of time.

Yoni and his colleagues were saved.

With President Bill Clinton during first visit to the White House as prime minister, 1996.

Sara and Yair with President Clinton, assessing nearly two-year-old son Avner's pillow pile, Oval Office, 1996.

Waving to Sara during first speech to Congress, with Vice President Al Gore and Speaker of the House Newt Gingrich, 1996.

On the beach in Caesarea with Avner, 1997. King Herod the Great's ancient port is in the distance.

A well-guarded moment on the Caesarea beach with Yair, Sara and security detail, 1997.

"Pray for the peace of Jerusalem." Depositing a written wish at the Western Wall with Yair, 1998.

"A Polska."
Meeting Pope
John Paul II at
the Vatican, 1997.

"Your loss is my loss." King
Hussein of Jordan between
Prime Minister Netanyahu and
Foreign Minister David Levy,
comforting the grieving mother
of an Israeli schoolgirl slain by a
Jordanian soldier, Bet Shemesh,
Israel, 1997.

"To King Hussein, get well
soon." A painting by seven-
year-old Yair for the "Good
King" upon learning of
his illness, showing an
extraterrestrial with a
magical cure, 1998.

Discussing peace
with Egyptian
president Hosni
Mubarak,
Washington, 1998.

"Don't read the press."
With former British
prime minister Margaret
Thatcher, at the prime
minister's office in
Jerusalem, 1998.

"We stand with Israel." With
the Reverend Jerry Falwell,
rallying evangelical support for
Israel before a meeting with
President Clinton, Washington,
1998.

"Now you've really upset
the president!" With
Clinton at the Wye River
Conference, Maryland,
1998.

"Fiasco." Clinton
with PLO leader
Yasser Arafat and
Israeli prime minister
Ehud Barak at
the failed Camp
David peace talks,
Maryland, 2000.

15

"We can unleash Israel's economy." Finance Minister Netanyahu with Prime Minister Ariel Sharon in the Knesset, 2004.

16

Tel Aviv before Israel's economic revolution, 1990s, and after, 2020.

17

Benzion and Bibi playing chess at the family home on Haportzim Street, Jerusalem, 2008.

Discussing Iran with President Barack Obama in the Oval Office, 2010.

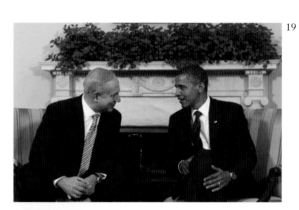

"It's a boy." Holding grandson Shmuel, son of Noa (in blue, left of Sara), at his brit ceremony with Chief Rabbi Israel Meir Lau, Yair, and Minister of Justice Yaakov Ne'eman looking on, Jerusalem, 2010.

"Study the Torah day and night." Congratulating son Avner on winning the National Bible Contest, Jerusalem, 2010.

Preparing with staff at presidential guest quarters Blair House before meeting President Obama, Washington, 2011.

"Remember when we were the new kids on the block?" With Vice President Joe Biden and Speaker of the House John Boehner before second speech to Congress, 2011.

Overlooking the Jordan Valley with Israel Defense Forces (IDF) officers on a border tour, 2011.

Mourning at Benzion's funeral with Sara, Yair and Avner, Jerusalem, 2012.

"The red line." Taking a stand against Iran's race toward nuclear weapons in a speech at the UN General Assembly, 2012.

With Israeli president Shimon Peres, 2012.

"Jackets off." Receiving Obama at Ben Gurion Airport on his first visit to Israel as president, 2013.

"Clearly, the boys got their looks from their mother." Obama with Yair (left) and Avner at the prime minister's residence, Jerusalem, 2013.

Sending Avner off to the IDF, Jerusalem, 2014.

With Russian president Vladimir Putin at the UN Climate Change Conference, Paris, 2015.

Visiting Chinese president Xi Jinping in Beijing, 2017.

Wading in the Mediterranean with Indian prime minister Narendra Modi on his visit to Israel, Givat Olga beach, 2017.

With Oman's Sultan Qaboos in his study, pointing to future rail links between the Arabian Peninsula and Israel, Oman, 2018.

Reviewing draft of third speech to Congress with Israeli ambassador to the US Ron Dermer, Washington, 2015.

"Even if Israel has to stand alone, Israel will stand!" Addressing the impending Iran nuclear deal during third speech to Congress, 2015.

"Never again!" Elie Wiesel taking a bow during a standing ovation in his honor while attending Prime Minister Netanyahu's speech to Congress, 2015.

"If you want a friend, get a dog." Caring for beloved family dog Kaya, Jerusalem, 2015.

"We liked the hamburgers best." Dessert with President Donald Trump, First Lady Melania Trump and Sara during dinner at the prime minister's residence prepared by Chef Moshe Segev, Jerusalem, 2016.

Visiting Kenya during first Israeli prime ministerial tour of four African countries, Nairobi, 2017.

Waving to avid supporters on first Israeli prime ministerial visit to Brazil, Brasilia, 2018.

"It was the happiest day of my life." Cancer-stricken Alon watching a World Cup soccer game with Sara and cancer survivor Mika, Moscow, 2018.

Visit to India, New Delhi, 2018.

44

Visiting Israeli counterterrorism unit (left) and border police (below), Israel, 2018.

45

46

"Iran lied!" Unveiling Iran's secret atomic archive, brought to Israel by the Mossad after a daring operation, IDF headquarters, Tel Aviv, 2018.

"The worst deal I ever saw." President Donald Trump withdrawing from the Iran nuclear deal, White House, 2018.

47

President Trump recognizes Israel's sovereignty over the Golan Heights, White House, 2019.

Relaxing with Sara on the Golan Heights, 2020.

"First jab." Receiving the first Covid injection in Israel from personal physician Dr. Zvi Bercovich, Tel Aviv, 2020.

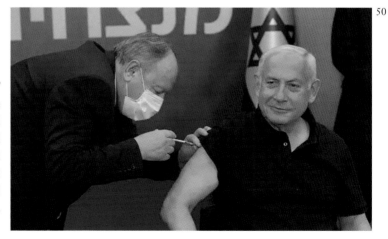

"Pivot of history." At the Abraham Accords signing ceremony with President Trump, UAE foreign minister Sheikh Abdullah bin Zayed Al Nahyan (right), and Bahrain foreign minister Abdullatif bin Rashid Al Zayani, White House, 2020.

With family on snowy days at the prime minister's residence, Jerusalem, 1997 and 2015.

47

PASSING THE TORCH

2012

I drew much inspiration from the wellsprings of our heritage. If that sounds overly dramatic, it wasn't. For years I studied the weekly portion of the Torah every Sabbath morning with Avner. Up until he was twelve, I taught him. From then on he taught me, surprising me again and again with his knowledge of the Scriptures, geography and history.

Unless war broke out, Sara would let nothing interfere with these sessions. She guarded my private moments with our boys as a lioness guards her cubs.

When I was reelected prime minister in 2009, Sara told me, "Let's not repeat the mistake of the first term. We gave everything to the job and neglected our boys. At the end that's all we'll have left. We can't bring back those early years but let's not waste the coming years while the boys are still young."

We followed this sound advice. Friday night dinner and Saturday lunch with the family became sacrosanct, a tradition we kept throughout my years in office.

Continuing the tradition of Prime Ministers Ben Gurion and Begin, I set up a Bible study group that met in the prime minister residence every few months. I later named it in honor of my late father-in-law Shmuel Ben Artzi, who had dedicated his life to the study of the Bible.

In 2003 I had befriended the great Talmudic scholar Rabbi Adin

Steinsaltz, who translated the Talmud into modern Hebrew and wrote a brilliant commentary on it. Several times I had the pleasure of studying portions of that ancient text with him, alone in his charming home on Agron Street in Jerusalem.

These were discreet meetings between old neighbors. Older than me by a few years, it turned out that Steinsaltz and I had grown up in the same secular Jerusalem neighborhood a hundred meters apart. Our discussions were fun and far-ranging. He who had found religion peppered his studies with humor and scholarship, delving into history, theology, archaeology and philology.

On one occasion when we argued about the particulars of a historical incident, Steinsaltz said, "Ask your father."

Great scholars usually recognize one another's expertise. What characterizes this unique group of people is their unceasing sense of curiosity and wonder.

During one Purim holiday I sat with Father and Avner at a café next to my Jerusalem home on Gaza Street.

"Imagine!" said Father, referring in wonderment to the Book of Esther. "The ruler of Persia, the greatest power of its day, appoints a Jew, Mordechai, as his deputy."

"What's so special about that?" said ten-year-old Avner. "It happened at least two other times."

"When?" I asked.

"When Pharaoh appointed Joseph as his number two," Avner said.

"And when else?" I pressed.

"When Lenin appointed Trotsky," Avner answered.

Father and I looked at each other. We could have come up with Joseph, but Trotsky! That was bewilderingly original.

I was proud of my two boys. Like his two grandfathers, Avner could become a great Biblical scholar or historian if he chose. He would eventually turn to the study of archaeology.

Yair from a young age was a precociously sharp-witted observer of the political scene. He could spot absurdity and weaknesses in opposing arguments as few people could. Completing undergraduate studies in international relations and graduate studies in government, he began writing impassioned political columns and commentary in defense of Zionism, and in defense of his father, and hosted his own radio show.

This earned him quite a few enemies, but also hundreds of thousands of internet followers who admired his combative directness and his refusal to bend to political fashions.

I was glad my sons were able to spend time in their early years with Sara's parents, who showered them with much love and affection. Both of their grandmothers died when the boys were very young, but they managed to spend some years with their grandfathers, especially with Shmuel, whose sensitive soul gave them comfort and solace in overcoming the challenges of being the children of parents under constant public scrutiny and criticism.

Shmuel and Father would often join us for Shabbat dinner. Between both grandfathers there were nearly two centuries of Jewish wisdom around the table. One evening after dinner, the boys wanted to show their grandfathers the wonders of the digital age.

"Look, Grandpa," Yair said to Shmuel, pointing to Google Earth, "here is your hometown of Bilgoray in Poland."

"*Saba* Ben Zion, say something in Hebrew," Avner said.

Father did.

"Here's how it sounds in Korean."

The two grandfathers nodded in appreciation but they weren't overly impressed.

"That's all well and good," they said gently, "but remember there are more important things in life."

They didn't have to say more. The boys understood what these "more important things" were, coming as they did from these two sages who devoted their lives to preserve our people's heritage and thereby ensure its future.

Shmuel passed away in 2011 at age ninety-seven. In the last year of his life, Sara brought him to the prime minister's residence. Alert until his last moment, Shmuel asked for a book and to be joined in prayer. Sara tended to him as she had before to her mother, Chava, on her sickbed. She never left their bedside, and lit memorial candles in their honor for years after their passing.

"I have never seen such devotion of a daughter to her parents," said Dr. Eliezer Rachmilevitch, who had been head of the Cancer Treatment Department at Hadassah Hospital. This was echoed by the other doctors and nurses who treated Sara's parents.

Father remained sharp and alert until a few months before his death in 2012 at 102 years of age. When I returned from one of my speeches at the UN, he suddenly said to me, "Jabotinsky couldn't give such a speech." Coming from someone who was always precise and measured in his assessments, and who had personally heard Jabotinsky's speeches, that was the ultimate compliment.

In March 2010, on Father's one hundredth birthday, the Begin Memorial Center in Jerusalem had convened a gathering in his honor. For hours learned scholars and writers spoke of his groundbreaking scholarship in Jewish history and his political activity in America on behalf of Zionism during World War II.

At the end of the evening, Father rose to speak. After walking unaided to the podium, he spoke for four minutes. This is what he had to say:

> I am much moved by the fact that you have gathered to express your well wishes on my hundredth birthday. You've said many fine things that stirred my heart and whose implications could be expanded upon, but since time is short, I will limit my remarks to one general comment.
>
> The existence of the Jewish people [is put into question] by the threats to annihilate us which are openly declared by our enemies. On the one side, Iran vows that soon Zionism will be destroyed when Iran will possess nuclear weapons.
>
> On the other, the people of Israel are showing the world how a nation should behave when faced with an existential threat: stare unflinchingly at the danger, calmly consider what needs to be done and what can be done, and be ready to enter the fray when the chances of success are reasonable.
>
> A powerful stance requires tremendous inner strength. The people of Israel show today that they have such strength, and this leads to my certain belief that our people will roll back this

danger to its existence. With the expression of this belief, I end my remarks.

When Father passed away two years later, I felt an indescribable sadness and emptiness. Did he leave the world despondent? Did he believe that his life's work, for which his eldest son gave his life, would endure? Did he truly believe that I would succeed in leading Israel in rolling back Iran's threat to our existence?

A man of his prodigious learning and intellectual rigor surely saw the pitfalls awaiting our people, yet he never gave in to either false hope or futile despair. He seemed to me like the rock of the ages, and he was my rock, always bringing me back to the basic values for which we fought. And now he was gone.

An enormous crowd attended his funeral. President Shimon Peres, who had eulogized Yoni, now eulogized Father. Turning to me, he said, "Bibi, your father wrote history. You are *making* history."

In my parting words I described his tenderness as a father and his love for Mother. But I also spoke of his enduring legacy and his confidence in our ability to safeguard the Jewish state:

> You taught me, Father, to look at reality head-on, to understand what it holds in store and to come to the necessary conclusions.
>
> You were not only endowed with the ability to see into the future but also to uncover the secrets of the past, and of course the two are related. Many times you told me that those who cannot understand the past cannot understand the present, and those who cannot understand the present, how can they portend what the future will hold?
>
> There were always those who did not see what you saw and dismissed your accomplishments. In this, too, you taught me to stick to the essential things, to separate the wheat from the chaff.
>
> As I say farewell, I use the same words Yoni wrote to you forty-six years ago: "I never told you how proud I am of the man that you are, and that I am your son."

Years later I was shown a graph of internet traffic in Israel during Father's final year. It spiked to incredible heights on the day of his funeral. Somehow this man, whose scholarship and activities on behalf of the Jewish people were never publicized, aroused extraordinary admiration among multitudes of people.

Without knowing all the details of his life and work, the people sensed what mattered.

In a hill overlooking the entrance to Jerusalem, Father was brought to rest next to Mother, ten meters away from Shmuel and Chava. Our boys were blessed to have such grandparents in life, now gathered together for eternity.

48

THE RED LINE

2012

On September 21, 2011, I met Obama at the UN General Assembly. In the ebb and flow of our unceasing conflicts and crises, this would be one of our better meetings.

Obama was entering his reelection year. He had invested a great deal of political capital during his first term in office trying to get the Palestinian-Israeli negotiations off the ground. The freeze, the battle over Jerusalem, the summit meetings in New York, Washington, Sharm el-Sheikh and Jerusalem all failed to get Mahmoud Abbas to the table.

Obama decided to ease off the pressure on me for now and concentrate on getting reelected. His speech in the General Assembly reflected this apparent shift. It would be the most pro-Israel speech he would give. He said there would be no "shortcuts to peace" and that peace must be negotiated directly by the parties. Neither the UN nor the US could impose it. In a statement, he reaffirmed his commitment to a two-state solution but stressed that it must ensure Israel's security.

"Israel, a small country of less than eight million people, looks out at a world where leaders of much larger nations threaten to wipe it off the map," he said, before proceeding to touch on themes of exile, persecution, and the Holocaust. "Israel deserves recognition," Obama summed up. "It deserves normal relations with its neighbors."

Ahead of the UN General Assembly, I responded to this statement with a positive reference to Obama's call for direct negotiations. Now in my own UN speech I proceeded to drive home a direct message to Abbas.

"Let's talk *dugri*," I called on Abbas, using the colloquial word used by Israelis and Arabs alike to denote straightforward speech. "The Arab proverb says you can't clap with one hand. The same goes for peace. I can't make peace with the Palestinians without you. Tear up your pact with Hamas. You're in this building, I'm in this building. Let's meet right now."

Once again Abbas did not come.

Back in Israel, I was at last gearing up for a real and impending possibility of a military operation against Iran's nuclear facilities. The main enrichment site at Natanz was well known and being monitored by the International Atomic Energy Agency, but we had now been alerted by foreign intelligence to a new, secret underground enrichment site under a mountain near the holy city of Qom.

Many in the upper echelons of Israel's security apparatus opposed an offensive strike. This was predictable. In many major decisions about security during my long tenure I would encounter their opposition. The top brass would later oppose me on the Sinai border fence that completely stopped infiltration from Africa.

They would also oppose me on the underground barrier that completely stopped the terror tunnels from Gaza. And before my time they had opposed the Iron Dome project, which would later protect Israel from deadly missiles and rockets. They were wisely overruled by Amir Peretz, who was defense minister at the time. These were defensive measures, so it was no surprise that in many offensive actions the nation's top generals and security officers were often equally or more hesitant.

This is not unique to Israel. In many democracies the military chiefs are naturally cautious and do not like unpredictable actions that could upset their carefully laid and budgeted plans. In Israel, where a political career can beckon after military and security service, there is extra reason not to rock the boat. Bold actions can result in failure, and failure can get you dishonorably discharged and derail a promising political career.

Since the Commission of Inquiry that had followed setbacks during the 1973 Yom Kippur War and cost senior officers their careers, there were many other inquiries, and they had a paralyzing effect on bold and imaginative military leadership.

It was thus exceedingly tough to carry out any dramatic military operation when the heads of the IDF, the Mossad and Shin Bet were united to oppose it.

I had tried to pass such a decision to attack Iran's nuclear facilities a year earlier, in 2010, and met a brick wall. The heads of the security services had adamantly opposed the action.

In that case, they argued that the delay to the Iranian nuclear program that would result from a strike would only be a few years and that in any case we could not operate without the prior consent of the United States.

I disagreed.

"They said the same thing about our attack on the Osirak reactor," I said, repeating the argument I had made to Robert Gates. "Yet thirty years later it hasn't been rebuilt. No one can take into account the psychological and political effects of a powerful strike. Imagine an Iranian attack on one of our key installations. Even if we could rebuild it quickly, we'd think again and again about how to protect the new installation from an enemy determined to destroy it. That could add many years of delay."

I also argued that the mere fact that we were willing to risk retaliation for an attack would communicate to the Iranian regime how dangerous it would be to continue threatening us with nuclear weapons. It would ingrain in their minds that such an attack would mean the destruction of Iran and their own deaths. Without an attack on their facilities, that wasn't at all obvious.

Third, I said, asking for prior American agreement and coordination was tantamount to killing the strike. Most of the American public overwhelmingly supported Israel and overwhelmingly opposed Iran. If Israel acted alone to safeguard its existence, I believed we could mobilize American public and congressional opinion to support us and this would in all likelihood induce the administration to support us after the fact, or at least not oppose us.

In any case, I summed up, by waiting we were giving Iran time to harden the targets, which would make any attack in the future much more difficult. Better to act now against an existential threat than face it later on worse terms, when we could do little or nothing about it.

Barak and Avigdor Lieberman—who was now foreign minister—had agreed with me. Presented with these arguments, the security chiefs came up with a new angle. The head of the Mossad contended that we would need a vote in the security cabinet to make such a decision legal. A decision by the prime minister, the defense minister and the foreign minister was not enough. Even the small "kitchen cabinet" of a select few ministers wasn't enough. But bringing such a decision to the much larger security cabinet could result in leaks that would derail the mission.

I realized that at the very least I could not avoid a vote in the kitchen cabinet and possibly, if I could figure out a way to overcome the leaks, in the full security cabinet. To overcome opposition from the security chiefs and to ensure a majority in a future vote, I would have to strengthen my standing with the Israeli public.

IN 2011, I faced one of the toughest decisions of my career. In June 2006, Hamas had abducted an Israeli soldier named Gilad Shalit. A Hamas force had penetrated Israel under the Gaza security fence through an underground tunnel, killed two IDF soldiers, and taken Shalit into Gaza back through the tunnel before the IDF could react. Hamas had been demanding an exorbitant price in the form of a prisoner exchange for his release ever since, first from the Olmert government and then from mine.

Shalit was alive, we knew that. I of course wanted to bring him home to his parents. Reclaiming people in captivity is a basic tenet of Judaism and a powerful ethos of the IDF. But at the same time, the release of dangerous killers for his freedom could claim the lives of more innocent Israelis and create an incentive for additional kidnappings.

Lacking intelligence that could enable a rescue operation, our only hope of bringing Shalit home was to bring Hamas's price down to a tolerable level. This meant releasing fewer and less dangerous Hamas prisoners in Israel than Hamas demanded.

The organized public campaign for Shalit's release merely encouraged Hamas to keep the price high. Most of the cabinet favored closing a deal, knowing that the blame for any negative aftereffects would fall on me anyway. For a long time, I stood in the breach almost alone and refused to do so.

But suddenly Hamas eased up on some of its demands. It would still be painful, but I could go for a deal.

I discussed this with Dermer.

"This may be our last opportunity to get Shalit out. I need more political capital for Iran. The only way to get it quickly is to bring Shalit home. I'm thinking of doing it," I said.

"Prime Minister, you'll be going against your own convictions," Ron said, knowing of my long-standing opposition to cutting deals with terrorists on hostages.

"I know," I said, "but there is also the opposing value of bringing back a captive soldier. Besides, do you see any other way to quickly gain the public support we'll need for an operation against Iran?"

"What if the public support for the release evaporates quickly?" Ron asked. "You'll come up short on both ends—caving in to terror *and* being weakened politically."

"That's a risk I'll just have to take," I answered.

I gave the order for our negotiators to tell the German intermediaries that, given Hamas's recent flexibility, I was prepared to relax our terms as well. This led to an immediate acceleration of the negotiations and a quick resolution of the swap.

On October 18, 2011, I received Shalit at an Israeli air base. He was quiet and frail but seemed to be in reasonable shape given the horrible torment he had been through. In a fatherly impulse I put my arm on his shoulders. He could have been my own son. I took comfort in the fact that I had rescued him from his hellish underground dungeon. His halting steps to freedom moved me deeply.

Shalit's return was welcomed by most of the public. As my poll numbers shot up, Dermer remarked, "I was wrong on the political impact of the deal. The public didn't see it as a left or right issue but about leadership. And you showed *leadership*."

Despite the short-term boost in public opinion, I was well aware of the long-term implications of the Shalit swap. Those were somewhat mitigated when the mastermind of the abduction and the perpetrator of many rocket attacks against Israeli civilians, Ahmed Jabri, was later targeted by the IDF on my orders and taken out before he could launch more planned attacks.

Armed with added political capital, I tried again to pass a decision to attack Iran's nuclear facilities. Barak and Lieberman were again firmly on my side but the military and security chiefs remained against any operation.

Again I argued that the longer we waited, the more difficult it would be to carry out an operation. When I sought to bring it to a vote in the kitchen cabinet, two members who I had hoped would support the decision balked. I didn't have a majority even in this smaller forum. I would have to try again.

ON MARCH 5, 2012, I met Obama in the Oval Office. Reviewing the deteriorating situation in Syria under its dictator, Bashar Assad, son of the previous dictator, Hafez Assad, Hillary said, "Apparently Bashar's mother is telling him, 'Your father would have done this, your father would have done that.'"

"I didn't know Bashar had a Jewish mother," I said, and then, looking at Secretary of Defense Leon Panetta, I corrected myself: "Sorry, an Italian mother." (Actually, except for my education, my mother never nudged me on anything.)

Everybody laughed, Leon the loudest. A former congressman, he was savvy and down-to-earth, lacking any of the ideological antipathies that animated many of his colleagues. He liked Israel and I liked him.

The atmosphere softened, but only a little. Our conversation centered mostly on Iran. My intention was to move the US to a tougher stance while maintaining our right to attack Iran's nuclear facilities. Obama assured me he was building a military capacity and said that it should be given a chance to work.

"I strongly believe a preemptive strike would be a mistake," he said. "Iran is weak. We will lose legitimacy and oil prices will spike. An Israeli attack would not achieve anything. In six to nine months, maybe the world will recognize the need for action."

He was clearly trying to get me to kick the can forward and postpone any action until after the presidential election in November 2012.

"I am the prime minister, you are the president," I said. "If I were in your shoes, I would probably think like you. But you are big and we are small. Acting early for me is not a question of trust in you; it's a question of my responsibility as the leader of Israel. In matters of survival and security Israeli prime ministers often disagree with American presidents."

I described how Ben Gurion disagreed with Secretary of State George Marshall on declaring Israel's independence, Eshkol disagreed with Lyndon Johnson on the Six-Day War, and Begin disagreed with Ronald Reagan on the need to destroy Saddam's nuclear reactor.

"I've recently been to the Villa Wannsee near Berlin, where the Nazis held the conference to coordinate the Final Solution," I said. "We're not going back to the brink of annihilation. Iran says Israel is a one-bomb country. They believe that with nuclear weapons they can wipe us out. We will act if there is no choice, with or without your support. In the meantime I believe it's important that you put forward clear demands on Iran to stop enriching uranium and to dismantle the Qom facility."

Obama responded by saying that if we attacked, the sanctions he had orchestrated would collapse. He explained that the reason so many countries agreed to them was that the US told them the alternative was Israeli military action. If Israel acted, these countries would immediately lift all sanctions.

I had heard this before in the *Mavi Marmara* affair. Once again Obama minimized the power of America and chose to "lead from behind." It was clear to me that if countries had to choose between doing business with the small Iranian economy or the $20 trillion American economy they would choose the latter. If the United States maintained sanctions following an Israeli attack, other countries would maintain them, too.

"I haven't yet decided to act militarily," I told Obama. "But I want you to know that I reserve the full right to do so."

"I can't decide that for you," he answered. "I can only tell you what I think: it would be a mistake."

"I hear you," I said. "But I didn't come here to get a green light."

In consultation with Defense Minister Barak, we postponed the decision on a potential strike by a few months.

Undoubtedly, however, I assumed US intelligence picked up enough signals to reveal that preparations were taking place. American anxiety that Israel would act against Iran dominated the rest of the year leading to the presidential elections.

Before the elections, Mitt Romney, the Republican candidate for president, visited Israel. As I had done with Obama when he visited Israel as a presidential candidate, I met Romney to discuss Iran, the Palestinians and the American-Israeli alliance.

I could easily imagine Romney, who was handsome and fit, with only a bit of gray hair, at BCG thirty-five years earlier. We never actually mingled during our time there because Mitt was a senior manager and I was a junior consultant, and we also never worked on the same case. Nonetheless, like anyone who had been at BCG in those days we reminisced about Bruce Henderson. All BCG graduates spoke in a common code when it came to economic matters. On the economy Romney spoke passionately and authoritatively.

He was knowledgeable about political and defense matters as well, but spoke about them with a bit less passion. Passion and conviction are the foundation of strength, which is what most people look for in a leader. Obama had these in abundance, even if his convictions and his reading of reality were often in direct conflict with my own.

As the months passed by during 2012, Obama sent a string of envoys to try to convince me not to act militarily. These included Leon Panetta and National Security Council director Tom Donilon, a straightforward professional. Both described to me in detail the developments in America's military preparations, hoping to curb Israel's activities.

I was noncommittal. Israeli preparations were real, and if they prompted similar preparations by the Americans, so much the better.

Still, the balance of American policy was to avoid concrete action, and even more than that, to make sure that *I* avoided it. Administration spokespersons constantly briefed against the wisdom and efficacy of such an attack. On August 30, 2012, General Martin Dempsey, the chairman of the Joint Chiefs of Staff, went further, saying, "The US will not be *complicit* in any Israeli action."

His choice of words outraged me. It both imputed an illegitimate, even criminal, nature to a potential Israeli action and signaled to Iran that the United States did not support Israel.

This was putting blinding daylight between the US and Israel. What better way to reassure Iran that it was not in any danger if it continued to pursue its nuclear program?

Worse signals of America's passivity would soon follow. On the eve of the eleventh anniversary of 9/11, I said on Bloomberg Television: "Iran will not stop unless it sees a clear determination by the democratic countries and a clear red line. They don't see a clear red line and I think the sooner we establish one, the greater the chances that there won't be a need for other types of action."

Barely a few hours passed before Secretary of State Clinton, while being interviewed on Canadian television, said emphatically, clearly in response to me, "The US is not setting deadlines for Iran."

Stunned by the speed in which the American administration rushed to distance themselves from Israel and assuage Iran's fears, we briefed the press: "Without a clear red line Iran will not cease its race toward a nuclear weapon."

The next day, September 11, I used a press conference during a visit by the Bulgarian prime minister, Boyko Borisov, to push back with my own words.

"The world tells Israel, 'Wait, there's still time,' " I said. "And I say, 'Wait for what? Wait until when?' Those in the international community who refuse to put red lines before Iran don't have a moral right to place a red light before Israel.

"If Iran knows that there is no red line and no deadline, what will it do? Exactly what it's doing. It's continuing, without any interference, towards obtaining nuclear bombs."[1]

I had a challenging phone call with Obama following my speech. My agenda was clear—get tough on Iran. Obama's agenda was centered on something else—making sure I didn't meet with Romney when I came to the UN a few days later.

A month earlier, Ron Dermer—whom I had appointed as Israel's ambassador to Washington in 2013—told Dan Shapiro, who had been appointed US ambassador to Israel, that in my coming visit to the UN I would want to see Obama. Obama didn't want to have the meeting, believing it would prompt a parallel meeting with Romney, who had asked to meet me when I came to the US. At the same time, Obama did not want it to look like he was snubbing me so close to the election.

He argued that meeting opposing presidential candidates so close to an election would politicize the discussions. I thought differently. I wasn't concerned with politics but rather with Israel's survival. Four years later I met with both candidate Donald Trump and candidate Hillary Clinton on the eve of the 2016 elections. I spoke to both about Iran.

But now I felt boxed in by a direct plea from the president of the United States.

"C'mon, man, work with me on this," he said.

His plea was so direct and so candid that I was left with little choice. Would I force upon the president of the United States a meeting he didn't want?

I instructed National Security Advisor Yaakov Amidror to tell the press that we hadn't asked for a meeting with Obama, even though Dermer had. Amidror said it was the only time he had lied in all his years of public service. I offered a lame excuse to Mitt Romney on why we couldn't meet. He accepted it graciously.

In my September 11 phone conversation with Obama, I weighed in on the statements by Hillary and General Dempsey.

"These statements convey that the US has no deadline and undermine Israel's right to self-defense. The number one terror regime in the world calls for the annihilation of my country and my people, and most of the criticism is reserved for whether Israel should act or not act."

Obama pushed back on this: "We've imposed the toughest sanctions ever on Iran. The idea that we're spending more time convincing Israel not to act than on Iran is not true. Some of the concerns we raised were raised by your military people, too."

Ouch! I had wondered when he would get to that one.

"We don't need to get into the deliberations of our military but they are more nuanced than that," I said. "At least they don't speak out publicly, while the head of your military did speak out against us, which is extraordinary."

But my main point was reserved for something else.

"I believe that if Iran sees a clear red line, they will not cross it," I said to the president.

"I can't give a red line," he replied, "that says that if they have X amount of centrifuges on Y date, then I'd bomb a week later. The red line I gave is no nuclear weapons."

That, I thought, would be too late.

When the conversation ended, I put the phone down and looked at my staff. As in all such conversations with foreign leaders, they had sat around the table and heard the exchange, occasionally handing me notes with suggestions.

"I guess we have no choice," I said. "*We'll* have to be the ones to draw the red line. We'll do that when I next speak at the UN."

We had two weeks to prepare. The most important question was, Where do you draw the line? Iran had two hundred kilograms of low-enriched uranium at the 3 percent level. If it crossed the 20 percent enrichment level we would be in the danger zone. The time it takes to enrich uranium to bomb-grade quality shrinks rapidly after 20 percent. Once there, Iran would be 90 percent of the way to having enough enriched uranium for a bomb. That is where I would draw the red line.

The next question was how to present this red line visually.

Answer: by actually *drawing* a red line.

This suggestion came from Gary Ginsberg, an American whom I had gotten to know a few years earlier through a mutual friend. We struck an immediate friendship. A lawyer by training, Gary had worked with both Bill Clinton and Rupert Murdoch.

He knew politics and he knew the media. Politically moderate, he would sometimes temper my words, yet at other times he could toughen them. He had an uncommon ear for language and an uncommon ability to weed out imprecision.

He, Ron Dermer, my friend Spencer Partrich and my cousin Nathan Mileikowsky became my sounding board before speeches in the UN and in Congress. A wonderful camaraderie emerged among us. In our preparatory meetings I enjoyed the input of these four incredibly incisive minds who helped me hone the text of my speeches in America. But these sessions were more than intellectual exercises. They were fun. We often broke out in bellyaching laughter by trying out Jackie Mason–like alterations of the text, incorporating vulgar or comical expressions.

"Bibi, on second thought, cut that out! You might actually say it," they would warn me, howling merrily.

I seldom enjoyed myself so much as with these four who were united in their love of Israel and their support for me. I couldn't hope for better or more capable friends.

Now, before the UN speech, it was only Gary who could come from the States to Israel for a preparatory meeting. Spencer and Nathan would meet us in New York before the speech. Gary's first suggestion was that I physically draw the bomb while standing on the podium. After some quick trials I passed on that idea. I would have the bomb diagram prepared in advance.

Not since my design of Yoni's scout troop pennant almost fifty years earlier did my drawing skills come in so handy. I sketched some diagrams and settled on a drawing of an old-style bomb topped by a caricature fuse at the top. Dermer, Gary and my spokesman Mark Regev broke out in laughter.

"That looks like the bomb that Wile E. Coyote would use against the Road Runner," Ron said.

"Beep-beep," I responded.

The staff got me the thickest red marker I had ever seen. I practiced drawing a line underneath the fuse while holding the diagram toward the audience. It folded in two so I could bring it unnoticed into the General Assembly, where props weren't allowed.

What the hell, I thought. Who's going to stop me?

The UN speech was carried by television channels worldwide. The front page of most of the leading newspapers in the world featured a photo of me holding the diagram on the UN podium. A zillion memes blossomed mocking the bomb presentation. This was fine with me. As long as they got my red line right.

An especially warm response came from an avid listener of my UN speeches, the towering UN security officer Matthew Sullivan. After each speech he would offer his candid opinion. Commenting a few years later on another one of my UN speeches, he said, "It was okay, but I liked your red line speech better."

While I appreciated the feedback, my most important audience was the tyrants of Tehran. The red line held for seven years.

49

"YOU'RE NEXT"

2012-2013

Obama called me after the red line speech. He was doubly pleased: I hadn't met his adversary Romney, and since Iran wasn't likely to cross the red line in the sixty days before the elections, the threat of an imminent Israeli strike was pushed beyond November.

A few weeks after my return from the UN, my Knesset coalition dissolved. The tottering Kadima party had joined my coalition a few months earlier under the new leadership of Shaul Mofaz. Mofaz had been Yoni's deputy in the Unit and later served as IDF chief of staff. Now he and his colleagues were pressured by the media to bolt from the coalition because of a disagreement on an abstruse law.

Before the Knesset was dissolved, I tried in vain to persuade seven members of Kadima (the legally required minimum of the party's Knesset members) to break away, form a new party and stay in the government. That would prevent new elections. I got six Kadima members to agree but failed to get the seventh.

"You're walking to certain political death," I said to the potential candidates for the seventh slot. "If you don't join us, Kadima will disappear. Yair Lapid will launch a new party and displace the lot of you." Lapid was a left-of-center television presenter who was warming up on the sidelines for a political career.

Even if some Kadima members believed me, they could not stand a few days of media opprobrium. They went quietly to their political graves.

Preparing for the elections, I formed a joint Knesset list between Likud and Avigdor Lieberman's Yisrael Beiteinu Party, hoping to cement the next coalition. This was a huge mistake. I was fighting the previous war. The joint list brought down our combined numbers. Some Likud and Russian voters so disliked each other as to prefer not to vote for a list that included those they disliked.

This political error would soon come back to haunt me. I won the elections on January 22, 2013, but barely, with the right getting sixty-one seats. But the seemingly rightist party, Naftali Bennett's Jewish Home, formed an alliance with Lapid and the two said they would join my government only on condition that I excluded the Orthodox religious parties.

Bennett had worked for me from the end of 2006 until February 2008 as my chief of staff when I was Opposition leader. After a year I let him go. Though he postured as right-wing, I gradually understood that this was an empty pose. He craved fame and power, and his willingness to exclude an important segment of the right for an opportunistic alliance with Lapid underscored this.

Lieberman, who had also worked for me, would eventually turn on me as well. Though he ostensibly held positions further to the right of Likud, he later joined Bennett's coalition, which included a far-left party and an Islamist Muslim Brotherhood party that opposes Israel as a Jewish state.

In 2012, lacking any other option, I agreed to let Bennett and Lapid join my coalition. My third government was sworn in on March 18, 2013, with Lapid as finance minister and Bennett as economics minister. This "Brotherly Alliance" between Bennett's supposedly hard-right party and Lapid's party on the center left was peculiar. Their platforms shared few goals, if any. The only thing that united them was a desire for power, and a willingness to shed their commitments to their voters to achieve it.

TWO MAJOR MILITARY events occupied my attention during the months leading to the 2013 elections, one unpublicized and one overt.

The clandestine operation was aimed at stopping the mass smuggling of advanced Iranian weapons to Hamas from Sudan. Some of the weapons would come by sea to Port Sudan, others by air to Khartoum's international airport. From both destinations the weapons would be transported by trucks up the Nile Valley and into the Egyptian Sinai, and from there smuggled through underground tunnels into Gaza.

Military intelligence and Mossad alerted us to a particularly large shipment of lethal missiles intended for Hamas that would land in Khartoum. If we acted quickly we could destroy it from the air, thus also sending a powerful message to Sudan's dictator, Omar al-Bashir, that we meant business.

I convened a meeting of the defense minister, the top army chiefs and the Mossad to authorize the operation. Israeli fighter bombers would fly along the Red Sea, veer into Sudan, and destroy the containers at Khartoum airport. The distance was substantial—five thousand kilometers round-trip—but Israel's air force could handle it.

While the IAF and intelligence officers supported the strike, military chief of staff Benny Gantz voiced strong reservations. He argued that an action of this magnitude could lead to war and therefore required full cabinet approval.

"What war?" I asked Yohanan Locker, still my military secretary. "What's the problem? That the Sudanese will send rubber boats up the Nile?"

Sudan's nonexistent war-making capability didn't worry me. Nor did I think that the strike would elicit any response from Iran or its proxies. I asked Attorney General Yehuda Weinstein to issue an opinion that since there was no realistic risk of war involved, a general cabinet meeting was unnecessary. But to avoid these pitfalls in the future I also asked him to prepare a bill that would enable Israel to decide on an action that *might* lead to war in the security cabinet alone, without the need for a meeting of the entire cabinet, from which leaks were more likely.

Unlike the full cabinet, with close to thirty ministers and an equal number of aides, security cabinet meetings were smaller and more discreet, and their meetings were never publicized. (With a view to Iran, I was able to pass a law as one of my first acts in the next government to enable critical decisions on war to be made there.)

Armed with Attorney General Weinstein's legal opinion, I ordered the air strike on Khartoum. Executed in the middle of the night on October 23, 2012, it was precise and brilliantly carried out by Israel's air force pilots. The weapons and munitions in the airport exploded in an enormous conflagration in the heart of Sudan's capital, sending towering plumes of fire and smoke into the sky. Forty containers filled with weapons and explosives were destroyed. Two Sudanese lives were lost, but in military terms this was as surgical as a massive air strike could be.

Just to make sure Sudan's ruler got the message, I sent him a brief addendum through discreet channels:

"You're next."

The Sudan smuggling route was quickly shut down.

Though the press reported explosions in Khartoum airport, we kept mum, as is often Israel's practice.

This was decidedly not the case in a far bigger operation against Hamas a month later. Hamas's military wing was led by the mercurial and pugnacious Ahmed Jabri, who earlier had organized the abduction of Gilad Shalit. Jabri regularly ordered the unprovoked firing of rockets on Israeli civilians in cities and communities bordering Gaza, making life hell for their residents.

As soon as the rockets were fired, he and his fellow Hamas commanders would go to their underground bunkers, immune to our retaliation. When things calmed down, they would emerge from their bunkers and the cycle would start anew. The only way to put an end to this was to take him out by surprise during one of these interludes of calm. A month after Khartoum, our intelligence services located Jabri. We could target the car he was in without harming his family and with minimal civilian casualties.

I knew such a strike would lead to another round of rockets launched by Hamas on our cities and then counterstrikes by us. We were now equipped with newly operational Iron Dome antimissile batteries. In nonbattle exercises their performance was promising. It had been first used seven months earlier, but would this miraculous system work under a heavy barrage of rockets? No one knew for sure.

I gave the order to strike. Jabri was hit in the center of Gaza on November 14, 2012. This was the beginning and main objective of what became known as Operation Pillar of Defense. The message to the terrorist leaders was clear: you can run but you can't hide. Sooner or later, Israel will get you. This message would need to be periodically reinforced.

As predicted, the strike on Jabri was followed by thousands of rockets fired into Israel's cities. We responded by targeting missile launchers, Hamas terrorist infrastructure and Hamas personnel when they came out of their bunkers. The Iron Dome proved effective against roughly 90 percent of the enemy's projectiles, a remarkable achievement. Still, a million Israelis living inside the arc from Ashdod to Beer-Sheba to Ashkelon had to constantly run into shelters to protect themselves from the missiles that did get through.

As the battle progressed, our supply of Iron Dome interceptors dwindled.

"Without this shield, we're going to enter a pissing match with Hamas," senior officers told me.

Since we had achieved our major objective, knocking out the top Hamas commander Jabri right at the start of the campaign, there was no point in continuing. But ending these kinds of operations is much harder than starting them. The public invariably expects the government to continue the battle and "flatten Gaza," believing that with enough punishment the Hamas regime would collapse.

Yet that would only happen if we sent in the army. The casualties would mount: many hundreds on the Israeli side and many thousands on the Palestinian side. Did I really want to tie down the IDF in Gaza for years when we had to deal with Iran and a possible Syrian front? The answer was categorically no. I had bigger fish to fry.

With emotions running so high, stopping a battle like this was enormously costly politically. The Hamas leaders would come out from their holes and declare victory among the ruins. Though hollow, this spectacle would exact heavy political costs in Israel. Political opponents would castigate me for "not finishing the job," as they did four years earlier to the Olmert government in the Gaza campaign of that time. Though as Opposition leader I had forcefully supported Olmert during that operation, defending it often on international television, I too criticized the government after the operation ended. I could hardly expect anything different in my case.

It was late 2012, with the 2013 elections on the near horizon, and I knew this criticism would be directed at me as well, but I decided to end the fighting nonetheless after a week of battle. We had lost two soldiers and four civilians; the Palestinians lost 233 lives, of which 155 were identified as terrorists, including several leading commanders.

Most of the civilian casualties were brought about because Hamas used them as human shields, thus committing a double war crime of indiscriminately firing at Israeli civilians while hiding behind Palestinian ones.

Hamas also wanted to end the fighting, but it needed to save face. Given that by now, Egypt was led by an Islamist government affiliated with Hamas, I thought that the new government in Cairo could give Hamas the necessary public cover.

I called Obama from the Prime Minister's Office and asked if he could dispatch Secretary of State Clinton to the region. He agreed. Coming from a visit to Indonesia, she quickly shuttled between Jerusalem and Cairo and brokered a cease-fire. I was grateful to her. Nine days after the strike on Jabri a cease-fire was declared.

Egyptian president Mohamed Morsi's government was receptive to playing the role of intermediary because it wanted to purchase American goodwill. And for good reason. A few months earlier, in June 2012, it had taken over Egypt after an election fraught with difficulties.

One of the first things Morsi did was to violate the Israel-Egypt peace treaty by sending dozens of tanks and armored personnel carriers into the Sinai without receiving our permission. I sent Morsi a stern message. If you don't remove these forces within seven days, I warned, I will appeal to the American Congress to stop the annual $2 billion in US aid to Egypt.

Egypt was in dire economic straits. Since I didn't publicize the threat, Morsi didn't lose face. Precisely a week later he pulled the tanks and armored personnel carriers out of the Sinai. Now he could use the opportunity of helping with a cease-fire to bolster his credentials with the Obama administration, which was sympathetic to the new regime.

Though our intelligence picked up that Morsi, once in office, planned to dissolve the emerging democratic institutions in Egypt and impose an authoritarian Islamic regime, the Obama administration didn't voice any criticism toward him. They reserved that for the new defense minister, Abdel Fattah el-Sisi, when he toppled Morsi in the summer of 2013 and saved Egypt from radical Islamist rule.[1]

Operation Pillar of Defense gave Israel two years of quiet. I had no illusions that we would not have to fight again, but for now there was calm.

50

"NOBODY LIKES GOLIATH"

2013

The American-brokered cease-fire agreement cost the Likud politically, as I had predicted. Naftali Bennett's party won twelve seats in the 2013 elections, with many of his votes coming from disgruntled Likud voters who were disappointed with the quick conclusion of Operation Pillar of Defense.

Lapid shot up to nineteen seats and replaced Kadima. The Kadima party disintegrated and Tzipi Livni formed her own party, which got six seats.

While Bennett and Lapid haggled with me, I told Livni I would give her the Justice Ministry portfolio if she joined my coalition and I ended up forming a government. This decision would have momentous consequences later because of her choice of appointments in the Justice Ministry.

In Israel's parliamentary system, with the limited time allotted to form a government, those who come aboard a coalition first usually get better terms, regardless of the size of their parties. A premium is often paid to start the coalition-building process. Livni joined and did take on the justice minister position, but her primary interest lay elsewhere. She wanted a front seat in the negotiations with the Palestinians.

During the previous year, Itzik Molcho, my able and discreet negotiator, had established a secret channel with Dr. Hussein Agha, a prominent Lebanese Shi'i who was close to the Fatah Movement in Lebanon and especially to Mahmoud Abbas. The two of them met regularly, mostly in London, in an effort to advance a realistic framework for peace negotiations.

Agha secretly came to see me several times in the Balfour residence, and such meetings were known to Abbas. I discussed with him openly my vision of a peace settlement and he seemed to indicate that there is a basis for advancing negotiations with Mahmoud Abbas.

I shared this information with Livni. She was skeptical of the "London Track," as we called it, and wanted to concentrate on negotiations through the US. Since she was concerned that she would be sidelined by Molcho, I agreed with her that the two of them would work together on Palestinian matters and that Molcho would share with her all the information from London.

They would brief each other and report to me, the final arbiter of policy. Distrustful at first, Livni and Molcho settled into a less-than-comfortable but working relationship.

Information was shared as promised, but there was constant tension between Livni, who continually wanted to offer generous territorial and other concessions to the Palestinians, and the more cautious Molcho, who insisted on tough reciprocity. He was concerned that Livni would undermine his negotiation strategy by offering these concessions in *her* back channels, or even frontally with the US negotiations.

There was now a new American negotiating team led by John Kerry, who had succeeded Hillary Clinton as secretary of state. I knew Kerry from years earlier when I served in Washington as deputy chief of mission and he was a senator from Massachusetts. He was intensely interested in international affairs, believing after repeated visits to Damascus that he could sway the likes of Bashar Assad toward peace. His confidence was not borne out by realities on the ground.

On a visit years earlier to Israel with his friend Senator Joe Biden, I invited both of them to a Jerusalem restaurant. They focused on the Palestinian issue.

"C'mon, Bibi," Kerry said in exasperation. "Everybody knows what the solution is. *You* know what it is. You just have to admit it and get on with the program."

They assumed the role of friends telling the facts of life to a younger colleague, who obstinately refused to accept those facts and abide by them. I looked at my two American friends. They were not seeking to harm Israel. They were absolutely convinced that the obstacle to peace lay in Israel and in people like me. I felt that my counterarguments about the continued Palestinian rejection of the Jewish state's existence largely fell on deaf ears.

But both Kerry and Biden had one quality that I appreciated. In moments of frustration they would lower their guard and say what they actually thought. I would reciprocate with equal frankness. An open verbal brawl between friends is better than delicate dissimulation between enemies. As Biden would later put it, "Bibi, I love you but I don't agree with a word you say." On many occasions the feeling was mutual.

Kerry soon appointed Martin Indyk as his Middle East envoy. Before doing so he asked for my consent. Indyk's previous stint as US ambassador to Israel from 1995 to 1997 and 2000 to 2001 didn't portend well. A devoted believer in the conventional narrative about Palestinians and Israel, he was exceptionally hostile to me. But I figured that anyone that Kerry sent would share the same attitude, so I didn't make an issue of it.

The new negotiation team was composed of many of the same people from the old one: Indyk on the American side, Molcho and Livni on our side, and Saeb Erekat on the Palestinian side.

All this would produce the same old nonresult. The involvement of the Americans would scuttle the potential progress of the London track. Abbas now could revert to relying on American pressures to produce Israeli concessions without being asked to offer corresponding Palestinian ones.

In hindsight, it was clear that the real "no daylight" policy under Obama was not between the US and *Israel* but between the US and the *Palestinians.*

Despite this, or because of it, Obama chose to begin his second term with a charm offensive with me and the Israeli public.

SOON AFTER HIS reelection, the president announced that he would be coming to Israel for his first official presidential visit.

I welcomed this opportunity to recalibrate our personal relationship. We pulled out all the stops in preparation for the visit. I saw eye to eye with Obama's staff on the need to avoid a speech by Obama in the Knesset. In Israel's intense and freewheeling political atmosphere he could encounter hecklers there from both the right and the left.

Obama landed in Israel on March 20, 2013, and his visit was a great success. President Peres and I, along with an A-list of Israeli VIPs, received Obama in a red-carpet reception in Ben Gurion Airport. After the official speeches, Obama and I walked to a nearby Iron Dome battery specially positioned for the president's inspection. As we marched on the tarmac, Obama took off his jacket and swung it casually over his shoulder. Instinctively I did the same.

If someone takes off his tie in your presence, you do the same. Why not with a jacket, too?

The world press now had a photo of the president of the United States and the prime minister of Israel walking chummily in the sunshine.

This was a good beginning.

Obama came that evening to a private dinner at the prime minister's residence. Sara, Yair and I greeted him warmly at the entrance. Standing for a photograph with Sara in the middle, he quipped: "A rose among the thorns."

When Avner came a little later and told him he had attended the Lollapalooza music festival in Obama's hometown of Chicago, Obama was genuinely pleased.

In the brief press conference outside, he was gracious about the hospitality he received and thanked Sara especially, noting about the boys, "I informed the prime minister that they are very good-looking young men who clearly got their looks from their mother."

We all laughed. Obama was at his best.

This congenial spirit continued through dinner. We discussed Iran and the Palestinians, mixing in personal stories from our lives, all in a nonconfrontational manner. Sara joined us for dessert, which was accompanied by a special concert by a leading Israeli songwriter.

But the visit wasn't all roses. The next day Obama gave a speech at Tel Aviv University to a carefully chosen young crowd. Extolling the virtues of an Israeli-Palestinian peace, he more or less encouraged the audience to rise above their leaders. My staff wanted to issue a statement to rebuff but I let it go.

"He said rise *above*, not rise *against*," I joked, not wishing to get into an unnecessary fight.

In the evening, at a large dinner at President Peres's residence, Obama reverted to a more moderate tone, even winking at Sara and me when some of the speeches given by the Israelis in attendance got particularly long-winded.

For me, the visit was marked by two important Obama statements, one public, the other private.

The Syrian civil war was raging at this time. When we faced the press in the prime minister's residence, Obama was asked point-blank about reports that the Syrian government had possibly used chemical weapons against opponents of Assad's regime a day earlier.

"Is this a red line for you?" a journalist asked.

"I have made clear that the use of chemical weapons is a game changer,"[1] he said, a reaffirmed threat heard round the world.

He had first drawn a red line on this issue a few months earlier in a White House statement. Would he make good on it if it were proven that chemical weapons were actually used in Syria? Time would tell.

And it did. Five months later, Assad's forces carried out a horrific chemical attack that killed 1,500 civilians. Obama called it "the worst chemical weapons attack of the twenty-first century."[2] The entire world was shocked by the footage of little children suffocating to death. All eyes were on Obama. He was scheduled to make a dramatic announcement.

Minutes before going on-air, he called me.

"Bibi," he said, "I've decided to take action but I need to go to Congress first."

I was astonished. American law did not require such an appeal. Syria was not about to go to war with the United States but Congress was unlikely to approve military action anyway. I hid my disappointment and rebounded with an idea that Energy Minister Yuval Steinitz had raised earlier with Ron Dermer and me in the event that Obama wouldn't attack.

The Russian military was in Syria to shore up the Assad regime and protect Russian assets in Syria, such as the strategic Russian naval base in Latakia. That was a fact we could do little to change. But Putin shared with us and the United States a desire to prevent chemical weapons from falling into the hands of Islamic terrorists who posed a threat to Russia, too.

"Why don't you get the Russians with your approval to take out the chemical stockpiles from Syria?" I suggested to the president. "We would back that decision."

This is in fact what transpired in the coming months, though some materials for chemical weapons were still left in Syria. Yet, despite these positive results, the lingering effect of Obama's last-minute turn to Congress was the impression that red lines can be crossed with impunity and that Obama would not employ America's massive airpower even when the situation warranted it.

I should have expected this. The second important and telling exchange between Obama and me during his visit to Israel happened in private, and gave me a heads-up on how he viewed the use of American power. The day after the intimate dinner at the prime minister's residence we met at a King David Hotel suite overlooking the Old City of Jerusalem.

I argued again for an American strike on Iran's nuclear facilities. America could still stop Iran from developing atomic bombs that would endanger America, Israel and the peace of the entire world. An American action now would give an enormous boost to the standing of the US and its president.

Obama's response floored me and Itzik Molcho, who sat beside me.

"Bibi," he said, "Nobody likes Goliath. I don't want to be an eight-hundred-pound gorilla strutting on the world stage. For too long we acted that way. We need to lead in a different way."

I was stunned. In the Middle East as I knew it, with Iran racing to nuclear weapons, and with the shifting geopolitical balance toward Asia, I would want to be a 1,200-pound gorilla, not an 800-pound one.

Often when I met officials of the Obama administration they waxed lyrical about the marvels of soft power. Culture, values, even Hollywood can do wonders to change the world, they said.

"Soft power is good," I acknowledged, "but hard power is even better."

By hard power I meant the judicious use of formidable military or economic power, or both.

The values of individual liberty and national freedom give meaning and strength to free societies. But they are not enough.

Power has the unfortunate quality of not being limited to the morally superior and the well intentioned. If malign forces amass enough of it and have the will to use it, they will overcome the less well-armed forces of good, especially if the good lack the tenacity to fight. Being a moral people won't save you from conquest and carnage, which was the history of the Jewish people for two thousand years.

Being perfect victims who harmed no one, we were perfectly moral. Being utterly powerless, we were led to the slaughter again and again. The rise of Zionism was meant to correct this flaw by giving the Jewish people the power to defend themselves. Enhancing this capacity was the central mission of my years in office.

Great empires throughout history, including the Romans and the Mongols, could rise and rule for centuries because they understood the need for overwhelming power. The United States, the most powerful force in modern times, could only ensure the constancy of its own superiority and the supremacy of its values if it continually nurtured its power and the will to use it when necessary.

Obama's extraordinary statement confirmed for me two things. First, he wanted to depart from the postwar American policy of peace through strength. He wanted peace through understanding.

This wasn't a result of personal weakness. It stemmed from his belief that the projection of American power had caused more harm than good. He truly viewed himself as "a citizen of the world." As such he wanted to reach a broad international consensus on pivotal issues that he believed would be shared by all or most major powers. This necessarily detracted from America's traditional global prominence and was interpreted as weakness by Iran and other powers that didn't share his view.

My second take from this conversation was that the chances of an American military action against Iran's nuclear facilities under Obama were practically nil. Even if he built an American military option, he was unlikely to use it preemptively. And the Iranians would know it. This meant he would conduct negotiations with them on their nuclear capabilities without the most important card up his sleeve.

Hiding my despondency, I accompanied Obama to Ben Gurion Airport. Before he boarded Air Force One, we had one more stop.

The Americans had urged us to finish the *Mavi Marmara* affair. We had already reached a compensation agreement with Turkey for the families of the Turks killed in the operation. What was needed now was a carefully worded script for a concluding conversation between Erdogan and me. As extra insurance against a future abandonment of the agreement by Erdogan, I asked Obama to be in on the phone conference. He did so from a special mobile cabin at the airport.

"Recep, how are you, my friend?" the president said to Erdogan. "How's the wife, how's the family?"

The genuine camaraderie in his voice tallied with what I had heard: One of Obama's closest friends among foreign leaders was the Turkish president, possibly because in Obama's eyes Turkey was an example of a modern, successful and democratic Islamic state. Presumably this friendship later weakened when, following an attempted coup against him on July 15, 2016, Erdogan transformed Turkey into a rigidly authoritarian regime, locked up all his political opponents, and threw more journalists in jail than almost any other ruler on earth.

Erdogan and I each read our lines. I thanked Obama. The *Marmara* affair was finally settled.

Despite this, and despite the fact that the Mossad provided intelligence to Turkey that prevented at least half a dozen terrorist attacks on Turkish soil, our relations with Turkey did not fully recover. Though trade continued at relatively high levels, Israeli tourism—once booming—tapered off. Erdogan kept attacking Israel and me on a regular basis as enemies of Islam. This was good politics in Turkey and he probably believed it. Close to a decade later, as Turkey's economy began to wobble, he would begin to change his tone and soften somewhat his attitude to Israel.

51

"COME ON A CLANDESTINE VISIT TO AFGHANISTAN"

2013

Obama let Kerry handle the negotiations with both Iran and the Palestinians. In late June 2013, Kerry came to Israel. It was now his turn to search for the Holy Grail.

We reminisced about one of our first meetings during a visit to Harvard when I was Israel's ambassador to the UN and he was a senator from Massachusetts. Since then we had met periodically, bonded by the common experience of schooling in Boston and a keen interest in international affairs. This passion naturally led Kerry to the post of chairman of the Senate Foreign Relations Committee. It was in this capacity, about a year before he became secretary of state, that I invited him to dinner when he visited Jerusalem.

Believing in Bashar Assad's readiness for peace, he had urged me to change my skeptical views on Syria and "show some imagination," a suggestion that quickly dissipated with the outbreak of the horrific Syrian civil war.

Rebounding quickly from his disappointment over Syria, Kerry was now enthusiastic over the possibility of a breakthrough with the Palestinians. He was certain that it could be achieved by generous gestures from me, and the gesture he had in mind was the release of pre-Oslo Palestinian terrorists from Israeli jails.

"Trust me, Bibi," he said. "Abu Mazen [Abbas] wants to come. But you've got to help him out."

Where had I heard that before? First settlement freeze, then Jerusalem freeze, now prisoner release. This stuff just goes on and on, I thought. Every Palestinian excuse and delay was accepted at face value by the Americans. They never asked the Palestinians for anything, whether substantive or even trivial.

With such automatic American backing, my demands for the Palestinian Authority to stop its systemic incitement of terror and dismantle terrorist cells couldn't get very far. But I could ask for something from *the Americans* in exchange for the concessions they were asking of Israel.

The freeze was over. Each time Israel built even the most modest housing project in Judea and Samaria, a small crisis in Israel-US relations ensued.

"John," I said, "releasing Palestinian prisoners is enormously difficult for me. It rewards terrorism and depresses Israeli morale. So Israel has to get something in return. Here's my proposal. We'll release some prisoners, not Hamas and all pre-Oslo. We'll do it in four tranches. Simultaneous with each tranche we'll announce housing starts in Judea and Samaria. We'll let you know the exact number of housing units and their location beforehand, and you won't agree or disagree."

Kerry stressed that the US could never formally agree to housing starts, but he went along with this suggestion. After some give-and-take, we agreed on releasing ninety prisoners over the next several months in four tranches. With each release we announced a corresponding building start that was met with muted American criticism.

The fourth tranche, however, didn't end up going through because of a disagreement. Despite my explicitly telling Kerry the opposite, the Americans said we had agreed to release some prisoners who were Israeli citizens. We denied that we did, having said from the start that since this could entail a violation of Israeli law, we couldn't guarantee it.

Abbas used this as an excuse to break a long-standing commitment. Under the Oslo Accords he was obliged not to ask for formal Palestinian membership in international organizations without our agreement, thereby negating the possibility of unilateral attempts to establish a Palestinian statehood.

He now did just that. This precipitated a crisis in the trilateral talks between the Israeli, American and Palestinian teams, effectively halting the negotiations.

Kerry adopted the Palestinians' blame narrative in full. On April 9, 2014, he told the Senate Foreign Relations Committee, "Unfortunately, the [Palestinian] prisoners weren't released on the Saturday they were supposed to be released, and—and so day [one] went by, day two went by, day three went by, and then in the afternoon, when they were about to maybe get there, seven hundred settlement units were announced in Jerusalem, and poof!"[1]

"Hasn't he learned anything?" I ranted at my staff.

One of them was particularly incensed. "We released scores of Palestinian prisoners, built housing with his tacit approval, Jerusalem is not a settlement, and Abbas violates his commitments by unilaterally joining fifteen international organizations."

"And who does Kerry blame?" I complained to my staff. "Israel of course!"

Kerry was indeed unrelenting. We had been continually meeting in Israel, the US and Rome, a favorite middle ground for both of us. We talked endlessly on the phone and conducted repeated videoconferences. With Molcho and Livni flanking me on either side, we dived into substance and parsed out language with finely honed verbal scalpels.

Kerry drew up a framework for peace that he wanted Israel and the Palestinian Authority to agree to "in principle." Introduced in December 2013, it covered many of the central topics but not always to our satisfaction. We disagreed on several of its core provisions, first among them security.

I asked the IDF's planning department to draw up a comprehensive plan addressing Israel's security requirements in a final peace settlement. They did a fine job addressing possible threats from the ground and the air, dealing with everything from protecting Israel against terror tunnels to safeguarding our crucial airspace.

Though Kerry didn't accept our threat assessments and our solutions, I would later use this important work in my discussions with the Trump team on a new peace plan.

In my discussions with the secretary, I repeatedly focused on the need to have Israel control our eastern border along the Jordan. I also insisted that we maintain the right of the IDF and Shin Bet to root out terror cells and armament production within the Palestinian-controlled areas.

"The Palestinians," I said, "simply do not and will not do the job."

Kerry brought in US general John Allen to suggest an alternative.

I called in Boogie Yaalon, whom I had recently appointed as defense minister, to hear the American proposal with me. Allen laid out a presentation of US technological monitors that would be placed along the border. He said this would obviate the need for permanently stationed Israeli forces along the Jordan. As for the internal policing against terrorism within the Palestinian areas, the US would train the Palestinian security forces to do the job.

I responded that shortly after Israel left Gaza, those same Palestinian Authority security forces caved to Hamas terrorists.

"This is different," Kerry said. "These forces would be trained by us."

He then made an extraordinary proposal.

"Bibi, I want to arrange a clandestine visit for you to Afghanistan. You'll see with your own eyes what a great job we did there to prepare the Afghan army to take over the country once we leave."

Yaalon and I looked at each other. Our glances said everything.

"John," I said, "the minute you leave Afghanistan the Taliban will mop up the force you trained in no time." Boogie concurred completely.

In 2021, that is exactly what happened. Once the US withdrew its last forces, the US-trained Afghan military crumbled into dust in a matter of days.

I remembered a similar discussion with another secretary of state, George Shultz, who made the same argument to encourage our withdrawal from Lebanon. The US was training the Lebanese Army to take over the country. I argued that once we left Lebanon, radical forces would grab control. Lacking the cohesive zealotry of the radicals, the American-trained forces would collapse or become irrelevant. That's exactly what happened when we withdrew from Lebanon in May 2000. Hezbollah took over the country in no time.

The United States could afford to leave Afghanistan, albeit with tragic consequences for the Afghan people, who would again be subjugated by the Taliban, because that country was *thousands of miles* away from America. But an Israeli withdrawal from large areas in Judea and Samaria would place the Islamists a few thousand *meters* from all of our major cities.

We would hand the hills around Jerusalem and Tel Aviv to Hamas. A terrorist organization supported by Iran and committed to our destruction would take over the heart of our homeland and threaten our survival.

US officials repeatedly underestimated the power of the Islamists and overestimated the power of their non-Islamist allies. Unless you have forces with an equal commitment to fight and die to defend their country, the Islamists eventually win.

As long as Israeli forces held on to territories adjoining Israel, the Islamists would be kept at bay. The minute we vacated those territories, the Islamists would take over, as did Hezbollah in Lebanon and Hamas in Gaza.

Kerry and I ended our conversation with a disagreement that was never really resolved. What to do to prevent an impasse?

Molcho and Dermer suggested a way out that was conceived during earlier discussions with Tony Blair, when he served as the representative of the Quartet, an association of the US, Russia, the UN, and the European Union that sought to advance peace negotiations in the Middle East.

We would say that we were willing to enter the negotiations on the basis of Kerry's framework while adding that we have some reservations about some of its specific provisions. The Palestinians would do the same. This would get both of us to the table and we would take it from there.

In a meeting with Obama in September 2013, I had discussed this idea as well as the ongoing negotiations with Iran.

Obama reiterated his "absolute commitment to prevent Iran from acquiring nuclear weapons."

"We entered negotiations with our eyes open and we'll consult with Israel during the negotiations," he said.

In my next meeting with Obama, on March 31, 2014, I gave him Israel's formal consent to begin negotiating with the Palestinians on the basis of Kerry's framework with the reservations clause.

Two weeks later, Obama invited Abbas to the Oval Office.

"Netanyahu has agreed to sign on," he is reported to have told Abbas. "What is your position?"

Abbas refused to answer. He now demanded new conditions for commencing the talks: final and formal American recognition of a Palestinian state on the 1967 lines with East Jerusalem as its capital and the release of 1,200 prisoners, many mass murderers among them.

Pressed by Obama for an answer on returning to negotiations with Israel, Abbas reputedly said, "I'll think about it."

He never came back with an answer.

Instead he ordered the Palestinian Authority to demand Palestinian membership in fifteen other UN organizations, further deepening the divide between us.

Tzipi Livni, who had invested much hope and effort in the talks with the Palestinians via Kerry's framework, called this a "traumatic day" for her.

"Abu Mazen refused to answer Obama on the framework for peace," she said. "I advanced it with Prime Minister Netanyahu but Abu Mazen ended the matter by refusing to negotiate and going after Israel internationally."

I was surprised she was surprised.

A few days later, Abbas signed a pact with Hamas, prompting us to formally suspend the talks.

ON JANUARY 1, 2014, Ariel Sharon died after having been in a coma for eight years. His body lay in state in the Knesset, where President Peres, Vice President Biden, and I eulogized him. He was later buried on a hilltop on his farm, a few miles from the Gaza strip, in a modest ceremony also attended by Biden. At its end Sara approached the vice president.

"Joe, do you have any plans for the evening?" she asked.

"No, I just came to pay our respects. I have no special plans," Biden answered.

"Why don't you come to our place for a quiet dinner?" Sara offered.

"Be glad to."

Sara organized a table for two in the patio of the prime minister's residence. Before she left us Joe protested, his sense of humor never waning:

"Don't leave me alone with this guy," he joked.

"Why?" Sara said. "He's not so frightening."

We had another friendly dinner. Biden, always the gentleman, sent Sara a bouquet of flowers and a thoughtful note the next day.

52

"BIBI, PLEASE HELP US"

2013

During 2013, Israel was beset by a growing stream of illegal migrants from Africa. These were primarily able-bodied young men leaving Eritrea, Sudan and other countries in search of better income.

Unlike their counterparts who braved the Mediterranean to reach Europe, often with tragic results, these migrants usually had an easier job. Israel was the only first-world country they could *walk* to from Africa. Once they crossed the Sinai, all they needed to do was cross the Egyptian-Israeli border and sit down.

The courts told us that under international law, once they were a meter inside Israel's territory, we were obliged to care for them. The number of illegal immigrants grew from month to month, filling first Israel's Negev communities and then other cities, with the biggest concentration in southern Tel Aviv.

Though many migrants were hardworking and law-abiding, some were not. Crime and violence abounded in the neighborhoods they entered. On a visit to Eilat, I went to see one such neighborhood.

"Prime Minister," one mother wept before me. "Help me. I cannot go out to the street. Until a year ago we had a happy life. Now we're living in hell. Please, Bibi, please. Help us!" she sobbed.

Aside from this widespread misery, there was an even bigger issue involved. Israel's existence as a Jewish and democratic state was predicated on the maintenance of a solid Jewish majority. By 2013 some forty thousand illegal migrants had entered the country. If this flow continued to grow, as it showed every sign of doing, the whole foundation of the state would be undermined.

This challenge did not come only from Africa. Since 2014, some twenty thousand illegal job migrants, also with no connection to Israel or Judaism, had come from Eastern Europe, and we made every effort to return them to their home countries.

If the rate of migration continued to grow we'd have in a short order 100,000 to 200,000 migrants a year. Within a decade Israel could be overwhelmed with well over a million illegal migrants total, equivalent to some 40 million in the United States on a relative population basis. Israel's Jewish majority could disappear and Israel's future as a democratic Jewish state with it.

Israel was a tiny country with a small population. It wasn't Western Europe, with a population of half a billion people. We would be demographically overrun. International law, which we respected, required us to accept *refugees* fleeing for their lives. It didn't oblige us to accept job migrants who came to earn a living, and the overwhelming number of these migrants fell into that category.

This, of course, wasn't a question of race. As prime minister I personally ordered several airlifts of thousands of Ethiopian Jews to Israel. This had been done earlier by other prime ministers as well, including Begin, Rabin and Shamir. We each contributed our share in bringing members of one of the lost tribes of Israel to their homeland.

Some of the most emotional moments in my life occurred when I went to receive Ethiopian Jews arriving in Israel. I was deeply moved seeing our Ethiopian brothers and sisters getting off the plane, carrying little babies named Zion and Jerusalem, kissing the ground of the Holy Land. This forgotten tribe of our people in the heart of Africa had kept the faith through centuries of persecution. Thousands of them died in perilous marches through the Sudan, pillaged, raped and murdered by brutal gangs as they made their way to Zion.

Some of the non-Jewish African migrants that were now streaming by foot into Israel also suffered tribulations en route, but by now there was a burgeoning and profitable smuggling industry that facilitated their passage. In any case, unlike our Ethiopian brothers and sisters, they had no cultural affinity to the Jewish state or the Jewish people. And unlike the illegal job migrants from Eastern Europe, whom we deported by the thousands, they were sheltered from deportation by claiming that going back to their home countries would endanger their lives.

Overwhelmingly this was not true. The real reason they wanted to stay was different: in *one day's* labor in Tel Aviv, they could earn the equivalent of *three hundred* days of labor in their home countries.

I was fully aware of the fact that blocking or deporting this illegal immigration would exact a human cost. Some of the illegal migrants had families with children born in Israel, speaking Hebrew and knowing no other country. At Sara's urging, I met a few of these children at the prime minister's residence. My heart went out to them.

Ultimately, many of these families stayed in Israel. My main focus and responsibility as prime minister was to prevent the breach of our borders by *future* illegal migrants.

I remembered a visit to the Great Wall of China.

Convening a special cabinet meeting with the army's leadership and various experts, I announced my intention to build a barrier along the Israeli-Egyptian border to prevent illegal migration from Africa. I wanted the IDF Engineering Corps to do it.

The military objected. Chief of Staff Gabi Ashkenazi and his Deputy Benny Gantz explained that the fence would not work.

"Why not?" I asked. "It worked pretty well for the Chinese."

"This is different," a staff officer explained. "They could tunnel under the barrier, as in Gaza."

"I doubt it," I said. You need buildings to hide entry and exit points. This was barren desert with no buildings in sight for many kilometers.

"So they'll climb over it," came the retort.

"Then we'll figure out how to make sure they won't be able to," I said in exasperation. This barrier would not just be a fence. We could use drones, mobile forces, fire hoses.

"Just get the job done," I said.

"Prime Minister," Ashkenazi said in a last-ditch effort, "we should build a virtual fence."

"What's that?" I asked.

"We'll have a physical barrier in the south and in the north of the border, but in between there'll be forces using visual means to intercept infiltrators."

"Yeah," I said, "you'll need half the army to monitor and seal two hundred kilometers. I want a real fence, not a virtual one."

The next obstacle the army put before me was cost. Showing diagrams of an enormously complicated multilayered barrier, they said the cost would run into many billions of shekels.

"I think it could be much cheaper," I said.

I instructed the cabinet secretary to bring to the next cabinet meeting a competing bid from the Public Works Department of the Transportation Ministry.

Faced with competition, the army cut its costs estimate for the fence by roughly half. I drafted a proposal to build the barrier. The cabinet approved the resolution in March 2010.

Once the order was given, the chief of staff, to his credit, went into high gear. He appointed Colonel Eran Ophir, an exceptional project leader whom I later called "Herod" because he built on a scale worthy of that famed builder-king. Every three months I would fly to the Egyptian-Israeli border to monitor the work in progress. Invariably Eran's deliverables came in ahead of schedule and under budget.

During the construction, in August 2011, an incident occurred that underscored an additional reason to erect the barrier. Several terrorists from the Sinai crossed the border near Eilat and murdered six Israeli civilians and two soldiers.

It was a reminder that building the fence was not only vital to stopping illegal job migrants. It would also block the growing number of terrorists coming in from the Sinai.

Less than two years after the beginning of its construction, the fence was complete.

Like the Great Wall of China that inspired it, it went up and down gullies and chasms and closed the border.

The rate of illegal infiltration into Israel went down to zero!

Israel was thus the first Western country to effectively seal its borders.

53

TUNNEL WAR

2014

The quiet we had purchased from Gaza in Operation Pillar of Defense was about to be broken by a chain of events that began with the brutal slaughter of three innocent boys and escalated into a full-scale war.

On June 12, 2014, three Israeli teenagers—Naftali Frenkel, sixteen; Gilad Shaer, sixteen; and Eyal Yifrah, nineteen—hitchhiked a ride near their yeshiva in the Gush Etzion region of Judea. Sitting in the backseat of the car, they belatedly understood that they had been abducted by Palestinian terrorists masquerading as Israelis. One managed to whisper a distress call to his parents on his mobile phone before being suddenly silenced. We learned later that they were murdered on the spot, their bodies hidden in a well in a Palestinian village. Hamas took "credit" for the kidnapping.

Shin Bet and the army went into a massive search for the boys and their abductors. They closed off entire parts of the Palestinian-controlled areas, conducted house-to-house searches, and shut down Hamas front organizations.

Eighteen days later, the bodies of the three teenagers were found. The entire country mourned. Like so many others, Sara and I tried to comfort their parents. They bore their grief with incredible dignity, arousing the admiration of the nation.

Shin Bet tracked down the killers to the environs of Hebron. Visiting the tracking headquarters, I was impressed by the systemic and unrelenting professionalism of the young men and women there. They homed in on the safe house where the terrorists were hiding. The border police and the special antiterror unit, the Yamam, surrounded the building. When the call to surrender was answered with gunfire, the Yamam stormed the premises and killed the terrorists.

This was only the beginning.

During the course of the manhunt, Hamas fired rockets into Israel. They were responding to the dismantling of Hamas infrastructure in the Palestinian areas that accompanied the search operation. Though we hoped that they would cease their attacks with the conclusion of the IDF operation, they didn't.

I convened the security cabinet several times.

"Our goal is not to enter a war," I said. "But we don't control Hamas. If they continue to escalate, we won't have a choice but to hit them very hard to restore deterrence and calm."

We instructed the IDF to prepare for an all-out battle.

Hamas disregarded our messages appealing for calm that were sent through discreet channels and continued to fire at Israel at an ever-growing pace.

Worse, our intelligence had previously discovered that Hamas had dug dozens of terror tunnels meant to cross under the border fence. Their specially trained forces could emerge from below ground and infiltrate unseen into the very heart of Israeli communities to kill and kidnap civilians and soldiers alike. Though we had encountered isolated tunnels in the past, such as the one used to abduct Gilad Shalit, this was a threat of a different magnitude. It was tunnel warfare on a grand scale. Hamas intended to surprise Israel by initiating the simultaneous penetration of *hundreds* of terrorists into the country. They planned to enter kindergartens and schools, murder Israelis and whisk dozens of hostages to Gaza back through the tunnels.

This could spell disaster.

In the two years prior I had convened Israel's technological units several times.

"We've got to find a way to identify the digging of tunnels and their precise locations," I instructed them.

I personally called heads of state and heads of multinational companies, including satellite operators, in search of a solution.

None was found.

"Goddamnit," I said to a group of experts, standing in front of the whiteboard in my military headquarters in Tel Aviv. "We're no more advanced than the Babylonians, the Romans and the Ottomans."

Just to make sure we weren't missing anything, we studied their methods in detail, too.

"What do the Americans have?" I asked. "What did they learn in Vietnam?"

"Prime Minister," came the despondent answer from the chief technologist, "they suggest sending in rats and things like that. But that doesn't help identify unknown tunnels and determine their precise location. For that we'll need a few more years of R&D."

A stark reality hit me. Israel would have to be a world pioneer in this field. For the moment, the only way to get the job done was by sending in ground troops.

On July 4, 2014, shortly after the abduction of the three teenagers, we were able to deal with one tunnel from the air. By other means, our intelligence identified the precise location of another terror tunnel that was nearing the Gaza border with Israel. We needed to stop the Hamas diggers before they penetrated Israel.

In a special security cabinet meeting, I authorized the IDF recommendation for an air strike on the tunnel. On July 7, the IAF drilled several bombs into it. Seven Hamas terrorists were killed in the tunnel, and it became unusable.[1]

The next day, Hamas escalated with massive rocket fire on Israeli civilians. The cabinet authorized the mobilization of forty thousand reservists. We were effectively at war. Operation Protective Edge, as it became known, was under way.

I called Defense Minister Yaalon and military Chief of Staff Gantz to my office in the IDF headquarters in Tel Aviv.

"The three of us are the iron triangle," I said. "There'll be a lot of challenges, a lot of criticism, and a lot of recriminations. I expect this not only from abroad but also from within. As long as things go well, everyone will be with us. When things don't, which is bound to happen, they'll go against us. But as long as the three of us stand together, they won't break us and we'll win this war."

Boogie and Benny agreed. Benny even suggested that when the fighting ended, we would go to a nearby burger place called BBB.

The first phase of the war was led by the IAF. It targeted Hamas rocket launchers, commanders and command posts that Hamas deliberately embedded in Gaza's densely populated civilian neighborhoods. It placed its main headquarters in a hospital and its stockpiles of rockets and missiles in hospitals, schools and mosques, often using children as human shields. Before bombing these Hamas targets, in an effort to minimize civilian casualties the IDF issued warning to civilians to evacuate the premises.

Hamas continued to rocket Israeli cities.

I instructed the army to prepare for a ground operation to take out the tunnels. Our soldiers would be susceptible to Palestinian ground fire, booby traps, land mines and antitank missiles, some fired by terrorists emerging from underground. As casualties would inevitably mount on both sides in this door-to-door warfare, I realized that Israel would face growing international criticism. But there was no other choice.

I called Obama, the first of many phone conversations we had during the operation. He said he supported Israel's right of self-defense but was very clear on its limits.

"Bibi," he said, "we won't support a ground action."

"Barack, I don't *want* a ground action," I said. "But if our intelligence shows that the terror tunnels are about to penetrate our territory, I won't have a choice."

I repeated this conversation with the many foreign leaders whom I called and who called me, thus setting the international stage for a ground action. Most accepted what I said.

The same could not be said for the international media. It hammered Israel on the growing number of Palestinian casualties from our air attacks, conveniently absolving Hamas of targeting Israeli civilians while hiding behind Palestinian civilians. The media also bought Hamas's inflated numbers of Palestinian civilian casualties, and even its staging of fake funerals. We unmasked many of those being claimed as civilians as Hamas terrorists by providing their names, unit affiliation and other identifying data.

I visited the IDF's Southern Command to meet the brigade commanders who would lead the ground action. They were feverishly working on the means to locate and destroy the tunnels. They were brave, resolute and smart. They knew very well the dangers they and their men would face. So did their soldiers, many of whom did not return.

"Good luck, may God be with you," I said as I shook the hands of the commanders.

On July 17 we began the ground phase of Protective Edge. Ground forces entered Gaza with tanks and armored personnel carriers and by foot. There were more tunnels than expected and the task of neutralizing them with explosives, water and cement was more complicated than anticipated. It took three weeks instead of the expected three days to complete the mission. During this time our casualties mounted. The daily casualty reports were painful, but I was determined that the mission to destroy the tunnels would be completed.

When it was, I convened the cabinet.

"We'll withdraw the ground forces. We don't need to put them at risk any more than necessary," I told them, communicating what I had already agreed on with the chief of staff and the minister of defense.

"We'll now begin the third phase of the operation, an aerial war of attrition," said the IDF chief of operation.

"Hamas rockets and mortars will be pitted against our Iron Dome missile defense and our airpower. They have limited means to hit us. We have overwhelming means to hit them. We're bound to win."

Hamas was determined to achieve its goals, from the release of jailed terrorists to the opening of an airport and seaport in Gaza through which they could bring in an endless supply of weapons. Pointedly, they included a demand that their senior commanders not be targeted in the future.

I was determined that they would get nothing, except a beating they would never forget.

Unlike during the previous Gaza operation in 2012, the Iron Dome supply did not run out. After Operation Pillar of Defense I had instructed the army to accelerate production of Iron Dome projectiles and batteries. We accomplished this with our own funds and with generous American financial support.

I now asked the Obama administration for an additional $225 million package to continue the production line after Protective Edge. He agreed, and with the help of Tony Blinken, the deputy national security advisor who later became Biden's secretary of state, the funding provision sailed through both houses of Congress. I deeply appreciated this support and said so publicly.

I was therefore very disappointed when the administration held back on the IDF's request for additional Hellfire rockets for our attack helicopters. Without offensive weapons we could not bring the Gaza operation to a quick and decisive end. Furthermore, as the air war lingered, the administration issued increasingly critical statements against Israel, calling some of our actions "appalling"[2] and thereby opening the moral floodgates against us.

Hamas took note. As long as it believed that we couldn't deliver more aggressive punches, and that international support was waning, it would continue to rocket our cities.

Unfortunately, it was aided in this belief by an international tug-of-war. On one side: Israel and Egypt. On the other: Turkey and Qatar, which fully supported Hamas. I worked in close collaboration with Egypt's new leader, el-Sisi, who had deposed the Islamist Morsi a few months earlier. Our common goal was to achieve an unconditional cease-fire. The last thing el-Sisi wanted was a Hamas success in Gaza that would embolden their Islamist allies in the Sinai and beyond. Hamas's exiled leader, Khaled Mashal, who escaped the Mossad action in Jordan, was now in Qatar. Supported by his Qatari hosts and Erdogan and ensconced in his lavish villa in Doha, Mashal egged Hamas to keep on fighting.

To my astonishment, Kerry urged me to accept Qatar and Turkey as mediators instead of the Egyptians, who were negotiating with Hamas representatives in Cairo for a possible cease-fire.

Hamas drew much encouragement from this American position. El-Sisi and I agreed to keep the Americans out of the negotiating loop. In the meantime the IDF would have to further degrade Hamas's fighting and crush their expectations of achieving anything in the cease-fire negotiations.

During the war, Naftali Bennett—with support from Avigdor Lieberman—broke a norm that had been respected in Israel since its establishment. Even as a security cabinet member, Bennett constantly and publicly attacked the government's handling of the war while IDF soldiers were under fire. He publicly advocated a full-scale ground invasion to "conquer Gaza." That could only be done with the wholesale destruction of Gaza, with tens of thousands of civilian deaths. After destroying the Hamas regime, Israel would have to govern two million Gazans for an indefinite period. I had no intention of doing that, especially since I had my gaze fixed on Iran, a much greater threat. Boogie Yaalon also referred to Bennett as the "Leaking Minister," who leaked information from the "holy of holies," referring to secret cabinet meetings.[3]

Midway into the conflict, I convened the cabinet and asked the chief of staff to lay out the invasion plans and assess the toll in lives. Then I asked the Defense Ministry to assess the resources needed for the postwar administration of Gaza.

I believed the cost in blood and treasure was not worth it. My clear impression was that all the cabinet ministers agreed with my assessment, though they were reluctant to say so publicly.

I shrugged off this hypocrisy.

In war, people expect their leaders to make the right decisions. Yet some allow themselves to irresponsibly take contrarian positions which they know are wrong. I decided against a full-scale ground invasion.

Lieberman and Bennett continued public briefings to point out that they were in favor of invading Gaza and destroying Hamas, though in the cabinet they remained largely silent. Bennett even advanced the absurd claim that he was the one who forced the destruction of the terror tunnels, notwithstanding that the entire IDF was preparing for the task well before the war.

In each of the war's fifty nights I would sit with the chief of staff and the head of Shin Bet to authorize that night's actions. I would then typically stay up until 3 a.m. to see the results.

After a few hours of sleep in Jerusalem, I would wake up for the following day's business. I convened the security cabinet every two days, briefed the Israeli public, and talked with foreign leaders.

The UN urged us to accept several twenty-four-hour humanitarian cease-fires for food, medicine and repairs of electricity lines for Gaza's residents. We always agreed, and Hamas always violated them. In one such cease-fire during the ground action, Hamas terrorists killed twenty-three-year-old Lieutenant Hadar Goldin and disappeared with his body into a tunnel. A brave fellow soldier pursued Goldin's killers as far as he could. Sergeant Oron Shaul had met a similar fate at the beginning of the operation. Hamas cruelly refused to return the bodies of these two fine soldiers for years.

As Hamas's rocket stockpiles dwindled, it reduced the number of rockets launched nightly but increased the range to Tel Aviv and beyond. Several of my conversations with Obama were interrupted by sirens.

"Sorry, Barack," I'd say. "I'm afraid we'll have to resume our conversation in a few minutes."

With the rest of the staff I had forty-five seconds to go into underground shelters, returning after getting the all-clear sign. These live interruptions strengthened my argument for taking increasingly powerful actions against Hamas.

And so we did.

The IAF destroyed more and more enemy targets. Hamas panicked and became careless. Our intelligence identified the locations of their commanders. We targeted them and delivered painful blows to their hierarchy. Hamas then shifted their command posts to high-rises, believing they would be immune to our strikes.

Using a technique called "knock on roof," the air force fired nonlethal warning shots on the roofs of the buildings. Along with phone calls to the building occupants, these warnings enabled them to leave the premises unharmed. The IDF flattened several high-rise buildings with no civilian casualties. The sight of these collapsing towers sent Hamas a powerful message of demoralization and fear. This was literally "you can climb but you can't hide."

Desperation was seeping through Hamas ranks. Arguments began to flare between Mashal in Qatar and the ground command in Gaza, which was suffering the brunt of our attacks. Eventually they caved. In the talks with Egypt they rescinded all their demands and agreed to an unconditional cease-fire that went into effect on August 26, 2014.

After fifty days, Protective Edge was over.

Sixty-seven IDF soldiers, five Israeli civilians, including one child, and a Thai civilian working in Israel lost their lives in the war. There were 4,564 rockets and mortars fired at Israel from Gaza, nearly all from civilian neighborhoods. The Iron Dome system intercepted 86 percent of them.[4] The IDF killed 2,125 Gazans,[5] roughly two-thirds of whom were members of Hamas, Palestinian Islamic Jihad and other Palestinian terrorist groups. A third were civilians who were often used by the terrorists as human shields. Colonel Richard Kemp, the commander of British forces in Afghanistan, said that "the IDF took measures to limit civilian casualties never taken by any Western army in similar situations."

At least twenty-three Palestinian civilians were executed by Hamas over false accusations of colluding with Israel. In reality many had simply criticized the devastation of Gaza brought about by Hamas's aggression against Israel.[6]

Hamas leaders emerged from their bunkers. Surveying the rubble, they predictably declared victory. This is what all dictatorships do. They are not accountable to the facts or to their people.

Less predictably, Palestinian Authority chairman Mahmoud Abbas admitted that Hamas was severely weakened and achieved none of its demands.[7]

With the conclusion of the fighting, I convened a nationally televised press conference with Boogie Yaalon and Benny Gantz.

"Hamas has been dealt a heavy blow," I said. "We set a clear goal to inflict serious damage to Hamas and the other terrorist groups, and by doing so to bring extended quiet to Israel's citizens. We destroyed the tunnel system which Hamas built for years. Hamas is diplomatically isolated. Will we reach our goal of long-term quiet? That's still too early to tell, but the severe damage caused to Hamas and to the other terror groups will increase the chances for achieving this goal."

Many in the public were not convinced. Roughly half believed there was no clear winner in the war.[8] After nearly two months of rocketing, in which millions of civilians stayed in shelters, this was understandable.

Israelis appreciated our soldiers' courage but had hoped for a more decisive victory in which the Hamas regime would be destroyed.

Still, it was a decisive victory. In total, thirty-two terror tunnels were dismantled or neutralized during Operation Protective Edge.[9] This heralded an accelerated effort to develop the intelligence and technological means to perfect the destruction of terror tunnels. Four years later, in December 2018, in Operation Northern Shield shocked Hezbollah. To its consternation the IDF located and destroyed a dozen terror tunnels on the Lebanese border that Hezbollah had been digging for years. Not a single soldier crossed the border. This greatly dismayed Hezbollah, ten times more powerful than Hamas, thwarting its plans to invade northern Israel and capture communities in the Galilee as part of an opening move in a future war. For the moment that large-scale war was averted.

Two years after that, in Operation Guardian of the Walls in 2021, the IDF shocked Hamas and the world by destroying miles of Hamas's underground tunnel network laced throughout the interior of Gaza. This "terror metro" of command-and-control bunkers and connecting tunnels was accurately bombed from the air. This had never been done before in the history of warfare.

There was one more "tunnel ace" up our sleeve.

After Protective Edge in 2014, I ordered the cabinet to authorize the building of a seventy-kilometer underground barrier on the Gaza-Israel border to defend against the completion of future attack tunnels. The IDF command opposed its construction because of the cost involved. As in the case of the border fence with Egypt, I insisted. The cabinet overruled the military's objection. Colonel Eran Ophir was again up for the task.

In the 2021 Gaza operation, the underground barrier, equipped with sophisticated sensors, worked perfectly. Not a single attack tunnel crossed into Israel.

We had neutralized the tunnel threat.

But I had no doubt this advantage would have to be maintained by continuous innovation to keep Israel several steps ahead of its enemies.

54

"NEVER AGAIN"

2015

Operation Protective Edge had led to an increase in Israel's security, but my main focus continued to be blocking Iran's path to nuclear weapons.

In October 2013, in a speech at the UN General Assembly, I lambasted Iran's new president, Hassan Rouhani. He began his tenure with a charm offensive meant to lull the West into signing a nuclear agreement favorable to Iran.

"Rouhani doesn't sound like Ahmadinejad," I said, referring to his fiery predecessor. "But when it comes to Iran's nuclear program, the only difference between them is that Ahmadinejad is a wolf in wolf's clothing and Rouhani is a wolf in sheep's clothing—a wolf who thinks he can pull the wool over the eyes of the international community."[1]

I read from a 2011 book Rouhani had written in which he bragged about his successful deception of Western negotiators in earlier nuclear talks when he served as Iran's chief nuclear negotiator.

"While we were talking to the Europeans in Tehran, we were installing equipment in Isfahan," he boasted about the nuclear facility where uranium ore called "yellowcake" was converted into an enrichable form that can be used in nuclear bombs.

"By creating a calm environment, we were able to complete the work in Isfahan," he wrote.

"He fooled the world once. Now he thinks he can fool it again," I said to the UN delegates. "You see, Rouhani thinks he can have his yellowcake and eat it, too."

"Iran doesn't need to violate the agreement," I added; it could simply keep it. To illustrate this point I quoted from a speech Rouhani gave to Iran's Supreme Cultural Revolutionary Council that was published in 2005: "A country that can enrich uranium to about 3.5% will also have the capability to enrich it to about 90%. Having fuel cycle capability virtually means that a country that possesses this capability is able to produce nuclear weapons."[2]

Precisely. Now the world powers were negotiating a nuclear agreement that would give Iran the critical capacity for uranium enrichment Rouhani had spoken about in 2005. And more.

"The agreement," I said, "also doesn't cover the other elements in producing nuclear bombs—not the weapon, not the warheads, not the ballistic missiles."

All these generous terms were showered by the world powers on a terrorist regime that was clearly pursuing nuclear weapons.

"It's not that it's hard to find evidence that Iran has a nuclear weapons program," I summed up. "It's hard to find evidence that Iran *doesn't* have a nuclear weapons program."

This didn't stop the great powers of the UN Security Council's five permanent members—the United States, China, Russia, Britain and France—plus Germany, the so-called P5+1, to sign an interim nuclear agreement with Iran in November 2013 in Geneva.

Now, in September 2014, this flawed interim agreement was about to be extended in preparation for the signing of a permanent agreement. Once again I used my speech at the UN General Assembly to warn of the dangers of a nuclear Iran.

"It's one thing to confront militant Islamists on pickup trucks, armed with Kalashnikov rifles," I said, referring to the ISIS terrorist threat that still captured the world's attention. "It's another thing to confront militant Islamists armed with weapons of mass destruction. Imagine how much more dangerous the Islamic state of ISIS would be if it possessed chemical weapons. Now imagine how much more dangerous the Islamic state of *Iran* would be if it possessed nuclear weapons."[3]

But there was a silver lining.

"I believe we have an historic opportunity," I said. "After decades of seeing Israel as their enemy, leading states in the Arab world increasingly recognize that together we face the same dangers, a nuclear-armed Iran and militant Islamist movements."

Foreshadowing the Abraham Accords, I said, "Many have long assumed that an Israeli-Palestinian peace can help facilitate a broader rapprochement between Israel and the Arab world. I think it may work the other way around: a broader rapprochement between Israel and the Arab world may help facilitate an Israeli-Palestinian peace. To achieve that peace, we must look not only to Jerusalem and Ramallah, but also to Cairo, Amman, Abu Dhabi, Riyadh and elsewhere."[4]

Two days later I repeated these themes in my meeting with Obama in the White House. As usual, my main emphasis was on Iran.

"As you know, Mr. President," I said, "Iran seeks a deal that would lift the tough sanctions that you worked so hard to put in place and leave it as a threshold nuclear power, and I fervently hope that under your leadership that will not happen."[5]

While my warnings on Iran didn't move Obama, they registered loud and clear in American public opinion and in Congress. This was soon to have momentous consequences.

BACK IN ISRAEL, I faced a political crisis. My coalition began to wobble over an antidemocratic bill threatening free speech. The left-wing parties, with the help of several right-wing members of the coalition, advanced a bill to effectively shut down Sheldon Adelson's free newspaper *Israel Today*, then the only significant right-wing media outlet in the country. Its competitor, *Yedioth Ahronoth*, used its muscle to ply members of Knesset from the right and even from Likud to support this outrageous bill.

When this assorted gaggle passed the first stage of getting the bill approved in the Knesset, I sprang to my feet.

"Shame on you!" I scolded them and stormed out.

Since I had lost control of my coalition, I decided to dissolve the Knesset. Having received prior information that Livni and Lapid had plotted to overthrow my government in a no-confidence vote, I fired both. I didn't want them as ministers in my government during an election.

I acted quickly, in retrospect perhaps too quickly.

To this day I'm not completely sure that the information provided to me on the impending plot was rock solid. But it was compelling enough. The deed was done.

My alliance with Lieberman's Yisrael Beiteinu also had broken apart. It never truly worked. Though I personally enjoyed strong support in the Russian community, some Russian and Likud voters simply did not mix well. Our combined poll numbers began to sink.

IN THE MIDST of the election campaign, on January 7, 2015, Islamist terrorists in Paris murdered twelve workers and journalists at the office of the satirical magazine *Charlie Hebdo*. The following day, one of the terrorists murdered a French policewoman, and, the day after he murdered four Jewish shoppers at a kosher supermarket. This brutal slaughter outraged millions around the world. A few days later, on January 11, I joined a solidarity march of world leaders that the French government organized on the streets of the capital. That evening I addressed a packed Jewish audience in the Grand Synagogue of Paris.

"Brothers and sisters, Jews of France," I said. "You have the full right to live in safety and tranquility as citizens with equal rights wherever you wish, including here in France. But Jews of our time have been blessed with another right that did not exist for previous generations: the right to join their Jewish brothers and sisters in our historic homeland, the Land of Israel; the right to live in our free country, the one and only Jewish state; the right to stand tall and proud at the walls of Zion, our eternal capital of Jerusalem.

"Any Jew who wishes to immigrate to Israel will be welcomed with open arms and warm hearts. They will not arrive in a foreign land but in the land of our forefathers. God willing, they will come, and many of you will come to our homeland."[6]

This was considered by the French prime minister and foreign minister as an undue call by an Israeli leader to members of the French Jewish community to leave France and come to Israel. "French Jews," they said, "belong in France."

Though I believed that any person's decision to immigrate was a matter of individual choice, I also believed that it was my duty as the prime minister of Israel to make it clear to my fellow Jews that they would be warmly embraced in our country.

Normally such a statement would be praised in Israel as a proud reaffirmation of Zionism, but during a stormy campaign this, too, was criticized as an election ploy. Yet it was instructive that the four slain Jews were brought by their families to be buried in Israel. I attended their funeral.

FACING A TOUGH election, I also saw that the P5+1 and Iran were racing to a dangerous nuclear agreement that would pave Iran's path to the bomb. Under the impending agreement, Iran would be able to freely enrich uranium within a few years. Becoming a threshold nuclear power with a nuclear arsenal, Iran would jeopardize the very existence of Israel.

I had to fight this.

But how could I possibly do it? The polls showed I could soon be out of office.

On Friday, January 8, 2015, I received a fateful call from Ron Dermer from our embassy in Washington. He told me that Speaker of the House John Boehner had called him asking whether I would be willing to address a joint meeting of Congress on the dangers of the impending nuclear deal.

It was a monumental decision. This would not just be another speech. I would be going into the lion's den in Washington to challenge a sitting American president. Stirring up such a hornets' nest on the eve of an Israeli election could have devastating political consequences.

The nuclear deal was *Obama's* top priority.

Blocking it was *my* top priority.

Placing this conflict on such a global stage would put me on a head-on collision course with the president of the United States.

Yet I was given the opportunity to speak before Congress and the

American people on a matter vital to Israel's very survival. I felt the pull of history. Such an invitation could not be declined.

"The answer is yes, in principle," I said to Ron.

That still left me time to think everything through. Dermer began working on the details with Boehner.

We settled on March 3 as the date of the speech, to coincide with AIPAC's annual conference. I would have six weeks to prepare the most important speech of my life.

Word spread that I would be giving the speech just a few days after we picked the date, and a chorus of condemnation erupted like a volcano. Statements like "Netanyahu is destroying our alliance with the United States" and "an act of enormous irresponsibility" flooded the press, the media, and the Knesset.

In the US, Dermer personally met with dozens of Democratic members of Congress, including most members of the Congressional Black Caucus, some of whom complained that the speech would be an insult to the first Black president. Jewish members of Congress complained that I would endanger the Jewish community's standing in America. One, a respected Democratic congresswoman whom I'd known and liked over the years, called me.

"Prime Minister," she said, "I strongly urge you not to come. But if you do, at least speak in a closed session."

A closed session could get me an important audience but not the most important one, the American public. Without the pressure of public opinion, my words would carry an incomparably weaker punch.

I explained to my congresswoman friend that I was not going to divulge any secrets but rather lay out for all to see the great dangers inherent in the proposed nuclear deal.

The fearful critiques came from within my government, too.

A senior minister said to me, "You can't stand up to America. Don't fight a fight you are not going to win. You won't stop the deal; you'll only rupture relations with our most important ally. Ask for added defense appropriations, but don't go."

Another minister argued that we should ask to be at the negotiating table.

"You forget that we *have* been at the table with the Americans for the last two years," I answered. "They listen politely to our comments, occasionally make minor modifications, but as far as making real changes—they haven't done a damn thing. We've gotten to the point where even the French are tougher than the Americans, but they too don't call the shots."

As the pressure mounted from abroad and from within, most of my staff joined in urging me to reconsider giving the speech or at least to do it at a later date. I was practically the only holdout.

"Why don't you push it beyond the elections? That way no one could say that it was political," was the most common suggestion.

"We may not *be* here after the elections," I answered.

As long as doubt lingered whether I would actually go through with the speech, I couldn't focus my efforts on preparing it properly.

Since I would be directly challenging a Democratic president, I assumed that my speech would be portrayed as breaking Israel's long-standing bipartisan support in Congress and eroding Democratic sympathies for the Jewish state. Though poll numbers later clearly showed that this wasn't the case, I didn't know that at the time.

All the reasons not to go weighed heavily on my mind. The move I was contemplating had never been done before. I felt uneasy about it. There was only one countervailing consideration: Could I sit idly by as an agreement was being hatched that would pave Iran's path to the bomb and which I could possibly help avert?

It was time to make a decision.

In mid-February I asked Ron Dermer to come back from Washington. Sitting in my office at the prime minister's residence, the two of us discussed for the nth time all the pros and cons.

Finally, Ron asked, "If you don't do the speech, what's the point?"

"The point of what?"

"The point of you sitting in that chair," he said, more a statement than a question.

At that moment the immortal words of the great Jewish sage Hillel from two thousand years ago hit me with full force.

"If I'm not for me, who will be for me? And if not now, when?"

If I don't take a stand on a nuclear deal that could threaten Israel's survival, I thought, what the hell am I doing here?

That clinched it.

"Let's get on with it," I told him.

In the two weeks before the speech, we met every morning for several hours, punching out drafts. In the afternoons and evenings I would go campaigning, sometimes holding as many as six campaign rallies in one day. My speeches were totally extemporaneous. In each stop I acknowledged the local Likud activists whom I knew from many years of our political work together. This was their moment to shine in the political sun. They were smart and proud, unfazed by the media campaign that sought to disparagingly portray them as "Bibi's baboons."

Some of the supporters moved me to tears. A ninety-year-old Yemenite woman brought me flowers, saying she prayed for me every day. People called and promised they would leave their hospital beds to vote for me, and they did.

Yet throughout this hectic campaign, my main focus was my upcoming appearance in Washington.

Unlike my campaign speeches, in which I planned a few main messages in my head but spoke off the cuff, the speech in Congress would be precise. Every syllable would be planned and, ideally, rehearsed. I would even deviate from my lifelong habit of making last-minute changes from the podium.

Israel is a small country. The superhighway network my government launched in 2009 was progressing well. Except for Eilat, in Israel's southern tip, everywhere else was easily accessible by car within two hours. I used the driving time between campaign stops to go over the latest draft of the speech and prepare for the next working session with Ron. Once in a while I would stop and look out of the car window. In the glorious sunlight of late February, the Galilee was decked in green and the Negev bloomed. But even more enthralling was the tremendous construction boom. Cranes sprouted everywhere. The underdeveloped periphery was being feverishly developed and connected to the country's center, a direct result of our mass investments in fast rail and road, our more liberal land policy, and our incessant war against red tape. It was a different country from what it had been just a few years earlier.

Except for brief pit stops at outdoor cafés in the glistening new shopping arcades, there was no time to bask in the early spring sun. Even then I pored over the speech drafts.

Obama cleverly refused to define the nuclear agreement as a treaty, which would have necessitated a two-thirds approval by the Senate, a hurdle he couldn't pass. He wanted to bypass Congress altogether but pressure was mounting to give it a say. This came in the form of the Corker Bill, which established a mechanism for Congress to approve or disapprove any nuclear deal. The downside was that it would require two-thirds of Congress to override Obama's inevitable veto, a hurdle that would be almost impossible for opponents of the deal to reach, even though Republicans controlled both the House and the Senate. But I set a more realistic goal to get a solid majority in the Congress, thereby cementing public opposition to the deal. Besides, I knew that since the deal would not be classified as a treaty, it would be easier for a future president to reverse it.

The key to undermining support for the disastrous deal was to convince the American people and their representatives in Congress why it was so dangerous. I knew that I couldn't ask people to be more pro-Israel than Israel. If Israel accepted or resigned itself to the deal, it was just a question of time before the nearly unanimous Republican opposition cracked and the dissenting Democrats in Congress disappeared along with them. This meant that in my speech I would have to tear into the proposed deal and expose its flaws for all to see.

It also meant offering an alternative course of action to curb Iran's nuclear program that would make sense to most people.

But there was also a third requirement.

A longtime friend and great supporter of Israel, Mort Zuckerman, the publisher of *U.S. News & World Report*, called me.

"You're going into a political tinderbox. Democratic sensibilities are at their height. I tell you, Bibi, I've known Washington for many years and I've never seen anything like this tension," he said. "So I have one suggestion for you. Be as respectful as possible to Obama." I took that to heart.

The weeks before the speech heightened the drama. The debate over the speech produced great expectations on a global scale. The whole world was watching.

How many Democrats would boycott the speech? Would those who would attend greet it coldly? Would there be heckling in the gallery?

On March 2, I arrived in Washington.

"No Blair House this time," I said to Sara.

We stayed at the Willard hotel, where Gary and Nathan joined me and Ron. The speech was the following day, March 3.

Unlike the day before any of my previous speeches at the UN or Congress, unlike my confrontation with Obama in the Oval Office, this time I was filled with apprehension.

Stage fright wasn't exactly it.

The last time I had that was in my first impromptu speech as UN ambassador in 1984. No great lover of alcohol, I nonetheless downed a few drinks.

When asked to address the assembled guests, I went to the podium.

Suddenly my head was spinning. About to pass out, I gripped the podium. In those precious seconds my head cleared. Somehow I managed to deliver my remarks. I vowed never to drink alcohol again on an empty stomach before a speech.

Now, in the bowels of the Willard hotel, something worse than alcohol got in my way. I had a terrible cold. Suffering from a chronic sinus condition for years, I regularly used antihistamine spray. It usually worked, but not this time. The more I injected the damn drops, the more congested I became. Trying to read the speech in a practice run, I choked in midsentence. Every midsentence.

Sara, Ron and the prime minister's medic offered various remedies, from bowls of steam to anticongestion pills. Nothing worked.

Worse, I found it hard to breathe even when I wasn't trying to speak. As I well knew, this periodically happened with an overdose of antihistamines. The trick was *not* to overdose, something I had clearly failed to do.

Was this a panic attack? Well, try this. Shut both nostrils with your fingers for a few minutes and see how long you remain calm. Then try reading out loud from a book.

"I can't believe this is happening to me," I said to Sara. "The most important speech of my life and I'm going to be foiled by this?" I threw away the nose spray dispenser in disgust.

"Try getting some sleep," she said, trying to calm me down. "This usually passes in the morning."

But it didn't pass this time.

After a sleepless night, I got up on the morning of March 3, showered, and shaved. Okay, I said to myself, there's no "survival tube" from the Hermon this time, no hand to pull me out of the water, as in Suez.

You'll just have to make do as is, I commanded myself.

As I sniffed and wiped my nose, we set out to Boehner's office. Then, suddenly, miracle of miracles! My sinuses cleared. They would stay that way until the evening.

Entering the Capitol Building, I was all smiles.

Boehner received us graciously. He was an urbane and thoughtful man, an old-school gentleman Republican. The congressional protocol officer rehearsed the routine of entering the hall, which I remembered from my two previous appearances.

"You realize, Prime Minister," Ron said, "that you and Winston Churchill are the only foreign leaders who have spoken three times before a joint meeting of Congress."

"Well, I'm sure Churchill's third speech had an audience more united in appreciation," I said.

I don't know if Boehner heard this, but just then he pulled out a little box.

"There's a small bust of Churchill there for you," he said.

"I'll put it in my office," I replied, much moved by this gesture.

The clarion call sounded.

"Mr. Speaker, the Prime Minister of Israel!"

I went through the aisles to loud cheers and a standing ovation, shaking hands with senators and US representatives, many of whom I had known for decades.

Even though some fifty Democrats did not attend, the hall was packed. Sara was seated in the crowded gallery next to Elie Wiesel and his wife, Marion. I nodded to them and they nodded back.

"He'll be like the uncle from Sicily," I said earlier that day to Ron, referring to a scene in *The Godfather: Part II*. Just by being there, Elie would remind everyone of the need to prevent another Holocaust.

Taking the podium, I noticed that, as expected, Vice President Joe Biden was absent this time.

I looked directly opposite me at the Seal on the back wall, with the engraving of Moses, the great lawgiver who took the Israelites out of bondage in Egypt.

I waited for the applause to subside, took a deep breath and began. Here is a short version of what I said.

> I want to thank you all for being here today. I know that my speech has been the subject of much controversy. I deeply regret that some perceive my being here as political. That was never my intention.
>
> I want to thank you, Democrats and Republicans, for your common support for Israel, year after year, decade after decade.
>
> Israel is grateful for the support of America's people and of America's presidents, from Harry Truman to Barack Obama. We appreciate all that President Obama has done for Israel.

I went on to detail Obama's assistance to Israel in several junctures.

All this was met with resounding applause and several standing ovations.

Encouraged by the warm welcome, having successfully crossed the first hurdle, the preamble, I plunged into Part One of the speech, Iran.

> I've come here today because as the prime minister of Israel I feel a profound obligation to speak to you about an issue that could well threaten the survival of my country and the future of my people: Iran's quest for nuclear weapons.
>
> We're an ancient people. In our nearly four thousand years of history many have tried repeatedly to destroy the Jewish people. Tomorrow night, on the Jewish holiday of Purim, we'll read in the Book of Esther of a powerful Persian viceroy named Haman who plotted to destroy the Jewish people some 2,500 years ago. But a courageous Jewish woman, Queen Esther, exposed the plot and secured for the Jewish people the right to defend themselves against their enemies. The plot was foiled. Our people were saved.
>
> Today the Jewish people face another attempt by yet another Persian potentate to destroy us. Iran's Supreme Leader Ayatollah Khamenei spews the oldest hatred of antisemitism with the newest technology. He tweets that Israel must be annihilated.

But Iran's regime is not merely a Jewish problem, any more than the Nazi regime was merely a Jewish problem.

At a time when many hope that Iran will join the community of nations, Iran is busy gobbling up the nations.

We must all stand together to stop Iran's march of conquest, subjugation and terror.

The battle between Iran and ISIS doesn't turn Iran into a friend of America. Iran and ISIS are competing for the crown of militant Islam.

In this deadly game of thrones, there's no place for America or for Israel and no freedom for anyone.

So when it comes to Iran and ISIS, *the enemy of your enemy is your enemy.*

Applause was accompanied by laughter.

As I was speaking I noticed that nearly all the Democrats were joining their Republican colleagues in the standing ovations, at first reluctantly and then often full-heartedly. But not in every case. Minority House Leader Nancy Pelosi turned her back on me.

When speakers spot indifferent or hostile members in an audience, they often get dejected. Not me. Nothing energizes me more. It steels my resolve and deepens my determination to argue Israel's case with all the force of conviction I can muster.

Now I was ready for Part Two, The Deal.

We must always remember: the greatest danger facing our world is the marriage of militant Islam with nuclear weapons.

But that is exactly what could happen if the deal now being negotiated is accepted by Iran. That deal will not prevent Iran from developing nuclear weapons. It would all but guarantee that Iran gets those weapons.

Any deal with Iran will include two major concessions to Iran. The first would leave Iran with a vast nuclear infrastructure, providing it with a short breakout time to the bomb. Not a single nuclear facility would be demolished. Thousands of centrifuges used to enrich uranium would be left spinning.

But the second major concession creates an even greater danger. Iran could get to the bomb by *keeping* the deal. Because virtually all the restrictions on Iran's nuclear program will *automatically* expire in about a decade. A decade may seem like a long time in political life, but it's the blink of an eye in the life of a nation and in the life of our children.

The foremost sponsor of global terrorism could then be weeks away from having enough enriched uranium for an entire arsenal of nuclear weapons and this with full international legitimacy.

Iran could have the means to deliver that nuclear arsenal to the far-reaching corners of the earth, including to every part of the United States. That's why this deal is so bad. It doesn't block Iran's path to the bomb. It *paves* Iran's path to the bomb.

If Iran is gobbling up four countries right now while it's under sanctions, how many more countries will Iran devour when sanctions are lifted? Many of its neighbors say they'll respond by racing to get nuclear weapons of their own.

This deal won't be a farewell to arms. It would be a *farewell to arms control*. The Middle East would soon be crisscrossed by nuclear tripwires. A region where small skirmishes can trigger big wars would turn into a nuclear tinderbox.

The hall was silent and attentive. I could feel my arguments sinking in. I was in my stride. With growing confidence, I proceeded to Part Three, The Alternative, during which the applause continued and the number of standing ovations increased.

We can insist that restrictions on Iran's nuclear program not be lifted for as long as Iran continues its aggression in the region and in the world.

Before lifting those restrictions, the world should demand that Iran do three things. First, stop its aggression against its neighbors in the Middle East.

Second, stop supporting terrorism around the world.

Third, stop threatening to annihilate my country, Israel, the one and only Jewish state.

If Iran changes its behavior, the restrictions would be lifted. If Iran doesn't change its behavior, the restrictions should not be lifted.

If Iran wants to be treated like a normal country, let it *act* like a normal country.

For over a year, we've been told that no deal is better than a bad deal. Well, this is a very bad deal. We're better off without it. Now we're being told that the only alternative to this bad deal is war. That's not true.

The alternative to this bad deal is a *much better deal*.

A better deal that doesn't leave Iran with a vast nuclear infrastructure and such a short breakout time, that keeps the restrictions on Iran's nuclear program in place until Iran's aggression ends.

A better deal that won't give Iran an easy path to the bomb and that Israel and its neighbors may not like, but with which we could live, literally.

Having laid out an alternative course of action, I was ready for the Finale.

I now turned to Elie Wiesel, to momentous applause.

Elie, your life and work inspires to give meaning to the words "Never Again."

I can guarantee you this. The days when the Jewish people remained passive in the face of genocidal enemies, *those days are over*. We are no longer scattered among the nations, powerless to defend ourselves. We restored our sovereignty in our ancient home. And the soldiers who defend our home have boundless courage. For the first time in one hundred generations, we, the Jewish people, can defend ourselves.

This is why as prime minister of Israel I can promise you one more thing: even if Israel has to stand alone, *Israel will stand*.

But I know that Israel does not stand alone. I know that America stands with Israel. I know that *you* stand with Israel.

You stand with Israel because you know that the story of Israel is not only the story of the Jewish people but of the human spirit that refuses again and again to succumb to history's horrors.

Facing me right up there in the gallery, overlooking all of us in this chamber, is the image of Moses, who led our people from slavery to the gates of the Promised Land. Moses gave the people of Israel resolve for thousands of years. I leave you with his message today: "Be strong and resolute, neither fear nor dread them."

My friends, may Israel and America always stand together, strong and resolute. May we neither fear nor dread the challenges ahead. May we face the future with confidence, strength, and hope.

May God bless the state of Israel and may God bless the United States of America.

I left the chamber to sustained applause, again shaking hands with the senators and representatives lining the aisles.

"What did you think?" I asked Ron Dermer.

"Mr. Prime Minister, you left it all out on the field," he said.

"What does that mean?" I asked, not familiar with the idiom.

"It means you rose to the occasion and did everything you could to make your case."

"I was never prouder of an Israeli prime minister," Elie Wiesel said to Sara.

In a reception of select members in a nearby room after the speech, Senate Minority Leader Chuck Schumer came over to me and told me that I had just moved six Democrats to support the Corker Bill, giving Congress a role in reviewing the nuclear deal with Iran.

I was relieved. I might not be able to stop Obama from signing a bad deal, but my speech had at least strengthened opposition to the nuclear deal in Congress and among the American people. It also helped turn Iran into the number one foreign policy issue of the 2016 American presidential election.

Every Republican running for the presidency opposed the deal and several leading Democrats did as well, including Senators Chuck Schumer and Bob Menendez, the ranking member of the Senate Foreign Relations Committee.

Two hours after I left the hall, Obama dismissed my speech as "nothing new."[7]

That was clearly not the case. In fact I had offered a completely different approach, tying a potential nuclear deal to a change in Iran's *behavior* and not to a mere change in the calendar.

The world press covered the speech with full force. The *Financial Times* in London wrote that my argument about the time frame of the deal "is likely to resonate with members of Congress from both parties who tend to be deeply critical about Iran."[8]

CNN described it as "combative and at times poetic."[9] Fox News said that I delivered a "strong message to Congress about [the] Iran deal."[10]

The *New York Times* wrote that I "used one of the world's most prominent venues to denounce a 'bad deal' being negotiated with Iran and to mount an audacious challenge to President Obama." It was "an extraordinary spectacle pitting the leaders of two close allies against each other."

The media in Israel did their best to criticize the speech and minimize its impact. But I was glad that, for a change, many Israelis had the opportunity to hear me directly on live television, over the heads of the snide commentators in the studios.

Back in the hotel, I was drained of energy, like a boxer after a bruising fight. I spent a few quiet hours with Sara. I thought of my grandfather Nathan, of my father, and of Yoni. I thought of Aaronsohn and Jabotinsky and of generations of Jews who fought to rekindle the flame of the Jewish national revival.

Seventy years after the Holocaust, the Jewish state had taken a powerful stand among the nations for its survival and its future. I called in the embassy staff and thanked them and singled out Ron Dermer.

Before I left Washington, an old colleague who was a Churchill buff approached me.

"Mr. Prime Minister," he said, "I've been following your activity for years, but now I want to tell you something.

"This was *your* finest hour."

5 5

LAST-MINUTE VICTORY

2015

After the speech, in America public opinion was firmly against the deal. This was true of Congress as well as the Senate, where 58 senators opposed it. While Obama avoided taking the deal to Congress for ratification, he could not stamp out this enduring public sentiment[1] that would legitimize a future withdrawal from the deal.

Back in Israel, the press and the opposition were in full swing to minimize this achievement.

"You don't know America," Yair Lapid patronized me in the media. "You've done irreparable damage to our relations with the United States."

This charge would be repeated ad nauseam by my political opponents in America and Israel alike: that my speech to Congress had wrecked bipartisan American support for Israel and made it a partisan issue. This became accepted as obvious truth. There was only one problem. It wasn't.

Each February, Gallup does a poll of American partisan attitudes toward Israel. Gallup polled Democrats in February 2015, a month before my appearance in Congress. Sympathy for Israel stood then at 49 percent. A year later, it had risen to 53 percent.[2]

There is a wide gap between the hostile attitude toward Israel of those in the political class, who had become more radical, and the general sentiment of Democratic voters, whose favorable attitude remained stable. This stability of Democratic favorability toward Israel is often misunderstood because it is overshadowed by Republican favorability, which has skyrocketed in the last decade.

While Israel faces a serious problem of vilification and slander on America's college campuses, which have veered sharply to the far left, it's worth noting that its favorability among the overall American public went up from 63 percent to a robust 75 percent during the twelve years I served in office from 2009 to 2021.[3]

Few countries enjoy such American support.

Of course, none of that mattered to my detractors. When I came back from Washington, an endless array of foreign policy and security experts who supported the nuclear deal were summoned to the television studios to buttress the argument that I had destroyed our relations with America. Since Israel's positive standing in the US was important to Israeli voters, the goal of these attacks was to lessen public support for my position. And it worked.

The incessant repetition of this allegation and the passage of a few days' time dissipated any immediate political boost I might have otherwise gained from the speech.

Likud now stood to lose the next election, scheduled for March 17, 2015. We had sunk into the twenty-seat range in the polls, well behind the newly named Zionist Camp, now headed by Isaac Herzog and Tzipi Livni, who together were projected to get thirty seats.

What to do? Rather than speaking optimistically about my chances for reelection and expressing confidence in Likud's victory, I did the opposite.

I pivoted right into the storm.

"If you don't come to vote, we're definitely going to lose," I told my supporters, making no attempt to hide my exasperation.

For close to four years, I had given almost no interviews to the Israeli press. Now, five days before the elections and with nothing to lose, I pulled out all the stops. I gave a firestorm of interviews to the mainstream and local media, from Radio Eilat to Radio Galilee.

The interviewers were initially shocked. They were used to politicians who expressed confidence in their party's prospects during elections, and so my dark forebodings were an unexpected twist. Some interviewers were happy to amplify my message of desperation, which they thought would demoralize Likud voters.

"Netanyahu is at wit's end."

"Netanyahu knows he's finished."

"This is the end of Likud."

This was music to my ears. When Likud voters understood the stakes involved, they rallied back to the party. Our numbers climbed.

Our opposition pulled out all the stops, too. A thinly disguised political NGO called V15, with a staff that included former Obama advisors, fueled an anti-Likud campaign with millions of dollars from abroad, including $300,000 given by the US State Department.[4]

This was highly questionable legally. The attorney general gave it a pass, however, arguing that V15 was not subject to campaign fundraising laws because it only *opposed* a particular party instead of *supporting* a specific one. Such flexibility was never shown to anyone on the right.

"They have V15," I said to my supporters in campaign rallies. "We have you."

Then I would invariably add, "But if you don't come out to vote on election day, we'll lose."

As our poll numbers began to recover, V15 began to worry. It worked doubly hard to mobilize voters from the left. On election day V15 went into full gear, concentrating on specific Arab and Jewish communities where there was practically no support for the Likud.

I took to the internet and the press to urge my supporters to come out and vote. At midday I received field reports of massive turnout for the Arab parties, which were always anti-Likud and anti-Zionist. In an eleventh-hour appeal to our voters, I sounded the alarm bell. The actual words I used were "Arab voters are flocking to the voting booths en masse." A much better formulation would have been "the voters of anti-Zionist Arab *parties* are flocking to the voting booths en masse and if you don't come to vote we will lose the election."

What I said was widely misrepresented as a slur against the right of Israeli Arabs to vote. It wasn't. Israeli Arabs voted for the Likud as well, and I consistently appealed to them in this election and in all elections.

But given my regret over the inconsiderate phrasing and my absolute conviction that every citizen, Arab and Jew, should have the right to vote, I called a meeting with pro-Zionist Arab leaders within forty-eight hours to apologize for any misunderstanding my words may have caused. Still, this incident has been used against me to this day.

Apparently many Israeli-Arab voters understood this distinction and appreciated the massive investment of my governments in their communities, because in future elections I would receive close to ten percent of their vote, an impressive showing for a Zionist party. Many Arab citizens want to be an integral part of the State of Israel and its success, and view the Likud under my leadership as the best vehicle for achieving a prosperous and secure future for themselves and their children.

This was in line with the liberal view of my father's mentor and the founder of my movement, Jabotinsky. He said about the future Jewish state, "There will dwell in abundance and bliss the son of Arabia, the son of Nazereth and my own son."[5]

At noon on election day, a holiday in Israel, I went to city centers and in the afternoon to Israel's beaches, literally pulling Likud voters out of the water to come and vote. As the hour neared for the closing of the polls, close friends and campaign staff crowded the prime minister's residence, but I still continued these exhortations to voters nonstop in live conversations on Facebook, right up to ten minutes before the polls closed.

"You're five minutes away from the polling station, Dina," I said in one of the last calls to a voter who thought she had missed her turn to vote.

"You can still make it. As long as you're in the voting hall before ten o'clock, your vote counts!"

"Okay, Bibi, I'm on my way!" she said. Many others did the same.

Five minutes before ten, I asked everyone to leave my small office. As was my custom, I stayed alone with Sara and the boys to hear the initial results of the exit polls.

At ten o'clock, the news programs reported the breaking information.

Likud had shot up well ahead of Livni and Herzog's Zionist Camp. A loud cheer shook the residence.

By morning the final results were Likud with 30 seats to 24 for the Zionist Camp. We had won decisively. With a few other parties, I was confident I could form a solid conservative block of 67 seats.

A week earlier, John McLaughlin, our able American pollster who became a personal friend, had said we were polling at "a weak twenty seats." Within seven days we had increased that number by 50 percent. Our Gevalt (Desperation) Campaign, as it came to be known, had won the day.

A month later I formed the government. It was not as easy as I had hoped. Lieberman decided not to take his six seats of predominantly right-wing Russian-speaking voters into the government, so my coalition was now sixty-one, hanging by a hair on one vote.

THE DEFECTION OF Lieberman, whose political career was launched after I appointed him director general of the Prime Minister's Office in my first term, was not the only time that I had experienced setbacks created by people who had worked with me.

A long political career like mine, spanning decades, inevitably produces personal disappointments. Close staff grow apart. Political allies whom I had nurtured later developed personal aspirations to lead the Likud or form their own parties, often after failing to replace me in party primaries. Disregarding their professed right-wing ideology, they would join the left in a quest for personal power.

Yet the overwhelming majority of my staff and supporters remained remarkably loyal to me for my close to forty years in public service. In many ways we've become a kind of family, from Eli Iluz, who has been my driver for thirty-five years, to the youngest additions, like the digital whiz kids Jonathan Urich and Topaz Luk, who joined me in their twenties shortly after their military service.

Topaz does hilarious impersonations of me. Once on an official visit to China, he called the Foreign Ministry office that had been set up in a Beijing hotel for my visit.

"Look," began Topaz, using a perfect rendition of my voice, "the manager of the Beijing Zoo wants to give me a panda as a personal gift. Please make the necessary arrangements to bring the panda on our return flight."

Fortunately this was stopped in time, before the press could concoct the "Panda Affair."

ON JULY 14, 2015, two months after forming my new government, the Iran nuclear deal was finalized. Dubbed the Joint Comprehensive Plan of Action (JCPOA), it laid out steps that would give Iran the unlimited right to enrich uranium, the critical component of nuclear bombs, within twelve years. It kept Iran's nuclear facilities intact with no effective inspection regime. It enabled Iran to continue developing ballistic missiles, including those that could potentially delver a nuclear payload to the US. By lifting sanctions it gave megabucks to the world's foremost practitioner of terror.

I attacked the deal mercilessly, calling it "a capitulation and a mistake of historic proportions." I said that Iran "will receive a sure path to nuclear weapons. Israel is not bound by this deal. We will always defend ourselves."

In my speech at the UN General Assembly a few months later, on October 1, 2015, I again ripped into the deal.

"Will the money now given to Iran by this agreement cause this leopard to change its spots? A rule of thumb I learned in life is that when you reward bad behavior, it gets worse."

I then went for the jugular, calling out the representatives before me, whose governments had praised the agreement to the gills.

> Seventy years after the murder of six million Jews, the rulers of Iran have promised to destroy my country, to murder my people. And the response from this body, the response of almost every country represented here has been . . . nothing!
>
> Complete and utter silence!
> Deafening silence!

I then stopped my speech and remained silent.

The audience moved uneasily in their chairs.

I remained on the podium and stared at the delegates for a full forty seconds, twenty seconds more than I had planned.

The delegates began looking at each other. They were literally squirming in their seats.

Finally, to rapt attention, I broke my silence.

"It's not easy to resist something that has been accepted by the leading powers of the world," I said. "Believe me, it's much easier to remain quiet. But over our long history, the Jewish people have learned the price of staying quiet. As the prime minister of the state of Israel, *I re-fuse to remain silent.* No matter what decision you reach here or in your capitals, Israel will do whatever it needs to do to protect itself and its people."

A few days earlier, I had voiced the same message in Moscow. Putin didn't particularly care about any action we took against Iran or its proxies in Syria. But he did care about the safety of his own military forces on Syria's soil, in its airspace, and especially its naval facilities in the Syria port of Latakia, on the Mediterranean.

The last thing Israel needed was a military clash with Russia. Once, in the crowded skies of Syria, our pilots nearly clashed with Russian pilots when we sent the IAF to destroy Iranian and Hezbollah military targets on Syrian soil. We tightened the screws on a deconfliction mechanism we had been refining between our armies to ensure that our forces would not clash inadvertently with each other.

At different times I brought to these coordination meetings in the Kremlin Israel's chief of intelligence, IAF commander, and the IDF chief of staff. Putin had their Russian counterparts present, too. We set up a hotline between the IDF and the Russian forces command in Syria. Just to make sure there were no miscommunications, we put native Russian speakers on our end of the line.

A few days after my visit to Moscow, just ahead of going to New York for my speech at the General Assembly, I went to Washington for my customary meeting with Obama at the White House.

He had one year left in his second term. The tension between us had subsided somewhat. We had settled into a routine in which each of us had staked out our positions. He had passed the JCPOA agreement with Iran, and I criticized it and vowed to do everything to roll it back and defend Israel against its consequences.

There was no point belaboring our differences over the Iran agreement. Obama was still intent on pushing for a Palestinian-Israeli deal. Most plans for a final settlement envisioned Israel trading unpopulated territory in its pre-1967 borders for populated Jewish areas in Judea and Samaria.

While not agreeing to the size of the "swaps," the delineation of the final borders, and the allocation of sovereign powers, I offered a conceptual twist that could introduce some flexibility into future negotiations: a three-way swap.

This idea was not new. Why not throw it back in the mix? It was better than a unilateral Palestinian state on the 1967 lines, which was something that I feared Obama would try to pass in a UN Security Council resolution before he left office.

I raised this three-way swap proposal in the Oval Office.

What if Israel stepped the Sinai border fence back into Israeli territory by a kilometer or two, all along its two-hundred-kilometer length? That would provide Egypt 200–400 square kilometers, which it could then give in equivalent territory to crowded Gaza, assuming the Palestinian Authority would one day replace Hamas.

A similar swap could be made along Israel's two-hundred-kilometer eastern border with Jordan along the Arava Valley. Jordan could then offer the Palestinians an equivalent amount of territory east of the Jordan. These swaps along Israel's two long borders would give the Palestinians additional territory while enabling Israel to keep valuable strategic lands within Judea and Samaria and maintain the Jewish communities and the Biblical sites in the heart of our historical homeland.

Secretary of State Kerry thought the three-way swap was worth a try, and Obama agreed. Three months later, in February 2016, I secretly met Jordan's King Abdullah, Egypt's President el-Sisi and Secretary Kerry in Aqaba.

Pleasant though the meeting was, the idea didn't get off the ground. When push came to shove, neither Abdullah nor el-Sisi would agree to it.

There was an eerie feeling in these collective meetings. Whenever I met with el-Sisi discreetly in Sharm el-Sheikh and with Abdullah in Amman, the talk was much more open and frank. But in the presence of our "American uncle," they reverted to traditional Arab positions that left little room for creativity.

Neither leader wanted to be exposed before his own people, let alone before another Arab leader, ceding on territorial negotiations with Israel of any sort. This of course didn't prevent cash-strapped Egypt from selling two islands in the Red Sea to Saudi Arabia in 2016. Though we knew we were making progress in our relations with the Arab world, there was still a ways to go.

Coming back from Aqaba, I decided to hold a primary in the Likud party to minimize internal strife in the party over the next few years. I insisted on holding direct, democratic elections among the Likud's 120,000 registered voters for Knesset candidates and for party leader. I didn't want to mirror most other parties, which had shifted to one-man rule and eliminated party primaries. Lapid and Lieberman, for example, named themselves as heads of their Knesset lists and appointed the list members without any party electoral body choosing the candidates. This didn't prevent them from castigating me as a dictator.

But this time no opposing candidate emerged to challenge me. It was the most unsatisfactory victory I had, but it saved the party more than one million dollars.

In May 2016, Lieberman finally decided to join the government as defense minister, giving the coalition a comfortable and secure majority. I breathed more freely. It seemed I now had a clear horizon of governance for the next four years.

But it was not to be.

The press was rife with rumors of a police investigation that would soon open up against me. For the next six years I would be subject to successive outlandish and politicized investigations.

Since I was winning one election after another, many believed this was the only way to remove me from Israel's political scene.

IN JUNE 2016, Putin invited Sara and me to Moscow for the twenty-fifth anniversary of the reestablishment of relations between Russia and Israel.

A few decades earlier we were shooting each other's planes over the skies of Suez. Now we were coordinating on how *not* to do so over the skies of Syria.

This event marked another great change. In the decades since the fall of the Soviet Union, a million Russian speakers had migrated to Israel, forming the largest community of Russian speakers outside the former Soviet Union.

These Russian-speaking Jews, whose release had been at the heart of our conflict with the former Soviet Union, now formed a cultural bridge between Israel and Russia. Even before their arrival in Israel, we who grew up in Israel were well familiar with Russian songs from World War II and from the Komsomol (the Soviet youth organization) that had been turned into Hebrew folk songs.

Our Russian hosts put up a production to celebrate these common bonds through music. A succession of Israeli and Russian artists sang the songs onstage.

Putin and I then went onstage to thank the artists. When we joked about where Russian Jews should live, I blurted: "May the best economy win."

Putin didn't seem to mind. Later I asked him to help us retrieve the remains of Israeli MIAs scattered in Syria. His forces succeeded in finding the remains of IDF soldier Zachary Baumel, who had fallen in the 1982 Lebanon War. Zachary's family and the entire nation were grateful. Baumel was buried on Mount Herzl in 2019, thirty-seven years after his death.

Given our successful cooperation in avoiding an Israeli-Russian clash in Syria, I decided to be frank with Putin.

I told him I expected that Obama would bring a strong anti-Israel resolution to the Security Council in the two months, between the end of his second term and the inauguration of the next American president.

Such a resolution could ultimately lead to sanctions against Israel's economy and would undermine our security.

Given reports I had heard of Obama's pledge to Mahmoud Abbas that he would recognize a Palestinian state before he left office, and with the American president soon to be free of any electoral considerations, I thought a move against Israel was inevitable. To protect the interests of my country, I could only hope that Putin would use his influence to delay or prevent such a move.

Putin heard me out. What he would do about it remained to be seen.

56

RISING POWER

2015–2020

Despite the buzz of press leaks that I would soon undergo a criminal investigation, I returned from Russia and continued business as usual, or more precisely business *unusual*.

Fifteen years earlier I had laid out a vision for ensuring Israel's future by significantly enhancing its national power. I fought in the trenches as finance minister to revolutionize its economy. I used the extra cash generated by free market reforms to bolster its military and intelligence capabilities.

Now it was time to combine our economic and security prowess to achieve a flourishing in international relations. These new partnerships would in turn open up new markets to further strengthen our economy and our military. Capitalizing on Israel's proven economic and technological achievements, and leveraging my personal standing on the world stage, I planned to reach out to countries on every continent and to all the great powers, thereby breaking once and for all the noose of isolation that the Arab economic boycott and its Palestinian successors had tried to place around Israel's neck.

But I was also aiming much higher than that.

It was time to establish Israel as a rising power in the world.

I began in Africa.

On July 4, 2016, the fortieth anniversary of the Entebbe Rescue, I visited Entebbe once again, this time with a large governmental delegation.

Climbing the control tower next to the Old Terminal I could still see the bullet holes left by Yoni's men. After a brief ceremony in the airfield, I went to a meeting at Ugandan president Yoweri Museveni's residence in Kampala, where he hosted a meeting with the leaders of Ethiopia, Kenya, Rwanda, South Sudan, and Zambia and a senior representative from Tanzania.

After the 1973 Yom Kippur War, Israel was kicked out of nearly every African country, but in recent years, its experts in agriculture, water management, public health, and telecommunications became increasingly sought after on the continent.

"Israel is coming back to Africa, and Africa is coming back to Israel," I said to the assembled leaders.

Opening up Africa as a market for Israeli goods and services was important, but even more important in my eyes was opening it up *politically*. African countries comprised some fifty of the UN's 192 members. Nearly all these countries automatically voted against Israel at the UN's various bodies. By prying away half a dozen countries I could begin to crack that anti-Israel bloc.

Within three years I visited Africa *four* times. In addition to Uganda, I visited Kenya, Rwanda, Chad, and Ethiopia. In Liberia I attended the annual conference of the Economic Community of West African States (ECOWAS), the only non-African leader to be invited. The same was true of the inauguration ceremony of Uhuru Kenyatta's second term as president of Kenya.

Those visits reverberated throughout the continent. Many countries became interested in making partnerships with Israel to better the lives of their people. Israeli condensation technology enabled Africans to produce water in their villages instead of walking miles each day to distant water sources; Israeli agricultural know-how multiplied the productivity of their crops; Israeli diagnostic methods helped them arrest the spread of HIV/AIDS.

The Palestinian Authority grew agitated. I was pleased to read the reports about its concern that "Israel is cutting into our traditional support in Africa."

Indeed we were. But the Palestinians were powerless to prevent many African countries from acting in their own self-interest. Visiting Chad, a huge country in the center of Africa battling Islamist terrorists, I quickly established full diplomatic relations, prying another Muslim country out of the anti-Israel coalition.

All these visits were firsts for an Israeli prime minister. But the trip that resonated most with symbolism was my visit to Ethiopia.

The contacts between the Jewish and Ethiopian peoples dated back to the Queen of Sheba's visit to King Solomon in Jerusalem three thousand years ago.

"This is a long-overdue reciprocal visit," I said to the Ethiopian parliament at Addis Ababa. "I'm sure it won't take another three thousand years until the next visit."

Joining me on the trip to Ethiopia were Ethiopian Jews who had emigrated to Israel, and who were deeply moved by the visit.

Many African leaders visited Israel at my invitation. Sara had wisely told me to do away with the large dinners that we held for visiting foreign leaders during my first term as prime minister. Hundreds of people would attend these mass events during which my guests and I could barely get a word in edgewise.

"Invite them to intimate dinners at the residence instead," Sara said. "That's how you build real personal bonds."

This was by far the best piece of advice I got on fostering personal diplomacy. During these quiet evenings, sometimes attended by our spouses, my guests and I would let our guard down in ways not possible in official meetings. We were naturally curious about each other's lives, what motivated our entry into politics, how we viewed the future of our countries and our own contributions to it. No briefing papers from the Foreign Ministry or the Mossad even came close to offering such insights.

Nearly always the talk would eventually turn to the United States.

"Could you help us with the administration? With Congress? With the American Jewish community? With the evangelicals?"

My responses were always measured and truthful. Sometimes we could help, at other times we couldn't. I was careful not to promise what I couldn't deliver. But clearly, my clash with the US president in Congress in 2015 had not diminished my standing in the eyes of international leaders. To the contrary. More than anything else, that speech and the multiple standing ovations it received increased it beyond what I could have expected.

Israel's international standing was boosted by the fact that I was repeatedly ranked by *Forbes* magazine among the most powerful people in the world, one of only four political leaders to consistently appear in each listing for over a decade.

FROM THE START I believed that a strong economy was vital to create Israeli power and to sustain it. I now focused my efforts on rapidly expanding Israel's economic potential.

There are basically two ways to expand a country's economy. You either create new products or you create new markets. Israel, I believed, could do both.

In the recently liberated Israeli economy, ingenious entrepreneurs were creating new and exciting products and services. I believed the government's role should be to interfere as little as possible in their activities and aid them with tax cuts, export credit guarantees, subsidized R&D and deregulation.

I squelched overregulation by requiring government ministries to give a cost estimate and a source of funding for each new regulation, and demanded the removal of an old regulation in exchange for any new one proposed.

The Chief Scientist's Office concentrated on encouraging innovation. I gave an annual prime minister's prize for innovation and an annual prize for advances in carbon-free transportation, generously provided by the Samson family from South Africa.

I was repeatedly invited to speak at the World Economic Forum in Davos, Switzerland, where I met some of the world's greatest tech entrepreneurs. With Bill Gates I discussed my goal of giving Israeli children who came from low-income homes access to affordable computers under a program I called "A Computer for Every Child." Gates approved of the initiative and gave the impression of being easygoing as well as eminently practical. Alternatively, a T-shirt-clad Mark Zuckerberg, then in his twenties, struck me as unusually intense and totally focused on his mission, a man in a hurry. After meeting in Davos, on one or two occasions in later years, we spoke on the phone on matters relating to internet regulations, something that as a believer in market forces and freedom of speech I was naturally loath to do.

I was delighted when both Microsoft and Facebook recognized Israel's technological prowess and established vibrant R&D centers in the country. Google, Apple and the other technological giants would do the same. Many bought Israeli companies, as did Warren Buffett, whose first acquisition outside the United States was an Israeli precision blade company named ISCAR, established by the visionary Stef Wertheimer. When I visited ISCAR's plant on a remote hill in the Galilee, I was amazed. The robotized facility was shipping precision blades to Japan! Talk about selling snow to the Eskimos.

Another memorable encounter was with Elon Musk. Over breakfast at the Balfour residence in 2018, I was deeply impressed by the clarity and boldness of his vision for the future.

Discussing Israel, he made some startling suggestions for developing solar energy and for revolutionizing inner-city transport with novel tunnel technology that he was working on. If proven practical, this could complement my vision of connecting Israel with north–south bullet trains that would eliminate the concept of periphery and would further interlink the vast network of highways and railways that we were already in the process of building.

Musk, though clearly aware of his exceptional capabilities, was down-to-earth and spoke matter-of-factly about things he was doing that were changing the world. All these inspiring entrepreneurs clearly appreciated Israel as a force for innovation.

And no wonder: with our free market policies, Israeli innovation thrived. Israel produced hundreds of agrotech start-ups, some specializing in precision agriculture. Why irrigate an entire field equally when you can use a drone and sensors on the ground to tell you which part of the field is parched and which is not? Relaying this information to computerized drip irrigation systems that Israel had already developed saved water and improved yields.

Sometimes agricultural innovation popped up in surprising places. My friend Shlomi Fogel, a successful entrepreneur of varied companies, developed a taste for blueberries, a fruit thought to be hard to grow in Israel. Applying ingenious technology, he built a largely robotic farm on the Golan Heights that grows blueberries and raspberries that compete with the best producers in the world.

This is but one small example of ingenuity by many thousands of Israeli start-ups. Such inventiveness opened doors worldwide.

Hundreds of water technology start-ups sprang up in Israel, many piggybacking on the massive investments we had made in desalination. In 2009, facing a severe water shortage, I had passed a decision in the government to build three huge desalination plants on the Mediterranean. If we needed more water, we could simply make it, and with surprising efficiency. Israel also led the world in treating sewage, recycling roughly 90 percent of our wastewater. The runner-up, Spain, recycled some 20 percent.

Meeting foreign leaders around the world, I would present these facts, and then ask a question.

"Which country produces the most milk per cow?" I asked.

"Holland, France, the US," were the common answers. But here too Israel was ahead of the pack.

"You see," I would tell the leaders, "the Israeli cow is special. Every *moo* is computerized. After all, we are the Land of Milk and Honey."

Visiting Japan in May 2014, I formed a close personal bond with its dynamic prime minister, Shinzo Abe. At the time very few Japanese companies invested in Israel.

"Why so few?" I asked him.

He explained that Japan's Foreign Ministry was weary of the Arab boycott.

"What boycott?" I asked. "Don't they know it's finished? Many Arab countries are trading with us, some even without intermediaries."

After visiting an automotive innovation site in Tokyo, I approached Abe.

"You know, we have a car industry, too."

"I didn't know that," he answered.

"Well, it's not called a car industry but there are hundreds of Israeli start-ups developing the software that is the future of automobiles."

Israeli companies had developed such groundbreaking technologies as the crowdsourcing GPS navigation system Waze, which had been sold to Google in 2014, and Mobileye's autonomous driving system, which was sold to Intel in 2017 for $15 billion.

"The Americans, Germans and French carmakers are already investing in Israel. Why should Japan be left out? Come to Israel and see for yourself," I suggested to Abe.

He did, making two visits. He immediately grasped the opportunities for Israeli-Japanese cooperation in automotive technology, financial technology, and many other fields. On his second visit he brought with him many leading Japanese CEOs, a clear signal to Japan's private sector that doing business with Israel was, well, kosher.

Within four years, many of Japan's leading companies had invested billions of dollars in R&D and joint ventures with Israeli companies.

The visits of most foreign leaders in Israel were barely mentioned by the Israeli media, for fear such coverage would strengthen me politically. But Abe's second visit was an exception. The creative chef we invited to prepare dinner for Abe and his wife had placed the salad in a ceramic dish in the shape of a shoe.

"Netanyahu Insults Japan's Prime Minister," ran one headline. Abe laughed.

When he was tragically assassinated in Japan in mid-2022, I was dumbfounded. Israel and I had lost a true friend. When I left office in 2021 and before his own departure from office for reasons of health, Abe asked me to address by phone a special cabinet meeting in which he thanked me for my friendship and expressed his appreciation for our joint efforts to cement relations between Israel and Japan. What a loss. What a man.

HAVING HELPED UNLEASH Israel's technological ingenuity by liberalizing the economy, most of my other job was to help sell it to the world.

But there were two areas that required direct intervention on my part. The first was natural gas. Israel was always an energy importer, highly dependent on foreign supply. If we could become an energy exporter, we would help the Israeli economy, lower energy costs for citizens and industry alike, clean up the air and strengthen our diplomatic ties.

For decades a government-run company searched for offshore gas.

It found nothing. Shortly after we enabled private companies to join the search, they found significant gas reserves off our Mediterranean coast.

A battle now ensued on two fronts: I needed to increase the government's share in the gas revenues, and to overcome environmental objections to taking the gas out of the sea.

To resolve the first issue I authorized Energy Minister Yuval Steinitz to set up a special public commission headed by a respected economist. Though it suggested changing the terms of the original government contract with the private gas firm, something I would normally be loath to do, I nevertheless adopted the commission's recommendations. The gas belonged to the people, and the gas revenues for the private companies were still enormous, even after the commission's adjustments.

Now came the second battle, truly incredible even in the twisted world of the Israeli left. A vast public campaign was launched to keep the gas in the seabed. The argument was not simply environmental preservation, since this could be addressed without keeping the treasured gas buried under the sea, but also to "maintain the gas for future generations."

This approach was applied in several countries, stalling the economic benefits of gas exploration for many years. After endless battles, and after many discussions with the American company Nobel Energy, which invested in a gigantic gas rig, Steinitz and I got the legislation and agreements approved.

Israel would soon sell gas to its neighbors in Egypt and Jordan.

We also laid plans for an underwater pipeline that would supply gas in the future from Israel and Cyprus to Europe. In 2020 we started selling gas to Europe through Egypt's liquefied natural gas facility. For the first time in its history, Israel would become energy independent and an energy exporter.

THE SECOND AREA I directly intervened in was cyber.

In 2011, I was approached by Professor Isaac Ben Israel, an ex-military officer who often advised me on scientific matters.

"I want you to read this book," he said.

"What is it?" I asked.

"It's a novel," he said.

"I don't read novels," I answered. I was a reader of history, biographies, books on political philosophy, archaeology and natural history, technology and economics.

"You'll want to read this one," the professor insisted.

The book described a future cyber war between the US and China. To me it didn't sound all that fictional.

I called Ben Israel the next day.

"I stayed up all night and finished reading the book. Come over as soon as you can."

While Israel had certain cyber capabilities already in place, the book convinced me we had to move forward much faster. We could not afford to be left behind.

I formed a steering committee with Ben Israel and my military secretary, Yohanan Locker, to develop the organizations, funding and procedures to jump-start Israel into cyberspace.

The first reason for this cyber drive was security. We could not be left defenseless against this powerful new technology. In remarks I gave at Tel Aviv University in June 2011, I said: Within five years Israel must be among the top five cyber powers in the world.

The introduction of cyber warfare was akin to the introduction of airpower in World War I. It required setting up an entirely new force with an entirely new *doctrine*. This entailed massive investment in the military, the Mossad and Shin Bet, alongside programs to recruit the most talented students from a young age and create new university departments.

It also necessitated the setting up of a national center of cyber defense to protect Israeli companies.

I appointed Professor Eviatar Matania, a graduate of the Talpiot program, to head this effort and met with him regularly.

Where do you start?

You can defend the IDF or the Mossad, but how do you defend against cyber penetration of the company that cleans their offices? Or the health clinics that service their personnel? How do you defend the electricity grid from cyberattacks that can shut down the country? Do you mandate cyber defense for private sector companies or leave it on a volunteer basis?

These were but a tiny fraction of the challenges we faced, along with the inevitable turf wars between security agencies as to who should do what.

There was no blueprint for any of this. All the advanced countries were grappling with the same questions, looking over each other's shoulders for clues on what to do.

I decided that the only way to move forward in this vast uncharted terrain was . . . *to move forward*.

I fell back on a well-known drill in the military. When Jeeps, tanks and armored personnel carriers are scattered aimlessly in the field, the commander issues an order.

"Follow me. Fall in line as you advance."

You decide on a direction, go forward, and let others follow. Sometimes a movement in a clear direction, even though not perfectly organized, is better than stagnation. Things sort themselves out and corrections are made as you go along.

This is what we now did.

Settling the bureaucratic turf battles between our security agencies, I established a National Cyber Headquarters on August 7, 2011, allocated responsibilities and tasks and appointed people to carry them out.

The massive government investment in cybersecurity helped spawn hundreds of new cyber companies. They fiercely competed with each other to recruit graduates from the intelligence units of the IDF and the security agencies.

What began as a security challenge now evolved into a great economic opportunity. In a digital world, cyber protection was needed everywhere and cyber companies mushroomed. But this growth could be easily stunted by overregulation.

One area where we did install regulation was in foreign sales of cyber capabilities. We made sure that such sales, especially to governments, would be carefully regulated by a special arm of the defense department, each sale requiring its strict approval.

But there were other areas in which we could help Israel's cyber companies. I let these companies import foreign specialists for special "fellowships" in Israel, thus helping address their number one problem—human capital. Many companies brought in people from Cyprus, Eastern

Europe and elsewhere to further fill the shortage, and also expanded their activities abroad. Soon the demand for Israeli cyber services was outstripping supply.

By 2017, Israel accounted for the second-largest number of cybersecurity deals globally, behind the US and ahead of the UK.[1] We had reached my target.

Being familiar with the growing cyberattack capabilities of enemies and friends alike, I studiously avoided using cell phones. They were banished from my office, as were computers, television screens and other gadgets that could give adversaries audio and visual access to Israel's most sensitive discussions.

Little did I imagine that just a few years later, the most advanced Israeli spyware on the planet would be used against my inner circle in order to illegally penetrate their lives and help coerce them to come out against me. Additional legal restrictions wouldn't have made a difference. This was already illegal. But in the race to oust me from office, overzealous police investigators committed this criminal act just the same.

Of course, I had no foreknowledge of any of this. But I was subjected to an increasing trickle of press leaks from the police about my purported wrongdoings. These illegal leaks later turned into a veritable flood, but even this did not distract me from my grand plan. I was on a mission.

WITH THE ENTREPRENEURIAL and technological revolution well under way, I moved with great speed to further open new economic and political markets for Israel, thereby creating the foundation for new international alliances.

In addition to my four visits to Africa, I forayed into Latin America, visiting Brazil, Mexico, Colombia and Argentina, the first time a sitting Israeli prime minister had visited those countries.

Targeting Asia, I visited China, India, Japan, Australia and Singapore.

In Thessaloniki, Greece, I met the leaders of Greece and Cyprus to solidify a tripartite East Mediterranean alliance.

I visited Azerbaijan and Kazakhstan, two large Muslim countries, and discussed with them, and later with Russia, Israel's entry as an associate into the fifteen-member Asian trading bloc known as the Regional Comprehensive Economic Partnership (RCEP).

In Vilnius, Lithuania, I met the leaders of the three Baltic countries: Lithuania, Estonia and Latvia. In Budapest, hosted by Hungary's unabashedly pro-Israel prime minister, Viktor Orban, I met the other leaders of the Visegrad Group countries—Poland, the Czech Republic, and Slovakia.

With many of these countries, we signed a host of agreements simplifying tax treaties, trade investment, and technological exchanges. I usually brought along delegations of Israeli businesspeople who met with their local counterparts, and when foreign leaders visited Israel many of them did the same.

In a closed meeting in Budapest in July 2017 with the leaders of the four Visegrad countries, I railed against the European Union policy of conditioning technological treaties with Israel on political progress with the Palestinians.

"Are these people in Brussels mad?" I asked. "We live in a technological age and Israel is a technological powerhouse. They're cutting their own nose to spite their face."

Because of a technical error, my scathing remarks on the EU bureaucracy were heard over the earpieces of the journalists waiting outside the hall. They were quickly broadcast for all the world to hear.

Rather than retreat, I again went straight into the line of fire. In Brussels a few months later I delivered the same message, albeit in more polite language, to twenty-eight European foreign ministers.

These world-encompassing tours to promote Israeli technology and prestige contrasted sharply with practices by past Israeli prime ministers. In the previous six decades, Israeli leaders focused their travels mostly on North America and Western Europe, believing that these places constituted the heart of the international community. Israel usually went there as a supplicant, asking for political and economic favors.

I was bent on changing this equation. And as Israel's power grew, it changed beyond recognition.

Countries were now coming to Israel for things *they* wanted from *us*, from groundbreaking civilian technology to security assistance and counterterrorism intelligence. Most of their governments couldn't be bothered with the traditional Palestinian political straitjacket. At most, some of the leaders would perfunctorily read some obligatory lines about the need to solve the Israel-Palestinian conflict, occasionally adding the need for a two-state solution.

Then we would get to the real business of cementing the ties between our countries.

This gradually became true even of the last holdouts, the Western Europeans. Though they still gave weight to the Palestinian issue, they too wanted to enjoy the benefits of Israeli technology.

In London, Paris, Berlin and Rome, I now asked to see the leaders of their respective business communities, many of whom eagerly came to meet me. When European leaders came to Israel, they in turn brought with them business delegations to specially organized exhibits of Israeli technology.

Israel, known in its early years as an exporter of Jaffa oranges and diamonds, was rapidly becoming recognized as one of the world's premier high-tech powers.

"How do we replicate the Israeli miracle?" many foreign leaders kept asking me.

"Oh, that's easy," I would answer. "Take a hefty dose of free market reforms, mix in heavy investments in military technology, shrink your country to a tiny area in which everyone meets everyone, and add a questioning ancient culture that is never satisfied with the status quo."

This was usually met with laughter.

SOMETIMES THE LAUGHTER came from an unexpected source, totally unrelated to the weighty subjects we discussed.

On a visit to Rome early in my second term as prime minister, I had met with its mercurial prime minister, Silvio Berlusconi.

"So, Bibi," he asked me, "how many television stations do you have?"

"Israel has three stations," I answered.

"No, I mean how many of them work for you?" asked Silvio, who owned Italy's largest media empire.

"None," I said. "Actually, all of them work against me."

"So how can you win elections with both hands tied behind your back?" he asked, bewildered.

"The hard way," I said.

Berlusconi's occasional pranks and lighthearted manner masked a sharp intelligence. Many of his ideas about reforming Italy's economy were right, but they met an iron wall of union and special interest obstacles that neither he nor any other Italian leader was able to crack.

He was decidedly pro-Israel and friendly. On his visit to Jerusalem in February 2010, he movingly told the Knesset of his mother's courageous stand against an SS officer, by which she saved a Jewish train passenger from certain death.

Berlusconi had a proclivity for provocation. In a press conference in a splendid Italian villa with both of us onstage facing the cameras, he gave a brief description of the site's historical background.

Flashing a slide that showed an erotic Renaissance scene, he said, "Here they did the bonga-bonga."

Toasting our delegation at lunch, he discussed his own standing in Italian public opinion.

"They published a poll the other day," he said, "asking Italian women, did you sleep with Silvio Berlusconi? Thirty-six percent said they had, the rest answered with a question: 'Just once?' "

So outrageous was this statement that it induced paroxysms of awkward laughter by many of those present, men and women alike.

As Israel was becoming a rising power in the world, heads of state from nearly all major countries visited it. One notable exception was the British royal family. It took seventy years after Israel's independence for a member of the British royal family to make an official visit to Israel. This glaring omission was probably advised by the hopelessly Arabist British Foreign Office, which had no problem sending royals to other countries in the Middle East. (State funerals provided the sad exception—Prince Charles had attended the funerals of Rabin in 1995 and Peres in 2016.)

I thought it offensive that the one true democracy in the Middle East was not a suitable destination for a royal visit from the mother of modern democracies. I communicated this to the British government in meetings with their officials and diplomats in 2017 and 2018.

"You're among the last to know that in today's technological world visiting Israel is an asset, not a liability," I said to a senior British official.

This was corrected in 2018 when Prince William visited Israel, making a great splash. The public loved him.

Sara, the boys and I greeted him in Balfour.

William was surprised by Avner's mastery of detail about William's favorite soccer team, Aston Villa. Avner's favorite team was Manchester United. I recounted my positive impression of its legendary coach, Sir Alex Ferguson, whom I had once met at a New York restaurant. William and I discussed the role of helicopters in military search and rescue operations, a topic he as a pilot was familiar with and I had experience in as a special forces officer in need of heliborne extraction.

We then discussed three extraordinary women who had great influence on William's life and heritage. Sara told him how much her mother admired his grandmother, Queen Elizabeth.

"My mother always told me that the Queen was very intelligent because she knows how to listen," Sara said.

Williams eyes lit up. "She is very much that, and an excellent listener," he responded.

In a private moment in my study, Sara also told William how much she identified with his mother, Princess Diana.

"I think about her every day," said William softly.

Perhaps the most moving part of the visit for me involved William's great-grandmother, Princess Alice. While a nun in Athens during the Nazi occupation of Greece in World War II, she sheltered Jewish refugees and was later honored by Yad Vashem, Israel's Holocaust memorial, with the title of Righteous Among the Nations—a designation for non-Jewish individuals who risked their lives to aid Jews. We brought some of the descendants of the families saved by Alice to meet her great-grandson. They expressed their deep appreciation for the woman who made their lives possible. William was visibly moved. Princess Alice died in 1969, but per her request, her remains were later moved from England to Jerusalem.

Two years after William's visit, in January 2020, Prince Charles attended a ceremony in Jerusalem marking the 75th anniversary of the liberation of Auschwitz. The prince, whom I had first met at King Hussein's funeral in 1999, approached me.

"Don't you *ever* age?" he joked.

These visits were a symbolic expression of the close relations between Britain and Israel—countries which exchanged billions of dollars in trade and over time increasingly cooperated in fighting terror—and did a great deal to correct a historical omission.

57

WALKING AMONG THE GIANTS

2016–2018

In January 2016, I was invited for my third official visit to China as prime minister.

The China of 2016 was certainly a far cry from what I had seen nearly two decades earlier, on my first visit. The bicycles and dilapidated buildings had been replaced by rivers of cars and forests of skyscrapers, serviced by a network of modern highways.

Reformist Chinese leader Deng Xiaoping's decision to liberate the Chinese economy in the 1980s had led to the reinstatement of China's position as an economic superpower, steadily encroaching on the US for the top spot. While no one should sell short the awesome power of America and its free market creativity, it was still wise to heed Kissinger's observation that, except for the last three centuries, China had the largest GDP on earth going back two millennia.

Could anyone seriously discount its ascendancy in the twenty-first century?

China was now led by Xi Jinping, a very different man from his predecessor, the jovial Jiang Zemin.

Xi was quiet and serious, totally focused on his mission to make China a leading, or more precisely *the* leading, power in the world. But he was also fully aware of the fact that China's rapid growth exacted a great price on its people, including heavy urban smog, water pollution and many related health problems.

He clearly understood that Israel was a fount of technology that China could not afford to overlook in seeking to solve these problems. Why else would he roll out the red carpet, ceremonies and all, and host an intimate dinner with the leader of a small country that comprised a tiny fraction of the world's population?

Over dinner I described to him Israel's unique health care system, which had computerized medical records for 98 percent of the population. If Israelis from Tel Aviv needed emergency treatment in a hospital in Beer-Sheba, their medical histories were instantly available, often saving lives and ensuring correct treatment.

One of my aides took out his computerized medical card to illustrate this point.

Xi asked to see the card and held it his hand.

"Mr. Chairman," I said, "I'm afraid you'll need another billion of these to make it work in China."

As the laughter subsided, I thought of another difference that I didn't mention. In Israel the government had no access to personal files, and patient privacy was strictly observed.

Like most Western leaders, I walked a fine line with China. On the one hand, I wanted to open the enormous Chinese market to Israel and also lure Chinese investments to Israel, particularly in physical infrastructure.

On the other, I was totally frank about setting clear limitations on what types of technologies we would share with China, stopping when it came to military and intelligence fields. This was our solemn commitment to our great ally the United States, with whom we shared much of this technology, as well as our cherished values as democratic societies.

The visit to China was a great success. In addition to China's political leaders, I met with the heads of its mammoth tech companies and was given the special honor of being invited to address a special college where China's future leaders were being trained.

"What's Israel's secret recipe?" the up-and-coming young Chinese bureaucrats asked me. I gave a truthful if diplomatically worded answer: "It's the freedom to innovate." After giving several interviews to Chinese television and media outlets, I was surprised to see people pointing to me on the streets. I suppose that an audience of hundreds of millions was a reasonable explanation for this.[1]

A few years later, in October 2018, China sent its senior vice president, Wang Qishan, to Israel. Our goal was to complete a technological and economic cooperation agreement between China and Israel, something we had been working on for years.

Wang's visit started with a private dinner at the Balfour residence. Even in this intimate setting, it began stiffly.

"Israel and China have much in common," I said, trying to break the ice.

"Population," I said.

No laughter.

"Size."

Still no laughter.

"Geography."

A third failed try.

Then the Chinese vice president suddenly spoke up, saying, "Sometimes nations can overcome the limitations of geography."

"What?" I said. "That sounds like something from Will Durant."

Wang became all excited. "Do you read Will Durant? I've read all his books," he said.

"So have I," I responded.

Rising from my chair, I went into my study and brought back a copy of Durant's *Lessons of History*.

Sure enough, there on page 17 was the quote, written perceptively by Durant almost fifty years earlier, with its reference to Israel: "The influence of geographic factors diminishes as technology grows.... Only the imagination and initiative of leaders, and the hardy industry of followers . . . as in Israel today can make a culture take form over a thousand obstacles. Man, not earth, makes civilization."

From that point on, the conversation flowed freely. We spent three days together, visiting R&D centers that specialized in agriculture, medicine, robotics, and other technologies.

The visit had far-reaching consequences. The two of us presided over the signing of the economic cooperation agreement, a goal many nations had sought and failed to reach—at the time, Switzerland was the only other country that had a similar agreement in place with China.

There was also a personal postscript to the visit. Later, when Avner completed his military service, he went trekking for six months in Australia and New Zealand. Bringing the role of Jewish mother to new heights, Sara joined him for three weeks. Mercifully, he spared her the experience of seeing him bungee-jump off a bridge and also cut his grueling treks to ten kilometers a day.

Coming back to Israel, Sara made a stopover in China. The Chinese government gave her a VIP tour of the Forbidden City. They also took her to a specially established Museum of Innovation, filled with photos of China's technological developments.

Sara couldn't believe her eyes. Right opposite the entrance, below a photograph of Xi, was a photograph of Vice President Wang Qishan and me at the signing of the China-Israel agreement, the only foreign leader featured in the museum.

When I saw that photo, I was grateful once again to Father for having introduced me to Will Durant half a century earlier. Just to make sure I wasn't being starry-eyed, I asked our ambassador in Beijing to visit the museum six months later. The photo was still there.

In the months before Wang Qishan's visit, direct flights between China and Israel had already been opened. I believed this was critical: even in the digital age, there was no substitute for face-to-face meetings between technologists, entrepreneurs, and businesspeople. We also already had in place the most important direct flight, from Tel Aviv to San Francisco, connecting innovators in Israel's Silicon Wadi to their counterparts in America's Silicon Valley.

In addition to China, I had and continued to make a concerted effort to open up two other gigantic markets—India and Brazil—to Israeli products and services as well. Together with China these countries comprised a full third of the world's population.

Brazil was historically cool to Israel. Meeting its president, Michel Temer, at the United Nations in 2017 right after my visit to Mexico, Colombia, and Argentina, I was pleasantly surprised to receive an invitation to visit the country.

"Why didn't you come to visit us as well?" asked the president.

"I wasn't invited," I replied.

"You are now," said the president.

I learned that Brazil had the fastest-growing evangelical community on the planet, with a larger-than-life reconstruction of the Second Temple.

When Temer was succeeded by President Jair Bolsonaro in 2018, the latter reissued Temer's invitation to visit Brazil and also attend his inauguration on January 1, 2019. I accepted.

The controversial and conservative Bolsonaro, who had visited Israel twice, was a strong supporter of fostering ties with Israel. Coming to Rio de Janeiro, I took a break to stroll along Copacabana Beach and joined an impromptu soccer game in the sand.

The people on the beach greeted me with supportive chants, and probably not because of my rusty soccer skills. This expression of support was loudly repeated by thousands of Brazilian evangelicals who saw me outside the palace in Brasilia during the inauguration ceremony.

The Bible can do wonders for diplomacy.

So can technology. When Narendra Modi, India's prime minister, visited Israel in July 2017, I accompanied him for four days. Having seen Israel's agricultural expertise when he was the governor of Gujarat, Modi was already favorably disposed to Israeli agricultural technology such as drip irrigation, but now he would see with his own eyes how far it had advanced.

Modi exuded warmth and directness. A practitioner of yoga, he expounded upon its spiritual and physical benefits. We hit it off immediately. On a beach in Givat Olga, near Hadera, I brought him a gift for the people of India, an Israeli outdoor vehicle fitted with a portable desalination unit.

It took water from the sea and a few minutes later, we were drinking desalinated water. At the urging of one of my aides, I took off my shoes. Modi did the same. The photograph of the two of us wading barefoot in the shallow water became iconic.

Even the Israeli press had to carry that one.

Six months later, in January 2018, I visited India with a huge business delegation. He accompanied me for four days, as I had done for him.

We visited Mumbai and Gujarat and R&D exhibits and met with Indian farmers.

"Prime Minister," said an Indian farmer, "Israeli experts increased my yield twofold."

"Mine threefold," chimed in her neighbor.

We visited Mahatma Gandhi's inspiring memorial and the home where he spun wool. The Indian government threw in a magnificent song-and-dance appearance by Bollywood stars and an unforgettable visit to the Taj Mahal for Sara and me.

In a private dinner at his residence, Modi and I sealed several important deals. I told him I never forgot the courage of the Indian soldiers who gave their lives to liberate Haifa from Ottoman rule a hundred years earlier.

IN SEPTEMBER 2017, I had made a speech at the UN that summed up the historical shift in Israel's international position.

> We're in the midst of a great revolution in Israel's standing among the nations. This is happening because so many countries around the world have finally woken up to what Israel can do for them. Those countries now recognize that Israel is *the* innovation nation—the place for cutting-edge technology in agriculture, in water, in cybersecurity, in medicine, in autonomous vehicles—you name it, we've got it.
>
> They also recognize Israel's exceptional capabilities in fighting terrorism. In recent years Israel has provided intelligence that has prevented dozens of major terrorist attacks around the world. We have saved countless lives.
>
> In one year hundreds of presidents, prime ministers, foreign ministers and other leaders have visited Israel, many for the first time, and I had the honor of representing my country on six different continents.
>
> One year, six continents.

Since this was the UN, I couldn't resist taking a swipe at the anti-Israel hypocrisy still prevailing in its various bodies.

"I haven't yet visited Antarctica," I said, "but I want to go there, too, because I've heard that penguins are also enthusiastic supporters of Israel. They have no difficulty recognizing that some things are black and white, right and wrong."

Yet it was the moments of deep historical reflection that moved me most in my journeys to foreign lands.

In Lithuania I stood atop the death pits where thousands of Jewish men, women and babies were shot. In Ukraine I visited Babi Yar, where Kyiv's Jews were massacred.

How far we had come!

Seventy years after the Holocaust, the Jewish state had finally rediscovered the capacity to resist the would-be destroyers of the Jewish people and to once again reassert Jewish power after undergoing incomparable suffering and savagery. Miraculously, the Jewish people had risen from the dead to take their place on the stage of history, just as Jeremiah, Isaiah and Ezekiel had prophesized.

Each year from 2015 to 2020, the University of Pennsylvania asked some seventeen thousand opinion leaders in twenty countries to rank the world's most powerful countries. With one-tenth of 1 percent of the world's population, tiny Israel now consistently ranked as the eighth most powerful country in the world.

58

PARTING SHOT

2016

O ne year earlier, I had made a very different sort of speech at the UN General Assembly.

It was September 2016, and I was acutely conscious of the fact that we were a mere four months away from the end of Obama's term. Anticipating that the president would bring an anti-Israeli resolution to the Security Council immediately after the US elections, when he would be freed of all political constraints, I wove this contingency into my speech.

I first ridiculed the unchanging, reflexive anti-Israel majorities at the UN, while the attitudes toward Israel on the part of so many of the individual states represented there had since moved on.

"Today's automatic majority against Israel at the UN reminds me of the incredible story of Hiroo Onoda," I said. I then told the story of a Japanese soldier who fought in the Philippines in World War II. Refusing to believe the war had ended, he lived in the jungle, scavenging for food, while Japanese tourists were vacationing in American-built hotels in nearby Manila. His former commanding officer finally convinced him in 1974 that he could come out of hiding and lay down his arms.

I then turned to the delegates.

"I have one message for you today: lay down your arms. The war against Israel at the UN is over."

By then some twenty countries that a few years earlier had supported anti-Israel resolutions no longer did so. But my main interest in that speech was to flag Obama's parting shot, which I believed was coming down the pike.

"I know there might be a storm before the calm," I said to the delegates. "I know there is talk about ganging up on Israel at the UN later this year. Given its history of hostility towards Israel, does anyone really believe that Israel will let the UN determine our security and our vital national interests?"

Beyond my conversation in Moscow and my hopes for a last-minute change of fortune, there was little I could do to stave off this ominous possibility. Earlier that summer, I had decided to concentrate instead on the one remaining item of business with the Obama administration: securing a Memorandum of Understanding for a ten-year military assistance program.

The first such MOU was forged during my initial term as prime minister. In the wake of my speech to Congress in 1996 calling for the end of economic assistance to Israel, I negotiated with the Clinton administration a deal in which an annual $1.2 billion of economic assistance was reduced by $120 million per year for ten years, at which point it would be done. At the same time, our $1.8 billion in annual military assistance was increased by $60 million per year, rising to $2.4 billion at the end of the ten-year period and ensuring the IDF the constancy of American support for a decade.

In 2007, when this ten-year MOU was expiring, Olmert had negotiated a new ten-year program with President George W. Bush for an increased amount.

The large security assistance to Israel was enthusiastically supported in Congress on both sides of the aisle. Many viewed it as a solid investment in an American ally that never asked for American troops, rolled back militant Islam in the heart of the Middle East, gave the US incomparable intelligence and jointly developed with America the most advanced weapons.

"Hell," one Southern senator told me, "if we had an Israel in Afghanistan, we'd save ourselves a trillion dollars and have a reliable ally against the bad guys."

Now it was my turn to seek a third MOU extension, this time with President Obama.

This was one of the reasons that some of the senior IDF staff had urged me not to speak to Congress on the Iran nuclear deal but to negotiate for a new MOU instead.

"No amount of money will protect us against atomic bombs," I responded. "We have to resist the deal *and* go for the MOU later."

"But speaking in Congress will jeopardize the MOU," they persisted.

"No, it won't," I said.

I thought that if anything, my confrontation with the president over the Iran deal and my public demonstration of how bad it was for Israel would lead him to extend the MOU, thus demonstrating the continuity of America's support for Israel under his administration.

Some suggested waiting for the next president. I shot that one down, too. You never know who or what might come next.

After some negotiations, Obama agreed to a new MOU that gave Israel $36 billion over ten years. It was strongly supported by Congress.

The MOU was signed on September 14, 2016, less than two months before the presidential elections. It was not the last time that I had to impose my judgment and familiarity with American politics over the advice of so-called American experts in our bureaucracy.

While I was in New York that same month to give my speech at the UN General Assembly, I asked to see both presidential candidates, and took Ambassador Dermer with me.

Hillary met us with her aide Jake Sullivan at a hotel where she was giving a speech. She was clearly focused on the debate she was about to have with Trump. Nothing annoys politicians fighting for their political lives more than a busybody who takes up their time while they're facing judgment day.

I spoke as briefly and as succinctly as I could.

I knew that Hillary supported the Iran deal, so I reiterated my position briefly and instead focused on the opportunities for peace with Arab countries that I believed were opening up. Hillary nodded and seemed to recognize the possibility.

Trump received Ambassador Dermer and me in his gilded apartment in Trump Tower. We had met several times over the years and he had endorsed my candidacy for prime minister a few years earlier. He was warm, affable and confident.

He didn't need much convincing about the Iran deal.

"That's the lousiest deal I've ever seen," he said. "I'm going to get out of it."

I agreed with that sentiment and told him so, and also repeated my belief that we could have a breakthrough for peace with several Arab countries.

My confidence was not theoretical. For years the Mossad had maintained security contacts with its counterparts in many Arab states.

These relations suffered a setback with the United Arab Emirates after the targeting of the Hamas terrorist operative Mahmoud al-Mabhouh in Dubai in 2010. Though the Mossad agents got out of the country, the subsequent public exposure of the Mossad's role in the operation caused a great embarrassment to the Emiratis and an enduring crisis in the ties between Israel and the UAE.

But all this began to change as the clouds of a nuclear Iran began to gather on the horizon, a Sword of Damocles over the heads of the Sunni Arab states, and it became apparent that I was the only leader willing to openly oppose the deal. Tony Blair, who shuttled back and forth between the Gulf and Israel in a private capacity, lobbied to have me meet the Gulf leaders. With his help, between 2016 and 2018, Itzik Molcho met with trusted representatives of the leaders from the key Gulf states as well as with Mohamed bin Zayed (MBZ), president of the United Arab Emirates, and other leaders.

Molcho arranged secret meetings with these representatives in Cyprus, in his home in Caesarea, and in the prime minister's residence in Jerusalem. This was followed by phone calls between me and the leaders, which in turn led to secret meetings between us.

We met in the Gulf several times. In one meeting I landed in a helicopter with Molcho, who initiated the meeting on the deck of a yacht in the Red Sea. I decided to hold the meeting there despite concerns raised by security officials.

The Arab leaders I met were smart and savvy, and we spoke openly and directly about our concern with the waning American readiness to confront Iran and its growing desire to accommodate it. We also spoke of how we could cooperate with each other militarily, economically, and diplomatically.

They told me that my speech in Congress against the Iran deal and my willingness to stand up to an American president was a turning point in their willingness to strengthen ties with Israel.

These meetings laid the foundations for what would ultimately be a breakthrough of historic proportions, the Abraham Accords.

THE US ELECTION day arrived.

Eight years earlier, I woke up to President Obama.

Now I woke up to President Trump.

My world had just changed. Remembering my conversation with Trump on the eve of the election, I realized that I would now have a great ally in my battle against Israel's greatest foe.

But there were still two months to go before the new president took office and I knew I would have to dodge Obama's parting shot at the UN Security Council.

"Who will they get?" I asked Ron.

"Get for what?" he asked.

"To front the anti-Israel resolution for them," I said. "They'll get some country to do their bidding. Then they'll abstain and avoid applying the veto. They'll then say they didn't vote against Israel."

"That won't fool anyone," Ron said.

"Maybe not, but I'm sure that's what they'll do."

And they did just that.

It didn't take more than a few days for the intelligence to flow in. Two normally Israel-friendly governments let us know that they were secretly approached by the US to support this hostile resolution and that they had no choice but to go along with it.

Egypt was chosen by the US as the country to submit the anti-Israeli resolution at the UN Security Council. I spoke to el-Sisi but he replied with a "what can I do" shrug of the shoulders. Trump's people were powerless to help but the president-elect did issue a statement decrying the imposition of terms by the UN and underscoring that direct negotiations were the only way forward.

I knew definitively that I had lost this round. UN Security Council Resolution 2334 passed on December 23, 2016, with the US abstaining. It mandated that "Israel stop immediately and completely all settlement activity in the Occupied Territories, including East Jerusalem."

In a speech at the Western Wall on the eve of Hanukkah, I ripped into the resolution. "The UN resolution is twisted and shameful but we'll overcome it. It says that the Jewish Quarter is occupied. That's absurd. It says that the Western Wall is occupied territory. That is absurd, too. We reject this outright just as we rejected the absurd resolution that equated Zionism with racism."

To express Israel's consternation, I called our ambassadors to New Zealand and Ukraine back, as those countries had joined Egypt in sponsoring the resolution; cut back support for Senegal, which had voted for it; and suspended Israel's annual membership fee payment to five UN bodies.

"Prime Minister, don't you think you're overreacting?" asked a Foreign Ministry official.

"Not in the least. This is merely a prelude to the real thing," I said.

I had received word that in the final months remaining until the inauguration of the new US president, a new and even harsher Security Council resolution was being prepared. This one would be a binding resolution calling on Israel to withdraw to the 1967 lines and establishing a Palestinian state with East Jerusalem as its capital.

In an unusual phone call that Obama made to a sympathetic Israeli journalist on October 14, 2016, three weeks before the presidential election, he may have been speaking of this possible resolution. "Before I leave office," Obama told the journalist, "I would like to bring a resolution to the UN Security Council that would set parameters for Israeli-Palestinian peace, stating the guidelines for the principles of a peace agreement, a Palestinian state, the final status of Jerusalem, and overall permanent borders based on the 1967 lines."[1]

I communicated to Moscow my extreme disappointment with Russia's vote on the previous resolution.

"We hear you" was the answer I received.

I was not disappointed again.

The second resolution never materialized.

*　　　*　　　*

OBAMA WAS ONE of the most gifted political leaders I had met. He was intellectually sharp, knew what he wanted to achieve, and was focused on his mission. Contrary to common lore, I never believed that the core of our conflict derived from a personality clash, at least not from my end.

We had a policy clash.

Though our personalities were decidedly different in many respects, it was noted by some commentators that in one sense they were oddly similar. We both tended to the cerebral, and we came to politics to realize ideological convictions, viewing political power as a means to achieving our ends. But given our ideological divide, we differed sharply on what those ends should be.

We clearly differed on the Palestinian issue, which Obama viewed through the distorted prism of the Palestinian narrative. He truly believed the Jews of Israel were neocolonials usurping the land from native Arab inhabitants, when the facts not only of ancient history but of modern times showed that things were the other way around. The Palestinian Arabs joined five Arab armies in their attempt in 1948 to uproot the Jews from their ancestral homeland and since then opposed any arrangement that would leave the Jewish state in place.

In the extreme, Obama's espousal of the Palestinian narrative manifested itself not only in flawed policy but also in personal attacks. He disregarded our history and disrespected Israel's elected leader, who dared to disagree with him. I doubt that he applied the language and tactics he used against me to many, if any, other world leaders. In this I differed from him. No matter how deep the disagreement, I tried as best I could to avoid showing personal disrespect to democratically elected leaders.

The biggest difference between us was our approach to the role of power in international affairs. Obama believed that much of history's ills were caused by the unjust exercise of *too much* power, specifically by the European colonial powers and their successor, America.

Believing, as Martin Luther King Jr. said, that "the arc of history bends towards justice," he held that the continued betterment of the world would be achieved by appealing to humanity's "better angels," as Lincoln put it. Hence the stress he put on the need for international consensus and his desire to "lead from behind," with the US taking a less prominent and less assertive role on the world stage.

I have a profoundly different view. Appealing to "better angels" can only work in a world governed by well-meaning liberal democracies. Assuming that world exists, when in fact it doesn't, is folly.

I believe that the rise of totalitarian regimes and murderous dictatorships necessitates resolute American global leadership of the democracies to roll back this aggression in order to protect our cherished freedoms, and sometimes our very existence. Even Lincoln's appeal to our "better angels" had to wait a few years for the crushing defeat of the Confederacy in America's bloodiest war.

This difference came to a head on the question of Iran. Obama believed that a conciliatory approach might moderate Iran's aggressive tendencies and that, at worst, a nuclear Iran could be contained.

I believed that preventing this genocidal regime from acquiring nuclear weapons was an absolute imperative and that once it possessed these weapons its aggressions would multiply a hundredfold.

I strongly disagreed with Obama on policy. I didn't think Obama was weak. He was willing to fight for his convictions, such as in his domestic battle over health care reform. But when his policies could endanger my country, as did those concerning Iran and the Palestinians, I had no choice but to fight back. And to do so, I had to rally not only public opinion in Israel but in America as well.

Since Obama knew well the power of public opinion, my continual appeals to the American public during his time in office caused considerable resentment on his part.

"The noise orchestrated by Netanyahu," he wrote in his memoir *A Promised Land*, "had the intended effect of gobbling up our time, putting us on the defensive, and reminding me that normal policy differences with an Israeli prime minister—even one who presided over a fragile coalition government—exacted a domestic political cost that simply didn't exist when I dealt with the United Kingdom, Germany, France, Japan, Canada or any of our other closest allies."

That was the whole point in a nutshell. None of those countries faced existential threats. While I genuinely appreciated Obama's help in maintaining Israel's qualitative military edge and signing the ten-year MOU, I could not look aside when he signed the Iran deal.

The claim that the deal would prevent Iran from developing nuclear weapons was simply not true. At best the deal would delay this by a few years, while giving Iran the means, the funds, and the legitimacy to become a ferocious nuclear power.

In a moment of candor, Obama admitted as much. Asked in a 2015 NPR interview what Iran's breakout time to a bomb would be from year 13 on of the agreement, he answered: "What is a more relevant fear would be that in year 13, 14, 15, they have advanced centrifuges that enrich uranium fairly rapidly, and at that point the breakout times would have shrunk almost down to zero."[2]

In other words, after year 12 of the agreement Iran would become a threshold nuclear power and could produce the critical components for nuclear bombs in no time.

That is why in my 2015 speech to Congress I said that the only deal that made sense with Iran was one that would remove economic sanctions and limitations on Iran's nuclear program only in exchange for dismantling Iran's *military* nuclear capacities and a demonstrable change in Iran's aggressive behavior.

Iran would have to dismantle its centrifuges—which serve the sole purpose of enriching weapons-grade uranium—shut down its underground nuclear bunkers, terminate its weapons development program, and cease its terror campaigns throughout the Middle East and beyond.

The 2015 deal with Iran had none of these requirements.

Any deal with Iran would be problematic because of the regime's tendency to cheat and the difficulty of monitoring its compliance. But the worst problem with Obama's 2015 deal and the subsequent attempts to revive it was that it gave Iran a sure path to become a threshold nuclear state while also providing it with immunity from attack.

With or without that agreement, Iran could get to breakout within a few years. The real difference is the de facto immunity that the deal gave Iran.

Iran without the nuclear agreement is a poor, isolated and illegitimate regime that is vulnerable to legitimate military action to prevent it from developing nuclear weapons. Iran with the agreement becomes rich, legitimate and immune to attack from any of the signatories.

No deal by itself would prevent Iran from breaking out to nuclear weapons. Only a credible military option can do that, and that option is precisely what the Obama deal suppressed. My stance was that no deal would be better than this bad deal because deterrence and freedom of action, the only things that ultimately can stop the Iranian regime from going nuclear, are preserved when there isn't a deal.

I believe that Obama understood this, but preferred containing a nuclear Iran to preventing it.

Obama and members of his administration constantly disparaged the motives for my opposition to the deal in briefings to the press. To them, I was a narrow-minded small-time politician maneuvering for my personal political survival. One even briefed an American journalist that I was little more than a "chickenshit." This from people who never risked their lives a day on a battlefield and whose political survival in America's presidential system could be challenged only once in four years and not every week, as in Israel's parliamentary system.

WHEN SHIMON PERES passed away in September 2016, many world leaders came to his funeral, including Bill Clinton, Obama and Kerry.

Kerry, who led the negotiations with Iran, had a message for me that he passed through one of the Israelis who had attended the funeral.

"Tell Bibi," he said, "that if he wants a funeral like this one, he'd better change his policies."

"Tell Kerry," I replied to the messenger, "that it's not my funeral I'm concerned with but Israel's."

For me, the clash with Obama was not personal. It was ideological. If he had confronted Iran, recognized our sovereignty in the Golan and Jerusalem, and dealt realistically with the Palestinian issue, I would have praised him to the gills. But since he went in an entirely different direction that could imperil Israel's future, I was left with no alternative but to confront him and his policies.

I never faced a tougher challenge.

59

NEW DEAL

2017

A day after the US elections, I phoned Donald Trump to congratulate him on his victory.

"Hey, Bibi," he said, "why don't you come over to see me next week?"

I thanked him for the invitation but, respectful of the one-president-at-a-time rule in America, decided to wait until after his inauguration. Instead I sent Ron Dermer and Yaakov Nagel, the Israeli national security advisor, to begin discussions with Trump's national security advisor, Michael Flynn, and his assistant K. T. McFarland. (Flynn would resign less than a month after Trump's inauguration, to be replaced by H. R. McMaster.)

At my request, they focused on Iran and on moving the American embassy from Tel Aviv to Jerusalem, a long-overdue recognition of our capital promised by successive American presidents but never fulfilled. This was also a Trump campaign pledge that I hoped he would keep.

However, a concerning early signal that the new administration would be less eager to break with conventional thinking occurred when Jared Kushner, Trump's son-in-law, whom I had met in his teens when I visited his parents' home in New Jersey, soon told Ron that Israel should freeze settlements for a couple of years to enable a peace deal with the Palestinians.

After Jared's request for a freeze, Ron called me anxiously on the secure phone from the embassy.

"Prime Minister, we have a problem," he said.

"Tell Jared we've already been down that rabbit hole."

"I already did," Ron answered.

We were in a good place on Iran, given President-elect Trump's clearly stated position, despite the tendencies of his senior team. But we were clearly in a bad place on the Palestinian issue, given the enduring hold that the Palestinian narrative had on Washington policy makers.

I later learned that a Jewish mutual friend of Trump and mine with whom I had severed my personal ties had bad-mouthed me in front of the president. Eager for a diplomatic role in the Middle East and having been told by the Palestinians that he had an opportunity to be a great peacemaker, he promised Trump that he could help deliver the "Deal of the Century" between Israel and the Palestinians. Mahmoud Abbas wants peace, he assured the incoming president and Bibi does not.

Once this false allegation had been implanted in the president's mind, it was hard to remove. Trump was naturally drawn to the challenge of achieving a deal where everyone else had failed. After all, he literally wrote the book on the art of the deal. He had already achieved the impossible by being elected president against all odds. Could he not do the impossible here as well?

Normally, I don't give in to despondency. But I did now. I had already had to deal with two presidents who unquestioningly bought the Palestinian canard and saw me as the obstacle to peace. Was I now condemned to another four years of this nonsense?

Shaking loose this dark mood, I repeated to myself the lesson I often imparted to others: "Things are never as good and never as bad as they seem."

But this depended on what we *did* in the down times.

In mid-February 2017, I flew to Washington for my first visit with the newly elected president. Donald and Melania Trump warmly greeted Sara and me on the South Lawn of the White House, a clear gesture of friendship that I had never received before.

"That's a good start," I said to Sara as we came out of the limo.

This continued in a friendly four-way chat in the Oval Office, which was also a refreshing departure from the past. Trump clearly enjoyed being president and his buoyant attitude was infectious. He was very courteous to Sara.

"Aren't we lucky, Bibi, to have such smart and beautiful wives," he said.

"We sure are," I agreed.

When we later got down to business with our staffs in the Cabinet Room, the conversation was freewheeling. With Trump, it couldn't be otherwise. He drove the conversation to the things that interested him and not what interested the bureaucrats. Most of our first meeting focused on Iran. The president repeated his intention to leave the Iran nuclear deal, and then suddenly popped a question.

"Why didn't you bomb them?" he asked about Iran's nuclear facilities.

"Because I didn't have the votes at the time," I answered frankly. "But it's still an option, as are other things."

This was accurate. In the intervening years and as my authority grew, I had authorized increasingly daring Mossad operations against Iran's nuclear program. I also ramped up Israel's military capacities to strike Iran's nuclear facilities. By the time I met Trump in the White House, I was confident that I would have both the means and the votes to carry out what was necessary to impede Iran's nuclear aspirations.

I raised the importance of moving the embassy to Jerusalem and the request was registered. At the end of the meeting I asked Ron to explain why American recognition of our sovereignty on the Golan Heights was an American win.

"It would be a nonmilitary blow to the Iranians, who are trying to entrench themselves in Syria," Ron said. "And we're not going to leave the place anyway."

No one objected, but no one volunteered to do anything about it, either. It's not that I expected an immediate answer. But coming out of the gate, I wanted to lay down markers on both issues, Jerusalem and the Golan.

When we were one-on-one in the Oval Office, I raised another subject.

"Donald, there's a tremendous opportunity for an historic breakthrough with the Arab states," I said. "They're terrified of Iran. I propose we begin with a Middle East security alliance led by you and including Israel, Saudi Arabia and the Emirates. This could quickly lead to formal peace agreements."

Remembering FDR's meeting with the Saudi king Ibn Saud on board an American warship after the Yalta Conference in 1945, I suggested a new version of shipboard diplomacy.

"Donald, you and I, MBZ and MBS can change history," I said. "Why don't you bring one of your aircraft carriers to the Red Sea and invite Mohammed bin Salman of Saudi Arabia, Mohamed bin Zayed of the UAE and me to a security summit on board? You can also invite President el-Sisi of Egypt and King Abdullah of Jordan. Anyone you invite will come. This will jump-start a new order in the Middle East."

For some reason, the president didn't embrace the idea. At the time, he was focused on reaching a narrower arms deal with the Saudis. He may have also thought I was just trying to avoid concessions to the Palestinians.

Regardless of his reasons, what I saw as ripe low-hanging fruit President Trump saw as a distraction from the real prize: the Holy Grail of an Israel-Palestinian peace.

Echoes of all this appeared in our press conference with the president after our meeting.

PRESIDENT TRUMP: Our administration is committed to working with Israel and our common allies in the region toward greater security and stability. That includes working toward a peace agreement between Israel and the Palestinians. The United States will encourage a peace and, really, a great peace deal. We'll be working on it very, very diligently. It's very important for me also. Very important to me also—something we want to do. But it is the parties themselves who must directly negotiate such an agreement. We'll be beside them. We'll be working with them. As with any successful negotiation, both sides will have to make compromises.

Trump then turned to me.

PRESIDENT TRUMP: You know that, right? (*Laughter*)

Prime Minister Netanyahu: *Both* sides.

When my turn came, I repeated my main points:

Prime Minister Netanyahu: Mr. President, you have said that the United States is committed to preventing Iran from getting nuclear weapons. You call for the defeat of ISIS. Under your leadership, I believe we can reverse the rising tide of radical Islam.

In rolling back militant Islam, we can seize an historic opportunity because for the first time in my lifetime and in the life of my country, Arab countries in the region do not see Israel as an enemy, but increasingly as an ally. I believe that under your leadership this change in our region creates an unprecedented opportunity to strengthen security and advance peace.

Questioned on the settlements, Trump answered with an oblique reference to the arrangement we were in the process of working out.

President Trump: As far as settlements, I'd like to see you hold back on settlements for a little bit. We'll work something out.

I reinforced my position when my turn came:

Prime Minister Netanyahu: I believe that the issue of the settlements is not the core of the conflict, nor does it really drive the conflict. It's an issue that has to be resolved in the context of peace negotiations. I think President Trump and I can arrive at an understanding so we don't keep on bumping into each other all the time on this issue.

Asked about a Palestinian-Israeli peace, Trump repeated his desire to see it through.

President Trump: I would like to see a deal be made. I think a deal will be made. I know that every president would like to. Most of them have not started until late because they never thought it was possible. And it wasn't possible because they didn't do it.

But Bibi and I have known each other a long time—a smart man, great negotiator. And I think we're going to make a deal. It might be a bigger and better deal than people in this room even understand. That's a possibility. So let's see what we do.

PRIME MINISTER NETANYAHU: Let's try it.

PRESIDENT TRUMP: Doesn't sound too optimistic, but (*Laughter*) he's a good negotiator.

PRIME MINISTER NETANYAHU: That's the "art of the deal." (*Laughter*)

The president then deflated the hopes that he would impose a two-state solution on Israel.

PRESIDENT TRUMP: So I'm looking at two-state and one-state, and I like the one that both parties like. (*Laughter*) I'm very happy with the one that both parties like. I can live with either one.

I seized on that.

PRIME MINISTER NETANYAHU: I read yesterday that an American official said that if you ask five people what two states would look like, you'd get eight different answers. Mr. President, if you ask five Israelis, you'd get twelve different answers. (*Laughter*)

But rather than deal with labels, I want to deal with substance. There are two prerequisites for peace.

First, the Palestinians must recognize the Jewish state. They have to stop calling and educating their people for Israel's destruction.

Second, in any peace agreement Israel must retain the overriding security control over the entire area west of the Jordan River. If we don't we'll get another radical Islamic terrorist state in the

Palestinian areas which will explode the peace and explode the Middle East.

Unfortunately, the Palestinians vehemently reject both prerequisites for peace. They even deny, Mr. President, our historical connection to our homeland. Why are Jews called Jews? The Chinese are called Chinese because they come from China. The Japanese are called Japanese because they come from Japan. Well, Jews are called Jews because they come from Judea. This is our ancestral homeland. Jews are not foreign colonialists in Judea.

LEAVING WASHINGTON, I realized I had a problem. The president of the United States opposed the Iran nuclear deal, as I did, but he had also become convinced that I was the obstacle to a Palestinian-Israeli peace that Mahmoud Abbas was ready for.

I had to hand it to the Palestinians. They outflanked me by embracing a friend from whom I had grown apart, promising him that he would be the great peacemaker. Trump had known this person for many years and considered him a reliable source on the Middle East. How could I not see that coming?

Admittedly, I wasn't so much worried that Trump would cozy up to the Palestinians with the same vindictive zeal as Obama. Most of the senior officials in his administration did not buy the Palestinian line. Besides, I knew that Trump would come to appreciate the great support Israel and I had in the evangelical community, the most important element of his political base.

Every time he mentioned "Jerusalem" or "Israel" in a speech, the evangelical crowd roared with approval. The unstinting evangelical support for Israel was nothing short of extraordinary and gave me much comfort.

But it still bothered me that a Palestinian wedge was introduced between the president and me.

I consulted with Ron and Nagel. The first order of business was to eliminate the constant American-Israeli friction around the settlements. In March 2017, I proposed a new understanding with the new administration.

We would replace the monthly announcement of new planning and construction in Judea and Samaria, which frequently produced public friction with the US, with a quarterly announcement that allowed for longer interludes of quiet. During these interludes we would show the Americans exactly where and how much we planned to build. We would moderate the territorial expansion of the settlements by building high-rises within existing communities. If we went beyond the communities' physical boundaries, we would limit construction to contiguous lots.

This addressed the long-standing American charge of "land grabbing" while ensuring the market-based growth of these communities.

By May 2017, this understanding was agreed upon, putting to bed for the next four years a contentious issue that had soured US-Israel relations for decades.

The appointment of David Friedman as US ambassador to Israel on May 15 helped implement this understanding since the American embassy in Israel received and vetted this quarterly report.

I had met David years before in Trump's New York office when he served as Trump's business lawyer. An Orthodox Jew, he was forthright and blunt about his support for Israel and the Jewish people's right to live in their historic homeland. Quick-witted and sharp-tongued when needed, he was a refreshing change from a long line of career diplomats who reflexively pushed the pro-Palestinian line.

A man after my own heart, he couldn't care less what the press wrote about him. But he definitely cared about what the president thought of him.

The other thing I could do to address the Palestinian wedge was to try to seed doubts in the president's newfound conviction that I was the obstacle to peace. The next opportunity to make that happen would be during his forthcoming visit to the Middle East.

Unlike Obama, whose first foreign visit was to Cairo, Trump chose to make his first visit abroad to Saudi Arabia and Israel, America's two most important allies in the region.

The Saudis greeted him on May 20 with an impressive reception, inviting him to join them in a ceremonial sword dance.

The president's first meeting in Israel two days later was less entertaining. As protocol required, he visited Israeli president Reuven Rivlin before meeting with me. When he was with Rivlin, Trump blurted out, "Bibi doesn't want peace."

For some unfathomable reason, this bombshell wasn't leaked.

Dermer, who accompanied Trump to that meeting, was flabbergasted. This was not "Houston, we have a problem." This was "Houston, we *are* the problem!"

When I met the president and his team shortly afterward in the King David Hotel, I flipped on a video that I hoped would help adjust his thinking about Mahmoud Abbas, and about me.

The video showed Abbas extolling peace in English for Western audiences and then a string of his statements in Arabic intended for Palestinian audiences and calling for the destruction of Israel and glorifying the Palestinian terrorists who murdered our people.

"Mahmoud Abbas pays the families of terrorists sitting in our jails. The more Israelis they murder, the more money they get," I said.

I could see that the video registered with Trump, at least momentarily.

"Wow," he said. "Is that the same guy I just met in Washington?" (Abbas had visited Washington in early May.) "He seemed like such a sweet, peaceful guy."

Naturally, Trump didn't like being taken for a fool. I hoped the video might mitigate further bonding during his scheduled meeting with Abbas in Bethlehem on the last day of his trip.

To address Israel's security needs, I prepared a simple slide for the president. It showed the distance from Tel Aviv to the 1967 lines to which the Palestinians demanded we retreat.

Superimposed on the map was the distance from Trump Tower to the George Washington Bridge. The two distances were identical.

"Mr. President," I said, "would you let a regime that wants to annihilate you set up a state at the George Washington Bridge? Of course not. Neither would we."

Ron also reached for an analogy that would resonate with the president: golf.

"Mr. President," he said, "peace with the Emirates is a five-foot putt. Peace with the Saudis is a thirty-foot putt. And peace with the Palestinians is a hole-in-one through a brick wall."

The president got it. For the time being, at least, we had certainly moved him to a better place.

Following our meeting at the King David Hotel, Trump went to the Western Wall, the first American president to do so.

During a long dinner in the prime minister's residence that evening, he, Melania, Sara and I spoke at length about the challenges we were all facing from a hostile press. Trump, who generally says what's on his mind, is even more candid in private. He waxed on about the reception he received from the Saudis.

"I gotta tell you, Bibi," he said, "they put on one hell of a production."

He was already eyeing lucrative deals for the United States with Saudi Arabia. I tried to nudge the conversation to the great political deal of peace with the Arab states that I believed was around the corner.

Still: a no go.

Trump loves hamburgers. So do I. The chef prepared hamburgers but insisted on also serving a five-course dinner. That would have been fine at any other time, but after getting through the hamburgers—the part of the meal we liked best—it wasn't necessary.

The next day the president gave a moving speech at the Yad Vashem Holocaust memorial. As with Obama, I agreed with his staff not to have the US president speak at the Knesset, where he would assuredly encounter jeers from the left.

Instead, we arranged an event in the Israel Museum. Trump was greeted enthusiastically and dazzled the crowd.

The next day he went to see Abbas in Bethlehem. In their meeting in DC a few weeks earlier, Trump had taken to the Palestinian leader, at one point referring to him as a "father figure." But our preparatory work exposing his double talk took the bloom off that rose, at least for a while.

Friedman, who accompanied Trump to Bethlehem, wrote in his 2022 memoir that "Trump leveled into Abbas over the tape, demanding to know who he really was, a peacemaker as he claimed in Washington or a terrorist as he proclaimed on the tape."[1]

When the president left Israel, I knew we had four great tasks before us. The first three were to get the US to leave the Iran deal, to get it to recognize Jerusalem as Israel's capital, and to get America to recognize Israel's sovereignty over the Golan Heights.

If we were lucky, we would also achieve a fourth mission, one that had eluded Israel for a quarter of a century: peace with more Arab states.

I knew there would be bumps along the way, but I was convinced that Trump's presidency offered an incredible opportunity to achieve these goals.

THROUGHOUT THEIR CHILDHOOD the boys pleaded with Sara to have a dog.

"Absolutely not," she replied. "Who will take care of it? Who will clean up after it? No way!"

In 2015 Avner, by then a soldier in the IDF, raised the matter again. He came to know a beautiful nine-year-old Alaskan Malamute dog named Kaya. Because of a death in the family that had kept her, she was going to be "put to sleep" if no household would take her in.

"Imma," Avner said, holding up his cell phone with Kaya's photo, "in five days this dog will die. Only you can save her."

That did it.

We took her in and publicly called on others to adopt aging dogs and save them from being euthanized.

Though beautiful, Kaya was aging and ailing, receiving medicine to ease the pain in her bad back. She blissfully spent the last three years of her life roaming the spacious courtyard of the Balfour residence, beloved by the security guards and going on walks with Yair and Avner, who cared for her.

In this they were joined by one other person—Sara. From a determined "never dogger" Sara became a doting "dog mother."

"Did Kaya take her medicine today?" she'd call the residence staff when we traveled abroad. "And don't forget to give her the vitamins."

In the last months of her life Kaya's health deteriorated and she could no longer walk. Sara went to great expense and arranged two operations on Kaya's spine by the finest veterinary surgeons, followed by hydrotherapy in a special clinic. It was to little avail. Kaya failed to recover and began to fade away. Sara, Avner, Yair and I visited her on the day before she died. We were heartbroken, feeling we had lost a family member.

Our years with Kaya reminded me of my own joy as a child playing with our dog, Bonnie. I could once again relate to the affections of millions of people to their pets. As an adult I could more fully appreciate the cognitive and emotional world of animals, which had hitherto been little understood by me.

It turned out President Harry Truman was right. In the cruel world of politics if you want a friend, get a dog.

I did.

And now I had lost a loyal friend.

60

MISSIONS ACCOMPLISHED

2017–2019

I met Trump again at the UN General Assembly in September 2017, four months after his trip to Israel.

He gave a scathing speech about North Korea, which at the time was rattling its nuclear sabers. For the first and only time as Israel's prime minister, I sat with Sara in Israel's seating area on the floor of the General Assembly. This was a way to signal our respect to the president while he was delivering his remarks.

In our meeting at the UN, I showed Trump a map of Hezbollah's 130,000 rockets aimed at Israel, which were embedded in civilian neighborhoods throughout Lebanon's towns and villages. He was amazed at the numbers and the concentration.

"Bibi, how do you sleep at night?" he asked me.

"By making sure *they* don't sleep at night," I answered. "They know what will happen to them if they attack us."

Then I added, "Donald, just think how much worse our situation will be if Iran gave Hezbollah a nuclear umbrella. They'd believe they could rocket our cities with impunity."

Iran was determined to build in Syria a Shiite militia of eighty thousand fighters commanded by Iranian generals, duplicating the Shiite Hezbollah organization in Lebanon. I was equally determined to prevent them from doing so.

"We will act to prevent an Iranian military presence in Syria on land, sea or air and to block entry into Syria of lethal weapons against us," I proclaimed in my UN speech.

In practice, this meant continual sorties by Israel's air force against Iranian military targets in Syria. This campaign escalated a year later on May 10, 2018, after Iran fired twenty rockets into the Golan Heights. We intercepted most of them and responded ferociously against Iranian and Syrian military targets.

In this battle of wills, Israel eventually got the upper hand. The Hezbollah-like capability Iran hoped to build in Syria never materialized. To ensure our freedom of action, I conducted periodic meetings with Putin, mostly in the Kremlin but twice also on the Black Sea. On one such visit I said to him flat out, "You don't want Iran in Syria any more than I do." I knew Russia didn't want the Islamic Republic as a military and economic competitor in Syria as it emerged from its civil war.

"Since we can't tolerate an Iranian base in Syria, we're going to continue our air attacks. I just wanted you to know that," I added, indicating that I was sharing with him our policy and not seeking his approval for it.

Putin didn't say anything. He merely spread his arms nonchalantly in a gesture that could only be interpreted as "be my guest."

I verified in other ways that I correctly interpreted that gesture.

The IDF and the Mossad acted vigorously against Iran's efforts to develop precision-guided missiles in Syria and Lebanon. Such missiles, capable of targeting Israeli airfields, power stations, communication centers and other strategic targets posed an even greater threat to Israel than the thousands of inaccurate rockets already pointed at our cities.

Neutralizing these precision-guided weapons was my second priority in Israel's national defense. The first priority remained blocking Iran's development of nuclear weapons.

"We can't just limit ourselves to striking the cat's paws in Lebanon, Syria or Gaza. We must be able to go after the cat itself: Iran," I said to Israel's security chiefs.

This meant developing new weapons for the IDF, alongside the Mossad's ongoing campaign against Iran's nuclear capabilities. The foreign press reported on continual assaults on Iran's nuclear scientists, as well as periodic explosions and malfunctions in its nuclear installations, including a cyberattack attributed to the Stuxnet malware.

No one ever took credit for anything specific.

There was one important exception to this rule. In 2017, Mossad chief Yossi Cohen presented me with a covert operation aimed at bringing Iran's secret nuclear archive to Israel.

Fearing an American action against it after the Iraq War, which was just beginning, the Iranian regime decided in 2003 to hide the documents detailing its military nuclear program in a secret stash in Tehran that only a handful of people knew about. The nuclear archive contained valuable documentation of nuclear know-how that the regime could retrieve at will.

In the meantime, the regime continued its military nuclear program under the SPND organization, a research arm of the Iranian Defense Ministry that operated several military nuclear research arms under academic guise.

Since Iran denied that it ever worked to develop an atomic bomb, it did not want to draw attention to its secret trove of documents that would prove it was lying. The officials in charge decided to forgo elaborate protective measures for fear that they could be detected by foreign intelligence services. They chose instead to cover the atomic archives with a cloak of secrecy and anonymity.

The scientific records were stored in several vaults in a dilapidated warehouse in Tehran watched over by two guards.

The first question I asked Yossi after he finished his presentation was, "Do they have a copy?"

"I don't know," he said. "But they're so sure that nobody knows about this archive that they may not have made a copy."

"You think they didn't put all this information on computerized files?" I asked.

"Not if they believed we'd get to these computerized files. Maybe they believed hiding the original paper files was the best protection," Yossi posited.

If that were the case, we would have a double win by exposing Iran's lies *and* depriving Iran of important documents.

I authorized the mission.

It was successfully carried out in early 2018. The Mossad agents broke into the warehouse, neutralized the guards and took out an enormous amount of material: 55,000 pages in paper files and another 55,000 files on 183 CDs.

The agents had a lead time of a few hours to bust the vaults open before Iranian security was alerted to the raid. Within hours the Iranians mobilized thousands of men to give chase. By the time they reached one location, our agents had skipped to the next. Cohen kept me informed hourly as the chase progressed. I bit the proverbial fingernails. It was that close.

Compared to this, Argo was child's play.

Incredibly, the Mossad agents succeeded in bringing *half a ton* of material to Israel. I went to see them personally, shook their hands warmly and thanked them for their courage.

"You have performed a magnificent service to Israel and to the world," I said. Not a word of hyperbole there. One day we'll be able to tell the world more about these silent heroes.

It took our analysts and scientific experts several weeks to go through the atomic archive. It contained documents detailing Project Amad, the secret Iranian program to develop nuclear weapons.

Right up front was a document with the project's mission statement: "Design, produce, and test five warheads each with ten-kiloton TNT yield for integration on a missile." This meant that as early as 2003, Iran was working to produce five Hiroshima-size atomic bombs capable of being delivered by ballistic missiles!

The files and CDs documented yellowcake production, centrifuge development, underground facilities for the development of nuclear cores, warhead development, implosion simulations, testing sites—the works.

On March 5, 2018, I went to see Trump in the White House. The president had his key aides with him. We showed them a short video clip describing what we found.

After seeing the clip, the president pointed to the other senior officials in the Oval Office and said, "Maybe they needed to see this. I didn't. I've already decided to leave the deal."

But it didn't hurt to give the president additional tailwind in world public opinion.

I told Trump that I would shortly present these findings to the public, thus giving advance backing to his decision to withdraw from the nuclear deal. I prepared a slide presentation and showed it before the world in a televised news conference on April 30.

After a short introduction that quoted solemn statements by Iran's leaders that they never had any plans to develop nuclear weapons, I said, "Tonight, I'm here to tell you one thing: *Iran lied.*"

These two words were emblazoned in huge letters on a large screen behind me. I walked through the brief presentation, which exposed those lies with documents, videos and diagrams discovered in Iran's secret atomic archives. All this received worldwide coverage.

Predictably, my detractors in Israel were unhappy.

"Why is the prime minister divulging a Mossad operation?" they sneered.

"Tell them the Iranians already know about this operation," I said to spokesman Mark Regev. "I'm not divulging details of *how* the Mossad pulled it off. I'm divulging the *results* of the operation to expose Iran's deceptions before the entire world."

"Why didn't the prime minister just share this information with other intelligence agencies?" said another grump.

"Tell these geniuses that I'm not trying to bury this stuff in Western security bureaucracies. I'm trying to alert the world to a grave danger."

Only after this international exposure did I authorize the Mossad to show the detailed archive material to other Western intelligence agencies, other than the Americans, with whom we had already shared the material.

Before then, Yossi Cohen had wanted to give his European counterparts the intelligence information in the hope that they would influence their governments to support Trump in leaving the deal.

"No way," I said. "Their governments would merely say, 'Ho hum, nothing new here,' and focus all their efforts to persuade Trump *not* to leave the deal."

Indeed, a few days before my presentation in the Oval Office, German chancellor Angela Merkel and French president Emmanuel Macron had visited the White House to plead with the president to do just that.

But I knew that exposing the nuclear archive after those European leaders visited DC would counteract any influence, if any, they might have had on President Trump.

I ended the April 30 press conference with these words: "In a few days President Trump will decide what to do with the nuclear deal. I'm sure he'll do the right thing for the United States, for Israel and for the peace of the world."

Eight days later, President Trump announced that the US was leaving the Iran deal and reimposing sanctions on Iran.

Mission number one accomplished.

SEVERAL MONTHS EARLIER, in November 2017, the president had called me up.

"Bibi," he said, "I'm thinking of announcing that we recognize Israel's capital and that we'll move our embassy there. What do you think? You think anything serious will happen? Because that's what some of my guys say." Though I'm not prone to express unrestrained emotion, I was thrilled to hear the president's intentions.

I knew that a real battle was being waged in the administration around this question. Naturally, I supported those like David Friedman from the inside and Sheldon Adelson from the outside who sought to convince the president to uphold his campaign promise. I myself had urged him to do so many times. Still, he asked me a direct question and I owed him an honest answer.

"Look, you never know," I said. "But I don't see any particular problem in our intelligence. I don't think they'll burn down American embassies in Arab countries or anything like that. At most, we here in Israel will suffer pushback, but I don't see that coming, either. And in the unlikely event that happens, we're prepared to shoulder the cost."

We were close to a big win, but we weren't quite there yet. A few days later, as I was boarding a plane from Tel Aviv to Nairobi for one of my African visits, Ambassador Dermer called me urgently from Washington to inform me that after a meeting in the Oval Office about recognizing Jerusalem, those opposed had convinced Trump to let US security chiefs contact their Israeli counterparts about the possible fallout.

Uh-oh! If even one of the Israeli security chiefs balked, the whole thing might fall apart. With the plane engines already warming up, I asked National Security Advisor Meir Ben Shabbat, who had organized the trip, to disembark and stay in Israel. If I wouldn't act in this critical juncture the moving of the embassy might not take place.

"Meir, I know you've worked hard to prepare this visit," I told Ben Shabbat. "But right now this is more important. I want you to go one by one to the chief of staff, the head of intelligence and the heads of Mossad and Shin Bet and hold their feet to the fire. They just have to tell the Americans what they told me. No more, no less." Though I could see the disappointment on his face, Meir didn't argue. He disembarked and returned to the Prime Minister's Office.

The security chiefs held the line. A week later, on December 6, 2017, President Trump ended seventy years of diplomatic absurdity by recognizing a three-thousand-year-old truth. Jerusalem was the capital of the Jewish people from the time of King David to the present. President Trump declared that the US recognized it as Israel's capital and that he would move the American embassy there.

After the American announcement, *nothing* happened. No spontaneous storming of American embassies, and no significant demonstrations throughout the Arab world. As the president later said to the fearmongers, "the sky didn't fall."

This troubled Hamas greatly. For months it had been trying to get international traction for its campaign to storm the security fence separating Gaza from Israel. This had nothing to do with the announcement of the Jerusalem embassy. Every Friday for months, they had sent thousands of Palestinian rioters to approach the fence, some carrying weapons, grenades or combustible material. Their leaders promised to "rip the hearts out" of Israeli civilians beyond the fence.

The IDF had orders to prevent them from breaking into Israel. Whenever possible, the soldiers used nonlethal means to prevent the rioters from crossing the fence and carrying out attacks in Israel. Shooting was the last resort and orders were to aim at the rioters' legs.

But as the "fence jihad" heated up under deliberate Hamas incitement, the rioters increasingly tried to cross the fence and Palestinian casualties mounted.

Still, as there was little international traction for these fence charges, Hamas leaders decided to tie one of these assaults to the embassy issue. Hamas deliberately scheduled one of the weekly fence-charging dates to coincide with the US embassy opening in Jerusalem in May 2018, giving orders to Hamas militants to penetrate Israel and kill Israelis. In the ensuing clash, some sixty Palestinians were killed, including many Hamas activists.

Artificially concocted for the media, this assault was the first and only manifestation of violent protest around Trump's declaration on Jerusalem.

Most of the Arab governments didn't care one way or another. Guatemala and Honduras, as a result of strong evangelical influence, as well as Paraguay and Kosovo, followed the American example and recognized Jerusalem as Israel's capital. Others, including Hungary, the Czech Republic, Brazil and Australia, opened official trade and cultural offices in the city. Old habits die hard but this was a good beginning.

Yet there was one fly in the ointment. Under a new government subjected to pressure from the local Palestinian community, Paraguay returned its embassy to Tel Aviv a year later. In response I closed our embassy in their capital, Asunción.

The official opening of the US embassy took place in a location that David Friedman found in South Jerusalem. It was a few hundred meters from my childhood home in Talpiot. It dawned on me how much Jerusalem had grown in the intervening years, how much Israel had grown.

From the ridge where the new embassy stood, you could see the Temple Mount and David's City, the sloping hill on which he placed our capital three thousand years ago.

As the ceremony began, I whispered to my aide next to me in a mimicked British accent, "It's about bloody time."

Trump deserved all the credit for making that historic decision. Seventy years had passed before an American president had the gumption to do the right thing.

Sara and I joined Jared Kushner, Ivanka Trump, David Friedman and his wife Tammy to unveil the plaque, which read:

The Embassy of the United States
Jerusalem, Israel

Mission number two accomplished.

*   *   *

THE GOLAN WAS next.

In my first meeting with President Trump at the White House in February 2017, I had asked him to recognize it as part of Israel.

As in the case of Jerusalem, our historic connection to the Golan was often either overlooked or simply unknown. The Golan was where half the tribe of Menashe settled at the dawn of our history, 3,500 years ago, at the time of Moses. In 67 CE the Jewish residents of Gamla in the western Golan made a heroic stand against Titus's Roman legion but were slaughtered on the steep slopes of the camel-shaped hill. Yet even after the fall of Jerusalem three years later and up to the eighth century CE, the Golan remained populated by Jews.

It boasted some thirty synagogues, dating from the Second Temple period to the eighth century. Great Talmudic scholars prayed, taught and wrote in the Golan.

My government helped reconstruct some of these synagogues, none so brilliantly as the one in Ein Keshatot. Ravaged by an earthquake in the eighth century, all that was left of this magnificent structure was a pile of rubble. Using sophisticated software, Israeli archaeologists determined where each stone should go. When I attended the opening ceremony of the reconstructed Ein Keshatot synagogue, I could almost hear the prayer chants of our ancestors.

This and many other restoration projects were funded by the Moreshet (Legacy) program, which I launched when I came back to the premiership in 2009.

"A people who doesn't know its past will put its future in doubt," said the Israeli leader Yigal Alon.

I deeply believed this. Over the next decade the Legacy program funded the restoration of numerous ancient Biblical and Talmudic sites. It also built visitor centers in Biblical Lachish, the Judean city that fell to the Babylonians, and refurbished more modern sites that were important to the history of Zionism.

These included the Tel Hai fort in the Galilee, where the Jewish Legion commander Trumpeldor fell in 1920; the munitions factory under a fake kibbutz constructed to hide it during Israel's War of Independence; the camp in Atlit where "illegal" Jewish immigrants were interred by the British; and the British Mandate prison in Akko (Acre), from which Irgun prisoners broke out in one of history's most daring prison escapes; and the hall in Tel Aviv where Ben Gurion declared Israel's independence in 1948. Astonishingly, no restoration work on these and other historical sites had been done for decades.

I also went out of my way to help fund the restoration of Aaron Aaronsohn's home in Zikhron Yaacov and his experimental farm in Atlit.

The international community didn't care about our ancient roots in the Golan. It even forgot that Syria held that piece of land for only nineteen years, that during those years it shelled our villages and kibbutzim below, and that in 1967 we took the Golan in a war of self-defense.

At first, President Trump's policy on the Golan did not differ from that of his predecessors. An opportunity to change that came suddenly in December 2018 when he publicly announced he was removing US military forces from Syria.

I asked to speak to the president, concerned that a precipitous American withdrawal of forces could further destabilize the situation there and undermine our security. But I decided not to try to change the president's mind for two reasons.

First, as a policy Israel does not ask for the US to put its troops in harm's way. That was an internal US decision. Second, the chances of Trump reversing his decision after publicly making it known were minimal.

Instead, I explained to Trump how Israel's security could be undermined by such a withdrawal and asked him to take steps to minimize its negative impact. One of those steps would be to recognize Israeli sovereignty over the Golan Heights.

The president listened but didn't commit. Over the next several weeks, I made achieving US recognition a top priority. Ambassador Dermer focused on that mission in Washington and I pressed the issue at every opportunity.

I went with visiting senator Lindsey Graham, an old friend, up to the Golan Heights on March 11, 2019. Lindsey was a stalwart and consistent supporter of Israel, sometimes outflanking me in demanding more support for Israel from US administrations than we had actually asked for.

"I'm doing this for America's interest," he had previously told me. Now on a hill overlooking the Golan, he publicly called before the media for American recognition of Israeli sovereignty over this vital strategic territory.

Then, on his visit to Jerusalem on March 20, I spoke to Secretary of State Mike Pompeo about the Golan. Pompeo was a tremendous addition to President Trump's foreign policy team, having taken over from Rex Tillerson in April 2018. A former congressman and CIA chief, Pompeo possessed a keen understanding of diplomacy, politics and power. But while Pompeo and Friedman were in favor, the ultimate decision on the Golan would be made by Trump.

A few days before my visit to Washington in March 2019, all these efforts bore fruit.

On March 21, President Trump's office tweeted: "At a time when Iran seeks to use Syria as a platform to destroy Israel, President Trump boldly recognizes Israel's sovereignty over the Golan Heights."

The excitement swept all of Israel.

Some forty years earlier, in the 1973 Yom Kippur War, the IDF bravely defended the Golan at a high price. Yoni almost lost his life there in 1967 and risked his life there again in 1973 when he led his men in battle against Syrian commandos and then rescued his friend, the wounded tank commander Yossi Ben Hanan, behind enemy lines.

For me the Golan resonated with memories from my years in the military, including the time I almost froze to death climbing the steep slopes of the Hermon as I led my soldiers back from a clandestine mission on the Syrian side of the snow-swept plateau.

Now the most powerful nation in the world was about to recognize Israel's sovereignty over this historic battleground, without a shot being fired.

I attended the signing ceremony at the White House four days later.

Mission number three accomplished.

61

"BRING US BIBI'S HEAD"

2009-2022

In the years of struggle and accomplishment following my return to the Prime Minister's Office, I had to contend with a persistent challenge: an unrelenting defamation campaign in the media by the Israeli left and their supporters, falsely accusing me, and often Sara, of alleged wrongdoings, frequently accompanied by police investigations.

The genesis of their deep hatred for me often perplexed me. Most of my childhood friends came from left-of-center homes. My parents avoided discussing partisan politics at home. Ben Gurion consulted with Father and invited my father-in-law to his Bible study. My own views were conservative but decidedly not extreme. My service in the UN was widely appreciated across the Israeli political spectrum. Yet after my return to Israel from diplomatic service and my climb to the Likud leadership, I became the object of growing animosity.

The hostility toward me as a political leader resulted from the convergence of several factors.

First, past precedent: other strong leaders from the right had received similar treatment. Jabotinsky was at one time vilified as "Vladimir Hitler" by Ben Gurion.[1] Begin was slandered as "fascist" and "divisive." Even the historic peace treaty he signed with Egypt didn't protect him from the charge of being a "murderer" and a "warmonger" in the First Lebanon War. (Today Jabotinsky is held by the left as a model of a humanist leader while Begin is hailed as a great unifying figure, often by the same people who attacked them in the past.)

Second, I had been the leader of the Opposition during Rabin's tragic assassination, earning me the false charge of fomenting the murder and breaking the dream of an imminent peace that was anything but imminent, and that had in fact collapsed under a deluge of Palestinian acts of terror well before the assassination.

Third, my long stay in office undermined the left elite's hopes that they could maintain their hegemony over leading institutions in the country indefinitely.

Fourth, Israeli society itself had become more politically polarized with the rise of internet and social media, intensifying the sentiments of my opponents and supporters alike.

But yet another factor may have been even more potent. To many in the ruling elites I had betrayed my social class. Educated and politically influential, I led the "plebeians" to power. Worse, I led them in the wrong direction. The elites believed that if not for me, vast parts of the public would have acquiesced to far-reaching territorial withdrawals, the redivision of Jerusalem and other central items on the left's agenda. This patronizing attitude didn't consider the possibility that my supporters and I shared the same views. Broad swaths of the Israeli public supported me precisely because I held and defended *their* ideals and values. The elites expressed this contempt by dubbing my supporters "Bibists," people with no independent views of their own. But had I advocated a leftist agenda the so-called Bibists would have stopped supporting me instantly. Which is what they did time and again when right-wing leaders adopted a leftist agenda.

As time went on, all these factors resulted in me becoming the subject of an unrelenting campaign of character defamation—a combination of press calumny and legal harassment.

THE DEFAMATION CAMPAIGN had begun in earnest with the comical 1996 "CIA Affair" and reached new heights with the farcical "Movers Affair" and "Gifts Affair" in 1999. By 2009, when I returned to office, all these preposterous charges had collapsed. Indeed, I hoped at the time that the days of trumped-up legal and press harassment were behind me.

Yet, following the familiar pattern, a new "affair" would start out with bombastic "revelations" about this or that alleged wrongdoing, accompanied by a chorus of opposition and press demands for a police investigation. This, my opponents hoped, was a surefire way to end my political career. If one attempt failed, they would try another. Everything was fair game.

In 2011, I was accused of double-billing travel expenditures. The media exploded with sensational stories about the so-called Bibi Tours Affairs. Under heavy pressure the police began an investigation. An incredible six years later, the case was closed. There wasn't a single instance of double billing.

Next was the "Pistachio Affair" in 2013. I was accused of buying too much ice cream (pistachio, my favorite). The actual expenditure was equivalent to two ice cream cones a day (which I confess was a clear violation of my allowed caloric intake). Like the ice cream the accusation melted on further scrutiny.

Then there was the "Laundry Affair." In a series of appeals to the courts beginning in 2013 through 2016, Sara and I were falsely accused by a leftist NGO of ordering excessive laundry and dry-cleaning services in Israel and abroad. We didn't. The appellants demanded we reveal all our laundry expenditures, "including underwear." After years of litigation in the District and Supreme Court this charge too was quashed and the appellants were fined for court expenses.[2]

The "Garden Furniture Affair" got a bit more traction. In this one, Sara was accused of illicitly relocating three outdoor patio chairs from Balfour to our private home in Caesarea. This too was false. The garden furniture in question was purchased by us.

Still, it took a full three years for these "Garden Furniture" claims to collapse. Guests were flabbergasted when they saw the tawdry patio chairs that were the subject of so many claims that we were living in gilded luxury at the public's expense.

And on it went.

While these concocted "affairs" exacted a personal and public price I was still winning elections, in 2013 and again in 2015.

My political opponents decided to up the ante.

Starting in 2017, special activist organizations were formed, funded by NGOs and wealthy supporters of my political opponents. They organized continual demonstrations against me, but their main focus was elsewhere.

In a moment of candor, one of the initiators of these demonstrations, who was also a candidate for the Labor Party's Knesset list, was caught on camera saying this at a parlor meeting: "You want to take down Bibi? It'll be difficult to take him down in elections. . . . We don't have the Russian voters. We don't have a flagship issue. We don't have the Sephardic voters. We don't have the periphery [the Negev and the Galilee]. We're in deep trouble. You want to bring him down? Let's bring him down through corruption."

He was quite specific on how to do it: "Let's protest against the Attorney General in front of his home to force him to investigate Bibi, to kick him out."[3]

This plan was implemented.

For a full year, protesters held weekly demonstrations around Attorney General Avichai Mandelblit's home. They stalked him wherever he went, even when he was buying groceries. Their ubiquitous spokespersons attacked him as being a cowardly yes-man for not going after me.

Eventually Mandelblit caved.

As he said on a prime-time TV program, the moment he entered office "a multitude of odds and ends of trivial things, some bordering on gossip, were thrown at me. If they hadn't been directed at the Prime Minister nothing would have been done with them. Nevertheless, I authorized a police investigation."[4]

In other words the attorney general of Israel opened a criminal investigation against the prime minister of Israel based on claims he himself characterized as "bordering on gossip."

Once he opened the investigations, the demonstrators and the news media changed their tune. They now hailed Mandelblit as "a fearless fighter for the rule of law."

The first casualty of Mandelblit's campaign was Sara. A disgruntled former employee who had been responsible for ordering food in the prime minister's residence accused her of ordering in meals for official dinners from restaurants instead of using an in-house "cook." This became known as the "Meal Tray Affair."

Never mind that the "cook" was actually a cleaning lady with limited cooking skills. Never mind that the expenditure on food in the residence skyrocketed during the former employee's tenure and immediately sank after his departure. Never mind, too, that neighbors saw him regularly unpacking boxes of food at a relative's home.

Nothing was allowed to taint the credibility of the ex-employee, not even a housekeeper in the residence who filed a complaint to the police that he had sexually harassed her in our bedroom. A senior investigating police officer in the case tried to intimidate the housekeeper.

"Netanyahu won't be the prime minister anymore," he told her. "You have nothing to worry about."

When that failed, he turned to scare tactics. "He wanted me to say that Netanyahu paid me to file the complaint," revealed the housekeeper, "and if I wouldn't say that, he said I'd spend the night in jail."

Sara wasn't actually charged with inappropriately *ordering* the food, but with receiving it. The fair-minded judge noted that "this was the first time in history that someone was brought to trial on meal trays." During the trial, the judge said that since most of the food was ordered for hosting official guests, it was not clear to him what the problem was. He added about Sara that "criminal activity is not in her nature."

Nevertheless, the prosecution refused to close the case. To avoid years of litigation, a compromise was reached in which Sara would admit minor wrongdoing "with no intention to defraud anyone" and pay a modest fine. When an indignant NGO petitioned the Supreme Court to increase the fine, the court threw out the petition and fined the NGO, with court expenses to be paid to the state and to Sara.[5]

The "Meal Tray Affair" added to the toll but it also had a boomerang effect. Many saw it for what it was: an attempt to tarnish *me*.

Failing to bring me down with double billing, pistachio ice cream, garden furniture, underwear and meal trays, my opponents realized that something more substantial was needed. Thus, in 2016, began the so-called "Submarine Affair."

The story line claimed that I instructed the IDF to purchase unneeded submarines and ships from the German corporation Thyssen-Krupp in order to benefit a company in which my cousin Nathan held minor shares. The company allegedly produced a small component in the production of the steel purportedly used to make the vessels.

If true, the financial benefit to my cousin, and supposedly to me, would have been minuscule, at most a few thousand dollars. But the accusations were even more absurd because my cousin's company sold nothing to ThyssenKrupp's marine division. ThyssenKrupp explained that the type of steel used to manufacture the naval vessels could not even be physically produced with the components from my cousin's company.

For once, the normally zealous prosecutors stayed on the sidelines. They didn't have much choice. I wasn't even questioned in the affair.

But the debunking of the claims didn't prevent Benny Gantz's Blue and White party from implying in the 2019 elections that I was guilty of no less than treason.

Their campaign strategist later said in a television interview that since their poll numbers were tanking, they needed a "security" issue to use against me and therefore decided to depict me as a traitor.

"We raised the submarine issue for political reasons," the strategist admitted, later adding, "a lot of inaccurate things were said in the campaign."[6]

Despite the fact that I had nothing to do with the submarine investigation, for years the television stations showed footage of me descending into one of the subs in endless loops. At first Gantz and Bennett didn't join the charade: "The Attorney General determined there is no reason to open an investigation and I'm fine with that," said Gantz. Bennett, who had supported the deal, agreed: "There's no corruption in the submarines. I supported the deal." He also added "Netanyahu would never compromise Israel's security for money."

Apparently neither of these politicians had any compunction to later brush truth aside and join the submarine shooting gallery, politicizing the IDF and Israel's security in the process. Seeking to prolong the public besmirching of my character, Bennett and Gantz's new coalition government in 2022 decided to appoint an investigatory committee on the submarine purchase.

The "Submarine Affair" resulted in the delay of the Israeli Navy's purchase of the subs by several years. By then the price of the vessels had nearly doubled, costing Israel an additional one billion euros.

THE "SUBMARINE AFFAIR" did not suffice for my opponents. Once again, something more was needed.

This was provided in 2019 by an indictment combining three charges: that I illicitly received cigars and champagne from a friend ("Case 1000"); failed to dismiss a so-called bribery attempt from a press mogul though even according to the indictment I had no intention of playing along ("Case 2000"); and received positive coverage on a website while making regulatory decisions concerning the website owner ("Case 4000"). The last charge was framed as bribery.

Since at the time of this writing the trial is still ongoing, I am limited in divulging many details debunking these charges. But I can relate several illuminating points.

Most legal scholars agree that before the charge against me was leveled no modern democracy had ever charged a politician with bribery for receiving positive press coverage. What's more, as it became apparent that the coverage in question was mostly negative, the charge changed from receiving "positive coverage" to receiving "unusual access" to the publisher, mostly for routine press releases issued by my spokesman.

The State Prosecutor Shai Nitzan actually *invented* a new crime tailored for me. Asked about the unprecedented nature of a bribery charge involving press coverage, Nitzan answered, "Every legal precedent has to start somewhere."[7]

The fear of using the criminal code as a political weapon is shared by all democracies. Most provide immunity for elected officials to protect them from politicized charges while in office, thereby protecting the people's choice, which is the foundation of democracy. Israel does not provide such sweeping protection for its elected leaders.

Nitzan not only pushed for an indictment; his colleagues rushed to do so against a sitting prime minister forty days before the election of April 2019, an act that could and did tilt the results. On February 28, 2019, the prosecution announced its intention to indict me pending a hearing and published a draft of the charge sheet. Asked about the seemingly deliberate timing, Nitzan replied blithely that he gathered people will not want to vote for a candidate suspected of bribery.[8]

When the first round of elections failed to produce a governing coalition, the prosecution timed the announcement of additional critical decisions regarding my case before the next election cycles.

On January 28, 2020, thirty-three days before the elections of March 2, the prosecution formally submitted the indictment to the court. It did so an hour before a pivotal press conference I held in Washington with President Trump on his peace plan.

Though I still received far more votes than anyone else who could potentially lead Likud, polls showed that these announcements had a significantly adverse impact on voters, and Likud lost several opportunities to create winning coalitions as a result.

Later, my trial exposed revelations that shook the foundations of the bribery charge. Before that happened, the missing votes prevented me from forming a government.

Legal interference in Israeli politics was not new, but since the time of the Likud's first victory in 1977, it has gradually taken a decided slant against the right.

In the thirty years up to 1977, only three former Knesset members were prosecuted, all identified with Labor.[9] Since then, more than thirty acting Knesset members have been indicted, twenty-four of whom belonged to Likud and affiliated rightist parties; three others were members of Arab parties. Almost no left-wing Knesset members have been indicted.[10]

In the previous decade, attempts by the government and former judges to restore public trust by bringing impartial oversight to the prosecution and the police investigatory unit had been continuously scuttled by Nitzan and his colleagues. Several conservative candidates for justice minister and police chief who called for such oversight were themselves indicted, putting a quick end to their candidacies. They were all later found innocent.

During the unfolding of my case, the need for impartial oversight became more relevant than ever. When the chief of police committed an act of misconduct that Nitzan himself labeled "outrageous," Nitzan buried the incident, warning that highlighting police misconduct "will only do good to those who want our harm and I don't have to spell things out," [11] clearly referring to me.

Nitzan made repeated public statements against me. He clearly crossed the boundaries of his office when he sent an email to sixty-two former Justice Ministry officials providing them with anti-Netanyahu talking points for press interviews. [12]

The police were also unrelenting in their pursuit of me, dating back to the beginning of their investigations in June 2016. One by one, many members of my closest staff and confidants were hauled into investigations and asked to give something, anything, on me.

One of them was subjected to extreme police intimidation and dirty tricks. Kept for days in a flea-infested cell, he was told that his family would be destroyed if he didn't "cooperate." Just to make sure he got the point, the police arranged a chance encounter during the investigation with a certain female acquaintance of his who was unrelated to the case.

Under this duress he became a state witness.

Then, in 2022, a newspaper investigative report exposed illegal police phone hacking of witnesses and others in my case with cutting-edge spyware. At first the police denied the story. Faced with incontrovertible evidence, they later admitted that they illicitly hacked the phone of a person who became another state witness. [13]

This witness revealed in court that he "felt threatened by police investigators" who told him to "think of his wife and seven children." He recounted being effectively told, in his words, to "bring us Bibi's head." [14]

The abuse of such spyware shocked the nation. When I appointed a new chief of police in 2015, well before I knew I would be the target of these practices, I specifically warned against inappropriate and unmeasured use of intrusive technology against civilians.

"A democracy must find a balance between civil liberties and public security," I said. "Everyone has a right to privacy. It's a basic right that defines us as human beings. This is a foundational right of free societies, and it demands that we not abuse the technological prowess that was developed by the security agencies."

I said this because I believe that democracy and the rule of law require the utmost respect for individual rights. No one is above the law, including the prime minister. But equally, no citizen can be subjected to criminal practices by the law enforcement agencies, including the prime minister.

When I pointed out some of the most egregious abuses of the rule of law that were revealed in my case and others, I was accused of engaging in a scorched-earth policy against the rule of law and democracy. I was painted as a boorish right-wing potentate hell-bent on destroying the foundations of Israeli democracy.

Nothing is further from the truth. I've always been a staunch believer in liberal democracy and have immersed myself since my teens in its classical texts. I protected the courts but I believed that preserving Montesquieu's balance between the three branches of government required reforms in Israel.

All in all, in the period spanning the police investigations, between June 2016 and December 2019, there were 561 news stories on prime-time television covering the investigations against me, 98 percent of them negative.

This means one negative news story every other day for three and a half years! Such a prolonged media feeding frenzy vies for a Guinness World Record.

I kept my focus and my cool. A joke began to circulate in Israel that an elephant was found in Africa with Bibi skin.

I'm often asked how I managed to continue to lead the country under such protests and assaults. The simple answer: I know who I am.

You can criticize me for many things. Being laser focused on my missions, I can sometimes be inattentive to others in a way that gets confused for aloofness. I can be curt. But there's one thing those who know me best or have worked closest with me would *never* accuse me of, and that is being corrupt.

From my earliest days, Father told me never to touch money if I ever entered public life. This remained sacrosanct to me. Hundreds of investigators spent more than a hundred million dollars scouring the globe in search of my so-called corruption. All they found was champagne bottles and cigars (whose numbers they vastly inflated) and a few nonnegative press articles.

I could withstand the attempted character assassination directed against me. But it was excruciatingly difficult when it was leveled against my family, who endured continuous suffering. I drew strength from the courage of Sara and the boys, from the constancy of my supporters and from the knowledge that truth is on my side.

Though the vilification hurt, nothing would distract me from two great missions I would soon embark on: achieving the historic Abraham Accords and protecting Israel from a global epidemic.

62

NEW PATH TO PEACE

2020

President Trump's groundbreaking recognition of Israel's claims in Jerusalem and the Golan, as well as his withdrawal from the dangerous Iran nuclear deal, did not quench his thirst for the "Deal of the Century," a final peace settlement between Israel and the Palestinians.

Early in his term he appointed his son-in-law Jared Kushner, aided by the able Jason Greenblatt, to accomplish this task.

A religious Jew and one of Trump's lawyers, Jason didn't hide his sympathies for Israel. Refreshingly, I never saw in him the need to bend over backward to prove his supposed objectivity. Though it was obvious that Jared called the shots, Jason's wisdom often helped my peace efforts.

I tried to steer both to the path of regional peace treaties with the Gulf states. Jared, who had formed close relationships with these countries' leaders and ambassadors, eventually became acquainted with their changing attitudes toward Israel. But throughout Trump's tenure, Jared remained committed to the task that the president had charged him with: get a peace deal with the Palestinians.

Faced with the president's fixation on the Palestinian issue, I decided that the best strategy was not to fight him over it but to work with his administration in a way that would still enable us to reach a breakthrough with the Arab states.

I knew the Palestinians would reject any plan Trump put on the table. The question was whether the US could come up with a plan that neither

Israel nor the Arab states would reject out of hand. When such a plan was presented, Israel could accept it with reservations, the Arab states could point to it as a good beginning, and we could begin normalizing our relations with them despite Palestinian rejectionism.

The Trump plan might also serve as a template for a workable peace with the Palestinians for some time in the future. It could replace the many dangerous proposals that came before it and that would have compromised Israel's security and undermined our national interests.

This strategy was easier said than done. Simultaneously pursuing an Israeli-Palestinian peace and a broader regional peace required an enormous expenditure of energy in Washington, Jerusalem, and elsewhere in the Middle East.

On the one hand, we kept up our contacts with the Gulf states. Ron Dermer met regularly with their ambassadors in Washington and I intensified my contacts with their leaders in the region. At the same time, we began to discuss our ideas about peace with the Palestinians with Jared, Jason and David Friedman.

THE PURSUIT OF a wider peace was aided by the fact that the Arab leaders witnessed our continued efforts to roll back Iran's nuclear program and Iran's attempts to embed itself in Syria. In the Middle East people respect strength and make peace with the strong. Everyone watched how Israel and Iran, the two strongest powers in the region, slugged it out over the skies of Syria. When we repeatedly hit Iran's targets in Syria, Syrian air defenses responded with increasingly vehement and misdirected antiaircraft fire. Sometimes their antiaircraft missiles landed as far away as off the Tel Aviv coast or in the northern Jordan Valley. We responded by systematically destroying Syrian antiaircraft batteries.

The inaccuracy of the Syrian antiaircraft fire resulted in an uncomfortable diplomatic situation with Russia. On September 17, 2018, while Israeli pilots were hitting nearby targets, a Syrian antiaircraft missile downed a Russian Ilyushin intelligence-gathering plane on its way to land at the Syrian air base in Khmeimim. Fifteen Russian crewmen were killed. The outraged Russians accused Israel of downing the plane.

I called Putin and explained that the plane was brought down by Syrian fire. Though two days later Putin said in a press conference that Israel hadn't shot down the plane and the incident seemed to be a result of a tragic string of misunderstandings, the Russian military command persisted in accusing us. It took many weeks and a special air force delegation I sent to Moscow to begin to dispel this mistaken assumption.

But the doubt persisted, fueled by Russian officers sympathetic to the Syrian army. Our freedom of action in Syria was imperiled. In a ceremony in Paris on November 11, 2018, to mark the one hundredth anniversary of the end of World War I, I met Putin and other world leaders in a lunch hosted by France's President Emmanuel Macron. I waited for all the guests to leave and pulled Putin aside.

It was our first face-to-face encounter since the downing of the plane.

"It was a tragic mistake. I assure you once again it wasn't us," I began, and then added, "Please tell your men to rein in these crazy Syrians. They won't succeed in shooting down our planes, but if they continue their wild fire, they'll bring down a civilian airliner."

We agreed to ratchet up the coordination between our air forces in Syria. Israel's sorties in the skies of Syria were resumed.

All this was duly registered by the Arab leaders. My unique position of having strong ties with both the American and the Russian presidents was buttressed when I flew directly from a visit with Trump in Washington to one with Putin in Moscow on January 29, 2020. Within twenty-four hours I had intimate meetings with the leaders of two of the most powerful countries on earth.

These signs of Israel's growing reputation inside Russia had been evident for some time. On May 9, 2018, Putin had invited me to attend ceremonies marking the seventy-third anniversary of Russia's victory over the Nazis in World War II. I was the only foreign leader other than Prime Minister Aleksandar Vucic of Serbia to attend.

I stood in Red Square as a military band played our national anthem, "Hatikva." A shiver ran down my spine. On that day, seventy-three years earlier, the Jewish people had been ground into dust and ash. Three-quarters of a century later I stood proudly representing the resurgent Jewish state, a power among the nations.

Yet as I watched the Russian troops march by, another thought also preoccupied me.

Thousands of Russian soldiers had practiced for months for this day. As the tanks, S-300 antiaircraft batteries, and assorted other weapons rolled by, I noted to Putin, "I recognize many of these weapons from our skirmishes in Syria."

Putin laughed.

But it was no laughing matter.

With about 150 million people, Russia had a GDP only four times the size of Israel's GDP with 9 million people. Yet despite its limited economic resources, Putin had rebuilt Russia's military to what appeared to be a formidable force.

This was one of the subjects raised in my visits to the Baltic states, the Visegrad group and Ukraine. The leaders of all these countries respected Israel greatly and sought its friendship. I felt enormously proud that after the horrors of the Holocaust the Jewish people suffered on their soil, the Jewish state was now being looked up to by all these countries as a much-valued partner. Our innovations in such areas as cybersecurity, automotive technology, health management, agriculture and defense beckoned to them.

Yet we weren't omnipotent. What I had seen on the parade ground in Red Square reaffirmed my conviction that our policy of treading carefully in Syria when it came to Russia was the correct one.

On May 29, 2019, I convened an unprecedented meeting in Jerusalem of the national security advisors of the United States, Russia and Israel—John Bolton, Nikolai Patrushev and Meir Ben Shabbat.

While we had divergent interests in Syria, could we not agree on some common principles to advance the resolution of the conflict there? The first principle we all agreed upon was that Iran's military should leave Syria.

This was important in its own right, but I also wanted the Russian security bureaucracy to witness firsthand the level of intimate relations Israel had with the United States. That could never hurt.

ON MOST FRONTS Israel was doing exceedingly well. On August 9, 2018, it received its highest-ever credit rating from the S&P rating agency, AA, which had only been achieved by fourteen other countries.

Though we were still one rating level below the top tier occupied by the US and eight others, we had overtaken many economies. Israel's economy was roaring, our security situation in Gaza had stabilized, we had effectively blocked Iran's plans to embed itself militarily in Syria and American pressure on Iran's nuclear program had been resumed—as had our various activities to stymie its nuclear ambitions.

With regard to the Palestinians, I had already helped create a positive change in their economic well-being by adopting liberal policies on investment, transportation, commerce and employment. I cut the number of Israeli security checkpoints and slashed the time it took to go through them. I also avoided a general closure of the Palestinian areas even in times of tension, letting some 150,000 Palestinian workers continue traveling to their jobs in Israel.

Shopping malls and new neighborhoods popped up in Ramallah and in other Palestinian towns. I even encouraged Israeli high-tech firms to set up joint ventures with Palestinian counterparts. Palestinian GDP per capita, though still low as in other unindustrialized and unreformed economies of the Arab world, nonetheless rose by a whopping 70 percent during my tenure from 2009 to 2019.[1]

I wondered: Could we use the hiatus from terror and overbearing US administrations to craft a new and realistic framework for peace, and could we harness our growing relationship with the Arab states to support it?

I discussed this possibility with Trump's people. Dermer discussed it with Arab ambassadors in Washington from 2016 on.

"Don't the Americans realize the Palestinians don't want peace?" they asked Dermer.

"We're working on a plan that neither Israel nor the Arab states would *have* to oppose," Dermer answered, "and which we can use as a basis for normalizing relations between you and us."

I sat with Dermer and drafted the basic principles on the path to peace that would guide our discussions with the Americans. The list was headed by two consistent principles that I had advocated for years: the Palestinians would recognize Israel as the Jewish state and end all claims against it, and Israel would retain military and security control west of the Jordan River.

Israel would not return to the 1967 lines and no Palestinian refugee would be accepted in the Jewish state. Jerusalem would remain united as Israel's capital and for the first time, the United States would recognize Israel's sovereignty over all the Jewish communities in Judea and Samaria. These long-held goals were now within reach.

No one would be uprooted from their home—Jew or Arab. This would require a change in approach from *territorial* continuity in the Palestinian areas to *transportational* continuity. Docks, train links, overpasses and underpasses would enable the Palestinians to enjoy the free movement of people and goods. A designated airport could be located in Jordan or elsewhere to facilitate air travel for Palestinians, with appropriate security arrangements for Israel.

Finally, Gaza would need to be demilitarized and transferred from Hamas rule to the control of Palestinians committed to peace.

As for a wider peace, Israel would normalize relations with Arab states, creating diplomatic offices, consulates and embassies and enjoying overflight rights.

Zionism always sought to deepen our roots in our ancient homeland. This was a historic opportunity to do so.

The discussions with Trump's team went on for more than two years. By the beginning of 2019, the basic contours of the plan were in place and we hoped that it would be unveiled following the Israeli elections in April 2019.

My coalition was nearing the end of its four-year term. We faced Benny Gantz's new united, multi-headed, center-left Blue and White party. The left was greatly aided by an indictment brought against me a mere few weeks before the election date. We undoubtedly lost some votes because of the deliberate timing of the indictment. Still, I rallied my base, and many were energized to vote for me by what they saw as a blatant attempt by the prosecution to tilt the elections results.

Despite an overwhelming electoral victory that appeared to produce a right-wing coalition of 65 seats, Lieberman's small five-seat party refused to join my coalition. Instead of 65 Knesset members ready to join a Likud coalition, we were left with only 60, not enough to get a ruling majority. This triggered new elections. Why Lieberman suddenly switched horses midstream remains the subject of much speculation, mostly tied to the criminal investigations that were conducted at the time related to the misuse of his party's funds.

A man who had railed against the left suddenly joined the left to topple a right-wing prime minister.

These electoral shenanigans forced us to postpone the peace plan.

The next round of elections took place in September 2019. But neither the right-wing bloc I led nor the left-wing bloc opposing me won a majority. Electoral fatigue was beginning to set in. Over the next few weeks, neither side could form a government and a third round of elections was called for March 2020.

Stuck in this endless loop, time was running out on launching the peace plan. The Trump administration was now approaching the end of its term and was eager to put out the Israeli-Palestinian peace plan. But I knew that even with our great historical achievements, our agreement to negotiate on the basis of the plan would be challenged by some on the right, especially on the eve of elections. Despite this, I was willing to take the risk. I had been through two American administrations that refused to look at the Israeli-Palestinian conflict through a different lens. Yet here was a different administration that was open to an entirely new approach.

The Trump administration was heading into its final year, and if we waited, there was a real chance they would be preoccupied with their campaign and the benefits of the plan would be lost.

When I agreed to take the political risk of engaging the Trump plan, I added one overriding element that parted with the tradition of waiting for Palestinian consent before anything could move forward. The plan allocated 30 percent of Judea and Samaria to Israeli sovereignty. This territory included all the Israeli communities, strategic lands like the Jordan valley, and areas of historic Biblical Jewish sites.

I insisted that the territory that President Trump's plan envisioned as being part of Israel in the future be part of Israel in the present. In other words, I wanted to apply Israeli law to this land up front, regardless of later negotiations with the Palestinians and regardless of whether they agreed to negotiate at all. In exchange, I would agree to hold off on doing anything with the territory Trump had envisioned for a future Palestinian state—no construction, no new settlements—but I limited this commitment to a period of four years.

Still, even though I only agreed to *negotiate* on the basis of the Trump plan, it was dangerous for me politically, since it offered a conceptual map of a Palestinian state, however limited in Palestinian sovereign powers and however generous in sovereign Israeli territory compared to previous plans. Even if the Palestinians rejected it, my willingness to negotiate on its basis was fraught with risk. This could only be offset if I could receive an American assurance that regardless of the Palestinian reply, I could automatically and immediately incorporate into Israel the areas intended to be under Israeli sovereignty.

I decided to advance this idea with the US administration.

"Ron," I said, "this is key. I'm not going to Washington unless the Americans agree that if I agree in principle to negotiate on the basis of the plan Israel gets thirty percent of the land up front, regardless of the Palestinian response."

"So what do you want?" asked Ron.

"I want a clear and unequivocal American commitment that the US will recognize the incorporation of these territories into Israel right away."

"Prime Minister," Ron said, "the right should realize that they'll never get a better American peace plan. Never."

"Even if they should, they won't," I said. "They don't even remember that we just saved them from Obama's plan for a Palestinian state on the 1967 borders and zero security for Israel."

"But the Palestinians are sure to reject the deal and it has all the elements you've been fighting for over the past decade—Palestinian recognition of a Jewish state, Israeli security control of the entire area west of the Jordan, no refugees, a united Jerusalem, no uprooting of people. American backing for these positions is a huge achievement," Ron said.

"Sorry, Ron, it's not enough. I need a clear American guarantee on what we get regardless of the Palestinian answer."

This was unprecedented. "Can we get it?" I asked.

"We can try," said Ron.

I knew that there would probably never be a better opportunity and the upside was huge. The Palestinians would most likely say no, and we'd get 30 percent of what is rightfully ours. I decided to go for it.

Jared and David assured me that in exchange for Israel agreeing to negotiate on the basis of the Trump plan and setting aside the territory the U.S. designated for a potential Palestinian state for at least four years, President Trump would immediately recognize Israeli control over 30 percent of the territory.

On January 28, 2020, the day before the ceremony unveiling the Trump peace plan, I exchanged letters with President Trump. The president's letter stated that the US would support Israel's declaration of sovereignty over the territory envisioned as part of Israel in the peace plan and my letter made clear that Israel would move forward with a declaration regarding sovereignty "in the coming days."

On the basis of these understandings, painstakingly negotiated by Dermer, Jared and Friedman over several months, I came to Washington. Three Arab ambassadors of countries that had no formal relations with Israel—the UAE, Bahrain and Oman—attended the ceremony, a sign of what was soon to come.

Trump extolled the plan as the first "fact-based" realistic proposal to solve the Israeli-Palestinian conflict. It was certainly better and more realistic than all its predecessors, having incorporated all the principles I laid out with Ron. Praising me for my "courage to take this bold step forward," Trump then described the process that would lead to immediate American recognition.

"We will form a joint committee with Israel to convert the conceptual map into a more detailed and calibrated rendering so that recognition can be immediately achieved. . . . The United States will recognize Israeli sovereignty over the territory that my vision provides to be part of the state of Israel. Very important."

In my remarks I thanked the president for all he had done for Israel. I stressed the fact that he was the first US president to recognize Israeli sovereignty over any part of Judea and Samaria.

"Mr. President," I said, "because of this historic recognition, and because I believe your plan strikes the right balance where other plans have failed, I have agreed to negotiate peace with the Palestinians on the basis of your peace plan."

There, the deal was struck. I agreed to proceed to negotiations based on the Trump plan, and the president agreed to quick US recognition of Israeli sovereignty over the areas delineated in the conceptual map.

Back at Blair House, I started briefing the accompanying Israeli journalists that within days I would bring a "decision in principle" to the cabinet to apply Israeli sovereignty over the 30 percent. Obviously the detailed maps of these areas would have to await the rendering of geographic and topographic details not on maps with a scale of 1:250,000 but on maps of 1:20,000 scale, but that shouldn't take long.

David Friedman briefed several Israeli journalists as well about the deal we had struck. This was the first time in the more than half a century since the Six-Day War that the United States had recognized Israel's sovereignty over *any* territory in Judea and Samaria.

But then something went terribly wrong.

Within a couple of hours of the ceremony, as I was briefing the Israeli press, the administration backtracked. The White House told journalists that an impending US recognition of Israeli sovereignty was not in the immediate offing, but could happen in the future.

What transpired to bring about this change is still unclear. Did David and Jared not explain to the president the commitment that he had just proclaimed publicly and signed in an exchange of letters with me?

Whatever the reason, it was inappropriate and cost me a great deal. I had made a commitment and stood by it. I had agreed to negotiate on the basis of the Trump plan that had been unveiled at the White House. That was not easy for me politically but I did it. I upheld my end of the bargain. Unfortunately, the Americans did not.

This caused a major setback in Israel. I was accused by the right of making false promises. To overcome this disappointment, I agreed with the American negotiating team that before passing any government decision on sovereignty, we would first have to map out in detail the areas to be included, after which we expected the United States to recognize these areas as Israel's, a process that would require several months. Without such American support I wouldn't act unilaterally but I left that possibility deliberately vague in my public discourse.

In my subsequent coalition negotiations with the Blue and White party to form a government, both sides would have to agree on everything. Any government decision was subject to a veto by Blue and White.

There was one notable exception that I insisted on including in the coalition agreement with Blue and White. The exception stipulated that

I could incorporate these areas into Israel even without the agreement of Blue and White. I was determined to move forward.

As our discussions with the Trump team about America recognizing Israeli sovereignty over parts of Judea and Samaria continued, we simultaneously advanced a normalization agreement with the UAE. The Emiratis, who heard from the Americans that they were not about to approve annexation soon, could now also argue that signing an agreement with Israel would supposedly stave off the potential incorporation of territories in Judea and Samaria.

Sheikh Mohamed bin Zayed (MBZ) was a shrewd and visionary leader. Following his father's footsteps, he completed the transformation of the Emirates from several sleepy fishing villages into a robust free trade zone with excellent shopping and port facilities. He understood that a peace agreement with Israel would offer the Emirati economy the benefit of Israeli innovation and tourism, closer defense ties with Israel, and a tacit alliance with Israel and the US against the aggression of Iran, only a few kilometers away on the other side of the Strait of Hormuz.

The peace negotiations between us, the Emirates, and the Americans were conducted secretly in Washington over a six-week period in the summer of 2020. On the Israeli side, only three people were aware of the negotiations besides me—Ambassador Dermer, Minister of Tourism Yariv Levin, and National Security Advisor Meir Ben Shabbat.

Earlier, working on the Trump peace plan for an Israeli-Palestinian agreement, I shared information in a limited circle. Dore Gold, Israel's former ambassador to the UN and a trusted advisor, was involved in overseeing the map. Michael Herzog, a former brigadier general in IDF intelligence and a future ambassador to the US, reviewed the security-related sections of the plan. This leakproof circle in a country notorious for leaks enabled us to shock the world. I would now do the same with the Abraham Accords.

On August 13, 2020, the normalization agreement was announced in a three-way phone call between Trump, MBZ, and me.

Before convening the official ceremony in Washington, we set a goal of completing a similar agreement with Bahrain. Bahrain, a thriving city-state in the Gulf, was equally concerned with Iranian aggression and equally open to cooperating with Israeli entrepreneurs.

This readiness had deep roots. Five years earlier, during the Paris Climate Conference of November 2015, which I attended, I confidentially met a senior emissary from Bahrain in a meeting arranged at the Élysée Palace by President François Hollande. Already then we had discussed our common interests and the need to normalize the relations between our two countries, which to that point had been maintained mostly by the Mossad. In 2020 these seeds germinated. The agreement with Bahrain, like the preceding one with the Emirates, was reached with the prior knowledge and encouragement of Saudi Arabia.

We raced against time, knowing that the US elections were only a few weeks away. We knew that if Trump lost, the peace train would likely grind to a halt. Making history often requires beating electoral deadlines.

The signing ceremony of the agreements with the UAE and Bahrain, which were named the Abraham Accords, took place on September 15 on the White House lawn. Trump beamed. Despite his fixation with the Palestinians, he could justifiably take pride that he was the first president in a quarter century to sponsor not one but two peace deals, between Israel and two Arab states.

Standing in the White House terrace, overlooking a sunny South Lawn, with the two Arab foreign ministers and me at his side, the president spoke:

> We're here this afternoon to change the course of history. Together, these agreements will serve as the foundation for a comprehensive peace across the entire region—something which nobody thought was possible.
>
> These agreements prove that the nations of the region are breaking free from the failed approaches of the past. Today's signing sets history on a new course.

As we stood in that balcony, I saw Sara, Yair and Avner seated with the rest of the guests down below. I was glad my family was with me to experience this historic moment. They had suffered so much and had been pilloried for so long. Here was vindication for their unceasing travails. This was a day my sons would describe to their grandchildren.

Peace would be advanced by nurturing Israel's economic, military, and diplomatic strength. It would not be achieved by following the failed formula of offering dangerous concessions to the Palestinians that undermined Israel's security and brought war closer.

My policy reversed the order of achieving peace with the Arab world by bypassing the Palestinian veto. Instead of starting with the Palestinians, begin with the wider Arab world and only then tackle the challenge of achieving a final settlement of the Palestinian-Israeli conflict.

In the ceremony I began by thanking President Trump for his decisive leadership in brokering peace.

"This day is a pivot of history," I said. "It heralds a new dawn of peace." I went on to emphasize that strength was the first and most essential prerequisite to peace. It was also the vindication of what some referred to as the Netanyahu Doctrine, but in reality it was a culmination of Jabotinsky's "Iron Wall" theory, passed on from him to Father and from Father to me.

Then the foreign ministers of the UAE and Bahrain, Trump and I each signed the Abraham Accords.

Jackpot! Mission number four accomplished.

In a phone call with President Trump on September 4, 2020, on live television, the president took justifiable pride in the achievement, and then threw me a curveball.

"So what do you think, Bibi?" he said. "Do you think Sleepy Joe could have made this deal, Bibi? Sleepy Joe. Do you think he would have made this deal? Somehow I don't think so."

Professor Klausner's unexpected question to me almost seventy years earlier about the chocolates that he used to give my brother and me raced through my mind.

While deeply appreciative of President Trump's efforts, as the prime minister of Israel I couldn't get into the thick of America's politics.

"Well, Mr. President," I answered, "one thing I can tell you is that we appreciate the help for peace from anyone in America, and we appreciate what you've done enormously."

*   *   *

THE SIGNING OF the Abraham Accords released enormous positive energies. Flying over Saudi Arabia, Israelis poured into Dubai, Abu Dhabi and Bahrain. Business leaders in Israel and the Gulf were busy closing deals, while goods from the Gulf came to the ports of Haifa and Ashdod. Israelis and Gulf Arabs openly embraced one another. It was nothing short of miraculous.

The accords served as a platform to have two other Muslim countries join the circle of peace. The US now placed normalization very high on its agenda and was willing to offer concrete incentives for other countries to take the plunge.

The first was Sudan.

On February 3, 2020, I had visited Uganda to meet Sudan's military chief, Abdel Fattah al-Burhan, one of two Sudanese leaders who had led the movement to topple the dictator Omar al-Bashir. This meeting was discreetly arranged by Uganda's President Yoweri Museveni.

Over lunch with al-Burhan, I discussed the advantages that would accrue to Sudan from establishing relations with Israel, including being removed from the US list of terror-supporting states. Naturally, I didn't reminisce about my decision to bomb Khartoum airport a few years earlier.

Al-Burhan was clearly interested. But as the lunch progressed, I saw that he was having trouble releasing even the brief statement about our meetings that had been agreed upon beforehand.

"What's the problem?" I asked the able Ugandan diplomat Najwa Gadaheldam, who had done much to arrange the meeting.

"He's got domestic opposition," she said. "The other partner in his coalition is fearful that normalization with Israel would stir Muslim protest."

We eventually issued the statement about our meeting, but the obstacle of internal resistance to peace with Israel still needed to be overcome.

While we were having lunch, we discussed African and Israeli cuisine. For some reason Chinese cuisine also popped up in the conversation.

"You know they eat everything there," one of the guests said. "Even bats. That's supposedly where this new disease corona came from."

When we parted we warmly thanked Uganda's president and his assistant Gadaheldam.

A year later, Najwa was diagnosed with Covid. The emergency medical assistance I sent to Uganda failed to save her. I never knew if she received my final expression of thanks for her part in securing the third peace agreement between Israel and Sudan.

Resistance in the chronically unstable Sudan was ultimately overcome, and an agreement was formally concluded on January 6, 2021. The US agreed to remove Sudan from the list of terror-supporting states and Sudan agreed to open its airspace to aircraft bound to and from Israel, bringing my vision of direct flights to anywhere in Africa and South America one step closer.

The fourth peace achieved before the end of Trump's term was with Morocco.

The Mossad had continuous relations with its Moroccan counterpart agency and Israeli tourists had visited the country for years. But we had no official, normalized diplomatic relations and no direct flights between our countries.

During a UN visit in September 2018, I had met discreetly with Morocco's foreign minister, a meeting arranged by Dore Gold.

"It's time to come out in the open and formally establish normalization. Let's begin with direct flights from Tel Aviv to Rabbat," I said.

From Morocco's side, the foreign minister was interested in securing a closer relationship with the US, especially on the matter of Morocco's long-standing claim over Western Sahara. We agreed to see what we could each do for the other.

Once the Abraham Accords were signed in Washington, we focused on securing a peace treaty with Morocco. The US administration signaled its willingness to recognize Morocco's territorial claims and Morocco expressed its willingness to normalize relations with Israel, including the opening of embassies and the establishment of direct flights.

A three-way phone call on December 10, 2020, was arranged for President Trump, Morocco's King Mohammed VI and me in which we announced the normalization agreement between Israel and Morocco. The public announcement stirred many hearts in Israel, especially among those whose families came from Morocco. Given its historically benign treatment of the Jewish community, they retained a warm feeling for the country. Now, after the normalization agreements were in place, they could fly there without the hassle of connecting flights and endless delays.

In a separate phone call I reached out to the king of Morocco, using a mixture of English and my halting French.

What began as a stiff diplomatic conversation soon thawed into friendly banter. This being a call to Morocco, I ended it by alluding to the closing line of *Casablanca*, with which the king was familiar.

"Your Majesty," I said, "This is the beginning of a beautiful friendship."

The king laughed. "I agree," he said.

In Israel's first 72 years it achieved two peace agreements. Within four months in 2020 it achieved four more.

A short time before the US election, Kosovo, a fifth Muslim country, this time in Europe, was added to the list of countries making peace with Israel. This was entirely an American-led operation and it included a Serbian commitment to open an embassy in Jerusalem.

I HAD ACTUALLY hoped and planned for one more peace agreement with an Arab nation, which, due to regrettable circumstances, wasn't to be. The country I had in mind was Oman.

I visited in October 2018, and my meeting then with Oman's leader, Sultan Qaboos bin Said, was poignant and deeply moving. Unlike most of my other meetings about normalization with leaders of Arab countries, this visit was not clandestine but open for the world to see. Qaboos was frail and in advanced stages of the cancer that would claim his life fourteen months later. He greeted Sara and me with grace and dignity in his exquisite palace in Muscat. In my life I had visited grand palaces from the Élysée to the Kremlin, many much bigger than the one in Muscat, but I never saw such refined and minute attention to aesthetic detail.

This was clearly the work of the Sultan himself, who quietly escorted Sara and me through the corridors and halls that he had personally designed. The Sultan struck me as having the soul of an artist, an impression strengthened by a private concert he arranged for us of striking Arab music. We later joined him for a late-night dinner accompanied by European chamber music, with which he was also intimately familiar.

Qaboos was a wise leader who maintained a careful balance of relations with the surrounding Arab countries and Iran, across the Gulf.

In his study I described to him Israel's vision of a rail link between the Arabian Gulf and Israel's Mediterranean ports.

"This is the future," I said.

His eyes grew bright, yet there was deep sadness in them. We left in a warm embrace, understanding it was unlikely we would ever meet again.

Flying back to Israel, I turned to Sara.

"Why do you think he invited us?" I asked.

"He wanted to see you before he died," she said simply.

Qaboos died on January 10, 2020, leaving a sealed envelope with the name of his designated successor. Had he lived he probably would have been another signatory of the Abraham Accords.

TO ACHIEVE THE peace between Israel and Arab states we had overcome many obstacles, none more enduring than the obsessive belief in the centrality of the Palestinian issue and the need to achieve a Palestinian-Israeli peace before any other peace could be made.

John Kerry, like so many others, had held that belief, and he expressed it in December 2016 during a conference in Washington attended by many of my political opponents, invited especially from Israel to hear it:

> There will be no separate peace between Israel and the Arab world. I want to make that very clear to all of you. I've heard several prominent politicians in Israel sometimes saying "Well, the Arab world is in a different place now, we just have to reach out to them and we can work some things with the Arab world and we'll deal with the Palestinians."
>
> No, no, no and no . . . There will be no advance and separate peace with the Arab world without the Palestinian process and Palestinian peace. Everyone needs to understand that. That is a hard reality.

When Kerry finished delivering his remarks, he received thunderous applause.

It was only by breaking out of this flawed way of thinking, however, that true progress was made. In its first seventy-two years, Israel made peace with two Arab countries, Egypt and Jordan. In the span of four months, Israel had made peace with four more.

By building Israel's power and challenging Iran, we had made Israel an attractive ally to our Arab neighbors. By bypassing the Palestinians, we could now achieve four diplomatic breakthroughs and sign four historic agreements.

This was truly a New Middle East, one built on real strength and no false illusions.

TRUMP HAD MADE history.

He was able to do so because of his inherent irreverence. He was bound by few conventions. This is why he could brush aside the traditional thinking of the foreign policy elite on such matters as the Iran nuclear deal and recognizing Jerusalem and the Golan.

Yet, paradoxically, his initial fixation on that old axiomatic truth—that an Israeli-Palestinian peace would solve the problems of the Middle East and that the key to achieving that peace was overcoming Israeli intransigence—delayed the launch of the historic peace accords between Israel and Arab states to the end of his term rather than its beginning, as I had hoped. "By that time," as Ron Dermer told Jared Kushner, we were "running out of runway to get more peace treaties," which could have effectively ended the Israeli-Arab conflict.

Often described as a transactional president, Trump would approach an issue by asking, "Why do we need this?" invariably followed by, "What do we get for this?" Often this attitude got to the heart of many absurdities and iniquities, but sometimes it overlooked basic truths.

"Why do we need NATO?" a question that puts into doubt a critical foundation of the free world's security, is entirely different from "Why are the NATO partners not paying their fair share?" a legitimate Trump question that had long waited to be asked.

Trump's insistence on reciprocity in trade was also well overdue. Why should some countries be allowed to insist on free trade for themselves while closing off their markets to American goods and services?

Trump's unpredictability caused much discomfort among his frequently changing staff and among America's allies, who were used to automatic, reflexive support from American presidents. But it had its uses internationally by putting America's adversaries off balance and instilling fear in its enemies.

As Israel's prime minister, I saw it as my job to carefully navigate through the new reality Trump brought to Washington in order to advance Israel's security and vital national interests and to forge four historic peace agreements.

I could do so because Trump adopted an entirely new approach to peacemaking. He did not heed bureaucratic orthodoxy and was willing to go outside the box. For the first time in Israel's history, peace was achieved without ceding territory or uprooting Jews from their homes. It was based on mutual economic, diplomatic and security interests in which all sides benefited.

In addition to recognizing Jerusalem and the Golan, President Trump recognized the legality of Jewish communities in Judea and Samaria. In confronting Iran he was equally bold. Recognizing the absurdity of the Iran deal, he withdrew from it and did not hesitate to apply forceful economic and military pressures on Tehran.

In all this he was a true trailblazer.

Despite bumps in the road, our years together were the best ever for the Israeli-American alliance, strengthening security and bringing four historic peace accords to Israel and the Middle East.

They showed the world that great things happen when an American president and an Israeli prime minister work in tandem, with no daylight between them. We proved conclusively that if you pursue peace through strength, you get both.

63

COVID

2019–2021

The news of the coronavirus outbreak in China in December 2019 lit warning lights in many countries, including Israel. The great distance from China to Israel offered no protection.

Remembering the exponential growth of epidemics from my MIT statistics course some fifty years earlier, I knew it wasn't a question of *if* we would get hit by the virus but only *when*. Well before the World Health Organization said so, I told the Israeli public that we were in the midst of a global pandemic.

Brushing aside the usual criticism of my political opponents that I was being alarmist, I acted swiftly.

I instructed the government ministries and the health system to follow two simple rules: First, save lives. Second, overprepare rather than underprepare.

Under this policy, Israel was among the first countries in the world to restrict flights from China and place restrictions on incoming flights from other countries, while setting up a system of medical tests and isolation for Israelis returning from abroad.

When Covid cases soon began to spread in Israel, we diluted the presence of workers in both the government and the private sector, asked the public to wear masks, limited the number of people gathering in one place, and used court-approved digital means to track the sources of infections.

The IDF set up a Covid lab and its soldiers helped distribute food to "red cities" with restricted movement. Using their contacts abroad, the Mossad and the Ministry of Defense helped the government purchase life-support machines and other vital equipment.

The brunt of fighting the pandemic fell on Israel's dedicated doctors, nurses, and other caregivers who stood on the front lines. I expressed the nation's gratitude for their efforts in nightly broadcasts with the director general of the Health Ministry, Moshe Bar Siman Tov, and other officials.

In times of uncertainty, people need to see and hear their leaders. I spoke clearly and straightforwardly without minimizing the dangers ahead.

During the first few months of the disease, everyone was grasping at straws in the dark. I was no different.

I called eminent virologists around the world and picked their brains. I spoke twice to Dr. Deborah Birx, of President Trump's Covid team. I brought in experts from Israel's scientific community. Not all of them agreed on the severity of the disease. A Nobel Prize–winning biochemist told me that Covid was "a small anthill" that would soon disappear. I didn't buy it.

I got much better advice from my friend Larry Ellison, the brilliant founder and chairman of Oracle, who was working closely with experts at Oxford University on fighting epidemics.

"Bibi, get as many vaccines as you can, from as many sources as you can, as quickly as you can," Larry urged. As usual, he was spot-on.

I discussed with Larry and his advisors my intention to develop an Israeli vaccine. Israel's Biological Institute began working on this project. They did fine work, but because they were practically starting from scratch, they couldn't reach the finish line ahead of the pharmaceutical giants that had been working on vaccines for years. Still, the accumulated knowledge could serve Israel well in the future.

Alongside the virus itself, I had to confront disinformation campaigns from political opponents and sundry Covid deniers. The head of the Opposition, Yair Lapid, called on people to take to the streets against an "illegitimate government."[1] Yoram Lass, a former deputy minister of health in a Labor government, said "Covid is no more than a flu" and "the chances from dying from it are almost zero."[2] Benny Gantz said that my policies were politically geared to prevent people from voting. A fierce debate raged in the nightly news programs over government policy.

The disease killed tens of thousands in Italy, Belgium, Holland, Spain and other countries. As it spiked in Israel, threatening to collapse our hospitals' ability to care for the seriously ill, I tightened the screws. Enforcing a lockdown, we got the infection rate down, "flattening the curve," as the saying went.

Israel was ahead of the curve, seemingly able to bring the disease under control while others could not. It was then that I made a cardinal mistake. Responding to public pressure, the government lifted restrictions on public gatherings, restaurants, bars, eateries, large parks, swimming pools, and public transportation too quickly.

To make matters worse, I gave a press conference in which I thanked Israel's citizens for their cooperation and then added, "We want to help the economy and ease your lives, to make it possible for you to get out, return to normalcy. Go get a cup of coffee, a glass of beer, have fun."[3]

The public did just that and the infection rate soon began to rise again.

"Prime Minister, are we out of it?" I was asked by my staff.

"Of course not," I answered. "As long as there's even one infected person around, the disease will reappear and again spread exponentially."

"So what should we do?"

"You ever play an accordion?" I asked. "That's what we'll do. We'll open up and close down the country, depending on the infection rate and our hospitals' ability to handle the severely ill, until we can get this damn thing under control."

The "accordion policy" was an attempt to strike a balance between keeping the hospitals from crashing and keeping businesses from collapsing. We shelled out billions of shekels to help small businesses, employers, and laid-off workers.

This largesse was frowned upon by those who had previously supported my tight fiscal policies. Two prominent officials in the Finance Ministry unabashedly briefed reporters against the government's economic aid policy.

"Prime Minister Netanyahu is working against Finance Minister Netanyahu," carped my critics.

Not quite. Unlike in previous economic crises, the world was awash with cheap credit. The cost of an economic collapse from a general health breakdown would be far greater than the interest payments we would have to make to keep business alive.

During my long tenures as finance minister and prime minister I faced three global economic crises. Each one required its own diagnosis and treatment. Following the dot-com crisis of 2001–2002, I led Israel's free-market revolution. Following the subprime mortgage crisis of 2008, I pursued a policy of conservative restraint. And now in the economic crisis brought on by Covid in 2020 I instituted a policy of infusing the economy with cheaply available credit to stimulate economic activity, believing that we would recover rapidly once the pandemic was brought under control. In all three cases Israel's economy was among the first in the world to emerge from the crises.

Yet I knew that Covid required careful maneuvering between health and economic needs. Periodic lockdowns can't go on forever without severe cost to businesses and to the physical and mental health of citizens. Lockdowns could only buy limited time for the development of real solutions.

From the start of the pandemic I believed there were only two such solutions: the development of an effective vaccine or the development of an effective cure. Or both.

Several pharmaceutical companies were racing to develop vaccines. Remembering Ellison's sage advice, my policy was "Get as many vaccines from as many reliable sources for as many people as possible."

The Health Ministry made tentative initial contacts with several of these firms.

I instructed its officials to sign contracts with them as quickly as possible.

"Don't argue with them about the price," I said to them. "If a vaccine is developed, the price will skyrocket and we'd regret the fact that we didn't order enough vaccines in time."

Time was indeed of the essence. Once an effective vaccine was ready, we would have to compete with the largest and most prosperous countries in the world to get doses. What advantage can a tiny country with one-tenth of 1 percent of the world's population have over everyone else?

Every week or so I held videoconferences with the leaders of other small countries who had managed, like us, to control the disease. We shared information, seeking to learn from each other's experience.

My curiosity was piqued on November 11, 2020, in one of those conferences when the prime minister of Greece, Kyriakos Mitsotakis, noted that the head of Pfizer, which was working on the most promising vaccine, was a native of Thessaloniki.

"You know, Bibi, he's also Jewish," he said.

I went to my office in the Knesset immediately after the call.

"Google Pfizer's CEO," I told my staff.

I learned that his name was Albert Bourla.

"Like the Israeli writer Ofra Bourla-Adar," I noted with increasing interest. "Get him on the line now."

Within minutes, Albert Bourla was on the call.

"Prime Minister Netanyahu," he said, "I am thrilled to talk to you."

"I am delighted no less to talk to you," I replied.

Bourla shared his family's story with me. On the eve of Holocaust, Thessaloniki's Jewish community was 50,000 strong. Only 2,000 Jews survived. His parents and his wife's parents were among them.

"My wife is by my side," Albert said. "She is no less excited than I am."

Bourla knew of my visit with Sara to Thessaloniki two years earlier, including to the synagogue where he had married his wife, Myriam.

An instant chemistry was formed between us. Bourla was serious, smart and compassionate. He expressed his belief that Pfizer was en route to developing an effective vaccine. He was fully committed to the company he was managing and fully aware of the great service it could provide humanity. I knew that he was utterly professional, so despite his sympathy to Israel he could not single us out for favorable treatment.

We agreed to speak again shortly.

I racked my brain. Once the vaccine was developed, it would take many months to produce large quantities. A full-scale "vaccine war" could ensue between major countries. We had little time before leaders would face the gravest stage of the exponential spread of the disease and press the pharma companies to supply them with the vaccines. Israel would be pushed to the end of the line.

What could tilt the balance? What could Israel offer Pfizer to warrant a large supply of vaccines?

I immediately consulted Meir Ben Shabbat, the head of National Security Council; Moshe Bar Siman Tov, the director general of the Ministry of Health; Dr. Osnat Luxemburg, a senior official at the Health Ministry and, as always, Ron Dermer.

In talking to them, we hit upon an idea.

Israel had a computerized database containing the medical records of 98 percent of Israelis. It was a statistical database that rigorously protected the privacy of individual records. Before the outbreak of Covid, I passed a decision in the government to finance the use of this database for the development of generic drugs and medical treatments by Israeli companies dealing with life sciences. My goal was to make Israel a global biotech center, just as it had become a leader in other technological fields.

Now I put forth a sweeping idea. Israel could be the first country in the world to achieve herd immunity by a mass vaccination campaign. We could use the database for statistically evaluating the vaccine's effectiveness for people of different ages, different medical conditions and other factors. No other country had such a robust and all-encompassing database.

We also had a unique system of four health maintenance organizations (HMOs) that covered nearly everyone in the country and could be mobilized to administer the vaccines efficiently and swiftly to the entire population. We could be the model country for the world on nationwide vaccinations.

I called the HMO chiefs. They told me and the minister of health that they were up to the challenge.

"Prime Minister, with an all-out effort we'll be able to vaccinate one hundred thousand Israelis daily," they assured us.

Two days after our first conversation, I called Bourla back.

"I have a suggestion for you, Albert," I said, and told him of our idea. Bourla was intrigued.

He understood the possible breakthrough and asked, "Prime Minister, are you sure you'll be able to meet those numbers?"

"Albert," I said, "I give you my word. As prime minister I will personally take care of it. Israel is different from other countries. We are a small country but very effective in security and lifesaving matters. The HMOs and the public are accustomed to acting in crisis. There is no other country like us in the world."

In practice, Israel's vaccination rate reached a peak of 200,000 jabs a day, an astounding number in a country of nine million people.

As Bourla later wrote:

> Netanyahu was among the first to call me to advocate for earlier deliveries in his country and started me wondering if Israel could be the country to demonstrate the benefits of widespread vaccination.
>
> Two days later, I received another call. . . . [H]e hadn't even bothered to schedule it. He brought to my attention some legal issues related to our contract negotiations for delivery of the vaccine. I promised to come back to him. I looked at my watch and calculated the time in Israel.
>
> "Prime Minister, it is two thirty in the morning!"
>
> "Don't worry about that. I don't need much sleep," he replied. "Look, Albert. If we leave this just to the lawyers, we will never get it done. I will conference our head lawyer now. Can you do the same?"
>
> I felt a little bit uncomfortable, but . . . by 3:00 a.m. Israel time, most of the [legal] issues were resolved, with only a few of them remaining on the table. . . . I thought this was the last time I would hear from Bibi.

It wasn't. All in all, I called Bourla at least fifty times in the coming months. Recounting the events later, Bourla said, "Your Prime Minister was obsessive. He would call me at 3:00 in the morning to ask questions. He wanted to know every detail."

That was an accusation I readily accepted.

I also spoke many times with Stéphane Bancel, the CEO of Moderna, Pfizer's main competitor, with whom we signed a contract for the supply of several hundred thousand vaccines. But it was clear that only Pfizer could supply Israel with the needed millions, and the company was ready to do so once they were sold on Israel as the model country for mass vaccination.

"You know everyone will think we did this because we are Jews," Bourla writes that he texted Mikael Dolsten, Pfizer's head of research, who also happens to be Jewish.

"I know, but Israel is the right bet," Dolsten replied.[4]

On November 9, 2020, Pfizer announced that it had developed an effective vaccine for Covid-19.[5] On December 9, the first plane with Pfizer vaccines landed in Israel, and on December 11, the US Food and Drug Administration granted emergency approval of that vaccine. On December 19, I was the first Israeli to get jabbed, dispelling the fears of many and kicking off a mass vaccination campaign. I encouraged all eligible Israelis to get vaccinated and soon millions did so.

Following Albert's suggestion, the Ministry of Health signed a research collaboration agreement and formed a steering committee with epidemiologists from Israel, Pfizer and Harvard University.

As Israel exceeded a 90 percent vaccination rate for high-risk populations such as the elderly we dramatically reduced the infection rate and the number of seriously ill. Before vaccines we tragically lost six thousand lives to the virus. With vaccines we brought the death rate down to almost zero at the time.

Israel was vaccinated earlier and quicker than other countries. We were a success story and an international model. We made information about the efficacy of the vaccine available to Pfizer and the world.

Bourla summed it up best when he said, "Israel has done the most amazing job in mobilizing their health care system and delivering the most successful vaccination campaign in the world."

Of course, the story doesn't end here. Israel, like the rest of the world, must learn to contend with new Covid variants and future epidemics of other viruses. This will require new vaccines, new therapeutic drugs, and new techniques. But Israel showed how a determined nation can overcome such a seemingly impossible challenge.

64

ROLLER COASTER

2019-2022

While I was dealing with Covid and forging our four peace agreements I was also contending with ongoing political upheaval.

Between 2019 and 2020, Israel had experienced an electoral roller coaster. It went to the polls three times—in April 2019, September 2019, and March 2020—before I was able to form a government.

Even then it was a composite "rotation" government, multi-headed from the start, composed of Likud and a splintered Blue and White party. With 36 seats I would serve first as prime minister, to be followed a year and a half later by Benny Gantz with 15 seats.

It was a problematic union from the start. To form a government I had to agree to give Blue and White a veto on all cabinet decisions, a prescription for potential paralysis. Blue and White blocked most of my initiatives and some of its cabinet ministers openly criticized me, knowing that I couldn't fire them under the coalition agreement, which was anchored in legislation.

This quickly descended into daily recriminations, each side accusing the other of not adhering to its part of the coalition agreement. Having seen in the first two months of the government that Blue and White ministers were acting like an opposition within the coalition, I intentionally left them in the dark on crucial matters to prevent them from scuttling my initiatives.

On other matters we needed to go through the government or the Knesset, and we were often stymied. When Covid was still raging, Blue and White even objected to a government decision to fund the third dose of lifesaving vaccines that I ordered from Pfizer to stave off the resurgence of infections that would come sooner or later.

I got around them by getting approval for the funding in the Knesset finance committee, which had a committee head aligned with Likud. Cabinet meetings turned into excruciating debating sessions, sometimes lasting until the early morning hours.

Somehow we trudged along.

Yet there was one challenge that we met with unity and harmony. The Knesset was dissolved for a fourth time on December 22, 2020. In the ensuing elections on March 23, 2021, Likud got 30 seats, well ahead of the runner-up center-left party that got 17 seats. Still, given Israel's wobbly parliamentary system, the results were inconclusive and for weeks no one was able to form a new government.

My government had just completed the most secure and prosperous decade in Israel's history, brought it out of Covid before any other country in the world, and elevated Israel to be a power among the nations. Above all, the efforts of my successive governments rolled back, time and again, Iran's quest to develop nuclear weapons. Former IDF chief of staff Gadi Eisenkot summed it up succinctly in 2022 when he said, "Had Israel not implemented a multifaceted strategy of primarily covert operations, Iran would have become nuclear seven to ten years ago."[1]

It was precisely at this politically unstable stitch of time, when all the parties were haggling to form the next coalition, that we worked together when we faced a powerful challenge from Hamas.

The crisis was ostensibly sparked by a pending court decision to allow the eviction of a few Palestinian families from several houses owned by Jews in the Jerusalem neighborhood of Shimon Ha Tzadik.

Hamas protested that the Israeli government was "cleansing Palestinians from East Jerusalem." This was nonsense. The government was not involved in any way in this wholly civil dispute about private property rights.

Hamas declared that it was "the protector of Muslim Jerusalem" and incited daily riots by Palestinians. On May 6, 2021, escalating its rhetoric, it threatened Israel: "We cannot be silent on what is happening in Jerusalem. Israel should expect that we will act at any moment."

Things came to a head on May 9, one day before Jerusalem Day, an annual celebration of the reunification of our capital after the Six-Day War.

Muslim worshippers on the Temple Mount threw rocks on Jewish worshippers at the Western Wall below. When Israeli police intervened, they threw rocks at them, too, and used fireworks as projectiles to attack the officers. Twelve policemen and hundreds of rioters were wounded.

The following day, Hamas issued an ultimatum. It demanded that within six hours Israel withdraw the police from the Temple Mount and the Shimon Ha Tzadik neighborhood and that it release all the rioters arrested in the Temple Mount riots. If Israel didn't comply, it would suffer the consequences.

This was clearly out of the question.

All this coincided with the annual parade conducted on Jerusalem Day. The parade was scheduled to start at the Old City's Damascus Gate, pass through the crowded Muslim Quarter and reach the Western Wall. The Damascus Gate had been the scene of several recent incidents in which Palestinian terrorists stabbed Jews to death.

I was under considerable pressure from the press, the Opposition and the Palestinians to cancel the parade. Such a capitulation to Hamas extortion was not an option. But in an effort to avoid a violent clash, I was willing to change the parade route. The security services suggested that it be rerouted to the Jaffa Gate, reaching the Western Wall via a road that circumvented crowded neighborhoods. I agreed.

The parade began at five thirty in the afternoon.

Half an hour later, at six o'clock, Hamas fired dozens of rockets at Israel, seven of them at Jerusalem and twenty at the greater Tel Aviv area.

That was that. Enough was enough.

I convened the cabinet, which unanimously authorized a strong military response to this outrageous attack. Our goal in what would come to be known as Operation Guardian of the Walls was to degrade Hamas's fighting ability and to restore deterrence.

"Hamas will suffer blows they can't even imagine," I promised.

Rather than starting slow in the hope of deescalating, we struck hard, much harder than anyone anticipated. In the early hours of the campaign we hit senior Hamas commanders and technical experts. With minimal civilian casualties, we brought down several towers that served as Hamas command posts. The IDF destroyed Hamas naval and aerial units that had planned to attack us from the sea and the air. We also struck the Hamas cyber warfare unit.

Though Hamas was aware that we had been building a subterranean wall equipped with sensors around the Gaza perimeter, its effectiveness at blocking the terror tunnels shocked them. The underground route through which they planned to penetrate Israel was gone.

But the biggest shock of all were our pinpointed aerial strikes with bunker-busting bombs on the "terror metro," the underground web of tunnels and bunkers beneath the Gaza Strip that Hamas had built to provide shelter to its terrorist army. This was the first time in the history of warfare that tunnels were struck with such precision and effectiveness from the air, a major technological and intelligence coup that set Hamas back at least a decade.[2]

In the first day of the fighting, America's new president, Joe Biden, called me. We had known each other for close to forty years, from the time we both came to Washington, he as a young senator from Delaware and I as deputy chief of Israel's embassy to the United States. Four days after the 2020 elections Biden was declared president-elect. In the twenty-four hours after that declaration I followed twenty other world leaders in offering my congratulations. This elicited the ire of President Trump, who to this day believes that I was the first to do so.

Now in our phone call President Biden said that America stood by Israel's right to defend itself. But in the coming days, as the fighting escalated and the press reported on mounting Palestinian casualties, he began to push for a cease-fire.

"Bibi, I gotta tell you, I'm coming under a lot of pressure back here," he said. "This is not Scoop Jackson's Democratic Party," referring to the strikingly pro-Israel senator whose long tenure ended in the 1980s.

"I'm getting squeezed here to put an end to this as soon as possible."

I responded that I was getting squeezed by millions of Israelis in underground shelters who rightfully expected me to knock the daylight out of the terrorists. For this the IDF needed a few more days to complete the destruction of the Hamas terrorist infrastructure. Our intelligence could pick off more prime targets, especially since Hamas's underground bunkers were no longer secure.

Biden agreed but resumed the pressure to end the fighting the next day. As I did earlier with Obama during Operation Protective Edge in 2014, I asked and got from Biden during Operation Guardian of the Walls a commitment to fund the replenishing of Iron Dome interceptors, a defensive weapon system that enjoyed broad bipartisan support in the US Congress.

Each phone conversation with the president brought the end of the fighting closer. I could buy a little more time, but it was clear that we would not have the seemingly unlimited time we had in 2014. Nor did we need it. Within a little over a week, the IDF's main battle goals were achieved, but I had one more objective in mind. With some luck and a bit more intelligence work, we might be able to pick off Mohammed Deif, the Hamas terrorist chief who was responsible for the murder of hundreds of Israelis and who had managed to evade all our previous efforts to target him.

The air force targeted the suspected building. No one was killed and Deif escaped again. After that attempt, I agreed to let Egypt negotiate an unconditional cease-fire that Hamas was all too eager to accept.

Hamas had suffered a dramatic degradation of its capabilities via the destruction of the military infrastructure it had built for years. The so-called protectors of Jerusalem would think twice before firing rockets at Jerusalem again. And indeed, the following year the Jerusalem Day parade was held with no interference from Hamas, not even a whispered threat.

During the eleven days of battle, ending on May 21, I convened the security cabinet almost daily. The rancor and infighting with Blue and White disappeared, partly because the country faced a common security challenge, partly because we were clearly gaining the upper hand.

In war, setbacks often divide; successes usually unite.

Guardian of the Walls—thwarting the terror tunnel network and the naval and aerial capabilities that Hamas built over many years—was our most successful operation against Hamas to date.

Cumulatively, the best indicator of the success of our operations was that in the five years after Protective Edge in 2014 up to the end of 2019, the population in the Israeli communities adjacent to Gaza grew by 15 percent, compared to 9 percent in the rest of the country.[3] That robust growth continued after Guardian of the Walls.

Yet during that operation, in addition to Hamas and Islamic Jihad rockets on our cities, we faced another ominous threat. Israel has several cities with mixed Jewish and Arab populations. Normally they coexist peacefully and harmoniously. Now, in the midst of the fighting, groups of radicalized Israeli Arabs attacked their Jewish neighbors with automatic weapons, murdering them in apartment buildings and in the streets.

The shooters, often an amalgam of Islamic radicals and criminal elements, were using illegal weapons rampant in Arab communities. This lawlessness was a festering sore for decades.

When I came into office in 2009, I discovered that sixty years after the founding of Israel, we had only one police station in one Arab community, in the Galilean city of Nazareth. Over the next decade, my governments built eleven additional stations, added Arab policemen and appointed an Arab deputy chief of police. The police began to enter criminal strongholds to collect illegal weapons, sometimes engaging the outlaws in firefights.

One important positive development was the change in the attitude of the Israeli-Arab community. For years they had rejected the introduction of Israeli police into their communities. Many had integrated into Israeli society and wanted safe neighborhoods, like their Jewish counterparts. Most Arab citizens now *wanted* the police to intervene against the lawless gangs that were making their life hell.

In 2015, I had also budgeted $5 billion to the Arab community to bolster infrastructure, education and law enforcement. This was several times more than the combined spending of all previous governments.

But the task of dealing with the violent gangs in the Arab community was far from complete, and it confronted us with full force in the middle of the Guardian of the Walls campaign.

I went from the security cabinet meeting in Israel's military headquarters in Tel Aviv to the emergency police headquarters in nearby Lod.

I ordered the beefing up of police presence in the mixed communities with thousands of policemen and border guards and brought in Shin Bet to identify the ringleaders.

Though we soon brought the violence under control, the wound still festers and bursts periodically. Addressing it requires a major effort mobilizing national will and resources. I was prepared to lead the charge once the fighting ended.

I didn't get to do so.

As the fighting subsided on May 21, I warned that two small, ostensibly right-wing parties, whose leaders, Naftali Bennett and Gideon Sa'ar, had promised their voters that they would not form a government with the left, would do just that. I was branded a hysterical liar. Bennett even went on live television and signed a contract he had drafted for the viewers in which he pledged not to form a government with the left or with the Islamists under any circumstances.

Now he proceeded to brazenly violate this solemn pledge.

For the first time in Israel's history, a hodgepodge of parties with conflicting platforms formed a coalition with the Islamist Ra'am party, which is opposed to the very existence of Israel as a Jewish state.

With a party numbering only six members out of the Knesset's 120 members, Bennett served as prime minister.

With thirty seats, I was now again the leader of the Opposition.

The new government lasted only a year. Though hailed by leading columnists in the West as promoting unity in Israel, it did the very opposite. It excluded the majority of the Jewish electorate and made a pact with the Muslim Brotherhood party, whose charter and governing Islamist council is officially committed to the dissolution of the Jewish state.

Within months Israel experienced a wave of terrorist attacks that claimed the lives of twenty-two Israelis. In the cities and campuses of Israel, PLO and Hamas flags were hoisted. Israel's flag was burned on the Temple Mount. In the heart of Jerusalem, Israeli citizens hid the Israeli flag out of fear of Palestinian rioters brandishing PLO flags.

Though mouthing a tepid opposition to the Iran deal, which most of the public opposed, the government's stance on Iran was weak and indecisive. It did little to stem the global economic crisis that hit Israel too. Instead, it raised taxes on the economically disadvantaged and gave the

Muslim Brotherhood party a check of more than ten billion dollars with virtually no oversight.

Such a government was bound to fall, and it did.

Its leaders had assumed that once a government was established, the right-wing bloc would collapse and Likud would boot me out. The opposite happened. The bloc held and my support swelled among my supporters. It was the government bloc that caved and elections were called.

With the help of the able Yariv Levin I led a highly disciplined and united opposition, spending many days and nights in the Knesset. Though we were short a few seats, we began winning one vote after another. In the non-Knesset days I toured Israel's cities and met the people, much easier to do when you're not prime minister constrained by security. This was invigorating. Many expressed their support and their desire to see me return to office.

"We want our country back. We want to feel safe again. We want our pride restored," they said over and over again.

The year out of office was a time for reflection and recuperation. It honed my perspective about the great tasks still before Israel: Confronting Iran, stabilizing the economy and bolstering its competitive edge as a world leader in new technologies, and expanding the circle of peace to end the Israeli-Arab conflict.

The hiatus also gave me something I could never achieve while in office—the time to write this book. For this I will be forever grateful.

MY STORY, OUR STORY

When my parents were born, the tsars ruled Russia, the British Empire spanned the globe and the Ottomans ruled the Middle East. During their lifetime, all these empires collapsed, others rose and fell, and the destiny of the Jewish people swung from despair to triumph, from the Holocaust to the rebirth of the Jewish state.

But the enduring permanence of this triumph has never been guaranteed. My parents' generation was tasked with founding the state; my generation was tasked with securing its future. The arc of history may bend toward justice, but it is a brittle arc. It can break at any moment under the pounding of the darkest forces.

The founding of Israel did not stop attacks on the Jews. It merely gave the Jews the power to defend themselves against those attacks. As a soldier, I fought to defend Israel on battlefields, as a diplomat I fended off attacks against its legitimacy in world forums, as finance minister and prime minister I sought to multiply its economic and political power among the nations.

And indeed, Israel has become an international success story, a powerhouse of innovation, enterprise and strength. This newfound power gives us a future of promise and has led to four peace agreements. More will surely come if we continue to nurture our might, our resolve and our belief in the justice of our cause.

Yet I have never lost sight of the dangers that face us. A necessity for any living organism is the ability to identify danger in time to do something about it, a quality that was lost to our people over the course of centuries of exile. This is why I led the effort and took boundless risks to prevent Iran, which calls for our destruction, from arming itself with nuclear weapons, an effort that still requires unceasing tenacity.

If Iran were to acquire nuclear weapons, threatening not only Israel but the entire world, the skill, ingenuity and leadership required to fend off this threat would increase many times over.

In the thousands of years of the existence of the Jewish people, we enjoyed only three periods of independence in a united realm: eight decades under David and Solomon, eight decades under the Hasmonaeans, and eight decades since the establishment of the modern state of Israel.

Through three millennia we never gave up on our dream to live as a prosperous and free people in our homeland, the land of Zion. Having restored our independence, we cannot, we will not, let anyone bring an end to this miracle.

When I look back on my childhood in Jerusalem with Yoni and Iddo, my years in America, my service in the Unit and my escapes from near death, I realize they were all somehow woven together to prepare me for my life's mission.

Yet nothing is ever predetermined. If Yoni hadn't insisted on joining the Unit and if he had not fallen in Entebbe, my life would have taken a different course. Nor did I know that I would recover from the tragic death of my brother, whom I miss every day. And if Moshe Arens had not invited me to go to Washington, I would not have been thrust onto the world stage.

Who can unravel destiny in the unpredictable twists of fate? I for one cannot, but I can say that I have clearly lived a life of purpose: to help secure the future of my ancient people who suffered so much and have contributed so much to humanity. This mission will continue to inspire me until the end of my days.

I have been privileged to be guided by extraordinary parents, to be supported by a loving family, and to represent so many who shared my vision and followed me with open hearts through the turbulence of political life.

But is there truly such a thing as a life of purpose? Every age has its

Ecclesiastes and Lucretius, who tell us that all is ephemeral. "Vanity of vanity, all is vanity,"[1] says the Bible. "What profit hath a man of all his labor which he hath taken under sun?"[2]

Toward the end of his life, Will Durant, one of my favorite authors and a great admirer of the Jewish people, tried to comfort humanity by noting the value of human achievements, however temporary:

> We need not fret about the future . . . Never was our heritage of civilization and culture so secure, and never was it half so rich. We may do our little share to augment it and transmit it, confident that time will wear away chiefly the dross of it, and that what is finally fair and worthy in it will be preserved, to illuminate many generations.[3]

Durant was right.

The rebirth of Israel is a miracle of faith and history. The Book of Samuel says, "The eternity of Israel will not falter." Throughout our journey, including in the tempests and upheavals of modern times, this has held true.

The People of Israel Live!

ACKNOWLEDGMENTS

This book was written in longhand during nine months after my departure from the Prime Minister's Office in 2021.

Ophir Falk deserves my everlasting thanks for his companionship and labor, which helped make it possible. Typing the untypable, he made many valued suggestions in style, content and research, cutting into family time and occasionally accompanying me on my political forays. I don't know of many books written in the backseat of a car swirling on Galilean and Negev roads.

My friend of many years Gary Ginsberg gave his extraordinarily deft editorial advice in endless transatlantic phone calls. I could not hope for a more incisive critic. In a short but productive editing visit to Israel, he was joined by our old mate, the perceptive Spencer Partrich, the A Team reassembled.

I received equally committed and valuable editorial comments from my brother Iddo and from Ron Dermer, each scrupulously checking the facts about the periods of my life with which they were intimately familiar, having played important roles in them. This effort was helped by Sharon Dartwa, who indefatigably chased down even the most obscure facts, with references to boot.

Ron of course was also a valued partner in generating many of the ideas that guided Israel's relations with the United States and our new peace partners in the Middle East, while often standing in the line of fire when those ideas were opposed in Washington. He deserves not only my gratitude but also that of Israelis and Americans.

Will Murphy made many important edits, stressing among other things the need for clarifying historical context to non-Israeli readers. In this he was greatly aided by Max Meltzer, who also helped with the photographs and maps shown in the book. Howard Wolfson and Aaron Klein offered invaluable and nuanced perspectives on making the manuscript accessible to diverse segments of the reading public. Aaron's insights helped highlight innumerable crucial points in the manuscript.

I am deeply grateful to Jon Karp of Simon & Schuster for publishing my memoirs. His initial enthusiasm never waned. It was happily shared by Jennifer Long of Gallery Books, Jennifer Bergstrom, and other dedicated staff members of Simon & Schuster who helped prepare the book for publication.

Though some of the manuscript was written in the oddest of places, including in the Knesset plenary during impossibly long budget debates, I enjoyed the hospitality of good friends who offered me the use of their homes for more quiet introspection.

David Ellison kindly took us into his secluded home in Hawaii. The two weeks I spent writing there gave the manuscript a significant boost, aided by Maddie Giammona, who temporarily took on the daunting task of deciphering my handwriting.

The Edri family, our wonderful neighbors across the street in Caesarea, made their home, less frequented after the passing of my close friend Leon Edri, readily available to me at all hours.

Our dear friends the Falic family generously put up with my extended bursts of writing in the patio of their Jerusalem home. Its incomparable panoramic view of the Temple Mount never failed to inspire me and remind me of why I was writing this book.

To all these friends and colleagues I owe many thanks, but above all my greatest debt is to my wife, Sara, and to our sons, Yair and Avner. They gave me solace and support in the worst of times and stood by me at all times.

Often with great pain and personal cost, Sara sacrificed her finest years, the boys the innocence of childhood, to accompany me on my lifelong mission for Israel. I have never seen such courage in the face of vilification and adversity as Sara's. She drew strength from knowing that she, too, was serving a larger purpose. I drew comfort that as the years passed more and more people appreciated her sacrifice.

My final thanks go to the millions in Israel and around the world who never lost the sense of wonder at the realization of our ancient prophecies, the ingathering of the exiles, and the rebirth of the Jewish state. May their faith endure, may the flame continue to light our path.

NOTES

Chapter 1: Brothers

1 Sayeret Matkal in Hebrew is "General Staff Reconnaissance Unit."
2 Robert T. Holden. "The Contagiousness of Aircraft Hijacking," *American Journal of Sociology* 91, no. 4 (1986): 874–904, doi:10.1086/228353.ISSN 0002 -02.JSTOR2779961.S2CID144772464,1https://www.journals.uchicago.edu /doi/10.1086/228353.
3 Benjamin Netanyahu and Iddo Netanyahu, eds., *The Letters of Jonathan Netanyahu: The Commander of the Entebbe Rescue Force* (Jerusalem: Gefen, 2001), p. 13.
4 Shalom Yerushalmi, "I Was a National Hero, I Was Left with Nothing," *Maariv*, July 2, 2011, https://www.makorrishon.co.il/nrg/online/1/ART2/255 /490.html [Hebrew].
5 Drew Middleton, "Key to Raid's Success," *New York Times*, July 5, 1976.
6 Moshe Dayan, *Story of My Life* (New York: William Morrow, 1976), 488.
7 *Piers Morgan Live*, "One-on-One with Benjamin Netanyahu," CNN, March 17, 2011, https://transcripts.cnn.com/show/pmt/date/2011-03-17 /segment/01.

Chapter 2: Roots

1 Heda Bushes, "The Hebrew Encyclopedia and Israeli Books Abroad," *Haaretz*, October 16, 1959, https://www.nli.org.il/he/newspapers/?a=is&oid=ha retz19591016-01.2.133&type=nlilogicalsectionpdf&e=————-he-20—1— img-txIN%7ctxTI-%d7%94%d7%90%d7%a0%d7%a6%d7%99%d7% a7%d7%9c%d7%95%d7%a4%d7%93%d7%99%d7%94+%d7%94%d7 %a2%d7%91%d7%a8%d7%99%d7%aa+%d7%97%d7%95%d7%aa%

d7%9e%d7%99%d7%9d——————-1; Central Bureau of Statistics, *Statistical Abstract of Israel* (Jerusalem: Government Printer, 1950), 15 [Hebrew].

2 B. Netanyahu, *The Origins of the Inquisition in Fifteenth Century Spain* (New York: Random House, 1995).

Chapter 3: America

1 Protocols of Rishon LeZion Community Council meeting, November 7, 1910, as transcribed by Shoshelet, "The First Families of Eretz Israel." The descriptions relating to Abraham Marcus and his son-in-law Benjamin Segal taken from Shoshelet [Hebrew].

2 Most of the Urfalim community migrated to Ottoman Syria in December 1896, fleeing the Hamidian massacres of Armenians, instigated by Ottoman Sultan Abdul Hamid II. The massacres marked the end of the multicultural period, which had characterized Urfa and Anatolia in general for millennia. Yigal Moshe Israel, Yigal Baldgreen, and Zion Suleiman, "Across the river came our ancestors: The Jews in Urfa and southeastern Turkey, their immigration to Eretz Israel and their integration into it," Rishon Lezion Museum Publishing, 2013.

3 "Visits Holy Land, His Life's Dream," *Minneapolis Journal*, January 8, 1911.

4 Shoshelet, "The First Families of Eretz Israel."

5 The Rothschild family's critical role in sustaining the early proto-Zionist and Zionist communities—such as Rishon LeZion, where my maternal great-grandfather, Abraham Marcus, settled in 1896; Petach Tikva, where my mother was born 1910; and Rosh Pina (near Safed), where my grandfather Nathan served as a schoolmaster upon coming to Palestine in 1920, as well as many other communities—was often marginalized by the Labor movement in order to magnify the achievements of Socialist Zionism. This distortion is well documented in Simon Schama's, *Two Rothschilds and the Land of Israel* (1978).

6 Adi Armon, "Ben-Zion Netanyahu in the Red Carnage Sea," *Haaretz*, January 7, 2020, https://www.haaretz.co.il/literature/study/.premium-1.8369835 7.1.2020 [Hebrew].

Chapter 4: Back in Israel: Blissful Years

1 Leyada is the shorthand name of the school. Hebrew University High School website, https://leyada.net/; "Hebrew University Secondary School," Wikipedia, https://en.wikipedia.org/wiki/Hebrew_University_Secondary_School.

2 A. E. Housman, "To an Athlete Dying Young," originally published in his collection *Shropshire Lad* (1896), lines 1–4.

3 Dropsie College for Hebrew and Cognate Learning was a private institution that became part of the University of Pennsylvania in 1993.

Chapter 5: America Again: Nerds and Jocks

1 Benjamin Netanyahu and Iddo Netanyahu, eds., *The Letters of Jonathan Netanyahu: The Commander of the Entebbe Rescue Force* (Jerusalem: Gefen, 2001), 30.

2 Netanyahu and Netanyahu, 44.

3 Netanyahu and Netanyahu, 46.

4 Netanyahu and Netanyahu, 43.

5 Netanyahu and Netanyahu, 78.

6 Netanyahu and Netanyahu, 115.

7 Netanyahu and Netanyahu, 90.

8 Letter from Elizabeth Gentieu given to Israel's representative in Philadelphia.

Chapter 6: The Six-Day War

1 Netanyahu and Netanyahu, eds., *The Letters of Jonathan Netanyahu*, 134.

2 Netanyahu and Netanyahu, 133.

3 Netanyahu and Netanyahu, 137–38.

4 Netanyahu and Netanyahu, 140.

5 Netanyahu and Netanyahu, 212.

6 Netanyahu and Netanyahu, 226.

7 Arnan told Iddo Netanyahu of this meeting when he lived at our home in Jerusalem for roughly a year from 1974 to 1975.

8 Virginia Cowles, *The Phantom Major: The Story of David Stirling and the SAS Regiment* (New York: Collins, 1958).

Chapter 7: The Unit

1 Netanyahu and Netanyahu, eds., *The Letters of Jonathan Netanyahu*, 151.

Chapter 8: Combat

1 Letter from Israel Nir to Michael Maimon, who served with Nir and Netanyahu in the same team in the Unit and who also helped pull Bibi up to safety [Hebrew].

2 Netanyahu and Netanyahu, 161.

3 Letter from Shlomo Shatner to Benjamin Netanyahu, July 2018 [Hebrew].

4 Netanyahu and Netanyahu, Letter of Shlomo Shatner to Benjamin Netanyahu, 185.

Chapter 9: Commander

1 Personal account provided by Ruby Peled in letter to Benjamin Netanhayu, June 23, 2022.

2 Avi Dicter in Likud meeting at Knesset on October 20, 2021 [Hebrew].

3 Avner Schur, *Crossing Borders: Sayeret Matkal and Its Founder Avraham Arnan* (Kinneret: 2008) [Hebrew].

4 Netanyahu and Netanyahu, eds., *The Letters of Jonathan Netanyahu*, 200.

5 Adi Mendel and Nadav Zak, "The Late Captain Nehemiah Cohen," *Hamachaneh*, May 2017, https://www.idf.il/media/%D7%9E%D7%92%D7%96%D7%99%D7%9F/%D7%92%D7%99%D7%9C%D7%99%D7%95%D7%9F_%D7%9E%D7%90%D7%99/index.html#p=8 [Hebrew].

Chapter 12: The Yom Kippur War

1 Uri Ben Yosef, *The Angel: Ashraf Marwan, the Mossad, and the Surprise of the Yom Kippur War* (Tel Aviv: Zmora Bitan, 2010) [Hebrew].

2 Major General (ret.) Gadi Eisenkot, speech at Netanya Academic College, June 1, 2022.

Chapter 13: Hasbara

1 Hasbara literally means in Hebrew "explanation." The term is used to convey presenting Israel's case in public opinion.

2 Yaakov Erez, "So Young and Already an Ambassador," *Maariv*, October 5, 1984, https://www.nli.org.il/he/newspapers/?a=is&oid=mar19841005-01.2.318&type=nlilogicalsectionpdf&e=————-he-20—1—img-txIN%7ctxTI————1 [Hebrew].

3 Televised debate in the program "The Advocates" moderated by Marilyn Berger. The subject of the debate was: "Should the United States Support 'Self-Determination' for Palestinians in a Middle East Peace Settlement?" PBS, June 6, 1978, https://openvault.wgbh.org/catalog/V_98F4072381BB439F8ECE8DC747297DBE.

4 Gidi Weitz, *Haaretz*, October 7, 2021, https://www.haaretz.co.il/magazine/.premium.HIGHLIGHT-MAGAZINE-1.10272578?lts=1634036149343 [Hebrew].

5 Moshe Shemesh, "The Founding of the PLO 1964," *Middle Eastern Studies* 20, no. 4 (1984): 105–41, http://www.jstor.org/stable/4283033.

6 *The History of the Land of Israel*, Keter Publishing House—Yad Yitzchak Ben-Zvi, Volume Five: The Roman-Byzantine Period, Part I, 2. The Roman Empire and the Roman Administration in the Land of Israel (Moshe David Har, 1984), 19 [Hebrew].

7 Merriam-Webster defines "Mandate" as "an order or commission granted by the League of Nations to a member nation for the establishment of a responsible government over a former German colony or other conquered territory." In this case the designated territory was Palestine, which reverted from Ottoman to British administration.

8 "Golda Meir Quotes," *The Iron Lady of Israeli Politics*, Thames TV, 1970.

9 UN Security Council Resolution 242 was submitted to the council by the British ambassador to the UN, Lord Cardon, on November 22, 1967. It was drafted with the help of US representative to the UN Arthur Goldberg, Undersecretary of State Eugene Rostow, and others. It was later reaffirmed by Resolution 338 at the end of the Yom Kippur War on October 22, 1973.

Chapter 14: Father

1 Benzion Netanyahu, Hazeet Ha'am, June 2, 1933.

2 Anna Nordau, *Memoirs* (Jerusalem: Mitzpah, 1930), 159.

3 The *New York Times* reported that Professor Schweinfurth, "the king of botanical explorers," considered Aaronsohn's work to be "the most important botanical discovery which occurred during his lifetime, and one which scientists all over the world are saying may result in untold benefit to humanity in the indefinite increase it promises in the world's supply of wheat." "Prehistoric Wheat Found in Palestine," *New York Times*, October 20, 1912.

4 Richard Mienertzhagen's Army Diary, 1899–1926, 224–25; Sheffy, *British Military Intelligence*, 269–73; J. D. Grainger, *Palestine* (1917), 100–101.

5 Yvette Alt Miller, "Israel's Unknown Heroic Spies of World War I," AISH, November 9, 2017, https://aish.com/israels-unknown-heroic-spies-of-world-war-i/.

6 Balfour Declaration (2007). In *Encyclopædia Britannica*, https://www.britannica.com/event/Balfour-Declaration.

7 Christopher Simon Sykes, *The Man Who Created the Middle East: A Story of Empire, Conflict, and the Sykes-Picot Agreement* (London: Collins, 2017); Adam Ramsey, "When Britain Promised the Promised Land," ozy, June 22, 2017, https://www.ozy.com/true-and-stories/when-britain-promised-the-promised-land/78660/; Moshe Harpaz, "Did False Information about Deportation of the Jews of Jaffa and Tel Aviv Contribute to the Acceleration of the Balfour Declaration?" *Kesher* no. 56 (Spring 2021): 116–42.

8 A Western Union telegram from Louis Brandeis to Felix Frankfurter dated November 22, 1917, on learning of the signing of the Balfour Declaration, acknowledges Aaronsohn's and Weizmann's efforts but notes that Aaronsohn is to be credited for instigating the process. The Declaration "is sending the Message Aronson [*sic*] has started for Zionist work." Aaronsohn Archives, Bet Aaronsohn Museum, Zichron Yaakov, Israel.

9 Michael Posner, "The Spy from Palestine," *Queen's Quarterly* 115, no. 1, https://go.gale.com/ps/i.do?p=AONE&u=googlescholar&id=GALE|A179351991&v=2.1&it=r&sid=AONE&asid=1a5ff86a.

10 Articles by Ze'ev Jabotinsky appearing in the third chapter of Aryeh Naor, ed., *Jabotinsky's Writings: Eretz Israel B* (Jabotinsky Institute and the Menachem Begin Center, 2019); Ze'ev Jabotinsky, "The Manufacturer and Mer-

chant," speech at the Spring Exhibition of the Hebrew Industry, Tel Aviv, Spring 1929.

11 Articles by Ze'ev Jabotinsky appearing in the third chapter of the book, edited by Aryeh Naor, "Jabotinsky's Writings—Eretz Israel B," published by the Jabotinsky Institute and the Menachem Begin Center, 2019; Jabotinsky, "The Manufacturer and Merchant."

12 Iddo Netanyahu, "Implementation of Political Zionism: Benzion Netanyahu in the United States," Mida, February 29, 2020, https://mida.org.il /2020/02/29/%D7%99%D7%99%D7%A9%D7%95%D7%9E%D7%94 -%D7%A9%D7%9C-%D7%94%D7%A6%D7%99%D7%95%D7%A0 %D7%95%D7%AA-%D7%94%D7%9E%D7%93%D7%99%D7%A0 %D7%99%D7%AA-%D7%91%D7%A0%D7%A6%D7%99%D7%95% D7%9F-%D7%A0%D7%AA%D7%A0%D7%99/ [Hebrew]; Tal Shalev, "The Shadow of the Father: How Ben-Zion Netanyahu Influenced His Son's Wallachia," Walla, April 30, 2012, https://news.walla.co.il/item/2529053 [Hebrew].

13 United Zionists of America ad, "Partition Will Not Solve the Palestine Problem!" New York Times, September 12, 1947, https://pbs.twimg.com/me dia/EaMiRabU4AMtWoa?format=jpg&name=large; Ofer Aderet, "Ashes of WWI Jewish Legion Chief to Be Interred in Israel," Haaretz, October 13, 2014, https://www.haaretz.com/jewish/.premium-jewish-legion-chief-s -ashes-to-be-buried-in-israel-1.5314574; Douglas Martin, "Benzion Netanyahu, Hawkish Scholar, Dies at 102," New York Times, April 30, 2012.

14 John Henry Patterson, With the Zionists in Gallipoli (London: Hutchinson, 1916).

15 Rafael Medoff, Militant Zionism in America: The Rise and Impact of the Jabotinsky Movement (Tuscaloosa: University of Alabama Press, 2002). Medoff was the director of the David S. Wyman Institute for Holocaust Studies in Washington, DC.

16 Edward Alexander, University of Washington, review of Medoff, Militant Zionism in America, Middle East Quarterly (Winter 2003), https://www.mefo rum.org/1504/militant-zionism-in-america.

17 Arthur Schlesinger Jr., "How McGovern Will Win," New York Times, July 30, 1972.

18 PM Netanyahu's Eulogy for His Father, Professor Ben-Zion Netanyahu, April 30, 2012, Richard Stengel, "Benzion Netanyahu," Time, May 14, 2012.

19 B. Netanyahu, "Jacob B. Agus, Abravanel Statesman and Philosopher," Commentary, February 1954, https://www.commentary.org/articles/jacob -agus-2/don-isaac-abravanel-statesman-and-philosopher-by-b-netanyahu/.

20 Tom Segev, "What Did Benzion Suggest to Ben Gurion in 1956?" Haaretz, May 4, 2012, https://www.haaretz.co.il/magazine/1.1699750 [Hebrew].

Chapter 15: "One Day It Will Help Your Country"

1 Ray Kurzweil, *The Singularity Is Near* (New York: Viking, 2005).

2 "Israeli Prime Minister Benjamin Netanyahu Unveils Iran's Atomic Archive," Iran Watch, May 4, 2018, https://www.iranwatch.org/our-publications /policy-briefs/israeli-prime-minister-benjamin-netanyahu-unveils-irans -atomic-archive.

Chapter 16: Agony

1 Shimon Peres eulogy for Yoni, in Netanyahu and Netanyahu, eds., *The Letters of Jonathan Netanyahu*, pp. 299–300.

2 Benzion Netanyahu, letter to Shimon Peres, July 8, 1976, Israeli Ministry of Defense Archive.

3 Netanyahu and Netanyahu, eds., *The Letters of Jonathan Netanyahu*, v–xi.

4 Hillel Halkin, "Words of a Fallen Soldier," *New York Times*, January 25, 1981, https://www.nytimes.com/1981/01/25/books/words-of-a-fallen-sol dier.html?scp=1&sq=The%20Letters%20of%20Jonathan%20 Netanyahu&st=cse.

5 *Boston Globe*, quoted in J. Correspondent, "Historic 76 Entebbe Raid Remembered on the Web," June 22, 2001, https://www.jweekly.com/2001/06 /22/historic-76-entebbe-raid-remembered-on-the-web/, in Netanyahu and Netanyahu, eds., *The Letters of Jonathan Netanyahu*, back cover.

6 Netanyahu and Netanyahu, eds., *The Letters of Jonathan Netanyahu*, back cover.

7 Netanyahu and Netanyahu, 297–300.

8 Iddo Netanyahu, *Sayeret Matkal at Entebbe* (Tel Aviv: Yedioth Books, 2007) [Hebrew].

Chapter 17: Entebbe

1 "Holocaust Survivor Lived Through Auschwitz and Entebbe Idi Amin Hijacking," *Entebbe News*, April 9, 2001, https://entebbenews.net/holo caust-survivor-lived-through-auschwitz-and-entebbe-idi-amin-hijacking/; Netanyahu and Netanyahu, eds., *The Letters of Jonathan Netanyahu*, v–xi.

2 Quoted in Iddo Netanyahu, *Sayeret Matkal at Entebbe* (Tel Aviv: Yedioth Books, 2007), 476.

3 Iddo Netanyahu, *Yoni's Last Battle* (Jerusalem: Gefen Publishing House, 2002), 96.

4 Nehama Duak, "Entebbe—30 Years Later," *Yedioth Ahronoth*, May 2, 2006 [Hebrew].

5 Netanyahu, *Yoni's Last Battle*, 136. Shani also says, "This is the greatest warrior the country has ever had."

6 "Operation Jonathan in First Person," Intelligence and Political Policy Research Institute, 2016, 78–79.

7 Netanyahu, *Yoni's Last Battle*, 200.

8 Shimon Peres, *From These Men: Seven Founders of the State of Israel* (Jerusalem: Idanim, 1979).

Chapter 18: Terrorism

1 Eliyahu Lankin, *The Story of the Commander of Altalena* (New York: Hadar, 1967); Menachem Begin, *The Revolt* (Tel Aviv: Ahiasaf, 1950), 250–51 [Hebrew].

2 Ezra Zohar, *In the Grip of the Regime* (Jerusalem: Shikmona, 1974) [Hebrew].

3 Thomas Schelling, lecture in conference on "Termination of Wars," Jerusalem, June 1976.

4 Suzanne Weaver, "The Political Use of Terror," *Wall Street Journal*, July 26, 1979.

5 Paul Johnson, "The Seven Deadly Sins of Terrorism," in Benjamin Netanyahu, ed., *International Terrorism: Challenge and Response* (New Brunswick, NJ: Transaction Books, 1981), 11.

6 Weaver, "The Political Use of Terror."

7 Netanyahu, ed., *International Terrorism*.

Chapter 20: Diplomat

1 Eitan Rabin, "The Reagan Girl Is a Boy and He Is Not Amputated," *Davar*, August 20, 1982, https://www.nli.org.il/he/newspapers/?a=is&oid=dav19820820-01.2.11&type=nlilogicalsectionpdf&e=————he-20—1—img-txIN%7ctxTI-%d7%94%d7%99%d7%9c%d7%93%d7%94+%d7%94%d7%9c%d7%91%d7%a0%d7%95%d7%a0%d7%99%d7%aa+————1 [Hebrew].

2 Ze'ev Schiff & Ehud Ya'ari, *Israel's Lebanon War* (New York: Simon and Schuster, 1984), 233.

3 Iddo Netanyahu, "Judges Can Also Be Wrong," *Maariv*, April 3, 1983 [Hebrew].

4 Benjamin Netanyahu, *Fighting Terrorism: How Democracies Can Defeat the International Terrorist Network* (New York: Farrar, Straus & Giroux, 2001), 68.

5 Netanyahu, *Fighting Terrorism*, 67–74.

6 Benjamin Netanyahu, ed., *Terrorism: How the West Can Win* (New York: Farrar, Straus & Giroux, 1986), 175, and based on presentations to the Jonathan Institute conference held in Washington, DC, in 1984.

7 "How to Stop Terrorism," *Time*, April 14, 1986.

8 George Schultz letter to Benjamin Netanyahu, May 2, 1986.

9 George P. Shultz, *Turmoil and Triumph: My Years as Secretary of State* (New York: Charles Scribner's Sons, 1993), 730.

10 Netanyahu, ed., *Terrorism*, 14.

Chapter 21: Ambassador

1 Yaakov Erez, "So Young and Already an Ambassador," *Maariv*, October 5, 1984, https://www.nli.org.il/he/newspapers/?a=is&oid=mar19841005 -01.2.318&type=nlilogicalsectionpdf&e=———-he-20—1—img-txIN %7ctxTI—————1 [Hebrew].

2 "Sowing righteousness grows salvation," a collection of sayings by Rebbe Milowitz, Chabad graduate, New York, 1993, 75; https://www.youtube.com /watch?v=HjAvOedDFa8&t=22s, April 19, 1988.

3 "Shultz 'Admired' Netanyahu," *Maariv*, July 14, 1985.

4 Yaakov Roy, " 'All of Israel Guarantees Each Other': Activities for Soviet Jews Around the World Until the Gates Open," Beit Hatfutsot Publishing, Tel Aviv, 2007 [Hebrew].

5 Yaron London, "Europe Will Be German," *Yedioth Ahronoth*, November 24, 1989 [Hebrew].

6 Anat Berko, "The Moral Infrastructure of Chief Perpetrators of Suicidal Terrorism" (PhD diss., Bar-Ilan University, 2001).

7 Yuri Yalon, "In Prison, I Played Thousands of Chess Games in My Head," *Israel Hayom*, January 28, 2016 [Hebrew].

8 During dollar distribution ceremony, April 19, 1988. "Struggle with 119 MKs: What Exactly Did the Rebbe Say to Benjamin Netanyahu?" Chabad Online, March 4, 2019, https://www.youtube.com/watch?v=HjAvOedDFa8 (Rebbe).

9 Lubavitcher Rebbe letter to Benjamin Netanyahu, May 17, 1988, Brooklyn, NY.

Chapter 22: Politics

1 Yossi Sarid, "Netanyahu's Race to the Top," *Haaretz*, July 14, 1988 [Hebrew].

2 Channel 12, Ilan Lukach interview with Haim Yavin, https://www.mako .co.il/news-politics/2022_q2/Article-ef7f15e2672e081027.htm, televised May, 21, 2022 [Hebrew].

3 Amnon Abromovitch, "Netanyahu Project," *Maariv*, September 6, 1988.

4 Einat Berkovich and Biranit Goren, Kol Hair, June 21, 1996, https://www .zman.co.il/13462/ [Hebrew].

5 Member of Knesset, Dalia Itzik, during a debate in the Knesset plenum, "Who are you, Benjamin Netanyahu?," July 3, 1996.

6 Dan Lavie, "Shin Bet chief did not tell truth to Prime Minister Netanyahu," Israel Hayom, https://www.israelhayom.co.il/article/415541, September 25, 2016 [Hebrew]; Shai Gal, "Western Wall Tunnels: Who Gave the Recommendation?"; Channel 2 News, 2, September 24, 2016, https://www.mako.co.il /news-military/security-q3_2016/Article-465345c8eba5751004.htm [Hebrew].

7 Ehud Olmert, interview with Makor Rishon, October 29, 2020, https:// www.makorrishon.co.il/news/278195/.

8 Letters to the Editor, "7 Days," *Yedioth Ahronoth*, November 3, 2006 [Hebrew].

9 Interview with Linda Scherzer, CNN, January 17, 1991.

10 Interview with Linda Scherzer, CNN, January 17, 1991.

11 "Bibi Netanyahu: National Explains for Rent," *Yedioth Ahronoth*, November 18, 1991 [Hebrew].

12 Christiane Amanpour, "Hanan Ashrawi Explains Why She's Resigning from the PLO," PBS, December 15, 2020, https://www.pbs.org/wnet/amanpour -and-company/video/hanan-ashrawi-explains-why-shes-resigning-from -the-plo/.

13 PM Netanyahu's Speech in the Knesset, July 31, 2013, https://www.you tube.com/watch?v=fTo-d_gqttU; Jonathan Liss, "Netanyahu presents: The 140-character Israeli-Palestinian conflict," *Haaretz*, August 1, 2013, https:// www.haaretz.co.il/news/politi/1.2087190 [Hebrew].

14 Caracalla enacted the constitution *Antoniniana de civitate*, which accorded Roman citizenship to "free residents" of the empire. Salo Baron, *A Social and Religious History of the Jews*, vol. 11 (New York: Columbia University Press, 1952), 109. See also *Encyclopaedia Judaica*, vol. 5, 157.

15 Samuel Katz, *Battleground: Fact and Fantasy in Palestine* (New York: Bantam Books, 1973), 88.

16 Benzion Dinur, *Israel in the Diaspora*, vol. 1, *From the Conquest of the Land of Israel by the Arabs to the Crusades* (Tel Aviv: Dsvir, 1960), 27–30 [Hebrew].

17 Mark Twain, *The Innocents Abroad: Or, The New Pilgrims' Progress* (Hartford, CT: American Publishing Company, 1869).

18 Yasser Arafat, speech to the UN General Assembly, November 13, 1974, https://unispal.un.org/DPA/DPR/unispal.nsf/0/A238EC7A3E13EED 18525624A007697EC 152.

19 Arthur Penrhyn Stanley, *Sinai and Palestine in Connection with Their History* (New York: A. C. Armstrong & Sons, 1894), 184–86.

20 Kaiser Wilhelm II, quoted in Marvin Lowenthal, ed., *The Diaries of Theodor Herzl* (New York: Dial, 1956), 292.

21 Balfour Declaration, November 2, 1917.

22 Tamar Golan, "Netanyahu-Arafat Confrontation in Geneva over Small Money and Map of Israel," *Maariv*, May 27, 1990.

23 Labor Party Election Broadcasts, 1992 Elections, https://elections.walla.co .il/item/2581848; https://www.youtube.com/watch?v=Ymxwe2xGel8.

Chapter 23: Nathan

1 "Dreamer and Warrior: Lines the History and Actions of the Late Rabbi Milikowski," *Haaretz*, March 7, 1935 [Hebrew].

2 "Dreamer and Warrior."

3 "Dreamer and Warrior."

4 "Dreamer and Warrior."

5 *Nathan Milikowski, Nation and State* (Tel Aviv: Simania, 1994), 179 [Hebrew].

6 Jabotinsky, quoted in Joseph Schechtman, *The Vladimir Jabotinsky Story: The Early Years* (New York: Thomas Yoseloff, 1956), 89.

7 Benjamin Netanyahu, *A Place Among the Nations: Israel and the World* (New York: Bantam Books, 1993), 29.

8 Benzion Netanyahu, *The Founding Fathers of Zionism* (Jerusalem: Balfour Books and Gefen Publishing House, 2012), 89.

9 Theodor Herzl, *The Jewish State* (Vienna: M. Breitenstein, 1896).

10 Theodor Herzl, *The Interest of the Jews* (Jerusalem: Diary Books, 1985–1994, 1997–2001), I, 482.

11 Marvin Lowenthal, ed., *The Diaries of Theodor Herzl* (New York: Dial Press, 1956), 267–73, 339.

12 Theodor Herzl, *Altneuland* (Leipzig: Hermann Seemann Nachfolger, 1902), 49.

13 Obituary of Rabbi Avraham Yitzchak HaCohen Kook to Rabbi Natan Milkowski, February 4, 1935, "In a Nation and a State" (Tel Aviv: Simania, 1994), 179.

Chapter 24: Leader of the Opposition

1 An exchange in *The Crown* (TV series), episode "Scientia Potentia Est," aired November 4, 2016.

2 Netanyahu, *A Place Among the Nations.*

3 Benjamin Netanyahu, "The Great Danger," *Yedioth Ahronoth*, February 19, 1993.

4 Speech given at a rally marking twenty-five years of Israeli settlement on the Golan, June 10, 1992, https://www.youtube.com/watch?v=ldgyYenN9eA.

5 Benjamin Netanyahu, "Again in front of the Golan," *Yedioth Achronoth*, September 11, 1992.

6 Eitan Glickman, "Netanyahu: 'Rabin Hides Behind Shachak's Apron,' " *Yedioth Ahronoth*, June 28, 1995; and speech in the Knesset, June 28, 1995 [Hebrew].

7 Yasser Arafat speech in Johannesburg, https://www.youtube.com/watch?v=P8RRbPbIXe8; Jim Hoagland, "Arafat's Loose Lips," *Washington Post*, May 26, 1994, https://www.washingtonpost.com/archive/opinions/1994/05/26/arafats-loose-lips/ffd735a8-fe5f-4172-87fa-a77b4261c820/.

8 Nadav Haetzni, Oded Granot, and Shefi Gabay, "Faisal Husseini: We Have Not Given Up the Rifle," *Maariv*, Nov. 24, 1993 [Hebrew].

9 Zvi Alush, "Head of the Palestinian Security Services: We Will Not Keep Quiet until Israel Leaves East Jerusalem," *Yedioth Ahronoth*, May 29, 1994 [Hebrew].

10 "The War Against Terror," *Jerusalem Post*, April 17, 1995; *An-Nahar*, April

11, 1995; Cal Thomas, "Words to His People Reveal Arafat's Intentions," *South Florida Sun-Sentinel*, September 22, 1995.

11 Jon Immanuel, "Arafat Sworn In As PNA President," *Jerusalem Post*, Feb. 13, 1996.

12 Karsh Ephraim, "Oslo War: Anatomy of Self-Deception," Begin-Sadat Center for Strategic Studies, Bar-Ilan University, 2003, 7.

13 Netanyahu and Netanyahu, eds., *The Letters of Jonathan Netanyahu*, 226.

14 Benjamin Netanyahu, Knesset speech, May 11, 1994, https://www.knesset .gov.il/Tql/knesset/Knesset13/html/19940511@19940511001@001.html.

15 Yitzhak Rabin, Knesset speech, https://www.youtube.com/watch?v=bR LX8RiXS84; speech at a Joint Meeting of the Foreign Affairs and Defense Committee of the Finance Committee, Knesset, May 19, 1995.

16 Speech at a conference in the Golan Heights, April 17, 1995, https://www .youtube.com/watch?v=q8IrDX7m3RQ.

17 Mina Tzemach's poll for Nissim Mash'al program, Channel 2, February 2, 1995, https://www.youtube.com/watch?v=0pz3m8qkVAA&t=76s [Hebrew].

18 "A Change in Public Opinion," Tel Aviv University poll, *Yedioth Ahronoth*, March 26, 1995.

19 Haim Shibi, "The United States Will Help Rabin Not Lose the Election," *Yedioth Ahronoth*, January 29, 1995 [Hebrew].

20 Anshel Pfeffer, *Bibi: The Turbulent Life and Times of Benjamin Netanyahu* (Basic Books, New York, 2018), 313.

21 Joseph Tommy Lapid, on the *Popolitika* program, Channel 1, December 1995, https://www.youtube.com/watch?v=Po3J48v2nQw [Hebrew].

22 Yitzhak Rabin speech at Knesset, October 5, 1995.

23 Michael Kirk, Mike Wiser, and Jim Gilmore, "Netanyahu at War," *Front-line*, January 5, 2016, https://www.pbs.org/wgbh/frontline/film/netanyahu -at-war/.

Chapter 25: Prime Minister

1 Haim Shibi, "Clinton Disappointed, but Declared to Continue to Stand Behind Israel," *Yedioth Ahronoth*, May 31, 1996 [Hebrew].

2 Nehama Duak, "Is the Combine Trio Better: Barak, Shahak and Milo?" *Yedioth Ahronoth*, October 29, 1998 [Hebrew].

3 Haim Shibi, "Tonight at 6, Clinton will Shake Prime Minister Netanyahu's Hand," *Yedioth Ahronoth*, July 9, 1996 [Hebrew].

4 *The Human Factor*, television series by director Dror Moreh, Episode 2, Channel 8, 2020.

5 Netanyahu speech to US Congress, July 10, 1996, https://mfa.gov.il/mfa /mfa-archive/1996/pages/pm%20netanyahu-%20speech%20to%20us%20 congress-%20july%2010-%201996.aspx.

Chapter 26: First Reforms

1 This description is taken from the preamble of *A Durable Peace*, published by Warner Books in 2001.

Chapter 27: Sara

1 Note from Robert Asch, former Chief Psychologist of Israel's Ministry of Education, 2021.

2 Alon Izraev, https://www.facebook.com/photo/?fbid=901609376706075&set=a.145979088935778, July 20, 2018.

3 Yitzhak Kadman, Director of the National Council for Child Welfare, Radio interview, 1997.

Chapter 28: King Hussein

1 After two terrorist attacks in Jerusalem: In the Mahane Yehuda market, July 30, 1997—16 killed. And on Ben Yehuda Street in Jerusalem, September 4, 1997—5 killed.

2 Ophir Falk, *Targeted Killings, Law and Counter-Terrorism Effectiveness: Does Fair Play Pay Off?* (London: Routledge, 2020), 28.

3 A senior Mossad official who had developed a close relationship with the king described this all-night session, which he also attended: "Despite suffering that night from a flu with high fever, the prime minister was calm and totally focused. He listened to different views, took decisions and gave clear orders to make sure the decisions were carried out. The prime minister's sang-froid and clarity of thought in the midst of the chaos that night saved Israel from potentially serious international consequences."

Chapter 29: First Skirmish

1 Israel Security Agency database published on Shabak website (2010).

2 Yaron London, "Tide of Terror," *Yedioth Ahronoth*, September 2, 2001 [Hebrew].

3 Shimon Schiffer and Nehama Duak, "Clinton to Netanyahu: 'Appreciate Your Courage and Your Determination,' " *Yedioth Ahronoth*, January 1, 1997 [Hebrew].

4 James E. Patrick, *British Christian History and the Jewish People: Recovering an Ancient Spiritual Legacy* (Cambridge: Grove Books Limited, 2017), p. 15.

5 Yaari Ploskin, "Prof. William Hechler," *Haaretz*, February 20, 1931, https://www.nli.org.il/en/newspapers/?a=is&oid=haretz19310220-01.2.25&type=nlilogicalsectionpdf&e=————-en-20—1—img-txIN%7ctxTI————1 [Hebrew].

6 This description is taken from Walter Russell Mead, *The Arc of a Covenant:*

The United States, Israel, and the Fate of the Jewish People (Knopf, New York, 2022).

7 Rev. William Blackstone in 1891: "Palestine Belongs to the Jews!" on the FOZ Museum website, https://fozmuseum.com/blog/blackstone-in-1891/.

8 Lodge–Fish Resolution, September 21, 1922.

Chapter 30: Wye River

1 Wye River Agreement text: https://archive.is/20121218170902/www.mfa .gov.il/NR/exeres/EE54A289-8F0A-4CDC-93C9-71BD631109AB.htm https://archive.is/20121218170902/www.mfa.gov.il/NR/exeres/EE54A289 -8F0A-4CDC-93C9-71BD631109AB.htm.

2 Editor's Note, "Deri: Barak Spreads Hatred Among the People," *Walla*, August 31, 2000 [Hebrew].

3 Editors of *Globes*, "Olmert: Barak suffers from internal and mental collapse; he sells the State of Israel," *Globes*, December 24, 2000; Amir Tibon, "This is how Israel first agreed to the partition of Jerusalem," *Walla*, February 27, 2014 [Hebrew].

Chapter 31: Wilderness

1 Judge Eliezer Goldberg, State Comptroller Report for Year 2000, published April 29, 2001: "The listing of gifts that were received in the Prime Minister's Office started only in 1995 [a year before I was elected]," wrote the judge. "As for Prime Minister Netanyahu's tenure, the Prime Minister's Office has a list of presents received by Mr. Netanyahu, including detailed names of the persons who gave them and the dates they were given."

Chapter 32: Citizen Against Terror

1 Diana Bachur, Ali Waked and the Agencies, "Bush to Sharon: Israel Must Retreat Without Delay," *Ynet*, April 7, 2002, https://www.ynet.co.il/art icles/0,7340,L-1815408,00.html [Hebrew].

2 Speech made at rally in support of Israel in Washington, DC, on April 15, 2002.

3 Speech at rally in Support of Israel in London on May 6, 2002.

4 George W. Bush speech at the White House on June 24, 2002.

5 The War on Terror—Six Speeches, 9.

6 Donald Rumsfeld, *Rumsfeld's Rules: Leadership Lessons in Business, Politics, War, and Life* (New York: HarperCollins, 2013), pp. 227–28.

Chapter 34: Crisis

1 Guy Rolnik, "Silvan Shalom Returns to the Treasury," *Haaretz*—The Marker, June 22, 2006 https://www.themarker.com/markets/1.369540 [Hebrew].

Chapter 35: Fat Man, Thin Man

1 Quoted in Daniel Yergin and Joseph Stanislaw, *The Commanding Heights* (New York: Simon & Schuster, 2002), p. 408.

Chapter 36: "Don't Read the Press"

1 Labor Relations Unit, Ministry of Industry, Commerce, and Tourism, 2004 [Hebrew].
2 Bank of Israel report submitted to the Knesset, May 3, 2005 [Hebrew].

Chapter 37: "*This* Is Social Justice!"

1 Professor Moshe Sikron, "The Human Capital of the Population of Israel," in "Who and What in Israel," self-published, Kfar Saba, 2003 [Hebrew].
2 According to the Central Bureau of Statistics, Labor Force Survey, 2018, (Jerusalem: February 27, 2020).
3 Stated by a participant at the 35th Zionist Congress, Jerusalem, June 22, 2006.
4 Itay Zehoral, "Israel is among the top 20 global economies in GDP per capita for the First Time," *Forbes Israel*, May 5, 2021.
5 "Monitoring the implementation of government policy: A comparative review," Knesset Information and Research Center, October 22, 2020, https://fs.knesset.gov.il/globaldocs/MMM/4e14e373-5fbb-ea11-8116 -00155d0af32a/2_4e14e373-5fbb-ea11-8116-00155d0af32a_11_16414.pdf [Hebrew].
6 Real GDP, CIA—*The World Factbook*, 2021, https://www.cia.gov/the-world -factbook/field/real-gdp-purchasing-power-parity/country-comparison.
7 Merav Arlozorov, "Netanyahu's Tragedy," *Haaretz*, TheMarker March 4, 2019 https://www.themarker.com/opinion/2019-03-04/ty-article/0000017f -f23d-d8a1-a5ff-f2bfdf4b0000; Nehemiah Stresler, "The Catastrophe Law Works," *Haaretz*, December 7, 2005, https://www.haaretz.co.il/opinions /2005-12-07/ty-article/0000017f-db55-df9c-a17f-ff5d43960000 [Hebrew].

Chapter 38: A Clash of Head and Heart

1 Yoel Marcus, "Planned Withdrawal: Twenty Settlements in Gaza and West Bank within a Year or Two," *Haaretz*, February 2, 2004 [Hebrew].
2 Shlomi Golubinsky, Economist Milton Friedman to the Chairman of the

Knesset Finance Committee, Yaakov Litzman: Approved Recommendations of the Bachar Committee, *Haaretz*, July 17, 2005, https://www.haaretz.co.il/misc/1.1027942 [Hebrew].

3 Daniel Doron, "Appreciative policymakers," The Israel Center for Social & Economic Progress, http://icsep.org.il/support/appreciative-policy-makers.

4 Letter of resignation submitted to Prime Minister Sharon, August 7, 2005 [Hebrew].

5 Ammon Abramovich at the Van Leer Institute, February 25, 2005; https://www.youtube.com/watch?v=pQubYq46aW8 [Hebrew].

6 Amnon Abramovich, *Yedioth Ahronoth*, February 5, 2019 [Hebrew].

Chapter 39: "This *Is* Your Life!"

1 Bill no. 2299/17פ, banning investment in corporations that have a business relationship with Iran, was tabled by Benjamin Netanyahu on March 12, 2007 and was adopted on April 2, 2008, https://main.knesset.gov.il/Activity/Legislation/Laws/Pages/LawBill.aspx?t=lawsuggestionssearch&lawitemid=240795.

Chapter 40: "Not One Brick!"

1 According to the Foreign Ministry, in the second intifada, between 2000 and 2005, 1,090 Israelis were killed by Palestinian terrorism. https://www.gov.il/en/Departments/General/victims-of-palestinian-violence-and-terrorism.

2 Terrence McCoy, "The Roots of Why Obama and Netanyahu Dislike Each Other So Much," *Washington Post*, February 26, 2015, https://www.washingtonpost.com/news/morning-mix/wp/2015/02/26/the-roots-of-why-obama-and-netanyahu-dislike-each-other-so-much/; Peter Beinart, excerpt from *The Crisis of Zionism* in the *Times of Israel*, April 15, 2012, https://www.timesofisrael.com/the-crisis-of-zionism-by-peter-beinart/.

3 Transcript: Obama's Speech at AIPAC, June 4, 2008, https://www.npr.org/templates/story/story.php?storyId=91150432.

4 Obama says he used "poor phrasing" on Jerusalem, Reuters, July 13, 2008, https://www.reuters.com/article/us-usa-politics-obama-jerusalem-idUSN1337076120080713.

5 Amy Soberano, "McCain: If elected, I'd move US embassy to Jerusalem," *Jerusalem Post*, July 27, 2008, https://www.jpost.com/international/mccain-if-elected-id-move-us-embassy-to-jerusalem.

6 Roee Nahmias, "Haniyeh to Obama: Support our right to freedom," *Ynet*, https://www.ynetnews.com/articles/0,7340,L-3662245,00.html.

7 Shimon Schiffer, "We are not interested in how—an arrangement within 4 years," *Yedioth Ahronoth*, April 16, 2009 [Hebrew].

Chapter 41: "Lots of Daylight"

1 Orly Azulai and Itamar Eichner, "Obama and Netanyahu: A Talk from Dad to Dad," *Yedioth Ahronoth*, May 20, 2009 [Hebrew].

2 Patrick Healy, "Obama and Clinton Clash Over Iran," *New York Times*, Oct. 13, 2007, https://www.nytimes.com/2007/10/13/us/politics/13clinton.html.

3 Remarks of President Obama Marking Nowruz, March 20, 2010, https://obamawhitehouse.archives.gov/realitycheck/the-press-office/remarks-president-obama-marking-nowruz.

4 Barack Obama, Cairo speech, 2009, https://www.youtube.com/watch?v=B_889oBKkNU.

5 Ron Kampeas, "At White House, U.S. Jews offer little resistance to Obama policy on settlements," *Jewish Telegraphic Agency*, July 14, 2009, https://www.jta.org/2009/07/14/politics/at-white-house-u-s-jews-offer-little-resistance-to-obama-policy-on-settlements.

6 Barack Obama, *A Promised Land* (New York: Crown Publishing Group, 2020), chapter 25.

7 "With the Marchers," *New Yorker*, June 22, 2009.

8 "Obama to Iran: 'The whole world is watching,'" CNN, June 20, 2009, http://edition.cnn.com/2009/POLITICS/06/20/iran.obama/index.html.

9 President Obama's Press Briefing, June 23, 2009, https://www.nytimes.com/2009/06/23/us/politics/23text-obama.html.

10 Eli Lake, "Why Obama Let Iran's Green Revolution Fail," Bloomberg, August 3, 2016, https://www.bloomberg.com/opinion/articles/2016-08-24/why-obama-let-iran-s-green-revolution-fail.

11 Obama press briefing, June 23, 2009, https://www.nytimes.com/2009/06/23/us/politics/23text-obama.html.

12 Orly Azoulay, "Attack would endanger aid," *Yedioth Ahronoth*, April 24, 2009 [Hebrew].

Chapter 42: The Battle for Jerusalem

1 Ethan Bronner, "As Biden Visits, Israel Unveils Plan for New Settlements," *New York Times*, March 9, 2010, https://www.nytimes.com/2010/03/10/world/middleeast/10biden.html.

2 CNN interview, "Clinton: Israeli settlement announcement insulting," March 13, 2010, http://edition.cnn.com/2010/WORLD/meast/03/12/israel.clinton/index.html.

Chapter 44: *Marmara*

1 Turkel Report Summary, 2011, 9, https://web.archive.org/web/20110304072410/http://www.turkel-committee.gov.il/files/wordocs/7896summary

-eng.pdf; Turkel Report and Summary, https://www.gov.il/he/departments /general/turkel_committee.

2 Turkel Report Summary, 278.

3 Updated committee report, https://web.archive.org/web/20091007093730 /http://www2.ohchr.org/english/bodies/hrcouncil/specialsession/9/docs /UNFFMGC_Report.pdf.

Chapter 45: The Lecture

1 Josh Rogin, "Levin: White House pushing 60-day settlement freeze extension," *Foreign Policy*, September 29, 2010, https://foreignpolicy.com/2010 /09/29/levin-white-house-pushing-60-day-settlement-freeze-extension/.

2 Sara Miller, "Netanyahu: Nuclear-armed Iran Is the Greatest Danger Facing Israel," *Haaretz*, Nov 8, 2010, https://www.haaretz.com/2010-11-08 /ty-article/netanyahu-nuclear-armed-iran-is-the-greatest-danger-facing -israel/0000017f-f62c-d044-adff-f7fd0d8e0000.

3 Ari Shavit, "Netanyahu's Speech in Congress Missing His Life," *Haaretz*, May 25, 2011, https://www.haaretz.co.il/news/politics/2011-05-25/ty-article /0000017f-dba8-df9c-a17f-ffb8e8170000 [Hebrew].

Chapter 48: The Red Line

1 Karen DeYoung and Joel Greenberg, "Netanyahu: U.S. has no 'moral right' to stop Israeli action on Iran," *Washington Post*, September 11, 2012, https://www.washingtonpost.com/world/middle_east/netanyahu-with out-ultimatum-us-has-no-moral-right-to-stop-israel-from-attacking -iran/2012/09/11/cb56ac8a-fc12-11e1-a31e-804fccb658f9_story.html.

Chapter 49: "You're Next"

1 News Wires, "Obama 'strongly condemns' violence in Egypt," France 24, August 15, 2013, https://www.france24.com/en/20130815-barack-obama -reacts-egypt-violence-live.

Chapter 50: "Nobody Likes Goliath"

1 "Remarks by President Obama and Prime Minister Netanyahu of Israel in Joint Press Conference," White House, March 20, 2013, https://obama whitehouse.archives.gov/the-press-office/2013/03/20/remarks-president -obama-and-prime-minister-netanyahu-israel-joint-press-.

2 Paul Lewis, "US Attack on Syria Delayed After Surprise U-turn from Obama," *Guardian*, August 31, 2013, https://www.theguardian.com/world /2013/aug/31/syrian-air-strikes-obama-congress.

Chapter 51: "Come on a Clandestine Visit to Afghanistan"

1 Arshad Mohammed and Patricia Zengerle, "Kerry says willing to take blame for U.S. foreign policy failures," Reuters, April 8, 2014, https://www.reuters .com/article/uk-usa-diplomacy-kerry-idUKBREA371YD20140408.

Chapter 53: Tunnel War

1 Amos Harel, "Seven Hamas Operatives Killed in Tunnel Attack in Gaza," *Haaretz*, July 7, 2014, https://www.haaretz.co.il/news/politics/1.2367901; https://mfa.gov.il/MFA/ForeignPolicy/Terrorism/Pages/IDF-strikes -Hamas-tunnel-as-terrorists-plan-attack-7-Jul-2014.aspx [Hebrew].

2 Harriet Sherwood, "Israel calls partial truce amid outrage at third strike on UN school," *Guardian*, August 3, 2014; https://www.theguardian.com /world/2014/aug/03/gaza-israel-united-nations-school-strike-ban-ki -moon.

3 Tal Shalev, "Ya'alon Raises the Tone Against Bennett: 'The Damage Done by the "Leaking Minister" Is Considerable,' " January 26, 2017, https://news .walla.co.il/item/3035028 [Hebrew].

4 International Counter Terrorism Institute website, August 2014, https:// www.ict.org.il/Article/1262/Operation-Protective-Edge-A-Detailed-Sum mary-of-Events#gsc.tab=0.

5 Israel Ministry of Foreign Affairs, "Annex: Palestinian Fatality Figures in the 2014 Gaza Conflict," from report "The 2014 Gaza Conflict: Factual and Legal Aspects," June 14, 2015.

6 Ilene Prusher, "Israel and Palestinians Reach Open-Ended Cease-Fire Deal," *Time*, August 26, 2014.

7 "Palestinian Authority President Slams Hamas Claims of Victory," *Washington Free Beacon*, September 7, 2014; "Netanyahu: Hamas Suffered Its Greatest Blow Since It Was Founded," *Jerusalem Post*, August 27, 2014, https:// www.jpost.com/Arab-Israeli-Conflict/Netanyahu-Hamas-failed-achieved -nothing-except-sustaining-worst-blow-since-its-founding-372535.

8 A poll published in *Haaretz* found that 54 percent of those surveyed believed there was no clear winner in the fifty-day war. Yossi Werter, "First Survey After the Agreement," August 27, 2014, https://www.haaretz.co.il/news /politics/.premium-1.2418034 [Hebrew].

9 "Examination of the Names of Palestinians Killed in Operation Protective Edge: Part Ten," Israeli Intelligence & Heritage Commemoration Center, February 19, 2015.

Chapter 54: "Never Again"

1 Speech at UN General Assembly, October 1, 2013; "Netanyahu: Rouhani Is a Wolf in Sheep Clothing," *Wall Street Journal*, October 1, 2013, https://www

.wsj.com/video/netanyahu-rouhani-is-a-wolf-in-sheep-clothing/26D540BB
-2A44-4447-8FC9-C0D1DEE3C36D.html. Full text: https://mfa.gov.il
/MFA/PressRoom/2013/Pages/PM-Netanyahu-addresses-UN-General
-Assembly-1-Oct-2013.aspx.

2 Text of speech by Hassan Rohani to the Supreme Cultural Revolution
Council, September 30, 2005, http://www.bits.de/public/documents/iran
/Rahbord.pdf.

3 Netanyahu speech to the UN General Assembly, September 28, 2014,
https://embassies.gov.il/UnGeneva/NewsAndEvents/Pages/PM-Netan
yahu-addresses-the-UN-General-Assembly-29-Sep-2014.aspx.

4 Netanyahu speech to the UN General Assembly, September 28, 2014,
https://mfa.gov.il/MFA/PressRoom/2014/Pages/PM-Netanyahu-addresses
-the-UN-General-Assembly-29-Sep-2014.aspx.

5 "Remarks by US President Barack Obama and Prime Minister Benjamin
Netanyahu," Israeli Ministry of Foreign Affairs, October 1, 2014, https://mfa
.gov.il/MFA/PressRoom/2014/Pages/Remarks-by-US-President-Barack
-Obama-and-Prime-Minister-Benjamin-Netanyahu-1-October-2014.aspx.

6 "PM Netanyahu's Remarks at the Great Synagogue of Paris," January 11,
2015, https://www.gov.il/en/departments/news/speechparis110115.

7 Stephen Collinson, "Bad relationship gets worse for Obama, Netanyahu,"
CNN, March 4, 2015, https://edition.cnn.com/2015/03/03/politics/netan
yahu-speech-analysis-congress/index.html.

8 Geoff Dyer, "Iran deal would create 'nuclear nightmare,' Netanyahu warns,"
Financial Times, March 3, 2015, https://www.ft.com/content/b129f3b8-c1c6
-11e4-abb3-00144feab7de.

9 Collinson, "Bad relationship gets worse for Obama, Netanyahu."

10 Douglas E Schoen, "Netanyahu Speech: Bibi delivers strong message to Congress about Iran deal," Fox News, March 3, 2015, https://www.foxnews.com
/opinion/netanyahu-speech-bibi-delivers-strong-message-to-congress
-about-iran-deal.

Chapter 55: Last-Minute Victory

1 Alicia Parapiano, "Lawmakers Against the Iran Nuclear Deal," *New York
Times*, Sept. 10, 2015, https://www.nytimes.com/interactive/2015/09/09/us
/politics/lawmakers-against-iran-nuclear-deal.html.

2 Lydia Saad, "Americans' Views Toward Israel Remain Firmly Positive,"
Gallup, https://news.gallup.com/poll/189626/americans-views-toward-israel
-remain-firmly-positive.aspx.

3 Ibid.

4 Burgess Everett, "Senate report: State Dept. grant also aided campaign to
unseat Netanyahu," *Politico*, December 7, 2016 https://www.politico.com
/story/2016/07/state-department-grant-netanyahu-225414.

5 Ze'ev Jabotinsky's poem "Smol Hayarden," first published in *Palestine Daily Mail*, April 11, 1930, https://www.nli.org.il/he/newspapers/dhy/1930/04/11 /01/article/7?&dliv=none&e=————-he-20—1—img-txIN%7ctxTI—— ————1&utm_source=he.wikipedia.org&utm_medium=referral&utm _campaign=%22%D7%A9%D7%9E%D7%90%D7%9C+%D7%94%D 7%99%D7%A8%D7%93%D7%9F%22&utm_content=itonut [Hebrew].

Chapter 56: Rising Power

1 "Fifteen Alarming Cyber Security Facts and Stats," Cybint Solutions, December 23, 2020, https://www.cybintsolutions.com/cyber-security-facts -stats/.

Chapter 57: Walking Among the Giants

1 Boaz Bismuth and Eli Leon, "Israel-China Relations: A Historical Milestone," *Israel Hayom*, May 3, 2013, https://www.israelhayom.co.il/article /86687 [Hebrew].

Chapter 58: Parting Shot

1 David Ze'ev Jablinowitz, "Hi David, This Is Barack Obama," *Times of Israel*, October 19, 2020, https://blogs.timesofisrael.com/hi-david-this-is-barack -obama-part-2/.

2 NPR interview, April 7, 2015, https://www.npr.org/2015/04/07/397933577 /transcript-president-obamas-full-npr-interview-on-iran-nuclear-deal.

Chapter 59: New Deal

1 David Friedman, *Sledgehammer: How Breaking with the Past Brought Peace to the Middle East* (HarperCollins, New York, 2022), p. 76.

Chapter 61: "Bring Us Bibi's Head"

1 Shlomo Nakdimon, "The Story of the Disgust and Affection Between Begin and Ben-Gurion," *Haaretz*, January 12, 2013, https://www.haaretz.co .il/magazine/the-edge/2013-01-12/ty-article/0000017f-f181-da6f-a77f -f98f56530000; Madeleine Tress, "Fascist Components in the Political Thought of Vladimir Jabotinsky," *Arab Studies Quarterly* 6, no. 4 (1984): 304–24, http://www.jstor.org/stable/41857736 [Hebrew].

2 "Peek at laundry packages—invasion of privacy,' " *Ynet*, January 10, 2019, https://www.ynet.co.il/articles/0,7340,L-5444496,00.html; Or Ravid, "Bibi HaBayita": Thousands demonstrated in front of the House of Representa-

tives in Petah Tikva," *Walla*, August 13, 2017, https://news.walla.co.il/item /3088371 [Hebrew].

3 Aybee Binyamin, May 2017, https://youtu.be/BT3Z1rm4FBE [Hebrew].

4 Dana Weiss, Channel 12 News, January 19, 2019, https://www.facebook .com/watch/?v=2029933873710398 [Hebrew].

5 Matan Wasserman, "Petition Rejected: Sarah Netanyahu's Victory over the Movement for Quality of Government," *Maariv*, April 7, 2022, https://www .maariv.co.il/news/law/Article-909794 [Hebrew].

6 Ronen Tzur in an interview with Guy Zohar, Channel 11, October 6, 2019, https://www.facebook.com/watch/?v=767364687017500.

7 Netael Bendel and Yehuda Yifrach, "It Is Not the Voter Who Decides Whether a Person Is Guilty or Not," *Makor Rishon*, May 8, 2019, https:// www.makorrishon.co.il/news/137923/ [Hebrew].

8 Bendel and Yifrach, "It Is Not the Voter Who Decides."

9 The most celebrated indictment of a Knesset member before the rise of the Likud was the one that didn't happen. When it was revealed that Prime Minister Rabin and his wife had violated Israel's antiquated foreign currency laws, Rabin chose to resign rather than face a potential indictment.

10 Avishai Ben-Haim, *Second Israel—The Sweet Gospel, the Bitter Oppression* (Yedioth Books, Tel Aviv, 2022), p. 144 [Hebrew].

11 Kalman Liebskind and Matan Wasserman, "Shai Nitzan Recruited Judges and Attorneys for a Fight Against Criticism," *Maariv*, November 15, 2019, https:// www.maariv.co.il/news/law/Article-729698 [Hebrew]; Shai Nitzan's letter to the former prosecutor's office managers, November 13, 2019, https://pbs .twimg.com/media/EJXEgsFXsAAg6Yv?format=jpg&name=large [Hebrew].

12 Liebskind and Wasserman.

13 State Response to Court, February 16, 2022, https://www.haaretz.co.il/em beds/pdf_upload/2022/20220216-170616.pdf [Hebrew].

14 Gilad Morag, Haim Golditch, and Gilad Cohen, "Pilber: 'I Was Threatened with an Interrogation. They Put a Cross on My Back, and the Target— Netanyahu,'" *Ynet*, May 10, 2022, https://www.ynet.co.il/news/article/rke bqo8lq [Hebrew].

Chapter 62: New Path to Peace

1 World Bank report, 2020, https://www.worldbank.org/en/publication/wdr 2020.

Chapter 63: Covid

1 Yair Lapid, https://www.facebook.com/YairLapid/videos/211982180045 790/.

2 "Niv Raskin Morning Show," Channel 12, March 10, 2020, https://www

.mako.co.il/tv-morning-news/articles/Article-5417e5d3b13c071027.htm [Hebrew].

3 "Netanyahu to Israelis: Have Fun, We're Easing Coronavirus Restrictions," *Jerusalem Post*, May 26, 2020, https://www.jpost.com/israel-news/netanyahu -to-israelis-have-fun-were-easing-coronavirus-restrictions-629366.

4 Dr. Albert Bourla, *Moonshot—Inside Pfizer's Nine-Month Race to Make the Impossible Possible* (New York: HarperCollins, 2022), p. 150.

5 Dr. Albert Bourla, *Moonshot*, p. 78.

Chapter 64: Roller Coaster

1 Major General (ret.) Gadi Eisenkot, speech at Netanya Academic College, June 1, 2022.

2 Or Heller, Netanyahu: "We changed the equation—we will not tolerate a drip of rockets," Channel 13 News, May 21, 2021, https://13tv.co.il/item /news/politics/security/netanyahu-1253724/ [Hebrew].

3 Central Bureau of Statistics, Jerusalem & Report of the Knesset Research and Information Center, December 9, 2019, https://fs.knesset.gov.il/global docs/MMM/2bdd1284-f510-ea11-8102-00155d0aee38/2_2bdd1284-f510 -ea11-8102-00155d0aee38_11_13690.pdf [Hebrew].

Chapter 65: My Story, Our Story

1 Ecclesiastes 1, 2.

2 Ecclesiastes 1, 3.

3 Will Durant, *Greatest Minds and Ideas of All Time* (New York: Simon & Schuster, 2002), chapter 5.

INDEX

PHOTOGRAPH CREDITS

FIRST INSERT
1, 2, 3, 4, 5, 7, 8, 9, 10, 11, 15, 18, 21, 25, 29, 30, 31, 48, 49, 50: Courtesy of the author
6: Courtesy of Michoel Rotenfeld
12: Cheltenham High School
13, 17, 20, 22, 23, 24, 26, 28, 33, 34: Israel Defense Forces Archive (IDF)
14: Denis Cameron/Shutterstock and LIFE Magazine
16: Public domain/IDF Archive/Avraham Vered
19: -/AFP via Getty Images
27, 36, 40, 41, 55: Government Press Office of Israel (GPO)
32: The National Library, Dan Hadani Archive Photographer
35, 42: Sa'ar Ya'acov/GPO
37, 38: Public domain
39: Courtesy of Aaronson House
43, 44: Courtesy of Reagan Presidential Library
45: United Nations Photo Library/Saw Lwin
46: Halberstam, Chaim B./Jewish Educational Media Inc.
47: Don Emmert/AFP via Getty Images
51: Patrick Baz/AFP/Getty Images
52: Claude Farge
53: Menahem Kahana/AFP

SECOND INSERT
1, 4, 8, 19, 21, 28, 29, 33, 40, 41, 43, 44, 49: GPO
2, 24: Milner Moshe/GPO
3, 52: Sa'ar Ya'acov/GPO
5: Shaul Golan/AFP via Getty Images
6, 7, 9, 11, 14, 22, 25: Avi Ohayon/GPO
10: Zvika Tischler/Yedioth Ahronoth
12: William Philpott/AFP via Getty Images
13, 27, 32, 34, 36, 37: Reuters
15: AP/Lefteris Pitarakis
16: Beivushtang
17: Davidi Vardi/PikiWiki
18: Ziv Koren
20: Courtesy of the Netanyahu Family
23: Shawn Thew/European Pressphoto Agency
26: United Nations Photo Library/J Carrier
30, 45: Kobe Gideon/GPO
31, 46, 50: Amos Ben Gershom/GPO
35: Newscom/Shahar Azran
38, 42: Topaz Luk
39, 53: Efi Azoulai
47: AP Photo/Evan Vucci
48: AP/Manuel Balce Ceneta
51: Alex Wong/Getty Images

Renewals: (800) 471-0991

www.sccl.org

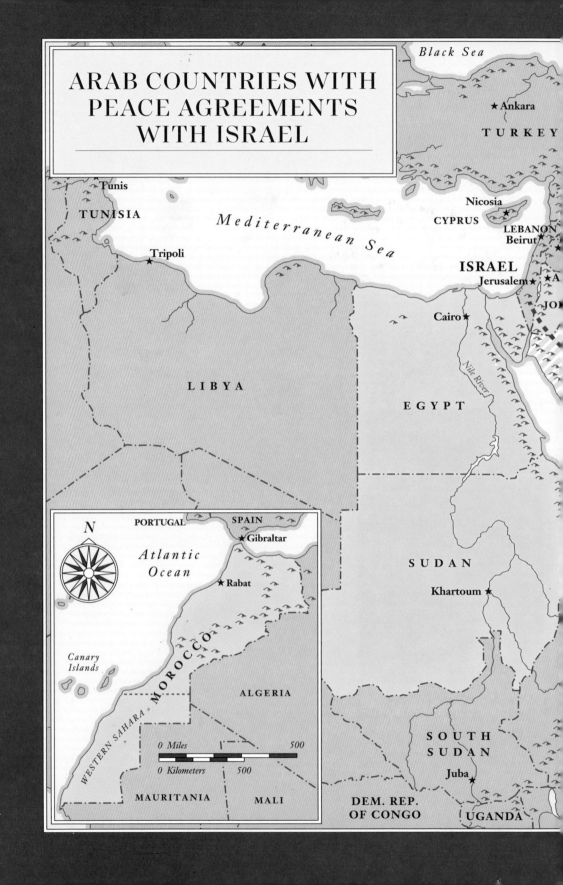

ARAB COUNTRIES WITH
PEACE AGREEMENTS
WITH ISRAEL